TEPS

서울대
텝스 관리위원회
최신기출
1000

서울대 텝스 관리위원회 최신기출 1000

문제제공 서울대학교 TEPS관리위원회
문제해설 양준희
펴낸이 임상진
펴낸곳 (주)넥서스

초판　1쇄 발행 2009년 8월 15일
초판 21쇄 발행 2017년 8월 20일

출판신고 1992년 4월 3일 제311-2002-2호
10880 경기도 파주시 지목로 5
Tel (02)330-5500 Fax (02)330-5555

ISBN 978-89-6000-547-1　18740

www.nexusbook.com

TEPS

서울대
텝스 관리위원회
최신기출
1000

서울대학교 TEPS관리위원회 문제 제공 | 양준희 해설

서울대학교
언어교육원
감수

넥서스

Preface

넥서스에서 이번에 출간하게 된 〈서울대 텝스 관리위원회 최신기출 1000〉으로 전국의 수험생들을 다시 만나 뵙게 되어 반갑습니다. 1999년 1월 제1회 TEPS 정기시험 실시 이후 10년이 지난 지금 TEPS는 대한민국 영어의 기준이 되는 대표 영어능력 검정시험으로 자리매김했으며, 아울러 실용영어 능력시험으로 특히 한국인의 영어 실력을 평가하는 데 높은 신뢰도를 인정받아 점차 채택하고 있는 기관이나 단체가 늘고 있는 추세입니다.

TEPS는 다른 공인 영어시험과 비교해 볼 때 요령이 통하지 않으며 수험자의 실질적인 영어 실력을 요구하는 시험으로 알려져 있습니다.

청해 – 문법 – 어휘 – 독해 각 영역별로 독특한 유형과 특징을 가지고 있으며, 전문적인 학술문에서 일상생활과 연관이 있는 실용문에 이르기까지 광범위한 지문과 다양한 난이도의 문제를 다루고 있습니다. 그만큼 준비하는 수험생들에게는 부담스러운 시험이기도 하지만, 조금 생각을 달리해 보면 TEPS 시험 준비가 곧 영어 실력 향상으로 이어지는 지름길이 될 수 있다는 뜻이기도 합니다.

본서는 위와 같은 TEPS 시험의 특징을 고려하여 최신 기출문제 출제 유형을 제대로 파악하고 각 영역별 전략을 코치해 주기 위해 기획되었습니다. 처음 TEPS 시험을 준비하는 수험생들에게는 표준 문제 유형 파악에 가장 유익한 교재로, 시험을 여러 번 본 사람들에게는 사전 점검용 모의고사 및 취약 파트별 전략 보충 교재로도 활용할 수 있을 것이라고 생각합니다.

TEPS 수험생들을 가르친 현장 강의 노하우와 저 또한 TEPS 수험생으로 고사장에서 체험한 경험들을 토대로 13개 파트별 전략을 소개했습니다.

이 전략들과 연계해서 기출문제를 철저히 분석, 실전 대비 능력 향상을 위해 모델이 될 만한 문제들로 이루어진 Model Test 1회분을 제공하였습니다. 또한 서울대 TEPS관리위원회에서 공개한 최신 기출문제 4회분을 Actual Test 형태로 해설과 함께 수록했습니다.

이 책이 나오기까지 넥서스와 서울대학교 TEPS관리위원회, 서울대학교 언어교육원의 여러 선생님들과 연구원들의 도움을 기획 단계부터 많이 받았습니다. 구체적인 피드백과 다양한 아이디어로 길을 제시해 주신 분들께 진심으로 감사드리며, TEPS 성적을 넘어 더 넓은 꿈과 비전을 향해 나아가는 TEPS 수험생들에게 이 책이 영향력 있기를 다시 한번 기원합니다.

양준희

Contents

All about the Book

1 / TEPS 파트별 전략

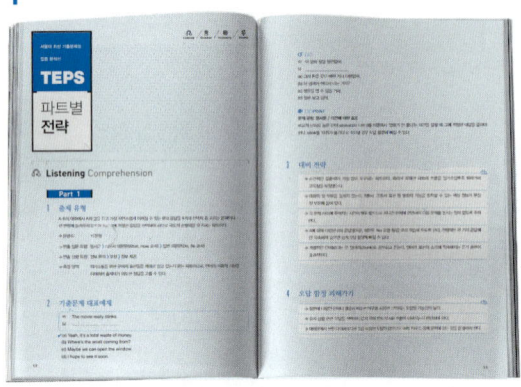

서울대 TEPS 기출문제 데이터 분석을 토대로 저자가 현장 강의에서
터득한 노하우를 접목시킨 TEPS 청해 – 문법 – 어휘 – 독해 13개
파트별 유형 분석, 대비 전략, 오답 함정 피해가기 소개

2 / Model Test

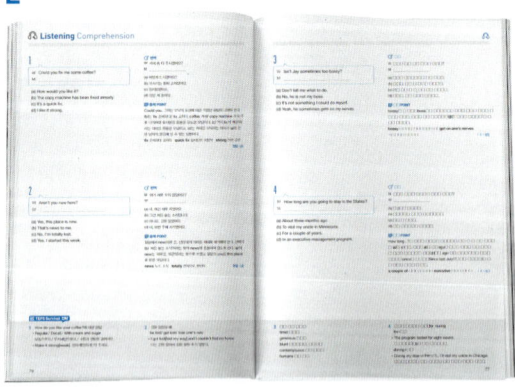

서울대 TEPS 기출문제 출제 원칙을 따르며 실제 시험 적응력 극
대화를 위한 모델 문제 200문항 1회분 및 확장 학습을 위한 TEPS
Survival 전략 추가

3 / Actual Test

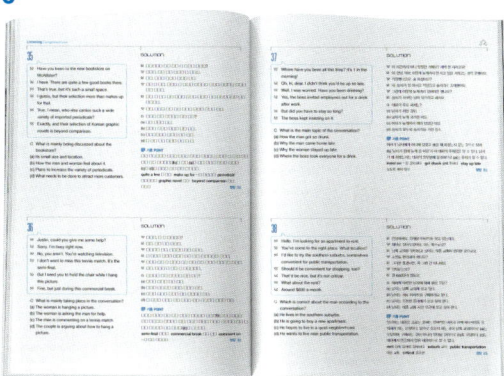

서울대 TEPS 시험과 동일한 환경을 구현한

문제집 및 기출문제 완전 해설, 청해 MP3 음원 제공

4 / 별책부록

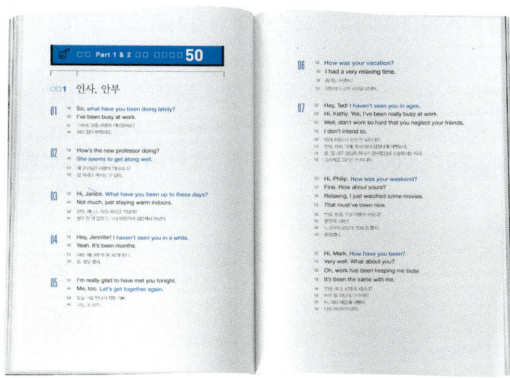

모바일 세대의 기동성 향상을 위해 서울대 TEPS 기출문제 중

청해 Part 1 & 2 기출 빈출표현 50개와 기출어휘 500개를 선별,

MP3 음원 제공

5 / 무료 동영상 강의

TEPS 스타 강사 그룹이 무료로 제공하는 TEPS 13개 파트별 대비

전략 강의 www.nexstudy.com

All about the TEPS

1 / TEPS란?

❶ Test of English Proficiency developed by Seoul National University의 약자로 서울대학교 언어교육원에서 개발하고, TEPS관리위원회에서 주관하는 국가공인 영어시험

❷ 1999년 1월 처음 시행 이후 연 12~16회 실시

❸ 정부기관 및 기업의 직원 채용, 인사고과, 해외 파견 근무자 선발과 더불어 대학과 특목고 입학 및 졸업 자격 요건, 국가고시 및 자격 시험의 영어 대체 시험으로 활용

❹ 100여 명의 국내외 유수 대학의 최고 수준 영어 전문가들이 출제하고, 언어 테스팅 분야의 세계적인 권위자인 Bachman 교수(미국 UCLA)와 Oller 교수(미국 뉴멕시코대)로부터 타당성을 검증받음

❺ 말하기 – 쓰기 시험인 TEPS Speaking & Writing도 별도로 실시 중이며, 2009년 10월부터 이를 통합한 *i*-TEPS도 실시 예정

2 / TEPS 시험 구성

영역	Part별 내용	문항수	시간/배점
청해 Listening Comprehension	Part I : 문장 하나를 듣고 이어질 대화 고르기	15	55분 400점
	Part II : 3문장의 대화를 듣고 이어질 대화 고르기	15	
	Part III : 6~8 문장의 대화를 듣고 질문에 해당하는 답 고르기	15	
	Part IV : 담화문의 내용을 듣고 질문에 해당하는 답 고르기	15	
문법 Grammar	Part I : 대화문의 빈칸에 적절한 표현 고르기	20	25분 100점
	Part II : 문장의 빈칸에 적절한 표현 고르기	20	
	Part III : 대화에서 어법상 틀리거나 어색한 부분 고르기	5	
	Part IV : 단문에서 문법상 틀리거나 어색한 부분 고르기	5	
어휘 Vocabulary	Part I : 대화문의 빈칸에 적절한 단어 고르기	25	15분 100점
	Part II : 단문의 빈칸에 적절한 단어 고르기	25	
독해 Reading Comprehension	Part I : 지문을 읽고 빈칸에 들어갈 내용 고르기	16	45분 400점
	Part II : 지문을 읽고 질문에 가장 적절한 내용 고르기	21	
	Part III : 지문을 읽고 문맥상 어색한 내용 고르기	3	
총계	13개 Parts	200	140분 990점

☆ **IRT** (Item Response Theory)에 의하여 최고점이 990점, 최저점이 10점으로 조정됨.

3 / TEPS 시험 응시 정보

현장 접수
❶ www.teps.or.kr에서 인근 접수처 및 준비물(응시료, 사진) 확인
❷ 접수처 방문: 해당 접수기간 평일 오후 12시 ~ 오후 5시

인터넷 접수
❶ TEPS관리위원회 홈페이지 접속 www.teps.or.kr
❷ 준비물: 스캔한 사진 파일, 응시료 결제를 위한 신용 카드 및 은행 계좌

4 / TEPS 시험 당일 정보

❶ 고사장 입실 완료: 9시 30분(일요일) / 3시(토요일)
❷ 준비물: 신분증, 컴퓨터용 사인펜, 수정테이프, 수험표, 시계
❸ 유효한 신분증
　성인: 주민등록증, 운전면허증, 여권, 공무원증, 현역간부 신분증, 군무원증, 주민등록증 발급 신청 확인서, 외국인 등록증
　초·중고생: 학생증, 여권, 청소년증, 주민등록증, 주민등록증 발급 신청 확인서, TEPS 신분확인 증명서
❹ 시험 시간: 2시간 20분 (중간에 쉬는 시간 없음, 각 영역별 제한시간 엄수)
❺ 성적 확인: 약 2주 후 인터넷에서 조회 가능

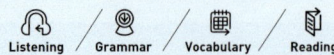

서울대 최신 기출문제를

집중 분석한

TEPS

파트별
전략

🎧 **Listening** Comprehension

Part 1

1 출제 유형

A-B의 대화에서 A의 말을 듣고 가장 자연스럽게 이어질 수 있는 B의 응답을 4개의 선택지 중 고르는 문제이다. 한 번밖에 들려주지 않으며 3초 내에 적절한 응답을 선택해야 하므로 극도의 순발력을 요구하는 파트이다.

➔ 문항수: 15문항

➔ 빈출 질문 유형: 평서문 〉 의문사 의문문(What, How 순서) 〉 일반 의문문(Do, Be 순서)

➔ 빈출 상황 유형: 정보 문의 〉 요청 〉 정보 제공

➔ 측정 영역: 의사소통을 위한 구어체 표현들을 제대로 알고 있는지 묻는 파트이므로, 언어의 사회적 기능을 이해해야 출제자가 의도한 정답을 고를 수 있다.

2 기출문제 대표 예제

> W   The movie really stinks.
>
> M   _____

✔ (a) Yeah, it's a total waste of money.

(b) Where's the smell coming from?

(c) Maybe we can open the window.

(d) I hope to see it soon.

☞ **번역**

W 이 영화 정말 형편없어.

M _____

(a) 그래 돈을 갖다 버린 거나 다름없지.

(b) 이 냄새가 어디서 나는 거지?

(c) 창문을 열 수 있을 거야.

(d) 얼른 보고 싶어.

⊞ **기출 POINT**

문제 유형: 평서문 / 의견에 대한 호응

비교적 난이도 높은 단어 stinks(질이 나쁘다)를 이용해서 '영화가 안 좋다'는 의견을 말할 때 그에 적절한 대답을 골라야 한다. stink를 '악취가 풍기다'로 착각할 경우 오답 함정에 빠질 수 있다.

3 대비 전략

→ 순간적인 집중력이 가장 많이 요구되는 파트이다. 따라서 최대한 대화의 흐름을 일거수일투족 따라가야 고득점을 보장받는다.

→ 대화의 첫 부분을 놓치지 않는다. 의문사, 조동사 표현 등 발화의 기능을 짐작할 수 있는 핵심 정보가 문장 첫 부분에 들어 있다.

→ 각 문제 사이에 주어지는 시간이 매우 짧으므로 지나간 문제에 연연하여 다음 문제를 놓치는 일이 없도록 주의한다.

→ A에 대해 다양한 B의 응답(평서문, 의문문, No 유형 등)을 미리 학습해 두도록 한다. 전형적인 한 가지 응답에만 익숙해져 있으면 쉽게 오답 함정에 빠질 수 있다.

→ 개별적인 단어보다는 구, 덩어리(chunk)로 공부하고 듣는다. 덩어리 표현의 소리에 익숙해지는 듣기 훈련이 효과적이다.

4 오답 함정 피해가기

→ 질문에 나왔던 단어나 발음이 비슷한 어구를 사용한 선택지는 오답일 가능성이 높다.

→ 유사 상황 관련 오답을 선택하지 않기 위해 반드시 A와 흐름이 이어지는지 판단해야 한다.

→ 대화문에서 쓰인 다의어의 다른 뜻을 이용한 오답이 많으므로 여러 가지 뜻 중에 문맥에 맞는 것을 잘 골라야 한다.

Part 2

1 출제 유형

A-B-A-B 대화에서 두 번째 A까지의 말만 듣고 4개의 선택지 중 가장 자연스럽게 이어지는 B의 응답을 고르는 문제이다. 한 번밖에 들려주지 않으며 3초 내에 적절한 응답을 선택해야 한다.

→ 문항수:　　　 15문항

→ 빈출 질문 유형: 평서문(부가의문문 포함) 〉 일반 의문문 〉 의문사 의문문

→ 빈출 상황 유형: 정보 문의 〉 요청 〉 정보 제공

→ 측정 영역:　　 Part 1과 더불어 구어체 표현에 대한 이해도를 측정하지만, 전체적인 대화의 흐름을 따라갈 수 있는 능력도 요구된다.

2 기출문제 대표 예제

> W　Have you heard that Jane got into the top university?
>
> M　That can't be. Peter was better than her in every respect and he wasn't accepted.
>
> W　I know, but it's true. I heard it from her sister.
>
> M　＿＿＿＿＿＿＿＿＿＿＿＿

   (a) What a small world!

   (b) Nice of you to say so.

   (c) Okay, I'll let her know.

✔ (d) I still can't believe it.

☞ 번역

W　제인이 최우수 대학에 들어갔다는 것 들었니?

M　그럴 리가 없는데. 피터가 어느 면에서나 그녀보다 나은데도 입학 허가를 받지 못했거든.

W　나도 알아, 하지만 사실인걸. 제인 여동생한테 들었어.

M　＿＿＿＿＿＿＿＿＿＿＿＿

(a) 세상 참 좁구나!

(b) 그렇게 말해줘서 고마워.

(c) 그래, 그녀에게 알려줄게.

(d) 아직도 믿을 수가 없네.

⊞ 기출 POINT

문제 유형: 평서문 / 정보 제공

첫 번째, 두 번째 대화에서 상황을 파악하고 세 번째 말에서 직접적인 단서를 얻어 정답을 선택해야 하는 Part 2의 특성이 잘 나타난 문제이다. 앞에서 최고 대학에 들어갔다는 사실에 대한 남자의 반응을 알고 있어야 (d)를 정답으로 찾아낼 수 있다. (b)는 칭찬받았을 때의 반응이고, (c)는 제인 여동생이 이 내용을 모른다는 가정 하에 할 수 있는 응답이다. 이처럼 Part 2에서는 상황이나 역할을 혼동시키는 오답이 많이 등장한다.

3 대비 전략

→ 세 번째 대화를 주의 깊게 듣는 것이 정답을 찾는 관건이다. 앞의 두 대화를 아무리 잘 들어도 세 번째 대화를
놓치면 답을 제대로 찾을 수 없다.

→ 자주 출제되는 구어체 관용표현 암기는 아무리 강조해도 지나치지 않다.

→ 대화를 듣고 전반적인 대화 상황을 판단할 줄 아는 능력을 기른다.

4 오답 함정 피해가기

→ Part 1과 마찬가지로 본문에 나왔던 핵심어와 유사 어구를 사용한 선택지는 오답일 가능성이 높다.
역으로, 주제나 내용은 어울리는데 새로운 단어가 등장하면 정답일 가능성이 높아진다.

→ 두 남녀의 입장과 역할을 구분해서 이해하도록 한다. 마지막 화자의 말에 이어져 상대가 아닌 같은 화자가
할 만한 말이 오답으로 제시되는 경우가 많다.

→ 선택지의 앞 부분은 그럴듯한데 엉뚱하게 끝나는 오답이 있으므로 끝까지 주의 깊게 들어야 한다.

Part 3

1 출제 유형

남녀가 3~4번 정도 주고받는 대화와 질문을 들은 후 네 개의 선택지 중 정답을 고르게 된다. 대화와 질문은 두 번 들려주며 선택지는 한 번 들려준다.

→ 문항수: 15문항

→ 빈출 질문 유형: 전체 대의 파악(6~7문항) 〉 세부 내용 파악(5~6문항) 〉 추론(3문항)

→ 빈출 대화 상황: 개인적 일상(정보 문의, 의견 교환 등) 〉 사회적 상황(업무, 예약 등)

→ 측정 영역: 표현을 주로 묻는 Part 1 & 2에서 한 단계 더 심도 있게 대화 내용에 대한 전반적인 이해와 대화 중 등장한 세부 내용, 추론 능력을 평가한다.

2 기출문제 대표 예제

W	Do you think this gray shirt is good for Tom?
M	This blue one looks better to me.
W	Blue doesn't suit him.
M	But he likes blue.
W	How do you know that?
M	Last year, I brought him a blue sweater and he liked it a lot.

Q What are the speakers discussing?
(a) What color suit Tom has.
(b) What their favorite colors are.
(c) What color tie they should buy.
✔ (d) What color shirt they should buy for Tom.

☞ 번역
W 이 회색 셔츠가 톰한테 잘 어울리는 것 같니?
M 나는 이 파란색이 더 좋아 보이는데.
W 파란색은 톰한테 어울리지 않아.
M 그렇지만 톰은 파란색을 좋아하거든.
W 그걸 어떻게 알아?
M 작년에 내가 파란색 스웨터를 사줬는데 아주 좋아했거든.

Q 화자들의 대화 내용은?
(a) 톰이 가지고 있는 양복의 색상.
(b) 두 사람이 좋아하는 색상.
(c) 두 사람이 구입해야 할 넥타이의 색상.
(d) 톰에게 사주면 좋을 셔츠의 색상.

⊞ 기출 POINT

문제 유형: 대의 / 일상 대화

대화의 전반적인 내용을 묻는 대표적인 대의 파악 유형이다. 대화 전체를 관통하는 중심 주제를 골라야 한다. 여자의 첫 번째 대화에서 주제가 암시되고 있다. 여기서 shirt라는 키워드와 그 이후 반복되는 color에 대한 이야기로 정답 (d)를 고를 수 있다. (a)와 (c)는 색깔이라는 비슷한 상황이지만, suit나 tie가 대화에서 전혀 언급되지 않았으므로 오답이다.

3 대비 전략

→ 첫 번째 대화와 질문을 들은 후 두 번째 들을 때 집중해야 할 부분을 구분한다. 가령, 대의 파악 문제는 대화의 흐름 파악에 집중하고, 세부 정보 파악은 구체적인 단서들을 놓치지 않아야 정답을 고를 수 있다.

→ 전체 대화 내용이 길어지므로 나만의 notetaking 기술을 개발하도록 한다. 못 알아듣는 단어는 발음나는 대로 우리말로 적어도 괜찮다.

→ 남자의 대화 내용과 여자의 대화 내용을 구분해서 기억해야 오답 함정에 휘말리지 않는다.

→ 선택지는 한 번만 들려주기 때문에 대화 내용 파악 후 특히 집중하고, 정답 가능성 여부를 ○ △ × 등으로 소거해 가며 듣는다.

→ 대화 속 등장한 단어나 구를 그대로 말하지 않고, 바꿔 말한(paraphrasing) 선택지 유형을 이해하자.

4 오답 함정 피해가기

→ 대의 파악 문제의 경우 대화 내용을 너무 일반화시킨 선택지나 지엽적인 사실만을 나열한 선택지는 오답이다.

→ 대화 속 단어나 구를 그대로 가져온 선택지는 오답일 확률이 높고, 다른 표현으로 바꿔 말한(paraphrasing) 선택지는 정답일 확률이 높다.

→ 특히 세부 내용 파악 문제에서는 남녀의 역할이 바뀐 오답 선택지가 많이 출제된다.

Part 4

1 출제 유형

80단어 내외의 담화문(monologue)을 들은 후 질문과 선택지를 듣고 정답을 고른다. Part 3와 마찬가지로 담화문과 질문은 두 번, 선택지는 한 번 들려 준다. 다른 어떤 파트보다 많은 정보가 빠르게 제시되고, 전문적인 어휘들이 등장하기 때문에 수험생들이 가장 어렵게 느끼는 파트이다.

→ 문항수: 15문항

→ 빈출 질문 유형: 대의 파악(7문항) 〉세부 내용 파악(5문항) 〉추론(3문항)

→ 빈출 담화문 유형: 학술문(인문과학, 사회과학, 자연과학) ≒ 실용문(공지사항, 방송, 광고)

→ 측정 영역: Part 3가 대화문에 대한 이해도 측정이라면, Part 4는 긴 담화문의 이해도 측정이다.
                  담화문의 요지, 대상, 화자, 구제적인 세부 내용, 사실, 추론 등을 묻는다.

2 기출문제 대표 예제

> Next Saturday is the annual Cancer Run. This event is in honor of Terry Fox, who died of cancer while raising money for cancer research. All money collected from the run will go to completing his dream of finding a cure. Races will take place at various times and places throughout the city. Please look for details in your local newspaper. Everyone is welcome.

Q What is the purpose of the announcement?
(a) To warn people of the dangers of cancer.
(b) To announce the death of Terry Fox.
(c) To inform people about cancer research.
✔ (d) To get people to join a fund-raising event.

☞ 번역

다음 주 토요일은 연례 암 퇴치 달리기를 하는 날입니다. 이 행사는 암으로 숨진 테리 폭스를 기리는 동시에 암 연구 기금을 마련하기 위해 준비된 것입니다. 이 달리기에서 모금된 돈은 치료법을 발견하려는 그의 꿈을 이루는 데 모두 쓰이게 됩니다. 달리기는 도시 전체에 걸쳐 다양한 시간과 장소에서 열릴 것입니다. 자세한 내용은 지역 신문을 참조하시기 바랍니다. 누구나 환영합니다.

Q 공지의 목적은?
(a) 암의 위험에 대한 경고.
(b) 테리 폭스의 죽음 발표.
(c) 암 연구에 대한 정보 제공.
(d) 기금 모금 행사 참여 권장.

문제 유형: 대의 / 실용문(안내방송)

공지사항의 목적을 묻는 전체 대의 파악 문제 유형이다. 이런 공지사항의 경우 주제는 흔히 담화문의 소개 부분(첫 번째와 두 번째 문장)에서 제시된다. This event is in honor of 이하에 이벤트의 목적을 제시하고 있고 그것이 결국 공지의 목적이다. 나머지 선택지는 지문에 나온 표현이나 지문과 관련된 상황을 이용한 전형적인 오답의 예이다.

3 대비 전략

→ 첫 번째 담화를 들을 때 전체 토픽을 파악하고, 질문을 들은 후 두 번째 들을 때는 질문 유형에 따라 집중해서 들어야 하는 부분에 유의한다.

→ 대의 파악 질문에서는 담화의 첫 두 문장을 중심으로 반복되는 개념을 이해하고, 세부 정보 질문 유형은 키워드를 메모해서 선택지를 들으며 정답을 소거해 나가도록 한다.

→ 사회과학, 자연과학 등 자신이 취약한 전문 분야의 용어들은 따로 암기해 두어야 낯선 토픽이 출제돼도 당황하지 않고 들을 수 있다.

→ 추론 문제 유형은 주로 전문적인 학술문에서 출제되므로 고난도 문제인 경우가 많다.

4 오답 함정 피해가기

→ Part 3와 마찬가지로 너무 일반적인 진술이나 담화문의 소재와 비슷한 상식적인 선택지, 지엽적인 사실들을 열거한 선택지는 오답일 경우가 많다.

→ 담화에 나오는 단어나 표현을 그대로 사용한 선택지는 오답일 확률이 높다.

→ 추론 문제의 경우 담화에 등장한 단순한 사실을 진술한 선택지는 오답이다.

→ 담화문의 내용을 유기적으로 잘 결합해서 바꿔 말한(paraphrasing) 선택지는 정답일 확률이 높다.

Grammar

Part 1

1 출제 유형

A-B 두 사람의 대화문을 읽고 빈칸에 알맞은 어법을 4개의 선택지 중에서 고르는 문제이다. 구어체 관용표현이 많이 출제되므로 청해 Part 1과 중복되는 부분이 있다.

→ 문항수: 20문항

→ 빈출 질문 유형: 문장 구조(어순) 〉 시제 〉 동사

→ 측정 영역: 일상적인 대화 표현 중에 녹아 있는 구어체 문법 사항들을 테스트한다.

→ 빈출 토픽: 구어체 문법 표현을 묻는 파트이므로 일상 생활, 학교, 사무실 관련 등 다양한 토픽이 출제된다.

2 기출문제 대표 예제

> A Do you think I'll pass the qualifying exam?
> B I _____.

(a) see not why

(b) see why not

(c) don't see not why

✔ (d) don't see why not

☞ 번역

A 제가 자격 시험에 통과할 것 같아요?

B 그러지 못하란 법이 어디 있어요?

⊞ 기출 POINT

문제 유형: 관용표현 / 문장 구조(어순)

동사 see는 understand의 의미가 있고, 여기서 I don't see why not은 I don't see why you will not pass the qualifying exam의 줄임이라 할 수 있다. 관용표현이라 할 수 있는 Why not 또는 I don't see why not의 쓰임에 익숙하거나 간접의문문의 문장 구조를 파악하고 있다면 풀 수 있는 문제이다.

3   대비 전략

→ 평소에 알고 있던 문법 지식들을 구어체 문장에서 적용해 보도록 한다.

→ 문법 네 파트 중에서 비교적 난이도가 낮은 파트이므로, 최대한 빨리 문제를 풀고 나머지 문법 파트에 시간을 할애한다.

→ 세부적인 문법 내용을 모두 공부하려 하지 말고 빈출 문법 영역(시제, 분사구문, 수 일치, 태 등)에 집중하고 시험에 자주 출제되는 선택지 패턴을 우선 익혀 둔다.

→ 전체적인 대화 내용을 완벽하게 파악하지 못하더라도 선택지를 중심으로 구조만 파악해도 풀 수 있는 문제가 많다.

4   오답 함정 피해가기

→ 빈칸이 들어가 있지 않은 A나 B의 질문이나 대답을 점검한 후 정답을 골라야 한다.

→ 한국인이 특히 취약한 문법 사항들(수 일치, 시제, 태)이 오답 선택지로 자주 등장한다.

→ 문장 구조를 묻는 문제는 선택지를 먼저 훑어보고 빈칸에 대입해서 소거해 나가는 방법이 효율적이다.

Part 2

1 출제 유형

20단어 내외로 이루어진 한두 개의 문어체 문장을 읽고 어법상 빈칸에 가장 알맞은 표현을 4개의 선택지 중에서 고르는 문제이다.

→ 문항수:　　　20문항

→ 빈출 질문 유형:　문장 구조(어순) 〉분사 〉수 일치

→ 측정 영역:　　　Part 1보다 심도 있게 문장 구조에 대한 이해력을 측정한다.

→ 빈출 토픽:　　　Part 1 토픽과는 구별되게 시사, 뉴스, 학술문 등 전문 분야의 글이 다뤄진다.

2 기출문제 대표 예제

> Most people are not aware of _____ racial prejudice exists in a society.

　(a) which extent
　(b) its extent of which
✔ (c) the extent to which
　(d) to which the extent

☞ 번역

대다수 사람들은 한 사회 안에 존재하는 인종 편견이 어느 정도인지 알지 못한다.

田 기출 POINT

문제 유형: 관계대명사

관계대명사는 Part 2에서 가장 많이 출제되는 문법 항목 중 하나이다. 빈칸 뒷부분을 보면 완전한 문장이 나오므로 빠진 부분은 관계부사(전치사+관계대명사)임을 선택지들을 통해 가늠할 수 있다. 또한, 빈칸은 앞에 나오는 are not aware of의 목적어가 되어야 하므로 명사인 the extent가 나와야 한다. 따라서 (c)가 정답이다.

3 대비 전략

→ 문장의 구조와 관련된 문법 영역(부사절, 도치 및 생략, 관계대명사, 수 일치, 부사의 어순, 완료 분사)의 개념을 이해한다.

→ 문장의 기본 구조를 익히기 위해 기출 문제를 풀 때도 정답만 확인하지 말고 문장을 분석해 보도록 한다.

→ 우리말과 근본적으로 다른 영어 문장 구조를 파악해 두자.

4 오답 함정 피해가기

→ 선택지와 더불어 문장의 주어와 동사를 가장 먼저 파악하도록 한다.

→ 선택지들의 형태(to부정사, 동명사 등)를 보고 테스트하는 문법 카테고리를 예측하며 빈칸 주위를 확인한다.

→ 한 가지 문법 사항만 묻는 문제도 있지만 두 가지 이상 입체적으로 문법을 점검해야 하는 선택지들도 출제된다.

Part 3

1 출제 유형

A-B-A-B의 구어체 대화문을 읽고 어법상 틀리거나 어색한 표현이 들어가 있는 문장을 고르는 문제이다.

→ 문항수:　　　 5문항

→ 빈출 질문 유형: 시제 〉어순 〉품사

→ 측정 영역:　　 Part 1 & 2가 단순하게 빈칸에 적절한 표현을 찾는 문제라면, Part 3는 여러 가지 문법 항목들이 포함된 대화문들 중 오류가 있는 문장을 찾아야 하므로 구어체 영어 표현에 대한 이해력을 보다 심도 있게 측정한다.

→ 빈출 토픽:　　 청해 Part 2에 나오는 표현들과 유사하게 일상 생활과 관련된 토픽들이 출제된다.

2 기출문제 대표 예제

> (a) **A** How come you're not at work today?
> ✔ (b) **B** Didn't you know that I apply for paternity leave?
> (c) **A** You mean you're staying home to take care of your baby?
> (d) **B** Of course. That is exactly what I mean.

☞ 번역

(a) 어쩐 일로 오늘 직장에 안 나갔나요?

(b) 육아 휴직 낸 거 몰랐나요?

(c) 애를 돌보려고 집에 있다는 말인가요?

(d) 그럼요. 제 말이 바로 그거예요.

⊞ 기출 POINT

문제 유형: 시제

육아 휴직을 낸 것은 과거 사실(applied for paternity leave)이므로 동사 apply를 과거형으로 질문해야 한다. 정답 (b) 외에도 나머지 선택지들에 관사, 현재 진행형, 명사절의 어순 등의 문법 요소들을 곳곳에 담고 있기 때문에 정답을 고르기가 Part 1 & 2보다 한 단계 어려워지는 것이다.

3 대비 전략

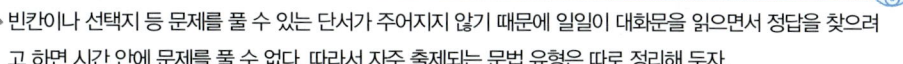

→ 빈칸이나 선택지 등 문제를 풀 수 있는 단서가 주어지지 않기 때문에 일일이 대화문을 읽으면서 정답을 찾으려고 하면 시간 안에 문제를 풀 수 없다. 따라서 자주 출제되는 문법 유형은 따로 정리해 두자.

→ 자주 출제 되는 문법 오류 – 시제 일치, 전치사, 관사, 명사 단·복수, 형용사 혹은 부사, 접속사 연관 구조, 간접 의문문의 어순 등

→ 대화문을 보고 출제자가 숨겨둔 문법 오류를 찾아내는 훈련이 필요하다.

4 오답 함정 피해가기

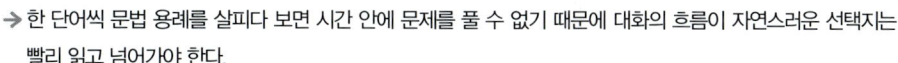

→ 한 단어씩 문법 용례를 살피다 보면 시간 안에 문제를 풀 수 없기 때문에 대화의 흐름이 자연스러운 선택지는 빨리 읽고 넘어가야 한다.

→ 자주 출제 되는 문법 카테고리를 기억해 뒀다가 그 부분을 우선 점검한다.

→ 선택지마다 문법적 요소들이 포함돼 있으므로 문장 구조적인 측면을 먼저 파악하고, 개별 품사를 확인한다.

Part 4

1 출제 유형

60단어 내외의 4~5개 문장으로 이루어진 단일 지문을 읽고 문법적 오류가 있는 문장을 고르는 문제이다.

→ 문항수: 5문항

→ 빈출 질문 유형: 문장구조 〉시제 〉품사

→ 측정 영역: Part 3와 마찬가지로 선택지와 빈칸 등 답을 고를 수 있는 단서들이 전혀 제공되지 않으므로, 지문에 대한 온전한 문법 이해력 측정이 가능하다.

→ 빈출 토픽: Part 2의 토픽과 유사하며 실용문보다는 학술문과 시사적인 지문이 주로 출제된다.

2 기출문제 대표 예제

(a) The evidence of global warming is still largely conjectural. ✔(b) True, global temperature has been risen by about 0.5℃ since the start of this century. (c) Most meteorologists, however, are uncertain as to whether the globe wasn't already warming before industrialization. (d) Untangling the greenhouse effect from other broad movements in the earth's temperature is extremely difficult.

☞ 번역

(a) 지구온난화에 대한 증거는 아직까지 대부분 추정에 머물고 있다. (b) 지구 기온이 금세기가 시작된 이후 0.5도씩 상승해 왔다는 것은 사실이다. (c) 하지만 대부분 기상학자들은 산업화 이전부터 지구가 이미 온난화되고 있었던 것은 아닌지 확신하지 못한다. (d) 지구 기온의 다른 큰 움직임에서 온실효과만을 분리해내는 것은 극히 어려운 일이다.

⊞ 기출 POINT

문제 유형: 태

동사의 태 문제는 Part 4에서 가장 많이 출제되는 분야 중 하나다. (b)에서 rise는 자동사이므로 수동형으로 쓸 수 없다. 따라서 global temperature has been risen은 global temperature has risen으로 바꿔야 한다. rise는 raise와 비교하여 태 문제로 자주 출제되므로 확실히 알아둔다. 이 문장의 True는 It is true that의 줄임말로 보면 된다.

3 대비 전략

→ Part 1 & 2를 먼저 풀다 보면 시간이 모자라서 Part 4를 위한 시간 할애가 안 될 때가 많다. Part 4는 점수 배점이 높으니, 문법 시간이 시작되자 마자 가장 먼저 푸는 것도 한 방법이다.

→ 지문과 단어 하나하나를 체크해 가며 정답을 찾는 것은 시간상 불가능하므로, 어떤 부분에 문법 오류가 숨어 있는지 미리 정보를 가지고 있어야 한다.

→ 자주 출제 되는 문법 오류 – 시제 일치, 문장의 어순, 분사구문, 간접의문문, 태, 전치사, 관사, 명사 단 · 복수, 형용사 혹은 부사, 접속사 연관 구조 등

4 오답 함정 피해가기

→ 문법 영역이 시작되면 빠르게 훑어 읽기를 하면서 주어와 동사를 먼저 점검하고 개별적인 품사 오류가 없는지 빠르게 읽어 내려간다.

→ 어디가 어떻게 틀렸는지 딱히 모르더라도 문장의 흐름이 어색한 선택지는 오답일 경우가 많다.

→ 복합시제, 분사구문, 태 등의 문법적 혼동 요소들이 선택지마다 숨어 있으므로 정답이 아닌 나머지 선택지들의 문법 요소들을 한번 더 점검하고 최종 정답을 고른다.

🗓 Vocabulary

Part 1

1 출제 유형

일상생활에서 많이 쓰이는 구어체 대화문에서 빈칸에 들어갈 적절한 어휘를 고르는 유형으로 다른 영역에 비해서 비교적 단순하게 답이 바로 나오는 문제들이 많다.

→ 문항수:　　　　25문항

→ 빈출 질문 유형: 구어체 관용표현 〉 연어 〉 2어 동사

→ 측정 영역:　　　짧은 시간 안에 많은 문제를 풀어야 하므로 구어체 표현에 대한 의미를 체화해서 알고 있는지 평가한다.

→ 빈출 토픽:　　　청해 Part 1, 문법 Part 1과 마찬가지로 일상생활과 관련된 토픽들이 등장한다.

2 기출문제 대표 예제

> A　Hey, what's _____?
> B　Not much. How about you?

(a) cool
(b) neat
✔ (c) new
(d) fresh

☞ 번역

A　이봐, 요새 별일 없어?
B　별로 없어. 너는 어때?

⊞ 기출 POINT

문제 유형: 회화 표현

What's new? 표현을 평소에 알고 있다면 바로 답을 고를 수 있지만 그렇지 않다면 선택지들을 소거해 보자.
Not much. How about you? 답변으로 봐 안부를 묻는 질문임을 알 수 있다. cool, neat, fresh 모두 어색하다.
여기서 new는 '새로운 일'을 의미한다.

3 대비 전략

→ 청해 Part 1 & 2 표현과 중복되는 부분이 있으므로 여기서 사용되는 관용표현을 주의 깊게 봐두자.

→ 개별적인 단어들의 의미 파악도 중요하지만 회화 표현이나 관용어구 등을 덩어리로 공부해야 감을 가지고 문제를 풀 수 있다.

→ 단어에 대한 단순한 지식을 평가하는 시험이 아니라 문맥에 맞는 구어체 어휘 사용법을 테스트하기 때문에 문장 속에서의 정확한 표현법을 알고 있어야 한다.

4 오답 함정 피해가기

→ 한국인에게 취약한 부분, 혼동하기 쉬운 단어들이 선택지로 나오기 때문에 우리말과 일대일 번역이 되는 선택지는 오답일 확률이 높다.

→ 문맥을 점검하지 않고 단어의 뜻만으로 선택지를 판단하면 오답 함정에 빠지기 쉽다.

→ 쉬운 단어의 다양한 의미가 정답으로 출제되는 경우가 많으므로 익숙한 단어의 쓰임새를 먼저 점검한다.

Part 2

1 출제 유형

신문 기사나 공고, 학술 지문 등 문어체 문장의 빈칸에 적절한 어휘를 고르는 문제 유형이다.

→ 문항수: 25문항

→ 빈출 질문 유형: 다의어 〉유의어 〉연어

→ 측정 영역: 독해 지문 수준의 문장을 통해 기초 어휘부터 고난도 어휘까지 문맥(context)을 통한 어휘 사용 능력을 평가한다.

→ 빈출 토픽: TEPS는 다른 영어능력 검정시험에 비해 어휘 출제 범위가 매우 넓으며 비즈니스 분야만 다루는 TOEIC이나 학술적인 내용을 묻는 TOEFL과 달리 다양한 토픽의 지문이 출제된다.

2 기출문제 대표 예제

St. Andrews, the oldest university in Scotland, was _____ in 1411.

(a) invented
✔ (b) founded
(c) operated
(d) produced

☞ 번역

스코틀랜드에서 가장 오래된 세인트 앤드루스 대학은 1411년에 세워졌다.

⊞ 기출 POINT

문제 유형: 유의어

선택지 모두 새로운 것을 만들어 낸다는 의미가 있다. 무엇을 만들어 내는가에 따라 서로 다른 동사를 사용해야 하는데, 회사나 학교, 기관 등을 설립하는 것은 found라고 한다.

3 대비 전략

→ 기출 어휘 리스트는 반드시 암기하도록 한다. 정답뿐만 아니라 선택지에 제시된 어휘들도 묶어서 기억하자.

→ Part 2를 위한 어휘 학습 분량이 워낙 방대하기 때문에 출제 유형별(다의어/ 유의어/ 연어/ 2어 동사/ 이디엄) 로 정리하거나 독해 지문에 나오는 고난도 어휘로 효율적으로 대비한다.

→ 영문 기사 등을 통해 이슈화되는 뉴스 관련 어휘를 정리한다.

→ 문맥에 따라 뜻이 달라지는 단어가 많이 출제되므로 단편적인 공부보다는 하나를 공부해도 쓰임을 정확하게 아는 것이 중요하다.

→ 가장 많이 출제되는 품사(동사 – 명사 – 형용사 순)를 우선 알고 대비한다.

4 오답 함정 피해가기

→ 문맥을 통한 단어 선택이 핵심 미션이므로 다른 선택지들도 대입해 보고 오답을 소거해 나가도록 한다.

→ 우리말로 번역하면 자연스러운 것 같은 오답 선택지들이 자주 등장한다. 영어 단어 용례로 정답을 찾아가야 한다.

→ 빈칸 다음에 전치사가 나올 경우 선택지와 전치사와의 어울림을 점검한다.

Reading Comprehension

Part 1

1 출제 유형

100단어 내외의 단일 지문을 읽고 글의 논리적인 흐름상 적절한 선택지를 고르는 유형이다. 구나 절을 고르는 문제(1~14번)와 연결어를 고르는 문제(15~16번) 두 가지가 있다.

→ 문항수:　　　16문항

→ 빈출 빈칸 위치: 마지막 문장 〉처음 문장 〉중간 문장

→ 빈출 지문 유형: 인문과학 〉사회과학 〉실용문(공지, 뉴스, 광고) 〉자연과학

→ 측정 영역:　　글의 전반적인 이해 능력 및 논리적인 흐름 파악 능력을 평가한다.

→ 빈출 연결어:　For example[instance], However, Rather, Yet, In addition

2 기출문제 대표 예제

This registration form must be completed and postmarked by the 25th of this month in order to be considered for the speech contest. In order to provide proper evidence of your current academic standing, the enclosed form is to be filled out and signed by an appropriate school official, usually a guidance counselor. The speech must be typed and have margins of no less than one inch. All other formatting should be standard. To summarize, make sure that the envelope you send us includes your _____.

(a) notarized registration form as filled in by the 25th
(b) first draft of the proposed speech you are to give
(c) list of all previous entries to this event and any awards won
✔(d) completed and signed registration form and typed speech

☞ 번역

웅변 대회에 참가하려면 등록 양식은 작성 후 이번 달 25일까지 우체국 소인이 찍혀야 유효합니다. 자신의 현재 학문적 위치에 대한 적절한 증빙을 위해 동봉 양식을 해당 학교 직원, 일반적으로는 안내 상담원이 작성하고 서명해야 합니다. 연설문은 타이핑해야 하며 1인치의 여백이 있어야 합니다. 이외의 포맷은 표준을 따릅니다. 요약하면 이곳으로 보내는 봉투 안에 작성 후 서명이 되어 있는 등록 양식과 타이핑된 연설문이 있는지 확인해 주시기 바랍니다.

(a) 25일까지 작성되어 공증된 등록 양식

(b) 연설 내용의 초안

(c) 본 이벤트에 대한 이전 참가 목록과 수상 경력

(d) 작성 후 서명이 들어간 등록 양식과 타이핑된 연설문

⊞ 기출 POINT

문제 유형: 대의 파악 / 실용문(안내)

안내 지문은 대개 정보를 나열하는 구성을 갖고 있다. 전체 대의를 파악해 보면 등록 양식이 갖추어야 할 조건을 밝히고 있다. 그런 다음 빈칸 문장과 바로 앞을 주의 깊게 분석해야 한다. 여기서 핵심 표현은 To summarize, 즉 앞에서 나열한 정보를 요약하는 표현이 나와야 함을 알 수 있다. 따라서 정답은 (d). 나머지 선택지는 지문에서 나왔던 표현들, 또는 연상된 표현들로 혼동을 유발하고 있는 오답들이다.

3 대비 전략

→ 절대 시간이 부족한 파트이므로 문장을 모두 해석하려 하지 말고 모르는 단어나 표현이 나와도 건너뛰고(skip) 문맥을 통해 흐름을 파악하는 연습을 한다.

→ 문제 푸는 순서를 연습한다. 먼저 지문을 훑어 읽고 대의를 파악한 후 빈칸 문장과 그 앞뒤를 분석하는 것이 정석이다. 그런 다음, 선택지를 소거해 나간다.

→ 15번과 16번에 출제되는 연결어 문제는 빈칸 앞뒤가 결정적인 단서가 된다. 예시, 결과, 역접, 첨가 등 다양한 연결어의 종류와 기능을 익혀두자.

4 오답 함정 피해가기

→ 지문에 나왔던 표현을 그대로 사용하지만 지문에 근거가 제시되어 있지 않은 선택지가 대표적인 오답 유형이다.

→ 지문 내용과 연상되는 내용이지만 논리적으로 연결되지 않는 오답 선택지들이 제시된다. Part 1의 핵심은 논리적으로 연결되는지 파악하는 것이다.

→ 상식 선에서 사실일 것 같은 선택지를 고르지 말고 주어진 지문으로만 유기적인 논리를 따져 봐야 한다.

Part 2

1 출제 유형

100단어 내외의 지문과 이와 연관된 질문으로 구성돼 있다. 실용문과 비전문적 학술문이 모두 지문으로 출제되고, 질문은 크게 세 가지 – 대의 파악(main idea), 세부 사항(correct), 유추(inference) – 로 분류된다.

→ 문항수:　　　21문항

→ 빈출 질문 유형: 세부 사항(10문항) 〉 대의 파악(6문항) 〉 유추(5문항)

→ 빈출 지문 유형: 사회 과학 〉 실용문(공지, 광고) 〉 인문 과학

→ 측정 영역:　　 단일 지문에 대한 전체 및 세부 내용 이해 및 유추 능력을 요구한다.

→ 질문 예:　　　 What is the passage mainly about?
　　　　　　　　Which of the following is correct according to the passage?
　　　　　　　　What can be inferred from the passage?

2 기출문제 대표 예제

Making plans for a dream vacation? Want to see the best the world has to offer? Why not let First Travel Agency take care of everything for you? Besides providing a wide range of services, from hotel and flight reservations, to exotic getaway tour packages, whatever we do for you will be first class all the way. Just one call to us and you will fly in first-class comfort, stay in the finest hotels, and eat in the most exclusive restaurants. If you want the best, we'll get it for you. You deserve it.

Q Which of the following is correct about the travel agency?

✔(a) It promises one-stop, high-quality travel services.

(b) It offers discounts for people on tour packages.

(c) It specializes in low-cost traveling for students.

(d) It provides first-class travel services for celebrities.

☞ 번역

꿈 같은 휴가 계획을 세우고 있나요? 세상에서 줄 수 있는 가장 멋진 것을 보고 싶으십니까? 퍼스트 여행사에서 고객을 위한 모든 것을 관리하도록 하세요. 호텔과 항공편 예약에서부터 이국적인 휴가 여행 패키지에 이르기까지 폭넓은 서비스를 제공할 뿐 아니라 모든 것을 1등급으로 제공해 드릴 것입니다. 전화 한 통이면 편안한 1등석 비행과 최고의 호텔 숙박, 최고급 레스토랑에서의 식사를 즐길 수 있습니다. 최고를 원하면 저희가 해드리겠습니다. 고객님은 그럴 자격이 있습니다.

Q 여행사에 대해 옳은 내용은?

(a) 원스톱 고품질 여행 서비스를 약속한다.

(b) 여행 패키지 이용객에게 할인을 제공한다.

(c) 학생들을 위한 저렴한 여행 전문이다.

(d) 명사들에게 1등급 여행을 제공한다.

문제 유형: 세부 사항 / 실용문(광고)

구체적인 정보가 많이 제공되는 광고 지문은 세부 사항 문제로 종종 출제된다. 세부 사항이라 해도 전체 주제(최고급 여행 서비스 제공)와 연관 있는 내용이 선택지로 제시되게 마련이다. 여기서도 (b), (c)의 할인, 저렴 등의 내용은 전체 주제와 어울리지 않으므로 오답인 것을 알 수 있다. (d)는 1등급 여행을 제공하는 것은 맞지만 명사들이라는 언급이 없으므로 오답이다. (d)와 같이 부분적으로만 옳은 내용을 제시하는 것도 흔한 오답 패턴이니 주의한다. 자세히 보면 지문에 나왔던 표현(tour packages)을 그대로 사용한 (b)는 오답인 반면, 지문에 나온 first-class, finest hotels 등을 one-stop, high-quality와 같이 다른 표현으로 바꾼 (a)는 정답임을 알 수 있다.

3 대비 전략

→ 지문 파악의 1단계 훈련은 주제 찾기이다. 문장 하나하나를 다 해석하려 하지 말고 키워드를 중심으로 훑어 읽기하면서 주제를 파악하는 연습을 해보자.

→ 세부 사항 파악 문제 유형은 질문을 먼저 읽고 지문을 읽은 후 선택지를 소거하는 방법으로 해보자. 이때 선택지가 언급된 문장을 찾아(scanning) 중점적으로 읽는 기술이 필요하다.

→ 영어 지문 구조를 파악해 두자. 두괄식, 즉 첫 문장에 중심 아이디어가 제시되는 경우가 대부분이므로 첫 문장에서 앞으로 전개될 내용을 가늠할 수 있어야 한다.

4 오답 함정 피해가기

→ 대의 파악 문제 유형의 경우 너무 일반적이거나 지엽적인 사실을 열거한 선택지는 오답 함정이다.

→ 세부 사항 문제 유형의 경우 지문에서 언급되지 않은 사실을 언급하거나, 지문과 연관 없는 상식적인 사실을 언급한 선택지가 오답으로 자주 등장한다.

→ 유추 유형 문제에서는 단순한 사실을 언급한 선택지나 지문 내용을 너무 광범위하게 상식선에서 진술한 오답 유형에 유의한다.

Part 3

1 출제 유형

4~5문장으로 된 한 단락의 지문을 읽고 글의 흐름상 어색한 선택지를 고르는 문제 유형이다.

→ 문항수:　　　3문항

→ 빈출 지문 유형: 인문과학 〉 사회과학 〉 자연과학

→ 측정 영역:　　　지문에 대한 논리적 흐름 파악 능력을 요구한다.

2 기출문제 대표 예제

> Sociologists do not agree completely on just what a social class is or what the class structure of modern capitalism looks like. (a) Traditional sociologists define class in terms of occupation and generally identify five classes: upper, upper-middle, lower-middle, working, and lower classes. (b) Marxist sociologists conceptualize class in terms of relations of property ownership and workplace authority. ✔(c) The English idiom "in a class by oneself" refers to the uniqueness of an individual. (d) The Marxist sociologist Erick Wright identifies six basic classes within contemporary capitalism.

☞ 번역

사회학자들은 사회 계급이 무엇인가, 혹은 현대 자본주의의 계급 구조가 어떻게 구성되어 있는가에 대해 완전한 의견일치를 보이지 않는다. (a) 전통적인 사회학자들은 계급을 직업에 따라 정의하여 일반적으로 다섯 개, 즉 상층, 중상층, 중하층, 노동자, 하층 계급으로 분류한다. (b) 마르크스주의 사회학자들은 재산 소유와 직무 권한의 관계에 따라 계급의 개념을 정의한다. (c) 영어 관용구 '타의 추종을 불허하는'은 개인의 고유성을 나타낸다. (d) 마르크스주의 사회학자 에릭 라이트는 당대의 자본주의 내에 여섯 개의 기본 계급이 있다고 규정한다.

⊞ 기출 POINT

문제 유형: 논리적 흐름 파악 / 사회과학

지문 전체 대의는 첫 문장에 드러나 있다. 사회학자들의 계급에 대해 동의하지 않고 있다는 것은 여러 견해가 있다는 뜻이며 이 단락에서 그 견해들이 나열될 것임을 암시한다. 선택지 (a), (b), (d)는 모두 사회 계급에 대한 견해들이며 이와 동떨어진 문장은 개인의 고유성을 언급하고 있는 (c)다.

3 대비 전략

→ 주제를 벗어나는 문장을 찾아내는 것이므로 전체 요지를 파악하는 연습은 아무리 강조해도 지나치지 않다. 주제문과 키워드를 찾는 연습을 통해 대의 파악을 하는 습관을 들인다.

→ 하나의 주제로 묶인 하나의 단락에서 각 문장의 역할을 따져보면서 공부한다. 보통 단락은 주제문과 주제를 뒷받침하는 보조 문장들로 이루어지며 보조 문장에는 예시, 근거, 결과, 반박 등이 있다.

→ 연결어에 유의하여 문장 간의 논리적 관계를 파악하는 공부를 해두도록 한다.

4 오답 함정 피해가기

→ 같은 소재를 다루고 있으나 전체 주제에서 벗어나는 문장이 오답으로 제시된다.

→ 글의 어조(찬성, 비판, 반박 등)가 갑자기 바뀌면 오답일 가능성이 높다.

→ 한 단락은 하나의 주제를 다루므로 새로운 주제의 문장이 나오면 오답이다.

Model Test

문제

Listening Comprehension CD1
Grammar
Vocabulary
Reading Comprehension

해 설 및 정 답

LISTENING COMPREHENSION

DIRECTIONS

1. In the Listening Comprehension section, all content will be presented orally rather than in written form.

2. This section contains 4 parts. In parts I and II, each passage will be read only once. In parts III and IV, each passage and its corresponding question will be read twice. But in all sections, the options will be read only once. After listening to the passage and question, listen to the options and choose the best answer.

Part I Questions 1—15

You will now hear fifteen conversation fragments, each made up of a single spoken statement followed by four spoken responses. Choose the most appropriate response to the statement.

Part II Questions 16—30

You will now hear fifteen conversation fragments, each made up of three spoken statements followed by four spoken responses. Choose the most appropriate response to complete the conversation.

Part III **Questions 31—45**

You will now hear fifteen complete conversations. For each item, you will hear a conversation and its corresponding question, both of which will be read twice. Then you will hear four options which will be read only once. Choose the option that best answers the question.

Part IV **Questions 46—60**

You will now hear fifteen spoken monologues. For each item, you will hear a monologue and its corresponding question, both of which will be read twice. Then you will hear four options which will be read only once. Choose the option that best answers the question.

GRAMMAR

Part I **Questions 1—20**

Choose the best answer for the blank.

1. A : I'm going to move to the Templeton area next month.

B : What a coincidence! _____.

(a) So I am
(b) So am I
(c) So do I
(d) So I do

2. A : Do you think the economy is getting worse in the new administration?

B : That is _____ recently.

(a) everyone's mind on
(b) everyone's on mind
(c) on mind everyone's
(d) on everyone's mind

3. A : Did you paint your bedroom yourself?

B : No, I _____.

(a) have painted it
(b) had it painted
(c) was painted
(d) had been painted

4. A : *Mamma Mia* is coming to the Sejong Center for the Performing Arts. Have you seen it?

B : Yes, I _____ it in London last year.

(a) see
(b) saw
(c) have seen
(d) had seen

5. A : I'm supposed to give a 5-minute speech on green energy and I don't know where to start.

B : I _____ a good book you would find helpful. Do you want to borrow it?

(a) am having
(b) have
(c) have had
(d) had

6. A : How was the Science Expo?

B : We had fun _____ with some of the exhibits.

(a) to look around and experiment
(b) looking around and experimenting
(c) looked around and experimented
(d) to looking around and experimenting

7. A : Something about you looks different.

B : I got my hair _____, actually.

(a) dye
(b) dyed
(c) dying
(d) to dye

8. A : Excuse me, but haven't we met before?

B : Yes, I think we go to _____ church.

(a) each same
(b) a same
(c) the same
(d) same

9. A : Excuse me. Do you work here?

   B : Yes, I do. Can I help you _____ something?

   (a) for
   (b) to
   (c) with
   (d) by

10. A : Are you going to the library this afternoon? I have a couple of books to return.

    B : I don't think so, but if I _____, I'll let you know.

    (a) will
    (b) could
    (c) would
    (d) do

11. A : We should have fixed the roof sooner.

    B : I know. _____, the house would not be in such bad shape now.

    (a) We did so
    (b) Had we done so
    (c) Have we done so
    (d) Did we do so

12. A : Can I move to a room with a better view?

    B : Sure. Would you like a room _____ the beach?

    (a) to face
    (b) facing
    (c) to face to
    (d) facing to

13. A : Do you happen _____ where my cell phone is?

    B : Oh, no. You've lost it again, haven't you?

    (a) knowing
    (b) to be knowing
    (c) to know
    (d) to have known

14. A : Which one would you prefer of these two shirts?

    B : I'd like the plaid _____.

    (a) one
    (b) it
    (c) that
    (d) thing

15. A : How do you like _____ here in New York?

    B : The people are very friendly and the cost of living is not as high as I expected.

    (a) yours
    (b) that
    (c) them
    (d) it

16. A : How long will it take to reinstall the software?

    B : It should be done _____ 3 or 4 hours.

    (a) until
    (b) by
    (c) in
    (d) for

17. A : How was Joan's wedding last weekend?

B : You _____ have seen it. It was the most beautiful wedding I've ever been to.

(a) should
(b) must
(c) could
(d) would

18. A : What do you want to know?

B : Who is the guy _____ with Julie?

(a) dance
(b) dances
(c) dancing
(d) danced

19. A : What is Mike doing? He was supposed to be here half an hour ago!

B : Speak of the devil. _____.

(a) Here comes he
(b) He came here
(c) So comes he
(d) Here he comes

20. A : Do you think Sue will accept the suggestion?

B : I'm not sure, _____.

(a) I hope
(b) hoping so
(c) so I hope it
(d) but I hope so

Part II Questions 21—40

Choose the best answer for the blank.

---

21. Whenever Laura feels depressed, she _____.

(a) to herself buys a pair of shoes
(b) buys herself a pair of shoes
(c) bought a pair of shoes for herself
(d) has bought a pair of shoes herself

22. He found _____ about the mistake he made at work.

(a) it embarrassing talks
(b) embarrassing it to talk
(c) talking embarrassment
(d) it embarrassing to talk

23. I have traveled to many places but _____.

(a) I've never been to Turkey
(b) never I've been to Turkey
(c) I've been never to Turkey
(d) I've been to Turkey never

24. All the equipment and medical instruments are cleaned and _____ thoroughly before reusing them.

(a) sterilized
(b) would have been sterilized
(c) be sterilized
(d) would be sterilized

25. _____ in a neighborhood coffee shop, she was completely absorbed by her book.

(a) Sitting
(b) To sit
(c) Sat
(d) Being sat

26. If _____, inflammation of the stomach can ultimately lead to an ulcer.

(a) left untreated
(b) leaving untreated
(c) having left untreated
(d) had been left untreated

27. Each group _____ twelve men and women.

(a) consist of
(b) consists of
(c) is consisting of
(d) has consisted

28. You will be shocked to see how many second-hand smokers die of _____ every year.

(a) lung cancer
(b) the lung cancer
(c) any lung cancer
(d) the lung cancers

29. I love this house, the windows and balconies _____ show the character and lifestyle of San Francisco through their Victorian style.

(a) that
(b) what
(c) of which
(d) to which

30. During the interview, applicants are asked to choose to answer _____ of the two questions they prefer.

(a) what
(b) which
(c) whatever
(d) whichever

31. _____ the support of his wife, he would never have become a lawyer.

(a) If it were
(b) Without
(c) Had it not for
(d) Except for

32. The President is likely _____ the agreement on tax reform next week.

(a) sign
(b) to sign
(c) to have signed
(d) being signed

33. He always wanted to do something to make _____ for the underprivileged.

(a) a world the better place
(b) the world a better place
(c) the place a better world
(d) a place the better world

34. For every fifty miles north that you go, the temperature gets lower _____ one degree Celsius.

(a) at
(b) for
(c) to
(d) by

35. Eating too much is _____ as malnutrition.

(a) every bit as harmful
(b) as harmful every bit
(c) as every bit harmful
(d) harmful as every bit

36. A chemical substance secreted by ants prevents them from _____ alive.

(a) being buried
(b) buried
(c) be buried
(d) burying

37. Only in your dreams _____.

(a) it will be possible
(b) will it be possible
(c) it is possible
(d) has been it possible

38. I'd rather _____ until we get the final decision from the Board of Directors.

(a) not tell you anything
(b) tell not you anything
(c) not to tell you anything
(d) do not tell you anything

39. This section lists the questions _____ about the product.

(a) most asked frequently
(b) frequently most asked
(c) frequently asked most
(d) asked most frequently

40. Because Mr. Bucks is a bit hard _____, you might have to repeat whatever you have to say.

(a) to hear
(b) by hearing
(c) of hearing
(d) hearing

Part III   Questions 41—45

Identify the option that contains an awkward expression or an error in grammar.

41. (a) A : We've run short of paper for the Xerox machine. Will you order some for us?

(b) B : Sure. It'll be delivered by tomorrow if I place the order now.

(c) A : Great. Would you let me know as soon as it will be here?

(d) B : No problem. If there is anything else I can do for you, let me know.

42. (a) A : It seems people are going to the movies less often these days.

(b) B : Actually, studies show people now go to the movies than ever.

(c) A : I thought with the Internet, people wouldn't bother getting out of the house to watch movies anymore.

(d) B : But seeing a movie at a movie theater is totally different.

43. (a) A : I'm going to the mall. Do you want to come?

(b) B : I'd like to, but I have a few things to take care of right away.

(c) A : Do you want to get something for you?

(d) B : No, I don't need anything, but thanks anyway.

44. (a) A : I totally forgot about the blind date Karl arranged for me!

(b) B : You mean you stood up your date?

(c) A : Yeah, and it was too late when I finally realized it.

(d) B : If I were in his shoes, I had been really pissed off!

45. (a) A : I can't put up with Dennis any longer.

(b) B : Can you tell me what is the exact problem?

(c) A : He always makes such a mess and just walks away.

(d) B : I think you should stop cleaning up after him and confront him about this.

Part IV **Questions 46—50**

Identify the option that contains an awkward expression or an error in grammar.

46. (a) Afrikaans is an Indo-European language that is derived from Dutch. (b) For the most part, it is spoken in South Africa and Namibia, and to outsiders sounds like a mix of German and Dutch. (c) Experts estimate that approximately 6.5 million people worldwide speak Afrikaans as a mother tongue. (d) Afrikaans has been seen long as a natural development from the South-Hollandic Dutch dialect.

47. (a) Someone with a learning disability does not necessarily have a low IQ or an inability to learn. (b) Countries such as the United States and Canada uses the term "learning disability" to refer to psychological and neurological conditions that affect a person's communicative capacities and potential to be taught effectively. (c) The term includes conditions like dysgraphia (writing disorder), dyslexia (reading disorder), dyscalculia (mathematics disorder), and developmental aphasia. (d) Alternatively, the term "learning disability" may be used more generally to refer to any developmental disability, as in the U.K.

48. (a) Society seems to be getting louder and louder. (b) This worries me because it is not only a huge disturbance, but it is also causing people to lose their hearing at a very young age. (c) It seems everywhere I go, to my office to the street to my local café, there has to be some form of dangerously loud sound. (d) If it's not construction or someone blaring music, then it's people arguing or trying to sell things.

49. (a) In the 1700s, philosophers such as Descartes and Hobbes shared a mechanistic view of human behavior. (b) They believed that the underlying reasons for behavior were the avoidance of pain and the quest for pleasure. (c) In later years, many psychoanalysts like Sigmund Freud supported the instinct theory, saying that human behavior could be explained by two major instincts. (d) These were the instinct to survive, such as a drive for sexual reproduction, and the instinct to avoid death, that causes aggression.

50. (a) Argentina has a federal, republican and representative form of government. (b) Executive power is vested in one person, the President, who is directly elected by universal suffrage for a term of four years. (c) The President and the vice-president are chosen by a runoff voting system. (d) If the candidate with the largest number of votes are not attained at least 45% of the vote in the first round of voting, a second round of voting is held.

This is the end of the Grammar section. Do NOT move on to the next section until instructed to do so. You are NOT allowed to turn to any other section of the test.

Vocabulary

Directions

This part of the exam tests your vocabulary skills. You will have 15 minutes to complete the 50 questions. Be sure to follow the directions given by the proctor.

Part I   Questions 1—25

Choose the best answer for the blank.

1. A : I can't see any _____ here.

   B : Me, neither. Do you think we can just jaywalk?

   (a) curb
   (b) crosswalk
   (c) lane
   (d) sidewalk

2. A : Thank you for coming so promptly on such short notice.

   B : No problem. My place is just a stone's _____ away.

   (a) drop
   (b) toss
   (c) fall
   (d) throw

3. A : Are there any women's shoes shops in this mall?

   B : Yes, we've got one on the seventh floor. They've got an excellent collection, and the prices are also quite _____.

   (a) reasonable
   (b) irrational
   (c) outrageous
   (d) plausible

4. A : I'm sorry, but there are no rooms available. May is our _____ season of the year.

   B : Can you tell me when the off season is, then?

   (a) pinnacle
   (b) height
   (c) peak
   (d) summit

5. A : I'm looking forward to working on the new project.

   B : But you can't _____ the possibility of Ronald being assigned to the job instead of you.

   (a) overlook
   (b) oversee
   (c) overthrow
   (d) override

6. A : Won't you stay with me for _____ support when the boss makes his decision?

   B : Sure thing. You know I'm always here for you.

   (a) ethical
   (b) morale
   (c) moral
   (d) upright

7. A : Great presentation!

   B : Thanks for the _____.

   (a) complement
   (b) compliment
   (c) compliance
   (d) completion

8 A : I heard the prisoner is still on the loose.

   B : Yeah, it seems that police dogs lost the _____ and he just disappeared in the darkness.

   (a) stink
   (b) scent
   (c) odor
   (d) reek

9. A : Sorry for dropping by. Were you in the middle of something?

   B : Not really. You've come at a(n) _____ time.

   (a) awkward
   (b) perfect
   (c) precise
   (d) hasty

10. A : Do you know how to format a hard drive?

    B : I'm sorry, but unfortunately I'm computer _____.

    (a) blind
    (b) savvy
    (c) illiterate
    (d) alien

11. A : Did you like the dress you ordered online?

    B : The pictures were deceiving. It didn't _____ my expectations.

    (a) answer for
    (b) come up to
    (c) live with
    (d) match with

12. A : Do you like tango?

    B : No, it's not _____. I much prefer salsa.

    (a) the tip of the iceberg
    (b) a hair of the dog
    (c) my cup of tea
    (d) the cream of the crop

13. A : How did you find your roommate?

    B : I put an ad in the _____ section of the school newspaper and he responded to it.

    (a) editorial
    (b) obituary
    (c) classified
    (d) personals

14. A : Do you know who is _____ the keynote address at the seminar?

    B : I heard it is Dr. Williams, the founder of the Field Robotics Center.

    (a) speaking
    (b) celebrating
    (c) delivering
    (d) fixing

15. A : He told me he forgot to bring his homework.

B : That's a _____ excuse. I don't buy it.

(a) steep
(b) lame
(c) low
(d) slight

16. A : Why was the soccer team's coach _____?

B : I'm not sure, but there's a rumor going around that he accepted bribes.

(a) restrained
(b) dismissed
(c) recruited
(d) dispatched

17. A : Why is Marian working overtime so much these days?

B : She not only has to pay _____ but also has to support her sick dad.

(a) rent
(b) loan
(c) money
(d) lease

18. A : I kept trying to call you last night, but I couldn't get through.

B : Sorry. While watching my _____ favorite show, I left the phone off the hook.

(a) all-time
(b) single
(c) unique
(d) well-versed

19. A : Hi, I wanted to apologize for being so crabby last night. I shouldn't have _____ on you.

B : That's fine. But I hope it won't happen again.

(a) picked it up
(b) taken it out
(c) put it down
(d) given it up

20. A : I'm so nervous. I don't think I can handle this interview.

B : Take a deep breath and _____.

(a) wind up
(b) straighten out
(c) loosen up
(d) burn out

21. A : I'm indebted to you. I couldn't have come this far without your help.

B : You're making me _____. It was nothing, actually.

(a) blush
(b) flush
(c) brass
(d) plush

22. A : What do you think of the government's new healthcare policy?

B : I hate their healthcare reform ideas. They're just another _____ scheme to deceive the public!

(a) delectable
(b) odious
(c) innocuous
(d) odorous

23. A : I have to get out of here. Where is the nearest _____?

    B : There is one down the hall.

    (a) retreat
    (b) exit
    (c) outlet
    (d) getaway

24. A : What do you say to my suggestion?

    B : Your idea sounds good, but I'd rather _____ my original idea.

    (a) drop in
    (b) lay out
    (c) stick with
    (d) carry off

25. A : The plague that hit Europe in the Middle Ages was horrible.

    B : Absolutely. I heard it _____ almost a third of the population.

    (a) passed away
    (b) cleaned up
    (c) wiped out
    (d) let down

Part II   **Questions 26−50**

Choose the best answer for the blank.

---

26. Richer countries are asked to take the initiative to stop greenhouse gas _____.

    (a) assuagements
    (b) recuperations
    (c) propagations
    (d) emissions

27. Through the _____ of fossils, paleontologists can learn more about dinosaurs.

    (a) reparation
    (b) restoration
    (c) reinstatement
    (d) reestablishment

28. The building was not as close as it looked, so it _____ me a while to walk there.

    (a) brought
    (b) had
    (c) cost
    (d) took

29. Companies should make customer _____ a top priority since happy customers tend to buy the same brand repeatedly.

    (a) approval
    (b) atonement
    (c) contempt
    (d) satisfaction

30. The ancient tomb has stood from time _____ on the hill.

(a) imminent
(b) immemorial
(c) impeccable
(d) impetuous

31. Even if you forget your lines, you can _____ on stage.

(a) render
(b) improvise
(c) forge
(d) contrive

32. Those who _____ the speed limit were responsible for more than half of all the car accidents last year.

(a) overcame
(b) outshine
(c) exceeded
(d) outpaced

33. A growing _____ of literature is showing a strong correlation between lack of sleep and memory.

(a) share
(b) bulk
(c) group
(d) body

34. Margaret Thatcher was first _____ the "Iron Lady" for her unrepentant and hard-line policies.

(a) titled
(b) dubbed
(c) recorded
(d) honored

35. The supermarket is _____ discount coupons to its customers to celebrate opening its fifth store in the area.

(a) throwing up
(b) putting through
(c) showing up
(d) giving away

36. _____ our website free for 7 days to decide if it satisfies your needs.

(a) Buy
(b) Try
(c) Experiment
(d) Hold

37. He faces life behind _____ for planting a bomb outside the embassy.

(a) prison
(b) bars
(c) wheels
(d) cell

38. A middle-aged man sued the tobacco company for giving him a fatal illness, but he lost his _____.

(a) file
(b) case
(c) charge
(d) sentence

39. The President made a(n) _____ threat to take health care away from Congress, which he has no power to do.

(a) blank
(b) free
(c) empty
(d) vacant

40. Try to consume the recommended daily _____ of vitamin C.

(a) taking
(b) dose
(c) number
(d) pills

41. The CEO will _____ next week a strategic alliance with eBay.

(a) renounce
(b) denounce
(c) pronounce
(d) announce

42. With vivid 3D graphics, the characters and the scenery in the new video game look astonishingly _____.

(a) realistic
(b) virtual
(c) fake
(d) truthful

43. You need a well-planned and strategic approach when you negotiate your _____.

(a) penalty
(b) salary
(c) fund
(d) income

44. She was smart enough to _____ herself into a managerial position in just three months.

(a) handle
(b) present
(c) maneuver
(d) operate

45. By doing away with the nation's culture, the colonialists _____ its treasured traditions.

(a) confronted
(b) relegated
(c) uprooted
(d) expedited

46. Brigit was embarrassed because she was completely _____ with Jack's novels.

(a) unacquainted
(b) valiant
(c) soothed
(d) deleterious

47. The heart-rending scene showed the character's _____ and her need for her husband's affection and understanding.

(a) satiety
(b) fragility
(c) incurability
(d) levity

48. Even if you're divorced, you still cannot _____ the debts incurred by your spouse during marriage.

(a) repudiate
(b) abdicate
(c) remand
(d) construe

49. Even the most _____ observer may fail to notice this flaw in the vase.

(a) astute
(b) vigorous
(c) insolent
(d) obsequious

50. The lecturer _____ a funny episode into his speech to keep the attention of the audience.

(a) abashed
(b) interjected
(c) condoned
(d) deluded

This is the end of the Vocabulary section. Do NOT move on to the Reading Comprehension section until instructed to do so. You are NOT allowed to turn to any other section of the test.

Reading
comprehension

Part I   **Questions 1—16**

Read the passage. Then choose the option that best completes the passage.

1.   A trade embargo is a strategic political move by one country to make another country either do something or refrain from doing something. For the most part, the country imposing the trade embargo will prohibit most or all people in their country from doing business with the country against which the trade embargo is imposed. One of the most famous trade embargoes in the modern era is the trade embargo the United States laid on Cuba. The embargo was established in 1962 in the hope that prohibiting trade with Cuba would _____, which would in turn inspire Cubans to overthrow Fidel Castro and implement a democratic government. The embargo failed in its mission and is still in place to this day.

(a) weaken the country's economy

(b) strengthen ties with the country

(c) incite hatred toward the United States

(d) grant asylum to political protesters

2.   Welcome to Loyal to Nature, your source for organic and natural products. Choose from a wide range of cosmetics, cleaning products, and much more. Be assured that at Loyal to Nature, our products _____. We are committed to the environment and everything we sell is 100% earth-friendly. After conducting many trials using various plants and fragrant essential oils, we are now proud to bring you our safe line of Loyal to Nature products. And of course, we never test anything on animals. Buy today and be glad to know that you are loyal to nature.

(a) are free of any scents

(b) remain on earth for years to come

(c) do not have any harmful substances

(d) contain a high percentage of water

3.   _____ *Lord of the Flies*, a novel by the British author William Golding. The story centers on a group of schoolboys stuck on a deserted island without any adults. They try to live on their own and govern themselves—with disastrous consequences. Some may be shocked by the violence in the novel, but Golding's message about human nature still resonates with current readers. Thus, it is required reading in classrooms around the world. The book discusses relevant themes such as individual welfare versus the common good, and civilization attempting to control chaos. In 2005, *Times* magazine chose it as one of the 100 best English-language novels from 1923 to the present.

(a) Fewer books have inspired so much wrath and criticism as
(b) An important work of fiction still read in many schools today is
(c) One of the more obscure and overlooked books is
(d) Students in the classroom rarely enjoy learning about

4. The Kaoshin government ended a nearly 2-week-old state of emergency Monday, following last week's violent political unrest. Prime Minister Vinisit Shamajiva lifted the emergency order for the capital city Phulong and nearby provinces, according to a government spokesman. National security agencies have also indicated that the threat of violence has eased. Immediately after Shamajiva's state-of-emergency declaration, scores of protesters stormed the Prime Minister's residence and pelted his car with sticks, stones, and debris. Fortunately for the Prime Minister, _____. Shamajiva acknowledged, "I was indeed afraid for my own life" when he was faced with the unruly crowd.

(a) he was not the focus of any violence
(b) he is familiar with animal pelts
(c) he brought a halt to the state of emergency
(d) he managed to escape unharmed

5. Told in an extraordinarily refreshing voice, *Yearning to Live* is an unforgettable novel about one woman's struggle to cope with tragedy and how she learns to love in the process. *Yearning to Live* is a love story unlike any other. Author Marta Kemmelman takes readers on an intense journey that allows them to see the painful reality of someone who must fight the odds just to survive. _____ will appreciate the sharp, complex insights on life's setbacks in the book. Now available in paperback for $12.95 online or at a fine bookstore near you.

(a) Those delighted by cheerful prose
(b) Anyone who has been stricken with grief
(c) Readers attempting to write their own novels
(d) People looking for a light read

6. People running addiction centers in the United States are seeing more and more women coming in for treatment for Internet addiction. Those seeking help are young and often new mothers. They are addicted to blogs, message boards, and virtual world sites such as Second Life. Sadly, these moms are part of a growing addiction seen globally. The increase of those who are dependent has psychiatrists trying to get Internet addiction recognized as an official mental disorder that can be treated just like alcohol dependency. One survey in the U.S. found that 14 percent of Internet users find it hard to stay away from it for several days at a time, and _____.

(a) officials are classifying the dependence as a serious illness
(b) the responses show signs that the addiction is waning
(c) that number is even higher in other countries around the world
(d) that they have little remorse for the effect it has on their lives

7.

Dear Mr. Luanda,

I am following up on the previous three letters we sent to you regarding your delinquent account. _____ in the amount of $312.93 for over six months. We are hoping that we will not be forced to forward your account to a collection agency. Unfortunately, if we do not receive payment by December 15, we are left with no alternative but to take action, which may permanently and adversely affect your good credit rating. We urge you in the strongest terms possible to resolve this matter immediately. We hope to receive your payment soon.

Sincerely,

Janis Robbins
Accounts Receivable

(a) You are collecting on a delinquent bill
(b) Your account has been unpaid
(c) We would like to offer you an increase
(d) A low interest rate will be applied

8. Teachers may make students spit out their gum, but chewing gum _____ _____. Recent studies show that munching on a stick of sugar-free gum can curb your appetite and improve your memory. Research funded by the Wrigley Science Institute shows more reasons to chew away on gum, including a finding that chewing gum can lead to better performance in classrooms. Teachers may have to rethink banning gum and might instead hand out a stick to each student.

(a) has been known to benefit children
(b) can provide necessary nutrients for kids
(c) can cure certain diseases
(d) may not deserve the bad reputation it has

9. When you get an itch, such as a mosquito bite, cells in the skin release chemical called histamine. Certain sensory neurons respond to the histamine and carry a message up to the spinal cord that alerts it to the itch. From there the message is sent to other neurons that run to the thalamus in the brain, which processes and relays sensory information. These neurons are part of a bundle of spinal neurons called the spinothalamic tract. From the thalamus, the "itch" message is passed to the cerebral cortex, which interprets the signals and _____.

(a) produces the itchy sensation   (b) releases the histamines
(c) the spinal cord receives the signals   (d) relieves the itch

10. You may have been told that it is wrong to judge people based on their appearance, but many social scientists say there are reasons why we quickly categorize people based on how they look. This kind of stereotyping is important to the way we function even when those judgments are very wrong. Judging people by their appearance means putting them quickly into impersonal categories, much like deciding whether an animal is a mouse or a squirrel. Stereotyping is how we make sense of the information before us. Long ago, this ability could have meant the difference between life and death. People had to ascertain whether a person appeared to have malignant or benign intent and _____.

(a) search for refuge in their vicinity
(b) shun those who seemed dangerous
(c) gravitate toward those who are muscular
(d) judge them for who they really are

11. In 1989, an oil tanker called the Exxon Valdez dumped about 11 million gallons of crude oil into Prince William Sound, Alaska. The spill, the largest in U.S. history, _____. In fact, thousands of birds, otters, fish, and other sea creatures died immediately, and scientists today are still seeing the lingering effects from the oil spill. They have found pollutants in the blubber of killer whales that swim in the area and a decrease in their population. Toxic substances may keep the whales from reproducing successfully. Scientists suspect that these whales will not recover for another 10 years.

(a) was particularly detrimental to animals
(b) was mediated by scientists studying wildlife
(c) took place in an area known to have many icebergs
(d) was quite costly for the residents of Alaska

12. A common problem among couples is that the woman wants to air her frustrations and just wants an open ear, but the man will try to deliver a solution instead. When two people are having trouble with communication, the one giving advice needs to develop new listening skills. At the same time, the person who wants to complain needs to be specific in what they want. One way to express that is to say, "I really want to get something off my chest. Is it okay if I just vent and you listen?" _____ will go a long way towards bridging misunderstandings.

(a) Bending the truth when necessary
(b) Being subtle with what you really want to say
(c) Stating your intentions up front
(d) Using sign language like this

13. Although historians credit the ancient Greeks, specifically Athenians, with forming the first democracy around 500 BC, _____. The important thing, and the biggest difference between Athenian democracy and almost all subsequent democracies, is Athenians practiced a remarkably direct—and not representative—form of democracy. With very few exceptions, Athenians did not vote for politicians to represent them, the citizens themselves voted on almost every policy, from war to taxes to construction.

(a) they did not live in the same kind of democracy as we now have
(b) the Greeks preferred a more dictatorial style of government
(c) elections were infrequent or unreliable for the most part
(d) only a handful of people were involved in the democratic process

14. The worst offense a presenter can commit is to bore his or her audience. These days, traditional lectures and slideshows _____. So some savvy presenters are now using high-tech pens to track presentations. Others display PowerPoint slideshows online. These technologically jazzed-up presentations are creating a lot of buzz about what the future of presentations might hold. One California startup company has conceived of "pencasts," which are made using the Pulse SmartPen and specially gridded paper. The pen goes beyond writing duties and has a voice recorder that "notes" which notes were taken and at which point in the recording. Expect to see other new gadgets meant to wow audiences during presentations in the near future.

(a) are barely able to launch products for companies
(b) often fail to convey what the presenter intends
(c) are not happening as often as they used to
(d) are not enough to keep people's attention

15. Swine flu is on the minds of many doctors and scientists. This strain of influenza does not usually infect humans, but several people have become afflicted in North America, particularly if they had exposure to pigs. This virus has genes from North American swine and avian influenza, human influenza, and swine influenza normally found in Asia and Europe. Scientists emphasize that eating pork will not lead to swine flu. However, someone afflicted with swine flu can spread it to other humans. _____, soldiers in Mexico handed out masks for people to wear and advised against kissing other people.

(a) By the same token   (b) Furthermore
(c) Therefore   (d) Thereafter

16. The Montessori Method is a child-centered alternative form of education, based on the child development theories of Maria Montessori (1870-1952). Montessori was an Italian doctor who devoted herself to teaching the children of Rome's ghettos. Her visionary methods launched an educational movement which has become popular around many parts of the world. The basic tenet of the Montessori approach is allowing children to learn on their own while being guided by the teacher. Teachers at Montessori schools diverge from traditional instructors who correct work and mark up assignments in red ink. _____, the teacher evaluates what the child has learned and then guides him or her into new areas of discovery.

(a) For all that   (b) Similarly
(c) Rather   (d) Yet

17. Tourists visiting South Africa will undoubtedly see a wide array of crafts being sold at curio markets or on a street corner. The handiwork displays the inventiveness of South African artists. In addition to carvings made from traditional stone and wood, and sculptures using beads, fabric, and clay, there are pieces made from bottle caps, beer cans, and telephone wires. Some craftsmen use labels from food cans to create colorful papier mache bowls. Wire is another favored medium, as seen in renderings of cars, motorcycles, and even radios that actually work.

Q : What is the best title for the passage?

(a) Tourism in South Africa   (b) The Ingenuity of South African Artisans
(c) Curio Markets of South Africa   (d) Branding the Art of South Africa

18. The 1967 World's Fair was originally scheduled to be held in Moscow to commemorate the 50th anniversary of the Russian Revolution, but financial concerns caused the Soviet Union to rescind itself from consideration and the bid was bestowed upon Montreal, Canada instead. The International and Universal Exposition, or Expo 67 as it is commonly called, was considered to be the most successful World's Fair of the 20th century. Over 50 million visitors and 62 nations participated. It also set the record for the most attendants in a single day for a world's fair, with 569,000 visitors on its third day.

Q : What is the passage mainly about?

(a) A large public exhibition in Montreal
(b) Financial woes of the Soviet Union
(c) Various sites of the World's Fair
(d) Links between the Russian Revolution and World Expos

19. Cold sores, those painful blisters that form around the mouth, are not just annoying—they are also highly contagious. These cold sores, also known as fever blisters, are the result of the herpes simplex virus one (HSV-1), a relatively harmless and common virus. The virus can spread through human contact but can also survive on towels, cups, and other household items. Unfortunately, once you have the virus, you have it for life and there is currently no cure for it. Sometimes the virus lies dormant in the body and is triggered by exposure to the sun, stress, or a toothache.

Q : What is the main idea of the passage?

(a) The proper treatment for cold sores
(b) How to prevent the herpes simplex virus one
(c) Mortality rates for people with cold sores
(d) The virus that causes cold sores

20. Children in previous generations seemed to have less to worry about than children and adolescents today. According to a study, terrorist attacks, war, and shootings are among the 20 most common fears for children. Experts say that overexposure to television news is to blame for creating anxiety in children. Young kids are not mature enough to understand events on the news such as kidnapping. They also advise that parents get counseling for children who show symptoms of anxiety, such as difficulty sleeping, headaches, and stomach pains.

Q : What is the passage mainly about?

(a) Concern among parents over violence   (b) How children are portrayed on television
(c) Anxiety among today's children   (d) Why the media should be censored

21. Wildfires have consumed thousands of acres and destroyed dozens of homes in Kansas. In a written statement, Governor Michael Ingram said, "This has already proved to be a devastating event for the area, and if the fires persist we will have to seek federal assistance." The hardest-hit area is Finger Valley, a region abundant with corn and wheat farms. The officials are estimating damage to crops worth hundreds of thousands of dollars. One farmer who helped his family evacuate in time said, "That was my life's work all gone in one fell swoop."

Q : What is the best title for the news report?

(a) Officials Raise Alert for Wildfires
(b) Kansans Assess Damages after Natural Disaster
(c) Governor Seeks Federal Assistance after Wildfire Damages
(d) Wildfires Finally Put Out in Kansas

22. Zakat, or "alms for the poor," is the Islamic principle of giving to charity. Today, it serves largely as the welfare contribution to poor and deprived people in the Muslim world. Muslims view zakat as a way of purifying themselves from their greed and safeguarding future business. Furthermore, zakat purifies the person who receives it because it keeps him from begging and envying the wealthy. According to the laws of Islam, those who do not pay zakat will not have their prayers accepted. Zakat can be demonstrated in many ways. For example, it is not uncommon to see families in Iraq cook food for the homeless or even invite them to dinner regardless of their level of wealth.

Q : What is the passage mainly about?

(a) A religious practice of helping those in need
(b) Traditional Muslim convictions in modern society
(c) The role of relief organizations in certain parts of the world
(d) The most important law of Islam

23. With the end of communism in Eastern Europe and the fall of the Soviet Union in the late 1980s and early 90s, North Korea's economy declined sharply. In fact, gross national income per capita is estimated to have fallen by about one-third between 1990 and 2002. The economy has since stabilized and shown some small improvements, especially in recent years, though that is due mostly to increased inter-Korean economic cooperation. North Korea passed some relatively modest wage and price reforms in 2002, and has increasingly tolerated markets and a small private sector as the state-run distribution system has deteriorated.

Q : Which of the following is correct according to the passage?

(a) South and North Korea have been collaborating with each other.
(b) North Korea was down to about 33% of its gross national income from 1990 to 2002.
(c) Aid from overseas has helped North Korea boost its economy.
(d) North Korea is following the example of Eastern Europe and the Soviet Union.

24. Votes were still being counted for Sangala's parliamentary elections, but the ruling Independent Party was already celebrating. People are predicting that Independent Party leader Mbeki Futu will be Sangala's next president, despite his checkered background. Futu has been accused of accepting bribes from lobbyists and was eventually acquitted after a lengthy trial. Futu continues to remain popular with the poor, who make up the majority of this poverty-stricken nation. As one voter said outside the booths, "Futu is one of us. He understands what we need." Pundits anticipate not only a win for Mbeki Futu but a full-on landslide.

Q : Which of the following is correct according to the passage?

(a) People like Futu because he is honest and ethical.
(b) Voters believe that Futu can identify with them.
(c) Experts predict Futu will win by a small margin.
(d) Futu was convicted of bribery charges in the past.

25. Plants absorb carbon dioxide more efficiently amidst pollution than they do in a clean atmosphere. The effects of atmospheric pollution seem to have enhanced plant productivity around the world by as much as 25% from 1960 to 1999. As a result, there was a 10 percent increase in the amount of carbon stored by the land. This has important implications for efforts to fight future climate change. When sunlight is reduced, photosynthesis in plants is reduced as well. However, clouds and atmospheric particles scatter sunlight. Plants are then able to convert more of the available sunlight into growth because fewer leaves are in the shade.

Q : Why does pollution enhance plant productivity?

(a) Particles in the air can disperse sunlight more effectively.
(b) It stimulates photosynthesis in plant life.
(c) It creates better conditions for increasing the number of leaves in the shade.
(d) It increases the amount of ultraviolet rays entering the Earth's atmosphere.

26. Current memory cards hold 10 to 100 gigabits of data per square inch in silicon chips, and they have an estimated life expectancy of only a few decades. Scientists are formulating a new computer memory device that consists of an iron nanoparticle (1/50,000 the width of a human hair) enclosed in a hollow carbon nanotube. When electricity is present, the nanoparticle can be shuttled back and forth with great accuracy, thus creating a programmable memory system that, like a silicon chip, can record digital information and play it back using conventional computer hardware. The device has a storage capacity as high as 1 terabyte per square inch (a trillion bytes of information) and a lifespan of one billion years.

Q : Which of the following is correct according to the passage?

(a) Future memory material will have greater storage capacity within an increased amount of space.
(b) A new memory device can store at least ten times more data than conventional silicon chips.
(c) Today's data storage devices hold a limited amount of data and do not last for more than ten years.
(d) The nanoparticle device can outperform current memory cards but it has some drawbacks.

27. Did you ever wonder how your ears can hear sounds? Inside the ear there are certain cells called "hair cells" that sense vibrations in the air. These cells have tiny hair-like projections, called stereocilia, arranged in rows by height, which in turn bend slightly when sound vibrations reach them. Scientists think the movement opens small pores, called ion channels. As positively charged ions rush into the hair cell, mechanical vibrations are converted into an electrochemical signal. This is what the brain interprets as sound. These ion channels also help protect the ear against sounds that are too loud. The ear adjusts the sensitivity of its ion channels to match the noise level in the environment.

Q : Which of the following is correct according to the passage?

(a) Hair cells are responsible for transforming vibrations into sound.
(b) Stereocilia are tiny hair-like projections containing hair cells.
(c) The ion channels cushion the environment to protect the ear from loud sounds.
(d) Sound is created when sound waves bend within small pores.

28. Mercury, as the smallest rocky planet, has weak gravity, and due to its proximity to the sun it is also scorching hot. These conditions make it difficult for the planet to hold on to its extremely thin atmosphere. However, a solar wind helps maintain the atmospheres, which otherwise may have vanished long ago. This thin gas of electrically charged particles, called a plasma, blows constantly from the surface of the sun and transfers sufficient energy to blast atoms from the surface of Mercury into its atmosphere, replenishing it.

Q : Which of the following is correct according to the passage?

(a) A solar wind blows rocks towards Mercury.
(b) Mercury's thinning atmosphere consists of charged particles.
(c) Plasma from the sun moves atoms into Mercury's atmosphere.
(d) Mercury has weak gravity because it is close to the sun.

29. The Checkers speech was an address delivered by then Republican vice-presidential candidate Richard Nixon on television and radio in 1952. The speech was Nixon's response to critics who had accused him of accepting gifts and misusing funds appropriated for the election campaign. The speech is so named because Nixon declared that he intended to keep one gift—a dog named Checkers. This reference to a pet touched the public and led to an outpouring of support for the senator. The speech has since been mocked, and now the term "Checkers speech" has come more generally to mean any emotional speech by a politician.

Q : Which of the following is correct according to the passage?

(a) Speeches like the Checkers speech have become a useful tool for politicians today.
(b) The current meaning of Checkers speech falls far from Nixon's original intent.
(c) Nixon was found guilty of misappropriating political funds.
(d) The mention of a dog engendered sympathy among voters.

30. Anti-governmentTaliban fighters will withdraw from the Buner district, just 87 kilometers from the Pakistan capital, Islamabad, a spokesman says. The move came soon after Pakistan's President, Asif Ali Zardari, told the national assembly that the military could stop the Taliban and that the country's nuclear weapons were safe. "If anybody challenges the will of the government, then we will react," Asif Ali Zardari said. He further backed up his conviction by saying, "The defense of the country is in capable hands and our nuclear program is in safe hands." It remains to be seen if the Taliban will make another attempt to enter the region.

Q : Which of the following is correct about the Taliban according to the news report?

(a) They will no longer endeavor to infiltrate Pakistan.
(b) They will continue to advance into the Buner district.
(c) They are part of Pakistan's military.
(d) They are opposed to the government of Pakistan.

31. A study suggests that global warming could lead to more human deaths. Researchers in Spain found an increase of cholera cases in Zambia that seem related to climatic factors. For the first time, the results confirm that an increase in environmental temperature six weeks before the rainy season increases the number of people affected by cholera by 4.9%. This disease has a marked seasonal component associated with the rainy season and thrives in high temperatures. Humans can contract the disease from contaminated water and food. Cholera has been known to cause great human, social and economic losses.

Q : Which of the following is correct according to the passage?

(a) Global warming led to more cholera deaths in Africa and Europe.
(b) Cholera is passed directly from one person to another.
(c) Higher temperatures impede the spread of cholera.
(d) Researchers examined the period before the rainy season.

32. Portuguese is one of the world's major languages, ranking 6th according to number of native speakers, 191 to 230 million people. Although Brazil is the only Portuguese-speaking nation in the Americas, it is home to half the population of South America. Portuguese is also widely spoken in other areas formerly colonized by Portugal, such as Mozambique. Nine countries list it as their official language, including Macau and Angola. The Portuguese diaspora has created large communities of Portuguese speakers in various regions along the east coast of the United States and in Ontario, Canada as well.

Q : Why is Portuguese spoken by so many people?

(a) It is an official language in every South American country.
(b) Colonization and immigration have widened its use.
(c) It is widely spoken throughout the United State.
(d) Portugal continues to exert a lot of influence on the Americas.

33. Those who believe that animals are capable of feeling remorse will be heartened by a recent study that examined brain scans of monkeys trying to win a large prize of juice by guessing where it was hidden. When the monkeys were incorrect in their selection and were then shown the location of the prize, the neurons in their brains clearly registered a form of regret. A researcher noted that the monkeys reacted to their losses by changing their subsequent guesses, much like humans shift strategies after missing opportunities. A capacity for regret could thus be advantageous evolutionarily in terms of foraging for food and finding partners who will share resources equitably.

Q : What can be inferred from the passage?

(a) Monkeys who guessed correctly showed similar changes in their brain scans.
(b) All animals are capable of feeling regret.
(c) Researchers rewarded the monkeys who exhibited signs of remorse.
(d) Regret in monkeys may help them to survive.

34. Valence Mutual recognizes the threat posed to both the health of employees and the interests of the company by life-threatening diseases such as, but not limited to, tuberculosis, typhoid, and meningitis. Therefore, Valence Mutual is committed to the promotion of awareness of such conditions among employees. The nurse's office will hold a workshop to educate people about diseases and administer vaccinations for a variety of conditions. The workshop will take place on Tuesday, June 3rd, from 10 am to 11:30 am and is mandatory for all employees. Please make every effort to attend this very important session. Thank you.

Q : What can be inferred from the passage?

(a) Employees will have their work interrupted on June 3rd.
(b) Those who do not attend the workshop will be able to reschedule.
(c) Valence Mutual has had serious illnesses at its office before.
(d) The vaccinations may not be suitable for all people.

35. Julian Asher has a condition called synesthesia. When he listens to music, he also sees it. The sounds of a violin make him see a burgundy color, reminiscent of red wine, while a cello's music evokes images of golden honey. Synesthesia is a neurological condition in which people experience a mixing of their senses. Those affected may see colors and movement in numbers, words or sounds. One study says that as many as 1 percent of people have the most recognizable form of synesthesia. This condition may not be well-known to many, but a number of famous people have been labeled as synesthetes, including individuals of many different artistic talents.

Q : What is most likely to be discussed next?

(a) How synesthesia is depicted in arts and literature
(b) Sources for further reading on synesthesia
(c) Some celebrities with synesthesia
(d) Scientific studies on synesthesia

36. Tortillas are the unleavened flatbread made from wheat or corn most commonly seen in Mexican food. They date back to pre-Columbian civilizations, around 10,000 BCE. When the Spaniards found unleavened flatbread in Mexico among the Aztecs, they named it "tortilla," from the Spanish word "torta," or "round cake." Tortillas are consumed all year round, on different occasions, with all kinds of meals. They are often filled with meat to make dishes such as tacos.

Q : What can be inferred from the passage?

(a) Tortillas are mostly consumed on special occasions.
(b) Spaniards replaced their bread with tortillas.
(c) Tortillas form the basis of the traditional Mexican diet.
(d) Most people today know of tortillas because of tacos.

37. Those who want to live long lives should perhaps look at how people in Andorra live. The average Andorran can expect to live at least 85 years. That is longer than anywhere else in the world. People in this small nation bordering Spain and France embrace healthy living. When talking to various people there, it becomes clear that the concept of living longer is not on everyone's mind, but the idea of living well and living healthy comes up in nearly every conversation. Many Andorrans follow exercise regimens that involve walking up and down the hillsides. Even those in their 80s and 90s can easily climb two or three flights of stairs built into the mountainside.

Q : What can be inferred about Andorrans?

(a) They aim to lengthen their lifespan.
(b) People in Spain and France also live very long lives.
(c) Conversations about living healthy are responsible for their longevity.
(d) Their active lifestyle is part of their longevity.

Part III Questions 38–40

Read the passage. Then identify the option that does NOT belong.

38. In 1953, America's CIA and the UK's MI6 helped pro-Western Iranians carry out a coup d'etat. (a) This covert operation deposed Prime Minister Mohammed Mosaddeq's democratically elected government and aided in installing a government in Iran that supported the British and American governments. (b) The Anglo-American coup, referred to as Operation Ajax, was initially considered successful, but is today seen as a grave political mistake on the part of the United States and Britain. (c) Madeleine Albright has expressed that sentiment, saying the operation was a failure that led to the seeds of anti-American terrorism in the country. (d) Some argue that while many of Mosaddeq's allies abandoned him, the withdrawal of support by the clergy was fatal to his cause.

39. Amazon's Kindle, a hand-held gadget for reading books, has revolutionized the literary world. (a) Publisher Hearst Corp. is hoping it can do the same for its newspapers and magazines with its own device. (b) These so-called "e-readers" display crisp text on a screen that closely approximates a paper, all the while saving money on paper, printing, and delivery. (c) Hearst Corp. partly owns several leading cable networks, as well as numerous TV station and web sites. (d) Cost-cutting measures are especially important for Hearst during a time when ads sales are dropping and people prefer to get their news and entertainment electronically.

40. Most people conceive of capital as assets that yield income and other useful outputs over long periods of time—for example, a bank account, shares of stock or factories. (a) However, such obvious forms of capital are not the only type of capital that exist in society. (b) Other types include real estate property, automobiles and other personal possessions. (c) Recently, economists have broadened the meaning of the term to include intellectual capital, or investments in intellectual property. (d) In classical economics, capital is one of three factors of production, the others being land and labor.

This is the end of the Reading Comprehension section. Please remain seated until the proctor has instructed otherwise. You are NOT allowed to turn to any other section of the test.

🎧 Listening Comprehension

1

> W Could you fix me some coffee?
> M _____

(a) How would you like it?
(b) The copy machine has been fixed already.
(c) It's a quick fix.
(d) I like it strong.

☞ 번역

W 커피 좀 타 주시겠어요?
M _____

(a) 어떻게 드시겠어요?
(b) 복사기는 벌써 고쳐졌어요.
(c) 임시방편이죠.
(d) 진한 게 좋아요.

▦ 출제 POINT

Could you...?라는 부탁의 표현에 대한 적절한 응답이 나와야 한다. (b)는 'fix 준비하다/ fix 고치다, coffee 커피/ copy machine 복사기'로 다의어와 유사발음 혼동을 유도한 오답이다. (c) 역시 fix의 '해결'이라는 의미를 활용한 오답이고, (d)는 커피를 부탁하는 여자가 (a)와 같은 남자의 물음에 할 수 있는 답변이다.

fix 준비하다; 고치다   **quick fix** 임시방편, 미봉책   **strong** 진한; 강한

정답_(a)

2

> M Aren't you new here?
> W _____

(a) Yes, this place is new.
(b) That's news to me.
(c) No, I'm totally lost.
(d) Yes, I started this week.

☞ 번역

M 여기 새로 오지 않았어요?
W _____

(a) 네, 여긴 새로 지었어요.
(b) 그건 처음 듣는 소리입니다.
(c) 아니요, 길을 잃었어요.
(d) 네, 이번 주에 시작했어요.

▦ 출제 POINT

질문에서 new(새로 온, 신임의)의 의미를 제대로 해석해야 한다. 선택지 (b) '처음 듣는 소식'이라는 뜻의 news와 혼동하지 않도록 한다. (a)의 new는 '새로운, 최근의'라는 뜻으로 쓰였고 질문의 you를 this place로 받은 오답이다.

news 뉴스, 소식   **totally** 전적으로, 완전히

정답_(d)

📖 TEPS Survival 전략

1 How do you like your coffee?에 대한 응답
• Regular./ Decaf./ With cream and sugar.
  보통으로요./ 무카페인으로요./ 크림과 설탕을 넣어서요.
• Make it strong[weak]. 진하게[연하게] 타 주세요.

2 길을 잃었을 때
be lost/ get lost/ lose one's way
• I got lost[lost my way] and I couldn't find my home.
  나는 길을 잃어서 집을 찾을 수가 없었다.

3

W Isn't Jay sometimes too bossy?
M _____

(a) Don't tell me what to do.
(b) No, he is not my boss.
(c) It's not something I could do myself.
(d) Yeah, he sometimes gets on my nerves.

☞ 번역

W 제이는 가끔 너무 나서지 않아요?
M _____

(a) 나한테 이래라저래라 하지 마세요.
(b) 아니요, 그는 제 상관이 아니에요.
(c) 그건 내가 할 수 있는 일이 아니에요.
(d) 그래요, 가끔 신경에 거슬려요.

⊞ 출제 POINT

bossy는 말 그대로 boss처럼 이래라저래라 시키는 사람의 성향을 나타내는 말이다. 성격에 대해 언급했으므로 (d)의 '신경에 거슬린다'는 답변이 적절하다.

bossy 으스대는, 이래라저래라 하는 **get on one's nerves**
~의 신경을 건드리다   **정답_(d)**

4

M How long are you going to stay in the States?
W _____

(a) About three months ago.
(b) To visit my uncle in Minnesota.
(c) For a couple of years.
(d) In an executive management program.

☞ 번역

M 미국에 얼마나 오랫동안 머무를 건가요?
W _____

(a) 약 3개월 전입니다.
(b) 미네소타의 삼촌을 방문하려고요.
(c) 이삼 년 정도요.
(d) 경영 프로그램에 있습니다.

⊞ 출제 POINT

How long...?은 기간을 물어보는 질문이므로 답이 될 수 있는 선택지는 (a)와 (c)이다. 하지만 (a)의 경우 ago가 있어서 기간이 아닌 과거의 한 시점을 나타내므로 정답은 (c)이다. ago 외에 과거로부터의 기간을 나타내는 since를 활용하여 Since last July(7월부터 있었어요)와 같은 오답도 출제될 수 있다.

a couple of 수개의, 두서넛의 **executive** 관리의, 경영의 **정답_(c)**

---

3 성격 관련 형용사
timid 소심한
generous 관대한
blunt 퉁명스러운, 무뚝뚝한
contemptuous 남을 얕보는
humane 인정 있는

4 기간을 나타내는 전치사 for, during
for+숫자
• The program lasted for eight weeks.
  그 프로그램은 8주 동안 계속되었다.
during+명사
• During my stay in the U.S., I'll visit my uncle in Chicago.
  미국에 머무르는 동안 시카고에 계신 삼촌을 방문할 거예요.

5

W It looks like it's going to rain.

M _____

(a) Yes, it has.
(b) Oh, no. I hope it won't.
(c) When it rains, it pours.
(d) I know. I hope it doesn't stain.

☞ 번역

W 비가 올 것 같은데요.

M _____

(a) 네, 그래요.
(b) 저런, 안 왔으면 좋겠어요.
(c) 비가 오기만 하면 퍼붓는군요.
(d) 알아요. 얼룩지지 않으면 좋겠군요.

⊞ 출제 POINT

'비가 올 것 같다'는 추측의 표현으로 대화가 시작된다. (a)는 동사 looks를 받아 Yes, it does가 되어야 질문에 맞는 답이 된다. (c)는 관련 상황을, (d)는 유사발음을 이용한 함정이다. '비가 퍼붓다'라는 표현으로 pour를 쓴다는 것도 기억해 두자.

pour 쏟다, 퍼붓다　**stain** 얼룩지다; 얼룩　　　　　　　정답 _(b)

6

M Would you like seconds?

W _____

(a) Sure. What's up?
(b) No, thanks. I'm stuffed.
(c) Of course I don't.
(d) I don't have any plans.

☞ 번역

M 한 그릇 더 드시겠어요?

W _____

(a) 물론이죠. 무슨 일이에요?
(b) 고맙지만 사양할게요. 배가 불러요.
(c) 물론 아닙니다.
(d) 아무 계획도 없어요.

⊞ 출제 POINT

seconds는 복수로 써서 '더 청해서 먹는 음식'을 뜻한다. 따라서 사양의 표현인 (b)가 가장 적절하다. (a)는 second의 다른 뜻, '순간, 잠깐'을 이용한 함정이고, (c)는 Do you like...?에 대한 답변으로 오답이다.

seconds 또 한 그릇　**stuffed** 배가 부른　　　　　　　정답 _(b)

📖 TEPS Survival 전략

5 비 관련 표현
- When it rains, it pours.
  비가 오기만 하면 억수로 쏟아진다. (설상가상)
- It rains cats and dogs. 비가 억수같이 온다.
- It's been raining on and off since last night.
  어젯밤부터 비가 오락가락하네.
- The rain is letting up. 빗방울이 약해지고 있어.

6 식사 관련 표현
- I'm so hungry I could eat a horse.
  (말이라도 먹을 수 있을 정도로) 굉장히 배가 고파.
- I'm full[stuffed]./ I've had enough[plenty]. 배불러.
- That soup is mouth-watering. 그 수프 정말 맛있어 보인다.
- Could I have seconds, please? 한 그릇 더 먹어도 될까요?

7

W The shuttle bus is still running, isn't it?

M _____

(a) No, I stopped running last month.
(b) I'm on my way.
(c) It left a minute ago.
(d) It is, but you'd better hurry.

W 셔틀버스가 아직 운행 중이죠, 그렇지 않나요?

M _____

(a) 아니요, 지난달에 달리기를 그만뒀어요.
(b) 가는 길이에요.
(c) 금방 떠났어요.
(d) 그래요, 하지만 서두르는 게 좋을 거예요.

출제 POINT

(a)는 다의어 run의 의미를 활용한 오답이다. The shuttle bus를 it으로 받아 No, it stopped running last month(아니요, 그 버스는 지난달에 운행이 중단됐어요)라고 하면 정답이 될 수 있다. (c)는 버스가 계속 운행되는지의 여부를 알 수 없으므로 오답이고, 운행 여부를 알려주는 (d)가 정답이다.

run 운행하다; 달리다   정답 _(d)

8

M You shouldn't take risks like that with your job.

W _____

(a) I found a job last week.
(b) That would be much too risky.
(c) I know. I should have known better.
(d) No, I need to take care of it now.

M 일자리를 가지고 그렇게 모험을 하면 안 돼요.

W _____

(a) 지난주에 일자리를 구했어요.
(b) 그건 너무 위험해요.
(c) 알아요. 좀 더 현명하게 처신했어야 했는데.
(d) 아니요, 지금 처리해야 합니다.

출제 POINT

(a)와 (b)는 각각 남자의 말에서 들린 job과 risks를 활용한 오답이다. shouldn't라는 책망, 경고, 우려하는 표현이 나왔으므로 그에 수긍하는 (c)가 어울린다.

take risks 모험을 하다, 위험을 무릅쓰다   **risky** 위험한; 모험적인

정답 _(c)

---

7 운행 관련 표현
- The trolley bus runs every 10 minutes.
  전차가 10분 간격으로 운행된다.
- Special buses will operate between downtown and stations. 시내와 역 사이 특별 버스편이 운행될 것이다.
- The truck will go off the road on Tuesday.
  화요일에 트럭이 운행을 중단할 것이다.

8 risk 관련 표현
take[run] a risk of/ take risks of ~의 위험을 무릅쓰다
at all risk/ at any risk 어떤 위험이 있더라도, 결단코
be at risk 위험한 상태에 처하다
- Millions of lives are at risk from cholera.
  콜레라로 인해 수백만 명의 목숨이 위험에 처해 있다.

9

W What are you up to this Friday?

M _____

(a) Nothing in particular.
(b) I was visiting my parents.
(c) Whatever you say.
(d) Something came up.

☞ 번역

W 이번 주 금요일에 뭐 할 거예요?

M _____

(a) 별일 없어요.
(b) 부모님을 방문했어요.
(c) 하라는 대로 할게요.
(d) 일이 좀 생겼어요.

⊞ 출제 POINT

What are you up to?는 예정이나 계획을 묻는 인사말로 '특별한 일이 없다'고 답하는 (a)가 정답이다. (b)와 (d)는 과거시제이므로 질문과 시제가 맞지 않고, Whatever you say는 상대방의 말에 별로 찬성하지 않거나 상대가 원하는 대로 하고 싶지 않으면서도 수긍하는 표현이므로 문맥에 어울리지 않는다.

up to ~할 예정인   **come up** 발생하다. 일어나다   정답_(a)

10

M When did you hear Jill moved out of town?

W _____

(a) Since yesterday.
(b) I last saw her a week ago.
(c) Not until this morning.
(d) For a month.

☞ 번역

M 질이 다른 동네로 이사 갔다는 소식을 언제 들었어요?

W _____

(a) 어제 이후로요.
(b) 일주일 전에 마지막으로 봤어요.
(c) 오늘 아침에서야 들었어요.
(d) 한 달 동안이요.

⊞ 출제 POINT

When으로 시작하는 의문문은 매우 자주 출제된다. 보통 답변으로 A week ago와 같이 과거의 특정 시점을 언급하는 표현이 나오지만 (c) Not until this morning과 같이 돌려 말할 수도 있다. (a)와 (d)는 시간을 나타내는 표현이지만 When과 어울려 쓸 수 없다.

move out 이사 가다   정답_(c)

📖 TEPS Survival 전략

9 whatever 관련 표현
whatever you do (명령문에서) 일러 두는데, 알았지?
• Whatever you do, don't go there again.
  너한테 일러 두는데 그곳엔 절대로 두 번 다시 가지 마.
  whatsoever: whatever의 강조형
• The campaign seems to have had no effect whatsoever.
  캠페인은 아무런 효과도 거두지 못한 것 같다.

10 move in with 이사해서 ~와 살게 되다
• Steve's parents want to move in with him.
  스티브의 부모님은 그의 집에 들어와 살고 싶어 한다.
  settle in 이사하다, 자리잡고 살다
• Hundreds of thousands of foreigners settled in Belgium between 1920 and 1930. 1920년에서 1930년 사이 수십 만 명의 외국인들이 벨기에에 자리를 잡았다.

11

W How did you find the reception last night?

M _____

(a) It was easy to find.
(b) I haven't decided yet.
(c) I didn't even notice.
(d) It was okay.

📖 번역

W 어젯밤 환영회는 어땠어요?

M _____

(a) 찾기 쉬웠어요.
(b) 아직 결정 못했어요.
(c) 알아차리지도 못 했어요.
(d) 괜찮았어요.

🎛 출제 POINT

(a)는 find의 다양한 의미를 사용한 오답이다. find는 '찾다'라는 뜻 이외에 '알다, 깨닫다'라는 의미가 있다. '~가 어땠어요?'라는 질문에 어울리는 응답은 (d)이고, (b)와 (c)는 유사 상황을 이용한 함정이다.

reception 리셉션, 환영회 **notice** 알아채다, 깨닫다   정답_(d)

12

M I owe you an apology.

W _____

(a) That's all right.
(b) My pleasure.
(c) You're welcome.
(d) That's a shame.

📖 번역

M 죄송합니다.

W _____

(a) 괜찮습니다.
(b) 오히려 제가 기쁩니다.
(c) 별말씀을요.
(d) 유감스러운 일이군요.

🎛 출제 POINT

감사나 사과 표현과 그에 대한 일반적인 응답은 반드시 익혀두어야 한다. owe는 원래 '빚지다'라는 뜻이지만 owe A an apology라고 하면 'A에게 미안하다'라는 사과의 표현이 된다. (b)와 (c)는 감사에 대한 응답이다.   정답_(a)

---

11 How+find/ take/ feel 상대의 의견 묻기
• How will your friends take it?
  이것을 네 친구들은 어떻게 받아들일까?
• How do you feel about that proposal?
  제안에 대해 어떻게 생각하세요?

12 사과 관련 표현
• I offer my sincere apology./ Please accept my sincere apology. 진심으로 사과 드립니다.
• How can I make it up to you? 어떻게 하면 보상이 될까요?
• Don't give it another thought. 신경 쓰지 말고 잊어버려.
• I'll let you off this time. 이번에는 봐준다.
• Sorry is not enough! 미안하다고 하면 다예요!

13

> W I'm debating whether I should go to Sean's farewell party.
>
> M _____

(a) I'd love to. Friday is good.
(b) It's not a big deal. I don't need to go.
(c) But I thought you two were good friends.
(d) That sounds like fun. I'll join you guys.

☞ 번역

W 션의 송별회에 가야 할지 말아야 할지 고민 중이에요.

M _____.

(a) 가고 싶어요. 금요일 괜찮아요.
(b) 별거 아니에요. 전 갈 필요 없어요.
(c) 두 분이 친한 줄 알았는데요.
(d) 재미있을 것 같아요. 저도 합류할게요.

⊞ 출제 POINT

I'm debating whether는 어떤 사안에 대해 결정하지 못할 때 쓸 수 있는 표현이다. 파티에 가기를 주저하므로 친한 친구가 아니냐며 의아해하는 (c)가 적절하다. (b)는 주어가 바뀌었고, (d)는 상황을 이용한 함정이다.

debate 토론하다, 논의하다 **farewell party** 송별회   **정답_(c)**

14

> M What's the current interest rate?
>
> W _____

(a) It depends on what kind of account you want.
(b) Are you interested?
(c) It's half past five.
(d) We don't change foreign currency.

☞ 번역

M 현재 이자율은 얼마인가요?

W _____.

(a) 원하시는 계좌에 따라 다릅니다.
(b) 관심 있으세요?
(c) 다섯 시 반입니다.
(d) 환전은 하지 않습니다.

⊞ 출제 POINT

이자율을 묻는 질문에 (b)는 '흥미있는'이라는 interest의 다른 의미를, (d)는 유사 상황을 이용하여 함정을 만들고 있다. 따라서, '원하는 계좌에 따라 다르다'는 (a)가 정답이다.

current 현재의 **interest rate** 이자율, 금리 **account** 계좌, 계정
foreign currency 외환, 외화   **정답_(a)**

📖 TEPS Survival 전략

13 파티 관련 표현
housewarming party 집들이
welcome party 환영회
mask party/ masquerade 가면 무도회
surprise party 깜짝 파티
baby shower 임신 축하 파티

14 은행 관련 표현
open an (checking) account
(당좌 예금) 계좌를 개설하다
an active[inactive] account 사용 중인[휴면] 계좌
get a loan 대출을 받다
draw money 돈을 인출하다

15

W Your cart is in the way.
M _____

(a) That's the way to go.
(b) Can you move over?
(c) I'm sorry. I'll move it.
(d) You have to go this way.

🔊 번역
W 당신의 카트가 길을 막고 있어요.
M _____

(a) 바로 그거예요.
(b) 좀 비켜주시겠어요?
(c) 미안해요. 치울게요.
(d) 이쪽으로 가야 해요.

⊞ 출제 POINT
'카트가 길을 막고 있다'는 말에 대해 카트를 치워 달라는 암묵적인 요청으로 받아들이고 답한 (c)가 정답이다. (b)는 여자가 남자에게 할 수 있는 말이고, (a)와 (d)는 way의 다양한 의미를 활용한 오답이다.
cart 수레, 카트 **move over** 이동하다   정답_(c)

16

M You're not headed uptown, are you?
W Actually, I am. Why do you ask?
M I was hoping to get a ride with you.
W _____

(a) But I'm going the opposite way.
(b) Then hop in.
(c) What took you so long?
(d) Of course, it is.

🔊 번역
M 주택가 쪽으로 가진 않죠?
W 실은 가는데요. 왜 물으세요?
M 같이 타고 갔으면 해서요.
W _____

(a) 하지만 저는 반대쪽으로 가는데요.
(b) 그럼 타세요.
(c) 왜 그렇게 오래 걸렸어요?
(d) 물론 그렇죠.

⊞ 출제 POINT
남자가 여자에게 차를 태워줄 것을 요청하는 상황이다. 여기서는 head 가 '~로 향하다'라는 뜻으로 쓰였다. hop in은 '(차에) 올라타다'라는 뜻이고 (a)는 이미 같은 방향으로 간다는 내용이 언급되었으므로 문맥에 맞지 않는다.
uptown 주택가 **opposite** 반대의, 맞은편의 **hop in** (차에) 올라타다   정답_(b)

---

15 way를 사용한 표현
get out of the way 피하다, 비키다
• I yelled at the cyclist to get out of the way.
  나는 자전거를 타고 있는 사람에게 비키라고 소리쳤다.
get in the way 방해하다
• Please tell Tom not to get in the way.
  탐에게 방해하지 말라고 전해줘.

16 town 관련 표현
uptown 주택가
downtown 도심지; 상업 지구
boom town 신흥 도시
college[university] town 대학촌
ghost town 유령 도시

17

W   It's so windy out there!
M   It sure is. My hat blew off my head this morning.
W   Were you able to get it back?
M   _____

(a) It's over my head.
(b) Don't get carried away.
(c) No, I won't be back till later.
(d) I grabbed it just in time.

☞ 번역

W   밖에 바람이 많이 불어요!
M   맞아요. 아침에 쓰고 있던 모자가 날아갔다니까요.
W   다시 찾았어요?
M   _____

(a) 무슨 말인지 모르겠어요.
(b) 그렇게 넋을 잃지 말아요.
(c) 아니요, 나중에야 돌아올 거예요.
(d) 가까스로 잡았어요.

▦ 출제 POINT

blow off(불어 날리다)라는 숙어를 알아야 풀 수 있는 문제로 바람에 모자가 날아갔는데 겨우 잡았다는 (d)가 정답이다. (a)의 over my head나 (b)의 carry away는 관련 어구로 상황 혼동을 유발하는 오답이다.

over one's head ~에게 이해되지 않는; ~의 경제력을 넘어선
get carried away 넋을 잃다   **just in time** 겨우 시간에 맞춰

정답_(d)

18

W   Mark, where have you been?
M   I went to see a movie. Why?
W   We were supposed to meet for dinner.
M   _____

(a) It completely slipped my mind.
(b) Thanks, but I already ate.
(c) Great. What are you in the mood for?
(d) The movie was forgettable.

☞ 번역

W   마크, 어디 갔었어요?
M   영화 보러 갔었는데, 왜요?
W   만나서 같이 저녁 먹기로 했잖아요.
M   _____

(a) 깜박 잊어버렸어요.
(b) 고맙지만 벌써 먹었어요.
(c) 좋아요. 어떤 걸 먹고 싶어요?
(d) 영화는 그저 그랬어요.

▦ 출제 POINT

'저녁 먹기로 약속했다'는 여자의 말에 '깜박 잊었다'고 답하는 (a)가 정답이다. slip one's mind(깜박 잊어버리다)는 단골로 출제되는 관용 표현이다. 나머지 선택지는 movie와 meet for dinner를 활용한 전형적인 상황 혼동 오답이다.

slip one's mind 깜박 잊다   **be in the mood for** ~하고 싶은 기분이다   **forgettable** 잊을 만한, 그저 그런

정답_(a)

📖 TEPS Survival 전략

17 날씨 관련 표현
scorching 타는 듯한/ muggy 찌는 듯이 더운
freezing 얼어붙은, 몹시 추운/ humid 습한
foggy, misty 안개가 긴/ murky 음산한
drizzling 이슬비가 내리는

18 slip 관련 표현
slip one's mind[memory] 깜박 잊다
• I was supposed to phone him, but it slipped my mind.
  그에게 전화하기로 했는데 깜박 잊어버렸어.
let something slip 비밀을 누설하다; 기회를 놓치다
• Megan let it slip that they were planning to get married.
  메건은 엉겁결에 곧 결혼할 거라고 말하고 말았다.

19

M Are you going by the pharmacy today?
W I wasn't planning to, but I can.
M Could you pick up a prescription for me?
W _____

(a) Where did you leave it?
(b) Of course it's open.
(c) It certainly will be.
(d) You can count on me.

☞ 번역

M 오늘 약국에 들를 건가요?
W 그럴 생각은 아니었지만 들를 수 있어요.
M 그러면 처방전 좀 받아 주시겠어요?
W _____

(a) 어디에 두었어요?
(b) 물론 문은 열었지요.
(c) 분명 그럴 겁니다.
(d) 저만 믿으세요.

⊞ 출제 POINT

(d)의 count on은 '~를 믿다, 의지하다'라는 뜻으로 여기서는 요청을 수락하는 표현으로 쓰였다. 약국에서 처방전을 찾아와야 하는 상황이므로 처방전을 어디에 두었냐고 묻는 (a)는 오답이고, (c)의 certainly는 확실한 긍정을 나타내는 말이지만 답이 되려면 주어를 바꾸어 I certainly will이라고 해야 한다.

go by ~에 들르다 **pharmacy** 약국 **prescription** 처방, 처방전

정답_(d)

20

W I'm never going to date again.
M Oh, come on. Someone better will come along.
W Tell me, how do you usually meet new people?
M _____

(a) I use an Internet dating service.
(b) Meeting new people keeps you young.
(c) Because I just broke up with my girlfriend.
(d) I hope everything turns out okay for you.

☞ 번역

W 다시는 데이트 안 할 거예요.
M 그러지 말아요. 더 나은 사람이 나타날 거예요.
W 보통 어떻게 새로운 사람들을 만나는지 말해 줘요.
M _____

(a) 인터넷 데이트 서비스를 이용해요.
(b) 새로운 사람들을 만나면 젊음이 유지돼요.
(c) 방금 여자친구와 헤어졌거든요.
(d) 모든 일이 다 잘되기를 바라요.

⊞ 출제 POINT

Part 2에서는 마지막 질문을 잘 들어야 한다. how do...? 부분을 제대로 들어야 유사 상황 오답인 (c)나 (d)를 고르는 실수를 피할 수 있다. 새로운 사람을 어떻게 만나느냐는 질문에 인터넷 데이트 서비스라는 방법을 제시하는 (a)가 정답이다.

come along 오다; 동의하다; 지내다 **break up with** ~와 헤어지다
turn out 결국 ~가 되다

정답_(a)

---

19 go by 유사 표현
go by/ drop by[in]/ stop by[in]/ come by 들르다
- Are you dropping by the museum next week?
  다음 주에 박물관에 들를 예정이니?
- Nathan stopped in to see me on his way home.
  네이선은 집에 가는 길에 나를 보기 위해 잠깐 들렀다.
- Please come by my office sometime this afternoon.
  오늘 오후 아무 때나 제 사무실에 좀 들러주세요.

20 date 관련 표현
- I'm with someone.
  만나는 사람 있어요.
- I'm not seeing anybody. 만나는 사람 없어요.
- I've been dating[going out with] Jocelyn for six months.
  조셀린과 6개월째 교제 중이에요.

21

W Have you been working out?
M I have. Can you tell?
W You look stronger and more toned overall.
M _____

(a) I feel a lot better, too.
(b) I really enjoy my job.
(c) Thanks for the tip.
(d) I can only imagine.

📖 번역

W 요즘 운동해요?
M 네, 알아보겠어요?
W 전체적으로 더 튼튼하고 탄력 있어 보여요.
M _____

(a) 컨디션도 훨씬 좋답니다.
(b) 일이 정말 재미있어요.
(c) 조언 감사드려요.
(d) 상상이 가네요.

⊞ 출제 POINT

(b)는 work out과 work 사이의 형태적 유사성을 이용한 오답이다. 운동을 통해 더 건강해졌기 때문에 '컨디션도 좋다'는 (a)가 자연스러운 응답이다. feel은 감정, 느낌을 표현하는 말이지만, 몸 상태를 표현할 때도 많이 쓰인다. 예를 들어, I'm not feeling well이라고 하면 '몸이 좋지 않아'라는 뜻이다.

work out 운동하다 **toned** (근육이) 발달한, 탄력 있는 **tip** 조언, 충고

정답_(a)

22

M Did you do anything fun yesterday?
W Yeah, I went shopping with Patty.
M Where did you guys go?
W _____

(a) On Saturday afternoon.
(b) We're best friends, actually.
(c) To the mall down the street.
(d) Patty is not very fashionable.

📖 번역

M 어제 뭐 재미있는 일이라도 했나요?
W 네, 패티하고 쇼핑했어요.
M 어디로 갔는데요?
W _____

(a) 토요일 오후에요.
(b) 사실 우리는 단짝 친구예요.
(c) 길을 따라 있는 쇼핑몰에요.
(d) 패티는 별로 유행을 따르지 않아요.

⊞ 출제 POINT

(a)는 Where/ When 의문사를 혼동시킨 전형적인 오답 패턴이다. (b)와 (d)도 friends와 patty를 이용해 그럴싸하게 들리지만 Where did you guys go?라는 남자의 물음에 대한 답변은 아니므로 오답이다.

go shopping 쇼핑을 가다 **fashionable** 유행을 따르는, 최신 유행의

정답_(c)

🗒 TEPS Survival 전략

21 운동 관련 표현
work out/ exercise/ go to the gym 운동하다
gym rat 운동광
regular exercise 규칙적인 운동
be a good[poor] athlete 훌륭한[형편 없는] 운동 선수이다

22 유행 관련 표현
the latest fashion[mode/ vogue] 최신 유행
a passing vogue 일시적인 유행
out of mode 유행이 지난
lead the fashion 최첨단 유행을 달리다
follow the fashion 유행을 따르다
be[fall] behind the fashion 유행에 뒤지다

23

M Maria's daughter called with an urgent message.
W Oh, she was on her way out just now.
M We should find her before she leaves.
W _____

(a) What time does she usually leave?
(b) Maria is one of our best workers.
(c) It's probably not that important, anyway.
(d) I'll see if I can catch her.

☞ 번역
M 마리아의 딸이 긴급한 용건으로 전화했어요.
W 마리아는 방금 막 나가던데요.
M 그녀가 가버리기 전에 찾아야 해요.
W _____

(a) 그녀는 보통 몇 시에 떠나죠?
(b) 마리아는 가장 훌륭한 직원 중 한 사람이에요.
(c) 어차피 별로 중요하지 않아요.
(d) 제가 찾아 볼게요.

⊞ 출제 POINT
긴급(urgent) 메시지로 온 연락이므로 당사자를 반드시 찾아 알려줘야 한다. (a)는 대화 본문에 나온 leave라는 단어를 사용하여 혼동을 주고 있으나 아예 같은 단어가 반복되는 경우는 정답이 아닌 경우가 많다. (c)는 남자가 언급한 urgent message와 상반되므로 오답이다.
urgent 긴급한 **on one's way out** 나가는 길   정답_(d)

24

W Did you hear what happened to John?
M Yeah, I heard he broke his leg skiing.
W Luckily, it's just a hairline fracture.
M _____

(a) He's over the hill.
(b) That's a shame.
(c) It could've been a lot worse.
(d) Yes, his skis are very expensive.

☞ 번역
W 존한테 무슨 일이 있었는지 들었어요?
M 네, 스키를 타다가 다리가 부러졌다더군요.
W 다행히도 살짝 금이 간 것 뿐이래요.
M _____

(a) 그는 한물갔어요.
(b) 유감이네요.
(c) 그나마 다행이네요.
(d) 그래요, 그의 스키는 아주 비싸요.

⊞ 출제 POINT
It could've been a lot worse는 직역하면 '더 나쁠 수도 있었다'인데 '그나마 다행이다'라는 뜻으로 위로나 안도할 때 쓰는 표현이다. 조동사 could와 have가 겹쳐 발음도 어렵고 초급자가 놓치기 쉬운 부분이므로 구문 전체를 입에 익혀두어야 한다. (a)는 이디엄을 이용한 오답이고, (b) 역시 Luckily라고 언급한 여자의 말과는 어울리지 않는다.
hairline 매우 가는 선 **fracture** 골절 **over the hill** 전성기를 지나서
That's a shame. 유감이네요.   정답_(c)

---

23 전화 관련 표현
telephone/ make a call 전화하다
give someone a call[ring] ~에게 전화하다
make an urgent[emergency] call 긴급 전화를 하다
transfer a call 다른 사람 번호로 전화를 돌려주다
return a call 답례 전화를 하다
collect call 수신인 요금 지불 전화

24 hill 관련 표현
over the hill 절정기를 지나서; 나이 먹어
• I'm not over the hill. 나는 아직 건재하다.
go downhill 쇠퇴하다(decline)
• Grandma broke her leg last month, and she went downhill quite rapidly after that. 할머니께서는 지난달 다리가 부러진 이후 병이 급속도로 악화되었다.

25

M   Karen, can I talk to you?

W   Uh-oh. Did I do something wrong?

M   You left the dog outside in the cold overnight.

W   _____

(a) Sorry to say that.

(b) I'm a complete idiot!

(c) Oh, no. Are you okay?

(d) How could you do that!

☞ 번역

M   카렌, 얘기 좀 할 수 있어요?

W   이런, 제가 뭘 잘못했나요?

M   추운데 밤새도록 개를 밖에 내 두었잖아요.

W   _____

(a) 그런 말을 해서 미안해요.

(b) 전 정말 바보예요!

(c) 저런, 괜찮으세요?

(d) 어떻게 그럴 수가 있어요!

⊞ 출제 POINT

여자의 잘못을 남자가 지적했으므로 여자가 자책하는 (b)가 정답이다. (c)는 밖에 내버려 둔 것은 남자가 아니라 개이므로 오답이다. (d)는 전형적인 적반하장의 오답 형태로, 대화하는 남녀의 입장이 뒤바뀌어 있다.

overnight 밤새   **idiot** 바보, 백치   정답_(b)

26

W   How are the renovations going on your apartment?

M   It's just one delay after another.

W   That's too bad. I hope the end is near.

M   _____

(a) It's close to you.

(b) You and me both.

(c) What took you so long?

(d) Thank you for your help.

☞ 번역

W   아파트 리모델링은 어떻게 돼가요?

M   이런저런 이유로 계속 늦어지고 있어요.

W   그것 참 안됐네요. 곧 끝나길 바라요.

M   _____

(a) 당신한테 가까워요.

(b) 저도 마찬가지예요.

(c) 왜 이렇게 오래 걸렸어요?

(d) 도와줘서 고마워요.

⊞ 출제 POINT

(a)는 문맥상 전혀 무관한 내용이고 (b)는 상대와 같은 생각을 할 때 쓰는 표현으로, 남자도 곧 끝나길 바란다는 뜻이므로 정답이다.

renovation 수리, 리모델링   **delay** 지연, 지체   정답_(b)

📋 TEPS Survival 전략

25 I'm a complete idiot! 관련 표현

- I was not myself today. 오늘 제정신이 아니었어.
- Are you out of your mind? 너 제정신이니?
- You must be out of your senses./ You must be not in your right mind. 너 제정신이 아니구나.
- He recovered[came to] his senses. 그는 정신을 되찾았다.

26 리모델링 관련 표현

be under renovation 리모델링 중이다

- The building is currently under renovation.
  건물은 현재 리모델링 중입니다.

refurbish 재단장하다

- The hotel down the street has been refurbished.
  도로가에 있는 호텔이 재단장했어요.

27

W Did you find a place to stay?
M Bob said he may go out of town so I might stay at his place.
W When exactly is he taking off?
M _____

(a) I think he's taking time off work.
(b) At the corner of Melrose and California Avenue.
(c) He's going to Dubai.
(d) In two days.

☞ 번역

W 머물 곳을 찾았나요?
M 밥이 도시를 떠날 것 같다고 해서 그의 집에 머물 것 같아요.
W 정확하게 언제 떠나는데요?
M _____

(a) 잠시 휴가를 내는 것 같아요.
(b) 멜로즈와 캘리포니아길 모퉁이에요.
(c) 그는 두바이에 가요.
(d) 이틀 후에요.

⊞ 출제 POINT

마지막 질문을 정확하게 듣는 것이 문제 해결의 포인트이다. (b)와 (c)는 Where에 대한 답으로 함정을 만들고 있다. (a)는 take off의 서로 다른 두 가지 뜻을 이용한 오답이다. take off와 같이 문맥에 따라 의미가 달라지는 관용표현에 유의하자.
take off 출발하다; 휴가를 내다   정답_(d)

28

M Here, have some pasta.
W I already ate, but I'll try a little bit.
M That's not too much for you, is it?
W _____

(a) It's absolutely delicious.
(b) Thanks, but I don't want any.
(c) No, that's perfect.
(d) Yes, it's quite pricey.

☞ 번역

M 자, 파스타 좀 드세요.
W 벌써 식사했는데 조금만 먹어 볼게요.
M 그 정도는 그렇게 많지 않겠죠?
W _____

(a) 너무 맛있어요.
(b) 고마워요. 하지만 조금도 먹고 싶지 않아요.
(c) 아니요, 딱 좋아요.
(d) 그래요, 꽤 비싸네요.

⊞ 출제 POINT

That's not too much는 경우에 따라 정도, 가격에 대해 쓰일 수 있으므로 (d)와 같은 오답이 나올 수 있다. Part 2의 경우 가장 중요한 부분은 마지막 질문이지만 여전히 앞의 두 대화에서 주어진 상황을 이해할 필요가 있다. (a)는 파스타를 먹는 상황을 이용한 오답이며, (b) 역시 앞서 한 말과 반대되는 내용의 오답이다.
absolutely 절대적으로   **pricey** 값비싼   정답_(c)

---

27 take off 관련 표현
　　take off/ leave/ set out 떠나다
• Let's take off before your father gets home.
　너의 아버지께서 돌아오시기 전에 떠나자.
　take off 이륙하다
• Our plane took off from the wrong runway.
　우리 비행기는 잘못된 활주로에서 이륙했다.

28 가격을 나타내는 표현
　　price 값
　　fare 교통수단의 요금
　　fee 수수료
　　tuition 수업료
　　rate 시세, (시간당) 급료, 운임
　　rent 임대료

29

W Look over there! It's an elephant.
M Quick! Get the video camera.
W I thought you were holding it.
M _____

(a) It's a once-in-a-lifetime opportunity.
(b) Did we leave it somewhere?
(c) You know I can't hold on forever.
(d) Do you want to go to the zoo?

☞ 번역

W 저기 좀 봐! 코끼리야.
M 빨리! 비디오 카메라를 가져와.
W 네가 들고 있는 줄 알았는데.
M _____

(a) 평생에 한 번 있을까 말까 한 기회야.
(b) 어딘가에 놔두고 온 거 아니야?
(c) 알다시피 나도 계속 버티고 있을 순 없어.
(d) 동물원에 가고 싶어?

⊞ 출제 POINT

대화에서 hold의 뜻을 정확하게 이해하는 것이 포인트이며 카메라를 찾고 있는 상황이므로 (b)가 정답이다. (c)의 hold on은 '유지하다; 버티다'라는 전혀 다른 뜻으로 사용되었다. (d)는 코끼리와 동물원의 연상을 이용한 오답이다.
once-in-a-lifetime opportunity 평생 한 번 있는 기회, 천재일우의 기회 **hold on** 유지하다; 버티다　　　　　　정답_(b)

30

W How are you getting to Tulsa?
M I think I'll just drive.
W What about taking the train?
M _____

(a) Yes, driving is faster.
(b) Actually, I don't have a car.
(c) When are you leaving?
(d) I find it's too dangerous these days.

☞ 번역

W 털사에 어떻게 가세요?
M 그냥 운전해서 가려고요.
W 기차를 타면 어때요?
M _____

(a) 맞아요, 운전이 빨라요.
(b) 사실, 저는 차가 없어요.
(c) 언제 떠나요?
(d) 기차는 요즘 너무 위험해요.

⊞ 출제 POINT

운전을 하겠다고 하는 사람에게 기차를 제안한다. 이런 상황에서 자연스러운 응답은 the train을 it으로 받아 기차가 위험하다는 (d)이다. (a)와 (b)는 driving에서 연상되지만 문맥에 맞지 않는 오답이다.
정답_(d)

📖 TEPS Survival 전략

29 기회 관련 표현
the chance of a lifetime 일생 일대의 기회
golden chance 황금 같은 기회
miss the boat 기회를 놓치다

30 get to/ arrive 도착하다
• How are you getting to your destination?
목적지까지 어떻게 가세요?
• I just arrived home.
지금 막 집에 도착했어요.

31

M Have you ever been to Amsterdam?

W A long time ago. Why?

M I'm thinking of going there for vacation.

W I think you'd like it there.

M It sounds like a really interesting city, but I heard it's expensive.

W I stayed on a houseboat to save money.

Q What are the speakers mainly discussing?

(a) Boats in Amsterdam.

(b) Things to do in another city.

(c) Travel plans.

(d) The cost of living.

☞ 번역

M 암스테르담에 가보셨어요?

W 오래 전이에요. 왜요?

M 휴가 때 거기 가려고요.

W 아마 마음에 드실 거예요.

M 정말 흥미로운 도시인 것 같아요. 하지만 물가가 비싸다고 들었어요.

W 저는 돈을 절약하려고 집배에 묵었죠.

Q 담화의 주된 내용은?

(a) 암스테르담의 배.

(b) 다른 도시에서 할 일.

(c) 여행 계획.

(d) 생활비.

⊞ 출제 POINT

주제를 묻는 문제이므로 대화 전체를 포괄하는 내용을 답으로 선택해야 한다. 주제 문제에서 흔히 제시되는 오답 패턴은 (a)와 (d)처럼 내용의 일부만을 제시하는 경우나 (b)와 같이 지나치게 범위가 넓은 경우 등이다. 따라서 정답은 (c)이다.

houseboat 집배 **cost of living** 생활비　　　정답_(c)

32

M This table is driving me crazy!

W What's the matter?

M It keeps wobbling and I can't type properly.

W Do you have any paper or cardboard with you by any chance?

M I only have today's newspaper. Why?

W You can wedge some paper under the shorter leg to make it stable.

Q What is the woman mainly doing?

(a) Offering a solution to a problem.

(b) Looking for today's newspaper.

(c) Complaining about an annoying matter.

(d) Taking the man's order.

☞ 번역

M 이 테이블 때문에 미칠 거 같아요!

W 뭐가 문제예요?

M 계속 흔들려서 타이프를 제대로 칠 수가 없어요.

W 혹시 종이나 판자 같은 거 있어요?

M 오늘자 신문밖에 없는데 왜 그러세요?

W 다리가 짧은 쪽에 종이를 좀 괴면 고정시킬 수 있어요.

Q 여자가 하고 있는 일은?

(a) 문제에 대한 해결책 제시.

(b) 오늘자 신문 찾기.

(c) 골칫거리에 대한 불평.

(d) 남자의 주문받기.

⊞ 출제 POINT

여자가 하고 있는 일, 여기서는 대화의 목적을 묻는 문제이다. 첫 대화에서 남자가 문제를 제시하고 두 번째, 세 번째에서는 여자가 해결책을 제안하고 있으므로 정답은 (a)이다. (b)는 지나치게 지엽적인 내용이며, (c)는 여자가 아닌 남자에 대한 설명이다.

drive A crazy A를 화나게 하다 **wobble** 비틀거리다, 흔들흔들하다

by any chance 혹시 **wedge** 쐐기로 고정하다　　　정답_(a)

---

31 I'm thinking of going…

　→ I plan to go…

　→ I have a plan to visit…

　go … for vacation

　→ go on a trip to…

32 is driving me crazy

　→ is driving me up the wall

　→ I can't put up with … any more

　Do you have … by any chance?

　→ Do you happen to have…?

33

M　Have you finished mailing out the invitations?

W　Not yet. I'm still waiting on some addresses.

M　Is there any way to get them sooner?

W　I suppose I could call them instead of waiting for an email from them.

M　Let's wait another day. If they don't get back to you by then, call them.

W　Some people were away for the holidays so they should be getting back now.

Q　What is the conversation mainly about?

(a) Holiday activities.

(b) Contacting people on vacation.

(c) How to address certain people.

(d) Following up on needed information.

☞ 번역

M　초대장 발송은 다 마쳤어요?

W　아직요. 아직 주소 몇 군데를 기다리고 있어요.

M　더 빨리 주소를 확보할 방법은 없나요?

W　이메일을 기다리는 대신 전화를 할 수 있겠죠.

M　하루만 더 기다립시다. 그때까지 답이 없으면 전화를 하도록 해요.

W　휴가를 떠난 사람들도 있는데 지금쯤이면 돌아올 거예요.

Q　대화의 주된 내용은?

(a) 휴가 활동.

(b) 휴가 중인 사람들에게 연락 취하기.

(c) 특정 사람들을 부르는 호칭.

(d) 필요한 정보 처리.

⊞ 출제 POINT

주제를 묻는 문제이다. 남녀의 첫 대화에서 주소가 없어 초청장 발송을 못하는 상황이 제시되고 두 번째, 세 번째에서 대응 방법이 논의되고 있다. (d) 주소, 즉 필요한 정보 처리가 정답이다. (c)는 address의 두 가지 뜻(주소, 호칭하다)을 이용하여 만든 함정이다.

be away 부재 중이다　**address** (직함 따위로) 부르다; 주소　**follow up on** 적절한 처리를 하다　　　　　**정답**_(d)

34

M　What time is the next shuttle into town?

W　The shuttle leaves every hour on the hour.

M　So the next one should be here in ten minutes?

W　Right. I wouldn't worry. The driver is usually on time.

M　And when does the shuttle come back?

W　It picks people up at half past every hour in front of the Sanderson Hotel.

Q　What is the main topic of the conversation?

(a) The shuttle schedule.

(b) The current time.

(c) A cancelled bus trip.

(d) A delayed bus.

☞ 번역

M　시내로 오는 다음 셔틀버스는 몇 시에 있나요?

W　셔틀버스는 매시 정각에 출발해요.

M　그렇다면 다음 버스는 10분 후에 오는 거네요?

W　맞아요. 걱정 마세요. 기사가 대개 시간을 잘 지켜요.

M　돌아오는 건 몇 시인가요?

W　샌더슨 호텔 앞에서 매시 30분에 사람들을 태워요.

Q　대화의 주제는?

(a) 셔틀버스 일정.

(b) 현재 시각.

(c) 버스 운행 취소.

(d) 버스 도착 지연.

⊞ 출제 POINT

항상 도입부를 놓쳐서는 안 되지만 특히 주제 문제의 답은 대부분 첫 부분에 제시된다. 여기서도 남녀의 첫 대화에서 셔틀버스 운행 일정에 대한 내용임을 짐작할 수 있다.

shuttle 셔틀버스　**every hour on the hour** 매시 정각에　**current** 현재의　　　　　**정답**_(a)

📖 TEPS Survival 전략

33 If they don't get back to you...

→ If you can't reach them...

Some people were away...

→ Some people were out of town...

34 What time is the next shuttle...?

→ When will the next shuttle arrive...?

The driver is usually on time.

→ The driver keeps good time.

→ The driver is usually punctual.

35

W What do you think is the fastest way to get to the airport?

M It depends on what time you're going.

W Well, I'll probably be leaving tomorrow morning at 8.

M There'll likely be really heavy traffic on the street, so I wouldn't take a taxi.

W Do you think it's better to take the subway there?

M The subway takes a long time, too, but at least it'll be cheaper.

Q What are the speakers mainly discussing?

(a) The best route to the airport.

(b) Modes of transportation to the airport.

(c) Traffic patterns during the day.

(d) The average cost of taxis.

📖 번역

W 공항에 가는 가장 빠른 방법이 뭐라고 생각해요?

M 몇 시에 가느냐에 달렸어요.

W 음. 아마 내일 아침 8시에 떠날 거 같은데요.

M 그렇다면 교통이 매우 혼잡할 테니 저라면 택시는 타지 않겠어요.

W 지하철을 타는 게 더 나을까요?

M 지하철도 오래 걸리지만 최소한 더 싸긴 하죠.

Q 대화의 주된 내용은?

(a) 공항으로 가는 가장 좋은 경로.

(b) 공항으로 가는 교통 수단.

(c) 하루 동안의 교통 패턴.

(d) 택시 평균 요금.

⊞ 출제 POINT

이 문제 역시 첫 번째 문답에 주제가 제시되어 있다. the fastest way to get to the airport를 paraphrase한 (b)가 정답이다. 이처럼 정답은 지문 일부의 표현을 바꿔 제시하는 것이 보통이다. (a)는 way/route 연상을 이용한 함정이다.

route 루트, 경로 **mode** 방법 **transportation** 교통. 운송 **정답** (b)

36

M Gail, did you have a chance to review my sales proposal?

W Sorry. I've been swamped with work.

M Could you just give it a quick look today?

W Sure. By the way, when are you leaving for London?

M I'm scheduled to leave on Thursday, but I may have to leave on Wednesday.

W Oh, then I'd better get right on that proposal.

Q What is the man mainly doing?

(a) Expediting a task.

(b) Complaining about work.

(c) Reviewing a proposal.

(d) Conferring with a client.

📖 번역

M 게일, 제 영업 제안서를 검토했나요?

W 미안해요. 일이 너무 많아서요.

M 오늘 좀 훑어 봐줄 수 있을까요?

W 물론이죠. 그런데 언제 런던으로 떠나세요?

M 목요일 출발 예정이에요. 하지만 수요일에 떠나야 할 수도 있어요.

W 아, 그러면 당장 그 제안서를 보는 게 좋겠군요.

Q 남자는 무엇을 하고 있는가?

(a) 일 재촉.

(b) 업무 불평.

(c) 제안서 검토.

(d) 고객 상담.

⊞ 출제 POINT

대화의 목적을 묻는 문제이다. 남자가 여자에게 상황을 설명하며 제안서 검토를 독촉하고 있으므로 (a)가 정답이다. 제안서를 검토하는 것은 남자가 아니라 여자이므로 (c)는 답이 될 수 없다.

be swamped with ～이 몰려 정신이 없다 **get right on** ～을 즉시 착수하다 **expedite** 재촉시키다. 진척시키다 **confer** 수여하다. 상담하다 **정답** (a)

---

35 It depends on what time you're going.

→ It depends on when you leave.

It'll be cheaper.

→ It'll cost less.

36 Did you have a chance to review my sales proposal?

→ Have you reviewed my proposal yet?

I've been swamped with work.

→ I've been tied up with work.

37

W Alex, I had the conference room booked but it looks like it's occupied.

M Mr. Collins is in there brainstorming with Kyle.

W I don't want to interrupt them, but I have a meeting scheduled in 10 minutes.

M How about I ask them to move?

W That would be great. Thanks so much.

M No problem. Let me know if there's anything else you need.

Q What is the conversation mainly about?

(a) Taking minutes at a meeting.
(b) Getting refreshments for a conference.
(c) The man's primary duties.
(d) Clearing a room.

☞ 번역

W 알렉스, 회의실을 예약해 두었는데 누가 쓰고 있는 것 같군요.

M 콜린즈 씨가 카일과 브레인스토밍을 하고 있어요.

W 그들을 방해하고 싶지는 않지만 10분 후에 미팅이 잡혀 있는데요.

M 그러면 제가 옮기라고 말해줄까요?

W 그러면 좋죠. 정말 고마워요.

M 뭘요. 또 필요한 게 있으면 알려주세요.

Q 대화의 주된 내용은?

(a) 미팅 동안 회의록 작성.
(b) 회의를 위한 다과 준비.
(c) 남자의 주요 임무.
(d) 회의실 비우기.

⊞ 출제 POINT

여자가 예약해 둔 회의실을 다른 사람이 쓰고 있다고 하자 남자가 이에 대한 해결책을 제시하고 있다. 전체 대화 내용을 포괄하는 주제는 (d) 회의실을 비우는 것이다. (a)의 minutes는 복수로 쓰여 '회의록'이라는 뜻을 나타낸다.

book 예약하다 **interrupt** 방해하다 **minutes** 회의록
refreshments 다과, 음료   정답 _(d)

38

M Do you know anywhere I can buy some stationery?

W Are you looking for something in particular?

M I just need some good quality paper and envelopes.

W In that case you should try Linda's Paper World.

M Where is it? Is it close to here?

W From here it's about a 15-minute walk.

Q Which is correct according to the conversation?

(a) The speakers are outside the stationery store.
(b) The man wants to buy some paper products.
(c) The man and woman cannot decide what to do together.
(d) The man is sorting some documents.

☞ 번역

M 문구류 살 수 있는 곳을 알아요?

W 특별히 찾는 것이 있나요?

M 그냥 질 좋은 종이와 봉투가 필요해서요.

W 그렇다면 린다네 페이퍼 세상으로 가보세요.

M 어디죠? 여기서 가까운가요?

W 여기서는 한 15분 걸어야 해요.

Q 대화에 따르면 옳은 것은?

(a) 화자들은 문구점 바로 밖에 있다.
(b) 남자는 종이 제품을 사고 싶어 한다.
(c) 화자들은 함께 무엇을 할지 결정하지 못하고 있다.
(d) 남자는 서류를 분류하고 있다.

⊞ 출제 POINT

(a)의 outside는 문구점 바로 밖에 있다는 의미인데, 남자의 첫 번째 대화에서 문구점의 위치를 문의하므로 오답이다. (d)는 document와 paper의 연상 작용을 이용한 함정이고 '남자는 종이 제품을 사고 싶어 한다'는 (b)가 정답이다.

stationery 문구류 **sort** ~을 분류하다 **document** 서류 정답 _(b)

🗐 TEPS Survival 전략

37 How about I ask them to move?
 → I could ask them to move for you.
 Let me know if there's anything else you need.
 → Is there anything else I can do for you?

38 Do you know anywhere I can buy some stationery?
 → Can you tell me where a stationery store is?
 From here it's about a 15-minute walk.
 → It takes about 15 minutes to walk there.

39

M What are you doing tomorrow?

W I'm going kayaking. I can't wait.

M I didn't know you liked to kayak.

W I just joined this new kayaking group for weekend outings.

M I've never gone kayaking. Is it very hard to learn how to kayak?

W It's not difficult, though after my first try last week I was sore.

Q Which is correct according to the conversation?

(a) The man enjoys kayaking.

(b) The woman has a new hobby.

(c) The man will join the woman's kayaking group.

(d) The woman is not very good at kayaking.

☞ 번역

M 내일 뭐 하세요?

W 카약을 타러 가요. 빨리 가고 싶어요.

M 카약을 좋아하는 줄 몰랐어요.

W 주말 나들이 삼아 새로운 카약 모임에 막 가입했어요.

M 카약은 한 번도 타본 적이 없어요. 배우기 많이 어려운가요?

W 어렵지는 않아요. 지난주 처음 해보고 나서 몸이 쑤시기는 했지만요.

Q 대화에 따르면 옳은 것은?

(a) 남자는 카약을 즐긴다.

(b) 여자는 새로운 취미가 생겼다.

(c) 남자는 여자의 카약 모임에 가입할 것이다.

(d) 여자는 카약을 그리 잘하지 못한다.

⊞ 출제 POINT

세부 사항의 일치 여부를 묻는 문제로 카약을 즐기는 것은 남자가 아닌 여자이므로 (a)는 오답이고 (c)와 (d)는 대화에서 제시되지 않은 내용이다. 새 카약 모임에 가입했고 지난주에 처음 카약을 타보았다는 여자의 말에서 (b)가 정답임을 알 수 있다.

outing 소풍, 산책   **sore** 아픈, 쓰린   정답_(b)

40

M How are you doing, Jessica?

W Not too well. I just wasn't prepared for this at all.

M Nobody was. Sal's death was a huge shock.

W We had a fight not too long ago and I said some terrible things to him.

M Hey, now. You can't think that way.

W I wish I could've apologized before he passed.

Q Which is correct according to the conversation?

(a) Sal is in the hospital.

(b) The woman is married to Sal.

(c) The man made a mistake at work.

(d) The woman regrets some things she said.

☞ 번역

M 어떻게 지내요, 제시카?

W 별로 잘 지내지 못해요. 이런 일에 전혀 준비가 되어 있지 않았거든요.

M 다 마찬가지예요. 샐의 죽음은 엄청난 충격이었어요.

W 얼마 전에 싸웠는데 샐에게 끔찍한 소리를 했어요.

M 자, 그런 식으로 생각하지 말아요.

W 그가 떠나기 전에 사과할 수 있었다면 좋았을 텐데요.

Q 대화에 따르면 옳은 것은?

(a) 샐은 입원 중이다.

(b) 여자는 샐과 결혼했다.

(c) 남자는 직장에서 실수를 했다.

(d) 여자는 자신이 한 말을 후회하고 있다.

⊞ 출제 POINT

여자가 샐의 죽음을 맞고 나서 안타까움을 표하고 있다. I could've apologized와 같이 〈조동사+have+p.p.〉가 나왔을 때는 유의해서 들어야 한다. '사과를 할 수 있었더라면'은 사과를 하지 못했다는 의미이므로 정답은 (d)이다. (b)와 같이 대화를 근거로 하지 않은 내용을 어림짐작으로 선택하지 않도록 한다.

pass 사망하다; 사라지다   정답_(d)

---

39 What are you doing tomorrow?

→ What is your plan for tomorrow?

→ What are you up to tomorrow?

→ Do you have any special plan tomorrow?

40 Sal's death was a huge shock.

→ His death shocked everybody deeply.

→ His death was shocking news for everyone.

→ It was totally unexpected.

41

W Are you ready to order, sir?
M Yes. I'd like the vegetable soup, but do you know if it's got flour in it?
W I'm not sure. I can check with the chef, though.
M Can you also find out about the grilled salmon? I'm allergic to wheat products.
W All right. And to drink?
M I'll take a glass of your house white wine.

Q Which is correct according to the conversation?
(a) The woman cannot decide what to eat.
(b) The restaurant does not serve fish.
(c) The man has dietary restrictions.
(d) The speakers are having an argument.

☞ 번역

W 주문하시겠습니까, 손님?
M 네. 야채 수프를 먹고 싶은데 수프에 밀가루가 들어가나요?
W 글쎄요. 주방장에게 확인해 볼 수 있습니다.
M 연어구이도 확인해 주시겠어요? 제가 밀 제품 알레르기가 있어서요.
W 네. 음료는요?
M 하우스 화이트 와인 한 잔 주세요.

Q 대화에 따르면 옳은 것은?
(a) 여자는 무엇을 먹어야 할지 결정하지 못한다.
(b) 식당에서 생선 요리를 팔지 않는다.
(c) 남자는 먹을 수 있는 음식에 제한이 있다.
(d) 화자들이 논쟁을 벌이고 있다.

⊞ 출제 POINT

세부 사항을 확인하는 문제이므로 오답 소거법으로 정답을 찾는다. 남자는 밀가루가 들어간 음식에 알레르기가 있어서 먹을 수 없으므로 '음식에 제한이 있다'는 (c)가 정답이다. (b)는 남자가 연어를 주문하려는 상황으로 보아 오답이다.

flour 밀가루 **be allergic to** ~에 알레르기가 있다 **wheat** 밀

정답_(c)

42

M Hi, I'm here to see Michael Whitmore. He was admitted yesterday.
W I'm sorry. Visiting hours are from 9 a.m. to 4 p.m.
M He's a very good friend of mine. Can't you bend the rules just a little bit?
W I'm afraid the hospital has a strict policy about visitors.
M Well, then, can I leave a note for him instead?
W Be my guest. I'd be happy to pass it on to him.

Q Which is correct according to the conversation?
(a) The woman is friends with the patient.
(b) The man will return another day.
(c) The woman is enforcing a rule.
(d) The man is being admitted to the hospital.

☞ 번역

M 안녕하세요. 마이클 휘트모어를 보러 왔는데요. 어제 입원했어요.
W 미안합니다. 방문 시간은 오전 9시부터 오후 4시까지예요.
M 아주 친한 친구예요. 규정을 조금만 완화해 주시면 안 될까요?
W 죄송하지만 병원은 방문객에 대해 엄격한 정책을 갖고 있습니다.
M 그렇다면 대신 메모를 남길 수 있을까요?
W 물론이죠. 기꺼이 전해 드리겠습니다.

Q 대화에 따르면 옳은 것은?
(a) 여자는 환자의 친구이다.
(b) 남자는 다른 날 다시 올 것이다.
(c) 여자는 규칙을 주장하고 있다.
(d) 남자는 병원에 입원 중이다.

⊞ 출제 POINT

문병 온 손님과 병원 직원 간의 대화 내용이다. 남자가 방문 시간에 대한 규칙 때문에 입원한 친구를 만나지 못하고 돌아가는 상황이므로 (c)가 정답이다. 입원한 사람은 남자가 아닌 남자의 친구이므로 (d)는 정답이 될 수 없다.

be here to ~때문에 왔다 **admit** 넣다, 수용하다 **bend the rules** 규칙을 왜곡해서 고치다 **Be my guest.** 그러세요, 좋을 대로 하세요. **enforce** 강경하게 주장하다

정답_(c)

📖 TEPS Survival 전략

41 I'd like the vegetable soup.
→ I'll have[take] the vegetable soup.

42 I'm afraid the hospital has a strict policy about visitors.
→ I'm sorry but the hospital is very strict about the visitors policy.

43

W Congratulations, Jamie. You must be so relieved to be done with law school.

M Yeah, it was three long years of studying, but I'm finally done now!

W What are you doing to celebrate? Do you have any special plans?

M No. I'm just going to hang out with some law school buddies.

W Well, enjoy this free time. You'll be pretty busy once you land a job as a lawyer.

M Thanks for the advice. You would know best from personal experience.

Q What can be inferred from the conversation?
(a) The man starts work tomorrow.
(b) The man already has a job lined up.
(c) The woman has just graduated from law school.
(d) The woman has experience working at a law firm.

44

W That exam was excruciating! How was it for you?

M The short answer section was okay, but I drew a blank on the essay.

W I totally thought Mr. Gonzalez would ask about the factors leading to World War I.

M Me, too! I didn't expect a question about the Great Depression.

W I'm afraid to get my test back. I think I failed.

M You probably still passed if you got most of the short answers correct.

Q What can be inferred from the conversation?
(a) The woman did not study for the exam.
(b) The exam had two parts.
(c) The man anticipated the essay question.
(d) The woman will pass the exam.

🗣 번역

W 축하해요, 제이미. 로스쿨을 마치게 돼서 한숨 돌리겠네요.

M 그래요, 3년간의 오랜 공부였는데 마침내 끝났네요!

W 축하하기 위해 뭘 하나요? 특별한 계획이라도 있어요?

M 아니요. 그냥 로스쿨 친구들 몇몇 하고 어울리려고요.

W 그래요, 지금 여유 있을 때 즐기세요. 변호사로 일하게 되면 꽤 바빠질 테니 말이에요.

M 충고 고마워요. 경험으로 가장 잘 아시겠네요.

Q 대화에서 유추할 수 있는 것은?
(a) 남자는 내일 일을 시작한다.
(b) 남자는 이미 결정된 일자리가 있다.
(c) 여자는 막 로스쿨을 졸업했다.
(d) 여자는 법률 회사에서 일한 경험이 있다.

⊞ 출제 POINT

대화에 제시된 내용을 바탕으로 유추해서 답을 찾아야 하는 문제이다. 반드시 대화 내용을 근거로 유추해야 한다. (a)와 (b)는 여자의 여유 좀 즐기라는 말로 보아 정답이 아니고, (c)는 남자에게 해당되는 내용이다. 남자의 마지막 말인 know best from personal experience에서 유추할 수 있는 (d)가 정답이다.

relieve 안도케 하다   **hang out with** ~와 어울리다, 사귀다   **line up** ~을 확보하다, 준비하다; 정렬하다   정답_(d)

🗣 번역

W 끔찍한 시험이었어! 넌 어땠어?

M 단답형 부분은 괜찮았는데 에세이에서 망친 것 같아.

W 곤잘레스 선생님이 1차 세계대전을 유발한 요인에 대해 물어볼 거라고 철석같이 믿었는데.

M 나도야! 대공황에 대한 질문이 나올 거라고는 예상 못했어.

W 시험 결과를 받기가 겁나. 낙제일 거 같아.

M 그래도 단답형을 거의 다 맞췄다면 통과했겠지.

Q 대화에서 유추할 수 있는 것은?
(a) 여자는 시험 공부를 하지 않았다.
(b) 시험에는 두 파트가 있었다.
(c) 남자는 에세이 질문을 예상했다.
(d) 여자는 시험을 통과할 것이다.

⊞ 출제 POINT

두 사람은 이미 치른 시험에 대해 이야기를 나누고 있다. 여자와 남자 모두 시험 내용을 잘못 예상했다는 말이 나오므로 (a)와 (c)는 답이 될 수 없다. 대화 내용 중에 short answer section과 essay, 즉 두 파트가 언급되었으므로 (b)가 정답이다. (d)와 같이 정확한 예측이 불가능한 선택지를 답으로 선택하지 않도록 주의한다.

excruciating 고통을 주는, 몹시 괴로운   **draw a blank** 허탕치다; 실패하다   정답_(b)

---

43 be done with law school
 → finish law school/ graduate from law school

44 I drew a blank on the essay.
 → I screwed[messed] up on the essay.

45

M Hi, Donna. Any news yet on selling your home?

W Nope. It's a really bad time now for people to buy.

M I thought you got an offer a couple of weeks ago.

W I did, but it was far below the asking price.

M And when are you planning to buy your new property?

W The closing date is March 15, but I'm not sure I'll sell my place before then!

Q What can be inferred from the conversation?

(a) The man is the woman's real estate broker.

(b) The woman's neighborhood is not considered very safe.

(c) The housing market has gotten better recently.

(d) The woman wishes to sell her home before she buys a new one.

46

Lizards and other cold-blooded creatures like to bask in the sun. But contrary to popular opinion, it's not just to keep warm. According to a recent study, chameleons alter their sunbathing behavior based on their need for vitamin D. Chameleons are like humans and most other vertebrates this way: they get vitamin D either by absorbing it from food or by producing it in their skin. However, the skin must be exposed to UV radiation to produce vitamin D. Researchers found that chameleons low in vitamin D increased their exposure to the sun's UV rays.

Q What is the speaker mainly talking about?

(a) Cold-blooded creatures.

(b) The health benefits of a vitamin.

(c) The reason chameleons sunbathe.

(d) Similarities between humans and reptiles.

📋 TEPS Survival 전략

45 It's a really bad time now for people to buy.
→ It's not a buyer's[buying] market.

☞ 번역

M 안녕, 도나. 당신 집 파는 것에 관한 새로운 소식이 있어요?

W 아뇨. 지금은 집을 사기에 아주 좋지 않은 시기예요.

M 몇 주 전에 샀다는 제안이 들어온 줄 알았는데요.

W 그래요. 하지만 제가 제시한 가격에 훨씬 못 미쳤어요.

M 새 부동산은 언제 구매할 예정인가요?

W 마감일이 3월 15일인데 그 전까지 집을 팔 수 있을지 모르겠어요!

Q 대화에서 유추할 수 있는 것은?

(a) 남자는 여자의 부동산 중개인이다.

(b) 여자의 동네는 별로 안전하지 않다고 평가된다.

(c) 주택 시장이 최근 나아졌다.

(d) 여자는 새집을 사기 전에 자기 집을 팔기를 바란다.

🏢 출제 POINT

여자가 집을 내놓고 팔리지 않아 걱정하는 내용의 대화이다. 남자가 여자에게 집이 팔렸는지의 여부를 묻고 있으므로 (a)는 답이 될 수 없다. (b)는 대화 내용만으로 추론할 수 없으며 (c)는 사실과 반대된다.

far below 훨씬 아래의 **asking price** 제시 가격; 호가 **real estate** 부동산

정답_(d)

☞ 번역

도마뱀과 같은 냉혈 동물들은 햇볕 쬐기를 좋아합니다. 하지만 일반적인 생각과는 달리 단순히 몸을 따뜻하게 하기 위해서만은 아닙니다. 최근 연구에 따르면 카멜레온은 비타민 D의 필요 정도에 따라 햇볕을 쬐는 행태를 바꾸는 것으로 알려졌습니다. 카멜레온은 인간이나 다른 대부분의 척추 동물과 마찬가지로 음식에서 비타민 D를 섭취하거나 피부에서 만들어 냅니다. 하지만 피부에서 비타민 D를 만들려면 자외선에 노출되어야 합니다. 연구자들은 카멜레온이 비타민 D가 부족할 때 자외선 노출 시간을 늘린다는 사실을 발견했습니다.

Q 화자가 주로 이야기하고 있는 것은?

(a) 냉혈 동물들.

(b) 비타민의 건강상 이점.

(c) 카멜레온이 일광욕을 하는 이유.

(d) 인간과 파충류의 유사성.

🏢 출제 POINT

담화문의 주제는 일단 단락의 첫 부분에 드러나 있는 경우가 대부분이므로 서두를 주의 깊게 듣는다. (a)는 범위가 너무 넓어 이 단락의 주제로는 부적절하며, (b)와 (d)는 초점이 어긋나 있다. 카멜레온이 일광욕을 하는 이유를 설명하고 있으므로 정답은 (c)이다.

lizard 도마뱀 **cold-blooded** 냉혈의 **creature** 생물 **bask** 햇볕을 쬐다 **vertebrate** 척추 동물

정답_(c)

46 by A or by B A에 의하거나 B에 의해서(선택)
by A and by B A와 B에 의해서
• The two most common ways to travel to Greece are by plane and by train.
그리스를 여행하는 가장 흔한 두 가지 방법은 비행기와 기차를 타는 것이다.

47

Ladies and gentlemen, may I have your attention, please? I regret to inform you that today's match between Selena Fritz and Marta Vladick will be canceled. Ms. Vladick has forfeited the match due to stomach cramps. Please present your ticket stubs at the box office to receive a full refund. You are eligible for 100 percent of the face value on the ticket. We apologize for the inconvenience. If you prefer, you can mail in your ticket stub to receive a refund. Further details are available on our website. Thank you for your understanding.

Q What is the announcement mainly about?
(a) The cancellation of a sporting event.
(b) Notice of a change of venue.
(c) Instructions on how to purchase tickets.
(d) Details about a person who has become sick.

48

The truth of the matter is that the world is changing at a rapid pace, and if the hospitality industry is to survive, we must do a better job of managing technology and addressing its challenges. Specifically, the industry must invest in technological infrastructure at both the corporate and the property levels. I get business travelers complaining to me all the time about the speed and cost of high-speed Internet at hotels. We have to learn to better utilize technology and meet customer demands, or we will simply lose their business.

Q What is the speaker mainly talking about?
(a) The changing nature of technology.
(b) Challenges for the hospitality business.
(c) The importance of high-speed Internet.
(d) The cost of running a business.

📖 번역

신사 숙녀 여러분, 잠시 주목해 주십시오. 유감스럽게도 오늘 셀레나 프리츠와 마타 블라딕의 시합은 취소될 예정입니다. 블라딕 선수의 복통으로 경기가 취소되었습니다. 매표구에서 입장권 반쪽을 제시하고 전액 환불을 받으시기 바랍니다. 입장권 액면가의 100%를 환급해 드립니다. 불편을 끼쳐 드려 죄송합니다. 원하신다면 입장권 절취 부분을 우편으로 보내 환급 받으실 수도 있습니다. 기타 자세한 내용은 홈페이지에서 확인하실 수 있습니다. 양해해 주셔서 감사합니다.

Q 안내 방송 대상은?
(a) 스포츠 경기의 취소.
(b) 장소 변경 공지.
(c) 입장권 구매 방법 안내.
(d) 아픈 사람에 대한 자세한 정보.

🎫 출제 POINT

장내 안내 방송의 목적을 묻고 있다. 이런 방송에서는 I regret to inform you that 뒤에 나오는 내용이 주제이자 방송의 목적이 된다. 따라서 today's match will be canceled를 바꿔 쓴 (a)가 정답이다. 블라딕 선수가 복통을 앓고 있다는 내용은 잠깐 언급되었을 뿐, (d)와 같이 담화 일부를 언급한 오답을 주의해야 한다.

forfeit 상실하다, 잃다 **stomach cramp** 복통 **stub** 입장권의 남은 반쪽 **eligible** 적격의, 자격이 있는   정답_(a)

📖 번역

사실 세계는 엄청난 속도로 변화하고 있고 서비스 산업이 살아남으려면 기술을 더 잘 다루고 도전에 좀 더 맞서야 합니다. 특히 서비스 산업은 기업과 자산 수준 모두에서 기술 인프라에 투자를 해야 합니다. 저는 출장 여행객들이 항상 호텔 고속 인터넷의 속도와 비용에 대한 불만을 털어놓는 것을 듣습니다. 기술을 더욱 잘 활용하고 고객의 요구에 부응하지 않는다면 비즈니스를 잃고 말 것입니다.

Q 화자가 주로 이야기하고 있는 것은?
(a) 변화하는 기술의 성향.
(b) 서비스 산업의 도전.
(c) 고속 인터넷의 중요성.
(d) 사업 운영 비용.

🎫 출제 POINT

주제를 묻는 문제이다. 역시 첫 문장의 to survive 이하에서 주제가 제시되고 있다. (a) 변화하는 기술의 성향은 주제를 너무 광범위하게 다루고 있으며, (c)와 (d)는 극히 일부분에 관한 내용이므로 오답이다. 빠르게 변화하는 세계 속에서 살아남기 위한 (b) 서비스 사업의 도전이 이 글의 주제이다.

hospitality industry 서비스업(호텔·요식업 등) **meet customer demands** 고객의 요구를 충족시키다   정답_(b)

---

47 안내 방송문에서 다음 구문 뒤에는 항상 중요한 내용, 즉 방송의 목적이 나오므로 주의 깊게 듣는다.
I regret to inform you that...
I am sorry to inform you that... 유감스럽지만 ~하다

48 The truth of the matter is that... 사실은 ~하다
연설문이나 발표문 등에서 강조하고 싶은 중요 내용을 말할 때의 도입 표현이다. 역시 이러한 표현 뒤에서 주제가 언급되는 일이 많으므로 놓쳐서는 안 된다.

49

Henry VIII is one of the most famous—and notorious—kings in British history. He became the King of England roughly 500 years ago. He's often portrayed in literature and movies as a cruel, womanizing monarch. He brutally suppressed the Protestant reformation of the church and eventually separated the Anglican Church from the Roman Catholic Church. He is also noted for his six wives, two of whom were beheaded. King Henry is notorious for his divorces, but he was actually never divorced from any of his wives. Rather, he founded a church to have his marriages annulled.

Q What is the speaker mainly talking about?
(a) The British royal family.
(b) The Roman Catholic Church in Britain.
(c) A famous event in British history.
(d) A controversial monarch.

50

Sudan is extremely diverse ethnically, with roughly 600 ethnic groups. It is also diverse linguistically, as people there speak over 400 languages and dialects. Sadly, some of Sudan's smaller ethnic and linguistic groups have disappeared over the years due mostly to migration, as migrants often forget their native tongue when they move to an area dominated by another language. Most Sudanese from differing linguistic groups can communicate with each other in Arabic despite the use of English by many of the elite.

Q What is the speaker mainly talking about?
(a) Migration patterns of Sudanese people.
(b) The effects of Sudan's civil war.
(c) How Sudanese people communicate.
(d) Sudan's many different peoples and languages.

☞ 번역

헨리 8세는 영국 역사상 가장 유명하고 악명 높은 왕 중 한 명입니다. 그는 약 500년 전 영국의 왕으로 즉위했습니다. 그는 종종 문학이나 영화에서 잔인한 바람둥이 군주로 묘사됩니다. 교회의 개신교 혁명을 잔인하게 억압했고 결국 영국 국교를 로마 카톨릭 교회로부터 분리시켰습니다. 그는 여섯 아내를 거느렸고 그 중의 둘을 교수대로 보낸 것으로도 유명합니다. 헨리 8세는 이혼으로 악명이 높지만 사실상 아내 중 그 누구와도 이혼한 적이 없습니다. 그는 교회가 그의 결혼을 무효화하도록 했습니다.

Q 화자가 주로 이야기하고 있는 것은?
(a) 영국 왕가.
(b) 영국의 로마 카톨릭 교회.
(c) 영국 역사의 유명한 사건.
(d) 논란이 많은 군주.

⊞ 출제 POINT

도입부에서 헨리 8세에 대한 이야기라는 것을 알 수 있다. 악명 높은 바람둥이로 알려진 헨리 8세는 영국 국교회를 로마 카톨릭에서 분리시켰고 여섯 아내 중 둘을 교수형시킨 왕이라는 설명이 이어지므로 (d)가 답이 된다.

notorious 악명 높은 **womanize** 바람둥이 짓을 하다 **annul** 무효로 하다, 취소하다   정답_(d)

☞ 번역

수단은 인종적으로 극히 다양한 국가로 600여 인종 집단으로 이루어져 있습니다. 또한 사용 언어도 매우 다양하여 400개가 넘는 언어와 방언이 사용됩니다. 슬프게도 수단의 소수 민족 및 언어 집단 중에는 시간이 흐르는 동안 대개 이주를 통해서 소멸한 경우도 있습니다. 이주민들이 다른 언어가 지배하는 지역으로 이주하면서 종종 모국어를 잊기 때문입니다. 서로 다른 언어 집단에 속하는 대부분의 수단인들은 사회 지배층 다수가 영어를 사용함에도 불구하고 서로 아랍어로 의사소통이 가능합니다.

Q 화자가 주로 이야기하고 있는 것은?
(a) 수단인의 이주 형태.
(b) 수단 내전의 영향.
(c) 수단인들의 의사소통 방법.
(d) 수단의 서로 다른 민족과 언어들.

⊞ 출제 POINT

첫 문장과 두 번째 문장이 also로 연결되면서 주제가 제시되고 있다. diverse ethnically와 diverse linguistically, 즉 인종, 언어의 다양성이므로 이 말을 풀면 (d) many different peoples and languages가 된다.

ethnic 인종의, 민족의 **dialect** 방언 **linguistic** 언어의; 언어학의 **due mostly to** 대체로 ~때문에 **dominate** 지배하다   정답_(d)

📖 TEPS Survival 전략

49 have+목적어+p.p. ~하도록 시키다, 당하다
- have his marriages annulled 결혼을 무효화시키다
- I had my car fixed. 나는 내 차를 정비시켰다.

50 despite+명사 ~에도 불구하고
 → despite the fact that+절
 → in spite of+명사
 → although+절
- despite the use of English by many of the elite
 → in spite of the use of English by many of the elite
 → even though[although] many of the elite use English

51

A new study followed women into menopause and found that those who breastfed were at lower risk for high blood pressure, diabetes and cardiovascular disease than those who did not breastfeed. Furthermore, the benefits were greater the longer they breastfed. Women who had breastfed for more than a year throughout their lifespan were almost 10 percent less likely than those who had never breastfed to have had a heart attack or a stroke in their postmenopausal years.

Q What is the speaker mainly talking about?
(a) Different methods for women to reduce the risk of serious diseases.
(b) One cause of female heart and stroke problems.
(c) The number of women who have children.
(d) The effects of breastfeeding.

☞ 번역

폐경기 여성을 대상으로 한 새로운 연구에서 모유 수유를 한 여성이 하지 않은 여성들에 비해 고혈압, 당뇨병, 심혈관계 질환에 노출될 위험이 적다는 사실을 발견했습니다. 더욱이 모유 수유 기간이 길수록 그 이점도 더 컸습니다. 전 생애에 걸쳐 1년 이상 모유 수유를 한 여성의 경우 전혀 모유 수유를 하지 않은 여성에 비해 폐경 후의 심장발작이나 뇌졸중에 걸릴 확률이 거의 10%나 적었습니다.

Q 화자가 주로 이야기하고 있는 것은?
(a) 여성들이 심각한 질병의 위험을 줄이는 다양한 방법들.
(b) 여성의 심장 및 뇌졸중 문제를 일으키는 하나의 원인.
(c) 자녀가 있는 여성들의 수.
(d) 모유 수유의 효과.

⊞ 출제 POINT

모유 수유를 한 여성과 하지 않은 여성의 폐경기 이후 질병 노출 결과를 대조하여 설명하고 있다. 질병을 줄이는 방법에 대한 설명은 없으므로 (a)는 오답이고, 모유 수유가 폐경 후 질병 노출도를 줄일 수 있다고 했으나 심장 및 뇌졸중을 일으킨다고 하지는 않았으므로 (b) 역시 오답이다. 정답은 (d)이다.
menopause 폐경기 **breastfeed** 모유로 키우다 **diabetes** 당뇨병
cardiovascular 심장 혈관의 **stroke** 뇌졸중   정답_(d)

52

The record-breaking heat wave will continue over much of the east today. Today's highs will hover above the 100-degree mark. People are making their way to local beaches and pools in droves. But fear not, as relief from the heat is on the way in the form of a cold front that is moving into the northeast today. In contrast to the scorching heat we've been experiencing, unseasonably cool temperatures are expected for much of the region by the weekend. That was a look at today's forecast. Now let's go back to Carol in the newsroom.

Q What is the speaker mainly talking about?
(a) The start of a heat wave.
(b) Places people should go swimming.
(c) The end of a period of hot weather.
(d) Activities people are taking part in locally.

☞ 번역

오늘 동부 지역 대부분에서 기록적인 이상고온이 계속되겠습니다. 오늘 최고 기온은 100도 이상을 기록하겠습니다. 인근 해변이나 수영장으로 인파가 몰려들고 있습니다. 하지만 오늘 북동쪽으로 이동하는 한랭전선과 함께 더위가 수그러들 것으로 예상되니 크게 걱정하지 않아도 될 것 같습니다. 현재의 찌는 듯한 무더위와는 반대로 주말에는 대부분 지역에서 이상저온을 경험하게 되겠습니다. 이상 오늘의 기상 예보였습니다. 이제 보도실의 캐롤을 다시 연결하겠습니다.

Q 화자가 주로 이야기하고 있는 것은?
(a) 무더위의 시작.
(b) 수영하러 갈 만한 장소.
(c) 무더운 날씨의 끝.
(d) 사람들이 근처에 참여하는 활동들.

⊞ 출제 POINT

동부 지역 일기 예보로 이상고온 현상 후 주말에는 이상저온 현상을 경험하게 될 것이라는 내용이므로 정답은 (c)이다. 중간에 But이라는 역접 접속사가 있으므로 그 뒷부분을 주의해서 들어야 한다.
heat wave 무더위, 폭염 **hover** 주위를 배회하다, 공중을 맴돌다
in droves 떼지어 **scorching** 몹시 뜨거운   정답_(c)

---

51 those who ~하는 사람들
- those who breastfed 모유 수유를 한 사람들
- Heaven helps those who help themselves.
  하늘은 스스로 돕는 자를 돕는다.
- There are those who say... ~라고 말하는 사람들도 있다

52 뉴스, 일기예보 관련 표현
- That was a look at.../ We had a look at...
  ~를 살펴 보았습니다
- Today is going to be...
  오늘 날씨는 ~하겠습니다
- Temperatures will reach...
  기온은 ~도까지 올라가겠습니다

53

With 4 billion copies sold, the Bible is the bestselling book of all time. Contrary to popular opinion, however, it is Agatha Christie—not William Shakespeare—who is the second bestselling author ever. Indeed, her detective novels have sold more than 2.3 billion copies in 56 languages since she published her first detective novel in 1920, *The Mysterious Affair at Styles*. In fact, her life was as full of mystery and intrigue as her novels.

Q Which is correct according to the talk?
(a) *The Mysterious Affair at Styles* was Christie's number-one bestselling book.
(b) More books by Shakespeare have been sold than books by Christie.
(c) Christie's life mirrored her novels to some degree.
(d) Christie's novels are more popular than the Bible.

☞ 번역

성경은 40억 부가 팔린 사상 최고의 베스트셀러입니다. 하지만 일반적인 생각과는 달리 두 번째 베스트셀러 작가는 윌리엄 셰익스피어가 아니라 아가사 크리스티입니다. 실제로 그녀의 추리 소설은 1920년 첫 작품인 〈스타일즈 저택의 죽음〉을 발표한 이래 56개 언어로 23억 부 이상 팔려나갔습니다. 사실 그녀의 삶은 그녀가 쓴 소설만큼이나 흥미로운 수수께끼로 가득했습니다.

Q 담화문에 따르면 옳은 것은?
(a) 〈스타일즈 저택의 죽음〉은 아가사 크리스티 최고의 베스트셀러이다.
(b) 셰익스피어의 책은 크리스티의 책보다 더 많이 팔렸다.
(c) 크리스티의 삶은 어느 정도 소설과 흡사했다.
(d) 크리스티의 소설은 성경보다 더 인기있다.

⊞ 출제 POINT

세부 사항을 묻는 문제이다. (a) number-one과 같은 표현들이 들어 있는 선택지는 답이 아닐 가능성이 높으므로 유의해서 본다. 마지막 말에서 크리스티의 삶이 소설처럼 수수께끼로 가득 찼다고 했으므로 정답은 (c)이다. (b)는 크리스티의 책이 셰익스피어의 책보다 더 많이 팔린 것이므로 오답이다.

intrigue 음모; 술책   **mirror** 반영하다, 흡사하다   정답_(c)

54

The United States Supreme Court will hear arguments on whether a school in Colorado violated the constitutional rights of a 13-year-old girl when officials strip-searched her. Officials from the school say they were looking for prescription-strength ibuprofen, a drug that treats minor aches and pains, after a classmate tipped them off that the girl sold the drugs to her. The strip-search failed to produce the drugs and when the parents of the girl found out what happened, they sued the school.

Q What does the girl claim happened to her?
(a) A teacher gave her the wrong mark on a test.
(b) She was searched illegally.
(c) A classmate assaulted her.
(d) She was suspended from school without just cause.

☞ 번역

미국 대법원은 콜로라도의 한 학교에서 교내 직원들이 13세 소녀를 발가벗겨 조사한 것이 헌법상 권리 위반인지 아닌지에 대한 논란을 듣게 됩니다. 직원들에 의하면 그들은 같은 반 급우에게 그녀가 가벼운 통증 치료제인 조제약 강도의 이부프로펜을 팔았다는 제보를 듣고 나서, 그 약을 찾고 있었다고 합니다. 조사한 결과 그 약은 발견되지 않았으며 이 일을 알게 된 그 소녀의 부모가 학교를 고소했습니다.

Q 소녀는 어떤 일이 일어났다고 주장하고 있는가?
(a) 교사가 부당한 시험 점수를 주었다.
(b) 불법적으로 수색을 받았다.
(c) 급우가 자신을 폭행했다.
(d) 정당한 사유 없이 학교에서 정학되었다.

⊞ 출제 POINT

세부 사항을 묻는 질문이므로 두 번째 청취 시 질문의 포인트인 girl's claim에 관한 부분을 잘 듣는다. 담화문에서 arguments on whether 이하에 답이 제시되어 있다. strip-search란 옷을 벗겨 몸을 수색하는 것이고 앞서 violated the constitutional rights라는 표현이 언급되었으므로 (b) '불법 수색'이 정답이다.

arguments on whether ~인지 아닌지에 대한 논쟁   **tip off** 비밀 정보를 누출하다   **strip-search** 발가벗기고 조사하다   **prescription-strength** 조제약 강도   **ibuprofen** 이부프로펜(항염증제)   정답_(b)

📖 TEPS Survival 전략

53 Contrary to popular opinion... 일반적인 믿음과는 달리 ~
• Contrary to popular opinion, women are not worse soldiers than men.
일반적인 견해와는 달리, 여성이 남성보다 군인 임무를 못하는 건 아니다.

54 약국 관련 표현
pharmacist 약사
fill a prescription 조제하다
without a prescription 처방 없이
over-the-counter medication 처방전 없이 직접 살 수 있는 약

55

Dr. Frank Drake devised the now famous equation that bears his name in 1961 while searching for artificial signals from two nearby stars. The Drake equation is a mathematical formula that allows people to estimate the number of civilizations in the Milky Way Galaxy that are capable of communication. People involved in the Search for Extra Terrestrial Intelligence (SETI) use the equation today. Due to the fact that the equation is relatively easy, amateur astronomers and scientists use it as well.

Q Which is correct according to the talk?
(a) Amateur astronomers created a famous equation in the 1960s.
(b) SETI astronomers thoroughly reject the Drake equation.
(c) The Drake equation is not considered very difficult.
(d) Frank Drake was a medical doctor whose hobby was astronomy.

56

Doctors are saying that the Acai berry is a "superfood" that can also help you lose weight. This small berry, which basically looks like a purple grape, is good for shedding pounds because it contains cyanidin, a highly antioxidant phytochemical compound. A Japanese study recently found evidence that cyanins carry out their magic by reducing fat absorption and draining body fat. We offer this amazing berry in juice and capsule form. Call us now to find out how you can get your free trial of the Acai Berry Capsule today.

Q What is one of the health benefits of the Acai berry?
(a) It makes people stronger.
(b) It increases people's appetite.
(c) It helps people lose weight.
(d) It reduces the risk of people getting cancer.

☞ 번역

프랭크 드레이크 박사는 1961년 두 개의 가까운 별들로부터 인공 신호를 찾던 중, 그의 이름을 딴 현재 유명한 방정식을 고안했습니다. 드레이크 방정식은 은하계에서 인간과 교신할 수 있는 문명의 수를 계산하도록 해주는 수학 공식입니다. 외계 지적 생명체 탐사계획(SETI)에 참여하고 있는 사람들은 오늘날 이 방정식을 사용합니다. 이 방정식은 비교적 쉽기 때문에 아마추어 천문학자나 과학자들도 사용하고 있습니다.

Q 담화문에 따르면 옳은 것은?
(a) 아마추어 천문학자들이 1960년대 유명한 방정식을 만들었다.
(b) SETI 천문학자들은 드레이크 방정식을 전적으로 부인한다.
(c) 드레이크 방정식은 크게 어려운 것으로 여겨지지는 않는다.
(d) 프랭크 드레이크는 취미로 천문학을 한 의사였다.

⊞ 출제 POINT

세부 사항에 대한 진위 파악 문제이므로 선택지를 하나하나 소거해서 답을 찾아야 한다. 방정식을 만든 것은 프랭크 드레이크이므로 (a)는 오답이다. (b)는 사실과 반대되는 내용으로 SETI에 참여하고 있는 사람들도 이 방정식을 사용한다고 했고, (d)는 언급되어 있지 않은 내용이다.
devise 고안하다, 발명하다 **equation** 방정식 **astronomer** 천문학자
정답_(c)

☞ 번역

의사들은 아사이베리가 체중 감량에도 도움이 되는 슈퍼푸드라고 합니다. 이 작은 딸기류 열매는 자주색의 포도 같은 모양을 하고 있는데, 고항산화 식물 화합물인 수아니딘을 함유하고 있기 때문에 체중을 줄이는 데 효능이 있습니다. 한 일본 연구는 최근 시아닌이 지방 흡수를 감소시키고 체지방을 유출시켜 그러한 효능을 발휘한다는 사실을 발견했습니다. 이 놀라운 베리를 주스 및 캡슐 형태로 판매합니다. 아사이베리 캡슐을 무료 시험하는 방법을 알아보시려면 지금 전화 주십시오.

Q 아사이베리의 건강상의 이점 중 하나인 것은?
(a) 체력을 강화시켜 준다.
(b) 식욕을 증진시킨다.
(c) 체중 감량을 돕는다.
(d) 암 발병 위험을 줄여준다.

⊞ 출제 POINT

광고 대상/ 광고하는 제품 특성/ 연락, 구입 방법 등의 순으로 전개된다는 점에 유의해서 청취한다. 여기서는 건강상의 장점을 묻고 있으니 is good for 뒤에 언급된 shedding pounds, 즉 체중 감소가 정답이다.
antioxidant 항산화(제) **phytochemical** 식물 화합물 **compound** 혼합물, 화합물
정답_(c)

---

55 due to the fact that ~라는 사실 때문에
　　 due to+명사 ~ 때문에
　• due to the fact that the equation is relatively easy...
　　 → because the equation is relatively easy...
　　 → due to[because of/ owing to] the simplicity of the equation...

56 광고 방송의 경우 보통은 다음과 같이 전화번호나 쇼핑몰을 알려주는 문장으로 방송을 마무리한다.
　　 Call us now to find out... 지금 전화해서 ~를 알아보십시오.
　　 Visit our website at www... 저희 홈페이지 ~에 접속해 보세요.
　　 You could either visit our offline store or shop online.
　　 오프라인 매장을 방문하시거나 온라인으로 구입하실 수 있습니다.

57

Downloading audio and video files without authorization may not be exactly the same as stealing someone's car, but it is still theft. Even though the copies cost nothing to produce for the record and film companies, the data in them has value. Some say they're not causing any real damage because they buy new copies of the downloaded files they like. However, the courts have ruled that this is not a valid rationalization.

Q Which is correct according to the talk?
(a) The courts are undecided on whether downloading material is illegal.
(b) Online movies are more popular than online music.
(c) Downloadable audio and video files cost a lot to make.
(d) Some people buy copies of the material they download.

☞ 번역

오디오 및 비디오 파일을 승인 없이 다운받는 것은 다른 사람의 차를 훔치는 것과 똑같지 않더라도 어쨌든 절도입니다. 사본을 만드는 데는 레코드나 영화 업체에 추가 비용이 들지 않지만 데이터 자체에는 가치가 있습니다. 다운로드 파일이 마음에 들면 제품을 구입하기 때문에 실질적으로 어떤 해를 가하는 것은 아니라고 말하는 사람들도 있습니다. 하지만 법원에서 이는 정당한 합리화가 될 수 없다고 판결했습니다.

Q 담화문에 따르면 옳은 것은?
(a) 법원은 자료 다운로드가 불법인지에 대해 결정하지 않았다.
(b) 온라인 영화가 온라인 음악보다 더 인기있다.
(c) 다운로드 가능한 오디오나 비디오 파일은 제작에 많은 비용이 든다.
(d) 다운로드 받은 자료를 구입하는 사람들도 있다.

⊞ 출제 POINT

담화문의 주제는 첫 문장 but 뒤에 제시되어 있다. 무허가 파일 다운로드는 불법이라는 것을 염두에 두고 선택지를 소거해 나간다. (a)는 마지막 문장에서 법원이 정당하지 않다고 판결했으므로 사실과 다르고, (b)와 (c)는 제시된 내용만으로 알 수 없다. 따라서 Some say ... they buy new copies of the downloaded files they like를 바꾸어 말한 (d)가 정답이다.

rule 지배하다; 판결하다   valid 근거가 확실한; 유효한   rationalization 합리화   정답_(d)

58

Hi, this is a message for Francis. This is Marley. You booked the package to Tahiti for me and my new bride. I just wanted to thank you for making the arrangements. The resort was beautiful and we enjoyed every minute of it. Our view from the room was stunning and the service was top-notch. The entire staff knew we were on our honeymoon so they treated us like royalty. I can't tell you how special we felt. I'll definitely recommend you to all our friends and family. Take care.

Q What can be inferred about the speaker?
(a) He will be going on a trip soon.
(b) His friends do not like to travel overseas.
(c) He is a travel agent.
(d) He was recently married.

☞ 번역

안녕하세요. 프랜시스 앞으로 보내는 메시지입니다. 저는 말리라고 합니다. 저와 제 부인을 위한 타이티 패키지 여행을 예약해 주셨죠. 수고해 주셔서 감사하다는 말씀을 드리려고요. 휴양지가 아름다워 있는 내내 즐거웠어요. 객실 전망도 너무 좋고 서비스는 최고였습니다. 전 직원들이 우리가 신혼여행 중이란 걸 알고 왕족처럼 대우해 주더군요. 얼마나 특별한 기분이 들던지요. 모든 친구들과 가족들에게 반드시 당신을 추천할 것입니다. 안녕히 계세요.

Q 화자에 대해 추론할 수 있는 것은?
(a) 곧 여행을 갈 것이다.
(b) 친구들은 해외 여행을 좋아하지 않는다.
(c) 여행사 직원이다.
(d) 최근 결혼했다.

⊞ 출제 POINT

전화 응답 메시지이므로 메시지 수·발신자와 용건을 먼저 파악한 뒤 두 번째 청취 시에 세부 사실을 집중해서 듣는다. 지난 여행에 대한 감사 내용이므로 (a)는 오답이다. bride와 honeymoon이라는 결정적 단서로 쉽게 정답 (d)를 찾을 수 있다.

bride 신부   stunning 놀라게 하는   top-notch 일류의   정답_(d)

🖹 TEPS Survival 전략

57 A와 B를 비교하면서 공통점을 강조할 때 사용하는 표현
A may not be exactly the same as B, but it is still...
A는 B와 똑같지는 않을지 모르지만 그래도 ~하다

58 강조의 표현
I can't tell you how... 얼마나 ~하는지 이루 말할 수가 없습니다
• I can't tell you how grateful I am.
말로 다할 수 없을 정도로 감사합니다.
You would never know how...
얼마나 ~한지 모르실 거예요.
• You would never know how sorry I am.
제가 얼마나 미안한지 모를 거예요.

59

The unemployment rate cannot ever be reduced to zero percent because, among other reasons, people are always being fired, being laid off or changing jobs. Thus, the term "full employment" does not mean 100 percent employment. Still, it is theoretically possible to make sure that anyone searching for a job can find one fairly quickly. Economists refer to this aim as "full employment." Early Keynesian economists believed that they could achieve full employment by having the Central Bank expand the money supply right up to the point where full employment was reached. After that, any monetary expansion would result in inflation.

Q What can be inferred about full employment?
(a) A country's Central Bank must play a passive role.
(b) Some people are briefly unemployed during full employment.
(c) The concept was invented by Keynesian economists.
(d) It is only possible with high inflation.

60

Hakarl is an Icelandic delicacy. Basically, it's a shark which has been cured with a particular fermentation process and hung to dry for four to five months. Hakarl has a distinct smell of ammonia and a very fishy taste. It's one of those foods that has an acquired taste. In fact, many Icelanders never eat it and the smell is so strong that Icelanders will suggest that those who eat it for the first time should hold their nose while taking their first bite. The accompanying beverage is a shot of brennivin, a local Icelandic spirit.

Q What can be inferred from the talk?
(a) Hakarl is a special type of food found in many northern countries.
(b) A lot of Icelandic food has some form of fermented shark in it.
(c) Many Icelanders do not like the taste of hakarl.
(d) Icelanders do not enjoy drinking brennivin.

☞ 번역

실업률은 결코 0%까지 낮아질 수는 없습니다. 이유 중 하나는 사람들이 항상 해고당하거나 구조 조정되거나 직업을 바꾸기 때문입니다. 따라서, '완전고용'이라는 용어는 100% 고용을 의미하는 것은 아닙니다. 하지만 구직자라면 누구나 꽤 빨리 일자리를 찾도록 하는 것은 이론적으로 가능합니다. 경제학자들은 이러한 목표를 '완전고용'이라고 부릅니다. 초기 케인즈 학파 경제학자들은 중앙은행이 완전고용에 도달할 때까지 통화공급을 증가시킴으로써 완전고용을 달성할 수 있다고 믿었습니다. 그 이상의 통화 확장은 인플레이션을 불러올 것입니다.

Q 완전고용에 대해 추론할 수 있는 것은?
(a) 한 국가의 중앙은행은 수동적인 역할을 해야 한다.
(b) 완전고용 중에도 잠시 동안 비고용 상태로 있는 사람들이 있다.
(c) 이 개념은 케인즈 학파 경제학자들이 창안한 것이다.
(d) 물가상승일 때만 가능한 일이다.

⊞ 출제 POINT

full employment(완전고용)에 관한 난이도 있는 담화문이다. 접속사 등의 연결어구를 잘 따라가는 것이 중요하고, 도입부의 Thus, Still 등 연결어구에서 단서를 얻으면 논리적 연결을 쉽게 파악할 수 있다. Thus 뒤에 이어지는 the term "full employment" does not mean 100 percent employment에서 정답 (b)를 찾을 수 있다.
lay off 정리 해고하다   monetary 통화의, 화폐의   정답_(b)

☞ 번역

하우카를은 아이슬란드의 별미입니다. 기본적으로, 이것은 상어를 특별한 발효 과정을 거쳐 처리한 다음 4~5개월간 널어 말린 것입니다. 하우카를에는 독특한 암모니아 냄새가 나며 매우 비릿한 맛이 납니다. 맛을 들여야 먹을 수 있는 그런 음식들 가운데 하나입니다. 사실, 아이슬란드인들 중에도 전혀 먹지 않는 사람들이 많으며 냄새가 워낙 강해서 처음 하우카를을 먹는 사람들은 처음 베어 물 때 코를 잡고 먹으라고 권할 것입니다. 함께 나오는 음료는 아이슬란드 지역의 독주인 브레니빈입니다.

Q 담화에서 추론할 수 있는 것은?
(a) 하우카를은 많은 북부 국가에서 발견되는 특별한 종류의 음식이다.
(b) 많은 아이슬란드 음식에는 발효시킨 상어가 어떤 형태로든 들어간다.
(c) 많은 아이슬란드인들이 하우카를의 맛을 좋아하지 않는다.
(d) 아이슬란드인들은 브레니빈 마시는 것을 즐기지 않는다.

⊞ 출제 POINT

하우카를이라는 음식에 대한 내용이다. 도입 부분의 Basically 뒤에는 정의가 따라 나오게 마련이므로 잘 듣는다. In fact 뒤에는 예상을 벗어나는 중요한 정보가 나오므로 주의해서 듣는다. 아이슬란드 음식이지만 뜻밖에 아이슬란드 사람 중에도 먹지 않는 경우가 많다는 언급이 있으므로 정답은 (c)이다.
delicacy 별미   fermentation 발효   beverage 음료   정답_(c)

---

59 up to a point 어느 정도까지
• I agree with him, but only up to a point.
나는 그에게 동의하지만 어느 정도까지만이다.
up to the point where ~한 시점까지

60 so ... that ~ can[cannot] 너무 …해서 ~할 수 있다[없다]
• She was so funny that I couldn't stop laughing.
그녀가 너무 재미있어서 나는 웃음을 멈출 수가 없었다.
so that ... may[can] ~할 수 있도록, 하기 위해서
• I make it a rule to go to bed early so that I can start my day early. 나는 하루를 일찍 시작할 수 있도록 일찍 잠자리에 드는 것을 규칙으로 하고 있다.

Grammar

1

> A I'm going to move to the Templeton area next month.
> B What a coincidence! _____.

(a) So I am
(b) So am I
(c) So do I
(d) So I do

📖 번역
A 다음 달에 템플턴 지역으로 이사할 예정이야.
B 정말 우연의 일치군! 나도 그래.

🎯 출제 POINT
어순/ 동사
'나도 그래'라는 동의 표현은 〈So+be동사+주어〉 또는 〈So+do동사+주어〉의 형태로 사용되는데, 이 문제에서는 A가 be going to를 사용하여 '~할 거야' 라고 말한 점이 힌트이다. '나도 이사를 갈 것이다'라고 해야 하므로 빈칸에는 So am I가 적절하다.
coincidence 우연의 일치   정답_(b)

2

> A Do you think the economy is getting worse in the new administration?
> B That is _____ recently.

(a) everyone's mind on
(b) everyone's on mind
(c) on mind everyone's
(d) on everyone's mind

📖 번역
A 새 행정부 하에서 경제가 더 악화될 거라고 생각하니?
B 최근 다들 그렇게 생각하고 있어.

🎯 출제 POINT
어순
'~의 마음 속에 있다, 생각하다'라는 뜻으로 on one's mind라는 표현을 쓴다.
administration 행정부   정답_(d)

3

> A Did you paint your bedroom yourself?
> B No, I _____.

(a) have painted it
(b) had it painted
(c) was painted
(d) had been painted

📖 번역
A 침실 페인트 칠은 직접 했니?
B 아니, 페인트 칠 시켰어.

🎯 출제 POINT
과거분사
페인트 칠을 스스로 했냐는 질문에 No라고 답했으므로 누군가에게 시켰음을 알 수 있다. 〈have+목적어+p.p.〉는 '목적어가 누군가에 의해 ~되게 하다'라는 뜻이다. 따라서 '침실이 페인트 칠 되게 누군가를 시켰다'는 의미가 되려면 빈칸에 (b) had it painted가 알맞다.
paint 페인트 칠하다   정답_(b)

📋 TEPS Survival 전략

1 앞 사람의 말에 동의할 때 긍정이면 〈so+조동사+주어〉, 부정이면 〈Nor[Neither]+조동사+주어〉로 받는다.
  • A: I can drive. 나는 운전을 할 수 있어.
    B: I can, too./ So can I. 나도 할 수 있어.
  • A: I can't drive. 나는 운전을 못해.
    B: I can't, either./ Nor[Neither] can I. 나도 못해.

2 get[become]+비교급: 점점 더 ~해지다
  • The patient was getting weaker every day.
    환자는 날이 갈수록 더 약해졌다.

3 have+목적어+p.p.: ~하게 시키다/ ~ 당하다[사역, 수동의 의미]
  • He had to have his house cleaned.
    그는 그의 집 청소를 시켜야만 했다.

4

A *Mamma Mia* is coming to the Sejong Center for the Performing Arts. Have you seen it?

B Yes, I _____ it in London last year.

(a) see
(b) saw
(c) have seen
(d) had seen

☞ 번역

A 〈맘마미아〉가 세종문화회관에 올 거래. 그거 봤니?

B 응. 작년에 런던에서 봤어.

⊞ 출제 POINT

과거와 현재완료 시제 구분의 문제로 현재완료로 물었다고 해서 답변도 현재완료로 해야 하는 것은 아니다. 답변 맨 끝에 last year라는 과거의 한 시점이 나와 있으므로 과거형을 써야 한다. **정답**_(b)

5

A I'm supposed to give a 5-minute speech on green energy and I don't know where to start.

B I _____ a good book you would find helpful. Do you want to borrow it?

(a) am having
(b) have
(c) have had
(d) had

☞ 번역

A 그린 에너지에 대한 5분 연설을 해야 하는데 어디서부터 시작해야 될지 모르겠어.

B 너에게 도움이 될 만한 책을 가지고 있어. 빌려 갈래?

⊞ 출제 POINT

시제

마지막 문장에서 Do you want to borrow it?이 있으므로 B가 지금 책을 소유하고 있음을 알 수 있다. 따라서 현재시제인 (b)가 정답이다.

be supposed to ~하기로 되어 있다   **give[deliver] a speech on** ~에 관한 연설을 하다   **정답**_(b)

6

A How was the Science Expo?

B We had fun _____ with some of the exhibits.

(a) to look around and experiment
(b) looking around and experimenting
(c) looked around and experimented
(d) to looking around and experimenting

☞ 번역

A 과학 엑스포 어땠어?

B 구경도 하고 몇몇 전시물을 가지고 실험도 하면서 재미있는 시간을 보냈어.

⊞ 출제 POINT

현재분사

We had fun의 문장 구조는 완벽하다. 그렇다면 문장 뒤에 올 수 있는 것은 부사나 분사구문이 와야 한다. '구경하기 위해서 재미있게 놀았다'는 (a)는 문맥상 어색하므로 '주위를 둘러 보고 실험도 하면서 재미있는 시간을 가졌다'는 (b)가 적절하다.

have fun 재미있는 시간을 보내다   **exhibits** 전시물, 진열품   **experiment** 실험(하다)   **정답**_(b)

---

4 go, come, leave, arrive 등의 왕래발착동사는 현재진행형으로 미래의 의미를 나타낼 수 있다.

• I'm leaving for Paris next Wednesday.
나는 다음 수요일에 파리로 떠난다.

5 have 동사가 '가지다'의 의미일 때는 진행형으로 쓸 수 없으나 '먹다, 마시다'의 의미일 때는 진행형을 쓸 수 있다.

• She is having lunch with her co-workers.
그녀는 동료들과 점심 식사 중이다.

6 수식하는 분사가 능동의 의미이면 현재분사를, 수동이면 과거분사를 사용한다.

• She just smiled, saying nothing.
그녀는 아무 말 없이 그냥 웃었다.

• Mark, shocked by the news, left without even saying goodbye. 그 소식에 놀란 마크는 작별 인사조차 없이 떠났다.

7

A Something about you looks different.
B I got my hair _____, actually.

(a) dye
(b) dyed
(c) dying
(d) to dye

☞ **번역**

A 너 뭔가 달라 보이는데.
B 사실 나 머리 염색했어.

⊞ **출제 POINT**

과거분사

〈get+목적어+p.p.〉는 '목적어가 ~되게 하다'라는 의미이다. 내 머리카락이 스스로 염색을 할 수 있는 것이 아니라 누군가에 의해 염색이 되는 수동의 의미이므로 과거분사 (b)가 정답이다.

dye 염색하다　　　　　　　　　　　　　**정답_(b)**

8

A Excuse me, but haven't we met before?
B Yes, I think we go to _____ church.

(a) each same
(b) a same
(c) the same
(d) same

☞ **번역**

A 실례합니다. 우리 전에 만난 적 있지 않나요?
B 네, 같은 교회를 다니는 것 같아요.

⊞ **출제 POINT**

관사

same은 명사를 수식할 때 항상 정관사 the와 같이 사용되므로 정답은 (c) the same이다.

go to church 교회에 가다　　　　　　　　**정답_(c)**

9

A Excuse me. Do you work here?
B Yes, I do. Can I help you _____ something?

(a) for
(b) to
(c) with
(d) by

☞ **번역**

A 실례합니다. 여기서 일하시나요?
B 네, 맞아요. 도와드릴까요?

⊞ **출제 POINT**

전치사

help someone with는 '~으로 누군가를 돕다'라는 표현이므로 정답은 (c)이다.

Can I help you with...? ~을 도와드릴까요?　　**정답_(c)**

📖 **TEPS Survival 전략**

7 get+목적어+p.p.: 목적어가 ~되게 하다 (수동)
　 get+목적어+to+동사원형: 목적어가 ~하게 하다 (능동)
　• How did you get her to pose for the painting?
　　그녀가 그림 그리는 데 포즈를 취하도록 어떻게 설득한 거야?
8 the same: (사물·성질·행동 등이) 똑같은 ~
　• People with the same career background should be paid
　　the same. 배경이 같은 사람은 동일한 급여를 받아야 한다.

9 help+목적어+with: 목적어가 ~하는 것을 돕다
　→ help+목적어+(to) do
　• Mary needs to help her children with their homework.
　→ Mary needs to help her children (to) do their homework.
　　메리는 그녀의 아이들이 숙제하는 것을 도와야 한다.

Grammar

10

> A Are you going to the library this afternoon?
>   I have a couple of books to return.
> B I don't think so, but if I _____,
>   I'll let you know.

(a) will
(b) could
(c) would
(d) do

📖 **번역**

A 오늘 오후에 도서관에 갈 거야? 반납해야 할 책이 두 권 있는데.
B 가지 않을 것 같은데, 가게 되면 알려줄게.

⊞ **출제 POINT**

시간·조건의 부사절

시간이나 조건을 나타내는 부사절에서는 현재시제가 미래시제를 대신한다. 주절에 미래를 나타내는 will이 쓰였지만 조건(if)을 나타내는 부사절이 있으므로 정답은 (d)이다.

return (책을) 반납하다   정답_(d)

11

> A We should have fixed the roof sooner.
> B I know. _____, the house would not be
>   in such bad shape now.

(a) We did so
(b) Had we done so
(c) Have we done so
(d) Did we do so

📖 **번역**

A 지붕을 더 빨리 고쳤어야 했는데.
B 알아. 그랬더라면 집 상태가 이렇게 나쁘진 않을 텐데.

⊞ **출제 POINT**

혼합 가정법

원문은 If we had done so인데 if가 생략될 경우 주어와 동사의 위치가 바뀐다. 따라서 정답은 (b)이다.

be in bad shape 건강이나 상태가 좋지 않다   정답_(b)

12

> A Can I move to a room with a better view?
> B Sure. Would you like a room _____ the
>   beach?

(a) to face
(b) facing
(c) to face to
(d) facing to

📖 **번역**

A 전망이 더 좋은 방으로 옮길 수 있을까요?
B 물론이죠. 해변이 보이는 방 괜찮으세요?

⊞ **출제 POINT**

현재분사

문맥상 '해변을 마주한 방'이라는 의미가 되려면 빈칸 이하가 room을 뒤에서 수식하는 구조가 되어야 한다. a room (which is) facing the beach에서 〈주격 관계대명사+be동사〉가 생략된 (b)가 정답.

view 시야; 경치   **room with a view** 전망 좋은 방   정답_(b)

---

10 if절에 동사의 현재형이 오면 어떤 가정이 아니라 조건을 의미한다.
 • If it rains tomorrow, the barbecue will be cancelled.
   내일 비가 온다면 바비큐 파티는 취소될 것이다.

11 과거 일이 현재까지 영향을 미칠 때 혼합 가정법을 사용한다.
   [If+주어+had+p.p., 주어+조동사 과거 (would/ should/
   could/ might)+동사원형]
 • If you had taken the shortcut, you would be home
   already. 네가 지름길로 왔더라면 벌써 집에 와 있을 텐데.

12 분사는 명사 앞이나 뒤에서 명사를 수식하는데 의미가 능동일
   경우 현재분사를, 수동일 경우 과거분사를 쓴다.
 • There is a free shuttle waiting in front of the hotel.
   호텔 앞에 무료 셔틀 버스가 대기 중이다. (능동)
 • The other injured man was carried to the nearest
   hospital.
   또 다른 부상자는 가장 가까운 병원으로 이송되었다. (수동)

13

A Do you happen _____ where my cell phone is?

B Oh, no. You've lost it again, haven't you?

(a) knowing
(b) to be knowing
(c) to know
(d) to have known

☞ 번역
A 혹시 내 휴대폰 어디 있는지 아니?
B 맙소사. 너 또 휴대폰 잃어버린 거 아니니?

⊞ 출제 POINT
관용표현

〈Do you happen to+동사원형〉 형태는 잘 외워 두도록 하자. 우리말로 '혹시 ~이니?'라는 의미로 생각하면 되겠다. 정답은 (c).

happen to 우연히 ~하다   정답_(c)

14

A Which one would you prefer of these two shirts?

B I'd like the plaid _____.

(a) one
(b) it
(c) that
(d) thing

☞ 번역
A 이 두 셔츠 중에 어떤 것이 더 마음에 드니?
B 나는 격자 무늬 셔츠가 맘에 들어.

⊞ 출제 POINT
부정대명사 one

plaid 앞에 정관사가 the가 있으므로 둘 중 특정한 하나를 지칭한다고 볼 수 있겠다. 형용사의 수식을 받으면서 앞에서 언급한 물건을 가리킬 수 있는 것은 부정대명사 one뿐이다.

plaid 격자 무늬의   정답_(a)

15

A How do you like _____ here in New York?

B The people are very friendly and the cost of living is not as high as I expected.

(a) yours
(b) that
(c) them
(d) it

☞ 번역
A 이곳 뉴욕에서 지내는 것이 어떤 것 같니?
B 사람들이 아주 친절하고 생활비도 예상했던 것보다 비싸지 않아.

⊞ 출제 POINT
관용표현

How do you like...?는 '~는 어떠세요?, ~을 좋아하세요?'라는 의미로 상대방의 의견을 물어볼 때 자주 사용이 된다. 여기서 대명사 it은 특정한 대상을 말하는 것이 아니라 어떻게 지내는지 막연한 것 혹은 상황을 의미한다.

friendly 우호적인   **cost of living** 생활비   정답_(d)

📖 TEPS Survival 전략

13 happen to는 It happens that 구문으로 바꿔 쓸 수 있다.
 • I happen to have some free time today.
 → It happens that I have some free time today.
   마침 오늘 여유 시간이 좀 있다.

14 부정대명사 one은 앞에 나온 가산명사의 반복을 피하기 위해 사용한다. 사람과 사물에 모두 쓰이며 복수형을 쓸 수 있고, 형용사의 수식을 받는다.

 • I want a donut. May I take one?
   도넛을 원해요. (도넛) 하나 가져가도 될까요?

15 특정 명사를 지칭하지 않는 it은 구어체에서 주로 쓴다.
 • How's it going? 요즘 어때? (사정/ 상황)
 • It looks like rain. 비가 올 것 같아. (날씨)
 • How long does it take to the station?
   여기서 역까지 얼마나 걸리나요? (시간)

16

A How long will it take to reinstall the software?
B It should be done _____ 3 or 4 hours.

(a) until
(b) by
(c) in
(d) for

📖 번역
A 소프트웨어를 다시 설치하는 데 얼마나 걸릴까?
B 서너 시간 안에 끝날 거야.

⊞ 출제 POINT
전치사
〈in+시간〉은 그 시간 안에 어떤 일이 발생함을 뜻한다. until과 by는 '~까지'로 미래의 정확한 시점이 나와야 하기 때문에 3 or 4 hours와 어울리지 않는다. 정답은 (c).
reinstall 재설치하다　　　　　　　　　정답_(c)

17

A How was Joan's wedding last weekend?
B You _____ have seen it. It was the most beautiful wedding I've ever been to.

(a) should
(b) must
(c) could
(d) would

📖 번역
A 지난 주말 조안의 결혼식 어땠어?
B 네가 봤어야 하는데. 내가 이제까지 가본 중에 가장 아름다운 결혼식이었어.

⊞ 출제 POINT
가정법
〈should+have+p.p.〉는 과거에 하지 못한 일에 대한 유감, 후회 등을 나타낸다. 문맥상 A는 결혼식에 가지 못했으므로 빈칸이 포함된 문장은 '네가 봤어야 했는데 안타깝다'는 뜻이 되어야 한다. 따라서 정답은 (a).
have been to ~에 가본 적이 있다　　　　　정답_(a)

18

A What do you want to know?
B Who is the guy _____ with Julie?

(a) dance
(b) dances
(c) dancing
(d) danced

📖 번역
A 무엇을 알고 싶은데?
B 줄리와 춤추고 있는 남자 누구야?

⊞ 출제 POINT
현재분사
'줄리와 춤추고 있는 사람'이라는 의미로 뒤에서 명사를 수식할 수 있는 것은 분사이다. 여기서는 남자가 춤을 추는 주체 즉, 능동의 관계이므로 dancing이라는 현재분사가 와야 한다.　　　　정답_(c)

---

16 until vs. by
둘 다 '~까지'라는 의미의 전치사로 사용되지만 until은 계속의 의미를, by는 완료의 의미를 나타내므로 구분해서 써야 한다.
• I studied for the final untill early morning.
　나는 이른 아침까지 기말고사를 위해 공부했다.
• You need to finish your report by this weekend.
　이번 주말까지 보고서를 완료하도록 하세요.

17 조동사+have+p.p. vs. 조동사+동사원형
• You should have seen it.
　그것을 보았어야 한다. ('보지 않았다'는 의미 내포)
• You should see it. 그것을 봐야 한다.

18 Who is the guy (who is) dancing with Julie?에서 〈주격 관계대명사+be동사〉는 생략 가능하다.

19

A What is Mike doing? He was supposed to be here half an hour ago!

B Speak of the devil. _____.

(a) Here comes he
(b) He came here
(c) So comes he
(d) Here he comes

📖 번역

A 마이크 뭐 하고 있는 거지? 원래 30분 전에 오기로 되어 있었잖아!
B 호랑이도 제 말하면 온다더니. 저기 오네.

⊞ 출제 POINT

도치구문

원래 부사가 앞으로 나오는 도치구문에서는 주어와 동사의 위치를 바꿔야 하지만 이 문장에서는 주어가 대명사 he이므로 도치되지 않았다.
Speak of the devil. 호랑이도 제 말하면 온다.   정답_(d)

20

A Do you think Sue will accept the suggestion?

B I'm not sure, _____.

(a) I hope
(b) hoping so
(c) so I hope it
(d) but I hope so

📖 번역

A 수가 그 제안을 받아들일 거라고 생각해?
B 잘 모르겠지만 그랬으면 좋겠어.

⊞ 출제 POINT

접속사

절과 절을 쉼표만으로 연결할 수 없으므로 접속사가 필요한데 앞뒤 절의 의미가 역접이므로 (d)가 정답.
accept the suggestion 제안을 받아들이다   정답_(d)

21

Whenever Laura feels depressed, she _____.

(a) to herself buys a pair of shoes
(b) buys herself a pair of shoes
(c) bought a pair of shoes for herself
(d) has bought a pair of shoes herself

📖 번역

로라는 우울할 때면 언제나 자신을 위한 신발을 한 켤레 산다.

⊞ 출제 POINT

시제/ 어순

Whenever ... feels 절이 현재이므로 주절의 시제도 현재가 되어야 하며, 'A에게 B를 사주다'의 뜻으로 buy A B의 어순이 적절하다.
feel depressed 우울함을 느끼다   정답_(b)

📋 TEPS Survival 전략

19 도치 구문
주어가 대명사일 때: 부사+주어+동사
주어가 명사일 때: 부사+동사+주어
• Here she comes.
• Here comes the teacher.

20 두 개의 절을 연결할 때는 접속사가 필요하며 구조와 의미에 따라 다양한 접속사를 구분하여 쓴다.

등위접속사: and, but, so 등
종속접속사: if, when, as, because 등

21 두 개의 목적어를 취하는 동사의 어순
• buy[make] A B = buy[make] B for A
  A에게 B를 사주다(만들어 주다)
• give[send] A B = give[send] B to A
  A에게 B를 주다(보내다)

22

He found _____ about the mistake he made at work.

(a) it embarrassing talks
(b) embarrassing it to talk
(c) talking embarrassment
(d) it embarrassing to talk

📖 **번역**

그는 직장에서 그가 한 실수에 대해 이야기하는 것을 난처해했다.

⊞ **출제 POINT**

가목적어 it
여기서 find는 〈동사+목적어+목적보어〉 순서여야 하는데 목적어
to talk about이 너무 길어 가목적어 it을 목적어 자리에 두고 실제 목
적어인 to talk about 이하를 뒤로 뺀 형태이다.
embarrass ~를 당황하게 하다, 난처하게 하다　　　　　정답_(d)

23

I have traveled to many places but _____.

(a) I've never been to Turkey
(b) never I've been to Turkey
(c) I've been never to Turkey
(d) I've been to Turkey never

📖 **번역**

나는 많은 곳을 여행해 보았지만 터키는 가본 적이 없다.

⊞ **출제 POINT**

부사의 위치
빈도 부사는 조동사 have 뒤에 위치하므로 정답은 (a)이다.
have been to ~에 가본 적이 있다　　　　　정답_(a)

24

All the equipment and medical instruments are cleaned and _____ thoroughly before reusing them.

(a) sterilized
(b) would have been sterilized
(c) be sterilized
(d) would be sterilized

📖 **번역**

모든 장비와 의료 기구는 재사용 전에 철저하게 닦고 소독된다.

⊞ **출제 POINT**

병렬구조
빈칸 앞 동사 부분을 보면 현재형(are cleaned)으로 기술하고 있고
and로 연결되어 있으므로 빈칸도 be동사 are에 묶여 sterilized가 되
어야 한다.
medical instrument 의료 기구　**sterilize** 소독하다　　정답_(a)

22 가주어와 마찬가지로 목적어가 너무 길 때 가목적어 it을 그 자리에 두고 실제 목적어(to take 이하)를 뒤로 보내는 형태의 구문이다.
• He makes it a rule to take a 30-minute walk every afternoon.
그는 매일 오후에 30분씩 걷는 것을 규칙으로 한다.

23 빈도 부사는 일반적으로 be동사나 조동사 뒤, 일반동사 앞에 위치한다.
• She is just 18, but has already been to many countries.
그녀는 아직 18살이지만 이미 여러 나라에 가보았다.

24 불변의 진리, 지침, 반복적인 습관 등은 현재시제로 나타낸다.
• The earth revolves around the sun.
지구는 태양 주위를 공전한다.

25

_____ in a neighborhood coffee shop, she was completely absorbed by her book.

(a) Sitting
(b) To sit
(c) Sat
(d) Being sat

☞ 번역
동네 커피숍에 앉아서 그녀는 책에 완전히 몰두했다.

⊞ 출제 POINT
분사구문
동시에 일어나는 상황을 나타내는 표현으로 부사절과 분사구문이 있다. 시제가 주절과 일치하므로 단순 분사구문이며 그녀가 앉아 있는 주체이므로 현재분사 Sitting을 쓴다.
absorbed 몰두한, 열중한; 흡수된   정답_(a)

26

If _____, inflammation of the stomach can ultimately lead to an ulcer.

(a) left untreated
(b) leaving untreated
(c) having left untreated
(d) had been left untreated

☞ 번역
치료를 받지 않을 경우 위의 염증은 결국 궤양으로 발전할 수 있다.

⊞ 출제 POINT
분사
If it is left untreated에서 접속사 If와 주절과 겹치는 부분을 생략할 수 있다. 여기에서 it is를 생략하면 남는 것은 left untreated이므로 정답은 (a)이다.
inflammation 염증 **ulcer** 궤양   정답_(a)

27

Each group _____ twelve men and women.

(a) consist of
(b) consists of
(c) is consisting of
(d) has consisted

☞ 번역
각 그룹은 12명의 남자와 여자로 구성된다.

⊞ 출제 POINT
수 일치
each는 단수 취급을 해야 하며 '~로 구성되다'라는 의미를 갖는 표현은 consist of이다. 그러므로 정답이 될 수 있는 후보는 (b)와 (c)이다. 이미 그룹이 구성되어 있는 상태이므로 정답은 (b)이다.
consist of ~로 구성되다   정답_(b)

📋 **TEPS Survival 전략**

25 완료분사구문: 분사구문의 시제가 주절보다 앞설 때
• Not having studied for the interview, I was totally lost when they asked me a difficult question. 인터뷰 준비를 하지 않았기 때문에 나는 어려운 질문을 받고 아주 당황했다.

26 주어+be동사가 생략된 분사구문 (수동)
• (As it is) written in simple English, this book can be read by anyone.

간단한 영어로 쓰였기 때문에, 이 책은 누구나 읽을 수 있다.

27 명사 앞에 one/ every/ each/ another 등이 오면 단수로 받아야 한다.
• Every one of the apples in the basket is rotten. 바구니 안의 사과는 모두 썩었다.

28

You will be shocked to see how many second-hand smokers die of _____ every year.

(a) lung cancer
(b) the lung cancer
(c) any lung cancer
(d) the lung cancers

☞ **번역**

얼마나 많은 간접 흡연자들이 매년 폐암으로 죽는지 보게 된다면 당신은 충격을 받을 것이다.

출제 POINT

관사

병명에는 관사를 쓰지 않으며 굳이 개수를 나타내지 않는 이상 복수로 쓰지 않는다.

second-hand smoker 간접 흡연자 **die of** ~로 죽다

lung cancer 폐암   정답_(a)

29

I love this house, the windows and balconies _____ show the character and lifestyle of San Francisco through their Victorian style.

(a) that
(b) what
(c) of which
(d) to which

☞ **번역**

나는 빅토리아 스타일을 통해 창문과 발코니가 샌프란시스코의 특징과 라이프 스타일을 보여주는 이 집을 좋아한다.

출제 POINT

소유격 관계대명사

두 문장을 이어 주는 관계대명사에 대한 문제이다. the windows and balconies (of this house) 즉 두 문장을 이어 주는 것이 매개가 this house이므로 of which가 정답이다.

Victorian 빅토리아 시대의, 빅토리아 풍의   정답_(c)

30

During the interview, applicants are asked to choose to answer _____ of the two questions they prefer.

(a) what
(b) which
(c) whatever
(d) whichever

☞ **번역**

인터뷰하는 동안 지원자들은 두 가지 질문 중 어느 것이든 그들이 선호하는 질문을 선택하여 답하게 된다.

출제 POINT

복합관계대명사

선행사를 포함하는 복합관계대명사를 묻는 질문이다. '두 개의 질문 중 어느 쪽이든 맘에 드는 것을 선택한다'는 뜻이므로 (d)가 정답으로 타당하다.

applicant 신청자, 후보자 **prefer** 선호하다   정답_(d)

---

28 질병, 운동, 학과, 식사명 등에는 관례적으로 관사를 쓰지 않는다.
 • have breakfast/ play tennis/ develop pneumonia/ study history

29 소유격 관계대명사 of which, whose
 • Everybody likes to work with the new manager.
  + Her attitude is always positive.
 → Everybody likes to work with the new manager, whose attitude is always positive.

긍정적인 새로운 매니저와 일하는 것을 모두 좋아한다.

30 선행사를 포함하는 복합관계대명사는 '어떤 ~라도, 무엇이든' 등으로 해석된다.
 • Whoever comes first will be served.
  누구든 빨리 오는 사람에게 음식이 제공될 것이다. (주격)
 • Do whatever you want to do.
  무엇이든 네가 원하는 것을 해. (목적격)

Grammar

31

_____ the support of his wife, he would never have become a lawyer.

(a) If it were
(b) Without
(c) Had it not for
(d) Except for

☞ 번역

아내의 지원이 없었다면 그는 결코 변호사가 되지 못했을 것이다.

⊞ 출제 POINT

가정법

가정법 과거완료 조건절에서 '~이 없었다면'의 의미로 쓰이는 Without을 묻고 있다. (c)는 주절이 과거완료이므로 Had it not been for가 되어야 답으로 가능하다.

except for ~을 제외하면

정답_(b)

32

The President is likely _____ the agreement on tax reform next week.

(a) sign
(b) to sign
(c) to have signed
(d) being signed

☞ 번역

대통령은 다음 주에 세제 개혁에 대한 협약에 동의할 것 같다.

⊞ 출제 POINT

be likely to

be likely 다음에는 to부정사를 써서 '~할 것 같다'라는 의미로 쓰인다. 따라서 (b)나 (c)가 답이 될 수 있는데 미래의 일을 예상하고 있으므로 (b)가 정답이다.

be likely to ~할 것 같다   **tax reform** 세제 개혁

정답_(b)

33

He always wanted to do something to make _____ for the underprivileged.

(a) a world the better place
(b) the world a better place
(c) the place a better world
(d) a place the better world

☞ 번역

그는 항상 세상을 소외 계층이 살기에 더 나은 곳으로 만들고자 무엇인가 하기를 원했다.

⊞ 출제 POINT

관사

문맥상 '세상을 더 좋은 곳으로 만들다'라는 내용이 되려면 정답은 (a)와 (b)로 압축된다. world는 정관사와 같이 쓰이는 단어이므로 정답은 (b).

the underprivileged 소외 계층

정답_(b)

📖 TEPS Survival 전략

31 if it were not for/ were it not for/ but for/ without
~이 없다면
if it had not been for/ had it not been for/ but for/ without
~이 없었다면

32 to부정사와 함께 쓰이는 동사구
• be about to: 막 ~하려는 참이다
• can't afford to: ~할 여유가 없다

• be supposed to: ~하기로 되어 있다
• be scheduled to: ~할 예정이다

33 하나밖에 없는 유일한 존재에는 정관사 the를 쓴다.
the sun, the sky, the sea, the ground, the world,
the environment, the earth

34

For every fifty miles north that you go, the temperature gets lower _____ one degree Celsius.

(a) at
(b) for
(c) to
(d) by

번역
당신이 북쪽으로 50마일을 갈 때마다 온도가 1도씩 낮아질 것이다.

출제 POINT
전치사
정도의 차이를 나타내는 전치사 by를 쓰는 것이 어울린다. lower to one degree Celsius는 '1도로 내려가다'라는 의미로 for every fifty miles(50마일마다)와 대구를 이루지 못하므로 오답이다.
Celsius 섭씨의 (*cf.* Fahrenheit 화씨의)   정답_(d)

Grammar

35

Eating too much is _____ as malnutrition.

(a) every bit as harmful
(b) as harmful every bit
(c) as every bit harmful
(d) harmful as every bit

번역
과식은 여러모로 보아 영양실조만큼 해롭다.

출제 POINT
동급 비교 어순
every bit은 부사로 해석되며 be동사 뒤에 위치하므로 is every bit as harmful 순으로 배열하는 것이 자연스럽다.
malnutrition 영양실조   **every bit** 여러모로 보아, 전적으로   정답_(a)

36

A chemical substance secreted by ants prevents them from _____ alive.

(a) being buried
(b) buried
(c) be buried
(d) burying

번역
개미들이 분비하는 화학 물질은 그들이 산 채로 묻히는 것을 막아준다.

출제 POINT
동명사
〈prevent+목적어+from -ing〉 구문으로 '목적어가 ~하는 것을 막다' 라는 뜻이다. (d)도 -ing 형태이긴 하지만 개미가 자신을 묻는 것이 아니라 묻혀지는 수동의 의미이므로 정답은 (a)이다.
secrete 분비하다   정답_(a)

---

34 정도, 차이의 의미로 쓰이는 전치사 by
- The number of people in the town decreased by 30%.
  마을 인구가 30%만큼 줄어들었다.

35 as+형용사+as: ~만큼 …한
- She was not as beautiful as I had imagined.
  그녀는 생각했던 것만큼 예쁘지는 않았다.

36 전치사의 목적어로는 명사 또는 동명사가 와야 한다.
- She is incapable of telling a lie.
  그녀는 거짓말을 못한다.

37

Only in your dreams _____.

(a) it will be possible
(b) will it be possible
(c) it is possible
(d) has been it possible

📖 **번역**

그것은 당신의 꿈속에서나 가능할 것이다.

🏛 **출제 POINT**

도치

부사구가 앞으로 나온 도치구문이다. only와 같은 부정어구가 앞에 나올 경우 〈부사구+조동사+주어〉의 형태가 되므로 정답은 (b)이다.

Only in your dreams. 불가능해.   정답_(b)

38

I'd rather _____ until we get the final decision from the Board of Directors.

(a) not tell you anything
(b) tell not you anything
(c) not to tell you anything
(d) do not tell you anything

📖 **번역**

이사회로부터 최종 결정을 받을 때까지는 제가 당신에게 아무 말도 하지 않는 편이 나아요.

🏛 **출제 POINT**

부정사 어순

had rather는 '~하는 편이 차라리 낫다'라는 뜻으로 뒤에 동사원형이 와야 하며 부정어와 같이 쓰일 때는 부정어가 had rather 다음에 위치한다.

Board of Directors 이사회   정답_(a)

39

This section lists the questions _____ about the product.

(a) most asked frequently
(b) frequently most asked
(c) frequently asked most
(d) asked most frequently

📖 **번역**

이 섹션은 제품에 대해 가장 많이 받는 질문을 나열하고 있다.

🏛 **출제 POINT**

분사구문 어순

명사 뒤에서 수식해 줄 수 있는 것은 분사구문이다. questions 자체가 질문하는 것이 아니라 누군가에 의해 질문이 던져지는 수동의 관계이므로 과거분사 asked를 쓴다. 문맥상 '가장 많이 물어보는'의 뜻이 되려면 부사 frequently가 asked 뒤쪽에 위치하고 most가 frequently를 앞에서 꾸며주는 형태가 되어야 한다.

list 목록에 기입하다; 열거하다   **frequently** 빈번히, 자주   정답_(d)

📋 **TEPS Survival 전략**

37 문법 영역에서 어순을 묻는 문제는 빈번하게 출제되므로 도치구문은 꼭 알아두어야 한다. only+after/ later/ when 등의 부사구가 문장 앞에 나오면 〈부사구+조동사+주어+동사〉의 순으로 도치된다.
• Only recently has the company started to make profits. 최근에서야 회사는 이익을 보기 시작했다.

38 to부정사 관련 표현
• have no choice but to: ~하는 수밖에 도리가 없다
• can afford to: ~할 (시간적·경제적) 여유가 있다
• leave nothing to be desired: 더할 나위 없이 좋다

39 부사의 위치
   often, occasionally, rarely: 일반동사 앞, be동사나 조동사 뒤
• I occasionally hear from her. 나는 가끔 그녀의 소식을 듣는다.
• He's rarely on time. 그는 거의 항상 지각한다.

40

Because Mr. Bucks is a bit hard _____, you might have to repeat whatever you have to say.

(a) to hear
(b) by hearing
(c) of hearing
(d) hearing

☞ 번역

벅스 씨가 청력이 조금 안 좋기 때문에 당신이 해야 할 말을 반복해야 할 수도 있다.

⊞ 출제 POINT

주절의 내용으로 보아 잘 듣지 못하는 사람은 벅스 씨, 즉 청력의 문제이므로 hard of hearing이 맞다. hard to hear라고 쓰면 '벅스 씨의 목소리가 작아서 잘 들리지 않는다'는 의미가 된다.
a bit 조금, 다소　　　　　　　　　　　　　　　　정답_(c)

41

(a) A　We've run short of paper for the Xerox machine. Will you order some for us?
(b) B　Sure. It'll be delivered by tomorrow if I place the order now.
(c) A　Great. Would you let me know as soon as it will be here?
(d) B　No problem. If there is anything else I can do for you, let me know.

☞ 번역

(a) 복사기 용지가 다 떨어졌어요. 당신이 주문 좀 해주시겠어요?
(b) 물론이죠. 지금 제가 주문하면 내일까지 배달될 거예요.
(c) 좋아요. 도착하자마자 저에게 알려주시겠어요?
(d) 문제 없어요. 달리 도울 일이 있으면 뭐든 말씀해 주세요.

⊞ 출제 POINT

시제
시간의 부사절에서는 현재시제가 미래시제 대용으로 쓰인다. 즉, as soon as it will be here를 as soon as it is here로 고쳐야 한다.
run short of ~이 부족하다, 떨어지다　**place an order** 주문하다
정답_(c) it will be here → it is here

42

(a) A　It seems people are going to the movies less often these days.
(b) B　Actually, studies show people now go to the movies than ever.
(c) A　I thought with the Internet, people wouldn't bother getting out of the house to watch movies anymore.
(d) B　But seeing a movie at a movie theater is totally different.

☞ 번역

(a) 요즘은 사람들이 영화를 자주 보러 가지 않는 것 같아.
(b) 사실 연구에 따르면 전보다 사람들이 영화를 더 보러 간다는데.
(c) 나는 인터넷 때문에 사람들이 영화 보러 집 밖에 나오기를 귀찮아 할 줄 알았어.
(d) 하지만 극장에서 영화를 보는 것은 완전히 다르거든.

⊞ 출제 POINT

비교급
'덜(less often) 보러 간다'는 표현이 나오고 그 말을 받아 '사실은 더 보러 간다'고 말하고 있으므로 more than ever라는 비교급 표현이 나와야 한다. 참고로 최상급은 more than ever before(그 어느 때보다 더)를 써서 표현한다.
bother 괴롭히다; 일부러 ~하다

정답_(b) than ever → more than ever

---

40 hard to+동사원형: ~하기 힘든
• She is hard to please. 그녀는 기쁘게 하기 어렵다.
= It is hard to please her.
41 시간부사절의 현재 시제 미래 대용은 part 3, 4에서 특히 많이 출제된다.
• You will fall in love with him as soon as you meet him.
당신이라면 그를 만나자마자 사랑에 빠질 거예요.
→ 미래의 일이지만 as soon as you meet him이라는 부사절이 있기 때문에 will meet 대신 현재형 meet을 사용함.

42 비교급으로 나타내는 최상급 표현
비교급+than any other+단수 명사: 그 무엇보다 더 ~한
• She is taller than any other girl in her class.
= No girl is taller than her in her class.
그녀는 학급의 어떤 소녀들보다도 키가 크다.

43

(a) A I'm going to the mall. Do you want to come?

(b) B I'd like to, but I have a few things to take care of right away.

(c) A Do you want to get something for you?

(d) B No, I don't need anything, but thanks anyway.

📖 번역

(a) 쇼핑몰에 가려고 하는데. 너도 같이 갈래?

(b) 그러고 싶지만 지금 당장 처리해야 할 일이 몇 개 있어.

(c) 뭘 좀 사다 줄까?

(d) 아니야, 아무것도 필요 없어. 어쨌든 고마워.

🔲 출제 POINT

to부정사의 주어

A가 mall에 가면서 B에게 사다 줄 것이 있는지 묻고 있다. (c)에서 to get something for you의 주체는 이 말을 하고 있는 A이다. to부정사의 주어가 문장 주어와 일치하지 않을 경우 내용상의 주어를 밝혀주어야 하므로 (c)는 Do you want me to get something for you?가 되어야 한다.

take care of ~을 돌보다, 처리하다

정답 (c) want to get → want me to get

44

(a) A I totally forgot about the blind date Karl arranged for me!

(b) B You mean you stood up your date?

(c) A Yeah, and it was too late when I finally realized it.

(d) B If I were in his shoes, I had been really pissed off!

📖 번역

(a) 칼이 주선해 준 소개팅을 완전히 잊어버렸지 뭐야!

(b) 데이트 상대를 바람맞혔다는 말이니?

(c) 맞아, 마침내 알아차렸을 때는 너무 늦어버렸어.

(d) 내가 그의 입장이라면 정말 화가 날 거야!

🔲 출제 POINT

가정법 시제

(d)에서 조건절과 주절의 시제가 다른 것을 확인할 수 있다. 일단 문맥상 현재 사실의 반대를 나타내므로 조건절에는 가정법 과거가 와야 한다. 따라서 주절의 시제 had been을 would be로 고쳐야 한다.

blind date 맞선 **stand up** ~를 바람맞히다 **be in one's shoes** ~의 입장이 되다 **piss off** 화나게 하다

정답 (d) had been → would be

📘 TEPS Survival 전략

43 부정사나 동명사가 있는 문장에서 주절의 주어가 내용상 주어와 일치하지 않을 경우 따로 내용상 주어를 밝혀 줘야 한다. Part 3와 4에서 가장 기본적으로 확인해야 하는 세 가지 문법 요소(주어와 동사의 수 일치, 시제 일치, 능동태와 수동태 적절성)와 더불어 주절의 주어와 내용상 주어 일치 여부 확인도 기억해 두자.

44 가정법 과거는 현재 실현 불가능한 바람이나 현재 사실에 반대되는 가정을 나타낸다.

• If it were cold, I would wear this jumper.
  만약 날씨가 춥다면, 나는 이 점퍼를 입을 텐데.

45

(a) A I can't put up with Dennis any longer.

(b) B Can you tell me what is the exact problem?

(c) A He always makes such a mess and just walks away.

(d) B I think you should stop cleaning up after him and confront him about this.

📖 **번역**

(a) 데니스를 더 이상 견딜 수가 없어.

(b) 문제가 정확히 뭔데?

(c) 걔는 항상 잔뜩 어질러 놓고 그냥 가버려.

(d) 내 생각에는 데니스가 간 뒤에 치다꺼리하는 건 그만두고 이 문제를 놓고 걔와 부딪혀야만 해.

⊞ 출제 POINT

간접의문문 어순

간접의문문인 경우 〈의문사+주어+동사〉의 구조를 취하므로 (b)의 어순을 what the exact problem is로 바로 잡아야 한다.

put up with ~을 참다, 견디다 **make a mess** 어질러 놓다

정답 (b) what is the exact problem
→ what the exact problem is

46

(a) Afrikaans is an Indo-European language that is derived from Dutch. (b) For the most part, it is spoken in South Africa and Namibia, and to outsiders sounds like a mix of German and Dutch. (c) Experts estimate that approximately 6.5 million people worldwide speak Afrikaans as a mother tongue. (d) Afrikaans has been seen long as a natural development from the South-Hollandic Dutch dialect.

📖 **번역**

(a) 아프리칸스는 네덜란드 공용어는 네덜란드어에서 파생된 인도 유럽 언어이다. (b) 대부분의 경우 이 언어는 남아프리카와 나미비아에서 사용이 되며 외부인들에게는 독일어와 네덜란드어를 섞어 놓은 것처럼 들린다. (c) 전문가들은 전세계적으로 대략 650만 명의 사람들이 이 공용어를 모국어로 사용하는 것으로 추정하고 있다. (d) 이 공용어는 오랫동안 네덜란드 남부 방언으로부터 발달된 것으로 여겨져 오고 있다.

⊞ 출제 POINT

부사 위치

〈have+p.p.〉 구문에서 부사는 조동사 have 다음에 위치해야 한다.

따라서 (d)의 has been seen long as에서 long의 위치를 has 뒤로 옮겨 주어야 한다.

Afrikaans 남아프리카의 공용 네덜란드어 **be derived from** ~에서 기인하다, 생겨나다 **Dutch** 네덜란드의, 네덜란드 말 **mother tongue** 모국어 **dialect** 방언

정답 (d) has been seen long as
→ has long been seen as

45 간접의문문이란 의문대명사(who, what, when, where 등)가 이끄는 의문문이 think, know, tell 등의 목적절로 쓰이는 경우를 말하며 〈의문사+주어+동사〉의 어순을 취한다.
• Do you know where his house is?(O)
  Do you know where is his house?(X)
  그의 집이 어딘지 아세요?

46 현재완료 구문에서 빈도부사는 조동사 have나 has 뒤에 위치한다.
• He has never been abroad. 그는 해외에 가 본 적이 없다.

47

(a) Someone with a learning disability does not necessarily have a low IQ or an inability to learn. (b) Countries such as the United States and Canada uses the term "learning disability" to refer to psychological and neurological conditions that affect a person's communicative capacities and potential to be taught effectively. (c) The term includes conditions like dysgraphia (writing disorder), dyslexia (reading disorder), dyscalculia (mathematics disorder), and developmental aphasia. (d) Alternatively, the term "learning disability" may be used more generally to refer to any developmental disability, as in the U.K.

☞ 번역
(a) 학습장애를 가지고 있다고 해서 반드시 IQ가 낮거나 배우는 능력이 떨어지는 것은 아니다. (b) 미국과 캐나다 같은 국가들은 '학습장애'라는 용어를 사람의 의사소통 능력과 효과적으로 배울 수 있는 잠재력에 영향을 주는 정신 및 신경적인 증상을 일컬을 때 사용한다. (c) 이 용어는 서자착오(글쓰기 장애), 난독증(글을 읽는 장애), 계산장애(수학 장애) 및 발육상의 실어증과 같은 증상들을 포함한다. (d) 이와는 달리 '학습장애'라는 용어는 영국에서와 같이 일반적으로 어떤 발달장애를 일컫는 말로 사용될 수도 있다.

⊞ 출제 POINT
수일치

가장 기본적이면서도 빈출되는 주어와 동사 수일치 문제이다. (b)는 주어가 countries로 복수이므로 동사도 uses가 아닌 use로 고쳐야 한다.
learning disability 학습 장애 **dysgraphia** 서자 착오 **dyslexia** 난독증 **dyscalculia** 계산 장애 **aphasia** 실어증

정답_(b) uses → use

48

(a) Society seems to be getting louder and louder. (b) This worries me because it is not only a huge disturbance, but it is also causing people to lose their hearing at a very young age. (c) It seems everywhere I go, to my office to the street to my local café, there has to be some form of dangerously loud sound. (d) If it's not construction or someone blaring music, then it's people arguing or trying to sell things.

☞ 번역
(a) 사회가 점점 더 시끄러워지는 듯하다. (b) 이점이 나를 우려케 하는데, 왜냐하면 이는 거대한 혼란일 뿐만 아니라 사람들로 하여금 매우 젊은 나이에 청력을 잃도록 하기 때문이다. (c) 내 사무실, 거리, 카페, 어디를 가든 위험할 정도로 시끄러운 어떤 종류의 소리가 있어야만 하는 것처럼 보인다. (d) 건축을 하거나 누군가 음악을 크게 틀어 놓는 것이 아니라면 다투거나 물건을 팔려는 사람들의 소리이다.

⊞ 출제 POINT
병렬구조

일단 (c) to my office to the street to my local café에서 세 장소가 나열되는데도 콤마(,)도 접속사도 없다는 점에 의문을 품어야만 한다. 문맥상 '사무실, 거리, 카페, 어디를 가도' 정도의 의미가 되어야 하는데, 'A부터 B까지'의 표현은 from A to B이다. from 뒤에 따라오는 to는 여러 개를 사용해도 무방하다. 따라서 (c)를 from my office to the street to my local café의 구조로 고쳐야 한다.
disturbance 방해, 걱정 **be associated with** ~와 관련이 있다
blare (나팔 경적 등을) 크게 울리다

정답_(c) to my office → from my office

📖 TEPS Survival 전략

47 주부가 긴 경우 주어와 동사의 일치를 묻는 문제가 많이 나오므로 실제 주어를 구분할 수 있어야 한다. 이때 수식어구를 괄호 안에 넣어보면 문장 구조 파악이 더 쉽다.

48 병렬어구는 형태를 일치시켜 주어야 한다는 점도 유의한다.
• Roy not only called, but came to meet her in person.
로이는 전화를 했을 뿐만 아니라 그녀를 직접 만나러 왔었다.

49

(a) In the 1700s, philosophers such as Descartes and Hobbes shared a mechanistic view of human behavior. (b) They believed that the underlying reasons for behavior were the avoidance of pain and the quest for pleasure. (c) In later years, many psychoanalysts like Sigmund Freud supported the instinct theory, saying that human behavior could be explained by two major instincts. (d) These were the instinct to survive, such as a drive for sexual reproduction, and the instinct to avoid death, that causes aggression.

☞ 번역

(a) 1700년대, 데카르트와 홉스 같은 철학자들은 인간 행동에 대한 기계적인 견해를 같이했다. (b) 그들은 인간 행동 밑에 깔려 있는 이유가 고통의 회피와 기쁨의 추구라고 믿었다. (c) 후년에 가서, 프로이트 같은 많은 정신 분석 학자들이 인간 행동은 두 가지 주요 본능으로 설명될 수 있다고 말하며 이 본능 이론을 지지했다. (d) 그 두 가지 본능이란 생식에 대한 욕구와 같은 생존 본능과 공격성을 불러 일으키는 죽음을 피하려는 본능이다.

⊞ 출제 POINT

관계대명사의 계속적 용법

(d)의 the instinct to avoid death, that causes aggression에서 관계대명사 that이 콤마(,)와 함께 쓰였다. 관계대명사의 계속적 용법에서는 that을 쓸 수 없으므로 which로 고쳐야 한다.

mechanistic 기계적인   **underlying** 기저의, 바닥에 깔린

quest 추구   **psychoanalyst** 정신 분석 학자   **instinct** 본능의

sexual reproduction 생식   **aggression** 침략, 공격

정답_(d) that causes aggression
→ which causes aggression

50

(a) Argentina has a federal, republican and representative form of government. (b) Executive power is vested in one person, the President, who is directly elected by universal suffrage for a term of four years. (c) The President and the vice-president are chosen by a runoff voting system. (d) If the candidate with the largest number of votes are not attained at least 45% of the vote in the first round of voting, a second round of voting is held.

☞ 번역

(a) 아르헨티나는 연방, 공화 및 대의 형태의 정부를 갖췄다. (b) 행정권은 4년 임기로 보통선거에 의해 선출된 대통령 한 사람에게 귀속된다. (c) 대통령과 부통령은 결선 투표 방식으로 선출된다. (d) 만약 가장 많이 득표한 후보가 1차 투표에서 적어도 45% 이상을 득표하지 못하면 2차 투표가 치러진다.

⊞ 출제 POINT

수동태/ 능동태

(d)의 주어는 candidate이며 문맥상 후보가 득표를 하는 것이기 때문에 능동태가 되어야 한다. 수동과 능동의 구분은 Part 3, 4의 단골 출제 포인트이며 특히 주어가 길어 구분이 어려운 경우 자주 출제된다.

vested 소유권이 정해진, 가득의   **universal suffrage** 보통 선거권

runoff 결선 투표   정답_(d) are not attained → does not attain

---

49 관계대명사에는 제한적 용법과 계속적 용법이 있는데 계속적 용법에서는 관계대명사 that 대신 which를 써야 한다.

• He designed two buildings in 1960's which[that] earned him famous architecture awards. (제한적 용법)
  그가 설계한 건물 중 두 개가 수상했다는 의미

• He designed two buildings in 1960's, which earned him famous architecture awards. (계속적 용법)
  그가 설계한 건물은 단 두 개인데 그 두 개가 수상했다는 의미

50 수동태로 쓸 수 없는 동사들
• 타동사: undergo, cost, resemble, become(어울리다), turn 등의 동사는 동사 자체에 수동 즉, '~하게 되다'라는 의미가 포함되어 있으므로 수동태로 쓸 수 없음에 유의하자.

Vocabulary

1

A I can't see any _____ here.
B Me, neither. Do you think we can just jaywalk?

(a) curb
(b) crosswalk
(c) lane
(d) sidewalk

📖 번역

A 여기는 횡단보도가 안 보이네요.
B 그러게요. 그냥 무단 횡단을 해도 될까요?

🏷 출제 POINT

jaywalk(무단 횡단하다)를 해야만 하는 상황은 횡단보도가 없을 때이므로 (b) crosswalk이 정답. 다른 선택지들 모두 공통적으로 도로와 관련된 표현의 오답이다.

jaywalk 무단 횡단하다 **curb** 인도와 차도의 연석 **crosswalk** 횡단보도 **lane** (도로의) 차도 **sidewalk** 인도   정답_(b)

2

A Thank you for coming so promptly on such short notice.
B No problem. My place is just a stone's _____ away.

(a) drop
(b) toss
(c) fall
(d) throw

📖 번역

A 그렇게 갑작스런 통보를 받고도 바로 와주셔서 감사합니다.
B 아무 문제 없어요. 저희 집이 엎어지면 코 닿을 데 있거든요.

🏷 출제 POINT

급한 연락에도 바로 와주어서 고맙다는 말에 No problem이라고 대답하므로 다음에 신속히 올 수 있었던 이유가 이어질 것을 짐작할 수 있다. a stone's throw away는 우리 말의 '엎어지면 코 닿을 데', 즉 '매우 가까운 거리'라는 의미의 관용표현이다.

promptly 신속히, 즉시 **on such short notice** 갑자기, 충분한 예고 없이 **a stone's throw away** 엎어지면 코 닿을 데; 매우 가까운 거리   정답_(d)

3

A Are there any women's shoes shops in this mall?
B Yes, we've got one on the seventh floor. They've got an excellent collection, and the prices are also quite _____.

(a) reasonable
(b) irrational
(c) outrageous
(d) plausible

📖 번역

A 이 쇼핑몰에 여성용 신발 가게가 있나요?
B 네, 7층에 하나 있어요. 신발 종류도 다양하고 가격도 아주 적당해요.

🏷 출제 POINT

가격(price)에 대해 말할 때 어울리는 어휘를 찾는 문제이다. 앞에서 excellent collection이라는 좋은 평가가 나오고 and로 연결되어 있으므로 역시 긍정적인 표현이 나와야 한다. 가격이 비싸지 않고 적당하다는 의미로 price와 함께 많이 쓰이는 reasonable이 정답. irrational이나 outrageous를 쓴다면 '터무니 없이 높은 가격'이라는 의미가 된다.

reasonable (가격이) 합리적인, 적당한 **irrational** 불합리한 **outrageous** 난폭한, 지나친 **plausible** 그럴 듯한, 정말 같은 정답_(a)

📑 TEPS Survival 전략

1 violate traffic regulations 교통 위반을 하다
   traffic ticket (citation) 교통 위반 딱지
2 within[at] a stone's throw of ~에서 매우 가까운 곳에
   within striking[walking] distance of
   ~에서 아주 가까운[걸어갈 만한] 거리에

3 floor plan 층별 안내도
   kiddie/ children's clothes 아동복 코너
   furniture shop 가구점

4

A I'm sorry, but there are no rooms available. May is our _____ season of the year.

B Can you tell me when the off season is, then?

(a) pinnacle
(b) height
(c) peak
(d) summit

📖 번역

A 죄송하지만 이용하실 수 있는 방이 없습니다. 5월은 1년 중 가장 성수기거든요.

B 그러면 언제가 비성수기인가요?

⊞ 출제 POINT

pinnacle, summit도 peak처럼 '절정, 정상'이라는 뜻을 갖는다. 하지만 '성수기'를 의미할 때는 season과 함께 써서 peak season이라는 표현을 사용한다.

off season 비성수기(의) **pinnacle** 절정, 정상 **height** 높음 **peak** 절정 **summit** 절정, 정상   정답_(c)

5

A I'm looking forward to working on the new project.

B But you can't _____ the possibility of Ronald being assigned to the job instead of you.

(a) overlook
(b) oversee
(c) overthrow
(d) override

📖 번역

A 새로운 프로젝트에 착수하기를 학수고대하고 있습니다.

B 그렇지만 로널드가 대신 일을 배정받을 가능성을 간과해서는 안 돼요.

⊞ 출제 POINT

A의 '학수고대하고 있다'는 말에 But으로 응답하고 있으므로 A가 한 말에 반대되는 내용이 와야 함을 알 수 있다. 따라서 '간과하다'의 (a) overlook이 정답이다.

look forward to -ing ~을 학수고대하다 **be assigned to** ~에 배치되다 **overlook** 간과하다; 감독하다 **oversee** 감독하다 **overthrow** 뒤집어 엎다 **override** ~보다 우위에 서다; 짓밟다   정답_(a)

6

A Won't you stay with me for _____ support when the boss makes his decision?

B Sure thing. You know I'm always here for you.

(a) ethical
(b) morale
(c) moral
(d) upright

📖 번역

A 사장님이 결정을 내릴 때 제 옆에 머물러서 정신적인 지지를 해주시지 않을래요?

B 물론이에요. 전 늘 당신 편인 걸 아시잖아요.

⊞ 출제 POINT

자칫 '사기'를 나타내는 morale을 답으로 선택할 수도 있지만 moral support는 '정신적 지지'라는 뜻이므로 답은 (c)이다. ethical은 '윤리적인'이라는 뜻으로 moral과 비슷한 의미를 갖지만 ethical support 하면 말 그대로 '도덕적 지지'라는 뜻이 되므로 문맥상 어울리지 않는다.

ethical 윤리적인 **morale** 사기; 도덕 **moral** 정신적인 **upright** 똑바로 선, 올바른   정답_(c)

---

4 절정, 최고조
peak/ height/ climax/ culmination/ apogee/ pinnacle/ summit/ apex/ crest/ zenith

• The democracy movements in China reached their apogee right before the Tiananmen massacre.
중국에서의 민주화 운동은 천안문 사태 바로 전에 절정에 달했다.

5 전복시키다
overthrow/ overturn/ upset/ capsize

• He completely overturned my preconceptions about geniuses. 그는 천재들에 대한 내 편견을 완전히 뒤집어 엎었다.

6 사기를 진작시키다
boost morale/ raise morale/ improve morale

• There are several wrong and right ways to raise morale. 사기를 높이는 데 몇 가지 옳고 그른 방법들이 있다.

7

A   Great presentation!
B   Thanks for the _____.

(a) complement
(b) compliment
(c) compliance
(d) completion

☞ 번역
A   발표 정말 좋았어!
B   칭찬해 줘서 고마워.

⊞ 출제 POINT
유사 형태의 단어에 관한 문제이다. '발표가 좋았다'라는 말에 대한 응답이므로 칭찬을 뜻하는 (b) compliment가 정답이다. complement와 compliment의 구분은 단골 출제 대상이므로 잘 구분해 두도록 하자.
complement 보충물   **compliment** 칭찬   **compliance** 승낙; 순종
completion 완성, 달성   정답_(b)

8

A   I heard the prisoner is still on the loose.
B   Yeah, it seems that police dogs lost the _____ and he just disappeared in the darkness.

(a) stink
(b) scent
(c) odor
(d) reek

☞ 번역
A   그 수감자가 아직 도망 중이라고 들었어.
B   맞아. 경찰견들이 단서를 놓쳐서 그가 어둠 속으로 사라져버린 것 같아.

⊞ 출제 POINT
lose the scent는 '단서를 놓치다'라는 의미의 관용표현이므로 정답은 (b)가 된다. stink, odor, reek은 냄새, 특히 '악취'를 뜻하는 단어이며 여기서는 중립적인 의미의 (b)를 쓰는 것이 적절하다.
on the loose 도망 중인   **lose the scent** 단서를 놓치다   **stink** 악취   **scent** 냄새, 향기   **odor** 악취   **reek** 악취   정답_(b)

9

A   Sorry for dropping by. Were you in the middle of something?
B   Not really. You've come at a(n) _____ time.

(a) awkward
(b) perfect
(c) precise
(d) hasty

☞ 번역
A   연락도 없이 들러서 미안해. 뭐 하고 있는 중이었어?
B   아니야. 아주 딱 좋은 시간에 왔어.

⊞ 출제 POINT
'미안하다'는 말과 함께 무언가를 하고 있는 중이었냐는 질문에 Not really라고 했으므로 답변은 '괜찮다' 내지는 '잘 와주었다'가 적절할 것이다. '완벽한 타이밍에 와주었다'는 의미의 (b)가 정답. (c)는 '정시에,' 즉 '약속한 시간에 꼭 맞추어 왔다'는 의미로 쓰일 수 있지만 A가 연락 없이 들렀으므로 문맥상 자연스럽지 않다.
awkward 어색한, 서투른   **perfect** 완벽한   **precise** 정확한   **hasty** 서두르는, 급한   정답_(b)

📖 TEPS Survival 전략

7 칭찬
compliment/ applause/ praise/ commendation
• The boss praised all the staff highly.
  상사가 모든 스탭들을 크게 칭찬했다.

8 prisoner/ inmate 죄수
death row inmate 사형수
behind bars 투옥 중이다

9 at ~ o'clock sharp 정각 ~시에
in time 시간 내에
on time 정각에

10

A Do you know how to format a hard drive?
B I'm sorry, but unfortunately I'm computer _____.

(a) blind
(b) savvy
(c) illiterate
(d) alien

✒ 번역

A 하드 드라이브 포맷할 줄 알아?
B 미안하지만, 안타깝게도 난 컴맹이야.

⊞ 출제 POINT

(c) illiterate은 '문맹의'라는 뜻이고 computer와 함께 쓰면 '컴맹의'라는 뜻으로 사용된다. blind는 정말 '눈이 보이지 않는다'는 의미이므로 부적절하다.

blind 장님의   **savvy** 정통하 있는   **illiterate** 문맹의   **alien** 이질적인, (성질이) 다른
정답_(c)

11

A Did you like the dress you ordered online?
B The pictures were deceiving. It didn't _____ my expectations.

(a) answer for
(b) come up to
(c) live with
(d) match with

✒ 번역

A 온라인으로 주문한 원피스가 마음에 들었나요?
B 사진에 속았던 것 같아요. 그 옷은 제 기대에 미치지 못했어요.

⊞ 출제 POINT

deceiving은 '속이는, 현혹하는'의 뜻이므로 결국 옷이 마음에 들지 않았다는 것이다. 따라서 기대에 부응하지 못했다(come up to one's expectations)는 표현이 와야 어울린다. answer for는 '책임지다', live with는 '~을 참고 지내다', match with는 '~와 어울리다'는 뜻이다.

deceiving 속이는, 현혹시키는   **expectation** 기대, 예상
정답_(b)

12

A Do you like tango?
B No, it's not _____. I much prefer salsa.

(a) the tip of the iceberg
(b) a hair of the dog
(c) my cup of tea
(d) the cream of the crop

✒ 번역

A 탱고 좋아하니?
B 아니, 내 취향은 아니야. 나는 살사를 훨씬 좋아해.

⊞ 출제 POINT

탱고를 좋아하느냐는 질문에 No라고 대답했으므로 부정하는 응답이 오는 것이 타당하다. (c) It's not my cup of tea가 '내 취향이 아니다'라는 뜻이므로 대화의 흐름에 적절한 응답이다.

the tip of the iceberg 빙산의 일각   **a hair of the dog** 해장술
my cup of tea 내 취향   **the cream of the crop** 알짜, 최상의 것
정답_(c)

---

10 literacy 읽고 쓰는 능력
    illiteracy rate 문맹률 (⇔ literacy rate 식자율)
    network illiterate 넷맹 (인터넷을 잘 못하거나 두려워하는 사람)
11 ~의 기대에 부응하다
    answer[meet] one's expectations
    come[live] up to one's expectations
    ~의 기대를 저버리다
    fall[come] short of one's expectations

12 • It's not my cup of tea. 내 취향이 아니야.
    • It's not for me.
    • It's not my type[taste].

13

A How did you find your roommate?
B I put an ad in the _____ section of the school newspaper and he responded to it.

(a) editorial
(b) obituary
(c) classified
(d) personals

☞ 번역

A 어떻게 룸메이트를 구했니?
B 학교 신문 광고란에 광고를 냈더니 그가 반응을 보였어.

⊞ 출제 POINT

put an ad, 즉 '광고를 냈다'고 말하고 있다. '신문의 광고란'은 classified section이므로 (c)가 정답.
put an ad 광고를 내다 **editorial** 사설의 **obituary** 부고의 **classified** 분류된, (광고가) 항목별인; 기밀 취급의 **personal** (신문의) 개인 소식란
정답_(c)

14

A Do you know who is _____ the keynote address at the seminar?
B I heard it is Dr. Williams, the founder of the Field Robotics Center.

(a) speaking
(b) celebrating
(c) delivering
(d) fixing

☞ 번역

A 세미나에서 기조 연설을 누가 하는지 아니?
B 필드 로보틱스 연구소의 설립자인 윌리엄스 박사님이라고 들었어.

⊞ 출제 POINT

'연설하다'라는 표현은 deliver[give] an address이므로 정답은 (c). '말하다'라는 의미의 speaking을 답으로 고르기 쉽지만 '연설'을 뜻하는 address나 speech는 deliver, give, make와 같은 동사와 함께 쓰인다.
keynote address 기조 연설
정답_(c)

15

A He told me he forgot to bring his homework.
B That's a _____ excuse. I don't buy it.

(a) steep
(b) lame
(c) low
(d) slight

☞ 번역

A 그가 나에게 숙제 가져오는 것을 잊어버렸다고 하더라.
B 구차한 변명이네. 나는 못 믿어.

⊞ 출제 POINT

buy는 구어로 '믿다, 받아들이다'의 의미가 있으므로 I don't buy it은 '믿지 못하겠다'라는 뜻이다. 따라서 빈칸을 포함한 부분은 숙제 가져오는 것을 잊어버린 것이 '신뢰성 없는 변명'이라는 의미가 되어야 한다. excuse와 어울려 '구차한 변명'이라는 뜻으로 쓰일 수 있는 단어는 lame, poor가 있다.
lame 절름발이의; 불충분한; 서투른
정답_(b)

📖 TEPS Survival 전략

13 business section 비즈니스면
obituaries 부고란
cultural section 문화면
international section 해외면

14 speech 연설
address 좀 더 격식을 차린 연설
opening speech 개회사
closing speech 폐회사
welcoming speech 환영사

15 • I don't buy it. 못 믿겠어.
→ I don't believe it.

16

A Why was the soccer team's coach
_____?

B I'm not sure, but there's a rumor going around
that he accepted bribes.

(a) restrained
(b) dismissed
(c) recruited
(d) dispatched

📖 **번역**

A 그 축구팀 코치가 왜 해임되었지?

B 확실하지는 않지만, 그가 뇌물을 받았다는 루머가 돌고 있어.

⊞ **출제 POINT**

'코치가 뇌물을 받았다'는 내용으로 보아 징계 또는 해임과 같은 부정적인 조치가 취해졌음을 짐작할 수 있다.

bribe 뇌물 **restrain** 삼가다, 억제하다 **dismiss** 해고하다; 해산시키다 **recruit** 모집하다, 스카웃 하다 **dispatch** 급파하다 **정답** (b)

17

A Why is Marian working overtime so much these
days?

B She not only has to pay _____ but also
has to support her sick dad.

(a) rent
(b) loan
(c) money
(d) lease

📖 **번역**

A 요즘 마리안이 왜 그렇게 초과 근무를 많이 하지?

B 집세를 내야 할 뿐만 아니라 병든 아버지를 부양해야만 하거든.

⊞ **출제 POINT**

not only A but also B(A뿐 아니라 B도) 구문이므로 A와 B가 같은 흐름의 내용이어야 한다. 병든 아버지를 부양한다는 내용, 즉 초과 근무를 해야만 하는 이유가 B에 왔으므로 A에도 그 이유에 해당하는 내용이 오는 것이 타당하다. (c) pay money는 돈이 필요한 이유로는 너무 막연하다.

work overtime 초과 근무하다 **rent** 집세 **loan** 대출 **lease** 임대차 계약 **정답** (a)

18

A I kept trying to call you last night, but I couldn't
get through.

B Sorry. While watching my _____
favorite show, I left the phone off the hook.

(a) all-time
(b) single
(c) unique
(d) well-versed

📖 **번역**

A 어젯밤에 통화하려고 계속 전화했는데 연결이 안 되더라.

B 미안해. 내가 가장 좋아하는 프로그램을 보느라고 수화기를 잘못 내려 놓았어.

⊞ **출제 POINT**

all-time favorite은 모든 때와 시대를 통틀어 가장 좋아한다는 의미로 함께 쓰이는 말이다. 따라서 정답은 (a).

off the hook (수화기가) 제자리에 안 놓여 **all-time** 전대 미문의, 불변의 **unique** 독특한 **well-versed** 정통한 **정답** (a)

---

16 there's a rumor going around는 there's word going around라고도 쓸 수가 있는데 여기서 word는 '소문'이라는 뜻이며 word가 '소문'이라는 뜻으로 쓰일 때는 관사를 앞에 붙이지 않는다.

17 loan 책[돈]을 대출하다
• He made a loan request for the new novel.
그는 새로 나온 소설에 대한 대출 신청을 했다.

18 get through 통화하다
put down the phone 전화를 끊다
• The line is busy. 통화 중이다.

19

A Hi, I wanted to apologize for being so crabby last night. I shouldn't have _____ on you.

B That's fine. But I hope it won't happen again.

(a) picked it up
(b) taken it out
(c) put it down
(d) given it up

☞ 번역

A 안녕, 지난 밤 내가 너무 화낸 것에 대해 사과하고 싶었어. 너에게 화풀이하지 말았어야 했는데.

B 괜찮아. 그렇지만 다시는 이런 일이 없었으면 좋겠어.

⊞ 출제 POINT

앞에 '사과하고 싶다'는 내용과 함께 〈shouldn't have+p.p.〉의 형태가 쓰여 '~하지 말았어야 했는데'라고 과거의 행동을 후회하는 내용이 나오고 있으므로 후회할 만한 행동을 찾는다. '화풀이하다'라는 의미의 (b)가 정답. crabby는 구어로 '심술궂은, 심통 난' 정도의 의미로 많이 쓰는 형용사이다.

crabby (사람들에게) 화를 내거나 불쾌하게 하는   **take it out on** ~에게 화풀이를 하다   정답_(b)

20

A I'm so nervous. I don't think I can handle this interview.

B Take a deep breath and _____.

(a) wind up
(b) straighten out
(c) loosen up
(d) burn out

☞ 번역

A 나 너무 긴장돼. 이 인터뷰를 해낼 수 없을 것 같아.

B 숨을 깊게 들이마시고 마음을 편하게 가져.

⊞ 출제 POINT

심호흡하라는 말 뒤에는 '긴장을 풀다'는 의미의 loosen up이 와야 자연스럽다.

wind up 결말을 내다. 마치다   **straighten out** 정리하다   **loosen up** 긴장을 풀다   **burn out** 다 써버리다   정답_(c)

21

A I'm indebted to you. I couldn't have come this far without your help.

B You're making me _____. It was nothing, actually.

(a) blush
(b) flush
(c) brass
(d) plush

☞ 번역

A 너한테 신세를 졌구나. 너의 도움 없이는 여기까지 못 왔을 거야.

B 쑥스럽다. 별거 아니었는데, 뭐.

⊞ 출제 POINT

빈칸 뒤에서 It was nothing이라고 한 것으로 보아 '쑥스럽네, 별거 아니었는데' 정도의 흐름이 적절하다. 따라서 정답은 (a). blush와 flush 모두 얼굴이 붉어지는 것을 의미하지만 flush의 경우 덥거나 병 때문에 얼굴이 붉어지는 경우에 사용된다.

indebted 부채가 있는; 신세를 진   **blush** 얼굴을 붉히다   **flush** 얼굴이 붉어지다   **brass** 놋쇠; 뻔뻔함   **plush** 호화로운   정답_(a)

📖 TEPS Survival 전략

19 화풀이하다
take it out on/ let off steam/ vent one's wrath/ wreak one's anger
• The man vented his anger on his daughter.
  남자는 그의 딸에게 화풀이했다.

20 • I'm nervous. 나 긴장돼.
  → I have butterflies in my stomach.

21 • I owe you one. 너에게 빚[신세]을 졌다.
  cf. How much do I owe you? 얼마예요?

22

A What do you think of the government's new healthcare policy?

B I hate their healthcare reform ideas. They're just another _____ scheme to deceive the public!

(a) delectable
(b) odious
(c) innocuous
(d) odorous

📖 **번역**

A 정부의 새 의료 정책에 대해 어떻게 생각하니?

B 나는 그들의 의료 개혁에 대한 생각들이 정말 싫어. 그건 대중을 속이기 위한 또 다른 더러운 책략이야!

⊞ **출제 POINT**

빈칸 앞에서 정부의 새 의료 정책을 hate한다고 했고 뒤에서도 scheme to deceive the public이 언급된 것으로 보아 빈칸에는 부정적인 단어가 와야 한다. odious와 odorous가 부정적인 의미의 단어인데 scheme과 어울려 의료 개혁을 받기에는 odious가 어울린다.

reform 개혁 **deceive** 속이다 **delectable** 즐거운, 기쁜 **odious** 가증한, 불쾌한 **innocuous** 악의 없는 **odorous** 악취 나는 **정답**_(b)

23

A I have to get out of here. Where is the nearest _____?

B There is one down the hall.

(a) retreat
(b) exit
(c) outlet
(d) getaway

📖 **번역**

A 나 여기서 나가야만 해. 가장 가까운 출구가 어디야?

B 복도를 따라가면 출구가 하나 있어.

⊞ **출제 POINT**

get out of here(여기서 나가다)라는 말에 이어지므로 출구를 묻는 내용이 적절하다. 정답은 (b). outlet도 비슷한 의미를 갖고 있지만 '배출구'라는 의미로 outlet for the repressed desires(억눌린 욕망의 배출구)와 같은 표현에서 쓰인다.

retreat 퇴각, 후퇴 **outlet** 배출구 **getaway** 도망, 출발 **정답**_(b)

24

A What do you say to my suggestion?

B Your idea sounds good, but I'd rather _____ my original idea.

(a) drop in
(b) lay out
(c) stick with
(d) carry off

📖 **번역**

A 내 제안 어떻게 생각해?

B 네 아이디어가 좋기는 한데 나는 내 원래 아이디어를 고수하고 싶어.

⊞ **출제 POINT**

빈칸 다음의 original idea와 어울리는 것은 '고수하다'라는 뜻의 stick with이다. 따라서 정답은 (c).

drop in 들르다 **lay out** 구성하다 **stick with** 고수하다 **carry off** 유괴하다, 낚아채가다 **정답**_(c)

---

22 What do you think of...? ~에 대해 어떻게 생각하니?
같은 표현으로 시험에 많이 등장하는 표현은
What do you say to -ing?이다.

23 fire exit/ fire escape 비상구
exit/ gateway 출구 (cf. getaway와 혼동 유의.)

24 들르다
drop by/ come by/ drop in on/ stop by
• I dropped by to see if you're feeling any better.
좀 나아졌는지 보려고 잠깐 들렀어.

25

A The plague that hit Europe in the Middle Ages was horrible.

B Absolutely. I heard it _____ almost a third of the population.

(a) passed away
(b) cleaned up
(c) wiped out
(d) let down

☞ 번역

A 중세에 유럽을 강타한 페스트는 정말 끔찍했어.

B 정말 그래. 인구의 거의 3분의 1이 죽었다고 들었어.

⊞ 출제 POINT

'페스트가 끔찍했다'는 말에 맞장구를 치고 있다. 인구의 3분의 1이 질병으로 인해 '죽었다'라는 의미가 되어야 하므로 (c) wiped out이 정답이다. pass away의 경우는 사람이 주어가 되어야 한다.

pass away 죽다 **clean up** 깨끗이 청소하다, 부패를 정화하다; (적을) 일소하다 **wipe out** 흔적 없이 지우다, 일소하다 **let down** 낙심시키다; 낮추다
정답 _(c)

26

Richer countries are asked to take the initiative to stop greenhouse gas _____.

(a) assuagements
(b) recuperations
(c) propagations
(d) emissions

☞ 번역

부국들은 온실 가스 배출을 막는 데 솔선할 것이 요청된다.

⊞ 출제 POINT

greenhouse gas emission(온실 가스 배출)처럼 자주 쓰는 표현은 덩어리로 알아 두는 것이 중요하다.

take the initiative 주도권을 갖다, 솔선하다 **assuagement** 완화물 **recuperation** 회복; 만회 **propagation** 보급 **emission** 배출
정답 _(d)

27

Through the _____ of fossils, paleontologists can learn more about dinosaurs.

(a) reparation
(b) restoration
(c) reinstatement
(d) reestablishment

☞ 번역

화석 복원을 통해 고생물학자들은 공룡에 대해 더 많은 것을 배울 수 있다.

⊞ 출제 POINT

paleontologist(고생물학자)라는 어려운 단어가 나왔지만 공룡에 대해 알기 위해서 하는 작업은 화석을 복원하는 것임을 유추할 수 있다. 선택지에 공통으로 들어가 있는 접두어 re는 '다시, 거듭하여, 새로' 등의 의미가 있어 모든 단어가 '~을 원상태로 되돌린다'는 뜻을 갖고 있다. 하지만 대상에 따라 쓰는 단어가 달라지므로 유의해야 한다. 화석이나 미술품 등 오래된 것을 복원하는 것은 (b) restoration이다.

fossil 화석 **paleontologist** 고생물학자 **reparation** 수리, 수선 **restoration** 회복, 복원 **reinstatement** 복직 **reestablishment** 재수립
정답 _(b)

📖 TEPS Survival 전략

25 plague 역병, 골칫거리
  be plagued with ~에 시달리다
  • Many Internet users were plagued with obscene mails.
  많은 인터넷 사용자들이 음란 메일에 시달렸다.

26 emit greenhouse gases 온실가스를 배출하다
  greenhouse gas reduction 온실가스 축소

27 reconstruction 재건, 개축; 복원
  reconstruction of the old historic building
  오래된 역사적 건물의 복원
  3D reconstruction 영상 복원

28

The building was not as close as it looked, so it _____ me a while to walk there.

(a) brought
(b) had
(c) cost
(d) took

☞ 번역

건물은 보이는 것만큼 가까이 있지 않아서 그곳까지 걸어가는 데 시간이 꽤 걸렸다.

⊞ 출제 POINT

'(시간·비용이) 들다'에 해당되는 동사는 (d) took이다. '～가 …하는 데 시간이 걸리다'의 뜻으로 〈take+사람+시간+to동사원형〉의 어순도 같이 알아두자. cost는 '(비용이) 들다'라는 의미이므로 정답이 될 수 없다.

a while 잠깐 동안   정답_(d)

29

Companies should make customer _____ a top priority since happy customers tend to buy the same brand repeatedly.

(a) approval
(b) atonement
(c) contempt
(d) satisfaction

☞ 번역

회사들은 고객 만족을 최우선으로 삼아야 한다. 왜냐하면 만족한 고객들이 동일한 브랜드를 반복해서 사는 경향이 있기 때문이다.

⊞ 출제 POINT

'고객 만족'으로 쓰이는 표현은 customer satisfaction이다. 또한 뒷부분의 happy customers라는 단어를 볼 때 의미적으로도 (d) satisfaction이 적절하다.

make A a top priority A를 최우선으로 하다   **repeatedly** 반복해서
approval 승인   **atonement** 보상   **contempt** 경멸   정답_(d)

30

The ancient tomb has stood from time _____ on the hill.

(a) imminent
(b) immemorial
(c) impeccable
(d) impetuous

☞ 번역

고대 무덤은 태고적부터 언덕에 있었다.

⊞ 출제 POINT

빈칸 앞의 from time에 자연스럽게 이어지는 표현을 찾는 문제이다. immemorial은 원래 '기억에 없는'이라는 뜻인데 from time immemorial이 덩어리로 '사람의 기억에 없을 만큼 오래된', 즉 '태고적부터'라는 의미로 쓰인다.

imminent 절박한   **immemorial** 기억에 없는, 태고의   **impeccable** 흠 없는   **impetuous** 맹렬한   정답_(b)

---

28 take A a while to: A가 ～하는 데 시간이 꽤 걸리다
 • It took me a while to finish the operation.
  작업을 끝내는 데 시간이 꽤 걸렸다.
29 satisfy customers 고객을 만족시키다
  meet customer demand/ meet the needs of customers
  소비자 요구를 만족시키다

30 immemorable 기억할 가치가 없는
  imminent/ impending 절박한, 임박한
  an impending storm/ danger/ disaster/ death
  임박한 폭우/ 위험/ 재해/ 죽음

31

Even if you forget your lines, you can _____ on stage.

(a) render
(b) improvise
(c) forge
(d) contrive

🖙 번역

설령 대사를 잊어버린다 하더라도 무대에서 임기 응변으로 대처할 수 있다.

⊞ 출제 POINT

미리 정해진 대사를 잊어버렸다면 즉석에서 만들어내어 대처해야 한다는 내용이 이어져야 자연스럽다. improvise가 '(연주·연설·공연 등을) 즉석에서 하다'의 의미이므로 (b)가 정답. forge는 '만들어내다'의 의미이긴 하지만 '거짓말을 꾸미다; 문서를 위조하다' 등의 부정적인 뉘앙스로 쓰인다.

render 묘사하다; 연출하다   improvise 즉석에서 하다   forge 거짓말을 꾸며내다; 문서를 위조하다   contrive 고안하다; 연구하다   정답_(b)

32

Those who _____ the speed limit were responsible for more than half of all the car accidents last year.

(a) overcame
(b) outshine
(c) exceeded
(d) outpaced

🖙 번역

지난해 자동차 사고의 절반 이상에 대한 책임은 제한 속도를 초과한 사람들에게 있었다.

⊞ 출제 POINT

'자동차 사고에 대한 책임이 있다'는 내용으로 보아 '제한 속도를 초과하다'라는 의미의 exceed the speed limit이 문맥상 적절하다. outpace는 '~보다 빠르다'라는 의미이지만 This car can easily outpace most cars(이 차는 대부분의 다른 차들을 쉽게 따돌릴 수 있다)와 같이 비교 대상이 뒤에 올 때 쓴다.

overcome 극복하다   outshine ~보다 빛나다   outpace ~보다 앞서다   정답_(c)

33

A growing _____ of literature is showing a strong correlation between lack of sleep and memory.

(a) share
(b) bulk
(c) group
(d) body

🖙 번역

점점 더 많은 연구 문헌들이 수면 부족과 기억력 사이의 깊은 상관관계를 보여주고 있다.

⊞ 출제 POINT

body는 많은 양을 나타낼 때 쓸 수 있는 표현으로 a body of water, a body of literature 등이 있다. a group of는 흔히 사람과 어울려 a group of people처럼 쓰인다.

literature 문헌; 문학   correlation 상관관계   lack 결핍   정답_(d)

📖 TEPS Survival 전략

31 off the cuff 즉흥적으로, 즉석에서
• The spokesman spoke off the cuff about the historic event to the reporters.
대변인은 역사적인 이벤트에 대해 즉석에서 리포터에게 말했다.

32 overspeed 과속(하다)
issue a ticket 교통위반 딱지를 발행하다

33 the correlation[connection/ link] between smoking and lung cancer 흡연과 폐암 간의 상관관계

34

Margaret Thatcher was first _____ the "Iron Lady" for her unrepentant and hard-line policies.

(a) titled
(b) dubbed
(c) recorded
(d) honored

📖 **번역**

마가렛 대처는 그녀의 완고한 강경 정책 때문에 처음 '철의 여인'이라고 불렸다.

🎫 **출제 POINT**

dub는 dub A B 형태로 쓰며 'A를 B라 부르다'라는 뜻이다. Iron Lady 앞에 전치사가 없는 것으로 보아 A is dubbed B로 쓸 수 있는 (b)가 답이다. title은 책의 제목이나 칭호, 작위 등과 함께 쓰이므로 문맥상 어울리지 않는다.

unrepentant 완고한 **hard-line policy** 강경 정책 　정답_(b)

35

The supermarket is _____ discount coupons to its customers to celebrate opening its fifth store in the area.

(a) throwing up
(b) putting through
(c) showing up
(d) giving away

📖 **번역**

그 슈퍼마켓은 이 지역에서 다섯 번째 상점 개업을 축하하기 위해 고객들에게 할인 쿠폰을 나눠주고 있다.

🎫 **출제 POINT**

discount coupon과 어울리는 단어는 '나눠주다'라는 의미의 give away[hand out/ distribute]이다.
throw up 급상승하다; 토하다 **put through** ~을 실행하다; 전화 연결하다 **show up** 돋보이다 **give away** 나눠주다 　정답_(d)

36

_____ our website free for 7 days to decide if it satisfies your needs.

(a) Buy
(b) Try
(c) Experiment
(d) Hold

📖 **번역**

저희 홈페이지를 7일 동안 무료로 사용해 보시고 여러분의 필요에 맞는지 결정하십시오.

🎫 **출제 POINT**

나중에 필요를 만족시키는지 결정하라는 말이 이어지므로, '시험 삼아 ~해보다'라는 의미의 try가 어울린다. buy는 뒤에 따라 나오는 free와 자연스럽게 연결되지 않는다.
satisfy one's needs 필요를 충족시키다(meet[accommodate] one's needs) 　정답_(b)

---

34 hard-line policy 강경정책
　soft-line policy 유화정책
　engagement policy 융화정책

35 throw away 내버리다, 낭비하다
　throw out 버리다
　throw up 토하다

36 try whether ~ or not ~할 수 있을지 시험 삼아 해보다
　• Try whether you can pass the test or not.
　테스트를 통과할 수 있을지 시험 삼아 해봐라.

Vocabulary

37

He faces life behind _____ for planting a bomb outside the embassy.

(a) prison
(b) bars
(c) wheels
(d) cell

📖 번역
그는 영사관 바깥에 폭탄을 설치한 혐의로 투옥 중이다.

⊞ 출제 POINT
폭탄 설치를 한 결과로는 '투옥되어', 즉 (b)의 behind bars가 적절하다. behind the wheel은 운전대 뒤에 있는 것, 즉 '운전 중'이라는 의미. (a)의 prison이 답이 되려면 life in prison과 같이 전치사 in이 나와야 한다.

plant 심다; 설치하다　**embassy** 대사관　**behind bars** 투옥 중인
cell (교도소의) 독방　　　　　　　　　　　　　　　**정답_(b)**

38

A middle-aged man sued the tobacco company for giving him a fatal illness, but he lost his _____.

(a) file
(b) case
(c) charge
(d) sentence

📖 번역
한 중년 남성이 그를 불치병에 걸리도록 한 혐의로 담배 회사를 고소했지만 패소했다.

출제 POINT
'고소했다'라는 내용 뒤에 but이 있으므로 결과가 좋지 않았다는 내용이 와야 하며 lose one's case가 '패소하다'라는 표현이므로 정답은 (b)이다. 반대로 '승소하다'는 gain[win] one's case이다. (a)의 file은 file a suit[complaint] 등과 같이 쓰여서 '소송[민원]을 제기하다'라는 뜻이다.

lose one's case 패소하다　**sentence** 선고하다　　　　**정답_(b)**

39

The President made a(n) _____ threat to take health care away from Congress, which he has no power to do.

(a) blank
(b) free
(c) empty
(d) vacant

📖 번역
대통령은 의료 정책을 의회에서 빼겠다고 하는데, 그에게는 그럴 만한 힘이 없다.

⊞ 출제 POINT
'말뿐인 협박'은 empty threat이라고 한다. make 동사를 써서 make empty threat을 덩어리째 기억해두자.

blank 정보가 없는; 기록되지 않은　**free** 무료의; 한가한　**vacant** 빈, 공석의　　　　　　　　　　　　　　　　　　　　　　　　**정답_(c)**

📋 TEPS Survival 전략

37 behind close doors (비밀을 지키기 위해) 사적으로 하는
behind one's back (~의) 뒤에서, 몰래
behind the scenes 무대 뒤에서; 남몰래

38 sue A for B/ accuse A of B　A를 B 때문에 고소하다
· John accused her of murder.
존은 살인 혐의로 그녀를 고소했다.

39 empty 힘이 없는, 내용 없는 (an empty glass, empty promise)
blank 정보가 없는, 기록되지 않은 (a blank tape, a blank CD)
free 무료의, 한가한 (free school meals, smoke free zone)
vacant 빈, 공석의 (a vacant position)

40

Try to consume the recommended daily _____ of vitamin C.

(a) taking
(b) dose
(c) number
(d) pills

☞ 번역

비타민 C 1일 권장량을 먹도록 하세요.

⊞ 출제 POINT

'1일 권장량'이라는 표현은 recommended daily dose이다.
dose 1회분 복용량 　　　　　　　　　　　　　정답_(b)

41

The CEO will _____ next week a strategic alliance with eBay.

(a) renounce
(b) denounce
(c) pronounce
(d) announce

☞ 번역

CEO는 다음 주에 이베이와의 전략적 제휴에 대해 발표할 것이다.

⊞ 출제 POINT

'이베이와의 전략적 제휴를 알리다, 발표하다'라는 내용이 되도록 (d) announce를 써야 한다. the strategic alliance가 아닌 a strategic alliance로 쓰여진 걸로 보아 기존에 있던 제휴가 아닌 이제 앞으로 하게 될 제휴를 나타내므로 renounce나 denounce는 맞지 않다.
alliance 연합　**renounce** (공식적으로) 포기하다　**denounce** 비난하다　**pronounce** 선언하다　　　　　　　　　　정답_(d)

42

With vivid 3D graphics, the characters and the scenery in the new video game look astonishingly _____.

(a) realistic
(b) virtual
(c) fake
(d) truthful

☞ 번역

새로운 비디오 게임 안의 캐릭터들과 장면은 선명한 3D 그래픽을 사용하여 놀랄 만큼 사실적으로 보인다.

⊞ 출제 POINT

vivid(선명한, 생생한), 3D graphics(3차원 입체 영상)라는 단어로 볼 때 빈칸에는 '진짜 같다'는 뜻의 realistic이 어울린다. truthful은 예술 작품이나 표현이 대상과 닮았다는 의미로 a truthful portrait(실제를 그대로 그린 초상화)처럼 쓰인다.
realistic 진짜 같은, 현실의　**virtual** 가상의　**fake** 가짜의, 모조의
　　　　　　　　　　　　　　　　　　　　　　정답_(a)

---

40 per capita consumption 1인당 섭취량
recommended per capita consumption for fruits
1인당 권장 과일 섭취량
42 fake/ replica/ imitation 모조품
• It's a perfect replica of the Titanic.
이건 타이타닉의 완벽한 복제품이군요.

41 give up/ renounce/ abandon 포기하다
• The king renounced the throne.
왕은 공식적으로 왕좌를 포기했다.

Vocabulary

43

You need a well-planned and strategic approach when you negotiate your _____.

(a) penalty
(b) salary
(c) fund
(d) income

📖 **번역**

연봉을 협상할 때는 잘 계획된 전략적인 접근 방법이 필요하다.

🏷 **출제 POINT**

연봉에 대해 협상하는 것이므로 '월급' 또는 '연봉'을 나타내는 salary가 가장 잘 어울린다.
penalty 벌금; 위약금   **salary** 급여   **income** 수입   정답_(b)

44

She was smart enough to _____ herself into a managerial position in just three months.

(a) handle
(b) present
(c) maneuver
(d) operate

📖 **번역**

그녀는 3개월 만에 교묘하게 매니저 직책으로 옮겨갔을 만큼 영리하다.

🏷 **출제 POINT**

maneuver A into B는 '교묘히 또는 영리하게 A를 B로 이동시키다'의 의미이므로 앞의 smart와도 잘 호응된다.
managerial 관리직의   **maneuver A into B** A를 B로 교묘히 이동시키다   정답_(c)

45

By doing away with the nation's culture, the colonialists _____ its treasured traditions.

(a) confronted
(b) relegated
(c) uprooted
(d) expedited

📖 **번역**

나라의 문화를 말살함으로써 식민주의자들은 그 나라의 귀한 전통을 뿌리째 뽑아버렸다.

🏷 **출제 POINT**

앞에서 문화를 말살한다는 내용이 등장하므로 빈칸에는 문화를 말살함으로써 의도하고자 한 내용이 와야 타당하다. 따라서 '뿌리째 뽑다'라는 의미의 uproot/ eradicate/ root out 등이 적절하다.
do away with 없애다, 폐지하다   **relegate** 내려 앉히다, 좌천시키다
uproot 뿌리째 뽑다   **expedite** 진척시키다; 신속히 처리하다   정답_(c)

📋 **TEPS Survival 전략**

43 make an approach 접근하다
• The US tried to make diplomatic approaches rather than military approaches.
미국은 군사적인 방법보다는 외교적인 접근 방식을 이용하려 했다.

44 maneuver ... into -ing 교묘히 ~가 …하게 만들다
• He maneuvered Jackson into agreeing.
그는 교묘하게 잭슨이 동의하도록 만들었다.

45 do away with/ get rid of/ remove/ abolish 제거하다; 폐지하다
• The government is planning to abolish the death penalty.
정부는 사형제도를 폐지하려고 계획 중이다.

46

Brigit was embarrassed because she was completely _____ with Jack's novels.

(a) unacquainted
(b) valiant
(c) soothed
(d) deleterious

🔁 번역
브리짓은 잭의 소설을 전혀 모르고 있었기 때문에 당황했다.

⊞ 출제 POINT
Part 2 마지막 다섯 문제는 고난도 어휘가 출제된다. 여기서는 embarrassed(당황한)라고 했으므로 소설에 대해 잘 모르고 있었을 것(unacquainted)이라고 내용을 추정하여 문제를 푼다.
unacquainted 낯선, 생소한 **valiant** 용맹스러운, 씩씩한 **soothe** 달래다(comfort) **deleterious** 해로운, 유독한   정답_(a)

47

The heart-rending scene showed the character's _____ and her need for her husband's affection and understanding.

(a) satiety
(b) fragility
(c) incurability
(d) levity

🔁 번역
그 가슴 아픈 장면은 인물의 연약함과 그녀가 남편의 사랑과 이해를 필요로 함을 보여주었다.

⊞ 출제 POINT
heart-rending(가슴 아픈)이라는 단어와 뒷부분의 남편의 사랑에 대한 필요라는 언급으로 미루어 빈칸에는 (b) fragility가 오는 것이 가장 적절하다.
heart-rending 가슴 아픈 **satiety** 싫증남, 물림 **fragility** 연약함 **incurability** 불치 **levity** 가벼움, 경솔함   정답_(b)

48

Even if you're divorced, you still cannot _____ the debts incurred by your spouse during marriage.

(a) repudiate
(b) abdicate
(c) remand
(d) construe

🔁 번역
설령 이혼한다 해도 당신은 여전히 결혼 기간 동안 배우자가 진 빚을 부인할 수 없다.

⊞ 출제 POINT
설령 이혼한다 해도(even if) 라는 말이 앞에 나왔으므로 논리적으로 볼 때 '그래도 부채에 대해 책임을 져야 한다', 또는 '피할 수 없다'는 내용이 와야 하므로 정답은 (a)이다.
incur 초래하다 **spouse** 배우자 **repudiate** 거절하다; 부인하다 **abdicate** 버리다 **remand** 송환하다 **construe** 해석하다   정답_(a)

---

46 soothe/ calm/ coax 달래다
- Michael tried to soothe his crying baby.
  마이클은 그의 우는 아이를 달래려고 했다.
- Bryan coaxed her into compliance.
  브라이언은 그녀를 달래 승낙하도록 했다.

47 heart-rending/ heart-breaking 가슴 아픈
  (⇔ heart-warming 가슴이 따뜻해지는, 흐뭇한)
- It is a heart-breaking experience for the staff.
  이것은 직원들에게는 가슴 아픈 경험이다.

48 incur 초래하다
  recur 재발하다, 반복되다
  occur 발생하다(happen)

Vocabulary

49

Even the most _____ observer may fail to notice this flaw in the vase.

(a) astute
(b) vigorous
(c) insolent
(d) obsequious

☞ 번역

심지어 가장 눈치 빠른 관찰자라도 이 꽃병의 결함을 알아채지 못할 수 있다.

⊞ 출제 POINT

even이 나왔으므로 '심지어 아주 기민한 사람이라도 알아채지 못할 수 있다'는 내용으로 전개되어야 논리에 맞다. 따라서 '명민한, 기민한' 의 뜻을 가진 (a) astute이 정답.
astute 명민한, 빈틈없는; 교활한(keen) **vigorous** 정력적인; 강력한
insolent 건방진, 오만한 **obsequious** 아첨하는   정답_(a)

50

The lecturer _____ a funny episode into his speech to keep the attention of the audience.

(a) abashed
(b) interjected
(c) condoned
(d) deluded

☞ 번역

그 강연자는 청중이 계속 집중하도록 하기 위해 그의 강연에 재미있는 에피소드를 끼워 넣었다.

⊞ 출제 POINT

청중이 강연에 집중하도록 하기 위해 할 수 있는 것은 재미난 이야기들을 연설에 '끼워 넣는' 것이다.
abash ~를 당황하게 하다 **interject** 끼워 넣다 **condone** 용서하다
delude 속이다, 착각하게 하다   정답_(b)

📖 TEPS Survival 전략

49 astute 명민한, 기민한(shrewd)
- The CEO made several astute business decisions for the company.
  CEO가 회사를 위해 몇 가지 명민한 사업 결정을 내렸다.

50 attract[draw] a person's attention ~의 관심을 끌다
pay attention to ~에 관심을 기울이다

📖 Reading Comprehension

1

A trade embargo is a strategic political move by one country to make another country either do something or refrain from doing something. For the most part, the country imposing the trade embargo will prohibit most or all people in their country from doing business with the country against which the trade embargo is imposed. One of the most famous trade embargoes in the modern era is the trade embargo the United States laid on Cuba. The embargo was established in 1962 in the hope that prohibiting trade with Cuba would _____, which would in turn inspire Cubans to overthrow Fidel Castro and implement a democratic government. The embargo failed in its mission and is still in place to this day.

(a) weaken the country's economy
(b) strengthen ties with the country
(c) incite hatred toward the United States
(d) grant asylum to political protesters

☞ 번역

무역 제재는 한 국가가 다른 국가로 하여금 무엇인가를 하게 만들거나 혹은 억제하도록 하는 전략적 정치 행위이다. 대부분의 경우 무역 제재를 가하는 국가는 그들 국가의 대부분 또는 모든 국민들로 하여금 무역 제재가 가해지는 국가와의 무역을 금지한다. 근세의 가장 유명한 무역 제재 중 하나는 미국이 쿠바에 가한 무역 제재이다. 이 무역 제재는 1962년, 쿠바의 경제를 약화시키고 이를 통해 쿠바 사람들을 고취시켜 피델 카스트로를 전복시키고 민주 정부를 세우도록 하는 바람에서 시행되어졌다. 그 무역 제재 조치는 목표 달성에 실패했으나 오늘날까지 여전히 시행되고 있다.

(a) 그 나라의 경제를 약화시키다
(b) 그 나라와의 관계를 강화하다
(c) 미국에 대한 적대심을 유발하다
(d) 정치적 시위자들에게 망명을 허가하다

⊞ 출제 POINT

무역 제재를 가하는 국가에서 무역 제재가 가해지는 국가와의 무역을 금지한다고 한 데서 '경제 약화'라는 무역 제재의 목적을 짐작할 수 있다. 또한 피델 카스트로를 전복시킨다는 내용과 연결해서 흐름이 자연스러운 것도 (a)뿐이다.
impose the trade embargo 무역 제재를 가하다   **overthrow** 전복시키다   **implement** 실시하다   **incite** 자극하다; 유발하다
hatred 증오, 원한   **asylum** 망명; 피난처   정답_(a)

📖 TEPS Survival 전략

1 A trade embargo is a strategic political move / by one country / to make another country / either do something or refrain from doing something.

무역 제재 조치는 전략적인 정치적 행위이다(A trade embargo is a strategic political move)까지가 기본 구조이고, 그 이하는 수식 어구로 보면 된다. 〈make+목적어(another country)+동사원형〉 구문으로 동사 do와 refrain이 either A or B로 연결되었다.

2

Welcome to Loyal to Nature, your source for organic and natural products. Choose from a wide range of cosmetics, cleaning products, and much more. Be assured that at Loyal to Nature, our products _____ . We are committed to the environment and everything we sell is 100% earth-friendly. After conducting many trials using various plants and fragrant essential oils, we are now proud to bring you our safe line of Loyal to Nature products. And of course, we never test anything on animals. Buy today and be glad to know that you are loyal to nature.

(a) are free of any scents
(b) remain on earth for years to come
(c) do not have any harmful substances
(d) contain a high percentage of water

☞ 번역

유기농 및 천연 제품을 구입하실 수 있는 로열 투 네이처에 오신 것을 환영합니다. 다양한 종류의 화장품, 세제를 비롯한 그 밖의 여러 가지 상품들 중 골라 보세요. 로열 투 네이처의 상품에는 유해 물질이 전혀 없다는 점을 믿으셔도 좋습니다. 저희는 환경 보호에 헌신적이며 판매되는 모든 제품은 100% 환경 친화적입니다. 다양한 식물과 향기나는 에센스 오일로 많은 실험을 거친 끝에 이제 여러분께 안전한 로열 투 네이처 상품을 내놓게 되었다는 사실에 자부심을 느끼고 있습니다. 물론 저희는 절대 동물 실험을 하지 않습니다. 오늘 바로 구매하시고 즐거운 마음으로 자연 사랑에 동참하십시오.

(a) 어떠한 향기도 나지 않는다
(b) 향후 몇 년간 지구상에 존재한다
(c) 유해 물질이 전혀 없다
(d) 높은 수분 함유율을 가지고 있다

⊞ 출제 POINT

첫 문장에 organic and natural products라는 말이 제품의 특성을 요약해주고 있다. 빈칸 뒷부분에서 제품의 특징이 구체적으로 나열(100% earth-friendly, safe line of products)되고 있으므로 이들 특징과 일치하는 (c)가 정답이다. (a)는 사실과 배치(fragrant essential oils)되며, (b)와 (d)에 대한 정보는 지문에 나와 있지 않다.

earth-friendly 지구[환경] 친화적인 (environment-friendly)
fragrant 향기로운

정답_(c)

3

_____ *Lord of the Flies*, a novel by the British author William Golding. The story centers on a group of schoolboys stuck on a deserted island without any adults. They try to live on their own and govern themselves—with disastrous consequences. Some may be shocked by the violence in the novel, but Golding's message about human nature still resonates with current readers. Thus, it is required reading in classrooms around the world. The book discusses relevant themes such as individual welfare versus the common good, and civilization attempting to

☞ 번역

오늘날 많은 학교에서 여전히 읽혀지고 있는 주요 소설 작품은 영국 작가인 윌리엄 골딩의 소설 〈파리대왕〉이다. 이 이야기는 어른들 없이 버려진 섬에 들어가게 된 한 무리의 남학생들에게 초점을 맞추고 있다. 그들은 자기들 스스로 살아가고 자신들을 스스로 통치하고자 하는데 이는 비극적인 결말을 가져온다. 어떤 사람들은 소설 속에 등장하는 폭력성에 충격을 받을지도 모르겠다. 그러나 인간의 본성에 대한 골딩의 메시지는 여전히 현대의 독자들에게 공감을 얻고 있다. 그 결과, 전세계적으로 교실에서 필독서가 되고 있다. 이 책은 개인의 복지 대 공익, 그리고 혼란을 통제하기 위한 문명화의 시도와 같은 적절한 주제를 다룬다. 2005년에 〈타임지〉가 1923년부터 지금까지 영어로 쓰여진 100대 베스트 소설 중의 하나로 이 작품을 선정하였다.

(a) 이렇게 많은 분노와 비판을 불러일으킨 책은 드물었다
(b) 오늘날 많은 학교에서 여전히 읽혀지고 있는 주요 소설 작품은
(c) 잘 알려지지 않고 간과되는 책들 중 하나는
(d) 학생들은 교실에서 배우는 것을 거의 즐기지 않는다

📖 TEPS Survival 전략

2 be assured that ~을 확신하다
• They are assured that their children will be safe with her.
그들은 그녀와 함께라면 자녀들이 안전하리라고 확신한다.

3 The story centers on / a group of schoolboys / stuck on a deserted island without any adults.
이야기의 중심은 한 무리의 남학생들이며 stuck 이하는 학생들을 꾸며주는 과거분사구이다. schoolboys (who were) stuck과 같이 〈관계대명사+be 동사〉가 생략된 것으로 보면 이해하기 쉽다.

control chaos. In 2005, *Times* magazine chose it as one of the 100 best English-language novels from 1923 to the present.

(a) Fewer books have inspired so much wrath and criticism as
(b) An important work of fiction still read in many schools today is
(c) One of the more obscure and overlooked books is
(d) Students in the classroom rarely enjoy learning about

4

The Kaoshin government ended a nearly 2-week-old state of emergency Monday, following last week's violent political unrest. Prime Minister Vinisit Shamajiva lifted the emergency order for the capital city Phulong and nearby provinces, according to a government spokesman. National security agencies have also indicated that the threat of violence has eased. Immediately after Shamajiva's state-of-emergency declaration, scores of protesters stormed the Prime Minister's residence and pelted his car with sticks, stones, and debris. Fortunately for the Prime Minister, _____. Shamajiva acknowledged, "I was indeed afraid for my own life" when he was faced with the unruly crowd.

(a) he was not the focus of any violence
(b) he is familiar with animal pelts
(c) he brought a halt to the state of emergency
(d) he managed to escape unharmed

4 The Kaoshin government ended / a nearly 2-week-old state of emergency / Monday, / following last week's violent political unrest.

〈주어+동사(end)+목적어(state of emergency)〉 뒤에 순서를 나타내는 부사구가 나오는 구문이다. following은 '~를 따라서, ~ 이후에'라는 뜻으로, 여기서는 정치 소요가 먼저 일어난 다음 계엄령을 해제했다는 의미이다.

5

Told in an extraordinarily refreshing voice, *Yearning to Live* is an unforgettable novel about one woman's struggle to cope with tragedy and how she learns to love in the process. *Yearning to Live* is a love story unlike any other. Author Marta Kemmelman takes readers on an intense journey that allows them to see the painful reality of someone who must fight the odds just to survive. _____ will appreciate the sharp, complex insights on life's setbacks in the book. Now available in paperback for $12.95 online or at a fine bookstore near you.

(a) Those delighted by cheerful prose
(b) Anyone who has been stricken with grief
(c) Readers attempting to write their own novels
(d) People looking for a light read

☞ 번역

유례없이 신선한 목소리로 풀어낸 〈Yearning to Live〉는 비극에 대처하는 한 여인의 몸부림과 그녀가 그 과정에서 어떻게 사랑을 배우는지에 대해 쓰여진 잊지 못할 소설이다. 〈Yearning to Live〉는 여느 작품과는 다른 러브 스토리이다. 저자인 마르타 케멀만은 오로지 생존을 위해 역경과 싸워야만 하는 이의 고통스러운 현실을 보여주는 강렬한 여정으로 독자들을 이끈다. 큰 고난을 겪어본 적이 있는 사람이라면 누구나 이 책이 담고 있는 인생의 장애에 대한 날카롭고 복합적인 통찰의 진가를 알아 볼 것이다. 근처의 대형서점이나 온라인을 통해 12.95달러에 구매 가능하다.

(a) 유쾌한 산문에 기뻐하는 사람들이라면
(b) 큰 고난을 겪어본 적이 있는 사람이라면 누구나
(c) 자기 스스로 소설을 쓰려고 시도하는 독자들은
(d) 가벼운 읽을거리를 찾는 사람들은

▦ 출제 POINT

빈칸 앞은 독자들이 책을 통해 다른 이의 고통스러운 현실을 맛보게 된다는 내용이다. 그러한 인생의 장애에 공감할 만한 사람들의 특징을 찾아 보면 (b)가 가장 자연스럽다. 고통스러운 현실과 (a)의 유쾌한, (d)의 가벼운 읽을거리는 내용은 글의 흐름과 맞지 않으며, (c) 또한 이 글의 내용과 거리가 멀다.

refreshing 상쾌한, 후련한 **yearning** 열망, 갈망 **odds** 불평등; 불화
setback 방해, 좌절   정답_(b)

6

People running addiction centers in the United States are seeing more and more women coming in for treatment for Internet addiction. Those seeking help are young and often new mothers. They are addicted to blogs, message boards, and virtual world sites such as Second Life. Sadly, these moms are part of a growing addiction seen globally. The increase of those who are dependent has psychiatrists trying to get Internet addiction recognized as an official mental disorder that can be treated just like alcohol dependency. One survey in the U.S. found that 14 percent of Internet

☞ 번역

미국의 중독자 치료센터 운영자들은 인터넷 중독 치료를 위해 들어오는 여성의 수가 점점 증가한다는 것을 느끼고 있다. 도움을 청하는 이들은 젊고, 이제 막 엄마가 된 여성들도 꽤 많다. 이들은 블로그나, 메시지 게시판, 또는 세컨드 라이프와 같은 가상 세계에 중독되어 있다. 슬프게도 이 어머니들은 전세계적으로 증가하고 있는 중독 현상의 일부이다. 인터넷 중독자들의 증가로 인해 정신과 의사들은 인터넷 중독이 알코올 중독과 같이 치료 가능한 공식적인 정신 질환으로 인식되도록 노력하고 있다. 미국의 한 여론 조사에 따르면 인터넷 사용자의 14%가 한 번에 며칠씩 인터넷을 멀리하기가 어렵다고 응답했으며, 세계적으로 다른 나라에서는 이보다 더 수치가 높다.

(a) 관계자들은 이러한 의존증을 중병으로 분류하고 있다
(b) 이러한 응답은 중독자가 줄어들고 있다는 것을 보여준다
(c) 세계적으로 다른 나라에서는 이보다 더 수치가 높다
(d) 그들은 이러한 중독성이 삶에 영향을 미치는 것에 거의 자책을 느끼지 않는다

📖 TEPS Survival 전략

5 Told in an extraordinarily refreshing voice, / *Yearning to Live* / is an unforgettable novel / about one woman's struggle to cope with tragedy...
주어는 *Yearning to Live*라는 소설 제목이며 앞의 분사구(Told 이하)가 주어를 수식하고 있다.

6 People running addiction centers in the United States / are seeing more and more women / coming in for treatment for Internet addiction.
주어인 People을 현재분사구(running ... States)가 꾸며 주며 〈지각동사(see)+목적어(women)+현재분사(coming)〉 구문을 이루고 있다. 이 문장은 More and more women are coming in과 같이 이 목적어를 주어로 바꾸어 쓸 수 있다.

users find it hard to stay away from it for several days at a time, and _____.

(a) officials are classifying the dependence as a serious illness
(b) the responses show signs that the addiction is waning
(c) that number is even higher in other countries around the world
(d) that they have little remorse for the effect it has on their lives

🔠 출제 POINT

빈칸 앞은 인터넷 중독자 수치에 대한 언급이 나왔고 and로 연결되고 있으므로 빈칸에는 이 수치와 관련된 내용이 와야 한다. (a)는 앞서 정신과 의사들이 인터넷 중독을 치료 가능한(that can be treated) 질병으로 본다고 했었고, (b) 역시 서론에서 중독자 수가 늘고 있다고 했으므로 둘 다 오답이다. 지문 중반에 언급된 a growing addiction seen globally와 연관지어 인터넷 중독이 미국에만 국한되지 않는다는 것을 보여주는 (c)가 정답이다.

be addicted to ~에 중독되다 **dependent** 의존하는 **mental disorder** 정신 질환 **wane** 감소하다 **remorse** 후회, 자책 **정답_(c)**

7

Dear Mr. Luanda,

I am following up on the previous three letters we sent to you regarding your delinquent account. _____ in the amount of $312.93 for over six months. We are hoping that we will not be forced to forward your account to a collection agency. Unfortunately, if we do not receive payment by December 15, we are left with no alternative but to take action, which may permanently and adversely affect your good credit rating. We urge you in the strongest terms possible to resolve this matter immediately. We hope to receive your payment soon.

Sincerely,
Janis Robbins
Accounts Receivable

(a) You are collecting on a delinquent bill
(b) Your account has been unpaid
(c) We would like to offer you an increase
(d) A low interest rate will be applied

📖 번역

루안다 씨,

귀하의 체납 계좌에 관해 저희가 이전에 보낸 3통의 편지에 이어 이 편지를 보냅니다. 당신의 계좌에서 지난 6개월간 312.93달러가 체납되었습니다. 본사는 귀하의 계좌를 미수금 처리 회사에 넘겨야만 하는 상황이 벌어지지 않기를 바라고 있습니다. 불행히도 12월 15일까지 지불이 이루어지지 않는다면 본사에서 조치를 취할 수밖에 없습니다. 이는 귀하의 신용등급에 영구적으로, 그리고 불리하게 영향을 미칠 수도 있습니다. 이 문제를 즉각 해결하기를 강력하게 촉구합니다. 귀하의 신속한 지불을 기대합니다.

미수금 계정팀
제니스 로빈스 드림

(a) 당신은 체납 고지서를 징수하고 있습니다
(b) 당신의 계좌가 체납되었습니다
(c) 우리는 인상을 제안하고 싶습니다
(d) 낮은 이자율이 적용될 것입니다

🔠 출제 POINT

빈칸 뒤에 312.93달러라는 액수가 나오는데, 이 돈의 정체와 관련된 힌트를 지문 곳곳에서 찾아볼 수 있다. 체납 계좌(delinquent account), 미수금 처리 회사에 넘긴다(forward your account to a collection agency), 당신이 지급해 주기를 바란다(We hope to receive your payment soon)에서 수신인이 체납액을 지불하지 않고 있음을 알 수 있으므로 (b)가 정답이다.

delinquent account 체납 계좌 **collection agency** 미수금 체납 처리 대행사 **credit rating** 신용등급 **adversely** 불리하게 **in the strongest term** 가장 강력한 어조로 **정답_(b)**

---

7 I am following up on / the previous three letters / we sent to you / regarding your delinquent account.
전체 문장의 목적어 the previous three letters를 we 이하가 수식해 주는 형태이다. we 앞에 목적격 관계대명사 that이 생략되었다고 볼 수 있다.

8

Teachers may make students spit out their gum, but chewing gum _____. Recent studies show that munching on a stick of sugar-free gum can curb your appetite and improve your memory. Research funded by the Wrigley Science Institute shows more reasons to chew away on gum, including a finding that chewing gum can lead to better performance in classrooms. Teachers may have to rethink banning gum and might instead hand out a stick to each student.

(a) has been known to benefit children
(b) can provide necessary nutrients for kids
(c) can cure certain diseases
(d) may not deserve the bad reputation it has

☞ 번역

교사들은 학생들에게 껌을 뱉도록 지시할 수도 있지만, 껌을 씹는 행위가 갖고 있는 나쁜 평판을 받지 않아도 될지 모릅니다. 최근 연구 결과들은 무설탕 껌을 씹는 것이 식욕을 조절해 주고 기억력을 향상시킬 수도 있다는 것을 보여줍니다. 링글리 과학 연구소가 재정 지원하는 연구는 껌을 씹는 것이 교실에서 더 좋은 성과를 가져올 수도 있다는 것을 포함하여 껌을 씹어야 할 보다 많은 이유를 제시합니다. 교사들은 껌 씹는 것의 금지를 재고하고 대신에 학생들에게 껌을 나눠주어야 할 수도 있을 것 같습니다.

(a) 아이들을 이롭게 한다고 알려져 있습니다
(b) 어린이들에게 필요한 영양소를 제공합니다
(c) 특정 질병들을 치료할 수도 있습니다
(d) 나쁜 평판을 듣지 않아도 될지 모릅니다

⊞ 출제 POINT

'교사들이 학생들에게 껌을 뱉으라고 할 수 있다'는 이 글의 첫 문장 뒤에 but이 있으므로 글의 흐름이 바뀐다는 것을 알 수 있다. 또한 빈칸 뒤에서도 껌이 줄 수 있는 긍정적인 효과에 대해 말하고 있다. (d)를 제외한 나머지 선택지 모두 껌에 대한 긍정적인 내용을 담고 있지만 빈칸 이하에서 언급된 껌의 효과인 better performance in classrooms와는 관련이 없거나 모호하므로 오답이다.

munch 우적우적 먹다   **curb** 억제하다, 구속하다   정답_(d)

9

When you get an itch, such as a mosquito bite, cells in the skin release chemical called histamine. Certain sensory neurons respond to the histamine and carry a message up to the spinal cord that alerts it to the itch. From there the message is sent to other neurons that run to the thalamus in the brain, which processes and relays sensory information. These neurons are part of a bundle of spinal neurons called the spinothalamic tract. From the thalamus, the "itch" message is passed to the cerebral cortex, which interprets the signals and _____.

☞ 번역

모기에 물린 것과 같이 가려움을 느낄 때는 피부에 있는 세포들이 히스타민이라는 화학 물질을 분비하게 된다. 특정 감각 뉴런들은 히스타민에 반응하게 되고 척수에 메시지를 전달해서 가려움에 대해 경계시킨다. 거기에서 이 메시지는 뇌에서 감각 정보를 처리하고 공급하는 신경상까지 이어지는 다른 뉴런들에게 전달된다. 이러한 뉴런들은 척추 시상계라고 불리는 척추 뉴런 다발의 한 부분이다. 신경상으로부터 '가렵다'는 메시지가 대뇌피질로 전달되면 대뇌피질은 신호를 해석하고 가려운 느낌을 만들어낸다.

(a) 가려운 느낌을 만들어낸다
(b) 히스타민을 분비한다
(c) 척수가 신호를 받는다
(d) 가려움을 완화시킨다

📖 TEPS Survival 전략

8 Research funded by the Wrigley Science Institute / shows more reasons / to chew away on gum, / including a finding / that chewing gum can lead to better performance in classrooms.
한눈에 잘 들어오지 않는 문장이지만 차근차근 분석해 보자. 주어(Research)가 더 많은 이유(more reasons)를 보여주고 있고, 그 이유에 관계대명사 that절의 발견(finding)이 포함되는 형태이다.

9 Certain sensory neurons / respond to the histamine / and carry a message up to the spinal cord / that alerts it to the itch.
등위접속사 and로 연결된 뒷부분을 보면 a message를 다시 관계대명사 that절이 수식하고 있고 that절의 it은 앞의 spinal cord를 가리킨다. 따라서 '척수에 메시지를 전달하고 그 메시지가 척수를 가려움에 대해 경계시킨다'는 의미가 된다.

(a) produces the itchy sensation

(b) releases the histamines

(c) the spinal cord receives the signals

(d) relieves the itch

🏷 출제 POINT

전문적인 내용을 다루고 있기 때문에 어렵게 느껴질 수 있지만 흐름을 잘 따라가면 쉽게 답을 찾을 수 있다. 가려움이 느껴지는 과정에 대해 기술하는 글이며 가렵다는 메시지가 전달되고 나서 대뇌피질이 가렵다는 메시지를 해석한다고 하였으므로 그 다음 과정은 쉽게 예측할 수 있다. 정답은 가려운 느낌을 만들어낸다는 (a)이다.

spinal cord 척수 **thalamus** 신경상 **spinothalamic tract** 척추 시상계 **cerebral cortex** 대뇌피질 **정답_(a)**

10

You may have been told that it is wrong to judge people based on their appearance, but many social scientists say there are reasons why we quickly categorize people based on how they look. This kind of stereotyping is important to the way we function even when those judgments are very wrong. Judging people by their appearance means putting them quickly into impersonal categories, much like deciding whether an animal is a mouse or a squirrel. Stereotyping is how we make sense of the information before us. Long ago, this ability could have meant the difference between life and death. People had to ascertain whether a person appeared to have malignant or benign intent and _____.

(a) search for refuge in their vicinity

(b) shun those who seemed dangerous

(c) gravitate toward those who are muscular

(d) judge them for who they really are

☞ 번역

외모로 사람을 판단하는 것은 잘못이라는 말을 들어본 적이 있으실 겁니다. 그러나 많은 과학자들은 우리가 사람을 금새 외모로 범주화해버리는 이유들이 있다고 합니다. 이러한 종류의 범주화는 심지어 이러한 판단들이 잘못되었을 때라도 우리가 기능을 하는 방식에 있어서 중요하다고 합니다. 외모로 사람을 판단한다는 것은 사람들을 재빨리 한 개인에서 벗어나는 범주에 둔다는 것을 의미합니다. 이는 한 동물을 쥐 또는 다람쥐라고 결정하는 것과 흡사합니다. 범주화는 우리가 눈 앞의 정보를 인식하는 방식입니다. 오래 전에는 이러한 능력이 삶과 죽음을 결정했을 수도 있습니다. 사람들은 어떤 사람이 악의적으로 보이는지 또는 호의적인 의도를 가지고 있어 보이는지 확인해야 했으며 위험해 보이는 사람들은 피해야 했습니다.

(a) 가까운 곳에서 피난처를 찾다

(b) 위험해 보이는 사람들은 피하다

(c) 근육질인 사람들에게 다가가다

(d) 그 사람이 어떤 사람인지 판단하다

🏷 출제 POINT

빈칸이 포함된 문장은 바로 앞문장의 this ability could have meant the difference between life and death에 대한 보충 설명이므로 두 문장이 논리적으로 연결되어야 한다. 빈칸 바로 앞에 '사람이 악의를 품고 있는지 호의적으로 보이는지를 판단해야 했다'는 내용이 나오므로 살기 위해 '위험해 보이는 사람은 피해야 했다'는 내용의 (b)가 적절하다. (a)의 경우 외모로 사람을 범주화한다는 글 전체의 내용과 연관이 없으므로 오답이다.

stereotype 고정관념; 정형화하다 **impersonal** 비개인적인 **malignant** 악성의, 유해한 **benign** 자비로운, 친절한 **vicinity** 가까운 곳, 주변 **shun** 피하다 **gravitate** 자연히 끌리다 **정답_(b)**

---

10 You may have been told / that it is wrong / to judge people based on their appearance, ...

that 이하를 들어본 일이 있을 것이라는 구문으로 시작되는 문장이다. that절을 살펴보면 〈it(가주어)+to(진주어)〉 구문으로, '사람을 외모를 기준으로 판단하는 것은 옳지 않다'는 의미가 된다.

11

In 1989, an oil tanker called the Exxon Valdez dumped about 11 million gallons of crude oil into Prince William Sound, Alaska. The spill, the largest in U.S. history, _____. In fact, thousands of birds, otters, fish, and other sea creatures died immediately, and scientists today are still seeing the lingering effects from the oil spill. They have found pollutants in the blubber of killer whales that swim in the area and a decrease in their population. Toxic substances may keep the whales from reproducing successfully. Scientists suspect that these whales will not recover for another 10 years.

(a) was particularly detrimental to animals
(b) was mediated by scientists studying wildlife
(c) took place in an area known to have many icebergs
(d) was quite costly for the residents of Alaska

☞ 번역

엑슨 발데즈라고 불리는 유조선이 1989년 1천 1백만 갤런의 원유를 알래스카의 프린스 윌리엄 사운드 지역에 버렸다. 미국 역사상 가장 최대인 이 기름 유출은 특히 동물에게 치명적이었다. 사실상 수천 마리의 새와 수달, 물고기 및 다른 바다 생물이 즉사했으며 오늘날 과학자들은 아직도 이 기름 유출의 계속되는 영향을 발견하고 있다. 그들은 이 지역을 헤엄쳐 다니는 범고래의 지방층에서 오염물질을 발견했고, 고래의 수가 감소했음을 밝혀냈다. 독성 물질로 인해 이 고래들이 새끼를 잘 낳지 못할 수도 있다. 과학자들은 향후 10년 동안 이 고래들이 회복하지 못할 것이라고 추정하고 있다.

(a) 특히 동물에게 치명적이었다
(b) 야생 생물을 연구하는 과학자들에 의해 중재되었다
(c) 많은 빙산을 가지고 있다고 알려진 지역에서 발생하였다
(d) 알래스카 주민들에게 매우 비용이 많이 들었다

⊞ 출제 POINT

미국 역사상 가장 최대 규모의 기름 유출이 어떠하다는 것일까? 빈칸 뒤를 보면 '많은 동물이 죽었고 오염물질이 고래에게 아직도 남아 있으며 이것이 고래 수를 감소시킨다'는 내용이 이어진다. 따라서 정답은 이에 대한 내용을 담고 있는 (a)이다. 글 전체를 읽지 않고 빈칸 뒤 In fact 이하의 한 문장만 읽어도 정답을 찾을 수 있는 유형이므로 이런 문제에서 시간을 소비하지 않도록 하자.

oil tanker 유조선 **dump** 버리다 **spill** 유출 **otter** 수달
lingering 오래 끄는 **blubber** 고래의 지방 **killer whale** 범고래
detrimental 해로운 **mediate** 중재하다   정답_(a)

12

A common problem among couples is that the woman wants to air her frustrations and just wants an open ear, but the man will try to deliver a solution instead. When two people are having trouble with communication, the one giving advice needs to develop new listening skills. At the same time, the person who wants to complain needs to be specific in what they want. One way to express that is to say, "I really want to get something off my chest. Is it okay if I just vent and you listen?"

☞ 번역

커플들 사이에 공통적인 문제점은 여성은 문제를 표출하고 상대방이 들어주기만을 원하지만 남자는 대신에 해결책을 제시하려고 한다는 것이다. 두 사람 사이의 의사소통에 문제가 있을 때에는 조언을 하는 쪽에서 이야기를 들어주는 기술을 새로이 개발할 필요가 있다. 동시에 불평하기를 원하는 쪽은 그들이 원하는 것에 대해 좀 더 구체적일 필요가 있다. 이를 표현하는 한 가지 방식은 "맘 속에 담고 있는 걸 다 털어놓고 싶어. 내가 다 털어놓을 테니까 당신이 들어주면 안 될까?"라고 말하는 것이다. 당신의 의도를 대놓고 말하는 것이 오해를 좁히는 데 큰 도움이 될 것이다.

(a) 필요에 따라 사실을 바꾸는 것
(b) 정말 말하고 싶은 것을 미묘하게 말하는 것
(c) 당신의 의도를 대놓고 말하는 것
(d) 이러한 수화를 사용하는 것

📖 TEPS Survival 전략

11 Toxic substances may keep the whales from reproducing successfully.
'목적어가 ~하는 것을 막다, 방지하다'라는 의미의 〈keep+목적어+from -ing〉 구문이다. from 뒤에 동명사 형태로 이어지는 문제가 자주 출제되므로 유의해야 한다.

12 have trouble with 앓다, 문제가 있다
• John is having trouble with his ear.
  존의 귀에 문제가 있다.
• Children with high blood pressure have trouble with memory as well as thinking.
  고혈압이 있는 어린이들은 사고뿐만 아니라 기억에도 문제가 있다.

_____ will go a long way towards bridging misunderstandings.

(a) Bending the truth when necessary
(b) Being subtle with what you really want to say
(c) Stating your intentions up front
(d) Using sign language like this

出題 POINT
'남녀 사이에 의사소통이 문제가 될 때 남자는 들어주는 연습을 하고 여자는 원하는 것을 구체적으로 말해야 한다'는 내용이다. 따라서 빈칸 이하와 같이 오해를 좁히는 데 도움이 되는 것은 바로 앞 문장처럼 (c) 하고 싶은 말을 구체적으로, 분명히 하는 것이다.
air 늘어놓다   get ... off one's chest ~을 털어놓다   vent 터뜨리다
go a long way towards ~에 크게 도움이 되다   bend 바꾸다
up front 솔직한   정답_(c)

13

Although historians credit the ancient Greeks, specifically Athenians, with forming the first democracy around 500 BC, _____.
The important thing, and the biggest difference between Athenian democracy and almost all subsequent democracies, is Athenians practiced a remarkably direct—and not representative—form of democracy. With very few exceptions, Athenians did not vote for politicians to represent them, the citizens themselves voted on almost every policy, from war to taxes to construction.

(a) they did not live in the same kind of democracy as we now have
(b) the Greeks preferred a more dictatorial style of government
(c) elections were infrequent or unreliable for the most part
(d) only a handful of people were involved in the democratic process

번역

비록 역사학자들은 고대 그리스인들, 더 정확히는 아테네인들에게 BC 500년경 처음으로 민주주의를 형성한 것에 대한 공로를 돌리지만, 그들은 현재의 민주주의와 동일한 민주주의 사회에서 살지 않았다. 아테네 민주주의와 그 뒤에 이어진 거의 대부분의 민주주의 사이에 중요하고도 가장 큰 차이점은 아테네인들은 매우 직접적인, 즉 대의 민주주의가 아닌 형태의 민주주의를 시행했다는 것이다. 아테네인들은 극히 미미한 예외를 제외하고는 그들을 대표할 정치인들을 뽑기 위해 선거를 하지 않았고, 아테네 시민들 자신이 전쟁에서부터 건설을 위한 세금에 이르기까지 거의 대부분의 정책에 대해 투표를 했다.

(a) 그들은 현재의 민주주의와 동일한 민주주의 사회에서 살지 않았다
(b) 그리스인들은 보다 독재적인 스타일의 정부를 좋아했다
(c) 선거는 자주 있지 않았고 대부분 신뢰성이 없었다
(d) 단지 몇 명의 사람들만이 민주적인 절차에 참여했다

出題 POINT
'비록 민주주의를 형성한 것에 대한 공로는 돌리지만'이라고 양보 구문을 썼으므로 글의 흐름에 반전이 있음을 알 수 있다. 또한 중간에 고대 민주주의와 그 후의 민주주의에 대한 차이점을 기술한 것으로 보아 고대 민주주의가 현재와 동일하지 않다는 데 초점이 맞추어져 있음을 알 수 있으므로 정답은 (a)이다. (b)는 지문에 언급되어 있지 않고 (c)와 (d)는 지문의 마지막 문장과 상반된 진술이다.
subsequent 뒤의, 차후의   dictatorial 독재적인   정답_(a)

13 historians credit / the ancient Greeks, (specifically Athenians), / with forming the first democracy
credit A with B는 'A에게 B에 대한 공로를 돌리다'라는 구문이므로 '민주주의 형성의 공을 고대 그리스인에게 돌리고 있다'라는 의미이다. 콤마를 사이에 두고 specifically Athenians라는 삽입구가 들어가 구문이 더 복잡해 보이지만 대의 파악을 할 때에는 삽입구를 제외하고 해석하면 더 쉽다.

14

The worst offense a presenter can commit is to bore his or her audience. These days, traditional lectures and slideshows _____. So some savvy presenters are now using high-tech pens to track presentations. Others display PowerPoint slideshows online. These technologically jazzed-up presentations are creating a lot of buzz about what the future of presentations might hold. One California startup company has conceived of "pencasts," which are made using the Pulse SmartPen and specially gridded paper. The pen goes beyond writing duties and has a voice recorder that "notes" which notes were taken and at which point in the recording. Expect to see other new gadgets meant to wow audiences during presentations in the near future.

(a) are barely able to launch products for companies
(b) often fail to convey what the presenter intends
(c) are not happening as often as they used to
(d) are not enough to keep people's attention

☞ 번역

발표자들이 저지를 수 있는 최악의 실수는 청중을 지루하게 하는 것이다. 요즘은 기존의 발표와 슬라이드 쇼로는 사람들의 관심을 유지하기에 충분하지 않다. 그래서 몇몇 발 빠른 발표자들은 이제 첨단 펜을 사용해 발표를 이끌어 나간다. 어떤 사람들은 온라인으로 파워포인트 슬라이드 쇼를 보여준다. 이렇게 기술적으로 다채로워진 발표는 발표의 미래가 어떻게 될지에 대해 많은 관심을 불러일으키고 있다. 한 캘리포니아 소재 신생 회사는 펄스 스마트펜과 특수하게 눈금이 그려진 종이로 만든 '팬캐스트'를 구상해냈다. 이 펜은 필기하는 능력을 뛰어넘어 어떤 메모가 어느 시점에 기록되었는지를 '기록하는' 음성 녹음기를 내장하고 있다. 가까운 미래에 발표 도중 청중을 놀라게 할 다른 새로운 장치들을 기대해 보자.

(a) 거의 회사를 위한 제품을 출시하기 힘들다
(b) 자주 발표자가 의도하는 것을 전달하지 못한다
(c) 예전만큼 자주 이용되지 않는다
(d) 사람들의 관심을 유지하기에 충분하지 않다

⊞ 출제 POINT

빈칸 다음 문장이 So로 이어지고 있으므로 빈칸의 결과로 '발 빠른 발표자들이 첨단 펜을 사용한다'는 의미가 된다. 첨단 펜을 사용해야만 하는 이유가 될 수 있는 것은 (b)와 (d)이나, 첫 문장에서 '청중을 지루하게 한다'는 내용과 자연스럽게 연결되는 (d)가 정답이다.

offense 실수   **savvy** 소식에 밝은   **jazzed-up** 다채롭게 한
gridded 눈금이 있는   **go beyond** ~을 능가하다   **gadget** 간단한 장치, 도구   정답_(d)

15

Swine flu is on the minds of many doctors and scientists. This strain of influenza does not usually infect humans, but several people have become afflicted in North America, particularly if they had exposure to pigs. This virus has genes from North American swine and avian influenza, human influenza, and swine influenza normally found in Asia and Europe. Scientists emphasize that eating pork will not lead to swine flu. However, someone

☞ 번역

돼지 인플루엔자는 많은 의사들과 과학자들의 걱정거리이다. 이 인플루엔자 변종은 보통 사람에게 감염되지 않지만 몇몇 사람들이 북아메리카에서 감염되었으며, 특히 돼지에게 노출되었을 경우 발병하였다. 이 바이러스는 북아메리카 돼지와 조류 독감, 일반 독감 및 보통 아시아와 유럽에서 발견되는 돼지 인플루엔자의 유전자를 갖고 있다. 과학자들은 돼지고기를 먹는다고 해서 돼지 인플루엔자에 감염되는 것은 아니라고 강조했다. 그러나 돼지 인플루엔자에 감염된 사람이 이를 다른 사람에게 전염시킬 수 있다. 그래서 멕시코에 있는 군인들은 사람들이 착용하도록 마스크를 나누어 주었고 다른 사람에게 키스를 하지 말라고 조언했다.

📖 TEPS Survival 전략

14 The worst offense (a presenter can commit) / is / to bore his or her audience.
주어부가 길어서 유의해야 할 문장이다. 주어 offense를 생략된 목적격 관계대명사 that절(a presenter can commit)이 수식하고 있고, be동사 뒤에 to 이하가 보어로 사용된 구문이다.

15 This virus has genes / from North American swine and avian influenza, human influenza, and swine influenza / normally found in Asia and Europe.
〈주어(This virus)+동사(has)+목적어(genes)〉에 긴 수식어구가 따라나오고 있다. normally 이하의 분사구는 바로 앞의 swine influenza를 수식하고 있다.

afflicted with swine flu can spread it to other humans. _____, soldiers in Mexico handed out masks for people to wear and advised against kissing other people.

(a) By the same token
(b) Furthermore
(c) Therefore
(d) Thereafter

(a) 동일한 방식으로
(b) 더욱이
(c) 그래서
(d) 그 후

16

The Montessori Method is a child-centered alternative form of education, based on the child development theories of Maria Montessori (1870-1952). Montessori was an Italian doctor who devoted herself to teaching the children of Rome's ghettos. Her visionary methods launched an educational movement which has become popular around many parts of the world. The basic tenet of the Montessori approach is allowing children to learn on their own while being guided by the teacher. Teachers at Montessori schools diverge from traditional instructors who correct work and mark up assignments in red ink. _____, the teacher evaluates what the child has learned and then guides him or her into new areas of discovery.

(a) For all that
(b) Similarly
(c) Rather
(d) Yet

☞ 번역

몬테소리 방식은 마리아 몬테소리(1870~1952년)의 아동 발달 이론을 기초로 한 아이들 중심 대안 교육의 한 형태이다. 몬테소리는 로마의 빈민가에서 아이들을 가르치는 데 헌신했던 이탈리아 의사이다. 그녀가 구상한 방식으로 인해 교육운동이 시작되었고 세계 곳곳에서 인기를 끌게 되었다. 몬테소리 방식의 주요 원칙은 교사들이 이끄는 동안 어린이 스스로 배우도록 하는 것이다. 몬테소리 학교의 교사들은 과제를 교정하고 빨간 잉크로 지적을 하는 기존 교사들과 다르다. 오히려 몬테소리 교사들은 아이가 배운 것을 검토하고 나서 아이가 새로운 발견의 세계로 가도록 인도해 준다.

(a) 그럼에도 불구하고
(b) 비슷하게
(c) 오히려
(d) 그러나

16 devote[commit] oneself to -ing ~에 헌신하다
· He devoted himself to training monkeys.
   그는 원숭이들을 훈련시키는 일에 헌신했다.

Reading

17

Tourists visiting South Africa will undoubtedly see a wide array of crafts being sold at curio markets or on a street corner. The handiwork displays the inventiveness of South African artists. In addition to carvings made from traditional stone and wood, and sculptures using beads, fabric, and clay, there are pieces made from bottle caps, beer cans, and telephone wires. Some craftsmen use labels from food cans to create colorful papier mache bowls. Wire is another favored medium, as seen in renderings of cars, motorcycles, and even radios that actually work.

Q What is the best title for the passage?
(a) Tourism in South Africa
(b) The Ingenuity of South African Artisans
(c) Curio Markets of South Africa
(d) Branding the Art of South Africa

☞ 번역

남아프리카를 방문하는 여행객들은 의심의 여지 없이 수많은 골동품들이 골동품 가게나 거리의 모퉁이에서 판매되고 있는 것을 보게 될 것이다. 이 수공예품들은 남아프리카 예술가들의 창조성을 보여준다. 전통적인 돌이나 나무 그리고 구슬, 천 및 점토를 사용한 조각품뿐만 아니라 병뚜껑, 맥주 캔 및 전화선을 이용한 작품들도 있다. 몇몇 공예가들은 화려한 색깔의 종이 반죽 항아리를 만들기 위해 음식 캔에 붙어 있는 라벨을 이용하기도 한다. 자동차, 오토바이와 실제로 작동하는 라디오를 표현한 데서 보여지는 바와 같이 철사도 또 하나의 인기 재료이다.

Q 지문의 가장 적합한 제목은?
(a) 남아프리카 관광산업
(b) 남아프리카 예술가들의 창의성
(c) 남아프리카의 공예 시장
(d) 남아프리카 예술의 브랜드화

⊞ 출제 POINT

도입부에서 여기저기에서 판매되고 있는 수공예품들이 남아프리카 예술가의 창의성(inventiveness)을 보여준다고 하였고 후반부에는 이러한 창의성을 보여주는 수공예에 사용되는 다양한 재료들에 대해 말하고 있다. 따라서 이 글은 전체적으로 '남아프리카 예술가들의 창의성'에 관해 기술하고 있음을 알 수 있다.

craft 기술, 공예 **curio** 골동품, 진품 **bead** 구슬 **fabric** 직물, 천 **papier mache** 종이 반죽으로 만든 **rendering** 표현 **ingenuity** 독창성 **artisan** 장인

정답_(b)

18

The 1967 World's Fair was originally scheduled to be held in Moscow to commemorate the 50th anniversary of the Russian Revolution, but financial concerns caused the Soviet Union to rescind itself from consideration and the bid was bestowed upon Montreal, Canada instead. The International and Universal Exposition, or Expo 67 as it is commonly called, was considered to be the most successful World's Fair of the 20th century. Over 50 million visitors and 62 nations participated. It also set the record for the most attendants in a single day for a world's fair, with 569,000 visitors on its third day.

☞ 번역

1967년 만국 박람회는 원래 러시아 혁명 50주년을 기념하기 위해 모스크바에서 개최될 예정이었다. 그러나 재정적인 우려 때문에 소련은 이러한 고려를 백지화했고 이 권한은 캐나다 몬트리올로 대신 넘어가게 되었다. 국제 세계 박람회 또는 흔히 Expo 67로 불리는 이 박람회는 20세기에 가장 성공적이었던 만국 박람회로 여겨졌다. 5천만 명 이상의 방문객들과 62개국이 참여하였다. 또한 세 번째 날 56만 9천의 방문객 수를 기록하면서 만국 박람회 사상 단일 최다 참석 기록을 세웠다.

Q 지문의 주된 내용은?
(a) 몬트리올에서 열린 대규모의 공식 박람회
(b) 소련의 재정상의 어려움
(c) 만국 박람회의 다양한 장소
(d) 러시아 혁명과 세계 엑스포 간의 연관성

📖 TEPS Survival 전략

17 Tourists visiting South Africa / will undoubtedly see / a wide array of crafts / being sold at curio markets or on a street corner.
주어는 Tourists이고 목적어인 crafts를 현재분사구(being 이하)가 꾸며주고 있는 형태이다. 뒤의 sold는 or로 연결된 두 장소가 수식하여 '골동품 가게나 거리 모퉁이에서 팔리는'의 의미가 되었다.

18 It also set the record / for the most attendants in a single day for a world's fair, / with 569,000 visitors on its third day.
set the record for는 '~의 기록을 세우다'라는 의미이다. for 이하에 대한 기록을 세운 것이므로 '하루 참가자 수에서 기록을 세웠다'는 뜻이 된다. with 이하는 구체적인 수치를 제시하는 부분이다.

Q　What is the passage mainly about?
(a) A large public exhibition in Montreal
(b) Financial woes of the Soviet Union
(c) Various sites of the World's Fair
(d) Links between the Russian Revolution and World Expos

전반적인 내용은 몬트리올에서 박람회가 열리게 된 배경과 그 성과 및 규모이다. 즉 몬트리올에 열린 박람회에 대해 설명하고 있으므로 정답은 (a)이다.

commemorate ～를 기념하다, 기리다　**rescind** 철회하다, 취소하다
bid 입찰　**bestow** 주다, 수여하다　**set the record for** ～에 대한
기록을 세우다　**woe** 불행, 재난　　　　　　　　　　　**정답_(a)**

19

Cold sores, those painful blisters that form around the mouth, are not just annoying—they are also highly contagious. These cold sores, also known as fever blisters, are the result of the herpes simplex virus one (HSV-1), a relatively harmless and common virus. The virus can spread through human contact but can also survive on towels, cups, and other household items. Unfortunately, once you have the virus, you have it for life and there is currently no cure for it. Sometimes the virus lies dormant in the body and is triggered by exposure to the sun, stress, or a toothache.

Q　What is the main idea of the passage?
(a) The proper treatment for cold sores
(b) How to prevent the herpes simplex virus one
(c) Mortality rates for people with cold sores
(d) The virus that causes cold sores

☞ 번역

고통을 수반하는 물집의 형태인 입가 발진은 괴로울 뿐 아니라 전염성 또한 매우 강하다. 이러한 입가 발진은 단순 포진으로도 알려져 있는데 비교적 무해하고 일반적인 바이러스인 헤르페스 심플렉스 바이러스 1 (HSV-1)로 인해 생겨난다. 이 바이러스는 사람과의 접촉을 통해 확산될 뿐만 아니라 수건, 컵 그리고 다른 가정용품에서 살아남을 수 있다. 불행히도 일단 이 바이러스를 갖게 되면 평생 지속되며 현재는 치료할 방법이 없다. 때때로 이 바이러스는 몸 안에서 잠복기를 갖기도 하며 태양에의 노출, 스트레스 또는 치통에 의해 나타나게 된다.

Q　지문의 주제는?
(a) 입가 발진에 대한 적절한 치료
(b) 헤르페스 심플렉스 바이러스 1 예방법
(c) 입가 발진을 가진 사람들의 사망률
(d) 입가 발진을 유발하는 바이러스

⊞ 출제 POINT

입가 발진에 대해 전반적으로 설명하면서 수건, 컵, 가정용품에서 바이러스가 옮겨질 수 있고 HSV-1 바이러스로 인해 병이 생긴다는 내용으로 보아 입가 발진을 일으키는 바이러스에 대해 말하고 있음을 알 수 있다. 따라서 정답은 (d)이다. 지문을 읽기 전에 (a) treatment, (b) prevent, (c) Mortality rates, (d) causes라는 핵심 어구들을 미리 파악해두면 문제 푸는 시간을 줄일 수 있다.

cold sore 입가 발진　**blister** 물집, 수포　**contagious** 전염성의
fever blister 단순 포진　**dormant** 잠복해 있는　　　　　**정답_(d)**

---

19 be triggered by는 '～에 의해 촉발되다'라는 의미이며 '결과 – 원인' 구문에서 자주 사용된다.
• The conflict in the area showed that wars could be triggered by climate change in the near future.
이 지역에서의 분쟁은 가까운 미래에 기후 변화에 의해 전쟁이 촉발될 수도 있음을 보여주었다.

20

Children in previous generations seemed to have less to worry about than children and adolescents today. According to a study, terrorist attacks, war, and shootings are among the 20 most common fears for children. Experts say that overexposure to television news is to blame for creating anxiety in children. Young kids are not mature enough to understand events on the news such as kidnapping. They also advise that parents get counseling for children who show symptoms of anxiety, such as difficulty sleeping, headaches, and stomach pains.

Q What is the passage mainly about?
(a) Concern among parents over violence
(b) How children are portrayed on television
(c) Anxiety among today's children
(d) Why the media should be censored

☞ 번역
이전 세대의 어린이들은 오늘날의 어린이들이나 청소년들보다 걱정해야 할 일이 적었던 것으로 보인다. 한 연구에 따르면 테러 공격, 전쟁 그리고 총격은 어린이들이 느끼는 20가지 가장 일반적인 공포에 포함된다고 한다. 전문가들은 텔레비전 뉴스에 과도하게 노출되는 것이 어린이들에게 걱정을 일으키는 원인이라고 한다. 어린 아이들은 유괴와 같은 뉴스를 충분히 이해할 만큼 성숙하지 않은 상태이다. 전문가들은 또한 수면장애, 두통 및 복통과 같은 불안으로 인한 증상을 보이는 아이들에 대해 부모들이 상담받을 것을 조언하고 있다.

Q 지문의 주된 내용은?
(a) 폭력에 대한 부모들의 우려
(b) 어린이들이 TV에서 묘사되는 방식
(c) 오늘날 어린이들 걱정거리
(d) 미디어가 검열되어야 하는 이유

⊞ 출제 POINT
과거에 비해 현대의 어린이들이 공포를 느끼는 일이 더 많은데 그 이유가 TV 때문이며 이로 인해 수면장애, 두통 및 복통까지 일으킬 수 있다고 기술하고 있다. 이는 오늘날 어린이들에게 나타난 걱정, 근심을 말하는 것이므로 정답은 (c)이다.
overexposure 과다 노출   **censor** 검열하다   정답_(c)

21

Wildfires have consumed thousands of acres and destroyed dozens of homes in Kansas. In a written statement, Governor Michael Ingram said, "This has already proved to be a devastating event for the area, and if the fires persist we will have to seek federal assistance." The hardest-hit area is Finger Valley, a region abundant with corn and wheat farms. The officials are estimating damage to crops worth hundreds of thousands of dollars. One farmer who helped his family evacuate in time said, "That was my life's work all gone in one fell swoop."

☞ 번역
산불이 캔자스 지역에서 수천 에이커를 불태우고 수십 가구를 파괴했다. 마이클 인그램 주지사는 서면을 통해 '이 화재가 이 지역에 엄청난 재해임이 이미 밝혀졌고 산불이 지속될 경우 연방 차원의 지원을 요청해야만 할 것이다'라고 밝혔다. 가장 큰 타격을 받은 지역은 많은 옥수수와 밀 농사를 짓는 지역인 핑거밸리이다. 관계자들은 농작물에 대한 피해가 수십 억 달러에 이를 것으로 추산하고 있다. 가족들이 제때 피신하도록 도왔던 한 농부는 '내 평생 쌓아온 일이 한꺼번에 날아갔다'고 말했다.

Q 뉴스 보도의 가장 적합한 제목은?
(a) 관료들이 산불에 대한 경고를 제기하다
(b) 캔자스 주의 사람들이 자연 재해 피해액을 추산하다
(c) 주지사가 산불 피해 후에 연방 지원을 요청하다
(d) 산불이 캔자스에서 마침내 진압되다

📖 TEPS Survival 전략

20 A is to blame for B A가 B에 대한 책임이 있다, B는 A 때문이다
• The President is to blame for the economic crisis.
대통령에게 경제 위기에 대한 책임이 있다.

21 The hardest-hit area / is Finger Valley, / a region / abundant with corn and wheat farms.
내용상 주어(area)가 모두 같은 지역(Finger Valley / a region)에 대한 이야기를 하고 있다. abundant 이하는 앞에 which is가 생략된 분사구로 region을 수식하고 있다.

Q What is the best title for the news report?
(a) Officials Raise Alert for Wildfires
(b) Kansans Assess Damages after Natural Disaster
(c) Governor Seeks Federal Assistance after Wildfire Damages
(d) Wildfires Finally Put Out in Kansas

산불 발생과 이에 대한 주지사의 발표 후 산불로 인해 가장 큰 피해를 입은 농사 지역 및 관계자들이 산출한 농작물 피해액이 소개되고 있다. 피해를 입은 캔자스 농부의 인터뷰로 마무리되는 것으로 보아 주된 내용을 담고 있는 (b)가 정답이다. 나머지는 모두 본문의 내용과 일치하지 않는다.

the hardest hit area 가장 큰 타격을 받은 지역 **abundant** 풍부한
in one fell swoop 일거에   정답_(b)

22

Zakat, or "alms for the poor," is the Islamic principle of giving to charity. Today, it serves largely as the welfare contribution to poor and deprived people in the Muslim world. Muslims view zakat as a way of purifying themselves from their greed and safeguarding future business. Furthermore, zakat purifies the person who receives it because it keeps him from begging and envying the wealthy. According to the laws of Islam, those who do not pay zakat will not have their prayers accepted. Zakat can be demonstrated in many ways. For example, it is not uncommon to see families in Iraq cook food for the homeless or even invite them to dinner regardless of their level of wealth.

Q What is the passage mainly about?
(a) A religious practice of helping those in need
(b) Traditional Muslim convictions in modern society
(c) The role of relief organizations in certain parts of the world
(d) The most important law of Islam

☞ 번역

'가난한 자들을 위한 자선'을 뜻하는 자카트는 자선을 베푸는 이슬람의 원칙이다. 오늘날 자카트는 무슬림 세계에서 가난하고 소외된 사람들을 위한 복지 분배에 크게 기여하고 있다. 무슬림들은 자카트를 그들 자신을 탐욕으로부터 정결하게 하고 미래 사업을 보호하는 방법으로 보고 있다. 그뿐만 아니라 자카트는 그것을 받는 사람들 또한 정결하게 하는데 왜냐하면 이들이 구걸을 하거나 부자들을 부러워하지 않도록 해주기 때문이다. 이슬람 법에 따르면 자카트를 지불하지 않는 사람들의 기도는 응답을 받지 못하게 될 것이라고 한다. 자카트는 많은 방법으로 행해질 수 있다. 예를 들면, 이라크에 있는 가정들이 그들의 부의 수준과 관계 없이 노숙자들을 위해 요리를 하거나 심지어 저녁에 초대하는 것은 흔히 볼 수 있다.

Q 지문의 주된 내용은?
(a) 어려운 사람들을 돕는 종교적 관행
(b) 현대 사회에서의 전통적인 무슬림의 신념
(c) 세계 특정지역에서 구호 단체들의 역할
(d) 이슬람의 가장 중요한 법

⊞ 출제 POINT

가난한 자들을 위해 자선을 베푸는 이슬람의 원칙인 자카트를 소개하는 글로 자카트가 사회에 어떻게 기여하는지와 그 실현되는 예를 보여주고 있다. 이러한 내용을 담고 있는 선택지는 (a)이다. (d)는 지문만으로는 알 수 없다.

alms 자선 **deprived** 가난한 **purify** 정화하다 **safeguard** 보호하다 **relief organization** 구호 단체   정답_(a)

22 Muslims / view / zakat / as a way / of purifying themselves from their greed
view A as B는 'A를 B로 보다, 간주하다'라는 뜻으로 여기서 A는 zakat, B는 a way이며 of 이하는 way를 수식하여 의미를 보충하고 있다.

23

With the end of communism in Eastern Europe and the fall of the Soviet Union in the late 1980s and early 90s, North Korea's economy declined sharply. In fact, gross national income per capita is estimated to have fallen by about one-third between 1990 and 2002. The economy has since stabilized and shown some small improvements, especially in recent years, though that is due mostly to increased inter-Korean economic cooperation. North Korea passed some relatively modest wage and price reforms in 2002, and has increasingly tolerated markets and a small private sector as the state-run distribution system has deteriorated.

Q Which of the following is correct according to the passage?

(a) South and North Korea have been collaborating with each other.

(b) North Korea was down to about 33% of its gross national income from 1990 to 2002.

(c) Aid from overseas has helped North Korea boost its economy.

(d) North Korea is following the example of Eastern Europe and the Soviet Union.

☞ 번역

1980년대 말과 1990년대 초에 있었던 동유럽의 공산주의의 종식 및 소련의 몰락과 함께 북한 경제는 극도로 위축되었다. 사실상 일인당 국민소득은 1990년과 2002년 사이 약 3분의 1이 감소했을 것으로 예상된다. 그후 경제는 안정되었고 비록 대부분 남북간 경제 협력 때문이기는 하지만 특히 최근 몇 년간 약간의 진전을 보여주었다. 북한은 2002년 몇 가지 비교적 적절한 임금 및 가격 개혁을 통과시켰으며 국영 유통 시스템이 악화되어 감에 따라 점점 더 시장과 작은 민간 분야를 보다 용인하게 되었다.

Q 지문에 따르면 옳은 것은?

(a) 남북한은 서로 협력해 오고 있다.

(b) 북한은 1990년에서 2002년 사이 국민소득이 약 33%로 감소하였다.

(c) 외국으로부터의 원조가 북한이 경제를 활성화하는 데 도움을 주었다.

(d) 북한은 동유럽과 소련의 전철을 따르고 있다.

⊞ 출제 POINT

북한의 경제가 나아졌다는 내용 뒤에 이러한 경제적 향상이 주로 남북 경제 협력 때문이라고(that is due mostly to increased inter-Korean economic cooperation) 했으므로 정답은 (a)이다. (b)의 경우 국민소득이 3분의 1이 감소했다고 했지 3분의 1 수준으로 감소한 것은 아니며 (c)와 (d)는 지문에 언급되지 않은 내용이다.

decline 감소하다   **stabilize** 안정되다   **inter-Korean economic cooperation** 남북 경제 협력   정답_(a)

24

Votes were still being counted for Sangala's parliamentary elections, but the ruling Independent Party was already celebrating. People are predicting that Independent Party leader Mbeki Futu will be Sangala's next president, despite his checkered background. Futu has been accused of accepting bribes from lobbyists and was eventually acquitted after a lengthy trial.

☞ 번역

상갈라의 의회 선거 결과가 아직 집계 중임에도 여당인 독립당은 이미 축하를 하고 있었습니다. 사람들은 독립당의 지도자 음베키 푸투가 곡절 많은 배경에도 불구하고 차기 상갈라의 대통령이 될 것이라고 예상하고 있습니다. 푸투는 로비스트들에게 뇌물을 받은 혐의로 기소되었으며 결국 긴 재판 끝에 무죄 판결을 받았습니다. 푸투는 가난으로 찌든 이 나라의 다수를 차지하는 빈곤층에게 여전히 인기를 얻고 있습니다. 투표소 밖에서 한 유권자가 '푸투는 우리 중 한 사람이다. 그는 우리가 무엇을 필요로 하는지 알고 있다'라고 말한 그대로입니다. 전문가들은 푸투가 그냥 승리하는 것이 아니라, 큰 격차로 압승할 것으로 예상하고 있습니다.

📖 TEPS Survival 전략

23 With the end of communism in Eastern Europe / and the fall of the Soviet Union in the late 1980s and early 90s, / North Korea's economy declined sharply.

With로 시작하는 전반부가 and로 연결되어 주절(North Korea's economy declined)의 내용을 보완해 주고 있는 부대상황 구문이다. 즉, '~하면서, ~와 함께'라고 해석한다.

24 Futu continues to remain popular/ with the poor, /who make up the majority of this poverty-stricken nation.

이 문장에서 쉼표로 연결되는 who는 계속적 용법의 관계대명사로 the poor에 대한 정보를 추가하고 있다.

Futu continues to remain popular with the poor, who make up the majority of this poverty-stricken nation. As one voter said outside the booths, "Futu is one of us. He understands what we need." Pundits anticipate not only a win for Mbeki Futu but a full-on landslide.

Q Which of the following is correct according to the passage?
(a) People like Futu because he is honest and ethical.
(b) Voters believe that Futu can identify with them.
(c) Experts predict Futu will win by a small margin.
(d) Futu was convicted of bribery charges in the past.

Q 지문에 따르면 옳은 것은?
(a) 사람들은 푸투가 정직하고 윤리적이기 때문에 좋아한다.
(b) 유권자들은 푸투가 자신들과 공감할 수 있다고 믿는다.
(c) 전문가들은 푸투가 적은 표차로 이길 것이라고 예상한다.
(d) 푸투는 과거에 뇌물 혐의로 유죄 판결을 받았다.

⊞ 출제 POINT

푸투가 빈곤층에게 인기가 있다는 내용과 함께 인터뷰한 유권자가 '그는 우리 중 한 사람이다(Futu is one of us)'라고 한 점으로 보아 유권자들은 푸투가 자신들과 공감할 수 있다고 믿는 것을 알 수 있다. 따라서 정답은 (b)이다. (a)는 언급되어 있지 않으며 (c)와 (d)는 지문과 상반되는 내용이다.

checkered 기복이 많은 **acquit** 석방하다, 무죄로 하다 **poverty-stricken** 매우 가난한 **landslide** 압승   정답_(b)

25

Plants absorb carbon dioxide more efficiently amidst pollution than they do in a clean atmosphere. The effects of atmospheric pollution seem to have enhanced plant productivity around the world by as much as 25% from 1960 to 1999. As a result, there was a 10 percent increase in the amount of carbon stored by the land. This has important implications for efforts to fight future climate change. When sunlight is reduced, photosynthesis in plants is reduced as well. However, clouds and atmospheric particles scatter sunlight. Plants are then able to convert more of the available sunlight into growth because fewer leaves are in the shade.

Q Why does pollution enhance plant productivity?
(a) Particles in the air can disperse sunlight more effectively.
(b) It stimulates photosynthesis in plant life.
(c) It creates better conditions for increasing the number of leaves in the shade.
(d) It increases the amount of ultraviolet rays entering the Earth's atmosphere.

⊂ 번역

식물은 깨끗한 대기에서보다 오염 상태에서 더 효과적으로 이산화탄소를 흡수한다. 대기 오염의 효과가 세계적으로 식물의 생산성을 1960년에서 1999년까지 25%만큼이나 향상시킨 것으로 보인다. 결과적으로 땅에 저장된 탄소의 양이 10% 증가되었다. 이는 미래 기후 변화와 싸우고자 하는 노력과 관련해 중요한 연관이 있다. 햇빛이 감소하면 식물 안에서의 광합성 작용 또한 감소하게 된다. 그러나 구름과 대기 입자들이 태양광을 분산시킨다. 그러고 나면 그늘에 가려진 잎의 수가 감소하기 때문에 식물은 보다 많은 태양 에너지를 변환시켜 성장하는 데 사용할 수 있다.

Q 오염이 식물의 생산성을 향상시키는 이유는?
(a) 공기 중에 있는 입자가 태양 빛을 보다 효과적으로 분산시킬 수 있다.
(b) 오염이 식물의 광합성 작용을 촉진한다.
(c) 오염이 그늘에 가려진 잎의 수를 증가시키는 데 더 좋은 환경을 만든다.
(d) 오염이 지구 대기로 들어오는 자외선의 양을 증가시킨다.

⊞ 출제 POINT

지문 마지막 부분에서 구름과 대기 입자가 태양광을 분산시키고 나면 그늘에 가려지는 잎이 감소하여 보다 많은 에너지를 변환할 수 있다고 하였다. 따라서 정답은 (a)이다. (b)와 (c)는 지문의 내용과 반대이며 (d)는 지문과 관련 없는 내용으로 오답이다.

carbon dioxide 이산화탄소 **admist** ~가운데 **enhance** 강화하다 **implications** 관련 **photosynthesis** 광합성 작용 **particle** 입자 **scatter** 흩뿌리다 **convert** 바꾸다 **disperse** 분산시키다   정답_(a)

25 Plants absorb carbon dioxide / more efficiently amidst pollution / than they do / in a clean atmosphere.
비교급 문장에서는 서로 비교되는 대상과 내용 두 가지를 파악하는 것이 중요하다. 여기서 비교 내용은 이산화탄소 섭취의 효율성이며 비교 대상은 오염된 대기(pollution)와 깨끗한 대기(a clean atmosphere)이다.

26

Current memory cards hold 10 to 100 gigabits of data per square inch in silicon chips, and they have an estimated life expectancy of only a few decades. Scientists are formulating a new computer memory device that consists of an iron nanoparticle (1/50,000 the width of a human hair) enclosed in a hollow carbon nanotube. When electricity is present, the nanoparticle can be shuttled back and forth with great accuracy, thus creating a programmable memory system that, like a silicon chip, can record digital information and play it back using conventional computer hardware. The device has a storage capacity as high as 1 terabyte per square inch (a trillion bytes of information) and a lifespan of one billion years.

Q Which of the following is correct according to the passage?
(a) Future memory material will have greater storage capacity within an increased amount of space.
(b) A new memory device can store at least ten times more data than conventional silicon chips.
(c) Today's data storage devices hold a limited amount of data and do not last for more than ten years.
(d) The nanoparticle device can outperform current memory cards but it has some drawbacks.

27

Did you ever wonder how your ears can hear sounds? Inside the ear there are certain cells called "hair cells" that sense vibrations in the air. These cells have tiny hair-like projections, called stereocilia, arranged in rows by height, which in turn bend slightly when sound vibrations reach them. Scientists think the movement opens small pores, called ion channels. As positively charged

📖 번역

최근의 메모리 카드는 실리콘 칩 안에서 평방 인치당 10에서 100기가 바이트의 데이터를 유지할 수 있으며 불과 몇 십년밖에 안 되는 예상 평균 수명을 가지고 있다. 과학자들은 속이 비어 있는 탄소 나노 튜브에 들어 있는 철 나노파티클(사람 머리카락의 5만분의 1의 폭)로 구성된 새로운 컴퓨터 메모리 장치를 구상하고 있다. 전기가 인가될 때, 나노파티클이 엄청난 정확도를 유지하며 앞뒤로 왕복함으로써 실리콘 칩처럼 디지털 정보를 기록하고 기존의 컴퓨터 장치를 사용하여 이를 다시 재생해 낼 수 있는 프로그램 가능한 메모리 시스템을 만들어 낼 수 있다. 이 장치는 평방 인치당 1테라바이트(1조 바이트의 정보)만큼이나 큰 저장 능력과 10억 년의 평균 수명을 가진다.

Q 지문에 따르면 옳은 것은?
(a) 미래 메모리 도구는 확장된 공간 안에 더 큰 저장 능력을 갖게 될 것이다.
(b) 새로운 메모리 장치는 기존 실리콘 칩보다 최소한 10배 많은 데이터를 저장할 수 있다.
(c) 오늘날의 데이터 저장 장치는 제한된 양의 데이터를 보관할 수 있고 10년 이상 지속되지 않는다.
(d) 나노파티클 장치는 기존 메모리 카드를 능가할 수 있지만 몇 가지 결함을 가지고 있다.

🏢 출제 POINT

현재의 10에서 100기가바이트보다 최소한 10배 많은 1테라바이트를 저장할 수 있다고 하였으므로 (b)가 정답이다. (a)는 an increased amount of space라는 표현이 본문과 다르며 (c)의 경우 지문의 a few decade와 맞지 않는다. drawback에 대해서는 지문에 나와 있지 않으므로
(d) 또한 정답에서 제외된다.

life expectancy 평균 수명   **hollow** 속이 빈   **shuttle** 왕복하다
back and forth 앞뒤로   **accuracy** 정확성   **outperform** 능가하다
drawback 결함   정답_(b)

📖 번역

당신의 귀가 어떻게 소리를 들을 수 있는지 궁금해한 적이 있나요? 귀 안쪽에는 공기 중의 진동을 감지할 수 있는 '헤어셀'이라고 불리는 특정 세포가 있습니다. 이 세포들은 높이별로 몇 줄로 배치되어 있는, 스테레오실리아라고 불리는 미세한 머리카락 같은 돌기를 가지고 있습니다. 스테레오실리아는 소리의 진동이 도달하면 차례로 살짝 꺾입니다. 과학자들은 이러한 움직임이 이온 채널이라고 불리는 조그만 구멍들을 열어준다고 생각합니다. 양으로 충전된 이온이 헤어셀로 들어가면서 기계적인 진동이 전기적인 신호로 변환이 됩니다. 이것을 뇌가 소리로 해석하게 되는 것입니다. 이러한 이온 채널들은 또한 너무 큰 소리로부터 귀를 보호하는 데 도움을 줍니다. 귀는 주변의 잡음 수준과 일치하도록 이온 채널의 감도를 조절합니다.

📋 TEPS Survival 전략

26 Scientists are formulating a new computer memory device / that consists of an iron nanoparticle(1/50,000 the width of a human hair) / enclosed in a hollow carbon nanotube.
긴 문장의 구문 분석은 일단 수식어구를 제외하고 기본 성분만을 파악한다. 여기서는 that절이 computer memory device를 수식하고, (which was) enclosed in a hollow carbon nanotube가 nanoparticle을 수식하고 있다. 괄호 안의 내용은 기본 요지를 파악한 다음 추가적으로 살펴본다.

27 This is what the brain interprets as sound.
관계대명사 what절은 '~하는 것'으로 해석한다. '이것이 뇌가 소리로 해석하는 것이다'라는 문장이며 This는 앞문장을 받아 an electrochemical signal(전기화학 신호)이 된다. 즉 '뇌가 전기화학 신호를 소리로 해석한다'는 뜻이다.

ions rush into the hair cell, mechanical vibrations are converted into an electrochemical signal. This is what the brain interprets as sound. These ion channels also help protect the ear against sounds that are too loud. The ear adjusts the sensitivity of its ion channels to match the noise level in the environment.

Q Which of the following is correct according to the passage?
(a) Hair cells are responsible for transforming vibrations into sound.
(b) Stereocilia are tiny hair-like projections containing hair cells.
(c) The ion channels cushion the environment to protect the ear from loud sounds.
(d) Sound is created when sound waves bend within small pores.

Q 지문에 따르면 옳은 것은?
(a) 헤어셀이 진동을 소리로 전환하는 역할을 담당한다.
(b) 스테레오실리아는 헤어셀을 포함하고 있는 머리카락 같은 작은 돌기이다.
(c) 이온 채널은 큰 소리로부터 귀를 보호하기 위해 주변을 완충시킨다.
(d) 소리는 음파가 조그만 구멍 내부에서 굽어질 때 생성된다.

▦ 출제 POINT
양이온이 헤어셀로 들어갈 때 진동을 뇌에서 소리로 인식하는 전기적 신호로 바뀐다고 했으므로 정답은 (a)이다. (b)는 스테레오실리아와 헤어셀의 관계가 반대로 설명되었고, (c)의 경우 지문에 주변을 완충시킨다는 내용은 나와 있지 않으므로 오답이다. (d)는 음파가 꺾어질 때 소리가 생기는 것이 아니라 양이온이 헤어셀에 들어갈 때 생긴다고 했으므로 오답이다.

projection 돌기 **pore** 작은 구멍 **positively** 양전기로
transform 전환하다   **정답_(a)**

28

Mercury, as the smallest rocky planet, has weak gravity, and due to its proximity to the sun it is also scorching hot. These conditions make it difficult for the planet to hold on to its extremely thin atmosphere. However, a solar wind helps maintain the atmospheres, which otherwise may have vanished long ago. This thin gas of electrically charged particles, called a plasma, blows constantly from the surface of the sun and transfers sufficient energy to blast atoms from the surface of Mercury into its atmosphere, replenishing it.

Q Which of the following is correct according to the passage?
(a) A solar wind blows rocks towards Mercury.
(b) Mercury's thinning atmosphere consists of charged particles.
(c) Plasma from the sun moves atoms into Mercury's atmosphere.
(d) Mercury has weak gravity because it is close to the sun.

☞ 번역
가장 작은 바위 행성인 수성은 중력이 작고 태양과 가깝기 때문에 찌는 듯이 덥습니다. 이러한 조건들이 수성이 극히 희박한 대기를 유지하기 어렵게 만듭니다. 그러나 태양풍이 대기가 지속되도록 도와주고 있습니다. 태양풍이 없다면 대기는 오래 전에 소멸했을 것입니다. 플라즈마라고 불리는 충전된 이 얇은 분자 가스들이 계속적으로 태양 표면으로부터 불어와서 수성 표면의 원자들을 대기로 날려 보내 복원하기에 충분한 에너지를 전달해 줍니다.

Q 지문에 따르면 옳은 것은?
(a) 태양풍이 수성을 향해 바위를 날려 보낸다.
(b) 수성의 얇은 대기는 충전된 분자들로 구성되어 있다.
(c) 태양의 플라즈마는 원자를 수성의 대기쪽으로 이동시킨다.
(d) 수성은 태양에 가깝기 때문에 약한 중력을 가지고 있다.

▦ 출제 POINT
태양풍 덕에 수성의 대기가 유지된다는 내용의 글이다. (b)는 충전된 분자들은 태양의 표면에서 나오는 것이고 수성의 대기는 원자들로 구성되어 있으므로 오답이다. 지문에서 plasma의 역할을 blast atoms from the surface of Mercury into its atmosphere, replenishing it이라고 설명했으므로 태양에서 배출된 플라즈마는 원자들을 수성의 대기 속으로 이동시킨다는 것을 알 수 있다. 따라서 정답은 (c). 태양에의 근접성과 수성의 중력 간의 관계에 대해서는 언급된 바 없으므로 (d)는 오답이다.

Mercury 수성 **scorching** 매우 뜨거운 **replenish** 채우다 **정답_(c)**

---

28 make it difficult for A to B A가 B하는 것을 어렵게 하다
it은 가목적어, to B 이하가 진목적어이다.
・Hypertension may make it difficult for children to think.
고혈압이 어린이들이 사고하는 것을 어렵게 만들 수도 있다.

29

The Checkers speech was an address delivered by then Republican vice-presidential candidate Richard Nixon on television and radio in 1952. The speech was Nixon's response to critics who had accused him of accepting gifts and misusing funds appropriated for the election campaign. The speech is so named because Nixon declared that he intended to keep one gift—a dog named Checkers. This reference to a pet touched the public and led to an outpouring of support for the senator. The speech has since been mocked, and now the term "Checkers speech" has come more generally to mean any emotional speech by a politician.

Q Which of the following is correct according to the passage?
(a) Speeches like the Checkers speech have become a useful tool for politicians today.
(b) The current meaning of Checkers speech falls far from Nixon's original intent.
(c) Nixon was found guilty of misappropriating political funds.
(d) The mention of a dog engendered sympathy among voters.

☞ 번역
체커스 연설은 1952년 공화당 부통령 후보였던 리처드 닉슨이 텔레비전과 라디오를 통해 했던 연설이었다. 이 연설은 뇌물수수와 선거용으로 모금된 기금을 잘못 사용했다는 혐의로 그를 비난했던 사람들에 대한 닉슨의 답변이었다. 닉슨이 선물 받은 체커스라는 개만큼은 간직하겠다고 밝힌 데서 이 연설의 이름이 붙여졌다. 이 개에 관한 언급은 대중에게 감동을 주었고, 이 상원 의원은 대중의 넘치는 지지를 받았다. 그 후 이 연설은 계속 모방되고 있으며 이제 '체커스 연설'은 정치인의 감정적인 연설을 통칭하는 말로 일반적으로 받아들여지고 있다.

Q 지문에 따르면 옳은 것은?
(a) 체커스 연설과 같은 연설들은 오늘날 정치인을 위한 유용한 도구가 되었다.
(b) 체커스 연설의 최근 의미는 닉슨의 원래 의도와는 매우 다르다.
(c) 닉슨은 정치자금을 횡령한 혐의로 유죄 판결을 받았다.
(d) 개를 언급한 것이 유권자들 사이에 동정을 일으켰다.

⊞ 출제 POINT
닉슨 부통령 후보의 Checkers Speech에 대한 글이다. 사실 확인 문제이므로 지문에서 명확하게 언급된 내용을 paraphrasing한 것을 골라야 한다. (a)의 유용한 수단(useful tool)과 (b)는 지문에서 언급되지 않았고, Nixon은 기소되었지(accused), 유죄 판결(found guilty)을 받은 것이 아니므로 (c)도 정답이 될 수 없다. (d)의 engendered sympathy among voters(유권자들의 동정을 불러 일으켰다)는 본문의 touched the public(대중에게 감동을 주었다)을 paraphrasing한 것이므로 정답이다.
electorate 유권자   **outpour** 흐르다, 넘치다   **mock** 흉내내다
engender 생기게 하다   정답_(d)

30

Anti-government Taliban fighters will withdraw from the Buner district, just 87 kilometers from the Pakistan capital, Islamabad, a spokesman says. The move came soon after Pakistan's President, Asif Ali Zardari, told the national assembly that the military could stop the Taliban and that the country's nuclear weapons were safe. "If anybody challenges the will of the government, then we

☞ 번역
반정부 탈레반 군사들이 파키스탄의 수도인 이슬라마바드에서 87킬로미터 떨어진 부네르 지역에서 퇴각할 것이라고 대변인이 밝혔다. 이 퇴각은 아시프 알리 자르다리 파키스탄 대통령이 국회에서 군대가 탈레반을 멈추게 할 수 있고, 파키스탄의 핵무기가 안전하다고 말한 뒤에 즉각적으로 이루어졌다. "만약 누군가가 정부의 의지에 도전한다면 그때는 우리가 행동을 취할 것이다"라고 아시프 알리 자르다리가 밝혔다. 그는 더 나아가 "국가는 방어 가능한 상태이며 우리의 핵무기 프로그램은 안전하다"라고 말함으로써 그의 결의를 뒷받침했다. 탈레반 전사들이 이 지역에 들어오려는 것을 다시 시도할지는 두고 볼 일이다.

☷ TEPS Survival 전략

29 The speech was / Nixon's response to critics / who had accused him of accepting gifts
여기서 who 이하는 critics를 수식하고 있다. who절의 him은 Nixon이며 of 이하에 비난하는 이유가 나온다. guilty of에서도 비슷한 구문을 볼 수 있다.
• Thomas was found guilty of murder.
  –〉 The court found Thomas guilty of murder.
토마스는 살인 혐의에 대해 유죄 판결을 받았다.

30 It remains to be seen if (whether) ～일지 아닐지는 두고 볼 일이다
• It remains to be seen whether Korean astronauts will actually get to the moon by 2032.
2032년까지 한국의 우주 비행사들이 달에 정말로 갈지는 두고 볼 일이다.

will react," Asif Ali Zardari said. He further backed up his conviction by saying, "The defense of the country is in capable hands and our nuclear program is in safe hands." It remains to be seen if the Taliban will make another attempt to enter the region.

Q Which of the following is correct about the Taliban according to the news report?
(a) They will no longer endeavor to infiltrate Pakistan.
(b) They will continue to advance into the Buner district.
(c) They are part of Pakistan's military.
(d) They are opposed to the government of Pakistan.

Q 뉴스에 따르면 탈레반에 대해 옳은 것은?
(a) 더 이상 파키스탄으로 침투하려고 하지 않을 것이다.
(b) 계속해서 부네르 지역으로 진격하고 있다.
(c) 파키스탄 군대의 일부이다.
(d) 파키스탄 정부와 대립한다.

⊞ 출제 POINT
군대가 탈레반을 멈추게 할 수 있다(the military could stop the Taliban)는 발표 후에 수도에서 퇴각한 것으로 보아 탈레반은 파키스탄 정부와 대립한다는 사실을 알 수 있다. 따라서 정답은 (d). 탈레반이 퇴각할 것이라고 하였으므로 (b)는 답에서 제외되며, 마지막 문장에서 탈레반 전사들이 이 지역에 들어오려 또 다른 시도를 할지는 두고 볼 일이라고 하였으므로 (a) 또한 사실과 다르다.
withdraw 퇴각하다 **conviction** 신념 **endeavor** 노력하다
infiltrate 잠입하다 　　　　　　　　　　　　정답_(d)

31

A study suggests that global warming could lead to more human deaths. Researchers in Spain found an increase of cholera cases in Zambia that seem related to climatic factors. For the first time, the results confirm that an increase in environmental temperature six weeks before the rainy season increases the number of people affected by cholera by 4.9%. This disease has a marked seasonal component associated with the rainy season and thrives in high temperatures. Humans can contract the disease from contaminated water and food. Cholera has been known to cause great human, social and economic losses.

Q Which of the following is correct according to the passage?
(a) Global warming led to more cholera deaths in Africa and Europe.
(b) Cholera is passed directly from one person to another.
(c) Higher temperatures impede the spread of cholera.
(d) Researchers examined the period before the rainy season.

☞ 번역
한 연구 결과에 따르면 지구 온난화가 보다 많은 인류의 죽음을 초래할 수도 있다고 한다. 스페인의 연구자들은 잠비아 지역에서 기후 요소와 관련이 있는 것으로 보이는 콜레라 발생이 증가했다는 사실을 발견했다. 이러한 결과들은 우기가 오기 6주 전 온도의 증가가 콜레라에 감염된 사람의 수를 4.9%만큼 증가시켰다는 점을 처음으로 확증하는 것이다. 이 질병은 우기와 관련된 현저한 계절적인 인자를 가지고 있고, 고온에서 번성한다. 사람은 오염된 물이나 음식으로부터 질병에 감염될 수 있다. 콜레라는 엄청난 인적, 사회적 그리고 경제적 손실을 야기한다고 알려져 있다.

Q 지문에 따르면 옳은 것은?
(a) 지구 온난화가 아프리카와 유럽에서 콜레라로 인한 사망자 증가를 가져왔다.
(b) 콜레라는 한 사람에서 다른 사람으로 직접적으로 옮겨진다.
(c) 높은 온도가 콜레라의 확산을 지연시킨다.
(d) 연구가들은 우기가 도래하기 전의 기간을 연구했다.

⊞ 출제 POINT
연구 결과에서 우기가 오기 6주 전의 온도 증가가 콜레라 감염자 수를 증가시켰다고 하였으므로 과학자들은 우기 도래 전의 기간을 연구했음을 알 수가 있다. 따라서 정답은 (d). 아프리카와 유럽이라는 내용은 언급되지 않았으므로 (a)는 오답이고, (c)는 지문과 반대되는 내용이며 (b)는 지문 내용만으로 알 수 없다.
lead to ∼한 결과로 이끌다, 야기하다 **contaminated** 오염된
impede 방해하다, 지연시키다 　　　　　　　　　　정답_(d)

---

31 lead to/ bring about/ cause/ give rise to ∼한 결과로 이끌다
• Financial uncertainty in the US could lead to a new world order.
　미국 내 경제의 불확실성이 새로운 세계 질서를 야기할 수도 있다.

32

Portuguese is one of the world's major languages, ranking 6th according to number of native speakers, or 191 to 230 million people. Although Brazil is the only Portuguese-speaking nation in the Americas, it is home to half the population of South America. Portuguese is also widely spoken in other areas formerly colonized by Portugal, such as Mozambique. Nine countries list it as their official language, including Macau and Angola. The Portuguese diaspora has created large communities of Portuguese speakers in various regions along the east coast of the United States and in Ontario, Canada as well.

Q Why is Portuguese spoken by so many people?
(a) It is an official language in every South American country.
(b) Colonization and immigration have widened its use.
(c) It is widely spoken throughout the United State.
(d) Portugal continues to exert a lot of influence on the Americas.

☞ 번역

약 1억 9천 1백만에서 2억 3천만 명에 달하는 원어민이 사용하는 포르투갈어는 6위에 해당하는 세계 주요 언어 중 하나이다. 미대륙에서는 브라질이 포르투갈어를 사용하는 유일한 국가이지만, 브라질은 남아메리카 인구 절반의 본거지이다. 포르투갈어는 또한 모잠비크와 같이 예전에 포르투갈 식민지였던 다른 지역에서 널리 쓰이고 있다. 마카오와 앙골라를 포함한 9개 국가가 포르투갈어를 공식 언어로 등록하고 있다. 포르투갈 이주자 집단은 미국 동부 해안의 여러 지역은 물론 캐나다의 온타리오에서도 커다란 포르투갈어 공동체를 형성하였다.

Q 많은 사람들이 포르투갈어를 사용하는 이유는?
(a) 모든 남미 국가에서 공식어이다.
(b) 식민화와 이민이 포르투갈어의 사용을 증가시켰다.
(c) 미국 전역에 광범위하게 사용된다.
(d) 포르투칼이 미대륙에서 큰 영향력을 계속 발휘하고 있다.

⊞ 출제 POINT

모잠비크와 같이 예전 식민지(colonization)였던 국가에서 널리 사용되며 포르투갈 이주자들이 여기저기 흩어져서 포르투갈 공동체를 형성하였다(immigration)고 했으므로 (b)가 정답이다.

diaspora 이주자 집단   **exert** 발휘하다   정답_(b)

33

Those who believe that animals are capable of feeling remorse will be heartened by a recent study that examined brain scans of monkeys trying to win a large prize of juice by guessing where it was hidden. When the monkeys were incorrect in their selection and were then shown the location of the prize, the neurons in their brains clearly registered a form of regret. A researcher noted that the monkeys reacted to their losses by changing their subsequent guesses, much like humans shift strategies after missing opportunities.

☞ 번역

동물들이 후회하는 감정을 느낄 수 있다고 믿는 사람들은 최근 한 연구에 의해 고무될 것입니다. 이 연구는 원숭이로 하여금 경품인 주스가 어디에 감춰져 있는지 맞추어 이를 얻도록 하는 방식으로 원숭이의 뇌의 움직임을 촬영한 실험입니다. 원숭이가 잘못된 선택을 하고 경품의 위치를 보여주었을 때 원숭이의 뇌에 있는 신경 세포들이 후회의 형태를 분명하게 나타냈습니다. 한 연구자는 원숭이가 그들의 차후 선택을 변경하며 그들의 손실에 반응을 나타냈고 이는 인간이 기회를 잃은 뒤에 전략을 수정하는 것과 매우 흡사했다고 기술했습니다. 그러므로 후회하는 능력은 음식을 찾고 자원을 공평하게 나누어 가질 짝을 찾는 진화적인 면에 있어 매우 유익할 것입니다.

Q 지문에서 유추할 수 있는 것은?
(a) 정확히 예측한 원숭이들은 뇌 촬영에서 유사한 변화를 보였다.
(b) 모든 동물들은 후회하는 감정을 가질 수 있다.
(c) 과학자들은 후회의 기미를 보인 원숭이들에게 보상을 주었다.
(d) 원숭이의 후회는 생존에 도움이 될지도 모른다.

📖 TEPS Survival 전략

32 Portuguese is one of the world's major languages, / ranking 6th according to number of native speakers, / or 191 to 230 million people.
ranking 이하는 포르투갈어를 부연 설명하는 부분으로, 동격의 or로 연결되어 있다.

33 Those who believe that animals are capable of feeling remorse / will be heartened by a recent study / that examined brain scans of monkeys trying to win a large prize of juice by guessing where it was hidden.
이 문장 분석의 핵심은 주어를 찾는 것으로 조동사 will 앞까지가 모두 주어부이다. 뒤의 study를 관계대명사 that 절이 다시 꾸며주고 있다.

A capacity for regret could thus be advantageous evolutionarily in terms of foraging for food and finding partners who will share resources equitably.

Q What can be inferred from the passage?
(a) Monkeys who guessed correctly showed similar changes in their brain scans.
(b) All animals are capable of feeling regret.
(c) Researchers rewarded the monkeys who exhibited signs of remorse.
(d) Regret in monkeys may help them to survive.

끝부분에 자원을 공평하게 나누어 가지게 하는 데(finding partners who will share resources equitably) 매우 유익하다고 했으므로 후회가 원숭이의 생존에 도움을 준다고 볼 수 있다. (a)는 지문에 언급되어 있지 않은 내용이며 (c)의 경우 실험을 위해 주스를 사용하기는 했지만 후회의 기미를 보인 원숭이에게 보상을 준 것은 아니다.

remorse 후회 **hearten** 고무하다 **neuron** 신경 세포 **forge** 뒤지며 찾다
정답_(d)

34

Valence Mutual recognizes the threat posed to both the health of employees and the interests of the company by life-threatening diseases such as, but not limited to, tuberculosis, typhoid, and meningitis. Therefore, Valence Mutual is committed to the promotion of awareness of such conditions among employees. The nurse's office will hold a workshop to educate people about diseases and administer vaccinations for a variety of conditions. The workshop will take place on Tuesday, June 3rd, from 10 a.m. to 11:30 a.m. and is mandatory for all employees. Please make every effort to attend this very important session. Thank you.

Q What can be inferred from the passage?
(a) Employees will have their work interrupted on June 3rd.
(b) Those who do not attend the workshop will be able to reschedule.
(c) Valence Mutual has had serious illnesses at its office before.
(d) The vaccinations may not be suitable for all people.

번역

발렌스 뮤추얼은 꼭 이 질병들에만 국한된 것은 아니지만 결핵이나 장티푸스 그리고 뇌수막염 같은 생명을 위협하는 질병이 직원들의 건강과 회사의 이익 모두에 위협을 가한다는 점을 인식하고 있습니다. 그래서 발렌스 뮤추얼은 직원들 사이에 이러한 상황에 대한 인식을 높이고자 노력하고 있습니다. 의료실은 사람들에게 질병들에 대해 교육하는 워크숍을 개최하고 다양한 질병에 대한 예방 접종을 실시할 것입니다. 워크숍은 6월 3일 화요일 오전 10시부터 오전 11시 30분까지 개최될 것이며 모든 직원들은 의무적으로 참석해야 합니다. 이 중요한 워크숍에 참석할 수 있도록 최대한 노력해 주시기 바랍니다. 감사합니다.

Q 이 지문에서 유추할 수 있는 것은?
(a) 직원들은 6월 3일 자신들의 업무를 중단하게 될 것이다.
(b) 워크숍에 참석하지 않는 사람들은 일정을 재조정할 수 있을 것이다.
(c) 발렌스 뮤추얼은 사무실에서 심각한 질병을 겪은 적이 있다.
(d) 예방 접종은 모든 사람에게 적합하지 않을 수도 있다.

출제 POINT

모든 직원이 의무적으로 참석해야 한다고 하였으므로 워크숍 당일인 6월 3일에 업무가 중단될 것이다. (b)는 워크숍 참여가 mandatory라는 언급이 있지만 그 외에 관한 내용을 찾을 수 없으므로 오답이다. (c), (d) 역시 이 글을 통해 알 수 없는 내용이다.

tuberculosis 결핵 **typhoid** 장티푸스 **meningitis** 뇌수막염
administer 실시하다 **penalize** 벌주다 **mandatory** 의무적인
정답_(a)

34 Valence Mutual recognizes the threat / posed to both the health of employees and the interests of the company / by life-threatening diseases / (such as, but not limited to, tuberculosis, typhoid, and meningitis.)

이 문장은 pose a threat to '~에 위협을 가하다'라는 기본 숙어를 바탕으로 분석해야 한다. 여기서는 수동태로 쓰여 threat posed to ... by ~ 즉, '~가 …에게 가하는 위협'이라고 해석한다. 중간에 들어간 both ... and ~, such as 등의 연결사에 유의해야 하며 such as 뒷부분은 예시이므로 일단 괄호로 묶었다가 나중에 해석을 해도 무방하다.

163

35

Julian Asher has a condition called synesthesia. When he listens to music, he also sees it. The sounds of a violin make him see a burgundy color, reminiscent of red wine, while a cello's music evokes images of golden honey. Synesthesia is a neurological condition in which people experience a mixing of their senses. Those affected may see colors and movement in numbers, words or sounds. One study says that as many as 1 percent of people have the most recognizable form of synesthesia. This condition may not be well-known to many, but a number of famous people have been labeled as synesthetes, including individuals of many different artistic talents.

Q What is most likely to be discussed next?
(a) How synesthesia is depicted in arts and literature
(b) Sources for further reading on synesthesia
(c) Some celebrities with synesthesia
(d) Scientific studies on synesthesia

✍ 번역

쥴리안 애셔는 공감각이라는 증상을 가지고 있습니다. 그는 음악을 들을 때 동시에 음악을 볼 수가 있습니다. 첼로 음악이 황금 꿀의 이미지를 만들어 내는가 하면 바이올린 소리는 붉은 와인을 연상시키는 적포도주 색을 보게 해줍니다. 공감각은 사람들이 감각의 혼합을 경험하게 되는 신경계의 증상입니다. 이러한 증상을 가진 사람들은 숫자, 단어 또는 소리에서 색깔을 보거나 움직임을 볼 수도 있습니다. 한 연구 결과에 따르면 무려 1%의 사람들이 가장 인식하기 쉬운 형태의 공감각을 가지고 있다고 합니다. 이 증상은 많은 사람에게 알려지지 않았을지도 모르지만 예술적 재능을 가진 사람들을 포함한 유명인들 중에도 공감각자로 구분되는 사람들이 있습니다.

Q 지문 뒤에 논의될 만한 내용은?
(a) 공감각이 예술과 문학에서 묘사되는 방식
(b) 공감각에 관한 더 많은 읽을거리의 출처
(c) 공감각을 가진 몇몇 유명인
(d) 공감각에 대한 과학적 연구들

⊞ 출제 POINT

끝부분에 다양한 재능을 가진 사람들을 포함한 소수의 유명인들 중에도 공감각을 가진 사람이 있다고 기술하고 있으므로 이러한 사람들의 예시가 이어질 가능성이 높다.

synesthesia 공감각 **burgundy** 적포도주 **reminiscent** 상기시키는 **evoke** 일깨우다; 자아내다 **label** 딱지를 붙이다; 분류하다 **depict** 묘사하다 **citation** 인용 정답_(c)

36

Tortillas are the unleavened flatbread made from wheat or corn most commonly seen in Mexican food. They date back to pre-Columbian civilizations, around 10,000 BCE. When the Spaniards found unleavened flatbread in Mexico among the Aztecs, they named it "tortilla," from the Spanish word "torta," or "round cake." Tortillas are consumed all year round, on different occasions, with all kinds of meals. They are often filled with meat to make dishes such as tacos.

✍ 번역

토르티야는 대부분의 멕시코 음식에서 볼 수 있는 밀 또는 옥수수로 만든 베이킹 파우더를 넣지 않은 평평한 빵이다. 토르티야는 기원전 10,000년경인 콜럼버스 이전 문명들로 거슬러 올라간다. 스페인 사람들이 아즈텍 문명에 있는 멕시코에서 베이킹 파우더를 넣지 않은 이 납작한 빵을 발견했을 때 스페인어로 '토르타', 즉 '둥근 빵'이라는 의미로 이를 '토르티야'라고 이름 붙였다. 토르티야는 일년 내내 다른 행사에서 모든 종류의 음식과 함께 먹는다. 토르티야는 종종 안에 고기를 채워 타코와 같은 음식을 만들기도 한다.

📖 TEPS Survival 전략

35 When he listens to music, he also sees it.
it은 앞 부사절의 music을 가리키는 대명사이다. '음악을 들을 때 동시에 음악을 본다'는 의미가 된다.

36 date back to pre-Columbian civilizations, around 10,000 BCE.
date back to는 '~까지 거슬러 올라가다'라는 뜻이며 pre-Columbian civilizations와 around 10,000 BCE 사이의 쉼표는 동격을 나타내어 두 시기가 같다는 의미이다.

• Erotica may date back to the Stone Age.
춘화의 역사는 석기시대까지 거슬러 갈지도 모른다.

Q What can be inferred from the passage?
(a) Tortillas are mostly consumed on special occasions.
(b) Spaniards replaced their bread with tortillas.
(c) Tortillas form the basis of the traditional Mexican diet.
(d) Most people today know of tortillas because of tacos.

Q 지문에서 유추할 수 있는 것은?
(a) 토르티야는 대부분 특별한 행사에만 먹는다.
(b) 스페인 사람들은 자신들의 빵을 토르티야로 대체했다.
(c) 토르티야는 전통 멕시코 식단의 근간을 형성한다.
(d) 오늘날 대부분의 사람들은 타코 때문에 토르티야를 알고 있다.

37

Those who want to live long lives should perhaps look at how people in Andorra live. The average Andorran can expect to live at least 85 years. That is longer than anywhere else in the world. People in this small nation bordering Spain and France embrace healthy living. When talking to various people there, it becomes clear that the concept of living longer is not on everyone's mind, but the idea of living well and living healthy comes up in nearly every conversation. Many Andorrans follow exercise regimens that involve walking up and down the hillsides. Even those in their 80s and 90s can easily climb two or three flights of stairs built into the mountainside.

Q What can be inferred about Andorrans?
(a) They aim to lengthen their lifespan.
(b) People in Spain and France also live very long lives.
(c) Conversations about living healthy are responsible for their longevity.
(d) Their active lifestyle is part of their longevity.

번역

장수하기를 원하는 사람은 어쩌면 안도라 지역의 사람들이 어떻게 살아가는지를 보아야 할 것이다. 안도라의 평균 수명은 최소 85세이다. 이는 전 세계 어느 지역보다 높은 수치이다. 스페인과 프랑스에 인접해 있는 이 작은 나라 사람들은 건강한 삶을 영위한다. 그곳에 있는 다양한 사람들과 이야기를 해보면 장수라는 개념을 모든 사람이 원하는 것은 아니라는 점이 분명해진다. 그러나 잘살고 건강하게 산다는 개념은 거의 모든 대화에서 나타난다. 많은 안도라인들은 언덕을 오르내리는 것을 포함한 건강 운동을 한다. 심지어 80대나 90대들도 산을 따라 만들어 놓은 계단을 2~3층 쉽게 올라간다.

Q 안도라 사람들에 대해 유추할 수 있는 것은?
(a) 그들은 자신들의 수명을 연장하는 데 목표를 둔다.
(b) 스페인과 프랑스에 사는 사람들 또한 매우 오래 산다.
(c) 건강하게 사는 것에 대한 대화가 그들의 장수를 책임지고 있다.
(d) 그들의 활동적인 생활 양식이 장수의 한 요소이다.

37 That is longer than anywhere else in the world.
단순해 보이는 문장이지만 앞 문장과 관련지어 해석해야 하므로 주의를 요한다. 주어 That은 앞 문장의 평균 수명이며, longer than의 비교 대상은 Andorra와 anywhere else in the world이다.

38

In 1953, America's CIA and the UK's MI6 helped pro-Western Iranians carry out a coup d'etat. (a) This covert operation deposed Prime Minister Mohammed Mosaddeq's democratically elected government and aided in installing a government in Iran that supported the British and American governments. (b) The Anglo-American coup, referred to as Operation Ajax, was initially considered successful, but is today seen as a grave political mistake on the part of the United States and Britain. (c) Madeleine Albright has expressed that sentiment, saying the operation was a failure that led to the seeds of anti-American terrorism in the country. (d) Some argue that while many of Mosaddeq's allies abandoned him, the withdrawal of support by the clergy was fatal to his cause.

☞ 번역

1953년에 미국 CIA와 영국의 MI6은 친서방 성향의 이란인들이 쿠데타를 일으키는 것을 도와주었다. (a) 이 비밀 작전은 모하메드 모사덱 총리의 민주적으로 선출된 정부를 무너지게 했고, 영국과 미국 정부를 지원하는 이란 정부를 설립하는 것을 도왔다. (b) 작전명 아작스로 일컬어지는 이 앵글로–아메리칸 쿠데타는 처음에는 성공한 것으로 여겨졌으나, 오늘날에는 미국과 영국 측의 중대한 정치적 실수로 여겨지고 있다. (c) 매들린 올브라이트는 이 작전은 반미 테러의 씨앗을 낳은 실패한 작전이라고 말하며 이 같은 의견을 표현했다. (d) 몇몇 사람들은, 비록 많은 모사덱 연합군이 그를 떠났지만, 성직자의 주도 하에 이뤄진 그의 퇴진 요구가 모사덱 총리의 운동에 치명적인 타격을 주었다고 주장하고 있다.

⊞ 출제 POINT

(b)에서 쿠데타가 오늘날 정치적 실수로 여겨지고 있다고 했고 (c)의 saying 이하에서 올브라이트 역시 실패한 작전이라는 의견을 내놓고 있다. 그러나 갑자기 (d)에서 성직자의 주도 하에 이뤄진 모사덱 총리의 퇴진 요구에 관해 언급하고 있으므로 글의 흐름상 적절하지 않다.

carry out a coup d'etat 쿠데타를 일으키다 **covert** 은밀한, 숨은
depose 물러나게 하다 **grave** 중대한 **sentiment** 감상; 의견
clergy 성직자 정답_(d)

39

Amazon's Kindle, a hand-held gadget for reading books, has revolutionized the literary world. (a) Publisher Hearst Corp. is hoping it can do the same for its newspapers and magazines with its own device. (b) These so-called "e-readers" display crisp text on a screen that closely approximates a paper, all the while saving money on paper, printing, and delivery. (c) Hearst Corp. partly owns several leading cable networks, as well as numerous TV station and web sites. (d) Cost-cutting measures are especially important for Hearst during a time when ads sales are dropping and people prefer to get their news and entertainment electronically.

☞ 번역

책을 읽기 위해 손에 들고 다닐 수 있는 장치인 아마존 킨들은 문학세계에 혁명을 일으켰다. (a) 허스트 신문사는 킨들처럼 자사의 제품으로 자사의 신문과 잡지를 읽을 수 있게 되기를 바라고 있다. (b) 이러한 소위 e-리더기는 신문, 인쇄 그리고 배달에 드는 비용을 줄이면서 화면에 신문과 거의 똑같은 또렷한 텍스트를 보여준다. (c) 허스트 사는 다수의 방송국과 홈페이지뿐만 아니라 주요 유선 텔레비전 방송망을 소유하고 있다. (d) 비용 절감 방식은 특히 광고 판매가 떨어지고 사람들이 전자 뉴스나 오락을 선호하는 때에 허스트 사에게 매우 중요하다.

⊞ 출제 POINT

처음 문장에서 아마존 킨들을 소개하고, (a)에서는 허스트 사에서도 신문과 잡지를 읽을 수 있는 장치를 개발하고자 한다는 내용이 이어진 뒤 (b)에서 킨들과 허스트 사의 제품, 두 제품을 These so-called "e-readers"로 받아 e-리더기가 문학세계에 가져온 변화와 그 기능에 관해 기술하고 있다. (c)에서 갑자기 허스트 사의 사업 영역에 대해 소개하는 것은 어색하다.

gadget 간단한 기계장치 **crisp** 또렷한 정답_(c)

📖 TEPS Survival 전략

38 The Anglo-American coup, / referred to as Operation Ajax, / was initially considered successful,
refer to A as B는 'A를 B라고 일컫다'인데 위 문장에서는 수동태로 쓰였고 A에 해당하는 것은 Anglo-American coup, B는 Operation Ajax이다.
• There are several reasons why they refer to their opportunities as the golden chances.

그들이 자신들이 가진 기회를 황금 같은 기회라고 부르는 데는 몇 가지 이유가 있다.

39 during a time / when ads sales are dropping ...
during a time when은 '~한 시기에'라는 의미이며 when이 시간을 나타내는 관계부사로 두 부분을 연결해주는 역할을 하고 있다.
• Eric lived during a time when blacks and women did not have the right to vote.
에릭은 흑인과 여성들이 선거권을 갖지 못한 시기에 살았다.

40

Most people conceive of capital as assets that yield income and other useful outputs over long periods of time—for example, a bank account, shares of stock or factories. (a) However, such obvious forms of capital are not the only type of capital that exist in society. (b) Other types include real estate property, automobiles and other personal possessions. (c) Recently, economists have broadened the meaning of the term to include intellectual capital, or investments in intellectual property. (d) In classical economics, capital is one of three factors of production, the others being land and labor.

 번역

대부분의 사람들은 자본을 수익을 내고 오랜 기간에 걸쳐 다른 유용한 결과를 가져오는, 예를 들자면 은행 계좌나 주식 또는 공장과 같은 자산으로 생각한다. (a) 그러나 이런 형태가 있는 자본만이 사회에서 존재하는 자본의 명백한 형태는 아니다. (b) 다른 형태의 자본에는 부동산, 자동차 및 기타 개인 재산이 포함된다. (c) 최근 학자들은 '자본'의 의미를 확장시켰는데 그것은 지적 자본 또는 지적 자산의 투자를 포함한다. (d) 고전파 경제학에서 자본은 토지, 노동과 함께 생산의 3요소 중 하나이다.

⊞ 출제 POINT

(a)와 (b)에서 부동산이나 자동차 및 개인 자산을 언급하며 이러한 형태의 자본 외에 다른 형태의 자본이 존재한다고 하였다. (c)에서는 자본의 넓은 의미를 소개하는데, (d)는 갑자기 고전파 경제학을 말하고 있으므로 적절하지 않다.

conceive of 생각하다, 이해하다   **real estate** 부동산   정답_(d)

---

40 Most people / conceive of capital as assets / that yield income and other useful outputs / over long periods of time ...

conceive of A as B는 'A를 B라고 여기다, 생각하다'라는 표현으로 여기서 A는 capital, B는 assets이며 assets를 that절이 다시 수식하고 있다.

• I often conceive of love as a fountain of energy.
나는 종종 사랑을 에너지가 솟는 샘이라고 생각한다.

Actual Test 1

 문 제

Listening Comprehension CD.2
Grammar
Vocabulary
Reading Comprehension

 해 설 및 정 답

LISTENING
COMPREHENSION

Part I **Questions 1—15**

You will now hear fifteen conversation fragments, each made up of a single spoken statement followed by four spoken responses. Choose the most appropriate response to the statement.

Part II **Questions 16—30**

You will now hear fifteen conversation fragments, each made up of three spoken statements followed by four spoken responses. Choose the most appropriate response to complete the conversation.

LISTENING COMPREHENSION

Part III　**Questions 31—45**

You will now hear fifteen complete conversations. For each item, you will hear a conversation and its corresponding question, both of which will be read twice. Then you will hear four options which will be read only once. Choose the option that best answers the question.

Part IV　**Questions 46—60**

You will now hear fifteen spoken monologues. For each item, you will hear a monologue and its corresponding question, both of which will be read twice. Then you will hear four options which will be read only once. Choose the option that best answers the question.

GRAMMAR

DIRECTIONS

This part of the exam tests your grammar skills. You will have 25 minutes to complete the 50 questions. Be sure to follow the directions given by the proctor.

Part I   **Questions 1—20**

Choose the best answer for the blank.

1.   A: What do you do for exercise?

    B: I really enjoy _____, so I do that almost every day.

(a) bike
(b) biking
(c) to bike
(d) to have biked

2.   A: Did you ever get in touch with Fred?

    B: No, _____, all I got was a recorded message.

(a) when I called
(b) when called
(c) I called
(d) calling

3.   A: John _____ on the 13th.

    B: Oh, that's tomorrow!

(a) arrived
(b) is arriving
(c) has arrived
(d) had arrived

4.   A: I've seen several productions of the famous ballet *Swan Lake*.

    B: _____, and they were great.

(a) I have so
(b) Have I so
(c) So I have
(d) So have I

5.   A: I'm sick of our computer. Let's buy a new one.

    B: Yes, ours _____ old and outdated by today's standards.

(a) is
(b) was
(c) will be
(d) had been

6.   A: Are you well enough to go to work?

    B: Yes, _____.

(a) think so me
(b) me so think
(c) I so think
(d) I think so

7.   A: Are you married, Dave?

    B: Yes. _____ married for two years.

(a) I'm
(b) I was
(c) I've been
(d) I'm being

8.   A: I have a job interview today.

    B: Good luck! Let me know _____ as soon as you find out.

(a) result
(b) a result
(c) the result
(d) this result

9. A: I'm going to Hong Kong for my vacation. How about you?

   B: I can't afford _____ a trip anywhere.

   (a) take
   (b) to take
   (c) for taking
   (d) being taken

10. A: Was it you making all that noise last night?

    B: No, it _____ have been me. I was out all last night.

    (a) mustn't
    (b) couldn't
    (c) mightn't
    (d) shouldn't

11. A: What's the hotel policy on room keys?

    B: They should _____ at the front desk.

    (a) leave
    (b) be left
    (c) be leaving
    (d) have been left

12. A: Our team needs more time to finish the class project.

    B: Our team _____, too.

    (a) needs to
    (b) does it
    (c) needs
    (d) does

13. A: The party got few votes in the election.

    B: Yes, _____.

    (a) more they didn't get it's a shame
    (b) a shame it's they didn't get more
    (c) it's a shame they didn't get more
    (d) they didn't get more it's a shame

14. A: When did the suspect finally talk?

    B: Only after they got him a lawyer _____ his mouth.

    (a) he opened
    (b) opened he
    (c) he did open
    (d) did he open

15. A: What did the professor ask you?

    B: He asked _____ my assignment.

    (a) how to me was I doing
    (b) me I was doing how with
    (c) me how I was doing with
    (d) how was I doing me with

16. A: Enrollment at this school seems to increase every year.

    B: True. Unfortunately, the number of teachers _____ the same.

    (a) are remained
    (b) is remained
    (c) remains
    (d) remain

17. A: I think Ann can be quite bossy.

    B: Yeah, she can't help but tell

    _____ .

    (a) what everyone to do
    (b) everyone what to do
    (c) what to do for everyone
    (d) everyone that is what to do

18. A: Should I do my essay on the first topic or the second?

    B: _____ you prefer to write on.

    (a) That
    (b) What
    (c) Which
    (d) Whichever

19. A: Have you seen my jacket anywhere?

    B: It's hanging _____ the hat stand.

    (a) in
    (b) at
    (c) on
    (d) with

20. A: Did your parents say okay to your auditioning for an acting job?

    B: No, they _____ see it my way.

    (a) mustn't
    (b) mightn't
    (c) wouldn't
    (d) shouldn't

Part II   **Questions 21—40**

Choose the best answer for the blank.

---

21. Joe found Annie in the kitchen _____ the dishes.

    (a) washing
    (b) washed
    (c) to wash
    (d) washes

22. The Enlightenment was a movement that started among a small elite group and slowly spread to make its influence _____ throughout Europe.

    (a) felt
    (b) to feel
    (c) feeling
    (d) having felt

23. The professor considered it an honor to have a scholarship named after

    _____ .

    (a) him
    (b) his
    (c) he
    (d) it

24. Sandra Blake is an award-winning writer _____ the *New York Times*.

    (a) in
    (b) for
    (c) over
    (d) across

25. Persistently late students, meaning those _____ have received more than five tardy slips, will be suspended.

(a) who
(b) which
(c) of which
(d) of whom

26. Many people think of dieting not just as a way to become thinner, but _____ control over their lives.

(a) a gaining of way
(b) gaining a way of
(c) as a way of gaining
(d) gaining as a way of

27. For centuries, humans have looked up at the sky and wondered _____ the confines of our planet.

(a) beyond what exists
(b) what exists beyond
(c) what beyond does exist
(d) beyond what does exist

28. Critics thought the new band would be successful, but not _____ successful as to break album sales records.

(a) very
(b) such
(c) too
(d) so

29. Once _____, harbor seals become less tolerant of contact with others of their kind.

(a) to wean
(b) weaned
(c) were weaned
(d) had been weaned

30. The lost cat had _____ white fur and blue eyes.

(a) long
(b) a long
(c) the long
(d) that long

31. According to school policy, clothing that is suggestive, vulgar or inappropriate _____ allowed on campus.

(a) have not been
(b) has not been
(c) are not
(d) is not

32. If the injured man _____ brought to the hospital sooner, doctors might have been able to save his life.

(a) be
(b) were
(c) has been
(d) had been

33. Immigration officials _____ of the fact that Mexican nationals enter the US illegally in large numbers.

(a) have been aware long
(b) aware have been long
(c) have long been aware
(d) aware long have been

34. _____ poaching continues to threaten tigers' survival significantly, their greatest long-term threat is habitat loss.

(a) If
(b) Since
(c) While
(d) Because

35. In the world of digital photography, _____ with computer software.

(a) taken pictures by you can be altered
(b) your pictures taken can be altered
(c) pictures you take can be altered
(d) can be altered your pictures

36. _____ in excessive quantities, caffeine may cause insomnia and headaches.

(a) Consume
(b) Consumed
(c) Consuming
(d) To consume

37. The manager demanded that the current project _____ done by the end of the week.

(a) had been
(b) is being
(c) be
(d) is

38. This website provides _____ on the causes of high blood pressure and treatment options.

(a) the informations
(b) an information
(c) informations
(d) information

39. The young mother _____ for only an hour when her baby's cries woke her.

(a) sleeps
(b) has slept
(c) will have slept
(d) had been sleeping

40. It was Audrey Hepburn's beauty, coupled with her vulnerability, that made her _____ presence.

(a) compelling such an on-screen
(b) such an on-screen compelling
(c) such a compelling on-screen
(d) on-screen compelling such a

Part III **Questions 41—45**

Identify the option that contains an awkward expression or an error in grammar.

41. (a) A: It seems like our experiment is a failure.

(b) B: Yeah, it isn't producing the results we expected.

(c) A: We must have done something wrong.

(d) B: Well, it might work good if we try it again with some changes.

42. (a) A: Alison is moving to Halifax in April.

(b) B: That's so sudden. Why did she decide to do that?

(c) A: She is offered a really good job there.

(d) B: I see. Well, we'll have to visit her sometime.

43. (a) A: Good evening. Do you have a reservation?

(b) B: My husband made one. He should be here already.

(c) A: What name is under his reservation?

(d) B: His last name is Chilton, Alan Chilton.

44. (a) A: I'm a bit nervous about going to the dentist this afternoon.

(b) B: Don't be. The dentist will make sure it's virtually painless.

(c) A: I guess you're right. Anyway, having a tooth pulled is a common procedure.

(d) B: That's right, but there's no sense in worrying about it.

45. (a) A: Who was the man you were talking to outside the library?

(b) B: He's the professor for which class I couldn't buy a textbook.

(c) A: What did he say you should do?

(d) B: He just said I could copy the relevant chapters from his book.

Part IV Questions 46—50

Identify the option that contains an awkward expression or an error in grammar.

46. (a) Behaviorists believe that the basis of all learning in animals is reinforcement. (b) Reinforcement occurs when an animal associates a behavior with a reward. (c) For example, if a hungry rat gets a food pellet after pushing a lever, it is likely to push the lever again. (d) Thus, having learned correctly what to do, food is then given to the rat as a reward.

47. (a) Dab Away is part of Ellen Lange's daily maintenance system designed to cleanse and balance the skin. (b) It works to remove dirt, excess oil, makeup and dead skin cells, keeping your skin clean and healthy. (c) You can also use Dab Away as a fast-acted spot treatment to reduce oily skin and clear clogged pores. (d) It comes with our patented hygienic applicator that allows for extra precision spot treatment.

48. (a) The main entrance to the ancient city of Babylon was called the Ishtar Gate. (b) It was constructed on the north side of the city in 575 BC by order of King Nebuchadnezzar II. (c) Dedicated to the goddess Ishtar, the great Ishtar Gate was made of beautiful blue tiles. (d) This gate also decorated with golden bulls and lions, considered to be the favorite

49. (a) By the early 1900s, astronomical standards for measuring time came to be regarded as problematic because of fluctuations in the Earth's rotation. (b) Scientists agreed that a new time standard was needed that would be independent of these fluctuations. (c) Because atoms of cesium emits a regular frequency, eventually cesium came to be used in the development of atomic clocks. (d) Eventually, in 1967, an international agreement confirmed that the cesium atomic clock would be the time standard for the world.

50. (a) Anthropologists say that rituals play a major role in societies around the world. (b) These rituals are primarily of two kinds—rites of passage and rites of affliction. (c) Rites of passage take place at important moments in a person's life, such as when a boy enters into a manhood. (d) Rites of affliction arise in times of crisis such as during an illness or a disaster.

This is the end of the Grammar section. Do NOT move on to the next section until instructed to do so. You are NOT allowed to turn to any other section of the test.

TEPS

Vocabulary

Part I Questions 1—25

Choose the best answer for the blank.

1. A: My son didn't get into the university he wanted to.

   B: Really? What a _____!

   (a) fail
   (b) pity
   (c) luck
   (d) grief

2. A: Hey, Iris! It's great to see you!

   B: Yeah, it's been _____ since I saw you last.

   (a) ages
   (b) dates
   (c) times
   (d) periods

3. A: Let's have dinner together tonight.

   B: I'd love to, but I already have _____.

   (a) fixes
   (b) plans
   (c) things
   (d) schemes

4. A: I didn't understand the lecturer's main point. Did you?

   B: No, I had no idea what he was trying to _____.

   (a) get across
   (b) make out
   (c) speak up
   (d) push in

5. A: May I speak to Bill, please?

   B: Sure, please _____ the line for a minute.

   (a) place
   (b) hang
   (c) hold
   (d) rest

6. A: Professor Lyndon is very opinionated.

   B: Yeah, and he doesn't like students with _____ views.

   (a) relating
   (b) differing
   (c) assuming
   (d) comparing

7. A: Oh, I forgot to bring my pen.

   B: Here, you can _____ mine.

   (a) borrow
   (b) handle
   (c) write
   (d) lend

8. A: Why don't you stop working on your essay and watch some football?

   B: No, it'll only be another half an hour before I _____.

   (a) halt
   (b) finish
   (c) complete
   (d) terminate

9. A: Is this stream very deep?

    B: No. You can _____ to the other side.

    (a) splash
    (b) wade
    (c) glide
    (d) pace

10. A: I'm so glad to finally have my diploma in my hand.

    B: Now you're _____ a college graduate!

    (a) officially
    (b) seemingly
    (c) indefinitely
    (d) consistently

11. A: Why don't you buy this bag?

    B: Because I want one with a shoulder _____.

    (a) strap
    (b) slack
    (c) string
    (d) strand

12. A: Anthony will turn out to be a great teacher.

    B: Absolutely. He's well _____ for the job.

    (a) cared
    (b) suited
    (c) affected
    (d) exposed

13. A: Doug says this poem is satirical.

    B: No, he has _____ it incorrectly.

    (a) impressed
    (b) speculated
    (c) conformed
    (d) interpreted

14. A: Honey, is the baby asleep yet?

    B: Yes, she just _____ to sleep.

    (a) caught on
    (b) looked up
    (c) threw away
    (d) dropped off

15. A: Excuse me, is this the administration office?

    B: No, that's at the other _____ of the hall.

    (a) point
    (b) limit
    (c) end
    (d) site

16. A: Have you heard from Jim lately?

    B: No, he's been _____ these past few days.

    (a) passive
    (b) indistinct
    (c) accessible
    (d) unreachable

17. A: Tim is making a big mistake joining the police force.

    B: Well, let him be the _____ of that.

    (a) judge
    (b) umpire
    (c) director
    (d) authority

18. A: I hear today's meeting was cancelled.

B: Yes, it's been _____ until next week.

(a) belated
(b) reissued
(c) updated
(d) postponed

19. A: The radio said the main highway is backed up.

B: I'll look for an alternate _____, then.

(a) route
(b) track
(c) curb
(d) lane

20. A: What did you do to make that dog you adopted less aggressive?

B: Nothing. She's just become

_____.

(a) sorer
(b) tamer
(c) looser
(d) brasher

21. A: I recently had knee surgery, so I'll need some special provisions on the flight.

B: Certainly. We'll do all we can to _____ you.

(a) preclude
(b) encounter
(c) contravene
(d) accommodate

22. A: Was the test hard?

B: No, it was _____.

(a) a piece of cake
(b) a stitch in time
(c) like getting a raw deal
(d) like a bull in a china shop

23. A: Hello. Can one of your staff here at the hotel organize a tour for me?

B: Yes, please see the _____ at that counter over there.

(a) server
(b) patron
(c) hotelier
(d) concierge

24. A: Take two of these pills every four hours, and you should feel better in no time.

B: Thanks, Dr. Zee. I hope they can help me _____ my cold.

(a) cut
(b) beat
(c) avert
(d) undo

25. A: I'd like to settle my bill and check out, please.

B: Sure. Just give me a moment to _____ your expenses.

(a) tally
(b) charge
(c) submit
(d) proclaim

26. The famous violinist Yehudi Menuhin _____ his first violin lesson at the age of three.

(a) took
(b) struck
(c) packed
(d) brought

27. In most kingdoms throughout history, a king's first-born son was the natural _____ to the throne.

(a) kin
(b) heir
(c) royalty
(d) attendant

28. Since the singer always looked calm and poised, no one ever guessed that she got _____ before every performance.

(a) mad
(b) tired
(c) bored
(d) nervous

29. To _____ the privacy of our customers, our company does not share any customer information.

(a) avoid
(b) protect
(c) resume
(d) determine

30. Fashion magazines _____ the unrealistic idea that a woman has to be skinny to be beautiful.

(a) notice
(b) extract
(c) promote
(d) compensate

31. Prices have been increasing quickly because of the high _____ of inflation.

(a) rate
(b) cost
(c) quality
(d) budget

32. The novelist traveled all his life, _____ 25 times to live in various cities around the world.

(a) settling
(b) turning
(c) moving
(d) housing

33. Car-seat manufacturer Safe-Co has announced that a new form of car seat will be _____ for toddlers.

(a) developed
(b) increased
(c) guided
(d) solved

34. A top Chinese space official stated that China's exploration plans will include a robotic moon _____ within the year.

(a) lift
(b) duty
(c) action
(d) mission

35. Instead of trying to solve the problems in her marriage, Judy took the _____ action of filing for divorce.

(a) drastic
(b) neutral
(c) dilatory
(d) amicable

36. In order to enjoy the delicate taste of fine wine, one must _____ it slowly.

(a) indulge
(b) permeate
(c) expend
(d) savor

37. Rooftop solar panels _____ sunlight and turn it into electricity that can be used to heat water or cool homes.

(a) install
(b) absorb
(c) radiate
(d) exercise

38. At the restaurant, a tank of lobsters was wheeled to our table and we were asked to _____ which of them we would like to eat.

(a) point
(b) select
(c) instruct
(d) promise

39. Graduates with degrees in English language and literature often _____ careers in teaching or in writing.

(a) pursue
(b) engage
(c) recognize
(d) apprehend

40. Eating too much salty food may _____ to high blood pressure.

(a) react
(b) adjust
(c) proceed
(d) contribute

41. The judge decided to _____ the contract between the two parties, canceling all commitments.

(a) annex
(b) dictate
(c) rescind
(d) mediate

42. After World War II, the United States and the Soviet Union _____ as the world's superpowers.

(a) upheld
(b) interned
(c) emerged
(d) witnessed

43. The company can continue to expand as long as we remain in _____ contact with industry leaders.

(a) delicate
(b) constant
(c) excessive
(d) redundant

44. An action or gesture considered rude in one culture might _____ perfectly acceptable behavior in another.

(a) accuse
(b) extend
(c) divulge
(d) constitute

45. Some panel monitors are _____ specifically for computer gaming.

(a) enlisted
(b) pictured
(c) designed
(d) compiled

46. The 14th Dalai Lama fled to India when the Chinese brutally _____ an uprising of the Tibetan people in 1959.

(a) expedited
(b) fraternized
(c) anticipated
(d) suppressed

47. In order to help protect the environment, many US states have _____ laws which forbid citizens from burning trash.

(a) enacted
(b) reneged
(c) depicted
(d) undermined

48. Users can download a program to fix the _____ in their new "OfficeSpace Software" package.

(a) maneuver
(b) seizure
(c) glitch
(d) hack

49. Corruption was _____ under the country's former prime minister, and unfortunately, little has changed under the new government.

(a) scanty
(b) rampant
(c) glutinous
(d) miscreant

50. Due to the overuse of antibiotics, bacteria are becoming _____ to many of the drugs designed to fight them.

(a) susceptible
(b) infectious
(c) malleable
(d) resistant

This is the end of the Vocabulary section. Do NOT move on to the Reading Comprehension section until instructed to do so. You are NOT allowed to turn to any other section of the test.

READING
COMPREHENSION

Part I **Questions 1—16**

Read the passage. Then choose the option that best completes the passage.

1. Have you heard about the new Ultrabody Fitness Center? No more hustle and bustle, no more hassles, and best of all, no more waiting! We offer a most convenient location, which is open 24 hours a day. At our gym, you'll find all the weight-training and aerobic-exercise equipment that meets your needs. Our professional trainers are also standing by round the clock to help you plan your workout regimen and offer nutritional advice. So, _____.

   (a) sign up and start improving your health
   (b) renew your membership before it expires
   (c) stop by for great discounts on our products
   (d) call to find out more about this new method

2. Gentle and polite people sometimes become quite the opposite when they go online, where they can be confrontational and aggressive. This is because they feel untouchable or protected through the anonymity the Internet provides. Anonymity gives them the sense that they can get away with things. It makes them bold. Thus, they _____ when they go online.

   (a) say things they usually would not dare to
   (b) are outgoing and friendly with everyone
   (c) prefer to remain anonymous instead
   (d) remain as shy as they are in real life

3. People lost in darkness or heavy fog, with only an inner sense of direction to guide them, will often walk in circles and sometimes return to the spot where they first became lost. This happens because no human body is perfectly balanced and individuals tend to favor either their right or left side. That favoritism then affects the direction of movement when they cannot see where they are going. Invariably, they will _____.

   (a) rely on memory to find the way
   (b) instinctively try to avoid the fog
   (c) compensate for a lack of balance
   (d) be unable to keep a straight path

4. Since laws have been enacted to protect children from questionable TV advertising, marketers have turned their attention to the Internet. The versatility of this new medium offers ample opportunities to influence the buying habits of children. One online advertising tool they use is the "bot-buddy." A bot-buddy is a computer-generated talking character designed to _____.

(a) protect children from online strangers
(b) teach children about using the Internet
(c) get children interested in certain products
(d) inform parents of the dangers of advertising

5. It was clear from the 1920s on that Hollywood studios _____. In fact, there were so many avid moviegoers in America, the studios could expect to retrieve their production expenses and turn a profit solely on US soil. With a domestic market larger than that of any other country, studios had large enough budgets for every aspect of filmmaking, thus creating what was then the world's biggest movie industry.

(a) were focusing on their global success
(b) did not pay their stars enough money
(c) benefited from a huge domestic market
(d) saw color movies as the future of cinema

6. Recent studies show that parental involvement with homework can help a child succeed in school. However, in a survey carried out in 2006, many parents said they were surprised by the difficulty of their child's homework. It required skills they did not have, and so they lacked the confidence to help out as much as they would have liked to. Surveyed parents said they would spend more time helping their children

_____.

(a) if their children wanted them to
(b) if the homework was not so difficult
(c) if teachers assigned more homework
(d) if they did not have to work long hours

7. _____ can be an exciting challenge, as you'll see in this month's *Do-It-Yourself* magazine. From re-plumbing pre-Civil War mansions to safely removing lead-based paint from late 19th-century brownstones, our experts in this month's issue will show you how. In addition, be sure to check out the special section entitled "Protecting a Historic Home" for information on products and tips on guarding your home against the elements.

(a) Updating your drab living space
(b) Choosing the right home security
(c) Restoring an old building or house
(d) Building a new house on your own

8. _____ in West Indian plantation colonies of the 18th century. Though up to 90% of the residents of these islands were black, the European minority owned most of the land and human resources. Some government officials and a handful of small farmers were not under European control; however, they depended just as much as everyone else upon the oppressive and exploitative plantation system. In short, everything revolved around the plantations and those who controlled them.

(a) Power was in the hands of the few
(b) Slave labor was the key to great wealth
(c) Racial segregation was the general rule
(d) High-level government corruption was rife

9.

Dear Customer,

This year marks BTC's 20th anniversary, and we would like to thank all of our customers for their support. We've come a long way in the boat building industry since 1988 with our Core-Bond, Poly-Bond and Core-Cell foam products. The demand for our foams has increased rapidly over the years. In fact, it looks like our products are set to become an industry standard. We have you to thank in helping to make us _____. We will continue to produce high-quality products, and we hope to enjoy your continued support.

Yours sincerely,
Thomas J. Brown, CEO

(a) the foam that we required for our boats
(b) the top custom-boat builder in the industry
(c) a leader in the manufacture of boating foam
(d) a regulator of industry standard specifications

10. Ion Talzan's lifelong fascination with extraterrestrials and outer space has influenced his bizarre drawings, paintings and sculptures. Black holes, stars, UFOs—these are just a few of his intergalactic subjects. However, his pieces are not mere flights of fancy: Talzan aims for realism. His UFO diagrams, for example, combine art with technical precision, even including notes on the mechanics of spacecraft and electromagnetic propulsion. His work, as he sees it, is _____.

(a) a means of describing all of his fantasies
(b) a combination of the scientific and artistic
(c) a step towards debunking the myth of UFOs
(d) a way of showing kids the benefits of science

11. Many couples in this country, like my wife and me, have what is called secondary infertility. That is when a couple has one child but cannot conceive another. Although the causes of this are almost identical to those of primary infertility, the emotional experience of secondary infertility can be very different. If we share our anguish with others, they often make us feel we are greedy and ungrateful. We cannot conceive a second child, but we are made to feel we have no right to complain. The fact is we

_____.

(a) have looked into other child care services
(b) may be worse off than many others think
(c) are lucky enough to have no complaints
(d) should really try to have another child

12. Perhaps more than any other alcoholic drink except wine, absinthe has had a reputation for being _____. Known as the "Green Fairy" for its emerald color, it was consumed in great quantities by them in the late 19th and early 20th century. Edgar Degas, Vincent van Gogh, Paul Gauguin and Pablo Picasso were all fans of the drink and its inspirational properties. Needless to say, absinthe also became synonymous with decadence, modernism and a bohemian lifestyle.

(a) a big part of the lives of the rich and famous
(b) associated with artists and artistic inspiration
(c) responsible for turning men into violent alcoholics
(d) the ruin of people who could have been great artists

13. Like Florence during the Renaissance, London in the 1800s or New York in the early 20th century, Shanghai has emerged as a global business hub. The tens of billions of dollars the Chinese government has poured into this city of 18 million residents have created one of the world's most business-friendly environments. The once rundown financial district, for example, is now an energetic strip of financial institutions, hip nightclubs, chic boutiques and trendy restaurants. Indeed, Shanghai has become

_____.

(a) a hot destination for budget travelers
(b) the center for the latest fashion trends
(c) the new capital of business journalism
(d) a business-savvy and cosmopolitan city

14. In fiction, a doppelganger is a double of a character, most often of the protagonist. This double or "evil twin" is sometimes employed by novelists as the representative of the dark side of a protagonist's personality or a sin they have committed, which they cannot escape from and inevitably have to confront. For instance, in Edgar Allan Poe's short story "William Wilson," the protagonist of questionable moral character is dogged by his doppelganger most tenaciously when his morals fail. When a doppelganger is around, then, it is often a moment when a protagonist _____.

(a) finds a new kind of inner strength
(b) admits to the limitations of human reason
(c) has to face an impure side of himself or herself
(d) sees the effects of having been double-crossed

15. At Sun Microsystems, we help businesses build, manage and profit from enterprise network computing. So it's no surprise that we offer a broad portfolio of support and network services. _____, through our Professional Services Organization, we help clients around the world manage their UNIX networks for maximum efficiency. With Sun, you can rest assured, knowing you've signed with a company dedicated to its clients' long-term success.

(a) Instead
(b) However
(c) Despite that
(d) For example

16. Last month's meeting of the International Monetary Fund in Singapore was held amid worry about the strain put on the Fund by two economic giants, China and the US. The strain is the result of the US borrowing approximately $3 billion a day coupled with China creating trade deficits and imbalances because of its artificially low currency. Neither country is willing to accept responsibility for the problem. _____, the US is criticizing China's undervalued currency for creating global economic concerns while China is blaming the US for habitually operating in the red.

(a) Hence
(b) Rather
(c) Likewise
(d) Meanwhile

Read the passage and the question. Then choose the option that best answers the question.

17. For years health experts have told the public to eat more fruits and vegetables because of their ability to prevent disease. The latest research in Europe once again supports this recommendation. It shows that people from Mediterranean nations, where a large percentage of daily caloric intake comes from vegetables, have lower rates of cancer and heart disease than do people in Western Europe, where fewer vegetables are eaten.

Q : What is the best title for the passage?

(a) Health Experts Urge a Change of Diet
(b) Fruits and Vegetables Help Reduce Disease
(c) Cancer Not Linked to Fruits and Vegetables
(d) Mediterranean Diets Are the World's Healthiest

18. The states of New Hampshire and Vermont are a paradise for nature enthusiasts. As a matter of fact, they were voted the nation's top two vacation destinations, abundant in colorful mountain retreats, scenic lakes and picturesque local villages. Both states are ideal for water skiing, fishing, golf, tennis and hiking. Sailing the lakes and canoeing the rivers are also fun pastimes. So why not visit one of these entrancing states for your next vacation? For more information, check out our website at tours.org.

Q : What is mainly being advertised about New Hampshire and Vermont in the advertisement?

(a) Their popular summer sports
(b) Their growing tourism industry
(c) Their attractions as vacation spots
(d) Their popularity for picturesque sightseeing

19. What is "good taste?" For most people, it is an adamantly subjective and highly changeable notion, yet somehow self-evident. This course explores "taste" as an abstract aesthetic sensibility and examines how it functions in the world of art and literature. We will investigate notions of aesthetics in readings ranging from the 18th-century Age of Reason through to modern critical thought. Writers to be observed include Jane Austen, David Hume, John Ruskin, Oscar Wilde and Harold Bloom.

Q : What is the passage mainly about?

(a) A course on aesthetics and literature
(b) A critical examination of famous authors
(c) A study of fiction during the 18th century
(d) A course on artworks throughout the ages

20. The Greenlake Outpatient & Acute Care Clinic will be celebrating its third birthday by holding a Children's Safety Fair on Saturday, March 15. There will be lots of fun activities and helpful demonstrations for the entire family from 10 a.m. to 1 p.m. Participants will be able to climb aboard a Greenlake Fire Department fire engine, see two police rescue simulations and watch an acute-care nurse demonstrate first aid for kids. Our clinic is located at 1475 Belvedere Road in Greenlake. Hope to see you there!

Q : What is the announcement mainly about?

(a) Fun activities for families
(b) A Safety fair at the clinic
(c) A day for firefighters' families
(d) Demonstrations at the fire department

21. As other countries have reached productivity levels similar to or greater than those of the United States over the past couple of decades, concern about the ability of US companies and their employees to keep up has increased. Some have found fault with the US education system for failing to equip students with the knowledge and experience they need to succeed in today's labor market. However, elements other than education also impact productivity, such as the low rate of investment in industrial plants and equipment, which in turn slows labor productivity.

Q : What is the passage mainly about?

(a) Reasons for the US losing competitiveness in productivity
(b) Countries that have surpassed US productivity levels
(c) Areas where more investments need to be made
(d) Links between US education and the economy

22. During the 1930s and 40s, the Nazis attempted to substantiate "Aryan" superiority through spurious interpretations of archaeology and biased archaeological theories. Nazi scholars conceived of a prehistory that located Germany as the origin of civilization, even to the point of suggesting that the ancient Greeks were Germanic. By using such pseudo-archaeology, the Nazi propaganda machine sought to prove that Germans were a superior race, which in turn was used to justify German domination of the world as something both desirable and inevitable.

Q : What is the best title for the passage?
(a) Nazi Distortions of History to Justify Tyranny
(b) Nazi-era Contributions to Historical Research
(c) German Superiority Disproved by Archaeology
(d) Using Archaeology to Refute Historical Inevitability

23. Noah Webster was born in 1758 in Connecticut to a family descended from Puritan governors. At the age of 16, he was admitted to Yale, and after his graduation he worked as a teacher. While teaching, he noticed numerous problems in the American school system, and he concluded that one solution was for Americans to learn from American textbooks. Hence, he compiled a grammar book, a reader and a spelling primer. As history now testifies, these represented the beginning of the standardization of American English.

Q : Which of the following is correct about Noah Webster?
(a) He taught while studying at Yale.
(b) His ancestry included Puritan governors.
(c) He returned to university after he quit his job.
(d) He wrote a book on the American school system.

24. The WWBF World Championship, sponsored by the World Wide Basketball Federation, is an international basketball tournament for men's national teams held every other year. A parallel event for women, the WWBF World Championship for Women, is also held biannually, concurrently with the men's tournament but in a different country. All participant teams contend for the Dolmen Trophy, the first of which was awarded in the 1967 men's games. The tournaments' structure is similar but not identical to that of the FIFA World Cup.

Q : Which of the following is correct about the men's WWBF World Championship according to the passage?

(a) It is no longer held once every two years.
(b) Its teams are mixed with players from different countries.
(c) It takes place at the same location as the women's tournament.
(d) Its tournament structure is similar to that of the FIFA World Cup.

25. The 1990s saw Paula Cole emerge from a supporting artist on Peter Gabriel's 1992-93 world tour to a pop sensation in her own right. Cole's first major breakthrough came with the success of her self-produced 1997 album *This Fire*, which included hit singles *"Where Have All the Cowboys Gone?"* and *"I Don't Want to Wait."* Cole went on to win the Grammy for Best New Artist in 1998. This was followed by her surprising eight-year hiatus from recording to raise her daughter. But Cole now finds herself in the spotlight again, thanks to her latest album *Courage* and an upcoming national tour.

Q : Which of the following is correct about Paula Cole according to the passage?

(a) The album *This Fire* was successful.
(b) She toured with Peter Gabriel in 1998.
(c) She took a long break from recording in 1996.
(d) A Grammy was awarded to her for her album *Courage*.

26. Canterbury Kennels specializes in breeding Chinese Shar Pei. Since 1979, we have been successfully breeding, raising and finding homes for these wonderful dogs. We have also run a carefully planned breeding program to produce healthy dogs with significantly minimized eye and breathing problems and with great dispositions. Whether you are looking for a good-natured family dog or a show dog to enter into competitions, we have the perfect puppy for you.

Q : Which of the following is correct about Canterbury Kennels according to the advertisement?

(a) They specialize in various Asian breeds.
(b) They are a newly established company.
(c) Their breeding program minimizes physical problems.
(d) Their kennel produces only prize-winning show dogs.

27. The region of Angkor was once at the center of the Khmer civilization, which flourished from the 9th century to the 15th century. It was from there that ruling Khmer god-kings once controlled a vast territory extending south to the Mekong Delta in Vietnam, north into Laos and west over large tracts of what is now Thailand. Angkor had a population exceeding 1 million and was home to over 1,000 temples, including the famous Angkor Wat, the world's largest single religious monument. However, in 1431, the Angkor region was invaded and conquered by the Thais, bringing the Khmer civilization to an abrupt end.

Q : Which of the following is correct according to the passage?
(a) Khmer territory once extended into present-day Thailand.
(b) The Khmer population exceeded 10 million at its peak.
(c) Khmer kings lived at the largest Angkor Wat temple.
(d) The Khmer people attacked the Thais in 1431.

28. In California, 100,000 reports of elder abuse have so far been filed, accounting for 20% of the 500,000 reports nationwide. It is an alarming situation for the state, but professionals argue that these numbers do not even accurately represent the extent of the problem. A 2005 study concluded that only one in 14 cases of physical abuse and neglect is likely to be reported to authorities. If this statistic holds true today, California is assuredly in the grip of a crisis that needs immediate attention.

Q : Which of the following is correct according to the passage?
(a) Today 20% of reported cases of elder abuse occur in California.
(b) One out of every 14 cases of elder abuse goes unreported.
(c) Elder abuse is in sharp decline according to a 2005 study.
(d) Physical abuse is reported less in California.

29. Van Gogh loved vivid colors and exaggerated texture because they helped him show what he felt when he looked at a landscape. Take, for example, his painting called *The Starry Night*, painted at Saint-Remy in the south of France in 1889. The colors used—purples, blues, whites, yellows and black—are brighter than those of a usual night sky, done with strong lines and applied with varying thicknesses. Sometimes the paint is so thick that it resembles layers of clay. To gain this kind of effect, Van Gogh would paint with a knife and even apply paint directly from a tube.

Q : Which of the following is correct about Van Gogh according to the passage?

(a) His *The Starry Night* was created with four colors.
(b) He used a knife to create texture in his paintings.
(c) He painted *The Starry Night* only with a brush.
(d) He favored purple, brown and yellow paints.

30.

Dear Householder,

Congratulations! You have been selected by our Awards Promotion Committee as the winner of a free two-day vacation at Holly Branch Resort in the beautiful Pocono Mountains. Upon confirmation of acceptance, you earn the right to stay in one of our extravagant condominiums where you can enjoy swimming, horseback riding and wilderness hiking. All we ask is for you to attend one informational meeting on time-share plans. There is no obligation to buy, and the meeting will last only 30 minutes. To claim your prize, please call (734) 323-6446 and proceed with your reservation.

All the best,
Jim Crock
Manager

Q : Which of the following is correct according to the notice?

(a) Holly Branch Resort is offering a rebate on all its vacations.
(b) The householder has won a no-strings-attached vacation.
(c) The householder must attend a meeting to get the prize.
(d) Jim Crock will soon contact the householder by phone.

31. Research shows that one in three people will be diagnosed with cancer at some point. Older people are statistically more likely to get it, but cancer can strike at any age. Some cancers, such as breast cancer, are becoming more common, while instances of lung cancer have declined due to a drop in the number of smokers. Excluding certain skin cancers and lung cancer, the rate of cancer appears to be increasing by about 1% a year. However, the good news is that nowadays treatments for common types of cancer are proving more successful.

Q : Which of the following is correct according to the passage?

(a) Cancer rates in older people are decreasing steadily.
(b) One in four people is likely to end up with cancer.
(c) Cases of skin cancer are rising by about 1% a year.
(d) Breast cancer rates have been increasing steadily.

32. In a study done on newborn infants, it was found that they are able to distinguish the human voice from other sounds. They also prefer to hear the human voice over other sounds. Female voices were what they liked most, and they preferred their mothers' voices to those of other women. However, they had no preference for their fathers' voices over those of other men. The infants tested responded equally well to live voices as they did to recorded ones, but they were much less responsive to non-speech sounds or instrumental music.

Q : Which of the following is correct according to the passage?
(a) Infants have trouble distinguishing different sounds.
(b) Infants prefer instrumental sounds over the human voice.
(c) Infants like female voices more than male voices in general.
(d) Infants like their fathers' voices more than those of other men.

33.

To the Editor,

The excellent article in your February edition entitled "A Land Free from Intrusion" reflected only too clearly the fragile nature of the delicately balanced Arctic ecosystem. I work with an NGO that is petitioning the United Nations to designate the entire Arctic region a zone free of any kind of oil exploration and military activity. With the aid of publications like yours, we are positive that we can make progress in this campaign and realize our goal. Thank you.

Sincerely,

Robert S. Moore

Q : What can be inferred about the writer?
(a) He supports environmental causes.
(b) He works for the United Nations.
(c) He was once an Arctic explorer.
(d) He works as an industrialist.

34. Nobody can perfect an organization overnight. If you happen to be an extremely charismatic and competent leader, your arrival may boost the morale of the group quickly and allow previously discouraged managers to confront problems they may have avoided under a different supervisor. However, such improvements are only immediate and temporary gains, much in the same way that an initial dose of drugs may have a short-term effect on a sick patient.

Q : What can be inferred from the passage?

(a) Charisma is critical for getting business ideas off the ground.
(b) Ineffective organizations typically lack charismatic leaders.
(c) Dispirited managers are often advocates of radical change.
(d) Leaders should take a long-term view on problem-solving.

35. The claim that America owes a debt for the enslavement and segregation of African-Americans has been debated for over 150 years. In recent times, a new movement has been attempting to receive monetary compensation by suing the US government for wrongs against their ancestors. However, this has attracted opposition even from African-American scholars, who say that while the government should acknowledge guilt, those in the movement would be unjustly enriched if compensated, since they never suffered the dire consequences of slavery.

Q : What can be inferred from the passage?

(a) Modern African-American scholars embrace the new movement.
(b) The US government can justly deny all the wrongdoings of slavery.
(c) Those suing for compensation are viewed by some as opportunistic.
(d) African-Americans will have a stronger say in government in the future.

36. The extinction rate for the world's 10,000 known bird species has been assessed at approximately one species every four years. However, according to Dr. Peter Lofton of Yale University, this rate falls short of taking into consideration elements such as the continual discovery of extinct bird species from fossil remains and the numerous "missing" species that scientists are hesitant to classify as extinct. Considering these factors, Dr. Lofton asserts that the extinction rate is currently approaching one bird species per year.

Q : What can be inferred from the passage?

(a) The extinction rate would be more accurate if fossil findings were ignored.
(b) The identification of all missing bird species is relatively easy.
(c) The extinction rate of bird species will most likely increase with time.
(d) The extinction rate of bird species has been underestimated.

37. Politicians are far more sophisticated now than they used to be in swaying public opinion and gaining votes. Now they target specific audiences, using complicated polling methods in order to address the right issues at the right time to the right people. They have speechwriters who can tailor speeches for any selected demographic. They have detailed knowledge of what kind of broadcasts particular voters listen to and when. It is a far cry from past political tactics, when speeches were given to everyone on broad issues affecting the nation as a whole.

Q : What can be inferred about today's politicians from the passage?

(a) They are focusing efforts primarily on attracting wealthy voters.
(b) They are more sensitive to the concerns of diverse voter groups.
(c) They are not as sincere in what they say as politicians of the past.
(d) They are less aware of broad national issues than their predecessors.

Part III **Questions 38–40**

Read the passage. Then identify the option that does NOT belong.

38. Most of us are aware of the dangers of skin cancer. (a) Recent studies suggest that up to one out of seven children will develop skin cancer as an adult. (b) This can be the result of a lifestyle with too much exposure to the sun or as little as just one incident of severe sunburn as a child. (c) Repeatedly apply sunscreen every two hours; more often if you get in the water. (d) So it is imperative to sun-proof your child every time he or she is out in the sun.

39. Fall foliage had little competition when I drove through the panoramic Blue Ridge Parkway. (a) There were no billboards or convenience stores to distract me from faraway mountains and neighboring valleys. (b) Nothing dampened the beauty of the greenery everywhere—the golden poplars, scarlet sourwoods and orange sassafras. (c) A few cluttered stretches notwithstanding, travelers can go for hours without passing anything more obtrusive than the occasionally emerging farmhouses. (d) Numerous hiking trails that are well worth following are detailed on free trail maps available at parkway headquarters.

40. It has become clear that Generation Xers are rejecting the distinction between Democrats and Republicans. (a) Even those who are actively engaged in national politics see partisan boundaries blurring into irrelevance. (b) Surveys suggest that no more than a third of the nation's population identifies with either political party. (c) This generation is focusing not on differences but on similarities between the two parties, seeing them both as corrupt and childish. (d) Not surprisingly, this group is least likely to favor the current two-party system and most likely to support independents.

This is the end of the Reading Comprehension section. Please remain seated until the proctor has instructed otherwise. You are NOT allowed to turn to any other section of the test.

Actual Test 2

문제

Listening Comprehension CD 2
Grammar
Vocabulary
Reading Comprehension

해설 및 정답

LISTENING
COMPREHENSION

Part I **Questions 1—15**

You will now hear fifteen conversation fragments, each made up of a single spoken statement followed by four spoken responses. Choose the most appropriate response to the statement.

Part II **Questions 16—30**

You will now hear fifteen conversation fragments, each made up of three spoken statements followed by four spoken responses. Choose the most appropriate response to complete the conversation.

Part III **Questions 31—45**

You will now hear fifteen complete conversations. For each item, you will hear a conversation and its corresponding question, both of which will be read twice. Then you will hear four options which will be read only once. Choose the option that best answers the question.

Part IV **Questions 46—60**

You will now hear fifteen spoken monologues. For each item, you will hear a monologue and its corresponding question, both of which will be read twice. Then you will hear four options which will be read only once. Choose the option that best answers the question.

GRAMMAR

DIRECTIONS

This part of the exam tests your grammar skills. You will have 25 minutes to complete the 50 questions. Be sure to follow the directions given by the proctor.

Part I Questions 1—20

Choose the best answer for the blank.

1. A : Is there something special you want for your birthday?

B : As long as it's _____, anything will be okay.

(a) expensive not so
(b) so expensive not
(c) too expensive not
(d) not too expensive

2. A : Did anyone call while I was away?

B : Yes, there _____ a call from your insurance company.

(a) is
(b) was
(c) will be
(d) is to be

3. A : You seem _____ talented at singing.

B : Thanks for the compliment.

(a) very
(b) well
(c) such
(d) that

4. A : May I speak to Dr. Wilson, please?

B : I'm sorry, _____ he isn't in.

(a) so
(b) yet
(c) but
(d) and

5. A : I have to pay my phone bill by tomorrow, but I've got no money.

B : I hope you don't expect me _____.

(a) of anything to do
(b) to do anything about it
(c) doing for that anything
(d) doing anything about it

6. A : I couldn't keep my eyes open throughout the lecture.

B : _____ I. It was really boring.

(a) Could either
(b) Either could
(c) Could neither
(d) Neither could

7. A : Isn't it time you _____ your homework?

B : Can't I do it after this TV show?

(a) started
(b) will start
(c) have started
(d) will be starting

8. A : Excuse me. Can I get my camera _____ here?

B : Yes, what seems to be the problem?

(a) repair
(b) to repair
(c) repaired
(d) repairing

9. A : Would you like us _____ your new computer?

    B : No, I'll take it with me now.

    (a) deliver
    (b) to deliver
    (c) delivering
    (d) to delivering

10. A : May I have tomorrow off?

    B : Sure. Tomorrow probably won't be _____.

    (a) busy day
    (b) a busy day
    (c) the busy day
    (d) any busy day

11. A : Are you a graduate student here?

    B : Yes, I'm working on my PhD _____ biology.

    (a) in
    (b) to
    (c) on
    (d) for

12. A : I think I deserve a higher salary.

    B : Why don't you _____?

    (a) ask a raise to your boss
    (b) your boss ask for a raise
    (c) ask your boss for a raise
    (d) for a raise ask your boss

13. A : Do you have to leave so soon?

    B : Yes, I _____ be going. I have another appointment.

    (a) can
    (b) may
    (c) must
    (d) would

14. A : Billy left a big mess in the kitchen this morning.

    B : I've _____, and he said it wouldn't happen again.

    (a) been speaking it to him
    (b) to him spoken about it
    (c) about it spoken to him
    (d) spoken to him about it

15. A : Why did you miss art class yesterday?

    B : I didn't _____, but my friends made me do it.

    (a) plan
    (b) plan to
    (c) plan do
    (d) plan to it

16. A : Do you want _____?

    B : Sure, I'd like that very much.

    (a) me going to a football game
    (b) to go a football game with me
    (c) with me go to a football game
    (d) to go to a football game with me

17. A : How did the conference go?

    B : Great. One of the good things _____ that no speaker went over their time.

    (a) is
    (b) are
    (c) was
    (d) were

18. A : Are you doing anything special tonight?

B : I'm _____ a play.

(a) thinking to go to
(b) going thinking of
(c) about to go I think
(d) thinking of going to

19. A : Thank you for coming to my concert on such short notice.

B : If I had known about it sooner, I _____ have brought my wife.

(a) shall
(b) must
(c) could
(d) should

20. A : Who would you recommend as our new chairperson?

B : John is the person _____ I believe is capable of getting the job done.

(a) who
(b) what
(c) which
(d) where

| **Part II** | **Questions 21—40** |

Choose the best answer for the blank.

---

21. Students found guilty of _____ inappropriate behavior as fighting or throwing things will be punished.

(a) so
(b) too
(c) such
(d) much

22. Our current CEO _____ by the company's Board of Directors last year.

(a) appoints
(b) appointed
(c) is appointed
(d) was appointed

23. _____ west in 1892, Gerald Clemens made sure all his prize possessions rode with him in the wagon.

(a) While having traveled
(b) To have traveled
(c) While traveling
(d) Traveled

24. _____ a balanced diet is one way to prevent tooth decay and gum disease.

(a) Eat
(b) Eating
(c) To be eating
(d) Having eaten

25. Many of the new policewomen _____ to take part in important assignments.

(a) not being allowed resented
(b) resented not being allowed
(c) being not allowed resented
(d) resented not to being allowed

26. _____ her work aside, the grandmother began to tell the story of her past to her grandchildren.

(a) Put
(b) To put
(c) Putting
(d) Being put

27. Blood _____ to the heart from the body is low in oxygen and high in carbon dioxide.

(a) returns
(b) to return
(c) returning
(d) to be returning

28. Wars leave painful memories _____ many veterans would rather forget.

(a) that
(b) what
(c) of whom
(d) by which

29. The increasing use of _____ has led to a reduction in the types of jobs people can perform.

(a) machinery
(b) machineries
(c) a machinery
(d) the machineries

30. As you progress through this course, you _____ all the skills needed to become a systems administrator.

(a) developed
(b) will develop
(c) have developed
(d) are about to develop

31. Jack can barely replace a fuse, _____ repair a broken TV set.

(a) yet
(b) while
(c) even so
(d) much less

32. The eye focuses light on the retina through an opening _____ size adjusts in order to change the amount of entering light.

(a) that
(b) what
(c) which
(d) whose

33. Steve hand-washed and rinsed his T-shirt and jeans thoroughly before hanging _____.

(a) up to dry them
(b) them up to dry
(c) to dry them up
(d) up them to dry

34. The manager's job was allocating work to _____ employee fairly.

(a) all
(b) both
(c) each
(d) some

35. It is incorrect to say that we are the only species _____.

    (a) that culture we depend to survive on
    (b) that depends on culture for survival
    (c) depend on culture for that survival
    (d) that survival depends on culture

36. Parents _____ not purchase the new uniforms this year if they do not wish to do so.

    (a) need
    (b) must
    (c) could
    (d) would

37. Her experience in prison was so traumatic for the young woman that she had a hard time _____.

    (a) describing it to anyone
    (b) for anyone describing it
    (c) to describe it for anyone
    (d) to be describing it to anyone

38. By January 15, we _____ over 100 applications for the technician position.

    (a) will process
    (b) have processed
    (c) have been processing
    (d) will have processed

39. No significant changes in the levels of hormone _____ in the patients.

    (a) observe
    (b) observes
    (c) was observed
    (d) were observed

40. _____ without passing the exam in this country.

    (a) Can a single teacher not be tenured
    (b) Not a single teacher can be tenured
    (c) A single teacher can be not tenured
    (d) No single teacher cannot be tenured

Part III **Questions 41—45**

Identify the option that contains an awkward expression or an error in grammar.

41. (a) A : So, tell me how your date went last night.
(b) B : It was horrible. I don't want to talk about it.
(c) A : But you want to meet her for a long time.
(d) B : Well, she was very different from what I had expected.

42. (a) A : We must take care of this financial problem right away.
(b) B : Yes, I have a team working on a solution as we speak.
(c) A : The board members wants it sorted out by tomorrow morning.
(d) B : Don't worry. We'll fix the problem by this afternoon.

43. (a) A : My head is throbbing with pain.
(b) B : Another headache? Did you take some aspirin?
(c) A : I did half an hour ago, but it's not working.
(d) B : Relaxing quietly helps usually my headaches.

44. (a) A : Hello. Is there anything in the reference section you need help with?
(b) B : It'd be grateful if you could help me find some old news articles about cloning.
(c) A : Are you interested in back issues of magazines or newspapers?
(d) B : I think I need to search through both.

45. (a) A : Hey, can't you drive more carefully? Now I have lipstick all over my face.
(b) B : Well, it's not my fault that your face got messy with lipstick.
(c) A : Not your fault? It's because you made sudden stop at the corner.
(d) B : Don't blame my driving. You should've put on your makeup at home.

Part IV Questions 46—50

Identify the option that contains an awkward expression or an error in grammar.

46. (a) Of all its accomplishments, the West is perhaps most proud of its scientific progress. (b) But this did not happen in isolation; its early progress was influenced by the Arab world. (c) Important discoveries made by Arab scholars published in texts that eventually made their way to Europe. (d) Medieval monks and scribes then made these discoveries accessible to Western scientists by translating the texts into Latin.

47. (a) On behalf of the school board, I would like to thank you for playing the piano at our reception. (b) Had it not been for your performance, I don't think our reception were half as successful. (c) You kept everybody entertained, and people simply did not want to leave. (d) I will certainly call you again for our next reception if you are available.

48. (a) Unlike other cancers, pancreatic tumors typically produce symptoms only after spreading throughout the body. (b) By then, drugs do not provide many relief, and patients die after a few pain-filled months. (c) Patients die so quickly that sometimes doctors do not even have time to examine their tumors properly. (d) Because it is difficult to diagnose early, pancreatic cancer is the fourth leading cause of cancer death.

49. (a) Baby hamsters are born blind, deaf and totally dependent on their mothers. (b) But they mature very quickly, reach full maturity in a little over a month. (c) Within seven days, they are covered in fur and begin to look more like their parents. (d) By day seventeen, they are old enough to leave the burrow and search for their own food.

50. (a) Over the last decade, scientists have saved at least 16 species from disappearing to captive breeding programs. (b) A number of these have been so successful that other programs are being launched around the globe. (c) Twenty more species are currently being seriously considered for breeding programs. (d) But conservationists and zoologists worldwide are working together to increase this number to 30.

This is the end of the Grammar section. Do NOT move on to the next section until instructed to do so. You are NOT allowed to turn to any other section of the test.

VOCABULARY

Part I Questions 1—25

Choose the best answer for the blank.

---

1. A : Do you still have those books on finance that I _____ you?

B : They're at home. I'll return them to you tomorrow.

(a) let
(b) lent
(c) sold
(d) owed

2. A : Excuse me, what's the best way to get downtown from here?

B : It's best to _____ bus number 602.

(a) pay
(b) take
(c) lead
(d) view

3. A : Do you know when Caroline will be back?

B : Sorry, I have no _____.

(a) idea
(b) goal
(c) mind
(d) sense

4. A : Did you get some sleep?

B : Yes. I had plenty of _____.

(a) rest
(b) snore
(c) amount
(d) moment

5. A : _____ me a call as soon as you arrive in Paris.

B : Sure. I'll call you when I get there.

(a) Give
(b) Drop
(c) Send
(d) Fire

6. A : Good morning, Service Department. Can I help you?

B : Yes, my Internet _____ is down. I can't get online.

(a) station
(b) detection
(c) admission
(d) connection

7. A : Shall we meet at noon?

B : That's _____ with me.

(a) fine
(b) neat
(c) sure
(d) right

8. A : Do you have enough money to go to Europe this summer?

B : Yes, I've been _____ for this trip for the past three years.

(a) saving up
(b) holding off
(c) starting over
(d) waiting around

9. A : We can't finish this report by five.

   B : No, there's no way it can be _____ by then.

   (a) ended
   (b) rounded
   (c) completed
   (d) terminated

10. A : How was your vacation in Rome?

    B : Great, except for being awakened every Sunday by the _____ of church bells.

    (a) hitting
    (b) ringing
    (c) banging
    (d) roaring

11. A : Could you take me for driving practice before my driving test?

    B : I'd rather not. You and I will probably _____ fighting.

    (a) end up
    (b) go after
    (c) run into
    (d) count on

12. A : It's a problem to have a busy road so close to the school.

    B : Well, the town council plans to _____ safety measures soon.

    (a) remit
    (b) transmit
    (c) implement
    (d) supplement

13. A : This soup doesn't have much taste.

    B : I know. It really is quite _____.

    (a) soft
    (b) salty
    (c) bland
    (d) smooth

14. A : Oh, no. I got three Cs this semester.

    B : Just _____ about it and move on.

    (a) forget
    (b) doubt
    (c) think
    (d) tell

15. A : They say the hotel shuttle bus won't arrive for at least 15 minutes.

    B : In that case, let's _____ a taxi. I'm too tired to wait.

    (a) elect
    (b) trace
    (c) catch
    (d) chase

16. A : Dr. Lewis said she hasn't seen a Northern Red Wolf for 20 years.

    B : I'm afraid they may now be _____.

    (a) extinct
    (b) hidden
    (c) sporadic
    (d) dormant

17. A : Can I have vegetarian meals on the flight?

    B : Certainly. There's no extra _____.

    (a) fare
    (b) price
    (c) ticket
    (d) charge

18. A : Would you like coffee or tea, sir?

    B : I'll have tea, please. No, on second _____, make it coffee.

    (a) choice
    (b) thought
    (c) decision
    (d) selection

19. A : Did you reserve a table at the restaurant?

    B : I couldn't. They were all _____.

    (a) sat down
    (b) filled out
    (c) phoned in
    (d) booked up

20. A : I usually don't have time to eat in the morning.

    B : But it's really bad for your health to _____ breakfast.

    (a) reject
    (b) jump
    (c) pass
    (d) skip

21. A : Why do you leave the car _____ for so long?

    B : Because it takes a long time to warm up.

    (a) idling
    (b) turning
    (c) steering
    (d) wheeling

22. A : What did your grandfather do during World War II?

    B : He _____ in the British Royal Navy.

    (a) served
    (b) existed
    (c) appeared
    (d) maintained

23. A : I checked all of my computer settings, but it still isn't working properly.

    B : Maybe you have _____ something.

    (a) overseen
    (b) overcome
    (c) overlooked
    (d) overpowered

24. A : I'm delighted to present you with this teaching award.

    B : It was a(n) _____ to have been a part of the competition. Thank you.

    (a) glory
    (b) virtue
    (c) award
    (d) privilege

25. A : I decided to shave off my _____. What do you think?

    B : You look great. Now I can finally see your cute chin.

    (a) goatee
    (b) tresses
    (c) whiskers
    (d) mustache

Part II　**Questions 26—50**

Choose the best answer for the blank.

26. After a ten-minute _____, the meeting continued for another two hours.

    (a) stop
    (b) time
    (c) break
    (d) gap

27. Feeding the farm animals was not as easy as it _____ at first.

    (a) meant
    (b) looked
    (c) expected
    (d) previewed

28. The French Foreign Minister hoped to _____ the crisis in trade negotiations with the US.

    (a) vanish
    (b) resolve
    (c) formalize
    (d) undermine

29. To prolong their life, _____ unused batteries in a cool, dry place away from heat or flame.

    (a) fix
    (b) add
    (c) store
    (d) prepare

30. Fashion magazines are now encouraging women over 40 to _____ a more feminine and youthful dress style.

    (a) meet
    (b) force
    (c) adopt
    (d) inhabit

31. Biologists often _____ different types of life forms based on their DNA.

    (a) inspire
    (b) classify
    (c) recollect
    (d) entertain

32. The old man was filled with _____ after he learned that he had won the lottery.

    (a) joy
    (b) deceit
    (c) victory
    (d) attitude

33. There are several ATMs inside the park that _____ major credit cards.

    (a) proceed
    (b) deposit
    (c) accept
    (d) utilize

34. Public buildings are often _____ with decorations that reflect their usage.

   (a) barred
   (b) tainted
   (c) granted
   (d) adorned

35. Even though crime may never be completely _____ from our community, it can be reduced.

   (a) deducted
   (b) dismissed
   (c) eliminated
   (d) subtracted

36. The recent revival of interest in Jane Austen owes a great deal to the successful film _____ of her novels.

   (a) adaptations
   (b) conversions
   (c) modifications
   (d) transformations

37. This new thermos is _____ to keep liquids cold for up to three hours.

   (a) engaged
   (b) designed
   (c) suggested
   (d) composed

38. The high cost of AIDS medication is a significant _____ on Britain's healthcare system.

   (a) burden
   (b) residue
   (c) inflation
   (d) depression

39. Cancellations of hotel reservations without 24 hours' notice are _____ to a penalty.

   (a) prior
   (b) subject
   (c) common
   (d) standard

40. The process of evaporation creates a cooling effect when it dries _____ on your skin.

   (a) irritation
   (b) alteration
   (c) perspiration
   (d) condensation

41. The meaning of the poem was so vague that few students _____ it at first.

   (a) grasped
   (b) clutched
   (c) swallowed
   (d) established

42. Hollywood movies _____ unrealistic images of Western culture that are accepted as accurate throughout the world.

   (a) assume
   (b) project
   (c) scatter
   (d) install

43. Internships at Sandern University are _____ to full-time students.

   (a) arranged
   (b) enclosed
   (c) attached
   (d) limited

44. Visitors to Vacaville should be warned that the area is sometimes affected by a _____ odor coming from oil refineries.

    (a) cruel
    (b) base
    (c) foul
    (d) thin

45. Even though the filmmakers proclaimed a commitment to _____, their film is seriously flawed with historical inaccuracies.

    (a) authority
    (b) objectivity
    (c) spontaneity
    (d) authenticity

46. The caste system, the traditional method of stratifying Hindu society, shapes nearly every _____ of life in India.

    (a) facet
    (b) class
    (c) status
    (d) vector

47. Tests show that ginger may enhance cancer treatment by _____ resistance to chemotherapy.

    (a) vacillating
    (b) brandishing
    (c) circumventing
    (d) substantiating

48. With a population made up of people from many different countries, New York City is one of the most _____ cities in the world.

    (a) infusive
    (b) enigmatic
    (c) provincial
    (d) cosmopolitan

49. Unfortunately, the results of the research cannot be accepted without considerable _____.

    (a) sobriety
    (b) symmetry
    (c) altercation
    (d) qualification

50. Many people regard capital punishment as a(n) _____ of the most fundamental human right.

    (a) salutation
    (b) retribution
    (c) infringement
    (d) embezzlement

This is the end of the Vocabulary section. Do NOT move on to the Reading Comprehension section until instructed to do so. You are NOT allowed to turn to any other section of the test.

READING
COMPREHENSION

Part I **Questions 1—16**

Read the passage. Then choose the option that best completes the passage.

1. Although you probably know that certain bacteria can cause harm, you might not be fully aware of the huge benefits bacteria can also provide. For instance, bacteria are crucial for a healthy balance in nutrition, since they produce essential elements such as nitrogen and sulfur for plants, which in turn are consumed by animals and humans. Bacteria are also instrumental in the manufacture of life-saving medicines. Thus, the presence of bacteria is

_____.

(a) likely to cause us harm
(b) linked to poor nutrition
(c) helpful for growing plants
(d) necessary in our daily lives

2.

Dear Editor,

My husband and I moved to this community last year. One day, while running some errands in Hooverville, we decided to have lunch at what we now consider one of our community's best tourist attractions, Bob Green's Bar & Grill. We have never tasted such good food—especially, their seafood dishes—and nothing beats the kind of service they offer. On top of this, Bob and the staff are very good-humored as well. We _____ this restaurant and hope you can find a spot in your magazine to publish this letter.

Sincerely,
Elaine E. Wilson
Parksville

(a) would like to visit
(b) highly recommend
(c) can hardly tolerate
(d) really advise against

3. _____ remains a major problem for the company. This is mainly because of an unexpected rise in resignations and retirements. The problem has been made worse because none of the company's existing employees have the experience or qualifications necessary to fill vacant positions. To prevent this from happening in the future, the company will provide training programs so that existing employees can advance where and when necessary. In the meantime, new staff will need to be sourced outside of the company.

(a) The training of new staff
(b) The government's new policy
(c) A reduction in company profits
(d) A lack of staff in key departments

4. Writing in Egypt goes back to about 3000 BC. Some historians speculate that the Egyptians learned how to write from the Sumerians, who had a flourishing civilization at the time. However, the Egyptian form of writing, hieroglyphs, does not look the same or work the same way as the Sumerian form of writing, cuneiform. So, it is possible that

_____.

(a) Egyptians must have copied them
(b) Egyptians invented their own writing
(c) Sumerians built schools and libraries
(d) Egyptians and Sumerians were at war

5. The Austin Air HE-3 was the best of the air purifiers we tested in terms of value for money. This model uses a true HEPA (High-Energy Particulate Air) filter, with a capacity to trap 99.97% of contaminants in a 700-square-foot room. While the Austin Air HE-3 is not as quiet as other models reviewed, it is half the cost. The warranty is also especially impressive, and with proper maintenance, you won't need to change the HEPA filter for five years. Our conclusion is that the Austin Air HE-3 is

_____.

(a) an excellent air purifier for the elderly
(b) the cheapest air purifier on the market
(c) the best model available in all categories
(d) an efficient and cost-effective air purifier

6. How can traditional art and culture _____? That's the idea behind the latest exhibit at Stokes Gallery, where traditional folk art is seen combined with 21st-century technology. One artist uses digital tapestries to simulate a loom; another combines a photo process with computer technology to make images inspired by her Mexican roots; while another uses recycled computer parts to create sculptures of cultural icons. You will find it surprising how a computer can be used to express traditional cultural ideas.

(a) be effectively promoted online
(b) change the way we view our future
(c) withstand the influence of globalized culture
(d) incorporate computers or modern technology

7. Korea's King Sejong was _____. He established the Jibhyeonjeon or "Hall of Worthies," early in his reign, where the Chosun Dynasty's best scholars flocked to pursue and conduct research. Simultaneously, he also demonstrated a keen interest in day-to-day government affairs, tenaciously seeking ways to improve the lives of the public by reforming the tax system and refining a wide range of government affairs. Consequently, during his rule, major progress was made in virtually every field: agriculture, astronomy, defense, diplomacy, geography, medicine, printing and science.

(a) a clever man who became famous for scholarship
(b) a great king who was admired in Asian countries
(c) the ruler who invented and widely spread Hangul
(d) an innovator who cared about social improvements

8. Obstetricians are looking to the government to intervene in their industry. Skyrocketing malpractice insurance costs have forced thousands of obstetricians to close their businesses, leaving many expectant women with nowhere to turn for medical care. However, legislation now being debated at state and national levels could deliver a much-needed solution. The new legislation is expected to_____.

(a) finance new hospitals throughout the district
(b) speed the process of getting licensed in obstetrics
(c) improve the quality of medical care for expectant women
(d) totally reform malpractice insurance practices in obstetrics

9. Mistaken notions—such as the idea that blood-letting cures the sick or that some races are inferior to others—have often been taken for fact and then rejected with fresh insights. Toward the end of the 20th century, science and government assured us that neither pesticides nor buried toxic wastes would harm human beings. Such false notions remind us that what we call facts _____.

(a) had an unexpected effect on scientific progress
(b) cannot be changed simply by what people say
(c) are the creations of human minds and fallible
(d) are valid if we have scientific proof

10. The Vision Award is an annual award recognizing _____. The award includes a crystal plaque, a special banquet honoring the recipient and a $10,000 cash donation toward furthering the winner's charity work. We are currently looking for nominees who are actively involved in any kind of service for the disadvantaged. They should work with minimal means and have a good record of helping those in need. Nominations will be accepted until January 31.

(a) significant volunteer work for the underprivileged
(b) substantial contributions toward curing blindness
(c) outstanding achievement in visual arts and design
(d) excellence in community planning and development

11. Archaeologists reported yesterday that they have finished uncovering a masterpiece of Mayan art that _____. This artifact, a 30-by-3-foot mural in vivid colors depicting the ancient culture's mythology of creation and kingship, is the centerpiece of a larger mural that, until recently, archaeologists dated to the culture's classical period. However, new tests have revealed that the centerpiece and larger mural are older than originally estimated, dating to about 100 BC. This indicates that the Mayan classical period, which was thought to have begun after AD 250, probably began much earlier.

(a) shows how authentic their use of color and shape was
(b) reveals an unusual use of symbols and writing methods
(c) suggests a surprisingly early flowering of the civilization
(d) proves that the Mayans knew their civilization was in decline

12. Ezra Pound played a large part in renewing English poetry in the Modernist era of the early 20th century. Yet he _____. He has been condemned as an elitist, an obscurantist and a charlatan—a man deficient in self-knowledge, with no real understanding of the modern world despite his Modernist posturing. And his fascist sympathies will forever taint his lofty conception of the artist and civilization.

(a) remains a flawed and controversial figure
(b) captured the spirit of his age like no other
(c) did not single-handedly revolutionize poetics
(d) defied the expectations of his literary colleagues

13. Early biologists who studied reflexes regarded these basic reactions to be inherited and common to all members of any given species. They also viewed instinct and learning as two separate aspects of automatic behavior. However, in some ingenious experiments, Josh Kalahan of the Milton University has demonstrated that certain automatic behaviors actually demand subtle forms of experience. In other words,

_____.

(a) some instinctive behaviors are partially learned
(b) instinctive behavior can lead to violent situations
(c) learned behaviors are not always taught by parents
(d) human behavior can be explained by genetics alone

14. In 1865 the sculptor Rodin submitted his bronze head called *Man with a Broken Nose* to the Salon, an art gallery in Paris. The piece demonstrated all the rugged strength and realism that is characteristic of Rodin's style, but the Salon's jury rejected it. Rodin was not deterred, and years later in 1877, he submitted his life-size sculpture of a man, called the *Age of Bronze*, to the Salon. It was accepted, yet it caused an immediate controversy, for it was so lifelike that people thought it to have been cast from the living model. People found _____.

(a) Rodin's realistic sculptures to be better than those of other artists
(b) Rodin too preoccupied with the evil side of human nature
(c) Rodin's kind of realism too confronting and radical
(d) Rodin to be a persistent and determined man

15. The English Language Institute at Whitford College caters to international applicants seeking admittance to graduate programs at American postsecondary schools. Through an intensive 25-hour-a-week curriculum, students enrolled are given the opportunity to prepare for the challenges in language and communication inside American classrooms. The objective of the Institute, _____, is to equip its ESL students with the necessary language skills to achieve academic success in any degree program at an American university.

(a) however
(b) therefore
(c) additionally
(d) nevertheless

16. Acid rain is primarily the result of the release of sulfur oxides into the atmosphere. The main sources of such emissions are most likely electrical plants, industrial boilers and large smelters. Gases that are vented into the air by tall industrial chimneys get caught up in prevailing winds where they are converted into dilute solutions of sulfuric and nitric acids. _____, the acid rain problem partially comes from earlier attempts to clear air pollution by raising the heights of smokestacks.

(a) However
(b) Ironically
(c) Particularly
(d) Consequently

Part II Questions 17—37

Read the passage and the question. Then choose the option that best answers the question.

17. In the past, the value of money was determined by the value of the material from which it was made, such as silver or gold. However, carrying around a lot of precious metal was cumbersome and often dangerous. As an alternative, banknotes were introduced. These were originally a kind of promissory note for an amount of precious metal stored in a vault somewhere. But eventually, as banknotes became more widely used, they were accepted as equivalent to precious metal and given the status of paper money.

Q : What is the passage about?

(a) What banknotes were once made of
(b) Why banks stored precious metals
(c) When cash became widely used
(d) How paper money originated

18. Preparing balanced, healthy snacks for children can be time-consuming, but a helpful tip is to get them used to eating cheese. Bread or crackers with cheese and an apple is a healthy snack which only takes 30 seconds to prepare. Moreover, your kids do not have to sit down to eat it; they can take it with them outside.

Q : What is the main idea of the passage?

(a) Children should eat at regular intervals.
(b) Making snacks can be time-consuming.
(c) Eating between meals makes children fat.
(d) Cheese is one of the best snacks for children.

19. Now, for the first time ever at the Apollo Museum, you can see the most accurately built representations of the famous machines envisaged by Leonardo da Vinci. The Apollo Museum is exhibiting over one hundred models of some of Leonardo da Vinci's unrealized machines and inventions created by artists and scientists from around the world. All models have been painstakingly based on Leonardo's original sketches. This amazing exhibition is at the Apollo from January 20 to March 10.

Q : What type of exhibit is the museum announcement about?

(a) Da Vinci's machine models
(b) Da Vinci's original sketches
(c) Models based on Da Vinci's designs
(d) The evolution of Da Vinci's machines

20. It is hard to believe that 19 computers can solve the problems of Dipichi, a tiny community in Haiti, where people battle daily against poverty, illiteracy and hunger. Yet that is exactly what US computer giant Hewlett-Packard (HP) and the Haitian government hope to achieve with a new IT lab being launched this month. The IT lab will provide information, education and training for Dipichi locals testing the theory that technology can tackle poverty. If successful, HP will introduce the lab concept to other destitute communities around the world.

Q : What is the best title for the passage?
(a) Heavy Cost of Bridging Digital Divide in Haiti
(b) Computer Literacy Guarantees Quality of Life
(c) Delivering Low-Cost Technology to the World
(d) Using Computer Technology to Combat Poverty

21.

Dear Sir,

I purchased a metal detector from your company for the amount of $225 and with a 30-day money-back guarantee. However, this product did not perform satisfactorily, so I decided to return it under the conditions of the guarantee. When returning the item, I opted to have the price of the product credited to my account. That was three weeks ago. Still, no credit has been applied to my account. Please look into this issue so that I do not need to take further action.

Sincerely,
George Barnes

Q : What is the writer's main point in the letter?

(a) He has been planning to buy a metal detector for weeks.
(b) He wants to know when his purchase will be delivered.
(c) He has not been given a refund for a returned product.
(d) He is going to take action if his money is not returned.

22. The revolutionary sentiments of the 60s gave rise to a new kind of politician in the West, and nowhere is this better exemplified than in Canada's Prime Minister, Pierre Elliott Trudeau. A charismatic individual who came to power in 1968 with tremendous public support, he served as a stark contrast to the older, more conservative generation of politicians who had been ruling Canada. Trudeau refused to be encumbered by conventional party policies, but rather left everything open to question and welcomed change, especially in policies concerning foreign affairs and national defense.

Q : What is the writer's main point about Pierre Trudeau?

(a) He represented a fresh and innovative approach to politics.
(b) He was passionate in his devotion to traditional party ideals.
(c) He focused his political strategy on foreign affairs and defense.
(d) He refused to let revolutionary attitudes influence his leadership.

23. An old people's home in Sibbhult, southern Sweden found itself under siege from two drunken elks Friday night. The elks had become drunk on fermented apples they found near the old people's home and had threatened residents. Police arrived at the scene quickly, but their attempts to chase the elks away proved unsuccessful until a police dog was brought in to help. The dog scared the elks back into a nearby forest.

Q : What scared off the elks?

(a) A police dog
(b) A police officer
(c) A drunken man
(d) Some neighbors

24. From ancient times, the Hawaiian island of Molokai was worshiped and feared as a center of mysticism and witchcraft. Then, starting in 1866, Hawaiians with Hansen's disease (leprosy) were abandoned on Molokai's Kalaupapa Peninsula to face death. The isolated settlement persisted in horrific circumstances until the arrival of Father Damien, a Catholic priest from Belgium, in 1873. He treated the settlers with dignity and gave them a sense of hope.

Q : Which of the following is correct according to the passage?

(a) Hansen's disease originated in Belgium.
(b) Father Damien contracted leprosy in Hawaii.
(c) Molokai used to have a large leprosy hospital.
(d) Molokai lepers were helped by Father Damien.

25. The Detroit Zoo is to hold its fourth annual Earth Day Festival this weekend. The festival promotes the importance of worldwide conservation and environmental education through Earth-friendly activities. Children can participate in crafts, face painting and even wall climbing, all while learning about the importance of preserving our natural world. "Smokey the Bear" will also be on hand to give children and adults tips about the environment. All proceeds from the festival go to the zoo's conservation program.

Q : Which of the following is correct about the Earth Day Festival?
(a) Its aim is to teach children the importance of education.
(b) It gives children information about the environment.
(c) It sells crafts that have been made by children.
(d) Its purpose is to promote the Detroit Zoo.

26. Ardente presents Immortelle, our newest winter coat. It has a sophisticated single-button wrap styling, with pockets to complement its clean lines. But this coat isn't just for show. It's as comfortable as it looks and also practical. Our Italian mill created a special blend of wools to bring you a coat that's soft, warm and elegant, yet durable enough to be worn as part of your daily wardrobe. Look for the Immortelle, available at all Ardente boutiques across Europe.

Q : Which of the following is correct about the Immortelle?
(a) It is suitable for everyday wear.
(b) It is made of polyester material.
(c) It is made by an Italian designer.
(d) It is designed for formal occasions.

27. There are two basic types of strengthening exercises: isotonic and isometric. Isotonic exercises are a type of resistance training that involves motion, expanding and contracting muscles in order to make them bigger and firmer. Weight lifting is the most common form of isotonic exercise. In isometric exercises, by contrast, there is little or no motion involved. You push as hard as you can against an immovable object or else tense your muscles for ten seconds. These exercises are usually used in physical rehabilitation for people who do not have the full range of motion.

Q : Which of the following is correct according to the passage?

(a) Isotonic exercises are less active than isometric exercises.
(b) Isotonic exercises are not effective for people who are active.
(c) Isometric exercises are most suitable for physically fit people.
(d) Isometric exercises are good for people with physical limitations.

28. The US Treasury Department has integrated several new anti-counterfeiting measures to combat increased counterfeiting with home computers and printers. One method is the use of special color-shifting ink that alters its hue when viewed at an angle. Another method is to randomly embed very small pieces of reflective plastic into the linen paper already used. The Department also incorporates a thin, metallic line that runs from the top to the bottom of the bills. None of these methods can be reproduced on home computers.

Q : Which of the following is correct according to the passage?

(a) Special paper with plastic implants can deter counterfeiting.
(b) Anti-counterfeiting methods have not changed significantly.
(c) Special ink is being used by counterfeiters on home computers.
(d) Home computers are now able to counterfeit any kind of bank note.

29. UN predictions paint a stunning picture of urban life in Asia in 2010. If current population growth and urban migration trends continue, 30 cities in Asia will have populations greater than 5 million (compared with 11 European cities and only two US cities). The largest will be Shanghai and Bombay, each with 20 million people. Beijing, Dhaka, Jakarta, Manila, Tianjin, Calcutta and Delhi will have more than 15 million people each. These figures will be the result of a shift from rural to urban living that is even now dramatically changing the face of Asia.

Q : Which of the following is correct about UN predictions for Asia in 2010?

(a) Asia's population will grow partly because of immigration.
(b) More than 5 million people will live in each of 30 Asian cities.
(c) New cities will be created because of Asia's growing population.
(d) The current number of people moving to urban areas will double.

30.

> Dear Sara,
>
> I was sorry to hear you couldn't make it to our high school reunion. It's unbelievable to hear that you're living in Perth, of all places. As you may know, I remained near our hometown after graduating, so I have always been curious about what it would be like to live abroad. I'm not sure whether you know, but Jim Frobish also lives in Australia, though I think he's in Brisbane working as a machinist. On the other hand, Anne Singer moved to Singapore, where she is a manager at an international export company. I can email you their contact information or other people's, so let me know if you're interested.
>
> Best wishes,
> Allison

Q : Which of the following is correct according to the letter?

(a) Jim is employed as a machinist.
(b) Sara manages an export company.
(c) Anne is currently living in Brisbane.
(d) Allison did not go to the school reunion.

31. Robert Schumann was a Romantic composer whose most notable masterpieces were in the areas of choral music, Lieder (German art songs) and piano music. He usually composed at the keyboard, and he included the piano in almost every single piece of work. In many of his Lieder, voice and piano go side by side, with the vocal line adding yet another layer of tone to the piano score. However, Schumann made the piano partake fully in the expression of emotions in such tunes, and his most characteristic music often came after the vocal parts had finished.

Q : Which of the following is correct according to the passage?

(a) Schumann's singing ability was one of his many talents.
(b) Piano played a crucial role in Schumann's compositions.
(c) Vocal components overrode the piano in Schumann's music.
(d) Piano pieces by Schumann are complex and difficult to play.

32. While most people think the fax machine is a modern invention, it was actually invented before the telephone. Scottish mechanic Alexander Bain patented his "electric printing and signal telegraph" in 1843, more than 30 years before the first phone was invented in 1876. Bain proposed using a scanning needle that could create an electrical signal when it touched a raised metal surface. The needle would be attached to a pendulum synchronized with another pendulum and needle on a receiving machine. Bain never built his machine, but Giovanni Caselli used much the same principle for a fax service between Paris and Lyon in 1863.

Q : Which of the following is correct according to the passage?

(a) Bain's fax machine was forgotten until the last century.
(b) A fax service existed before the phone was invented.
(c) The first fax machine was first patented by Caselli.
(d) Bain started the first fax machine company.

33. Conflict among siblings isn't unique to humans; it happens in every animal species that raises several young simultaneously. In most species, this rivalry is an important means of survival in the struggle for resources. However, that is not the case for human children who usually do not have to compete with each other for food and shelter. But other effects of sibling rivalry may prove crucial to their survival. For example, learning to cope with disagreements and disputes with siblings helps to promote important social skills, such as valuing another person's perspective, compromise and negotiation, and controlling anti-social behavior.

Q : What can be inferred from the passage?

(a) A child without siblings will often have violent tendencies.
(b) Sibling conflict can have a beneficial effect upon children.
(c) Wealthy families are much more prone to sibling conflicts.
(d) Sibling conflict originates from a lack of basic resources.

34. Having gone through application forms and witnessed firsthand what young adults have to bear in order to get admitted to university, I have to say, something is seriously wrong with our university entrance system. As it stands, youngsters desiring to attend university must accomplish more than what their parents had to in their days. As Dean of Admissions, I see young people who run their own businesses, own patents and do PhD-level research, just to get accepted. Their whole world is centered around studying, and they don't seem to know about anything else in life.

Q : Which statement would the writer most likely agree with?

(a) Youths are so focused on entering university that they lack other experience.
(b) It is difficult to select students among many equally qualified applicants.
(c) Teenagers waste too much time on things not associated with school.
(d) Exceptional achievements do not guarantee entrance to university.

35. The Tower of London, one of the most famous historical buildings in the world, was begun by the Norman King, William the Conqueror, who defeated Anglo-Saxon England in 1066. He built the Tower's central fortress not only to protect the city from invaders, but also to protect the conquering Normans from the people of London. It was begun in 1078 and was the most impressive structure most Anglo-Saxons had ever seen. It created a sense of fear and wonder for them that was intensified a century later when the tower was used to keep, torture and execute prisoners.

Q : What can be inferred from the passage?

(a) The tower gave Londoners a sense of pride in their city.
(b) The tower served the Normans as a symbol of their power.
(c) Londoners fiercely resisted the rule of the Norman conquerors.
(d) William the Conqueror eventually converted the tower to a prison.

36. In the past, it has been difficult to show a direct causal link between exposure to violence and violent behavior. However, a new study by US researchers claims to have isolated the independent contribution to violence. They compared 1,500 teenagers from a variety of socio-economic backgrounds with a similar likelihood of being exposed to violence. The results seem to confirm people's suspicions: exposure to violence in turn breeds violent behavior among youth.

Q : What can be inferred from the report?

(a) Acts of violence may be entirely justified in some cases.
(b) Watching violence and doing violence have no direct link.
(c) Teenage violence is an endemic problem throughout the United States.
(d) Ordinary individuals may commit violence if they are exposed to violence.

37. The government's failure to provide more funding for public housing is adversely affecting the working poor—those who are employed full-time but remain near or below the poverty line. And statistics back this up by clearly showing a direct correlation between affordable public housing and the ability to maintain employment. So the government needs to act quickly in resolving this public housing issue; otherwise, large scale, costly social problems associated with homelessness and unemployment are likely to emerge in cities across the country.

Q : What can be inferred from the passage?

(a) The government should increase the wages of the working poor.
(b) Increased funding for public housing now will save money later.
(c) The economy is suffering as a result of the government's policies.
(d) Better employment opportunities should be available for the poor.

Part III   Questions 38—40

Read the passage. Then identify the option that does NOT belong.

38. Noisy lawnmowers disturbing the peace of a Sunday afternoon are not a problem in Japan. (a) Nor are Japanese homeowners bothered by neighborhood children kicking a ball into their backyard. (b) Japanese society is known for its politeness. (c) It is simply because hardly anyone in Japan has enough lawn to need a lawnmower. (d) Houses with backyards and lawns are rare in this crowded country.

39. No one knows when alcohol was first produced by humans. (a) Early hominids could have begun making it after experiencing the effects of eating fermented fruit. (b) This theory is supported by the way monkeys have been observed piling fruit in rock crevices and waiting for it to rot so they could drink fermented juice. (c) Giraffes have not been observed to get drunk by eating fermented fruit. (d) In any case, throughout history, wherever humans have had access to fruit, they have tried to make fermented beverages.

40. Modeo's Supreme Single-Serve coffeemaker boasts a line of improvements that enable you to fully personalize your home coffee experience. (a) Unlike our previous Modeo coffeemaker, this new model allows you to select from various serving capacities. (b) Aesthetic improvements include a new chrome silver body and an LCD display. (c) We have also added the refinement of an adjustable nozzle to accommodate different size mugs. (d) And it has a 33% larger water reservoir, enough to brew coffee for family and friends without refilling.

This is the end of the Reading Comprehension section. Please remain seated until the proctor has instructed otherwise. You are NOT allowed to turn to any other section of the test.

Actual Test 3

 문 제

Listening Comprehension  CD 2
Grammar
Vocabulary
Reading Comprehension

 해 설 및 정 답

LISTENING COMPREHENSION

◐ 해설집 P 150

Part I **Questions 1—15**

You will now hear fifteen conversation fragments, each made up of a single spoken statement followed by four spoken responses. Choose the most appropriate response to the statement.

Part II **Questions 16—30**

You will now hear fifteen conversation fragments, each made up of three spoken statements followed by four spoken responses. Choose the most appropriate response to complete the conversation.

Part III Questions 31—45

You will now hear fifteen complete conversations. For each item, you will hear a conversation and its corresponding question, both of which will be read twice. Then you will hear four options which will be read only once. Choose the option that best answers the question.

Part IV Questions 46—60

You will now hear fifteen spoken monologues. For each item, you will hear a monologue and its corresponding question, both of which will be read twice. Then you will hear four options which will be read only once. Choose the option that best answers the question.

GRAMMAR

DIRECTIONS

This part of the exam tests your grammar skills. You will have 25 minutes to complete the 50 questions. Be sure to follow the directions given by the proctor.

Part I **Questions 1—20**

Choose the best answer for the blank.

1. A : What do students think of the library's new facilities?

   B : Most students I know _____ them useful.

   (a) find
   (b) finds
   (c) is found
   (d) are found

2. A : Did you buy some French bread?
   B : No, there was _____ left.

   (a) any
   (b) none
   (c) some
   (d) neither

3. A : Did you get that computer game?

   B : No. By the time I got to the store, every copy _____.

   (a) is sold
   (b) will be sold
   (c) has been sold
   (d) had been sold

4. A : Why were you at the supermarket for so long?

   B : There was _____ a long line at the counter that I was delayed.

   (a) so
   (b) too
   (c) such
   (d) much

5. A : Let me pay for the dinner.

   B : Absolutely not. _____ for it this time.

   (a) I'll pay
   (b) I had paid
   (c) I was paying
   (d) I'll have paid

6. A : I'm tired of Jake's screw-ups at work.

   B : Calm down, honey. There is nobody _____ doesn't have faults.

   (a) that
   (b) which
   (c) whom
   (d) whose

7. A : Alex is very knowledgeable about this town's history.

   B : He should be. He _____ here for years.

   (a) lives
   (b) was lived
   (c) is being lived
   (d) has been living

8. A : Is the coach worried about the team?

   B : Yes, their poor fitness is _____ concerns him most.

   (a) that
   (b) what
   (c) where
   (d) which

9. A : What's the rate for a double room?

B : A hundred dollars _____.

(a) night
(b) a night
(c) the night
(d) any night

10. A : What do you think of Mrs. Davis as a teacher?

B : She is _____ as anyone I've met.

(a) as a patient teacher
(b) as patient a teacher
(c) a very patient teacher
(d) a teacher that is patient

11. A : You should bring an umbrella in case it rains.

B : Good idea. It _____.

(a) looks it might
(b) looks like might
(c) might look like it
(d) looks like it might

12. A : What will you do _____ the park?

B : I'll just walk around for a while.

(a) at
(b) on
(c) for
(d) about

13. A : I want a handheld PC.

B : I'd like one, too, or something of _____.

(a) kind
(b) a kind
(c) the kind
(d) each kind

14. A : What does that article say men's average life expectancy is?

B : It says _____.

(a) it's about 78 years
(b) about 78 old years
(c) about 78 age of years
(d) it's age of about 78 years

15. A : Tell Sue I found her phone.

B : _____ her, I bet she has already bought a new one.

(a) To know
(b) Knowing
(c) Having known
(d) To have known

16. A : The concert tickets have sold out. We'll never get to see it now.

B : No, I _____.

(a) think it not suppose
(b) suppose we'll not so
(c) don't think I suppose
(d) don't suppose we will

17. A: Is it true Susan expanded her business?

B: Yes. _____ that she opened another.

(a) So successful her first store was
(b) Successful was her first store so
(c) Her first store was so successful
(d) Her first store was successful so

18. A : What do you think of the newcomer?

B : There is _____.

(a) about him no single thing I like
(b) no single thing I about him like
(c) a single thing that I don't like him
(d) not a single thing about him that I like

19. A : Why didn't you tell me you were going back to school?

    B : I _____ you if you had been willing to listen.

    (a) had told
    (b) was telling
    (c) will have told
    (d) would have told

20. A : It's so hot! Let's get out of this heat.

    B : Yeah, we shouldn't _____.

    (a) jog in the hottest part of the day
    (b) in the hottest part of the day jog
    (c) be jogging it's the day's hottest part
    (d) the hottest part of the day be jogging

Part II **Questions 21—40**

Choose the best answer for the blank.

---

21. Ink _____ for drawing as well as writing throughout history.

    (a) used
    (b) will use
    (c) has been used
    (d) was being used

22. After a half hour of rowing, the man stopped _____.

    (a) eat
    (b) to eat
    (c) eating
    (d) of eating

23. For most people, London is _____ an expensive city to live in.

    (a) so
    (b) very
    (c) even
    (d) quite

24. News sources state that there _____ have been a radiation leak at the nuclear power plant.

    (a) can
    (b) dare
    (c) need
    (d) might

25. The writer's latest novel _____ very differently from his earlier work.

    (a) has been reading
    (b) will be reading
    (c) is reading
    (d) reads

26. A girl _____ in the choir amazed the audience with her voice.

    (a) sings
    (b) to sing
    (c) singing
    (d) to be singing

27. Children under 8 are not allowed to use the swimming pool _____ they are with an adult.

(a) for
(b) yet
(c) unless
(d) whereas

28. The values of the Shinto belief system _____ many Japanese traditions.

(a) characterize
(b) characterizes
(c) is characterizing
(d) are characterizing

29. Grouping words _____ similar meanings may help language learners build vocabulary.

(a) to
(b) for
(c) with
(d) about

30. _____ for over 20 years, Bill and Angie know each other inside and out.

(a) To be married
(b) They are married
(c) Having been married
(d) They are being married

31. US political parties conduct national nominating conventions, _____ are held every four years.

(a) that
(b) what
(c) which
(d) where

32. A Wisconsin soda fountain owner _____ the first ice cream sundae in 1881.

(a) reputed to invent
(b) invented to be reputed
(c) is reputed to have invented
(d) has invented it being reputed

33. The need for mathematical and problem-solving skills _____ in many fields.

(a) has increased
(b) was increased
(c) have increased
(d) were increased

34. In 1878, an area which _____, was settled by Manoah Stevens and his family.

(a) Jacobston would be known as later
(b) later known as Jacobston would be
(c) would later be known as Jacobston
(d) later Jacobston would be known as

35. During the American Revolutionary War, _____ thousand British Loyalists returned to England.

(a) few
(b) every
(c) much
(d) several

36. Chinese law makes _____ his pregnant wife until well after her delivery.

(a) a man illegal to divorce
(b) illegal for a man to divorce
(c) to divorce illegal for a man
(d) it illegal for a man to divorce

37. _____ the archaeologists had located the ancient site, they organized its excavation.

(a) If
(b) Till
(c) That
(d) Once

38. The research has provided conclusive results, _____ in the table at the end of this document.

(a) details summarizing it are
(b) of which summarized are details
(c) the details of which summarizing it
(d) the details of which are summarized

39. Scarcely _____ the table when the doorbell rang.

(a) did he set
(b) had he set
(c) was he setting
(d) has he been setting

40. _____ Stalin's communist government, and those who did were sent off to labor camps.

(a) Few dared to speak out against
(b) Speaking out few dared against
(c) To speak against it were few daring
(d) Against were to speak few who dared

Part III   Questions 41—45

Identify the option that contains an awkward expression or an error in grammar.

41. (a) A : Did you go on a vacation last
                year?

   (b) B : No, I didn't. I couldn't afford to
                do.

   (c) A : How about this year? Do you
                have any vacation plans?

   (d) B : Yes, I'm thinking of going to
                Spain.

42. (a) A : Hello. This is Jim from Citiplex.
                Could I speak to Tom in sales,
                please?

   (b) B : I'm afraid his line is busy right
                now. Can I take a message?

   (c) A : Yes, I just want to request that
                he'll send me the list of this
                week's sales items.

   (d) B : No problem. I'll tell him as soon
                as he's free.

43. (a) A : Why do we have to get up so
                early tomorrow morning?

   (b) B : Because the traffic would be bad
                if we don't get an early start.

   (c) A : As long as we have good music,
                I don't mind being stuck in
                traffic.

   (d) B : You wouldn't say that if you had
                to do the driving.

44. (a) A : For how long did you study
                French?

   (b) B : I studied it in high school for
                three years.

   (c) A : Did you continue with French
                when you went to college?

   (d) B : Yes, but I stopped to take French
                in my second year.

45. (a) A : Hey, Jerry, do you think you can
                give me a hand on the weekend?

   (b) B : I'm not sure whether I'll have the
                time or not. What do you need
                help with?

   (c) A : I just need help rearranging some
                furnitures in my apartment.

   (d) B : That shouldn't take long. I could
                come over Sunday afternoon.

Part IV Questions 46—50

Identify the option that contains an awkward expression or an error in grammar.

46. (a) In the past, many food dyes were made from plants, animals or insects. (b) Some of these traditional dyes are being still used instead of synthetic dyes. (c) One example is cochineal, which is a crimson-colored dye made from tiny insects. (d) These cochineal insects, which live on cactus plants, are gathered by hand to make the dye.

47. (a) Cape Town and its surrounding areas once teemed with millions of workers. (b) They come to the region to earn a modest income by doing manual laboring jobs. (c) Often they worked under extreme conditions, with little prospect of getting anything better. (d) However, they kept working because they were supporting families hundreds of miles away.

48. (a) Daycare centers in this community are run by local authorities or by volunteer organizations. (b) Centers range from informal community-based groups setting up by parents to large-scale businesses. (c) The problem is that all of them are usually overfilled because people are in such desperate need of daycare. (d) So the government needs to expand existing centers or make new ones.

49. (a) The eyes of the chameleon are unique because they are not dependent on each other. (b) The eyes are not in sockets like ours but exist as slightly raised turrets on either side of a chameleon's head. (c) Chameleons can thus aim their eyes so that one eye can look ahead while the other looks back. (d) Moving independently, the world can be seen by a chameleon in almost 360-degree vision.

50. (a) During the 19th century, the focus of geographical exploration and mapping turned to the Arctic. (b) Many of the explorers who sailed to the Arctic sought a fabled Northwest Passage between Asia and Europe. (c) One of the most famous of them was British sailor called William Perry who made numerous voyages to the Arctic. (d) His trip to the Arctic Archipelago is considered to be one of the most important in the history of Arctic exploration.

This is the end of the Grammar section. Do NOT move on to the next section until instructed to do so. You are NOT allowed to turn to any other section of the test.

VOCABULARY

DIRECTIONS

This part of the exam tests your vocabulary skills. You will have 15 minutes to complete the 50 questions. Be sure to follow the directions given by the proctor.

Part I **Questions 1—25**

Choose the best answer for the blank.

1. A : Hi, Amanda. I'm so glad you could come to my party.

B : Oh, hi Tim. Thanks for _____ me.

(a) noting
(b) placing
(c) inviting
(d) showing

2. A : Excuse me, but how do I dial outside from this office phone?

B : Just press zero for an outside _____.

(a) line
(b) talk
(c) ring
(d) voice

3. A : Please turn down your music. I can hear it even in the other room.

B : Oh, I didn't think it was that _____.

(a) full
(b) loud
(c) huge
(d) strong

4. A : Hello. I have an appointment with Dr. Robins.

B : Certainly. Please _____ a seat.

(a) take
(b) wait
(c) hold
(d) bring

5. A : Kevin has shown amazing improvement in his music lessons.

B : Yes, he's very _____ in music.

(a) played
(b) talented
(c) oriented
(d) expressed

6. A : I really appreciate the pay raise the company gave me.

B : Well, you _____ it.

(a) deserved
(b) afforded
(c) charged
(d) claimed

7. A : Hello, I'm calling for Mr. Stone, please.

B : Yes, I'll _____ you to him now.

(a) deter
(b) usher
(c) locate
(d) transfer

8. A : Did you get Jennifer to join our gym?

B : No. She wasn't _____.

(a) included
(b) occupied
(c) interested
(d) concerned

9. A : I'm planning to live and work overseas. I think it'll be fun.

    B : Good idea. I wouldn't mind living _____, either.

    (a) abroad
    (b) beyond
    (c) outwards
    (d) worldwide

10. A : John and Mark are twin brothers, aren't they?

    B : No, but they do look very much _____.

    (a) alike
    (b) copied
    (c) parallel
    (d) matched

11. A : Was your cat all right after her ten-story fall?

    B : Yes. She _____ survived it.

    (a) tenderly
    (b) suddenly
    (c) reasonably
    (d) miraculously

12. A : Frank graduated from this school.

    B : Really? I didn't know he was a Hope College _____ !

    (a) faculty
    (b) prodigy
    (c) alumnus
    (d) associate

13. A : Sorry I forgot to pick up your suits from the dry cleaner.

    B : That's okay. I should've _____ you.

    (a) reminded
    (b) persuaded
    (c) advertised
    (d) memorized

14. A : Do you want to meet at the mall at 4?

    B : That's too early, but I can _____ it by 5.

    (a) see
    (b) meet
    (c) make
    (d) reach

15. A : I don't know what to do about the misplaced order.

    B : You need to at least try to _____ the problem.

    (a) sort out
    (b) stick up
    (c) switch off
    (d) saw down

16. A : Excuse me. Can you direct me to the Rand Hospital?

    B : I'm sorry, but I don't have a(n) _____ where that is.

    (a) opinion
    (b) locality
    (c) mind
    (d) clue

17. A : Should I tip taxi drivers here?

    B : No, it's not _____ to tip drivers in this country.

    (a) optional
    (b) customary
    (c) fundamental
    (d) rudimentary

18. A : Sandra is sad about her breakup.

    B : I know, but she'll _____.

    (a) pass it on
    (b) get over it
    (c) settle on it
    (d) slip it through

19. A : So, how has our business been performing since January?

    B : Not bad. Our sales _____ has increased by 15%.

    (a) addition
    (b) volume
    (c) depth
    (d) spot

20. A : Your statistics are extensive.

    B : Yes, they were _____ over many years.

    (a) inverted
    (b) compiled
    (c) fabricated
    (d) assembled

21. A : May I bring my baby's bottle on the plane?

    B : Yes, but it must pass through security in a(n) _____ bag to ensure it is safe.

    (a) takeout
    (b) well-being
    (c) airsickness
    (d) tamper-proof

22. A : So, your thesis is about the oppression of women in the Third World?

    B : Yes, that's the _____ of it.

    (a) gist
    (b) hub
    (c) tally
    (d) aspect

23. A : That doctor seems nice.

    B : Yes. He always treats patients _____.

    (a) timidly
    (b) cynically
    (c) ruggedly
    (d) courteously

24. A : I heard your blind date didn't work out.

    B : No, she _____.

    (a) pushed me through
    (b) dropped me down
    (c) turned me over
    (d) stood me up

25. A : The heat and humidity is so stifling that I don't feel like moving.

    B : Yeah, it makes me feel _____, too.

    (a) guileless
    (b) lethargic
    (c) distraught
    (d) overwrought

Part II   Questions 26—50

Choose the best answer for the blank.

26. Jane looks so young that people make the _____ of thinking she is a teenager.

(a) sum
(b) fault
(c) mistake
(d) memory

27. It is crucial that documents are carefully proofread and errors are _____.

(a) corrected
(b) accessed
(c) rubbed
(d) exited

28. We apologize for any inconvenience _____ by the train's late arrival.

(a) caused
(b) resulted
(c) bothered
(d) suspected

29. Our telescopes' mounts are capable of vertical and horizontal movement so that the telescope can be _____ in any direction.

(a) pointed
(b) viewed
(c) slipped
(d) framed

30. *Education News* is _____ six times a year and is aimed at teachers and parents.

(a) reviewed
(b) contained
(c) published
(d) subscribed

31. A leader's central responsibility is to _____ the conditions necessary for a society's growth and success.

(a) equip
(b) create
(c) handle
(d) donate

32. Acquiring insights into other countries' cultures is an essential _____ of a well-rounded education.

(a) component
(b) strategy
(c) layout
(d) tactic

33. Cut your caffeine intake by _____ non-caffeinated drinks for caffeinated ones.

(a) changing
(b) replacing
(c) purchasing
(d) substituting

34. The first half of the 20th century saw the world _____ in two global wars.

(a) broiled
(b) engaged
(c) mounted
(d) committed

35. Economic growth has increased in _____ contrast to the decline experienced last year.

(a) random
(b) morbid
(c) sharp
(d) lined

36. The minimum wage ensures that all entry-level workers _____ a fair base wage.

(a) obtain
(b) request
(c) bargain
(d) establish

37. The girl slept so _____ that the thunder did not wake her up.

(a) firmly
(b) wholly
(c) entirely
(d) soundly

38. The film is a reflection of the violence that _____ American culture.

(a) exudes
(b) spreads
(c) pervades
(d) subsumes

39. Industrialized nations should take the _____ and reduce greenhouse gas emissions.

(a) operation
(b) initiative
(c) example
(d) position

40. Some people say even friends can betray you and that you can only _____ on yourself in the end.

(a) check
(b) focus
(c) insist
(d) rely

41. The author dwells on _____ matters rather than on the essentials of medieval history.

(a) trivial
(b) relevant
(c) elemental
(d) invaluable

42. Berbers residing near the Mediterranean Sea make a(n) _____ as farmers.

(a) living
(b) existing
(c) provision
(d) occupation

43. Orangutans are closely _____ to humans genetically.

(a) placed
(b) related
(c) referred
(d) attributed

44. Research shows that there is a(n)
    _____ difference between the way
    problems are solved by experts and by
    novices.

    (a) stark
    (b) crass
    (c) obtuse
    (d) rotund

45. The government will _____ anyone
    hunting elephants illegally.

    (a) prosecute
    (b) institute
    (c) legislate
    (d) refute

46. Teaching disabled children is laborious
    yet rewarding, requiring determination,
    _____ and hard work.

    (a) rendition
    (b) distraction
    (c) pertinacity
    (d) infrastructure

47. From the remarks of the woman he was
    questioning, the detective _____
    that she must have committed the crime.

    (a) plied
    (b) reduced
    (c) deduced
    (d) conferred

48. The president felt _____ when he
    was accused unfairly by many reporters
    at the press conference.

    (a) piqued
    (b) felicitous
    (c) appeased
    (d) exonerated

49. Most of the damage caused by an
    earthquake results from seismic waves
    that _____ out from a fault line at
    8,000 or more miles per hour.

    (a) exhale
    (b) expunge
    (c) prolapse
    (d) propagate

50. A(n) _____ administration should
    be set up until a permanent governing
    body is established in the country.

    (a) interim
    (b) panoptic
    (c) subsistent
    (d) centrifugal

This is the end of the Vocabulary section. Do NOT move on to the Reading
Comprehension section until instructed to do so. You are NOT allowed to turn
to any other section of the test.

READING
COMPREHENSION

Part I   **Questions 1—16**

Read the passage. Then choose the option that best completes the passage.

---

1. A good résumé can only get you to the interview stage. In order to finally get a job, it is important to do well in the interview, beginning with a strong first impression. First impressions are critical because recruiters often make decisions based on them. So if you think your résumé is all that counts, think again. Right or wrong, final judgments

    _____.

    (a) can be affected by your work
    (b) can depend on who you know
    (c) are made based on your résumé
    (d) are influenced by initial meetings

2. Around 2000 BC, during the Shang Dynasty, people in China _____

    _____. There were gods that represented nature, such as weather and sky gods. There was also a higher god called Shang-Ti who ruled over all others. The ancient Chinese even believed that their ancestors became like gods when they died. Gods were clearly a very important part of their lives.

    (a) were fearful of God's wrath
    (b) worshipped many different gods
    (c) constantly disagreed over religion
    (d) praised some gods more than others

3. One of the sites I visited in Paris was the Alma Bridge over the Seine River, which is famous for a large statue of an infantry soldier that stands next to it. The statue is the only surviving part of the original Alma Bridge built in 1854, and Parisians used to use it as a gauge of river water levels. If the statue's toes got wet, Paris would be on flood alert. If his ankles went under water, riverside roads would be closed. If his hips were wet, that would mean _____.

    (a) the river water had lowered
    (b) the city might soon be flooded
    (c) the bridge was in need of repair
    (d) the statue would need to be moved

4. Welcome to Hermitage National Park. Visitors to the park are welcome to camp by the beautiful Lake Piron. However, please take caution not to harm the environment. Littering, cutting down trees and building unauthorized bonfires are strictly illegal, and those caught engaging in such activities face severe fines and penalties. A full list of prohibited activities is available at each ranger station or on our website. Please help us _____ .

    (a) stop people fishing in the lake
    (b) keep the new facilities clean
    (c) preserve the environment
    (d) stop all of the wastage

5. Disgraced journalist Lewis Landow has apologized today after a scandal concerning a falsified report. Last week Landow's column for *Life Today* magazine included a brief account of the Republican National Convention. The problem was that the convention had not taken place at the time. Landow's account was fictional, a fact exposed when *Life Today* magazines arrived in subscribers' mailboxes before the convention, earlier than he had thought they would. Landow was visibly upset _____ .

    (a) by *Life Today*'s account of his life
    (b) about the false reports against him
    (c) at not becoming a Republican candidate
    (d) when admitting that his report was fake

6. Carter carburetors were used on most GMC passenger trucks from 1941 to 1948. They were hardy contraptions, but they sometimes made trucks idle roughly. However, that was easily fixed. The float lever could be easily bent slightly upwards to lower the float level, or downwards to raise it. Nothing more was needed than a pair of nose pliers and a gentle touch. This same method is still used by owners and collectors of these old trucks today. It just goes to show that Carter carburetors _____ .

    (a) sell for a high price among collectors
    (b) are still durable and easy to maintain
    (c) perform as well as modern carburetors
    (d) can easily be replaced with newer ones

7. Certain advocates of vegetarianism in the 1800s believed that _____ _____. Consequently, their lifestyle was not just about physical health or the ethical treatment of animals. They saw carnivorism as something that transformed a person's behavior. It was deemed identical to cruelty and bad-temperedness; it was even regarded as leading to robbery, sycophancy and despotism. They went so far as to see meat eating as the source of all evil, blaming it for such abhorrences as the slave trade.

(a) cruelty to animals was uncivilized
(b) vegetables would guarantee a long life
(c) meat eating was against the word of God
(d) food formed character and affected the mind

8. Repressing sneezes may be harmful to your health. Air escaping from your nose and mouth during a sneeze can reach a maximum speed of 100 mph. Therefore, sneezing while holding your breath or blocking your lips or nose builds up enormous pressure in the nose and throat. Such pressure may push bacteria from your nose into your sinuses or into your ears through the Eustachian tubes. When you sneeze, you should cover your nose and mouth with a tissue. But it is recommended that _____.

(a) you use more than one tissue at such times
(b) you refrain from any measure to stifle a sneeze
(c) you do not sneeze in the direction of other people
(d) you seek medical advice if you are sneezing too often

9.

Dear Editor,

I'm very concerned about the rise in serious crimes being committed by youths. Many of these youths laugh at the justice system. That is because they get off lightly and receive sentences for children, which are often lenient, even though they have committed adult crimes. Since there are no serious consequences for their actions, the message sent to such juvenile criminals is that crime doesn't matter. At the moment,

_____.

Yours sincerely,
Tony Bundy

(a) juvenile offenders are treated inhumanely
(b) court procedures are being reformed
(c) victims of crimes are being ignored
(d) punishments do not fit the crimes

10. In ancient Egypt, a wide social rift separated the small group of rulers and the nobility from the majority of the populace at the bottom of the social ladder. To be more precise, pharaohs were at the top of the ladder and slaves and farmers were at the other end. This pyramid-like social stratification and top-down power structure governed every sphere of life. It meant that _____.

(a) society's rules were enforced by soldiers
(b) nobles were constantly fighting to gain power
(c) there were more slaves than there were farmers
(d) most wealth and power was in the hands of the few

11. Overwhelming evidence suggests that _____.
Studies have shown that children subjected to such treatment are significantly more likely to subject other people to physical punishments, both as children and as adults. In addition, the more violently children are punished, the more aggressive and violent they become later. One study found that among a group of children, the ones spanked the most as 3- to 5-year-olds exhibited more anti-social behavior than other children when observed 2 years later.

(a) parents should not spare children from spanking
(b) some punishments are more effective than others
(c) children should not be pushed too hard by parents
(d) corporal punishment increases aggressive behavior

12. Melatonin, a hormone found in all living creatures, is produced according to the daily patterns of light and darkness experienced by an animal. The production variation of melatonin acts as an internal seasonal clock for many animals, scheduling their mating or hibernation behaviors. This has been demonstrated in a laboratory with Siberian hamsters. As long as the light patterns of their natural environment are mimicked, the hamsters continue to follow seasonal eating, sleeping and mating patterns despite being in a laboratory because melatonin works like _____.

(a) a crucial hormone for human reproduction
(b) an internal timer that regulates different events
(c) a mechanism that governs night-time behavior
(d) a vital component for a healthy immune system

13. Back when the Tudors ruled England, the district in London currently known as Soho used to be a hunting ground of open fields and duck ponds where Londoners hunted wild game. Later, it became well known as London's shabby red-light district. Today, Soho still remains a hunting ground, only now people stroll through its lively streets, posh stores, cafés and clubs in search of food, drink and dancing. Its name now is synonymous with

_____.

(a) trendy attractions rather than raunchy entertainment
(b) disreputable and seedier sides of London night life
(c) exorbitantly high rents and high property prices
(d) one of the oldest traditions of English history

14. Haza Mining is a budding Mexican-based mining and exploration firm focused on extracting and developing gold, copper and industrial mineral substances. The company owns the Summit silver-gold property in southwest Mexico, which contains 117 acres of patented and 600 acres of unpatented mining claims; mineral lease rights to the Olego gold property near Mexico City; and a high-quality mica mine and processing complex in the eastern Sonora State. Haza plans to continue to _____.

(a) develop its extensive real-estate holdings in Mexico
(b) build a diverse portfolio of high-quality mineral assets
(c) proceed with its acquisition of international mining interests
(d) maintain its long-held industry lead with further exploration

15. The traditional values of many Asian cultures share the strong belief that adult children are responsible for the care of their aging parents. Such filial commitment is taken for granted, so failing to take care of one's parents is viewed in a very negative light. Regardless of the expenses, support of elderly parents should always be a priority. _____, an adult would be obliged not to accept a great job offer if it entailed a move that would negatively affect the care of his or her aging parents.

(a) For instance
(b) In addition
(c) However
(d) Then

16. English translations of literary classics can never match their originals. Nonetheless, translators strive to create definitive English versions out of the myriad of possible readings, which is why new translations of literary classics, such as Dante's *The Divine Comedy*, appear in every generation. These versions are always going to be provisional, limited and defined by the talents of translators. _____, in rare instances, translators do manage to produce a work of such excellence that it attains classic status itself.

(a) Yet
(b) Instead
(c) Furthermore
(d) Subsequently

Read the passage and the question. Then choose the option that best answers the question.

17. Our university's Teacher Training Program is an intensive eight-month program that enables liberal arts graduates to earn a teaching certificate at the elementary or secondary level. Teacher trainees gain field experiences in local schools, are paired up with teachers, attend classes and workshops, and go through 32 credit hours of practical coursework. Students in the program are eligible for student loans and are also awarded a stipend for their regular school work during the academic year.

Q : What is the advertisement mainly about?
(a) The details of a teacher training course
(b) The jobs currently available for teachers
(c) The rules for teachers working at a college
(d) The amount of work an average teacher does

18. Medical scientists now admit that little kids are not exclusively responsible for spreading the flu from daycares and classrooms to the rest of the community every year, as was once believed. New research on seasonal flu patterns indicates that working adults are more likely the culprits for the dispersion of flu nationwide. This discovery, published in the journal *Science*, could have profound implications for regulating annual flu outbreaks and any potential influenza pandemics.

Q : What is the main idea of the passage?
(a) Protecting children from flu is now more difficult.
(b) Seasonal flu patterns have changed dramatically.
(c) Flu pandemics will be more common in the future.
(d) Adults are spreading influenza more than children.

19. Toxic ammonia seeped from a cooling tube Wednesday as astronauts worked on mending the cooling system outside of the International Space Station. The astronauts, Mike Evans and Irvin Wilson, fortunately did not come in contact with the ammonia. The leak occurred towards the completion of an eight-hour spacewalk. Tests in the airlock afterward showed no sign of contamination. Ammonia is a big menace because it is highly poisonous and could cause respiratory problems if it makes its way into the space station.

Q : What is the best title for the passage?

(a) Leak Threatens Future of Space Station
(b) Spacewalkers Avert Collision in Outer Space
(c) Space Station in Danger Due to Cooling System
(d) Astronauts Avoid Toxic Substance Contamination

20. It has been known for some time that many animals learn by observation and imitation. In an early experiment that tested this idea, a cat was trained to obtain food by pressing a bar when a light went on. A second cat was then placed near the trained cat to watch how it obtained food. After a period, the second cat was placed alone near the bar and light. When the light went on, the second cat pressed the bar to get food. Apparently the cat had learned what to do from watching the trained cat.

Q : What is the passage mainly about?

(a) Ways that animals cooperate
(b) Training animals to get their own food
(c) Experimenting to change animal behavior
(d) Animals' ability to learn through observation

21. In times of famine, early intervention in the form of cash or vouchers with which food can be bought on the market can prevent the unintended ill effects of food aid. Food aid is detrimental when it is sent to a country for long periods because it can ruin local farmers. This in turn erodes a country's agricultural capacity. A case in point is Ethiopia, which received food aid equivalent to 15% of its annual cereal production in 2003, and today it has lower agricultural yields than it had prior to the famine. Cash or vouchers could have prevented this from happening.

Q : What is the main idea of the passage?

(a) Early intervention is ultimately the best method of famine relief.
(b) Belated food aid can have adverse side effects on local agriculture.
(c) Food aid has been the source of agricultural setbacks in Ethiopia.
(d) Cash or vouchers are more effective against famine than food aid.

22. Dance history is more advanced as a discipline in comparison to dance criticism. It boasts an increasingly refined methodology, an expanding body of literature and a growing number of experts devoted to it. More and more dance historians hold professional positions in academia than do exponents of dance criticism, and, interestingly, none of the best active dance critics in the US today holds an academic position. These factors, together with the rather weak formal training required for dance criticism, mean that dance history will keep advancing as a discipline in contrast to dance criticism.

Q : What is the passage mainly about?

(a) The benefits of scholars working in dance-related fields
(b) The opportunities available to dance experts in criticism
(c) The emerging growth of academic interest in the field of dance
(d) The academic prospects for dance history compared to dance criticism

23. A unique new book on art entitled *Inspired Children* focuses on the childhood art of great artists. Readers will gain a glimpse of budding talent from works such as a pencil drawing by a 4-year-old Keith Haring that has his signature polka dots, or the people and animals sketched by Vincent van Gogh at age 8. All drawings and paintings in this marvelous book are accompanied by excellent analyses and explanations by experts.

Q : Which of the following is correct about *Inspired Children*?

(a) It presents art featuring children.
(b) It shows famous works for children.
(c) It focuses on Van Gogh's late works.
(d) It contains expert analyses on child art.

24. In the 1800s, the high number of Irish, Polish and Italian immigrants settling in New York had a big impact on the social character of the city. Because they arrived in such great numbers, they changed the whole ethnic makeup of local populations. For example, hundreds of thousands of Irish immigrants led to one-third of New York's population born by 1855 being Irish.

Q : Which of the following is correct according to the passage?

(a) Few 19th-century immigrants were Irish.
(b) Many Irish immigrants settled in New York.
(c) Most Irish immigrants settled in rural areas.
(d) Irish immigrants first arrived in America in 1855.

25. Join the Clifford Hotel for a fun night when you can try out wines from all of the award-winning wineries in the prestigious 2008 Orange County Commercial Wine Competition. You can also treat yourself to gourmet food from a selection of Orange County's finest restaurants, enjoy live music, participate in a raffle to win a free bottle of fine wine, or join a silent auction! It's only $50 per person if you register by February 27, or $60 at the door. See you there on Sunday, March 9, 2 p.m. to 10 p.m., at the Clifford Hotel. Call (714) 708 - 1636 to register.

Q : Which of the following is correct about the advertised event?

(a) You get to vote in a wine competition.
(b) You can save money by pre-registering.
(c) You can taste food from around the world.
(d) You must register by March 9 for a discount.

26.

Dear Mom and Dad,

My sophomore year at college is off to a great start. I have finally found a better place to live! The two apartment mates I live with now share the same kind of lifestyle with me. They clean the apartment about once a month and do the dishes about once a week (or they wait until we run out of clean ones!). I get along with these guys much better than the guy in my old place who expected everything to be clean 24/7. It was simply unbearable! Anyway, I'll fill you in on more once I've settled in!

Love,
Matt

Q : Which of the following is correct according to the letter?

(a) Matt's last place was too hard to clean.
(b) Matt's new apartment mates are dirtier than he is.
(c) Matt's old apartment mate liked things to be clean.
(d) Matt's new apartment is shared by five people.

27. New beverage policies for schools will go into effect starting this fall semester. Under these new guidelines, elementary and middle school students will have a wider range of nutritious low-calorie beverage options, which include fruit juices, low-fat milk and bottled water. At high schools, these beverages will be available in addition to diet sodas, sports drinks and low-calorie teas. This initiative is all part of a broader effort to educate children about the significance of a healthy lifestyle and a balanced diet.

Q : Which of the following is correct about the new guidelines?

(a) Sodas are available in high schools.
(b) They have been in effect since last fall.
(c) Sports drinks are sold in middle schools.
(d) Some drinks are free of charge to students.

28. Huave is a language spoken by the native Huave people on the Pacific coast of Southern Oaxaca, Mexico. The language is used only in four villages in the Isthmus of Tehuantepec by some 18,000 residents. While still in use in the social life of these four villages, Huave is, nonetheless, a language in danger of extinction. Despite cultural fieldwork and linguistic revitalization projects sponsored and conducted by American universities in Huave communities, it is just a matter of time until only the elders will remember how to speak Huave.

Q : Which of the following is correct about the Huave language?

(a) It has become endangered despite its continued use.
(b) It continues to be spoken in most regions of Mexico.
(c) It is only spoken by the aged Huave population.
(d) It is now simply used for special ceremonies.

29. Lisa Turner has always had a problem with faces. As a child, she struggled to pick out her own face in school photos, and she has always been hard-pressed to describe her mother's features. Over the years, she has offended countless friends because she has passed them by as if they were strangers. "I lose friends because they think I'm ignoring them," says Turner. She is not ignoring them but has prosopagnosia or, more commonly, face-blindness. Once thought to be exceedingly rare and only the result of brain injury, a recent study has shown that prosopagnosia is inheritable and surprisingly common.

Q : Which of the following is correct about Lisa Turner?

(a) She had a brain injury when young.
(b) She had no pictures taken in school.
(c) She has a disorder that can be inherited.
(d) She has trouble remembering people's names.

30.

> Dear Mr. Green,
>
> I am writing to apply for the position of a full-time systems consultant posted in the *Times*. Please find attached my CV. Although I am a recent business school graduate, I have considerable work experience. While studying, I worked various part-time jobs involving software development. Also, the studies I undertook were practically oriented, so I have a good knowledge of current business systems and procedures. Should you require any further information, please do not hesitate to contact me.
>
> Best Regards,
> James Field

Q : Which of the following is correct about the writer?

(a) He gained his job experience after graduation.
(b) He has worked in software development.
(c) He is applying for a part-time position.
(d) He sent in his CV earlier.

31. It took nearly a year and a half after renowned novelist, professor and Nobel laureate Saul Bellow died, in April, 2005, for the last of his documents to arrive at Regenstein Library of the University of Chicago. The documents—comprising letters, notes, typewritten drafts, galley proofs, unpublished speeches and essays—filled approximately 150 boxes. Among the papers are Bellow's correspondences to and from authors like John Cheever, Bernard Malamud and Allan Bloom. There are also revisions of five novels Bellow had published. The library is extremely grateful to acquire this prized collection.

Q : Which of the following is correct about Saul Bellow according to the passage?

(a) He kept letters from other writers.
(b) He was writing a new novel when he died.
(c) He graduated from the University of Chicago.
(d) He left five unpublished novels among his papers.

32. At Shepherd's Menswear, we ship ordered items on the same business day if ordered by noon. Orders received in the afternoon are shipped the next business day. However, actual delivery time may vary. A delivery driver may decide not to leave a package at your door if you are not home. If you cannot wait for a delivery, we recommend that you leave us instructions as to where the delivery can be made instead.

Q : Which of the following is correct according to the passage?
(a) Every item ordered before noon is shipped the next day.
(b) Customers should contact delivery drivers when ordering.
(c) A delivery driver may not deliver your package if you are not home.
(d) Delivery instructions must be given by customers for every shipment.

33. Before the discovery of vitamins, people naturally protected their bodies from diseases caused by vitamin deficiency simply by consuming a wide variety of vegetables and fruit. There were some people, however, such as explorers and sailors, who often did not have access to their usual range of food choices for long periods of time. As a result, they fell sick with illnesses such as scurvy, which is caused by lack of vitamin C.

Q : What can be inferred from the passage?
(a) Sailors and explorers could not store fruit for long.
(b) Instances of scurvy never occur in today's world.
(c) There was no cure for scurvy in ancient times.
(d) Vitamin deficiency mainly affects children.

34. At Paramount High School, incoming teachers are required to spend some of their planning periods doubling as hall monitors. Desks are placed in the halls for teachers to use. All hall monitors will have an assigned partner, so they must check the schedule and coordinate with their partners on preferences for monitoring times. After two semesters, teachers will be exempt from hall monitoring duties unless special situations arise.

Q : What can be inferred about the monitoring policy from the passage?
(a) Not all teachers have the duty of monitoring halls.
(b) Unruly students must take time out at desks in the halls.
(c) Extra pay will be given to teachers who do the monitoring.
(d) Teachers are encouraged to remain standing while monitoring.

35. Zach Corporation has built its reputation for more than 30 years on an uncompromising commitment to sound systems. Now, Zach gives you even more lifelike sound in your own home with the new Zach 321 Home Entertainment System. This system can recreate full orchestral sound in your living room or the intricate arrangements of a jazz quartet in your den. Visit your local electronics store and hear the amazing Zach 321 for yourself. Also, order a Zach 321 before March 1 and save $75.

Q : What can be inferred about the Zach sound system?

(a) It is sold exclusively at Zach retail outlets.
(b) It is designed to work best in outdoor settings.
(c) It is able to reproduce a highly authentic sound.
(d) It is at the low end of the market in terms of price.

36. Eureka, an Internet encyclopedia, is not the paradise of clear and accurate knowledge one would hope to find. As a repository of user-generated content, it has errors in it, and although it is considerably larger than offline counterparts, it is far from being complete. Some people have tried to vandalize it by erasing or falsifying entries; at one point, the entire staff of Congress was barred from Eureka for sabotaging one another's profiles. In a way, this online encyclopedia is as much a litmus test of human nature as it is a reference tool.

Q : What can be inferred from the passage?

(a) User content sites are rarely consulted by professionals.
(b) Encyclopedias everywhere tend to have occasional errors.
(c) Workplace sabotage occurs more on the Internet than elsewhere.
(d) A certain level of skepticism is necessary with online information.

37. Ken Kesey's landmark 1962 novel, *One Flew over the Cuckoo's Nest*, helped shape the attitude of America's youth toward authority. The plot develops in a mental institution in which Kesey's main character, McMurphy, one of the inmates, is pictured as saner than the hospital's authorities. Anti-establishment youths throughout the 60s identified themselves with the novel and McMurphy's fight against authorities. They saw the upside-down, oppressive logic of McMurphy's keepers as similar to the official US government rationales for the war in Vietnam at the time. They also maintained the view that America itself was a kind of mental ward.

Q : What can be inferred about American youths in the 1960s according to the passage?

(a) They felt that mental patients should be released into society.
(b) They saw soldiers in Vietnam as equivalent to mental patients.
(c) They saw themselves as saner than those in charge of the country.
(d) They regarded everyday people as less enlightened than the insane.

Part III **Questions 38—40**

Read the passage. Then identify the option that does NOT belong.

38. In my experience, the key to being productive as a writer is sticking to a regular schedule.
(a) I make sure that I sit down to write by 10 a.m. each morning for five days a week.
(b) Of course, some people feel that writing is not about being a slave to a schedule.
(c) However, if you don't have that discipline, then maybe you're not cut out to be a writer. (d) I wrote my first book while seated at a small desk in the corner of my bedroom.

39. William Shakespeare was born in 1564 in Stratford-upon-Avon, England. (a) He spent the first 20 years of his life there, where a modest schooling barely prepared him for the theater. (b) He eventually married a young woman named Anne Hathaway, with whom he later had three children. (c) No one really knows how Shakespeare began his drama career after his academic training, but he started acting sometime around 1585. (d) What is certain, however, is that by 1592 he had established himself as an actor and a playwright of note.

40. The demand for copies of Martin Luther's works in the early 1500s was huge throughout Europe. (a) Between 1518 and 1521, no fewer than 800 editions of a hundred of his works were published in several languages. (b) Luther's works were censored and his adherents persecuted in many parts of Europe by the Catholic Church. (c) Thanks to the invention of the printing press, copies of his sermons, edifying tracts and vigorous polemics were all available to the public. (d) Without mass production, the popularity and impact of Luther across Europe would not have been nearly as great.

This is the end of the Reading Comprehension section. Please remain seated until the proctor has instructed otherwise. You are NOT allowed to turn to any other section of the test.

Actual Test 4

문 제

Listening Comprehension CD2
Grammar
Vocabulary
Reading Comprehension

해 설 및 정 답

LISTENING COMPREHENSION

DIRECTIONS

1. In the Listening Comprehension section, all content will be presented orally rather than in written form.

2. This section contains 4 parts. In parts I and II, each passage will be read only once. In parts III and IV, each passage and its corresponding question will be read twice. But in all sections, the options will be read only once. After listening to the passage and question, listen to the options and choose the best answer.

Part I **Questions 1—15**

You will now hear fifteen conversation fragments, each made up of a single spoken statement followed by four spoken responses. Choose the most appropriate response to the statement.

Part II **Questions 16—30**

You will now hear fifteen conversation fragments, each made up of three spoken statements followed by four spoken responses. Choose the most appropriate response to complete the conversation.

Part III **Questions 31—45**

You will now hear fifteen complete conversations. For each item, you will hear a conversation and its corresponding question, both of which will be read twice. Then you will hear four options which will be read only once. Choose the option that best answers the question.

Part IV **Questions 46—60**

You will now hear fifteen spoken monologues. For each item, you will hear a monologue and its corresponding question, both of which will be read twice. Then you will hear four options which will be read only once. Choose the option that best answers the question.

GRAMMAR

DIRECTIONS

This part of the exam tests your grammar skills. You will have 25 minutes to complete the 50 questions. Be sure to follow the directions given by the proctor.

Part I   **Questions 1—20**

Choose the best answer for the blank.

1. A: Can you get this report done in two hours?

   B: I _____ do my best.

   (a) will
   (b) may
   (c) need
   (d) might

2. A: Do you mind sharing your room with a guest for a few days?

   B: It won't bother me _____ much as long as she doesn't make a mess.

   (a) far
   (b) too
   (c) well
   (d) such

3. A: Should I apply for the managerial position?

   B: It _____.

   (a) will try not to hurt you
   (b) will try to hurt you not
   (c) won't hurt to try you
   (d) won't hurt you to try

4. A: The judge didn't seem to believe that the witness was telling the truth.

   B: I agree. He didn't look _____.

   (a) convinced
   (b) convincing
   (c) to convince
   (d) to be convincing

5. A: Mary, _____?

   B: My mother. Her birthday is next week.

   (a) you wrote to whom a letter
   (b) to whom you wrote a letter
   (c) to whom did you write a letter
   (d) whom did you write to a letter

6. A: Do you think Caroline was right to leave her job?

   B: No, she _____.

   (a) shouldn't
   (b) shouldn't do
   (c) shouldn't have
   (d) should have never

7. A: Where can I find some painkillers?

   B: I'm sorry. I didn't hear you. Could you repeat _____ you said?

   (a) that
   (b) how
   (c) what
   (d) which

8. A: That's a new cell phone, isn't it?

   B: Oh, you _____. I got it as a graduation gift.

   (a) will be noticed
   (b) were noticed
   (c) will notice
   (d) noticed

9. A: Where are you staying?

    B: I _____ in my uncle's apartment since I arrived.

    (a) live
    (b) am living
    (c) was living
    (d) have been living

10. A: What's all that noise outside?

    B: They are excavating land for a new building _____.

    (a) to our right next
    (b) next to our right
    (c) right next to ours
    (d) ours right next to

11. A: Have you ever been forced to do something you didn't want to?

    B: Fortunately no; _____ do that to anyone else.

    (a) I would ever
    (b) would I ever
    (c) nor would I ever
    (d) nor I would ever

12. A: I'm thinking of going to the Spiders concert.

    B: Make sure _____ in advance.

    (a) buying your tickets
    (b) your tickets you buy
    (c) you buy your tickets
    (d) tickets you are buying

13. A: What happened to your blouse?

    B: _____ the stairs, I accidentally fell and spilt coffee on it.

    (a) To walk up
    (b) Walking up
    (c) I walked up
    (d) To have walked up

14. A: Who left the lights on?

    B: Sorry. I _____ have done it.

    (a) will
    (b) shall
    (c) need
    (d) must

15. A: Why do all these Moorish houses have a courtyard?

    B: Because it's an integral part of a house _____ Moorish architecture.

    (a) in
    (b) at
    (c) to
    (d) on

16. A: Do you have any regrets about your decision?

    B: Yes. I _____ have accepted the offer.

    (a) had to
    (b) could
    (c) might
    (d) ought to

17. A: If you have any trouble with the instructions, please come and see me.

    B: Thanks, but I'm certain _____.

    (a) I'm to understand them
    (b) of them understanding
    (c) I can understand them
    (d) understanding them

18. A: What are you going to do with your bonus money?

B: _____ it all on books.

(a) I spend
(b) I'll spend
(c) I had spent
(d) I'll have spent

19. A: Is it true you have students who are often late to school?

B: Yes, some students in my class _____ easy access to transportation.

(a) hasn't had
(b) don't have
(c) haven't had
(d) doesn't have

20. A: How was the trip to China?

B: It was just fantastic! I loved the scenery, _____.

(a) the food to not mention
(b) not to mention the food
(c) the food not mentioning
(d) not mentioning the food

Part II	**Questions 21—40**

Choose the best answer for the blank.

---

21. Michael brought his books to school, _____ he forgot his pencils.

(a) but
(b) for
(c) as
(d) so

22. It is estimated that these days, 300,000 homeless people _____ on the streets of America's big cities.

(a) live
(b) lived
(c) were living
(d) had been living

23. The possibility that comets and large meteorites could collide with the earth in the future _____ serious consideration.

(a) that requires
(b) to require
(c) requiring
(d) requires

24. Omega-3 fatty acids in fish can modify the blood, _____ it less prone to clotting.

(a) make
(b) making
(c) to making
(d) and making

25. The group's original plan was to go _____ over the weekend.

(a) skied
(b) to ski
(c) skiing
(d) to skiing

26. Mencius is famous for his argument _____ most humans are inherently good.

(a) that
(b) what
(c) which
(d) whose

27. In the warm, crystal-clear waters of the tropics, coral reefs flourish, _____ vast areas.

(a) covered
(b) covering
(c) have covered
(d) to be covered

28. Poor prospects in the domestic job market have prompted many young people _____ for work overseas.

(a) search
(b) searched
(c) to search
(d) searching

29. Sandra really annoyed me, but I _____ and did not say anything.

(a) control myself managed
(b) managed to control myself
(c) myself controlling managed
(d) controlling myself managed

30. Last year, all the profits from the sale of the book _____ donated to a charity.

(a) is
(b) are
(c) was
(d) were

31. Animals that blend into their environment have the advantage _____ by predators.

(a) to be not easily detected
(b) not to be detected easily
(c) of not being easily detected
(d) of being not to be detected easily

32. People are not certain _____ the economy can improve in the near future.

(a) even
(b) since
(c) unless
(d) whether

33. Richard said that 25 dollars _____ considerably more than he expected to pay for a pair of socks.

(a) was
(b) were
(c) is being
(d) are being

34. It is the responsibility of parents or guardians to supervise _____ under their care while in the park.

(a) ones
(b) some
(c) those
(d) them

35. The professor gave _____ F to each student who did not turn in his or her term paper.

(a) a
(b) an
(c) any
(d) every

36. Conflicts between elephants are communicated by a display of aggression _____ they twirl their trunks or throw dust into the air.

(a) what
(b) which
(c) in what
(d) in which

37. Nowadays teachers consider themselves fortunate if they have just a few _____ studying.

(a) enjoying students in their class
(b) in their class students enjoying
(c) students in their class who enjoy
(d) students who enjoy in their class

38. There may be some decline in intelligence with age, but this is smaller and more limited in scope than _____.

(a) was once widely believed
(b) once being widely believed
(c) being widely believed once
(d) once widely it was believed

39. _____ to fit all head sizes, the hat is suitable for anyone.

(a) It is designed
(b) Designing
(c) To design
(d) Designed

40. _____ dates from an idea first conceived in the early 19th century.

(a) Computer
(b) The computer
(c) Any computer
(d) Each computer

Part III **Questions 41—45**

Identify the option that contains an awkward expression or an error in grammar.

41. (a) A: Hey, Iris, take a look at this article on nutrition in today's paper.
    (b) B: Don't tell me. It's the new National Institute of Health report, right?
    (c) A: That's right! It's all the latest on low-fat diets! How do you guess?
    (d) B: I read the article on the way home from work.

42. (a) A: Are you going out later?
    (b) B: I don't think so. I'm such tired.
    (c) A: Why? Were you up late last night?
    (d) B: Yes. I didn't go to sleep until 2 a.m.

43. (a) A: I don't think we can finish this project in time.
    (b) B: I agree, but what can we do about it?
    (c) A: We just need to tell the boss and explain why.
    (d) B: Then let's go now and sort things out to him.

44. (a) A: John, you're a T2 fan—are you going to the concert?
    (b) B: I don't know yet. I'm supposed you already have your tickets.
    (c) A: Actually, not yet. I'm going to buy them today.
    (d) B: Can I go to the concert with you? I don't know anybody else who's going.

45. (a) A: What do you think I should get Vanessa for Valentine's Day?
    (b) B: How about a card and a red rose?
    (c) A: Come on. Where's your imagination? All the guys buy flower.
    (d) B: I don't see anything wrong with that.

Part IV **Questions 46—50**

Identify the option that contains an awkward expression or an error in grammar.

46. (a) Recently, there have been protests about the cost of prescription drugs. (b) There has also been criticism about not having access to newly developed medicines. (c) Yet people are still not getting the medicines they need to stay healthily. (d) We need to do more to force the government to fix this problem.

47. (a) You need to be sensible if you intend to exert yourself in hot weather. (b) The hotter it is, the harder it is for you to get rid of excess heat, and the type of clothing you wear can make a big difference. (c) It is logical that if you wore lighter clothing when exercising, you will be cooler. (d) Everyone knows that, but few people realize that light clothing may actually save you from heat stroke and even death.

48. (a) Rocks provide clues about the nature and timing of the events that formed them. (b) Layer of rock, for instance, can tell us about an event that occurred millions of years ago. (c) Geologists are able to use this information to develop a larger picture of the processes that shaped the earth. (d) Then, they can better predict what geological events are likely to occur in the future.

49. (a) No one ever found out who murdered the old woman. (b) Many people thought it was Mr. Crawshank because he stood to gain the most from her death. (c) Certainly their animosity for each other was well known. (d) But if he be the murderer, surely he would have hidden his delight at the news of her death.

50. (a) Modern entertainment magic owes much to Jean Houdin, who opened a magic theater in Paris in the 1840s. (b) His specialty was the construction of machines that appeared to move and act as if were alive. (c) But he also displayed a gift for presentation which would set him apart from his peers. (d) In particular, his practice of appearing in a suit, rather than elaborate robes, has led many to see him as the first "modern" magician.

This is the end of the Grammar section. Do NOT move on to the next section until instructed to do so. You are NOT allowed to turn to any other section of the test.

VOCABULARY

DIRECTIONS

This part of the exam tests your vocabulary skills. You will have 15 minutes to complete the 50 questions. Be sure to follow the directions given by the proctor.

Part I   **Questions 1—25**

Choose the best answer for the blank.

1. A: I really like your new haircut.

    B: Thanks. It's _____ of you to say so.

    (a) nice
    (b) mild
    (c) ideal
    (d) pleasant

2. A: Can I help you _____ your groceries?

    B: Thank you. They are quite heavy.

    (a) buy
    (b) find
    (c) leave
    (d) carry

3. A: Is your teacher better today?

    B: No. He's still not in a very good _____.

    (a) sense
    (b) mood
    (c) manner
    (d) standard

4. A: What should I do if I can't keep my appointment?

    B: Let us know as soon as possible, and we'll _____.

    (a) repeat
    (b) return
    (c) respond
    (d) reschedule

5. A: I hope the hotel you booked has everything we need.

    B: Don't worry. It has great _____, such as a spa, bar and much more.

    (a) outfits
    (b) assets
    (c) services
    (d) facilities

6. A: I'm very sorry about the other day.

    B: There's no need to _____ an apology.

    (a) use
    (b) make
    (c) allow
    (d) spend

7. A: Why isn't the car moving?

    B: You have to _____ the parking brake.

    (a) start
    (b) release
    (c) position
    (d) accelerate

8. A: My skin is really _____ these days.

    B: You should apply moisturizing lotion right after you shower.

    (a) dry
    (b) soft
    (c) thin
    (d) tense

9. A: Could we have a table by the window?

B: I'm sorry, but the window tables are all _____.

(a) served
(b) shared
(c) crowded
(d) occupied

10. A: I know you're upset, but please don't cry.

B: I can't _____ it.

(a) help
(b) keep
(c) ensure
(d) save

11. A: Do you know where I should get off for the Stella Theater?

B: Sure, it's the third stop from here. Actually, I'm _____ there, too.

(a) posted
(b) headed
(c) directed
(d) forwarded

12. A: I thought that I _____ a better grade than this.

B: Well, go talk to the professor if you think it's too low.

(a) received
(b) intended
(c) deserved
(d) demanded

13. A: Can I _____ these trousers?

B: Of course. The fitting room's over there.

(a) try on
(b) put away
(c) wear out
(d) make over

14. A: How often do you _____?

B: I go to the gym every day.

(a) turn out
(b) take out
(c) work out
(d) figure out

15. A: Mount Seorak is breathtaking in the fall.

B: That's what I _____.

(a) hear
(b) plan
(c) meet
(d) grasp

16. A: Hello. Can I speak to someone about my account?

B: Everyone's busy right now. I'll have to _____ you on hold.

(a) ask
(b) tell
(c) put
(d) give

17. A: So, what did the judge decide?

B: The defendant was _____ and sentenced to 20 years in prison.

(a) acquitted
(b) convicted
(c) suspected
(d) prosecuted

18. A: Do you have any _____ to check in?

B: No, I only have one carry-on.

(a) luggage
(b) burden
(c) pack
(d) load

19. A: I think the office air conditioning is up too high.

B: Yeah. Let's go _____ it to the manager.

(a) call
(b) press
(c) lower
(d) mention

20. A: Hi, Charles. How's everything going?

B: Oh, I can't _____.

(a) argue
(b) dispute
(c) disagree
(d) complain

21. A: How soon will the curtain _____?

B: The performance will start in about five minutes.

(a) come down
(b) move over
(c) roll out
(d) go up

22. A: How are people prevented from sneaking guns into the building?

B: Guards at the entrance check everyone to see if they're _____.

(a) armed
(b) loaded
(c) equipped
(d) protected

23. A: Cathy is always fashionable, isn't she?

B: Yes. She has a(n) _____ for high fashion.

(a) legacy
(b) inkling
(c) penchant
(d) discipline

24. A: Jane isn't very sociable these days.

B: Well, she's been _____ with a lot of problems lately.

(a) getting through
(b) making away
(c) broken down
(d) caught up

25. A: Joseph thinks he's somebody since he got promoted.

B: I know. He's had a(n) _____ air about him ever since.

(a) acrimonious
(b) ignominious
(c) pretentious
(d) veracious

Part II Questions 26—50

Choose the best answer for the blank.

26. Woodwind instruments make sound when air is _____ through a mouthpiece.

    (a) opened
    (b) drawn
    (c) added
    (d) blown

27. Rest and proper care are needed to _____ from the flu.

    (a) return
    (b) excuse
    (c) recover
    (d) manage

28. High heels should be _____ since they can cause foot deformities.

    (a) muffled
    (b) checked
    (c) proposed
    (d) discouraged

29. Students can _____ greatly from regular use of dictionaries.

    (a) differ
    (b) benefit
    (c) instruct
    (d) motivate

30. People who eat a balanced, nutritious breakfast are usually _____ than those who do not.

    (a) frailer
    (b) denser
    (c) greedier
    (d) healthier

31. Every time your heart _____, blood is pushed through the arteries.

    (a) ticks
    (b) beats
    (c) turns
    (d) strikes

32. The house was _____ vacant for three months until a new owner moved in.

    (a) left
    (b) met
    (c) sold
    (d) taken

33. Parents should be _____ and treat every child equally.

    (a) biased
    (b) obedient
    (c) impartial
    (d) intolerant

34. Drawing pictures and telling stories were probably the earliest forms of creative _____.

    (a) expression
    (b) suggestion
    (c) application
    (d) preparation

35. At the last soccer game, the _____ called a lot of offsides.

    (a) referee
    (b) advisor
    (c) inspector
    (d) supervisor

36. The court _____ its original decision and freed the man.

(a) conformed
(b) restricted
(c) curtailed
(d) reversed

37. Understanding the links between culture and communication is _____ for passing this linguistics course.

(a) vital
(b) fatal
(c) secure
(d) delicate

38. Most people _____ a mortgage with a bank before they buy a house.

(a) entrust
(b) confine
(c) arrange
(d) delegate

39. The World Business Trade course is designed to teach you how to _____ sales deals successfully.

(a) hassle
(b) confer
(c) charm
(d) negotiate

40. In a(n) _____ and stable family unit, a child develops a sense of personal integrity and security.

(a) fragile
(b) dainty
(c) eligible
(d) affectionate

41. The protest became violent as demonstrators _____ with police.

(a) clustered
(b) pinched
(c) clashed
(d) raced

42. Body weight usually _____ throughout the day, such that people have different weights at different times of day.

(a) endures
(b) acquires
(c) preserves
(d) fluctuates

43. The baby _____ his arms toward his mother because he wanted to be picked up from his crib.

(a) enticed
(b) clutched
(c) stretched
(d) expanded

44. The first report on recent human rights abuses _____ in the country has just been published.

(a) crammed
(b) committed
(c) discharged
(d) appropriated

45. Electricity, water and other utilities will be _____ on your monthly bill.

(a) augmented
(b) transcribed
(c) solidified
(d) itemized

46. The word "music" _____ from "Muse," which is a Greek word for a goddess who presides over some form of artistic endeavor.

(a) derives
(b) conveys
(c) modifies
(d) formulates

47. Groundwater _____ has led to a national water crisis.

(a) depletion
(b) allowance
(c) conservation
(d) reinforcement

48. The venom of some species of spiders is so _____ that a victim can die within minutes if not treated immediately.

(a) lethal
(b) wicked
(c) terminal
(d) obnoxious

49. British authorities are readying new laws that will give police greater powers toward _____ terror attacks.

(a) debasing
(b) thwarting
(c) immolating
(d) deteriorating

50. Shopping for groceries at discount stores is one way to be _____ and save money.

(a) frugal
(b) scanty
(c) scabby
(d) meager

This is the end of the Vocabulary section. Do NOT move on to the Reading Comprehension section until instructed to do so. You are NOT allowed to turn to any other section of the test.

READING
COMPREHENSION

Part I **Questions 1—16**

Read the passage. Then choose the option that best completes the passage.

---

1. Harwood University is an accredited cyber university that offers the atmosphere and environment of a traditional classroom enhanced by the added flexibility of online education. We offer bachelor's degrees in some of the most highly competitive fields, such as business administration, education, human services and information technology. Now you can obtain a diploma even if you work full time or live a busy life. Harwood University can _____.

   (a) guarantee a high salary
   (b) fit education into your life
   (c) train you for a medical career
   (d) supply technological assistance

2. Aristotle once said that philosophy begins by _____.
   If this is so, then children must be the world's greatest philosophers because children are known to ask questions that are not always easy for adults to answer. For example, "Why do people exist? Why was I born a human and not a frog?" or "What was the name of the world's first person?" are questions a child might ask. Although these questions seem simple, they raise some very complex philosophical issues.

   (a) reading widely
   (b) asking questions
   (c) offering criticism
   (d) expressing wonder

3. In the past, a clearly defined political model existed, whereby it was easy to distinguish whether a political party was left-wing or right-wing. On the left side of politics, you had anarchism, communism and socialism, and on the right you had liberalism, conservatism and fascism. Today, this model _____. Several other ideologies have emerged that do not readily fit into either the left or right side of politics, such as populism, libertarianism and environmentalism.

   (a) is the standard used by the media
   (b) clearly represents public opinion
   (c) tends to be followed too closely
   (d) does not reflect current trends

4. Unemployment in America is on the rise while _____.
   Employers are hiring fewer workers because they can have their existing employees work
   longer hours. In the Detroit Metropolitan area, the average employee works 47.5 hours
   every week. But those working for the auto manufacturer Sazarn have a regular 50-hour
   week, and in some factories workers are putting in 60 hours a week. The United Auto
   Workers estimates that 59,000 automobile jobs would be created if the plants were on a
   recommended 40-hour week.

   (a) the hours of those with jobs are growing longer
   (b) the dependence on immigrant workers is rising
   (c) the number of low-paid auto workers is increasing
   (d) the amount of shareholder investment is decreasing

5. Although water is the only fluid that we need to stay alive, drinking certain other
   fluids provides many health benefits as well. Milk, for instance, can provide you with
   protein and calcium, while fruit juice can give you a little in the way of vitamins and
   fiber. However, other fluids, such as coffee, tea, beer and soda might be categorized as
   unhealthy. This is because they _____.

   (a) contain few or no calories
   (b) contain harmful ingredients
   (c) use very little artificial flavoring
   (d) give you other kinds of benefits

6. In 1829, a man by the name of Louis Braille _____. He
   developed an alphabet consisting of raised dots which represented letters and punctuation
   marks. By running their fingertips along the dots, blind people could read. Braille, as it
   later became known, was not readily accepted at first, but by 1932 it was used in many
   schools for the blind.

   (a) began to work on a new medical treatment
   (b) discovered a set of ancient writing systems
   (c) started a vocational school for illiterate adults
   (d) invented a system of communication for the blind

7. African art relics are increasingly valued and coveted for their intrinsic beauty and artistic merit. However, this greater appreciation has _____.
Gravesites have been robbed, archaeologically sensitive areas have been plundered, and precious relics have ended up in the hands of wealthy private collectors. The problem is not a new one; ancestral sites have been pillaged and artifacts stolen for decades, despite the bans on the exportation of cultural property that exist in many African states. Now, with the soaring demand for African relics, it is likely that much of Africa's cultural heritage will disappear into private hands.

(a) had a detrimental effect on the African economy
(b) meant that African art is too expensive for tourists
(c) been a windfall for museums displaying the treasures
(d) attracted the attention of a growing number of looters

8.

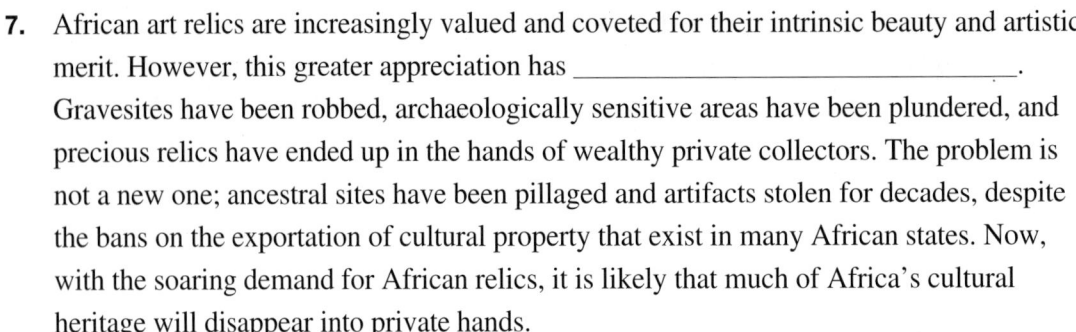

Dear Mr. and Mrs. Brown,

Since 1980, our organization, Rural Life, has been bringing underprivileged children from their crowded urban homes to a country ranch for two weeks of fresh air and sunshine. Our research shows that _____ enriches the lives of these inner-city children and leaves them feeling healthier and more fulfilled. For only $350, you can bring joy to an underprivileged child with the gift of a rural experience.
Please call our number or write to us today.

Sincerely,
Gerald R. Miller
President, Rural Life

(a) working in the inner city
(b) being exposed to rural life
(c) having a good summer job
(d) taking part in outdoor sports

9. Body temperature is controlled by the circulation of blood. The production and loss of body heat are balanced out by heat transfer through the bloodstream which is accomplished by _____. When the human body becomes overheated, the vessels dilate and an increased volume of blood flows through the skin. Heat is then able to spread more rapidly through the skin, dropping one's body temperature. When a person is cold, their blood vessels shrink, diverting blood from the skin to reduce heat loss.

(a) either perspiring or shivering
(b) adjusting the body's temperature
(c) varying the width of blood vessels
(d) changing the bloodstream's composition

10. Toronto will host the first in a series of anti-poverty concerts scheduled for this summer at multiple venues around the globe, which also include Tokyo and Johannesburg later in the summer. The announcement of the remaining host cities is due on Tuesday. Canadian organizers verified that the Toronto concert will be held on July 2 but would not provide any further information. The worldwide series of concerts _____. The events are aimed at those who might not otherwise fully recognize the seriousness of the issue.

(a) is likely to become an annual event
(b) should make a large profit for organizers
(c) has seen decreased attendance numbers
(d) is meant to help spread the anti-poverty message

11. Improvisation—spontaneous creation of musical passages—has been called "the lifeblood of jazz." Yet this central jazz concept is often misunderstood by laypeople. Often they see improvisation as unrelated to any musical structure or underlying composition as if it were a musical free-for-all, played without rules or any form of restraint. This is far from the truth however. Jazz improvisation invariably involves

_____.

(a) more playing from the heart than classical music
(b) following a chord sequence and preexisting melody
(c) radical experimentation beyond set musical patterns
(d) pulsating rhythms derived from African tribal melodies

12. I was naive to have thought that I'd find my "African-American" identity in Paris. But at that time, it seemed like a good idea. America was for me a country divided between black and white, a country that judged me only by the color of my skin. On the other hand, Paris represented liberation and equality—that is, until I got there. What I found was indifference and isolation. It's one thing to be wrongly judged because you are black, but to be completely ignored, well, that seemed somehow even worse. And it wasn't just in Paris. Generally, in Europe, a black American exile seeking freedom soon discovers

_____.

(a) much less prejudice and racism
(b) that equality exists in his mind alone
(c) a desire to adopt a European identity
(d) an identity that was not available at home

13. The revolution in art that impressionism represented did not arise solely from the artistic skills of key individual painters. Other historic forces were also at play. For one thing, impressionism emerged after half a century of some of the most dramatic innovations in pigment manufacturing that the visual arts had ever seen. This meant that new materials were presenting artists with new possibilities. Impressionist painters could not have produced what they did _____.

(a) without the introduction of new materials
(b) if the wealthy had not purchased their art
(c) without the ingenuity of masters like Monet
(d) if fine arts academies had not supported them

14. The Food and Drug Administration (FDA) is alerting healthcare experts and patients treated with Ruxate to reports of an increased risk of a fatal central nervous system viral infection. Patients presently being treated with Ruxate, who experience any significant changes in vision, balance or coordination, are advised to promptly consult their physician. While the medication has not yet been recalled, the FDA is working with Healthtech, the drug's sponsor, to gather data on risk potential. In addition, the FDA is also asking all healthcare professionals to _____.

(a) contact Healthtech regarding alternative drug and treatment options
(b) prescribe Ruxate for viruses afflicting the central nervous system
(c) report any adverse events associated with the drug
(d) administer the drug to prevent further complications

15. British ministers have been criticized for "misleading" the public regarding the success of their city academies program. An evaluation of the first 11 privately sponsored academies by consultants at Watson & Company shows that the academies are not functioning as effectively as expected. _____, the government dismisses such accusations, maintaining that academies a indeed bringing about "noteworthy changes" to conventional classroom culture. The academies, costing an average of 25 million dollars to build, were established to raise education levels in impoverished urban areas.

(a) However
(b) Similarly
(c) Therefore
(d) Otherwise

16. The way your goals are picked is as important as the goals themselves. If you allow others to pick your goals for you, your chances of not measuring up will increase greatly. _____, if you take a strong leadership role in setting your goals, you will have a better success rate because you will know better than anyone else what is right for you and what you can conceivably accomplish.

(a) On the other hand
(b) In the meantime
(c) For instance
(d) In any case

Part II **Questions 17—37**

Read the passage and the question. Then choose the option that best answers the question.

17. One day last May, photographers from across the US—rookies and Pulitzer Prize winners alike—were invited to tell the story of their lives, their communities and what it means to be American through digital photographs. The stunningly compelling images from this historic shoot, alongside essays by prominent writers, are now compiled in *One Day in America*, one of the most anticipated publications of the year.

Q : What is the advertisement about?

(a) A tourist guide for America
(b) A book of photos and essays
(c) A guide to good photography
(d) Pictures of celebrated landmarks

18. Preschool teachers must be aware of classroom dynamics and the ways children interact at all times. At the preschool level, groups should be small, with children in pairs or trios. In most cases, groups of four or more are too large. Note that group diversity should be maximized. Children of different ability levels, genders, language skills, and ethnic and cultural backgrounds should be mixed together.

Q : What is the topic of the passage?

(a) The types of afterschool activities for preschoolers
(b) The ideal size and composition of preschool groups
(c) The need to expose preschoolers to foreign cultures
(d) The problems preschoolers have in new environments

19. Trying to figure out which insurance plan is right for you? WowInsurance is a free service that allows you to compare hundreds of the nation's leading life insurance companies in just a few easy steps. We have the nation's fastest and easiest online service to compare insurance rates from the largest pool of life insurance companies available. Just log on to wowinsurance.com and see for yourself. Helping you make a smart and informed decision about your insurance needs is always our biggest priority!

Q : What is being advertised?

(a) An insurance company providing the lowest rates
(b) A company selling life insurance over the Internet
(c) A search tool for locating local insurance companies
(d) An online service offering insurance rate comparisons

20.

Dear Mr. Kim:

We received details from Mr. Lee, who has recently returned home from your country, stating that you would be interested in our electric fans. The enclosed catalogue will give you information on our complete product line. Please note that for payments we require that all transactions be based on an irrevocable letter of credit. We look forward to hearing from you soon.

Sincerely,
Tina Collins
Manager, Electric Fans Corporation

Q : What is the purpose of the letter?

(a) To return a shipment of a product
(b) To process import taxes and duties
(c) To check on a customer's line of credit
(d) To inform Mr. Kim about products and payment

21. Due to the easy access to so many images on the Internet, copyright owners' rights to these images are often forgotten. Pursuing offenders can be costly and has often not been undertaken. But now, technology is catching up with image thieves. Some copyrighted images are now encoded with a digital watermark so that it is possible to detect their unlawful use if they are published without the owners' consent.

Q : What is the passage mainly about?

(a) A new method for protecting copyrights
(b) The need to be careful about copyrights
(c) The best way to download images free
(d) Software for enhancing image quality

22. The next edition of Channel 10's most acclaimed program, *Insight*, looks at a highly classified spy agency in order to disclose how government organizations use surveillance technologies to monitor dissident citizens. Raw interviews with ex-spies, as well as with scientists who have developed voice recognition software, provide a flabbergasting insight into the new paradigm of "information warfare." Check your local listings for more details and the program schedule.

Q : What is the program mainly about?

(a) Personal confessions of former spies
(b) A look at warfare from a spy's point of view
(c) Methods for uncovering government secrets
(d) Technology now being used to spy on people

23. One of the oldest and simplest multi-cell forms of life on earth is worms, of which there are thousands of different kinds. Some worms eat small plants and animals, whereas others feed on decomposing matter. Still others exist as parasites inside various animals and plants, causing a number of diseases. Most types have a well-developed sense of touch and specialized organs that respond to chemicals in their surroundings. Also, many have a sense of sight, with eyes or eyespots on the head.

Q : Which of the following is correct about worms according to the passage?

(a) They are difficult to recognize.
(b) There are many kinds of them.
(c) They are poisonous to animals.
(d) They lack specialized organs.

24. A natural athlete, Terry Fox, after developing a form of bone cancer in 1980, had his right leg surgically removed from the knee down. During his recovery, he decided to do a cross-Canada run to boost cancer awareness. Terry began this "Marathon of Hope" on April 12, 1980, but his unyielding march was halted on September 1 of that year, after cancer spread to his lungs. He passed away on June 28, 1981. Today, Terry's heroic perseverance is commemorated through numerous awards, research fellowships and the annual Terry Fox Run, held in 60 nations around the world.

Q : According to the passage, why did Terry Fox end his "Marathon of Hope?"
(a) Cancer progressed to his lungs.
(b) His leg was amputated above the knee.
(c) His pace caused him to collapse.
(d) Not enough money was collected.

25. Renovated only six months ago, Sandy Beach Resort now has a viewing deck, a new restaurant and an extra swimming pool. All rooms have been refurbished, and inside each you will find a living room with a large sofa, big-screen TV, DVD player, coffee table and decorative fireplace. Serviced by an executive ferry from midtown Manhattan, Sandy Beach Resort is your own private getaway.

Q : Which of the following is correct about Sandy Beach Resort?
(a) It has different types of rooms.
(b) It was first built six months ago.
(c) It has an exclusive private beach.
(d) It provides transportation from Manhattan.

26. Midsummer's Eve is probably the most popular festival day in Sweden, together with Christmas. Midsummer is an old pagan celebration, dating back to the Viking era, and is celebrated on the longest day of the year (summer solstice), signifying that summer has reached its halfway point. It was originally a fertility rite to promote a good harvest in the autumn. These days it is better known as a national holiday, when family and friends meet to eat herring and fresh potatoes and to drink beer.

Q : Which of the following is correct about Midsummer's Eve?
(a) It is intended to promote a high birth rate.
(b) It has been celebrated since the Viking era.
(c) It is more popular than Christmas in Sweden.
(d) It is celebrated on the shortest day of the year.

27. In 1992, I was amazed to learn that Digitone had sent the first text message. So amazed, in fact, that in 1994 after my graduation, I did everything I could to get a job at Digitone. I was successful, and in two years I rose to become the company's product manager for text messaging. Text messaging was bigger than ever, but Digitone was not going in the direction I thought it should, and I felt confined by such a large organization. That's why in 1998, I left the company to write my book *Messaging for the Masses*. It sold 30,000 copies within a few months.

Q : Which of the following is correct according to the passage?

(a) In 1994, the writer became a product manager at Digitone.
(b) The writer did not expect text messaging to be so important.
(c) The writer quit working at Digitone to write about text messaging.
(d) Working for a large organization gave the writer a sense of accomplishment.

28. Despite the apparent chaos in the financial markets, authorities say donations are up at Crown University. Walter Knight, the university's chief financial officer and treasurer of the CU Foundation, says almost $214 million was given to the university and the foundation for the fiscal year ending June 30. Total private giving rose 12 percent from 2007, and giving among alumni and friends of the university increased by more than 15 percent—or nearly $13 million—from 2007. The university is in the midst of its largest fundraising campaign ever. The campaign, called Bright Futures, was launched in the summer of 2007 and has a target of $2.25 billion.

Q : Which is correct according to the passage?

(a) Private donations to the university rose 12 percent from 2007.
(b) Alumni and friends gave the university $13 million in 2007.
(c) Bright Futures is an institution that gave huge donations to the university.
(d) The university reached the target of $2.25 billion in its donation fund.

29. The following documents are required of minors when applying for a passport: birth certificate, marriage certificate of parents, identification cards of mother and father, and consent form signed by parents or legal guardian(s). Minors 15 or younger must come to the passport office accompanied by at least one parent or legal guardian. Minors over 15 may apply alone for a passport with a letter of consent signed by both mother and father or legal guardian(s).

Q : Which of the following is correct according to the requirements?

(a) A 14-year-old need not bring a guardian to apply for a passport.
(b) Minors must bring their parents' marriage certificate with them.
(c) Minors do not need a birth certificate if accompanied by parents.
(d) A 16-year-old can apply for a passport without a letter of consent.

30.

Dear Sir or Madam:

I read your letter yesterday from a woman seeking help for her depressed aging father. Her situation reminded me of my own, and I thought my experience could help her. In his last years, my father became depressed, and I did not know what to do to cheer him up. Then my sister-in-law came up with a wonderful idea. She assembled a collage of pictures from his life. He spent countless hours gazing at the collage with a faraway, happy expression on his face that let us know he was remembering happier times. Perhaps that woman's father would enjoy something like that as well.

Sincerely,
Mark in Westview

Q : What does the writer recommend to the woman with an aging father?

(a) Making a picture collage for him
(b) Coming up with a surprise for his birthday
(c) Talking with him for hours to cheer him up
(d) Writing a letter to help him overcome depression

31. Although the 5th centennial in 1992 of Christopher Columbus' first voyage to the Indies was viewed as a once-in-a-lifetime occasion to appreciate history and learn new truths, the actual event aroused more contention than enlightenment. Many arguments were discordantly raised and few discoveries were made. Surprisingly, the most controversial disputes were over this deceptively simple question: What was Christopher Columbus really like?

Q : What was supposed to happen at the Columbus anniversary?

(a) Columbus' first voyage to the Indies was going to be retraced.
(b) People were expected to celebrate the past and learn new facts.
(c) The event was expected to be more contentious than enlightening.
(d) People were supposed to debate about what Columbus was really like.

32. As a scientist, Leonardo da Vinci understood the importance of keeping scientific records better than anybody else in his time. So even if he never completed planned treatises on a variety of subjects, his undeveloped theories were contained in numerous notebooks. These were difficult for his contemporaries to comprehend, however, and that meant Da Vinci's findings were not well-known in his own lifetime. Had they been known, they would likely have revolutionized the scientific world of the 16th century.

Q : Which of the following is correct according to the passage?

(a) Da Vinci's records were based on scientific experiments.
(b) Da Vinci revolutionized the 16th-century scientific world.
(c) Da Vinci's scientific theories were not easy to understand.
(d) Da Vinci completed most of his planned scientific treatises.

33. There are many misunderstandings about Che Guevara's arrest. The US involvement in Bolivian affairs was far-reaching, but the US contribution to the military overthrow of Che's guerilla operations was minimal. To be exact, the US-trained-and-led Bolivian Rangers were responsible for capturing Che and almost routing his small forces in October 1967. However, Che's guerilla operations were already defeated prior to the arrival of the Rangers, so the role of the US was not crucial.

Q : What can be inferred from the passage?

(a) The Bolivian government was largely self-sufficient.
(b) Che would not have been captured without US help.
(c) US involvement in capturing Che tends to be exaggerated.
(d) Che had already surrendered before the Rangers intervened.

34. The Portuguese and Spanish were not the only ones pioneering the seas in the 1400s. In 1405 when the Portuguese and Spanish still believed that sailing past Cape Bojador on Africa's west coast meant burning in boiling seas, a Chinese sailor and explorer named Zheng He was sailing far and wide throughout the Indian Ocean. Zheng opened trade routes between China and more than 20 countries, including some in East Africa and Arabia, dealing in rare and foreign merchandise.

Q : What can be inferred from the passage?

(a) The Portuguese and Spanish traded with Zheng He.
(b) Zheng He brought many exotic animals back to China.
(c) The Portuguese and Spanish discovered Cape Bojador in 1405.
(d) Chinese sea exploration was once superior to that of the Europeans.

35. Our planet's environment is in a constant state of flux. While gradual natural changes impact species only slightly, rapid changes can endanger a species' existence. And the main cause of rapid changes is invariably some form of human activity. Loss of microbes in tropical forest soils, polluted aquatic habitats and global climate changes— these are all results of human activity, and all of these can lead to the loss of species.

Q : What can be inferred from the passage?

(a) Human activities need to be better managed to protect species.
(b) Rapid environmental changes are necessary for human survival.
(c) It is hard to gauge the impact of human activity on other animals.
(d) Industrial development does not affect already endangered species.

36. The Consumer Rights Center has revealed that a change in packaging milk is cheating consumers. Milk Factory's new plastic milk carton, modeled after the obsolete glass bottles, is the same price and height as its one-liter cardboard package, but holds 100ml less milk. Consumer Rights Center president David Russell criticized Milk Factory's packaging change "a cheap commercial trick that intends to deceive buyers" and is urging consumers to "fight back by refusing purchase of the given brand."

Q : What can be inferred from the news report?

(a) Old style milk container designs keep milk fresher.
(b) Customers prefer milk in glass than in plastic containers.
(c) People have been tricked into paying more money for milk.
(d) The milk packaged in the new container is lower in quality.

37. One of the most significant events affecting medieval European culture was colonization. Following Europe's discovery of the Americas, Europeans at first arrogantly regarded the New World as antithetical to all that was deemed civilized. Yet the discovery of other civilizations and cultures gradually provoked debate and self-reflection; European thinkers were forced to reassess Europe's position in the world and to question all Eurocentric assumptions. This reassessment of values influenced every aspect of European culture and effectively changed it forever.

Q : What can be inferred from the passage?

(a) The decline of Christianity in Europe began with colonization.
(b) Conquered American cultures regarded Europeans as uncivilized.
(c) The discovery of new cultures undermined Europe's sense of superiority.
(d) European colonization was fueled by the desire for cultural enlightenment.

Part III   **Questions 38—40**

Read the passage. Then identify the option that does NOT belong.

38. People have always used plants to treat diseases and other ailments. (a) Today, botanists continue to search for plants that may provide new medicines, but they do it with care. (b) Botany—the study of plants—was considered to be a branch of medicine until the mid-1800s. (c) Steps are taken to preserve plant species from the risk of extinction as a result of being over-harvested for medicines. (d) Fortunately, the medicinal ingredients of most plants used for medical purposes can be synthesized, which lowers the demand for plants in the wild.

39. The idea that humans are the only savagely violent primates that kill their own kind no longer holds. (a) Research has found that other primates also kill their own species. (b) Some primates show "semanticity," or the use of symbols, to signify objects and actions in their communications. (c) Some even demonstrate tool-making skills to design homemade weapons. (d) Others engage in what can only be referred to as warfare-organized, proactive group coercion directed at other populations.

40. Although Constantin Alajalov was born and studied art in Russia, the revolution there forced him to immigrate to the US. (a) During his lifetime, he was overlooked by art historians and considered a non-person by the Soviet Union. (b) He eventually established himself as a magazine cover artist, with drawings appearing on *The Saturday Evening Post* and *The New Yorker*. (c) This is a particularly remarkable achievement, as these magazines never used the same artists except Alajalov. (d) His career continued to thrive, and he became one of the most famous magazine illustrators of the 20th century.

This is the end of the Reading Comprehension section. Please remain seated until the proctor has instructed otherwise. You are NOT allowed to turn to any other section of the test.

Answer Keys

🎧 Listening Comprehension

1	(a)	2	(d)	3	(d)	4	(c)	5	(b)	6	(b)	7	(d)	8	(c)	9	(a)	10	(c)
11	(d)	12	(a)	13	(c)	14	(a)	15	(c)	16	(b)	17	(d)	18	(a)	19	(d)	20	(a)
21	(a)	22	(c)	23	(d)	24	(c)	25	(b)	26	(b)	27	(d)	28	(c)	29	(b)	30	(d)
31	(c)	32	(a)	33	(d)	34	(a)	35	(b)	36	(a)	37	(d)	38	(b)	39	(b)	40	(d)
41	(c)	42	(c)	43	(d)	44	(b)	45	(d)	46	(c)	47	(a)	48	(b)	49	(d)	50	(d)
51	(d)	52	(c)	53	(c)	54	(b)	55	(c)	56	(c)	57	(d)	58	(d)	59	(b)	60	(c)

🎙 Grammar

1	(b)	2	(d)	3	(b)	4	(b)	5	(b)	6	(b)	7	(b)	8	(c)	9	(c)	10	(d)
11	(b)	12	(b)	13	(c)	14	(a)	15	(d)	16	(c)	17	(a)	18	(c)	19	(d)	20	(d)
21	(b)	22	(d)	23	(a)	24	(a)	25	(a)	26	(a)	27	(b)	28	(a)	29	(c)	30	(d)
31	(b)	32	(b)	33	(b)	34	(d)	35	(a)	36	(a)	37	(b)	38	(a)	39	(d)	40	(c)
41	(c)	42	(b)	43	(c)	44	(d)	45	(b)	46	(d)	47	(b)	48	(c)	49	(d)	50	(d)

🔡 Vocabulary

1	(b)	2	(d)	3	(a)	4	(c)	5	(a)	6	(c)	7	(b)	8	(b)	9	(b)	10	(c)
11	(b)	12	(c)	13	(c)	14	(c)	15	(b)	16	(b)	17	(a)	18	(a)	19	(b)	20	(c)
21	(a)	22	(b)	23	(b)	24	(c)	25	(c)	26	(d)	27	(b)	28	(d)	29	(d)	30	(b)
31	(b)	32	(c)	33	(d)	34	(b)	35	(d)	36	(b)	37	(b)	38	(b)	39	(c)	40	(b)
41	(d)	42	(a)	43	(b)	44	(c)	45	(c)	46	(a)	47	(b)	48	(a)	49	(a)	50	(b)

📖 Reading Comprehension

1	(a)	2	(c)	3	(b)	4	(d)	5	(b)	6	(c)	7	(b)	8	(d)	9	(a)	10	(b)
11	(a)	12	(c)	13	(a)	14	(d)	15	(c)	16	(c)	17	(b)	18	(a)	19	(d)	20	(c)
21	(b)	22	(a)	23	(a)	24	(b)	25	(a)	26	(b)	27	(a)	28	(c)	29	(d)	30	(d)
31	(d)	32	(b)	33	(d)	34	(a)	35	(c)	36	(c)	37	(d)	38	(d)	39	(c)	40	(d)

TEPS 등급표

등급	점수	영역	능력검정기준(Description)
1+급 Level 1+	901~990	전반	**외국인으로서 최상급 수준의 의사소통 능력** 교양 있는 원어민에 버금가는 정도로 의사소통이 가능하고 전문분야 업무에 대처할 수 있음. (Native Level of Communicative Competence)
1급 Level 1	801~900	전반	**외국인으로서 거의 최상급 수준의 의사소통 능력** 단기간 집중 교육을 받으면 대부분의 의사소통이 가능하고 전문분야 업무에 별 무리 없이 대처할 수 있음. (Near-Native Level of Communicative Competence)
2+급 Level 2+	701~800	전반	**외국인으로서 상급 수준의 의사소통 능력** 단기간 집중 교육을 받으면 일반분야 업무를 큰 어려움 없이 수행할 수 있음. (Advanced Level of Communicative Competence)
2급 Level 2	601~700	전반	**외국인으로서 중상급 수준의 의사소통 능력** 중장기간 집중 교육을 받으면 일반분야 업무를 큰 어려움 없이 수행할 수 있음. (High Intermediate Level of Communicative Competence)
3+급 Level 3+	501~600	전반	**외국인으로서 중급 수준의 의사소통 능력** 중장기간 집중 교육을 받으면 한정된 분야의 업무를 큰 어려움 없이 수행할 수 있음. (Mid Intermediate Level of Communicative Competence)
3급 Level 3	401~500	전반	**외국인으로서 중하급 수준의 의사소통 능력** 중장기간 집중 교육을 받으면 한정된 분야의 업무를 다소 미흡하지만 큰 지장 없이 수행할 수 있음. (Low Intermediate Level of Communicative Competence)
4+급 Level 4	201~400	전반	**외국인으로서 하급 수준의 의사소통 능력** 장기간의 집중 교육을 받으면 한정된 분야의 업무를 대체로 어렵게 수행할 수 있음. (Novice Level of Communicative Competence)
5+급 Level 5	10~200	전반	**외국인으로서 최하급 수준의 의사소통 능력** 단편적인 지식만을 갖추고 있어 의사소통이 거의 불가능함. (Near-Zero Level of Communicative Competence)

i-TEPS 미리보기

2009년 10월 18일 첫 시행!
국내 최초 통합 영어능력 평가 *integrated*-TEPS

의사소통에 필요한 듣기, 말하기, 읽기, 쓰기 능력을 통합하여 평가한다.

듣기, 말하기, 읽기, 쓰기 능력은 서로 밀접한 관계를 가진 요소로 듣기, 읽기 능력 혹은 말하기, 쓰기 능력만을 단순히 측정해서는 정확한 영어능력을 평가하기 어렵다. *i*-TEPS는 유기적인 연관성을 지닌 이 네 가지 의사소통 능력을 통합적으로 측정하여 수험자의 영어능력을 정확하게 평가한다.

변별력과 신뢰도가 있는 시험이다.

i-TEPS는 국내 최고 권위의 영어능력 평가로 듣기, 읽기 분야에서 탁월한 변별력을 인정받은 TEPS와 국내 최초 CBT 방식의 영어 말하기·쓰기 시험인 TEPS-Speaking & Writing의 성공 노하우를 바탕으로 개발되었다. 실전 영어능력을 보다 정밀하게 측정할 수 있도록 세분화된 채점 요소를 적용하고 있으며, 출제자와 채점자를 어학 분야의 최고 전문가들로 선정하여 높은 신뢰도와 탁월한 변별력을 지니고 있다.

실전 영어능력을 측정한다.

간단한 대화를 할 수 있는 능력부터 도표를 보고 발표하는 분석력과 구성력까지, 접하는 상황에 따라 필요한 영어능력도 다양하다. *i*-TEPS는 유학이나 비즈니스 등 특정한 분야에서의 영어 활용 능력을 집중적으로 평가하는 타 시험과는 달리, 비즈니스 상황을 포함한 다양한 영어 사용 환경을 재현하여 실질적으로 활용 가능한 영어능력을 평가한다.

경제성과 효율성을 갖춘 시험이다.

i-TEPS는 타 통합 영어능력 평가시험에 비해 응시료가 저렴하다. 한 번의 시험으로 듣기, 말하기, 읽기, 쓰기 능력을 종합적으로 평가하여 각각의 영역을 별도로 평가해야 하는 타 시험과 비교해도 응시료 부담이 적다. *i*-TEPS는 최소의 시간과 비용으로 수험자의 영어능력을 정확히 측정하는 높은 효율성을 갖춘 시험이다.

2009년 *i*-TEPS 정기시험 일정

회차	시험일자	정기접수기간	추가접수기간	성적발표일
1회	10. 18(일)	8. 31 ~ 9. 27	10. 5 ~ 10. 12	11. 13(금)
2회	11. 8(일)	9. 21 ~ 10. 18	10. 26 ~ 11. 1	12. 4(금)
3회	12. 13(일)	10. 26 ~ 11. 22	11. 30 ~ 12. 6	1. 8(금)

☞ *i*-TEPS 영역별 유형 및 설명

i-TEPS는 기존의 TEPS와 TEPS-Speaking & Writing 시험을 토대로 듣기, 말하기, 읽기, 쓰기 능력을 종합적으로 측정하는 통합형 시험으로 개발되었다. Listening, Grammar & Vocabulary, Reading, Speaking, Writing의 5개 영역에 걸쳐 약 3시간 동안 진행되며, 총 143문항, 400점 만점으로 구성되어 있다.

영역		문제유형	문항수	시간		총점
Listening	Part 1	짧은 대화를 듣고 이어질 대화로 가장 적절한 답 고르기	15	35분		80점
	Part 2	긴 대화를 듣고 질문에 가장 적절한 답 고르기	15			
	Part 3	담화를 듣고 질문에 가장 적절한 답 고르기	10			
Grammar & Vocabulary	Part 1	대화문의 빈칸에 가장 적절한 답 고르기	15	20분		20점
	Part 2	단문의 빈칸에 가장 적절한 답 고르기	15			
	Part 3	대화문의 빈칸에 가장 적절한 어휘 고르기	15			20점
	Part 4	단문의 빈칸에 가장 적절한 어휘 고르기	15			
Reading	Part 1	지문을 읽고 빈칸에 가장 적절한 답 고르기	10	40분		80점
	Part 2	지문을 읽고 질문에 가장 적절한 답 고르기 (1지문 1문항)	19			
	Part 3	지문을 읽고 질문에 가장 적절한 답 고르기 (1지문 2문항)	6			
Speaking	Part 1	간단한 질문에 대답하기	1(3)		답변 10초	100점
	Part 2	소리내어 읽기	1	준비 30초	답변 45초	
	Part 3	일상 대화 상황에서 질문에 답하기	1(5)	준비 15초	답변 10초	
	Part 4	그림 보고 연결하여 이야기하기	1	준비 60초	답변 60초	
	Part 5	도표 보고 발표하기	1	준비 120초	답변 90초	
Writing	Part 1	받아쓰기	1	10분		100점
	Part 2	이메일 쓰기	1	15분		
	Part 3	의견 쓰기	1	30분		
계						400점

TEPS

Test of English Proficiency
developed by
Seoul National University

● 넥서스 수준별 TEPS 맞춤 학습 프로그램

기출·독해

서울대 기출문제

서울대 텝스 관리위원회 텝스 최신기출 1200제 2017 문제집 3 | 서울대학교 TEPS관리위원회 문제 제공 | 352쪽 | 19,500원
서울대 텝스 관리위원회 텝스 최신기출 1200제 2017 해설집 3 | 서울대학교 TEPS관리위원회 문제 제공 · 넥서스 TEPS연구소 해설 | 480쪽 | 25,000원
서울대 텝스 관리위원회 텝스 최신기출 1200제 2016 문제집 2 | 서울대학교 TEPS관리위원회 문제 제공 | 352쪽 | 19,500원
서울대 텝스 관리위원회 텝스 최신기출 1200제 2016 해설집 2 | 서울대학교 TEPS관리위원회 문제 제공 · 넥서스 TEPS연구소 해설 | 480쪽 | 25,000원
서울대 텝스 관리위원회 텝스 최신기출 1200제 문제집 1 | 서울대학교 TEPS관리위원회 문제 제공 | 352쪽 | 19,500원
서울대 텝스 관리위원회 텝스 최신기출 1200제 해설집 1 | 서울대학교 TEPS관리위원회 문제 제공 · 넥서스 TEPS연구소 해설 | 480쪽 | 25,000원
서울대 텝스 관리위원회 공식기출 1000 Listening/ Grammar/ Reading | 서울대학교 TEPS관리위원회 문제 제공 | 19,000원/ 12,000원/ 16,000원
서울대 텝스 관리위원회 최신기출 1000 | 서울대학교 TEPS관리위원회 문제 제공 · 양준희 해설 | 628쪽 | 28,000원
서울대 텝스 관리위원회 최신기출 1200/SEASON 2~3 문제집 | 서울대학교 TEPS관리위원회 문제 제공 | 352쪽 | 19,500원
서울대 텝스 관리위원회 최신기출 1200/SEASON 2~3 해설집 | 서울대학교 TEPS관리위원회 문제 제공 · 넥서스 TEPS연구소 해설 | 472쪽 | 25,000원

실전·어휘

실전 모의고사

How to TEPS 영역별 끝내기 청해 | 테리 홍 지음 | 424쪽 | 19,800원
How to TEPS 영역별 끝내기 문법 | 장보금 · 써니 박 지음 | 260쪽 | 13,500원
How to TEPS 영역별 끝내기 어휘 | 양준희 지음 | 240쪽 | 13,500원
How to TEPS 영역별 끝내기 독해 | 김무룡 · 넥서스 TEPS연구소 지음 | 504쪽 | 25,000원

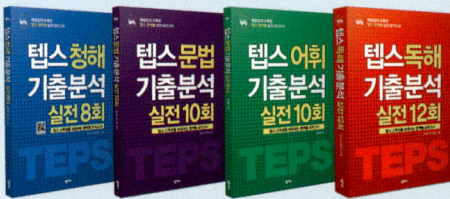

텝스 청해 기출 분석 실전 8회 | 넥서스 TEPS연구소 지음 | 296쪽 | 19,500원
텝스 문법 기출 분석 실전 10회 | 장보금 · 써니 박 지음 | 248쪽 | 14,000원
텝스 어휘 기출 분석 실전 10회 | 양준희 지음 | 252쪽 | 14,000원
텝스 독해 기출 분석 실전 12회 | 넥서스 TEPS연구소 지음 | 504쪽 | 25,000원

영역별

초급 (400~500점)

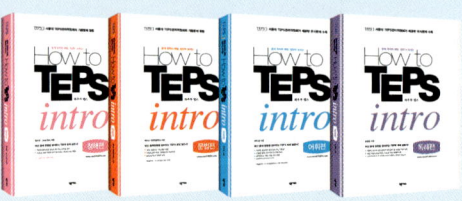

How to TEPS intro 청해편 | 강소영 · Jane Kim 지음 | 444쪽 | 22,000원
How to TEPS intro 문법편 | 넥서스 TEPS연구소 지음 | 424쪽 | 19,000원
How to TEPS intro 어휘편 | 에릭 김 지음 | 368쪽 | 15,000원
How to TEPS intro 독해편 | 한정림 지음 | 392쪽 | 19,500원

중급 (600~700점)

How to TEPS 실전 600 어휘편 · 청해편 · 문법편 · 독해편 | 서울대학교 TEPS
관리위원회 문제 제공(어휘), 이기헌(청해), 장보금·써니 박(문법), 황수경·넥서스 TEPS연
구소(독해) 지음 | 어휘: 15,000원, 청해: 19,800원, 문법: 17,500원, 독해: 19,000원
How to TEPS 실전 700 청해편 · 문법편 · 독해편 | 강소영 · 넥서스 TEPS연
구소(청해), 이신영 · 넥서스 TEPS연구소(문법), 오정우 · 넥서스 TEPS연구소
(독해) 지음 | 청해: 16,000원, 문법: 15,000원, 독해: 19,000원

종합서

한 권으로 끝내는 텝스 스타터 | 넥서스 TEPS연구소 지음 | 584쪽 | 22,000원
How to 텝스 초급용 모의고사 10회 | 넥서스 TEPS연구소 지음 | 296쪽 | 15,000원
How to 텝스 베이직 리스닝 | 고명희 · 넥서스 TEPS연구소 지음 | 320쪽 | 18,500원
How to 텝스 베이직 리딩 | 박미영 · 넥서스 TEPS연구소 지음 | 368쪽 | 19,500원

TEPS

서울대
텝스 관리위원회
최신기출
1000

서울대학교 TEPS관리위원회 문제 제공 | 양준희 해설

해설집

서울대학교
언어교육원
감수

넥서스

CD2

TEPS

서울대
텝스 관리위원회
최신기출
1000

1

M Excuse me, but do you have the time?
W _____

(a) It's twenty to seven.
(b) Right, it's on time.
(c) I won't be late.
(d) Yes, at 6:30.

SOLUTION

M 죄송하지만 몇 시죠?
W 7시 20분 전이에요.

⊞ 기출 POINT
Do you have the time?은 몇 시인지 묻는 말이다. 다른 표현으로
What time do you have?를 알아두자. 정관사 the가 없는 Do you
have time?은 '시간 있나요?'의 뜻으로 구분해 두어야 한다.
twenty to seven 7시 20분 전   **on time** 제시간에   정답 _(a)

2

W Ugh! I have such a terrible headache.
M _____

(a) I don't agree with that.
(b) Sorry to hear that.
(c) It isn't necessary.
(d) It'll be here soon.

SOLUTION

W 아휴, 두통이 너무 심해요.
M 안됐네요.

⊞ 기출 POINT
좋지 않은 일에 대한 유감의 표현을 묻는 문제이다. 상대방의 불행한 일
을 듣고 위로나 동정의 표현으로 (b) Sorry to hear that(그거 안됐네
요)을 쓴다. 위로 동정의 표현: Sorry to hear that./ It's a pity./
That's too bad.
such a terrible headache 아주 심한 두통   정답 _(b)

3

M How do you come to work?
W _____

(a) Let's take a taxi.
(b) It's an hour away.
(c) I came in a little late.
(d) I usually take the subway.

SOLUTION

M 출근은 어떻게 하세요?
W 보통 지하철을 타요.

⊞ 기출 POINT
일상적으로 반복되는 습관은 현재시제로 말하며 usually, often,
every day, always 등의 부사를 동반하는 경우가 많다. 질문과 같이
현재시제이며 usually를 사용한 (d)가 적절하다.
It's an hour away. 한 시간 거리이다.   **take a taxi/ the subway**
택시/ 지하철을 타다   정답 _(d)

4

W Guess what? I was promoted to office
manager.

M _____

(a) Maybe next time.
(b) I'm sorry about it.
(c) I'm happy for you.
(d) That's a good guess.

SOLUTION

W 있잖아요, 저 사무실 관리자로 승진했어요.
M 잘됐네요.

⊞ 기출 POINT

Guess what?은 You know what?과 같은 말로 의문형이지만 '저기, 있잖아'라는 뜻으로 이야기를 꺼낼 때 쓰는 말이다. 상대방의 기쁜 일을 함께 기뻐하는 응답으로 적절한 표현은 I'm happy for you이다. 반대로 좋지 않은 소식에 대한 응답으로는 (b)의 I'm sorry about it을 쓴다. **Guess what?** 있잖아. **promote** 승진시키다 **I'm happy for you.** 네가 잘되어서 기뻐.
정답 (c)

5

M Did anybody phone for me while I was out?

W _____

(a) Yes, a few showed up.
(b) No, not a single call.
(c) I have your number.
(d) I'll call later.

SOLUTION

M 제가 외출한 동안 저한테 온 전화가 있었나요?
W 아니요, 한 통도 없었는데요.

⊞ 기출 POINT

저한테 온 전화가 있었느냐는 말에 대한 응답으로 '한 통도 없었다'는 말이 적절하다. anybody라는 말에 집중하여 잘못 고를 수 있는 오답은 (a)의 '몇 명이 나타났다'는 말이다.
while ～하는 동안 **show up** 나타나다 **single** 하나의
정답 (b)

6

W Excuse me. You dropped your wallet.

M _____

(a) Oh, so I did. Thank you.
(b) That's not the one I wanted.
(c) Sorry, I forgot to bring mine.
(d) I have some money in my pocket.

SOLUTION

W 저기요. 지갑 떨어뜨리셨는데요.
M 이런, 그랬군요. 감사합니다.

⊞ 기출 POINT

누군가에게 지갑을 떨어뜨렸다고 알려 줄 때, 그 상황을 모르고 있었다면 '이런, 그랬군요'라는 말과 감사를 하는 것이 알맞다. Oh, so I did는 〈so+주어+조동사〉로 놀라면서 동의나 인정을 하는 표현이다.
So+조동사+주어: I visited Paris.—So did I. 나도 갔었어.
forget to ～할 것을 잊다
정답 (a)

7

M So, what have you been doing lately?

W _____

(a) It's been a while.
(b) I'll be just fine, thanks.
(c) I've been busy at work.
(d) That's nice of you to say.

SOLUTION

M 그래서, 요즘 어떻게 지내셨어요?
W 회사 일이 바빴어요.

⊞ 기출 POINT

요즘 근황을 묻는 질문에 질문과 같은 시제로 답한 (c)가 알맞다.
(a)는 시간이 얼마나 지났는지 묻는 질문에 대한 응답이 될 것이고,
(d)는 상대방의 친절한 말에 감사를 표시하는 말이다.
근황을 묻는 표현: How have you been doing lately?/ What have
you been up to lately?
lately 최근에 **while** (짧은) 동안, 잠시 **That's nice of you to say.**
그렇게 말해주니 감사해요. **정답** (c)

8

W Hello. This is Peggy. Is Mike home?

M _____

(a) He'll phone the office.
(b) Yes, I'm about to call him.
(c) Actually, he just stepped out.
(d) It was nice to hear from Mike.

SOLUTION

W 여보세요. 페기라고 하는데요. 마이크 집에 있나요?
M 실은 방금 나갔어요.

⊞ 기출 POINT

전화상에서는 자신이나 상대방을 가리키는 말로 인칭대명사를 쓰지 않
고 this를 쓴다. Is Mike home?에서 home은 부사로 쓰여서 집에 있
느냐는 말이 된다. '막 나갔다'는 (c)가 정답. be동사 의문문이므로 Yes
로 시작되는 (b)가 혼동을 줄 수 있는데 뒤의 내용이 맞지 않아 오답이다.
be about to 막 ~하려 하다 **step out** 밖으로 나가다 **hear from**
~에게서 소식을 듣다 **정답** (c)

9

M You're late! I always end up waiting for you!

W _____

(a) You wouldn't believe me anyway.
(b) I'm sorry I didn't wait longer.
(c) Let's change the role, then.
(d) That's not always the case.

SOLUTION

M 늦었잖아! 나는 항상 너를 기다리게 된다고!
W 항상 그런 건 아니잖아.

⊞ 기출 POINT

약속 시간에 늦은 사람에게 불만을 표시하고 있다. 가능한 응답은 (d) '항
상 그런 것은 아니다'이다. (a)는 '어쨌든 넌 날 믿지 않잖아'라는 뜻으로
내용과 무관한 말이다. '그럼, 역할을 바꾸자'는 (c)는 이 상황에서 의미
가 부정확하여 정답이 될 수 없다.
wouldn't believe 믿으려 하지 않다 **end up** 결국 ~하게 되다 **That's
not always the case.** 항상 그런 것은 아니다. **정답** (d)

10

W I don't think we can trust the salespeople at this dealership.

M _____

(a) But they're busy with another customer.
(b) I agree. They've been nothing but open.
(c) I've got a bad feeling about them, too.
(d) Buying a car is always a big decision.

SOLUTION

W 이 대리점 영업 사원들은 신뢰가 안 가는 것 같아요.
M 저도 이 사람들에 대해 안 좋은 느낌이 들었어요.

기출 POINT

좋지 않은 의견을 말할 때는 부정문의 형태로 I think we can't trust 라고 하지 않고 I don't think we can trust라고 쓰는 경우가 많다. 즉, not의 위치가 think 앞에 있다는 것에 유의해서 기억해 두자. 동의하는 내용의 (c)가 적절한 응답이다.

salespeople 판매원 **dealership** 판매 대리점 **nothing but+동사원형** ~만 할 뿐이다 **big decision** 결정하기 힘든 문제   정답_(c)

11

M I can't believe we have to work this Saturday.

W _____

(a) Well, I didn't.
(b) I'm working on it.
(c) No, I think we do.
(d) We have no other choice.

SOLUTION

M 이번 주 토요일에 일을 해야 하다니 믿을 수 없어요.
W 별 수 없잖아요.

기출 POINT

'토요일에 일을 해야 한다'고 불평하는 사람에게 해줄 수 있는 말로 적절한 것은 (d) '별 다른 수가 없잖아요'이다. (b)의 working on은 '~을 하는 중'이라는 뜻이므로 응답이 될 수 없다.

work on ~에 대한 일을 하다 **have no other choice** 다른 수가 없다   정답_(d)

12

W Now that you've visited my campus, what's your impression of it?

M _____

(a) It's bigger than I expected.
(b) I'll return the favor one day.
(c) It's not that far from my place.
(d) I couldn't agree with you more.

SOLUTION

W 우리 학교 교정에 와 보니까 인상이 어때?
M 기대했던 것보다 크네.

기출 POINT

Now (that)은 문장의 맨 앞에 서서 논리적이지는 않지만 이유를 나타내는 접속사로 쓰인다. 교정을 보고 느낀 자신의 감상을 말하는 (a)가 정답이다. '~에 대한 너의 인상, 감상'을 your impression of라고 말하는 것에 유의한다. (b)는 도움을 받았을 때 가능한 응답이고, (d)는 상대방의 말에 동의하는 표현으로 자주 나오니 기억해 두자.

now that ~이니까, ~인데 **return the favor** 은혜를 갚다 **couldn't agree with … more** ~와 전적으로 동감이다   정답_(a)

13

M	The door is locked, and I can't find the key!
W	_____

(a) See if it's unlocked.
(b) I'll lock it behind me.
(c) Don't forget to bring your key.
(d) There's a spare in the mailbox.

SOLUTION

M 문이 잠겼는데, 열쇠를 못 찾겠어!
W 우편함에 여분의 열쇠가 있어.

기출 POINT

'문이 잠겼다'는 말은 수동태를 써서 The door is locked라고 한다. 문이 잠겼고 열쇠를 찾을 수 없는 사람에게 해줄 말로 적절한 것은 '비상 열쇠가 있다'는 (d)이다. (b)는 '내가 나가면서 잠그겠다'는 말이므로 상황에 맞지 않는다.

be locked 잠기다 **see if** ~인지 보다 **lock it behind me** 내가 나가면서 잠그다 **spare** 예비품, 비상용품   정답_(d)

14

W	I'd like to put new carpeting in my living room.
M	_____

(a) Well, it does look good there.
(b) So, you've finished redecorating.
(c) Yes, it could do with re-carpeting.
(d) No, your carpeting is rather dingy.

SOLUTION

W 저희 집 거실에 카펫을 새로 깔고 싶어요.
M 맞아요. 새로 깔 때가 됐네요.

기출 POINT

could do with가 '~이 필요하다'는 뜻임을 알아야 풀 수 있는 문제이다. '새 카펫을 깔고 싶다'는 말에 동의하는 (c)가 가장 적절하다. (a)는 '거기에 잘 맞아 보인다'는 말이므로 부적절하다. (d)는 dingy의 뜻을 모르면 고를 수 있는 오답이다.

carpeting 카펫 깔기 **redecorate** 새 단장하다 **rather** 좀, 다소 **dingy** 때묻은   정답_(c)

15

M	Who should I take to the dance, Julia or Mary?
W	_____

(a) We'll all meet at the dance.
(b) Either one would be willing.
(c) I'd ask Julia or Mary first.
(d) That's a good decision.

SOLUTION

M 댄스 파티에 누구를 데려가야 할까? 줄리아, 아니면 메리?
W 둘 중 누구라도 기꺼이 승낙할 거야.

기출 POINT

둘 중 누구를 데리고 가야 할지 묻는 말의 응답으로 (b)가 가장 적절하다. '둘 중 누구라도'라는 의미로 either one을 쓴다는 것을 기억해 두자. 선택을 고민하는 말에 대한 응답이므로 (c)를 고르기 쉬우나 뒤에 이어지는 말이 맞지 않는다.

either 둘 중 어느 것이든 **willing** 마음이 내키는   정답_(b)

16

M I just heard Sam's back in town.
W Really? Then we should all get together.
M Good idea, but when?
W _____

(a) Over at my place.
(b) I'll do the cooking.
(c) Let's make it tomorrow.
(d) Everyone that we know.

SOLUTION

M 방금 들었는데 샘이 돌아왔대.
W 정말? 그럼 다 같이 한번 모여야지.
M 좋은 생각이야, 그런데 언제?
W 내일로 하자.

기출 POINT

마지막 말의 의문사에 집중하여 답을 찾는다. '내일'이라는 때를 명시하는 (c)가 맞는 응답이다. make it은 '도착하다, 해내다, 만나기로 하다' 등의 뜻으로 알아 두어야 할 표현이다. (a) Over at my place는 over 앞에 come이 생략된 표현으로 우리 집으로 오라는 말이다.

get together 모임을 가지다   **do the cooking** 요리를 하다
make it 만나기로 하다   **정답_(c)**

17

W Hello, is this Ted's Garage?
M Yes, Ted speaking. How can I help you?
W My car needs a tune-up.
M _____

(a) Bring it in anytime tomorrow.
(b) Yes, the repair comes to $145.
(c) Okay, but your car is still in the shop.
(d) It's important to keep your car clean.

SOLUTION

W 여보세요. 테드 정비소인가요?
M 네. 제가 테드입니다. 무슨 일이시죠?
W 제 차의 엔진 정비를 해야 해서요.
M 내일 아무 때나 차 가지고 들르세요.

기출 POINT

전화로 자동차 정비소에 수리를 맡기는 상황이므로 '내일 아무 때나 차 가지고 들르세요'라는 (a)가 알맞다. 수리 전에 수리비를 알 수는 없으므로 (b)는 맞지 않다. '가격이 ~이다'는 말로 〈come to+금액〉을 쓴다는 것도 기억해 두자.

garage 자동차 정비소   **tune-up** (엔진 등의) 철저한 조정   **anytime tomorrow** 내일 아무 때나   **come to+금액** 값이 ~가 되다   **정답_(a)**

18

M Is there a drugstore around here, Amy?
W Yeah, but it isn't open at this hour.
M Too bad. I need something for my cold.
W _____

(a) I'd speak with the pharmacist.
(b) I'll check my medicine cabinet.
(c) I can't stand seeing you in pain.
(d) You should try another medication.

SOLUTION

M 에이미, 이 근처에 약국 있니?
W 응, 그런데 이 시간에는 안 열지.
M 곤란하네. 난 감기약이 필요해.
W 내가 약품 선반을 확인해 볼게.

기출 POINT

감기약을 사기 위해 약국을 찾지만 이미 문을 닫은 시간이다. 곤란해 하는 남자에게 '약품 선반을 확인해 보겠다'고 한 (b)가 정답이며, 나머지 선택지들은 유사 상황과 연관 어휘(pharmacist, pain, medication)로 혼동을 유발하는 오답이다.

drugstore 약국   **pharmacist** 약사   **stand** 견디다, 참다
medication 약물 (치료)   **정답_(b)**

19

W How do you take your coffee, Steve?
M Cream and sugar, please.
W How about Caroline?
M _____

(a) Tea is fine for me.
(b) She likes it black.
(c) Thanks a lot.
(d) That will do.

SOLUTION

W 스티브, 커피를 어떻게 드세요?
M 크림과 설탕을 넣어주세요.
W 캐롤라인은요?
M 그녀는 블랙으로 마시는 걸 좋아해요.

⊞ 기출 POINT
'커피를 어떻게 드세요?'는 How do you take[like] your coffee?/ How would you like your coffee? 등을 쓴다. 캐롤라인은 어떻게 마시느냐는 질문이므로 커피 취향을 언급한 (b)가 알맞다. (a)는 캐롤라인이 직접 대답할 때 가능하고, (d)는 상대방이 골라준 경우 '그거면 좋겠네요'라고 답할 때 쓰는 말이다.
A is fine with[for] me. 저는 A가 좋겠어요. **That will do.** 그거면 좋겠다. 정답_(b)

20

M I heard you bought a car.
W I did. It's a brand-new sports car.
M How on earth could you afford that?
W _____

(a) Well, it's an expensive car.
(b) I'd better budget my money.
(c) I saved up for it, little by little.
(d) One day, I hope to do just that.

SOLUTION

M 차 샀다는 이야기 들었어.
W 응. 최신형 스포츠카야.
M 대체 돈이 어디서 났는데?
W 차 사려고 조금씩 모았지.

⊞ 기출 POINT
어떻게 최신형 스포츠카를 샀는지에 대한 응답을 찾는다. 〈afford+to 부정사(명사)〉는 '~할 경제적인 여유가 있다'는 뜻으로 꼭 알아두어야 할 표현이다. How on earth의 on earth는 How를 강조하기 위해 쓰는 말이다. (b)는 '돈을 규모 있게 쓰겠다'는 결심이므로 부적절하다.
brand-new 최신의 **how on earth** 대체 어떻게 **budget** 예산을 세우다 **save up** 모으다 정답_(c)

21

W I'll be a little late this evening, Dad.
M Why? What do you have planned?
W A dress rehearsal for our class play.
M _____

(a) Okay, but try not to be back too late.
(b) Yes, I heard you're seeing a play.
(c) I'll get dressed right away, then.
(d) I'd rather you went to rehearse.

SOLUTION

W 아빠, 오늘 저녁은 조금 늦을 거예요.
M 왜? 무슨 일인데?
W 우리 반 연극 총연습이 있어요.
M 알았다. 하지만 너무 늦지 않도록 해라.

⊞ 기출 POINT
What do you have planned?는 '무슨 계획이 있니?'라는 뜻이다. 연극 총연습이 있다는 딸의 말에 대한 아버지의 응답으로 늦지 않도록 하라는 (a)가 적절하다. (d) 〈I'd rather+주어+동사〉절에서 동사가 과거형인 것에 주의하며 이는 부드럽게 부탁하는 뜻으로 가정법과 같은 동사의 형태를 쓴다는 것을 기억해 두자.
dress rehearsal (의상을 갖춘) 총연습 **get dressed** 옷을 입다
I'd rather you went. 네가 가면 좋겠어. 정답_(a)

22

M This road is being repaired. We can't go any farther.

W Then how else can we get to Jodie's house?

M Go left and keep going until we reach the mall.

W _____

(a) I know she likes shopping there.
(b) Okay. I'll drive on straight ahead.
(c) I'll go about it the same way.
(d) I see. That's a good detour.

SOLUTION

M 이 도로는 보수 중이라 더는 갈 수 없어.

W 그럼 조디네 집에 어떻게 가지?

M 좌회전한 다음 쇼핑몰이 보일 때까지 직진해.

W 알겠어. 괜찮은 우회로인데.

⊞ 기출 POINT

도로가 공사 중이라 다른 길을 알려준 말에 대한 응답을 고른다. (d)의 detour(우회로)라는 단어가 힌트가 된다. (b)가 Okay로 시작되어 정답으로 고르기 쉬운데 알려준 길과 다른 방향이므로 오답이다. (c)에서 go about은 '~를 돌아다니다'라는 뜻으로 내용상 어울리지 않는다.

how else 어떤 다른 방법으로   **detour** 우회로   정답_(d)

23

W Hi, Philip. How was your weekend?

M Fine. How about yours?

W Relaxing. I just watched some movies.

M _____

(a) That must've been nice.
(b) Have a good evening.
(c) Serves you right.
(d) It might get better.

SOLUTION

W 안녕, 필립. 주말 어떻게 보냈니?

M 좋았어. 너는?

W 느긋하게 보냈어. 영화 좀 봤지.

M 좋았겠다.

⊞ 기출 POINT

'주말을 느긋하게 영화를 보면서 보냈다'는 여자의 말에 대한 응답으로 '좋았겠다'는 (a)가 정답이다. must have p.p.는 '~했음에 틀림없다'는 의미이다. (c) Serves you right은 맨 앞에 It이 생략된 것으로 '자업자득, 쌤통'이라는 말이므로 알아두자.

relaxing 느긋한, 편한   **must have p.p.** ~했음에 틀림없다
(It) Serves you right. 자업자득이다.   정답_(a)

24

M What do you think of your dorm room?

W It's very nice.

M Do you feel at home, then?

W _____

(a) I feel fine, thank you.
(b) Yes, it's nice to be home.
(c) I do. It has everything I need.
(d) All right. I promise to visit often.

SOLUTION

M 기숙사 방은 어때?

W 굉장히 좋아.

M 마음은 편하니?

W 응. 필요한 건 다 있으니까.

⊞ 기출 POINT

feel at home은 '편안하다'의 뜻임을 기억하자. 기숙사가 어떠냐고 묻는 첫 번째 여자의 질문에 nice라고 했으므로 (c)처럼 긍정의 답변을 예상할 수 있다. (a)는 기분이 어떤지 묻는 질문에 대해 '괜찮다'고 대답하는 말로 적절하며, (b)는 '집에 있는 것이 좋다'는 말이므로 부적절하다.

dorm 기숙사   **feel at home** 편안하다   **feel fine** 기분이 괜찮다
promise to+동사원형 ~하기로 약속하다   정답_(c)

25

W I'm worried about applying to a college.

M Just do some research and find a school that's a good fit for you.

W That's just it. What if there isn't one, even after I do a search?

M _____

(a) You'll need to apply to several.
(b) Then you must decide on a major.
(c) You'll have to figure out what to do first.
(d) I'm sure there's something out there for you.

SOLUTION

W 대학에 지원하는 일이 걱정돼.
M 그냥 조사 좀 하면서 너한테 잘 맞는 학교를 찾아봐.
W 그게 문제라니까. 조사를 해봤는데도 그런 학교가 없으면 어떻게 해?
M 분명 너에게 맞는 곳이 있을 거야.

기출 POINT
남자는 지원할 대학을 고민하는 여자에게 조언을 하고 있다. 자료 조사를 하고 잘 맞는 대학을 고르면 어딘가 맞는 곳이 있을 거라고 확신을 주는 내용이 적절하다. That's just it은 '바로 그거야. 그 문제야'라는 뜻이다.

apply to ~에 지원하다   **do research** 조사하다   **good fit** 잘 맞는 것   **What if…?** ~하면 어떻게 해?   정답 _(d)

26

M Have you noticed the attention Peter has been paying to Janet?

W I have. It's really too bad for Sally, though.

M What do you mean?

W _____

(a) Peter owes them both money.
(b) She was hoping to date Peter.
(c) Peter is used to more attention.
(d) She has been behaving strangely.

SOLUTION

M 피터가 재닛한테 신경 쓰는 거 눈치챘어?
W 그럼. 그런데 샐리한테는 정말 너무 안됐어.
M 무슨 말이야?
W 샐리가 피터랑 데이트하기를 바랐거든.

기출 POINT
피터가 재닛에게 관심을 보이는 상황에서 '샐리가 안됐다'고 말하는 사람에게 이유를 물었으므로 (b)가 적절하다. attention이라는 단어에만 집중하면 (c)로 잘못 고르기 쉬우니 조심하자.

pay attention to ~에게 주의를 기울이다   **owe A money** A에게 돈을 빌리다   **be used to+명사** ~에 익숙하다   정답 _(b)

27

M Ma'am, your visa is good for only three more days.

W Yes, I'm aware of that.

M So, how long will you be staying here in Canada on this trip?

W _____

(a) Till the day after tomorrow.
(b) As long as you can schedule it in.
(c) Not too long, but I quite enjoyed it.
(d) Well, I'll decide that when I get there.

SOLUTION

M 비자 유효기간이 겨우 사흘밖에 안 남았네요.
W 네, 저도 알고 있어요.
M 그럼 이번 여행에서 이곳 캐나다에 얼마 동안 머무를 건가요?
W 내일 모레까지요.

기출 POINT
'비자의 유효기간이 3일 남은 것을 알고 있다'고 말한 것으로 보아 내일 모레까지 머물 것이라고 답하는 (a)가 적절하다. (c)는 얼마나 오랫동안 여행을 갔었는지 묻는 질문에 여행을 다녀온 사람이 답하는 말로 알맞다.

be good 유효하다   **be aware of** ~을 알고 있다   **the day after tomorrow** 내일 모레   정답 _(a)

28

W Hey, Ted! I haven't seen you in ages.
M Hi, Kathy. Yes, I've been really busy at work.
W Well, don't work so hard that you neglect your friends.
M _____

(a) But it's my call.
(b) I don't intend to.
(c) Yes, I have been.
(d) You could say that.

SOLUTION

W 야, 테드! 너 한참 안 보이더라.
M 안녕, 캐시. 그래, 회사 일이 엄청나게 바빴어.
W 음, 일 너무 열심히 한다고 친구들한테 소홀하지는 마.
M 그러려고 그러는 건 아니야.

⊞ 기출 POINT

친구를 소홀히 할 정도로 열심히 일하지 말라는 충고의 말에 적당한 응답을 찾는다. '의도적인 것이 아니고 어쩔 수 없다'는 말인 (b)가 적당하다. (a)는 '내 마음이다, 내 결정이다'라는 뜻이고, (d)는 상대방의 말에 어느 정도 동의함을 나타낸다.
I haven't seen you in ages. 오랜만이야. **neglect** 소홀히 하다 **intend to+동사원형** ~할 의도이다 **You could say that.** 그렇게 볼 수 있죠.   정답_(b)

29

M Have you started looking for an apartment to rent in Florida?
W No. I want to wait until I get there before I start looking.
M Do you at least know the going rates?
W _____

(a) I know it's not cheap to rent there.
(b) No, I won't be staying for very long.
(c) Actually, I'm going to buy an apartment.
(d) That's because there's nothing in my price range.

SOLUTION

M 플로리다에서 렌트할 아파트를 알아보기 시작했니?
W 아니. 플로리다에 가서 알아볼 때까지 기다리려고.
M 시세는 알고 있니?
W 렌트비가 싸지 않다는 건 알고 있어.

⊞ 기출 POINT

플로리다에 가서 집을 구하겠다는 말에 대해 시세는 알고 있냐고 걱정하는 대화이다. 여자가 '가서 알아보겠다'고 한 것으로 보아 이어지는 답으로 '단지 값이 비싸다는 것만 알고 있다'는 내용이 어울린다. 렌트한다고 했으므로 아파트를 살 것이라는 (c)는 상황에 맞지 않는다.
at least 최소한 **going rate** 시세 **price range** 가격 범위 정답_(a)

30

W Excuse me, but when can I see Dr. Ashley?
M I'm afraid he's with a patient.
W But my appointment was an hour ago.
M _____

(a) I thought you were going to reschedule it.
(b) Of course. I'll call for the next patient.
(c) I know, but we're really backed up.
(d) In that case, I'll book you earlier.

SOLUTION

W 실례지만, 애슐리 선생님을 언제 뵐 수 있는 거죠?
M 죄송하지만 진료 중이십니다.
W 하지만 한 시간 전으로 진료 예약을 했는데요.
M 입니다만 환자가 많이 밀려서요.

⊞ 기출 POINT

예약한 진료 시간이 지나서 불만을 제기하는 환자와 담당자의 대화이다. 아직 환자를 보고 있는 중이라고 한 남자의 말을 통해 '환자가 많아서 밀려 있다'라는 대답을 추측해 볼 수 있다. I'm afraid (that)은 좋지 않은 내용을 말할 때 문장 앞에 써서 유감의 뜻을 나타낸다.
appointment 병원 예약 **call for** ~을 큰 소리로 부르다 **be backed up** 밀리다, 정체하다 **in that case** 그런 경우라면 정답_(c)

31

M Welcome to Commerce Bank. Can I help you?

W Yes. I'd like to open a savings account.

M Certainly. Could I see some ID, please?

W Sure. I have my driver's license and a state ID.

M Your driver's license will do, thank you.

Q What is the woman mainly doing in the conversation?

(a) Getting a driver's license.

(b) Paying her monthly bills.

(c) Opening a bank account.

(d) Withdrawing some cash.

SOLUTION

M 커머스 은행에 오신 것을 환영합니다. 도와드릴까요?

W 네. 예금 계좌를 개설하려고요.

M 알겠습니다. 신분증을 좀 볼 수 있을까요?

W 그럼요. 운전면허증과 주정부 신분증이 있는데요.

M 운전면허증이면 됩니다. 감사합니다.

Q 대화에서 여자가 하고 있는 일은?

(a) 면허증 발급.

(b) 월 청구서 지불.

(c) 은행 계좌 개설.

(d) 현금 인출.

⊞ 기출 POINT

예금 계좌를 개설하는 과정이다. will do는 많이 나오는 표현으로 '~면 된다, 좋다'는 뜻으로 쓰인다. 은행 관련 표현: open a savings account 예금 계좌를 개설하다/ cash a check 수표를 현금으로 바꾸다/ withdraw money 돈을 찾다/ ATM 자동 현금 인출기 (automated-teller machine)/ deposit 예금

savings account 예금 계좌 **ID** 신분증(identification) **withdraw** 인출하다

정답 _(c)

32

W What do you want for dinner tonight?

M I've been craving noodles, actually.

W Noodles, huh? Thai or Chinese?

M Both sound good. Which do you prefer?

W Thai is always good, but there's that new Chinese place.

M That's right! Let's give that place a try.

W Okay. I'll make a reservation for two.

Q What are the speakers mainly discussing in the conversation?

(a) What they will have for dinner.

(b) Meals that they like to prepare.

(c) A newly opened Chinese restaurant.

(d) How Thai food differs from Chinese.

SOLUTION

W 오늘 저녁 뭐 먹을래?

M 실은 국수가 당겼어.

W 국수라… 태국식 아니면 중국식?

M 둘 다 좋은데. 너는 어느 쪽이 더 좋니?

W 태국식이야 항상 좋지만, 새로 생긴 그 중국 식당 있잖아.

M 맞다! 거기 한번 가보자.

W 좋아. 내가 두 명으로 예약할게.

Q 대화에서 화자들이 논의하고 있는 것은?

(a) 저녁식사 메뉴.

(b) 두 사람이 만들고 싶어 하는 식사.

(c) 새로 생긴 중국 식당.

(d) 태국 음식과 중국 음식의 차이점.

⊞ 기출 POINT

주된 화제를 묻는 문제는 대화의 첫 질문에 집중해야 한다. 의견을 나눈 뒤 결국 중국식 국수를 먹자는 내용이므로 '무엇을 먹을지'가 주된 화제이다. 태국식과 중국식 국수 중에 고민하다가 새로 생긴 음식점에 가자고 했으므로 (c)는 주된 화제가 아니다. 둘 중 어떤 것이 더 좋은지 묻는 말로 Which do you prefer?를 기억해두자. give ... a try는 '~을 시도해보다'라는 뜻으로 give ... a shot/ take a shot at도 같은 의미이다.

crave 간절히 원하다 **reservation** 예약

정답 _(a)

33

W Who do you think will win the soccer game tonight?

M Probably Liverpool. They're a strong team.

W Stronger than Chelsea?

M Yeah, they're really having a good season.

W Chelsea hasn't been doing so badly. I'm rooting for them.

M Well, either way, it's going to be a good game.

Q What is mainly being discussed in the conversation?

(a) Who might win the game.

(b) The man's favorite team.

(c) Which game is on tonight.

(d) The woman's love of sports.

SOLUTION

W 오늘 밤 축구 경기에서 누가 이길 것 같니?

M 아마 리버풀이겠지. 잘하는 팀이잖아.

W 첼시보다 더 잘해?

M 응, 이번 시즌에 성적이 진짜 좋아.

W 첼시도 그렇게 못했던 건 아니잖아. 나는 첼시를 응원해.

M 음, 어찌됐든 좋은 경기가 될 거야.

Q 대화에서 논의되고 있는 것은?

(a) 우승할 팀.

(b) 남자가 제일 좋아하는 팀.

(c) 오늘 밤에 있을 경기.

(d) 여자의 스포츠에 대한 애정.

기출 POINT

첫 질문에 주제가 제시되어 있다. 리버풀과 첼시 중 어떤 팀이 경기에서 이길지 논쟁하고 있으므로 (a)가 정답이다. 여자는 '첼시도 나쁘지 않은 경기를 해왔다'며 첼시를 지지하는 이유를 말하고 있다.

have a good season 시즌에서 좋은 성적을 내다   **root for** ~을 응원하다

정답_(a)

34

W Hey, Bill. I've been looking for you.

M Well, you found me. What's up?

W I need to borrow your English 301 notes. Could I?

M But we're not in the same class. My notes are different.

W So? We're covering the same material.

M That's true. Well, if you think they'll help, here you go.

Q What is the woman mainly doing in the conversation?

(a) Comparing her notes with the man's.

(b) Returning the man's notes before class.

(c) Borrowing the man's English class notes.

(d) Finding out about a homework assignment.

SOLUTION

W 야, 빌. 널 찾고 있었어.

M 음, 나 여기 있잖아. 무슨 일인데?

W 네 영어 301 강의 노트를 빌릴 수 있을까?

M 그런데 우리 수업 같이 듣지 않잖아. 내 필기는 다르다고.

W 그래서? 같은 교재로 배우고 있잖아.

M 그건 그래. 음, 도움이 될 거라고 생각한다면, 여기 있어.

Q 대화에서 여자가 하고 있는 일은?

(a) 남자의 강의 노트와 비교하기.

(b) 수업 전 남자의 강의 노트 돌려주기.

(c) 남자의 영어 강의 노트 빌리기.

(d) 과제 확인하기.

기출 POINT

여자가 남자에게 영어 강의 노트를 빌리기 위해 찾아 온 상황이다. 수업은 다르지만 교재는 같으니 빌려 달라는 여자의 말에 남자는 승낙한다. 따라서 정답은 (c). 아직 빌리기 전이므로 노트를 비교한다는 (a)는 오답이다.

cover 학습하다   **material** 교재   **compare A with B** A와 B를 비교하다   **assignment** 과제

정답_(c)

35

M Have you been to the new bookstore on McAllister?

W I have. There are quite a few good books there.

M That's true, but it's such a small space.

W I guess, but their selection more than makes up for that.

M True. I mean, who else carries such a wide variety of imported periodicals?

W Exactly, and their selection of Korean graphic novels is beyond comparison.

Q What is mainly being discussed about the bookstore?
(a) Its small size and location.
(b) How the man and woman feel about it.
(c) Plans to increase the variety of periodicals.
(d) What needs to be done to attract more customers.

SOLUTION

M 맥알리스터 가에 있는 새 서점에 가봤니?

W 가봤어. 거기 좋은 책들이 꽤 많더라.

M 맞아. 그런데 공간은 굉장히 작지.

W 그런 것 같아. 그런데 책 종류가 다양해서 장소의 협소함을 보상하고도 남잖아.

M 맞아. 내 말은 어떤 서점이 그렇게 다양한 수입 정기간행물을 취급하겠냐고.

W 그래. 그리고 한국 극화 구색은 비교할 수조차 없어.

Q 서점에 대해 논의되고 있는 점은?
(a) 작은 규모와 위치.
(b) 남자와 여자의 서점에 대한 생각.
(c) 정기간행물의 다양성 증대 계획.
(d) 더 많은 고객 유치를 위해 할 일.

⊞ 기출 POINT

작은 서점이지만 다양한 종류의 책들을 구비하고 있다는 데 둘 다 감탄하고 있는 내용이므로 (b)가 정답. (a)는 세부 정보에 해당할 뿐이고 (c)와 (d)는 언급된 바가 없는 내용이다.

quite a few 꽤 많은 **make up for** ~을 보상하다 **periodical** 정기간행물 **graphic novel** 극화 **beyond comparison** 비교 불가인

정답_(b)

36

W Justin, could you give me some help?

M Sorry. I'm busy right now.

W No, you aren't. You're watching television.

M I don't want to miss this tennis match. It's the semi-final.

W But I need you to hold the chair while I hang this picture.

M Fine, but just during this commercial break.

Q What is mainly taking place in the conversation?
(a) The woman is hanging a picture.
(b) The woman is asking the man for help.
(c) The man is commenting on a tennis match.
(d) The couple is arguing about how to hang a picture.

SOLUTION

W 저스틴, 나 좀 도와줄래?

M 미안. 내가 지금 바빠서.

W 바쁘기는 무슨. 텔레비전 보고 있잖아.

M 이 테니스 경기는 놓치고 싶지 않아. 준결승이란 말이야.

W 하지만 내가 이 그림을 거는 동안 네가 의자를 잡아줘야 한다고.

M 좋아. 하지만 이 광고 할 동안만이야.

Q 대화에서 주로 일어나고 있는 일은?
(a) 여자가 그림을 걸고 있다.
(b) 여자가 남자에게 도움을 청하고 있다.
(c) 남자가 테니스 경기에 대해 논평하고 있다.
(d) 두 사람이 그림을 거는 방법을 놓고 실랑이를 벌이고 있다.

⊞ 기출 POINT

여자가 그림을 걸기 위해 도움을 요청하자 저스틴은 TV 테니스 경기를 보는 중이라며 거절하고 있다. 남자는 테니스 경기를 시청하고 있는 것이지 해설하는 것이 아니므로 (c)는 오답이다.

semi-final 준결승 **commercial break** 광고 시간 **comment on** ~에 대해 설명하다

정답 (b)

37

W Where have you been all this time? It's 1 in the morning!

M Oh, hi, dear. I didn't think you'd be up so late.

W Well, I was worried. Have you been drinking?

M Yes, the boss invited employees out for a drink after work.

W But did you have to stay so long?

M The boss kept insisting on it.

Q What is the main topic of the conversation?
(a) How the man got so drunk.
(b) Why the man came home late.
(c) Why the woman stayed up late.
(d) Where the boss took everyone for a drink.

SOLUTION

W 이 시간까지 어디 있었던 거예요? 새벽 한 시라고요!

M 어, 안녕, 여보. 이렇게 늦게까지 안 자고 있을 거라고는 생각 못했어요.

W 걱정했다고요. 술 마셨어요?

M 네. 상사가 일 마치고 직원들을 술자리로 초대했어요.

W 그런데 이렇게 늦게까지 있어야만 했나요?

M 상사가 자꾸만 남아 있으라고 해서요.

Q 대화의 주요 화제는?
(a) 남자가 취한 경위.
(b) 남자가 늦게 귀가한 이유.
(c) 여자가 늦게까지 깨어 있었던 이유.
(d) 상사가 모두와 술자리를 가진 장소.

⊞ 기출 POINT

여자가 남자에게 어디에 있었고 술을 왜 마셨는지 묻는 것으로 보아
(b) '남자가 집에 늦게 온 이유'가 이 대화의 주제임을 알 수 있다. 남자
가 왜 취했는지는 대화의 일부분에 불과하므로 (a)는 주제가 될 수 없다.

insist on ~을 강요하다   **get drunk** 술에 취하다   **stay up late**
늦도록 깨어 있다
정답_(b)

38

M Hello. I'm looking for an apartment to rent.

W You've come to the right place. What location?

M I'd like to try the southern suburbs, somewhere convenient for public transportation.

W Should it be convenient for shopping, too?

M That'd be nice, but it's not critical.

W What about the rent?

M Around $600 a month.

Q Which is correct about the man according to the conversation?
(a) He lives in the southern suburbs.
(b) He is going to buy a new apartment.
(c) He hopes to live in a quiet neighborhood.
(d) He wants to live near public transportation.

SOLUTION

M 안녕하세요. 임대할 아파트를 찾고 있는데요.

W 제대로 찾아오셨어요. 어느 쪽으로요?

M 남쪽 교외를 알아보고 싶어요. 대중 교통이 편리한 곳으로요.

W 쇼핑도 편리해야 하나요?

M 그러면 좋겠지만, 꼭 그런 건 아니에요.

W 임대료는요?

M 월 600달러 정도요.

Q 대화에 따르면 남자에 대해 옳은 것은?
(a) 남자는 남쪽 교외에 살고 있다.
(b) 남자는 새로 아파트를 구매하려고 한다.
(c) 남자는 조용한 동네에서 살고 싶어 한다.
(d) 남자는 대중 교통 시설 부근에 살고 싶어 한다.

⊞ 기출 POINT

일치하는 내용을 고르는 문제는 전체적인 내용과 함께 세부사항도 유
의해야 하는 유형이다. 앞으로 살고자 하는 곳이 남쪽 교외이므로 (a)는
오답이며, 구매하는 것이 아니라 임대할 것이므로 (b)도 오답이다. (c)는
대화에서 언급하지 않은 내용이므로 알 수 없다.

rent 집세, 임대료; 임대하다   **suburb** 교외   **public transportation**
대중 교통   **critical** 중요한
정답_(d)

39

W How's your ankle, Ken?

M It's much better, but it's still giving me trouble.

W You're getting it treated, right?

M I only started physical therapy recently.

W You left it a bit long, it seems.

M Yes, I wish I had gone earlier.

Q Which is correct about Ken according to the conversation?

(a) His ankle does not hurt anymore.

(b) He has not yet visited a therapist.

(c) He delayed treatment for his ankle.

(d) He is late for a doctor's appointment.

SOLUTION

W 켄, 발목은 좀 어때?

M 훨씬 나은데, 아직도 좀 신경이 쓰이네.

W 치료는 받고 있는 거지?

M 최근에서야 물리 치료를 받기 시작했어.

W 좀 오랫동안 방치해 둔 것 같구나.

M 응. 더 일찍 갔더라면 좋았을 텐데 말이야.

Q 대화에 따르면 켄에 대해 옳은 것은?

(a) 발목은 이제 더 이상 아프지 않다.

(b) 치료사를 아직 만나보지 않았다.

(c) 발목 치료를 미뤘다.

(d) 의사와의 약속에 늦었다.

⊞ 기출 POINT

대화 전체 내용과 세부적인 정보에 주의하여 답을 골라야 하는 유형이다. '치료를 오랫동안 방치해 두었다'고 했으므로 (c)가 정답이다. I wish 다음에는 가정법과 같은 동사 형태가 쓰인다는 것도 반드시 알아둘 사항이다.

ankle 발목 **get it treated** 치료받다 **physical therapy** 물리 치료
treatment 치료   정답_(c)

40

M Where are you from, Jenna?

W Me? I'm from all over.

M All over? So you moved around a lot, huh?

W Yeah. My dad was in the navy, so we never stayed in one place long.

M I bet you've lived in a lot of interesting places, then.

W I have, but it was hard to make friends.

Q Which is correct about the woman according to the conversation?

(a) She has lived in many different places.

(b) She recently joined the navy.

(c) She travels a lot for her job.

(d) She made friends easily.

SOLUTION

M 제나, 너 어디 출신이니?

W 나? 여기저기.

M 여기저기라고? 꽤 많이 옮겨 다닌 모양이구나?

W 응. 아버지가 해군이어서 한 곳에 오래 머무른 적이 없어.

M 그럼 흥미로운 곳에 많이 살아봤겠다.

W 그랬지. 그런데 친구 사귀기는 어려웠어.

Q 대화에 따르면 여자에 대해 옳은 것은?

(a) 여러 다른 곳에서 살았다.

(b) 최근 해군에 입대했다.

(c) 일 때문에 여행을 많이 한다.

(d) 친구를 쉽게 사귀었다.

⊞ 기출 POINT

출신을 묻는 질문에 I'm from all over라고 답했고 그 이유에 대해 설명한다. '아버지가 해군이어서 여러 곳으로 옮겨 다니면서 살았고 그래서 친구 사귀기가 힘들었다'는 세부 내용에 유의한다.

move around 돌아다니다 **make friends** 친구를 사귀다   정답_(a)

41

W Are you still running in the marathon this weekend?

M Sure. You know how much I enjoy marathons.

W I don't know if that's such a good idea.

M But I've been planning to enter it for a long time.

W Yes, but you've only just recovered from knee surgery.

M Don't worry about a thing. I'll be all right.

Q Which is correct according to the conversation?
(a) The woman is happy the man will run.
(b) The man's knee was recently operated on.
(c) The man suddenly decided to join the marathon.
(d) The woman wants the man to run in the marathon.

SOLUTION

W 이번 주말 마라톤에 여전히 출전하는 거니?

M 물론. 내가 얼마나 마라톤을 즐기는지 알잖아.

W 그게 그렇게 좋은 생각인지 잘 모르겠다.

M 하지만 이 대회에 나가려고 오랫동안 계획해 왔다고.

W 그래, 하지만 무릎 수술에서 회복한 지 얼마 안 됐잖아.

M 아무 걱정하지 마. 괜찮을 거야.

Q 대화와 일치하는 것은?
(a) 여자는 남자가 달리게 되어 행복하다.
(b) 남자는 최근 무릎 수술을 받았다.
(c) 남자는 갑작스레 마라톤 출전을 결정했다.
(d) 여자는 남자가 마라톤에서 달리기를 원한다.

🎏 기출 POINT

무릎 수술에서 방금 회복한 남자가 마라톤에 참가하려 하자 여자가 만류하는 대화이다. only just recovered from knee surgery에서 최근에 무릎 수술을 받았음을 알 수 있다. 마라톤은 남자가 오랫동안 바라던 일이었고, 여자는 남자가 무리해서 참가하는 것을 걱정하기에 (c)와 (d)는 모두 오답이다. 상대방 의견에 조심스럽게 반대를 나타내는 표현으로 I don't know if that's such a good idea를 기억해 두자.

surgery 수술 **Don't worry about a thing.** 아무 걱정하지 마.
operate 수술하다   정답_(b)

42

W Oh, no, I just remembered. We haven't paid this month's rent yet!

M I thought you paid it last weekend.

W No, it was due Saturday, but we had to visit your mother.

M Oh, yeah, that Saturday was really hectic.

W Yeah, and after that, I just forgot about it.

M Well, we'd better phone the landlord and explain.

Q Which is correct about the man and woman according to the conversation?
(a) They forgot to visit the man's mother.
(b) They have put off phoning the landlord.
(c) Their landlord has raised the rent again.
(d) Their rent was to be paid on a Saturday.

SOLUTION

W 어, 이런, 방금 생각났어요. 우리 이번 달 월세를 아직 안 냈어요!

M 지난 주말에 당신이 낸 걸로 생각했는데.

W 아뇨, 토요일까지 내야 했었는데 그때 당신 어머님 뵈러 가야 했잖아요.

M 아, 그래, 토요일 그날은 정말 정신 없었지.

W 그래요. 그리고 월세 내는 걸 잊었다고요.

M 음, 집주인한테 전화해서 설명해야겠군.

Q 대화에 따르면 두 사람에 대해 옳은 것은?
(a) 남자의 어머니를 찾아 뵙는 것을 잊었다.
(b) 집주인에게 전화하는 것을 미뤘다.
(c) 집주인은 임대료를 또 인상했다.
(d) 임대료는 토요일이 납부 마감이었다.

🎏 기출 POINT

두 사람은 월세를 내지 않은 일에 대해 얘기하고 있다. 토요일까지 지불했어야 하므로 올바른 것은 (d)이다. '~까지 지불해야 한다'는 be due Saturday on September 19처럼 be due 다음에 기한을 쓴다는 것도 기억해 둘 표현이다.

hectic 몹시 바쁜 **landlord** 집주인 **put off** 미루다 **raise** 올리다
                                                              정답_(d)

43

M   Hello. I'm calling about your cat.

W   Tell me you found her!

M   I did. She was lurking around my garden.

W   That's wonderful! Where is she now?

M   I lured her into my garage.

W   Thank you! When can I come for her?

M   Anytime. I live at 165 Oxford, the green house.

Q   What can be inferred from the conversation?

(a) The woman had been worried about her cat.

(b) The man would like to keep the cat himself.

(c) The woman did not know her cat was gone.

(d) The man is willing to look after the cat.

SOLUTION

M   여보세요. 당신 고양이 때문에 전화 드리는데요.

W   제 고양이를 찾았군요!

M   찾았어요. 제 정원 주변을 어슬렁거리고 있더라고요.

W   잘됐네요! 고양이는 지금 어디 있나요?

M   제 차고로 유인해 놨습니다.

W   감사합니다. 고양이를 언제 찾으러 가면 될까요?

M   아무 때나요. 저희 집은 옥스퍼드 가 165번지, 초록색 집입니다.

Q   대화에서 유추할 수 있는 것은?

(a) 여자는 그녀의 고양이를 걱정했다.

(b) 남자는 고양이를 가지고 싶어 한다.

(c) 여자는 고양이가 사라진 것을 모르고 있었다.

(d) 남자는 기꺼이 고양이를 돌봐 주려고 한다.

⊞ 기출 POINT

여자의 첫 번째 대화 Tell me you found her!를 통해 잃어버린 고양이에 대해 걱정했음을 유추할 수 있으며, 동시에 (c)는 오답이 된다. '언제 찾으러 갈까요?'를 When can I come to her?라고 말해 상대방의 입장에서 동사 go가 아닌 come을 쓴다는 것도 기억하자.

lurk 어슬렁거리다   lure 유인하다   정답_(a)

44

W   You're not going to sleep with the fan running, are you?

M   Yes, I am. Why do you ask?

W   Don't you know that it can make you sick?

M   I've never heard that. Why would it?

W   The fan lowers your body temperature and spreads dust.

M   That might be true, but it's probably not that bad.

W   Still, it's better to be safe than sorry.

Q   What can be inferred from the conversation?

(a) The man seldom sleeps with a fan running.

(b) The woman prefers fans to air conditioning.

(c) The man is unable to sleep in drafty spaces.

(d) The woman does not use a fan while sleeping.

SOLUTION

W   설마 선풍기를 틀어 놓고 잘 건 아니지, 그치?

M   그럴 건데. 왜 물어보는 거야?

W   그러면 몸에 탈이 날 수도 있다는 거 몰라?

M   그런 얘기는 못 들어봤어. 왜 그런데?

W   선풍기 때문에 체온이 낮아지고 먼지가 날린다고.

M   그럴 수도 있겠지만, 아마 그렇게 나쁘진 않을 거야.

W   그래도, 나중에 후회하느니 미리 조심하는 게 낫지.

Q   대화에서 유추할 수 있는 것은?

(a) 남자는 선풍기를 틀어 두고 자는 일이 거의 없다.

(b) 여자는 에어컨보다 선풍기를 선호한다.

(c) 남자는 바람이 드는 공간에서는 잠을 잘 수 없다.

(d) 여자는 잘 때 선풍기를 사용하지 않는다.

⊞ 기출 POINT

선풍기를 틀어 놓고 자려는 남자에게 건강에 해롭다는 조언을 하는 내용이므로 '여자는 잘 때 선풍기를 사용하지 않는다'는 것을 유추할 수 있다. (a)의 경우 남자가 첫 번째 대화에서 선풍기를 틀고 잘 것이라 했으므로 부정의 부사 seldom은 어색하다. (b)는 대화의 내용으로는 유추할 수 없다.

dust 먼지   (It's) Better safe than sorry. 유비무환, 나중에 후회하느니 지금 조심하는 게 낫다.   seldom 거의 ~않다   drafty 외풍이 심한

정답_(d)

45

W Hi, welcome to the Seattle Visitor's Bureau.
How can I help you?

M I just arrived from Sydney, and I don't have a
hotel reservation.

W Which part of town would you like to stay in?
And what price range?

M I'm here for an emergency business meeting
and would prefer a 5-star hotel downtown.

W That gives you a choice between the Marriott
and the Continental.

M I'll take the Marriott for three nights, please.

Q What can be inferred from the conversation?
(a) The man's flight arrived late.
(b) The meeting is at the Marriott.
(c) The Continental Hotel is booked up.
(d) The two hotels are located downtown.

SOLUTION

W 안녕하세요. 시애틀 여행 안내소에 오신 것을 환영합니다. 무엇을
도와드릴까요?

M 방금 시드니에서 도착했는데, 호텔 예약을 하지 않았어요.

W 도시의 어느 쪽에서 묵고 싶으세요? 그리고 가격대는요?

M 긴급 비즈니스 회의차 온 거라서 시내 중심가의 5성급 호텔이면
좋겠습니다.

W 그러면 메리어트와 콘티넨털 중에 고르실 수 있습니다.

M 그럼 메리어트에서 3박으로 해주세요.

Q 대화에서 유추할 수 있는 것은?
(a) 남자의 항공편이 늦게 도착했다.
(b) 회의가 메리어트에서 열린다.
(c) 콘티넨털 호텔은 예약이 끝났다.
(d) 두 호텔은 시내 중심가에 위치해 있다.

🎫 기출 POINT

출장 온 여행객이 여행 안내소에서 호텔을 예약하는 내용이다. 도심에
있는 5성급 호텔을 원하므로 안내소 직원이 추천한 두 호텔은 도심에
있을 거라고 유추할 수 있으므로 정답은 (d)이다.

호텔 관련 표현: What is the rate? 객실 요금이 얼마죠?/ peak
season 성수기/ Does the room have Internet access? 객실에서
인터넷을 사용할 수 있나요?

bureau 안내소 **price range** 가격 범위 **be booked up** 예약이 끝나다

정답_(d)

46

Although Benjamin Franklin was Philadelphia's
most renowned citizen, he was not so much known
for his achievements as his character. Despite
being a printer, author, inventor, scientist and
diplomat, he was most well-known for his sense
of humor. In fact, though he was on the council
to craft the Declaration of Independence, no one
would allow him to do the actual writing of the final
draft because they were afraid he would write a
joke into the document.

Q What is mainly being discussed about Benjamin
Franklin in the lecture?
(a) His sense of humor.
(b) His varied accomplishments.
(c) His popularity in Philadelphia.
(d) His work on the Declaration of Independence.

SOLUTION

벤저민 프랭클린은 필라델피아 출신으로는 가장 유명한 사람이기는 하
지만 그의 업적보다는 성격으로 더 잘 알려져 있었습니다. 인쇄업자, 작
가, 발명가, 과학자이자 외교관이었음에도 불구하고 그는 그의 유머 감
각으로 가장 잘 알려져 있었어요. 사실 그는 독립 선언서를 작성한 위원
회에 소속되어 있었지만, 그가 문건에 농담을 적을까 걱정돼서 아무도
그가 실제 독립 선언서의 최종본을 집필하게 두지 않으려고 했었죠.

Q 강의에서 벤저민 프랭클린에 대해 주로 논의하고 있는 것은?
(a) 그의 유머 감각.
(b) 그의 다양한 업적.
(c) 필라델피아에서의 그의 인기.
(d) 독립 선언서와 관련해서 그가 한 일.

🎫 기출 POINT

농담을 쓸까 봐 독립 선언서의 최종본에 글을 쓰지 못하게 했다는 일화
를 통해 벤저민 프랭클린의 유머 감각을 다루고 있으므로 정답은 (a)이
다. 그의 다양한 직업을 소개한 문장에 집중하여 (b)를 선택하지 않도록
주의한다.

renowned 잘 알려진 **achievement** 업적 **diplomat** 외교관
council 위원회 **craft** 작성하다 **Declaration of Independence**
독립 선언서 **draft** 초고

정답_(a)

47

Hey, Nicole! It's Ken. Where are you? It's 7 p.m. and I've been waiting for you in front of O'Malley's since 6:30. Call my cell phone when you get this message. If I don't hear from you by 7:15, I'm going to go to the party without you. Anyway, get back to me.

Q What is Ken's purpose for calling Nicole?
(a) To make plans to meet her at 7.
(b) To say that he is waiting for her.
(c) To let her know about a message.
(d) To tell her about the change of plan.

SOLUTION

이봐, 니콜! 나 켄인데 어디 있는 거야? 지금 7시고 6시 반부터 오말리스 앞에서 너를 기다리고 있어. 이 메시지 받으면 내 휴대폰으로 전화해 줘. 7시 15분까지 너한테서 연락이 안 오면 혼자 파티에 갈 거야. 어쨌든 연락 줘.

Q 켄이 니콜에게 전화한 목적은?
(a) 7시에 니콜과 만날 계획을 잡기 위해.
(b) 자신이 니콜을 기다리고 있다고 말하기 위해.
(c) 메시지에 대해 니콜에게 알려주기 위해.
(d) 계획이 바뀐 것을 니콜에게 말하기 위해.

기출 POINT
켄이 응답기에 남긴 내용이다. 니콜과 만나기로 약속하고 기다리고 있는데 나오지 않아서 7시 15분까지 연락이 없으면 혼자 파티에 가겠다고 하고 있다. 연락이 되지 않아 메시지를 남기고 있는 상황이지 어떤 메시지에 대해 알려주기 위한 것은 아니므로 (c)는 오답이다.
hear from ~로부터 연락을 받다   정답_(b)

48

This week on Tech World, we've traveled around the globe to bring you the latest in medical technology. Our destination was Paris, where a robot is in an operating room assisting with open heart surgery. For this surgery, however, the chief surgeon is not at his patient's side. He's conducting the procedure from the other side of the room. In other words, this is surgery via remote control.

Q What is mainly being introduced here?
(a) Surgeries made obsolete by modern technology.
(b) Paris leading the world in medical technology.
(c) The latest robot-assisted surgery technology.
(d) The dangers of remote-control surgery.

SOLUTION

이번 주 테크 월드에서는 여러분에게 최신 의학 기술을 선보이기 위해 세계를 누볐습니다. 우리의 행선지는 파리였는데요. 이곳에서는 로봇이 수술실에서 심장 절개 수술을 돕습니다. 하지만 이 수술에서는 담당 외과의가 환자 곁에 있는 것이 아닙니다. 담당 외과의는 수술실의 반대편에서 집도하고 있습니다. 다시 말해, 이 수술은 원격 제어를 통한 수술입니다.

Q 주로 소개되고 있는 것은?
(a) 근대 기술로 인해 쓸모없게 된 수술들.
(b) 의료 기술에서 세계를 선도하는 파리.
(c) 최신 로봇 지원 수술 기술.
(d) 원격 제어 수술의 위험성.

기출 POINT
파리의 로봇을 이용한 수술을 최신 의학 기술로 소개한 내용이므로 정답은 (c)이다. 의학 기술에서 선두인 파리의 면모가 아니라 로봇을 이용한 수술 기술이 주된 내용이므로 (b)는 답이 될 수 없다.
globe 세계 **destination** 행선지 **operating room** 수술실
surgery 수술 **surgeon** 외과의사 **via** ~에 의해서 **obsolete** 쓸모없게 된; 진부한   정답_(c)

49

If your child is becoming overweight to the point where it is a problem, you need to focus on establishing healthy habits. It rarely works to overemphasize physical appearance. Rather, establish regular patterns of balanced eating and a regimen of physical exercise to aid weight reduction. Of course, avoid fad diets as they may damage a growing child's health.

Q What is the main topic of the talk?
(a) Patterns of behavior parents should avoid.
(b) Why diets are unsuitable for young children.
(c) Reasons young children become overweight.
(d) How parents should help overweight children.

SOLUTION

만약 자녀의 비만이 문제가 되는 지경에 이르렀다면, 건강에 좋은 습관을 만드는 것에 집중할 필요가 있습니다. 겉모습을 지나치게 강조하는 것은 거의 효과가 없습니다. 그보다는 균형 잡힌 식사를 제때 하도록 양식을 정해 주고 운동 계획을 짜주어 체중 감량을 도울 수 있게 하세요. 물론 유행 다이어트는 성장기 어린이의 건강에 피해를 줄 수 있으므로 피하시고요.

Q 담화문의 주요 화제는?
(a) 부모가 피해야 할 행동 양식.
(b) 다이어트가 어린 아이들에게 적절하지 않은 이유.
(c) 어린 아이들이 비만이 되는 이유들.
(d) 부모들이 비만인 자녀들을 돕는 방법.

기출 POINT
아이들의 비만 문제에 대해 부모들이 취할 수 있는 방법에 대한 내용이다. 부모들은 아이들의 건강한 생활 습관을 만들어 주어야 하며 그 상세 방법을 설명하는 내용이므로 (d)가 적절하다. 마지막 문장에만 집중하여 (a)를 고르지 않도록 주의해야 한다.

focus on ~에 집중하다 **It rarely works to** ~하는 것은 거의 효과가 없다 **balanced eating** 균형 잡힌 식사 **regimen** 계획 **fad** 유행 **unsuitable** 부적당한 정답_(d)

50

We at Grace's Jewelry owe a lot to Pete Anderson, a long-time employee whose window displays have been as compelling as any work of art. In his 39 years on the job with us, he has designed well over 5,000 window displays, setting the bar for other local jewelry shops. Today, we the employees at Grace's honor you, Pete, as you leave us for retirement. Here's to Pete!

Q What is the speaker mainly doing in the speech?
(a) Celebrating an artist's new artwork.
(b) Paying tribute to an employee's service.
(c) Highlighting an employee's latest honors.
(d) Spreading the news of an employee's retirement.

SOLUTION

우리 그레이스 보석상은 피트 앤더슨에게 신세를 많이 졌습니다. 피트는 장기 근속 사원으로 그의 쇼윈도 상품 진열은 예술 작품만큼이나 흡인력이 있었습니다. 우리와 일했던 39년 동안 피트는 5,000건이 훨씬 넘는 쇼윈도 상품 진열을 디자인했고, 타 지역 보석상들의 귀감이 되었습니다. 오늘 피트 당신이 이곳을 떠나 퇴직하는 자리에 우리 그레이스 보석상 직원들은 당신에 대한 존경의 뜻을 표하기 위해 모였습니다. 피트를 위해 건배합시다!

Q 화자가 주로 말하고 있는 내용은?
(a) 예술가의 새로운 예술 작품 축하.
(b) 직원의 노고에 대한 경의 표현.
(c) 직원의 최근 표창 강조.
(d) 한 직원의 퇴직 소식 공지.

기출 POINT
화자는 퇴직 사원의 지난 근무 업적을 치하하고 있다. 그의 쇼윈도 디자인이 work of art(예술 작품)와 같고, 5천 개 이상의 쇼윈도 작품이 다른 보석상의 setting the bar(귀감이 된다)라는 표현을 통해 그의 역량을 높이 평가하고 있음을 알 수 있으므로 (b)가 정답이다.

compelling 흡인력이 있는 **window display** 쇼윈도 진열 **retirement** 퇴직 **pay tribute to** ~에 대해 경의를 표하다 **highlight** 강조하다 정답_(b)

51

Few doubt the correlation between the rising number of households headed by single working parents and our ever-growing problem with juvenile delinquency. Without both parents, more and more children are being left unsupervised as single parents attempt to make ends meet alone. The result is children raised according to values learned on the streets. Until society at large champions the traditional nuclear family, I fear the problem of juvenile delinquency can only worsen.

Q What is the main idea of the talk?
(a) Society is to blame for the problems of single parents.
(b) Juvenile delinquency is a major cause of broken families.
(c) Children of single-parent families are often well-adjusted.
(d) Child delinquency has resulted from the decline of the nuclear family.

SOLUTION

부모 중 한 사람만 일을 하는 가정 수의 증가와 늘어나는 청소년 범죄 문제 간의 상관관계를 의심하는 사람은 거의 없습니다. 부모가 모두 곁에 있지 못한 채 편부모가 생계를 꾸리기 위해 애쓰는 과정에서 점점 더 많은 어린이들이 방치되고 있습니다. 그 결과는 길에서 체득한 가치관에 따라 자라난 아이들입니다. 사회 전체적으로 전통적인 핵가족을 옹호하기 전까지 나는 이 청소년 범죄 문제가 악화될 것을 우려합니다.

Q 담화문의 주제는?
(a) 편부모 문제에 대해 사회가 비난받아야 한다.
(b) 청소년 범죄는 결손 가정의 주요 원인이다.
(c) 편부모 슬하에서 자란 아이들은 종종 정서적으로 안정되어 있다.
(d) 청소년 범죄는 핵가족의 쇠퇴로 인한 결과였다.

🎛 기출 POINT
요지를 묻는 문제이다. 일하는 편부모 가정에서 방치되는 청소년들이 거리로 나가고 범죄에 노출된다는 주장이다. 화자는 전통적인 핵가족, 즉 부모가 다 있는 가정을 지키려고 해야 청소년 범죄가 개선될 것이라고 말하고 있으므로 정답은 (d).
correlation 상관관계 **juvenile delinquency** 청소년 범죄 **make ends meet** 생계를 꾸리다 **champion** 옹호하다 **worsen** 악화하다
정답_(d)

52

The latest addition to rapid-deployment first aid kits is the algal bandage, which stops bleeding in seconds. The bandage is saturated with a complex carbohydrate solution produced by unicellular algae, which essentially accelerates blood clotting. Bleed time is cut by two-thirds. Currently, these are only used for emergency cases, but they may be used for other cases in the future.

Q What is mainly being discussed in the talk?
(a) A novel procedure for trauma victims.
(b) The future of medical research.
(c) A new emergency medical product.
(d) Time saved by a new treatment procedure.

SOLUTION

신속 배포형 구급 상자에 최근 추가된 것은 수초 내에 지혈해 주는 한천 붕대입니다. 이 붕대에는 단세포 조류에 의해 만들어지는 복합 탄수화물 용액이 배어 있어서 이것이 근본적으로 응혈을 촉진합니다. 출혈 시간의 2/3가 줄어듭니다. 현재 이 붕대는 응급 시에만 사용되고 있지만, 향후에는 다른 상황에서 사용될 수도 있습니다.

Q 담화에서 주로 논의되고 있는 것은?
(a) 외상 환자들에 대한 새로운 처치법.
(b) 의학 연구의 미래.
(c) 새로운 응급 의학 제품.
(d) 새로운 처치법으로 인해 단축되는 시간.

🎛 기출 POINT
빠른 시간 내에 지혈을 해주는 붕대에 대한 내용이다. 그 성분과 작용을 설명하고 있으므로 정답은 (c)이다. 출혈 시간을 줄여준다는 세부 정보에 집중하여 (d)를 고르지 않도록 주의한다.
first aid kit 구급 상자 **algal bandage** 한천 붕대 **saturate** 적시다 **carbohydrate solution** 탄수화물 용액 **unicellular algae** 단세포 조류 **accelerate** 촉진하다 **clotting** 응고 **trauma** 정신적 외상
정답_(c)

53

Veterinarians working for News 6 have uncovered shocking conditions in 25 of the 100 pet shops we visited during our investigation of animal cruelty in the pet industry. Conditions were so bad in these stores that the network lodged formal complaints against the store owners to have their licenses to sell animals revoked. Of the remaining 75 stores, conditions varied from excellent to acceptable. For those of you thinking of buying a pet, stay tuned for a list of stores deemed exemplary by our experts.

Q Which is correct according to the news report?
(a) Many pet stores operate without a proper license.
(b) News 6 experts do not recommend any pet stores.
(c) A number of store owners had their licenses revoked.
(d) The News 6 network filed complaints with authorities.

SOLUTION

뉴스 6에서 일하는 수의사들은 애완동물 업계의 동물 학대 조사 기간에 방문한 100개의 애완동물 업소 중 25개의 충격적인 상황을 폭로했습니다. 이들 업소에서의 상황은 너무나 열악해서 방송사에서는 이들 업주들의 동물 판매 허가를 취소해 달라는 공식 민원을 냈습니다. 나머지 75개 업소의 상황은 훌륭한 곳에서부터 허용할 수 있는 수준인 곳까지 다양했습니다. 애완동물 구매를 생각하시는 여러분들께서는 채널을 고정하시고 저희 전문가들이 모범업소로 생각한 곳들의 목록을 확인하십시오.

Q 뉴스 보도에 따르면 옳은 것은?
(a) 많은 애완동물 상점들이 적절한 허가증 없이 운영되고 있다.
(b) 뉴스 6 전문가들은 어떤 애완동물 상점도 추천하지 않는다.
(c) 여러 업주들의 허가가 취소되었다.
(d) 뉴스 6 방송사는 당국에 민원을 제기했다.

기출 POINT
애완동물 업소의 실태를 조사한 프로그램에 대한 내용이다. 이 방송사 측은 몇몇 업소의 허가를 취소해 달라는 공식 민원을 제출했으므로 (d)는 맞는 내용이다. 허가증이 없는 불법 업소나 이미 허가가 취소되었다는 언급은 없으므로 (a)와 (c)는 오답이다.
veterinarian 수의사 **investigation** 조사 **lodge** (고소장 등을) 제출하다 **revoke** 취소하다 **deem** ~으로 생각하다 **exemplary** 모범적인 **file** (민원 등을) 제기하다 　　　**정답 _(d)**

54

Attention all passengers for Aqua-Jet Airlines Flight 782, bound for Bali. Your flight is now boarding. Passengers traveling in first class or who need special assistance or are traveling with young children may board at this time. In a few minutes, we'll open boarding to passengers in rows 37 through 57. Until that time, we kindly ask that all other passengers remain seated.

Q Who may board right after the announcement?
(a) Passengers in rows 37 through 57.
(b) Passengers with no young children.
(c) Passengers who require assistance.
(d) Passengers traveling in economy class.

SOLUTION

발리 행 아쿠아 제트 항공 782편 탑승객 전원에게 알립니다. 여러분의 항공편은 현재 탑승 수속 중입니다. 퍼스트 클래스 승객이나 특별 도움이 필요한 분, 혹은 어린 아이들과 함께 여행하시는 분들은 지금 탑승하셔도 좋습니다. 몇 분 후, 37열부터 57열까지의 승객에 대해 탑승 수속을 진행할 것입니다. 그때까지 다른 모든 승객분들은 자리에 앉아 계실 것을 부탁드립니다.

Q 안내 방송 직후에 탑승할 수 있는 사람은 누구인가?
(a) 37열부터 57열까지의 탑승객.
(b) 어린 아이가 없는 탑승객.
(c) 도움을 받아야 하는 탑승객.
(d) 일반석 탑승객.

기출 POINT
탑승 안내 방송이다. 첫 번째 Question을 들은 후 두 번째 들을 때는 질문에서 묻는 세부내용만 메모해서 정답을 고르도록 한다. 탑승 순서에 대한 내용은 반드시 알아 두어야 한다. 1등석 승객과 휠체어 승객, 고령자, 신체 부자유자 등의 특별한 도움이 필요한 승객들과 어린이 동반자 승객들이 탑승하고, 그 다음으로 일반석 승객이 순서대로 탑승하도록 한다는 것을 기억해 두자. 방송 직후 탈 수 있는 사람은 (c) 도움이 필요한 승객이다.

bound for ~로 향하는 **board** 탑승하다 **row** 열 **announcement** 방송 　　　**정답 _(c)**

55

According to the federal Environmental Protection Agency, or EPA, lead contamination of tap water in two Washington homes was so high that the residents could taste it. Tests completed by the agency last week revealed that one of the homes has a lead level of 48,000 parts per billion, or ppb, and that the other has a level of 24,000 ppb, both far above the federal limit of 15 ppb. The EPA also reported that some city health officials may have known about the contamination some time ago.

Q Which is correct according to the report?
(a) Tap water throughout Washington has high lead levels.
(b) An acceptable level of lead in tap water is 15 ppb.
(c) Health officials were unaware of lead in tap water.
(d) Only one of the two homes had a high lead level.

SOLUTION

연방 환경 보호청 EPA에 따르면 워싱턴의 두 가구의 수돗물 납 오염도가 너무 높아 거주자들이 그 맛을 느낄 수 있을 정도였다고 합니다. 지난주 환경 보호청에서 완료한 실험에 따르면 이들 가구 중 한 곳은 납 수치가 48,000 십억 분율, 혹은 ppb였고, 다른 한 가구는 24,000 ppb로 두 가구 모두 연방 상한치인 15ppb를 훨씬 상회했습니다. EPA에서는 또한 몇몇 시 보건 관료들이 오염 사실에 대해 얼마 전부터 알고 있었을 수도 있다고 보고했습니다.

Q 보고서와 일치하는 것은?
(a) 워싱턴 전역의 수돗물은 납 수치가 높다.
(b) 수돗물 허용 납 수치는 15ppb이다.
(c) 보건 관료들은 수돗물 납에 대해 모르고 있었다.
(d) 두 가구 중 한 곳에서만 납 수치가 높았다.

기출 POINT
워싱턴 가구의 수돗물 납 오염도 조사에 대한 내용이다. 기준이 되는 연방 상한치는 15ppb라고 했으므로 (b)가 맞는 내용이다. 워싱턴의 두 가구를 조사한 것이고 시 보건 관료들이 그 사실을 알고 있다고 했으므로 (a)와 (c)는 오답이다. 차이는 크지만 두 가구 모두 높은 납 농도를 보였으므로 (d)도 틀린 내용이다.

federal 연방의 **lead** 납 **contamination** 오염 **tap water** 수돗물
ppb 10억 분의 1단위 (part per billion) 　　　　　　정답_(b)

56

Today's presentation is on periodontal disease, which attacks the gums and bones that support your teeth. If detected at an early stage, the disease can be treated with scaling and root-planing. Plaque is removed from around the tooth, and the surfaces of its roots are evened and polished. If the disease is not caught in a timely manner, however, the patient may need surgical treatment, which involves cutting the gums, eliminating plaque and restructuring damaged bone. In such a case, the worst-case scenario is that the disease may lead to tooth loss.

Q Which is correct about periodontal disease according to the lecture?
(a) Scaling is not needed if the disease is detected in time.
(b) Surgery is needed in the early stages of the disease.
(c) It may involve smoothing the surfaces of the roots.
(d) It is unlikely to damage bone at any stage.

SOLUTION

오늘의 프레젠테이션은 치주 질환에 대한 것인데요, 이 질병은 치아를 지탱하는 잇몸과 뼈를 공격합니다. 초기에 발견되면 스케일링과 치근 활택술로 이 질병을 치료할 수 있습니다. 치석을 치아 주변에서 제거하고, 치근의 표면을 고르게 하고 매끄럽게 합니다. 하지만 이 질병을 적시에 잡아내지 않으면 환자는 수술 치료를 받아야 할 수도 있는데, 이는 잇몸을 절개하고 치석을 제거한 후 손상된 뼈를 재조직합니다. 이 경우 최악의 시나리오는 이 질병으로 치아를 잃게 될 수도 있다는 겁니다.

Q 강의에 따르면 치주 질환에 대해 옳은 것은?
(a) 질병을 제때 발견하면 스케일링이 필요없다.
(b) 질병 초기 단계에서 수술이 필요하다.
(c) 치근 표면을 매끄럽게 하는 일이 수반될 수도 있다.
(d) 어느 단계에서라도 뼈에 손상이 갈 확률은 없다.

기출 POINT
각 시기별 치료 방법에 유의하여 정보를 파악해야 한다. 초기에 발견되면 스케일링과 치근 활택술을 통해 치료하고, 이후에는 수술 치료가 필요하며, 최악의 경우에는 치아를 빼야 한다는 내용이다. 치아 뿌리 부분을 매끄럽게 하는 치근 활택술 치료가 언급되었으므로 정답은 (c)이다.

periodontal 치주의 **gum** 잇몸 **scaling** 스케일링
root-planing 치근 활택술 **plaque** 치석 **even** 고르게 하다
polish 닦다, 윤내다 **eliminate** 제거하다 　　　　정답_(c)

57

In 15th-century North American colonies, constables were appointed by towns as peacekeepers. They were unpaid, had no uniform and were expected to carry out their chores while assuming their regular walks of life. Constables were highly unpopular, as part of their job involved reporting their neighbors' behavior to the courts. Arresting criminals and guarding them until trial was also their responsibility.

Q Which is correct about the constable's position according to the lecture?
(a) It required quitting regular work.
(b) People were appointed to it by lot.
(c) Most people admired the work it entailed.
(d) It partly required one to act as an informant.

SOLUTION

15세기 북미 식민지에서는 보안관을 마을의 조정자로 임명했습니다. 이들은 급여를 받는 것도 아니었고, 제복도 없었으며 자신들의 일상적인 직업을 이행하면서 잡일을 수행하도록 요구받았죠. 보안관들의 업무에는 이웃의 행동을 법원에 보고하는 것이 포함되어 있었기 때문에 보안관들은 매우 인기가 없었어요. 범죄자를 체포하고 이들을 재판 때까지 보호하는 것 역시 보안관들의 의무였습니다.

Q 강의에 따르면 보안관 직책에 대해 옳은 것은?
(a) 그 일을 하려면 정규 근무를 그만두어야 했다.
(b) 사람들은 추첨으로 그 직책에 임명됐다.
(c) 대부분 사람들은 그 직책이 수반하는 업무를 높이 평가했다.
(d) 그 일을 하려면 부분적으로 밀고자 역할을 해야 했다.

📊 기출 POINT

마을의 조정자인 보안관에 대한 내용이다. 마을에서 임명하여 무보수로, 일상적인 일과 병행하며 밀고자 역할도 해야 했기 때문에 사람들에게 인기가 없었다는 내용이므로 정답은 (d)이다.

colony 식민지 **constable** 보안관 **appoint** 임명하다
peacekeeper 조정자 **chore** 잡일 **criminal** 범죄자 **lot** 추첨
entail 수반하다 **informant** 밀고자 　　　　　　　**정답**_(d)

58

As the East-West Film Festival celebrates its 20th year, we, its founders, now reflect on where we've been and where we're going. The festival was part of our broader vision to bridge Eastern and Western cultures through the medium of film. However, we never imagined it would one day achieve such fame as a key international film festival. Now, 20 years later, the festival has carved out a niche as one of the best of its kind in the world.

Q What can be inferred about the festival?
(a) It has not grown in scale.
(b) It makes no profit for its founders.
(c) It will no longer take place annually.
(d) It features both Western and Asian films.

SOLUTION

동서 영화제가 20주년을 맞으면서, 우리 설립자들은 이제 우리가 걸어온 발자취와 현재의 행로에 대해 생각해 봅니다. 이 영화제는 영화라는 매체를 통해 동서양 문화 간에 가교 역할을 하겠다는 우리의 광범위한 비전의 일환이었습니다. 하지만, 우리는 이 영화제가 핵심 국제 영화제로 이 같은 명성을 얻게 되리라고는 전혀 생각하지 못했습니다. 20년이라는 세월이 흐른 지금, 이 축제는 세계 최고의 영화제 중 하나로 자리 매김했습니다.

Q 축제에 대해 유추할 수 있는 것은?
(a) 규모는 성장하지 않았다.
(b) 설립자들에게 이익을 전혀 창출하지 않는다.
(c) 더 이상 해마다 개최되지 않을 것이다.
(d) 서구 영화와 아시아 영화를 모두 상영한다.

📊 기출 POINT

언급되지 않은 내용을 유추하는 문제이다. '영화를 매체로 동서양 문화의 가교 역할을 하고자 했다'는 내용을 통해 이 영화제가 '서양과 아시아 영화를 모두 상영한다'는 사실을 추론할 수 있으므로 정답은 (d). 핵심 국제 영화제인데 '이익을 내지 않는다'는 추론은 부적절하므로 (b)는 오답이다.

founder 설립자 **reflect on** ~에 대해 깊이 생각하다 **medium** 매체
fame 명성 **carve out a niche** 자리매김하다 　　　　　　　**정답**_(d)

59

One might think that, of all the things we need to understand to function in the world, our own feelings would be among the easiest to grasp. Unfortunately, the truth is that many people mistrust their feelings and, as a result, have a hard time dealing with them. They either suppress or ignore them. What they do not realize is that becoming sensitive to their feelings is the first step towards a fuller knowledge of themselves and their world.

Q What can be inferred from the lecture?
(a) Suppressed feelings can limit self-understanding.
(b) More people are dealing with their feelings today.
(c) Feelings are easier to understand than people think.
(d) Modern life over-sensitizes people to their feelings.

SOLUTION

세상에서 역할을 하기 위해 우리가 알아야 하는 모든 것들 중에서 사람들은 우리 자신의 감정이 아마 가장 이해하기 쉬운 것이라고 생각할지 모릅니다. 불행히도 많은 사람들은 자신의 감정을 믿지 못하고, 그 결과 감정을 다루는 데 어려움을 겪는 것이 현실입니다. 사람들은 감정을 억누르거나 무시합니다. 사람들이 인식하지 못하는 것은 자신의 감정에 신경을 쓰는 것이 자기 자신과 세계에 대해 더 완전하게 알 수 있는 첫걸음이라는 것이죠.

Q 강의에서 유추할 수 있는 것은?
(a) 억눌린 감정은 자기 이해에 제약이 될 수 있다.
(b) 오늘날 더 많은 사람들이 자신의 감정을 다루고 있다.
(c) 사람들이 생각하는 것보다 감정은 이해하기 쉽다.
(d) 현대적인 삶 때문에 사람들은 자신의 감정에 과민해진다.

기출 POINT

강의 내용을 기반으로 언급되지 않은 것을 추론해 내는 문제이다. 사람들은 자신의 감정을 억누르고 이것은 자신과 세상에 대한 이해를 방해한다는 내용이다. 감정은 생각보다 이해하기 쉽다는 (c)는 정반대의 내용이다. 현대적인 삶이라는 외부 조건은 위의 내용과 무관하므로 (d) 역시 오답이다.

grasp 이해하다 **mistrust** 불신하다 **suppress** 억누르다
over-sensitize 과민하게 하다   정답 _(a)

60

Like other modernist writers, Virginia Woolf attempted to portray reality in an innovative way by rendering subjective experience as authentically as possible, as something relative and in a constant state of flux. She succeeds in meeting such a goal in *Mrs. Dalloway*, her fourth novel, with a masterfully interwoven texture of her protagonists' unique thoughts, emotions and dreams, adopting a style referred to as stream of consciousness. Her narrative flows from the conscious to the unconscious, from the fantastic to the real, and from memory to the present.

Q What can be inferred about the novel *Mrs. Dalloway* from the lecture?
(a) Its characters tend to have some semblance to Woolf herself.
(b) Woolf's personal outlook on consciousness is absent from it.
(c) It shows Woolf's grasp of contemporary philosophical ideas.
(d) The story's plot travels forward and backward in time.

SOLUTION

여타 모더니즘 작가들과 마찬가지로 버지니아 울프도 주관적인 경험을 최대한 믿을 만한 것, 상대적이면서 끊임없는 변화 상태에 있는 무언가로 그려냄으로써 현실을 혁신적인 방식으로 묘사하고자 시도했습니다. 버지니아 울프는 자신의 네 번째 소설인 〈댈러웨이 부인〉에서 의식의 흐름이라는 기법을 채택해서 주인공들의 독특한 생각, 감정과 꿈이 절묘하게 얽힌 짜임새를 사용해 이 같은 목표를 달성하는 데 성공하죠. 버지니아 울프의 서술은 의식에서 무의식, 환상에서 현실, 그리고 기억에서 현재로 흐릅니다.

Q 강의에서 소설 〈댈러웨이 부인〉에 대해 유추할 수 있는 것은?
(a) 등장 인물들은 울프 자신과 약간 닮은 성향을 보인다.
(b) 의식에 대한 울프의 개인적 견지가 빠져 있다.
(c) 현대 철학 사상에 대한 울프의 이해를 보여준다.
(d) 이야기의 줄거리가 시간을 넘나든다.

기출 POINT

모더니즘 작가로서의 버지니아 울프의 특성을 설명하는 강의이다. 그녀의 묘사 방식으로 의식의 흐름이라는 기법은 생각, 감정, 꿈이 얽혀서 의식과 무의식, 환상과 현실, 과거에서 현재로 흐른다고 했으므로 이야기가 시간을 넘나든다는 것을 유추해 볼 수 있다. 따라서 정답은 (d)이다.

portray 그리다 **innovative** 혁신적인 **render** 묘사하다 **relative** 상대적인 **flux** 끊임없는 변화 **protagonist** 주인공 **refer to** ~라고 부르다 **stream of consciousness** 의식의 흐름 **semblance** 유사함 **absent** 없는, 결여된 **contemporary** 현대의   정답 _(d)

🔊 Grammar

1

A What do you do for exercise?

B I really enjoy _____, so I do that almost every day.

(a) bike
(b) biking
(c) to bike
(d) to have biked

SOLUTION

A 운동은 뭘 하세요?

B 저는 자전거 타는 것을 즐겨서 거의 매일 탑니다.

⊞ 기출 POINT

enjoy는 동명사를 목적어로 취하는 동사이므로 biking의 형태로 써야 맞다. 동명사를 목적어로 취하는 동사: mind, give up, finish, avoid, consider, deny

exercise 운동　**bike** 자전거를 타다　　　　　　　　**정답** (b)

2

A Did you ever get in touch with Fred?

B No, _____, all I got was a recorded message.

(a) when I called
(b) when called
(c) I called
(d) calling

SOLUTION

A 프레드와 연락이 닿기는 했니?

B 아니. 전화하니까 녹음된 메시지만 나왔어.

⊞ 기출 POINT

all I got이 주어이고 was가 동사인 완전한 문장이므로 빈칸에 올 수 있는 것은 〈접속사+주어+동사〉 형태이다. 주어는 I로 all I got과 달라서 주어가 생략되는 분사구문인 calling은 불가능하며 when I called라는 부사절의 형태가 되어야 한다.

get in touch with ∼와 연락하다　**recorded message** 녹음 메시지
정답 (a)

3

A John _____ on the 13th.

B Oh, that's tomorrow!

(a) arrived
(b) is arriving
(c) has arrived
(d) had arrived

SOLUTION

A 존이 13일에 도착해.

B 와, 내일이네!

⊞ 기출 POINT

13일이 tomorrow라고 했다. 미래의 일에 대해 얘기하고 있으므로 미래시제를 써야 하지만 미래에 확실히 예정된 일은 현재진행형으로 나타내기도 한다. 따라서 빈칸에는 is arriving이 적절하다.

on the 13th 13일에　　　　　　　　　　　　　　　**정답** (b)

4

A I've seen several productions of the famous ballet *Swan Lake*.

B _____, and they were great.

(a) I have so
(b) Have I so
(c) So I have
(d) So have I

SOLUTION

A 나는 유명한 발레 〈백조의 호수〉를 여러 연출로 봤어.

B 나도 그랬는데, 다 훌륭했어.

⊞ 기출 POINT

'∼도 그러하다. ∼도 마찬가지이다'라고 말할 때 〈So+동사+주어〉를 쓴다. 조동사나 be동사의 경우 동사 자리에 그대로 쓰면 되므로 have를 써서 So have I가 된다.

production 연출　　　　　　　　　　　　　　　　**정답** (d)

5

A I'm sick of our computer. Let's buy a new one.
B Yes, ours _____ old and outdated by today's standards.

(a) is
(b) was
(c) will be
(d) had been

A 우리 컴퓨터 때문에 짜증나. 새 컴퓨터 하나 사자.
B 그래. 우리 컴퓨터는 요즘 기준으로 봤을 때 오래됐고 구식이지.

⊞ 기출 POINT
Let's buy나 old and outdated에서 내용상 미래나 과거로 혼동하기 쉽지만, our computer의 현재 상태에 대해 얘기하고 있으므로 빈칸에는 현재시제가 알맞다.
be sick of ~이 지겹다 **outdated** 구식의   정답 _(a)

6

A Are you well enough to go to work?
B Yes, _____.

(a) think so me
(b) me so think
(c) I so think
(d) I think so

A 출근할 수 있을 만큼 상태가 괜찮으세요?
B 네, 그런 것 같은데요.

⊞ 기출 POINT
상대방의 말을 받아서 대답할 때 긍정이면 so를, 부정이면 not을 붙이는 형태이다. Yes로 시작했으므로 I think so가 적절하다.
상대방의 말에 대한 응답: I hope not. 그렇지 않기를 바라요./ I suppose so. 그럴 거라 생각돼요./ I guess not. 그렇지 않을 것 같아요.
well 건강이 좋은   정답 _(d)

7

A Are you married, Dave?
B Yes. _____ married for two years.

(a) I'm
(b) I was
(c) I've been
(d) I'm being

A 데이브, 기혼이세요?
B 네, 결혼한 지 2년 됐어요.

⊞ 기출 POINT
과거의 상태가 현재까지 이어질 때 현재완료로 나타낸다. 현재 기혼자이므로 문맥상 결혼이 지금까지 이어져 왔다는 뜻이 되므로 빈칸에는 계속을 나타내는 현재완료인 I've been이 알맞다.
married 결혼한   정답 _(c)

8

A I have a job interview today.
B Good luck! Let me know _____ as soon as you find out.

(a) result
(b) a result
(c) the result
(d) this result

A 오늘 취업 면접이 있어.
B 행운을 빌어! 결과 나오는 대로 나한테 알려줘.

⊞ 기출 POINT
result라는 명사 앞에 올 한정사를 찾는 문제이다. result는 셀 수 있는 명사이므로 a나 the를 쓸 수 있고, 앞에서 이미 언급된 취업 면접의 result를 말하는 것이므로 the가 들어가야 한다. 관사는 우리말에 없는 개념이기 때문에 주의를 기울여 익혀 두어야 할 부분이다.
job interview 취업 면접 **as soon as** ~하자마자   정답 _(c)

9

A I'm going to Hong Kong for my vacation. How about you?
B I can't afford _____ a trip anywhere.

(a) take
(b) to take
(c) for taking
(d) being taken

SOLUTION

A 휴가로 홍콩에 갈 거야. 넌 어때?
B 나는 아무 데도 여행 갈 형편이 안 돼.

⊞ 기출 POINT

can[can't] afford는 '~할 형편이 [안]되다'라는 뜻으로 쓰인다. afford 다음에는 〈to+동사원형〉이 오므로 정답은 (b)이다.
to부정사를 목적어로 취하는 동사: happen, cause, swear, tend, want, pretend, ask, expect, demand, force, plan, offer, hope, arrange, manage

vacation 휴가 **afford** ~할 형편이 되다   정답_(b)

10

A Was it you making all that noise last night?
B No, it _____ have been me. I was out all last night.

(a) mustn't
(b) couldn't
(c) mightn't
(d) shouldn't

SOLUTION

A 어젯밤에 그렇게 소란스럽게 한 게 너였니?
B 아니, 나였을 리는 없어. 나는 어젯밤 내내 밖에 있었거든.

⊞ 기출 POINT

〈조동사(could/ might/ must)+have p.p.〉 형태에 대한 문제이다. '어제 밖에 있었으므로 시끄럽게 한 사람은 나일 리가 없다'라는 내용이 되어야 하므로 빈칸에는 가능성을 나타내는 could가 적절하다.
~일 리 없다: couldn't have p.p./ ~했어야 했는데: should have p.p.

make noise 소음을 내다   정답_(b)

11

A What's the hotel policy on room keys?
B They should _____ at the front desk.

(a) leave
(b) be left
(c) be leaving
(d) have been left

SOLUTION

A 방 열쇠에 대한 호텔 방침이 뭐죠?
B 열쇠는 접수처에 맡기셔야 합니다.

⊞ 기출 POINT

주어인 They는 room keys를 가리킨다. 방 열쇠는 남겨지는 것으로 의미상 수동태가 알맞다. 조동사 should 뒤에 오므로 be동사의 원형인 be가, 동사 leave의 과거분사형인 left가 쓰여 be left가 된다.

policy 방침 **front desk** (호텔 등의) 접수처   정답_(b)

12

A Our team needs more time to finish the class project.
B Our team _____, too.

(a) needs to
(b) does it
(c) needs
(d) does

SOLUTION

A 우리 팀은 반 프로젝트를 마치려면 시간이 더 필요해.
B 우리 팀도 마찬가지야.

⊞ 기출 POINT

짧은 대답은 앞에서 언급된 것을 최대한 생략하려고 한다. 일반적으로 짧은 대답형은 〈주어+조동사〉를 쓰며 일반동사인 경우에는 do/ does를 쓴다. need가 조동사로 쓰일 때도 있지만 여기에서는 주어에 따라 needs로 쓰인 것으로 보아 일반동사이다.

need 필요로 하다 **project** 과제   정답_(d)

13

A The party got few votes in the election.
B Yes, _____.

(a) more they didn't get it's a shame
(b) a shame it's they didn't get more
(c) it's a shame they didn't get more
(d) they didn't get more it's a shame

SOLUTION

A 그 당은 선거에서 거의 표를 못 얻었어요.
B 그러게요. 표를 더 많이 얻지 못한 건 유감이네요.

기출 POINT

표를 더 많이 얻지 못한 것은 유감스러운 일이라는 뜻이 되어야 한다. 안타깝거나 실망한 일에 대해 말할 때 〈It's a shame/ What a shame+(that절)〉을 쓴다.

party 정당 **vote** 투표 수 **election** 선거   정답_(c)

14

A When did the suspect finally talk?
B Only after they got him a lawyer _____ his mouth.

(a) he opened
(b) opened he
(c) he did open
(d) did he open

SOLUTION

A 용의자가 언제 입을 열었습니까?
B 변호사를 선임해 주고 나서야 입을 열었어요.

기출 POINT

도치 구문 문제이다. 강조 부사인 only, just가 이끄는 절이 문장의 앞에 나올 때 주절에 있는 주어와 동사가 도치된다. 이때 조동사나 be동사가 아닌 일반동사이면 opened he라고 하지 않고 조동사 do를 써서 did he open의 형태로 써야 한다.

suspect 용의자 **only after** ~후에야 **lawyer** 변호사   정답_(d)

15

A What did the professor ask you?
B He asked _____ my assignment.

(a) how to me was I doing
(b) me I was doing how with
(c) me how I was doing with
(d) how was I doing me with

SOLUTION

A 교수님이 너한테 뭘 물어보시든?
B 과제 잘하고 있냐고 물어보셨어.

기출 POINT

He asked me, "How are you doing with your assignment?"를 간접화법으로 나타낸 문장이다. 의문사 how가 있으므로 〈ask+목적어(사람)+의문사+주어+동사〉 순이 된다는 것을 기억해 두자.

professor 교수 **assignment** 과제   정답_(c)

16

A Enrollment at this school seems to increase every year.
B True. Unfortunately, the number of teachers _____ the same.

(a) are remained
(b) is remained
(c) remains
(d) remain

SOLUTION

A 이 학교의 등록자 수가 해마다 느는 것 같아요.
B 맞습니다. 불행히도 교사 수에는 변동이 없어요.

기출 POINT

동사 remain은 '~한 상태나 상황이 유지되다'라는 뜻이며 뒤에 silent/ unchanged/ friends와 같은 명사나 형용사가 보어로 올 수 있다. 단수 주어(the number)이므로 동사의 형태는 remains가 되어야 한다. the number of+복수명사: ~의 수 / a number of+복수명사: 많은 ~

enrollment 등록자 수 **seem to** ~하는 것 같다 **increase** 증가하다
unfortunately 불행히도   정답_(c)

17

A I think Ann can be quite bossy.

B Yeah, she can't help but tell _____.

(a) what everyone to do
(b) everyone what to do
(c) what to do for everyone
(d) everyone that is what to do

SOLUTION

A 앤은 꽤 으스대는 것 같더라.
B 응. 그녀는 모두에게 이래라저래라 할 수밖에 없어.

⊞ 기출 POINT

〈can't help but+동사원형〉은 '~할 수밖에 없다'라는 뜻이다. tell 다음에는 〈목적어(사람)+의문사〉가 있는 간접화법을 쓸 수 있다. 의문사구 what to do가 온 (b)가 정답이다.
bossy 두목 행세하는, 으스대는   정답_(b)

18

A Should I do my essay on the first topic or the second?

B _____ you prefer to write on.

(a) That
(b) What
(c) Which
(d) Whichever

SOLUTION

A 에세이를 첫 번째 주제로 써야 할까, 아니면 두 번째 주제로 써야 할까?
B 네가 쓰고 싶은 주제 아무거나.

⊞ 기출 POINT

응답으로 first topic과 second topic 둘 중에 어떤 것인지 말해 주어야 한다. 그래서 선행사인 topic을 포함하는 관계대명사를 써야 하는데 What과 Whichever가 가능하지만 두 가지에 대해 말하고 있으므로 '둘 중 무엇이든'의 의미인 Whichever가 적절하다.
prefer ~을 선호하다   정답_(d)

19

A Have you seen my jacket anywhere?

B It's hanging _____ the hat stand.

(a) in
(b) at
(c) on
(d) with

SOLUTION

A 내 재킷 어디선가 봤니?
B 모자걸이에 걸려 있어.

⊞ 기출 POINT

the hat stand라는 장소를 나타내는 명사 앞에 쓸 전치사를 고르는 문제이다. 모자는 모자걸이에 접촉하여 매달리는 형태가 되므로 in이나 at이 아니라 on을 쓴다.
hat stand 모자걸이   정답_(c)

20

A Did your parents say okay to your auditioning for an acting job?

B No, they _____ see it my way.

(a) mustn't
(b) mightn't
(c) wouldn't
(d) shouldn't

SOLUTION

A 네가 배우가 되기 위해 오디션 보는 걸 너희 부모님도 승낙하셨어?
B 아니. 부모님은 나처럼 생각하지 않으실 거야.

⊞ 기출 POINT

대답이 No로 시작하고 있어서 '내 생각을 이해하지 않으려 한다'는 문장이 되어야 하므로 빈칸에는 강한 의지, 고집을 나타내는 조동사 would의 부정형인 wouldn't가 알맞다.
audition 오디션을 보다   **see it my way** 내 생각을 이해하다   정답_(c)

21

Joe found Annie in the kitchen _____ the dishes.

(a) washing
(b) washed
(c) to wash
(d) washes

SOLUTION

조는 애니가 부엌에서 설거지를 하고 있는 것을 발견했다.

⊞ 기출 POINT
'애니가 설거지하는 것을 발견했다'는 말이므로 〈find+목적어+목적보어〉 형태이다. find의 목적보어 자리에는 동사가 올 때 현재분사나 과거분사를 쓰는데 목적어와 목적보어의 관계가 능동이면 현재분사를, 수동이면 과거분사를 쓰므로 빈칸에는 washing이 적절하다.
wash the dishes 설거지하다   정답_(a)

22

The Enlightenment was a movement that started among a small elite group and slowly spread to make its influence _____ throughout Europe.

(a) felt
(b) to feel
(c) feeling
(d) having felt

SOLUTION

계몽 운동은 소수 엘리트 집단 사이에서 발단되어 서서히 유럽 전역에 그 영향력을 행사할 정도로 확산된 운동이었다.

⊞ 기출 POINT
make는 〈목적어+목적보어〉를 필요로 하는 사역 동사이다. 목적보어는 목적어와의 관계가 능동이면 동사원형을, 수동이면 과거분사를 쓴다. 영향력은 느껴지는 것이므로 수동의 관계가 되어 빈칸에는 felt가 알맞다.
the Enlightenment 계몽 운동 **movement** 운동 **elite group** 엘리트 집단 **spread** 퍼지다 **influence** 영향력   정답_(a)

23

The professor considered it an honor to have a scholarship named after _____.

(a) him
(b) his
(c) he
(d) it

SOLUTION

그 교수는 자신의 이름을 딴 장학금이 생기는 것을 영광으로 생각했다.

⊞ 기출 POINT
〈consider+목적어+목적보어〉는 '~라고 생각하다'이며 considered it (to be) an honor의 it는 긴 목적어인 to have 이하를 대신하는 가목적어이다. have a scholarship named after도 〈have+목적어+목적보어(p.p.)〉의 형태이다. name after는 이어 동사로 다음에 목적어가 와서 '~를 따라 이름 짓다'라는 뜻이 되므로 교수를 가리키는 him이 정답이다.
honor 영광 **scholarship** 장학금   정답_(a)

24

Sandra Blake is an award-winning writer _____ the *New York Times*.

(a) in
(b) for
(c) over
(d) across

SOLUTION

샌드라 블레이크는 〈뉴욕 타임스〉의 수상 작가이다.

⊞ 기출 POINT
전치사 for는 어떤 회사나 단체, 팀에 소속되어 있는지 말할 때 사용한다. write for a local paper/ work for IBM/ play for the Team C 등으로 쓴다. '〈뉴욕 타임스〉에서 일하는 수상 작가'라는 뜻이 되도록 전치사 for를 써야 한다.
award-winning 수상 경력이 있는   정답_(b)

25

Persistently late students, meaning those
_____ have received more than five tardy
slips, will be suspended.

(a) who
(b) which
(c) of which
(d) of whom

SOLUTION

상습 지각생, 즉 다섯 번 이상 지각 표를 받은 사람들은 정학 처분을 받을 것입니다.

田 기출 POINT

관계대명사 문제이다. '~하는 사람들'이라는 일반인을 선행사로 하는 관계대명사로 those who를 쓴다. 관계대명사가 주어로 쓰이므로 주격인 who가 와야 하고 those는 복수이므로 동사가 have received가 된 것도 유의하자.

persistently 지속적으로   **tardy slip** 지각 표, 사유서   **suspend** 정학시키다

정답_(a)

26

Many people think of dieting not just as a way to
become thinner, but _____ control over
their lives.

(a) a gaining of way
(b) gaining a way of
(c) as a way of gaining
(d) gaining as a way of

SOLUTION

많은 사람들은 다이어트를 단순히 더 날씬해지기 위한 길이 아니라 자신들의 삶을 통제하는 방편으로 생각한다.

田 기출 POINT

not just A but B라는 접속사 형태에서 A와 B는 병렬구조를 이루면서 대등한 형태이어야 한다. 따라서 as a way to become과 같은 형태를 이루려면 as a way of gaining이 되어야 한다.

think of A as B A를 B로 생각하다   **thin** 마른   **gain** (체중이) 늘다

정답_(c)

27

For centuries, humans have looked up at the sky
and wondered _____ the confines of our
planet.

(a) beyond what exists
(b) what exists beyond
(c) what beyond does exist
(d) beyond what does exist

SOLUTION

수세기 동안 사람들은 하늘을 올려다보며 우리 행성 그 너머에는 무엇이 있을지 궁금해했다.

田 기출 POINT

wonder의 목적어로 의문사 what이 이끄는 절이 온 간접의문문이다. What exists beyond the confines of our planet?이라는 의문문이 wonder의 목적어 자리로 들어가 〈의문사 주어+동사〉의 어순이 되어 what exists beyond …가 된다.

century 세기   **confine** 범위, 영역   **planet** 행성   **exist** 존재하다

정답_(b)

28

Critics thought the new band would be successful,
but not _____ successful as to break album
sales records.

(a) very
(b) such
(c) too
(d) so

SOLUTION

비평가들은 새 밴드가 성공적이기는 하겠지만 앨범 판매 기록을 경신할 만큼 성공적이지는 않을 것이라고 생각했다.

田 기출 POINT

not so successful as to break는 〈not so+형용사+as to+동사원형〉 형태로 쓰였으며 '기록을 경신할 만큼 성공적이지는 않다'는 말이 된다. 이와 구별할 것은 가운데 형용사가 들어가지 않는 〈so as not to+동사원형〉인데 이는 '~하지 않도록'의 뜻이다.

critic 비평가   **sales records** 판매 기록

정답_(d)

29

Once _____, harbor seals become less tolerant of contact with others of their kind.

(a) to wean
(b) weaned
(c) were weaned
(d) had been weaned

SOLUTION

일단 젖을 떼고 나면, 점박이 바다표범은 다른 점박이 바다표범들과의 접촉에 대해 덜 관대해지게 된다.

⊞ 기출 POINT

Once는 때를 나타내는 접속사로 분사구문을 이끈다. 동사 wean은 '이유시키다, 젖을 떼다'의 뜻으로 주절의 주어인 harbor seals는 이유를 당하는 것이므로 과거분사가 와야 한다. Once weaned는 〈주어+be 동사〉가 생략된 형태이다.

harbor seal 점박이 바다표범 **tolerant of** ~에 관대한 **wean** 젖을 떼다

정답_(b)

30

The lost cat had _____ white fur and blue eyes.

(a) long
(b) a long
(c) the long
(d) that long

SOLUTION

잃어버린 고양이는 털이 하얗고 눈이 파랬다.

⊞ 기출 POINT

물질명사인 fur는 부정관사를 쓰지 못하고 복수형으로 만들지도 못 한다. 복수형 furs는 '모피제품'이라는 다른 뜻이 된다는 것에 주의하자. 여기에서는 물질명사로 쓰였기 때문에 long white fur의 형태로 써야 한다.

fur 털

정답_(a)

31

According to school policy, clothing that is suggestive, vulgar or inappropriate _____ allowed on campus.

(a) have not been
(b) has not been
(c) are not
(d) is not

SOLUTION

학교 방침에 따르면 선정적이거나 천박하거나 부적절한 의상은 학교 내에서 허락되지 않는다.

⊞ 기출 POINT

주어는 clothing이고 빈칸 뒤에 과거분사인 allowed가 있으므로 수동태임을 알 수 있다. 또한 명령이나 지시문에서는 현재시제를 쓴다는 것에 유의하자. clothing이 집합적 물질명사이기 때문에 단수 동사인 is가 온다. 집합적 물질명사: furniture, clothing, produce, baggage **suggestive** 선정적인 **vulgar** 천박한 **inappropriate** 부적절한

정답_(d)

32

If the injured man _____ brought to the hospital sooner, doctors might have been able to save his life.

(a) be
(b) were
(c) has been
(d) had been

SOLUTION

만약 그 부상자가 병원에 좀 더 빨리 호송되었더라면 의사들이 그의 생명을 구할 수 있었을지도 모른다.

⊞ 기출 POINT

가정법 과거완료 문장이다. 주절의 동사가 might have been이므로 과거에 일어난 일에 대해 다른 가정을 하는 가정법 과거완료임을 알 수 있다. 따라서 If절의 동사는 〈had+p.p.〉 형태를 써야 한다.

injured 부상당한

정답_(d)

33

Immigration officials _____ of the fact that Mexican nationals enter the US illegally in large numbers.

(a) have been aware long
(b) aware have been long
(c) have long been aware
(d) aware long have been

이민국 관료들은 멕시코인들이 때를 지어 불법으로 미국에 들어온다는 사실을 오래전부터 알고 있었다.

⊞ 기출 POINT

aware는 서술적인 형용사로 전치사 of와 함께 쓰인다. long은 형용사와 같은 형태로 부사로도 쓰이는데 이 문장에서 부사로 쓰여 형용사인 aware를 수식한다. 그러므로 aware 앞에 쓰거나 be동사 앞에 위치하는 것이 알맞다. 서술적 용법으로만 사용되는 형용사: afraid, alike, aware, asleep, worth, unable, pleased, glad
immigration 이민국 **national** 국민 정답_(c)

34

_____ poaching continues to threaten tigers' survival significantly, their greatest long-term threat is habitat loss.

(a) If
(b) Since
(c) While
(d) Because

SOLUTION

밀렵이 계속해서 호랑이들의 생존을 상당히 위협하기는 하지만 이들에게 있어 가장 큰 장기적인 위협은 서식지 소실이다.

⊞ 기출 POINT

밀렵이 생존을 위협한다는 사실과 가장 큰 장기적인 위협은 서식지 소실이라는 두 내용을 이어줄 접속사로 알맞은 것을 찾아야 한다. While은 문장 앞에서 '~라고는 해도, ~하지만'이라는 뜻으로 Although와 바꿔 쓸 수 있다.
poach 밀렵하다 **threaten** 위협하다 **significantly** 상당히 **long-term** 장기적인 **habitat** 서식지 정답_(c)

35

In the world of digital photography, _____ with computer software.

(a) taken pictures by you can be altered
(b) your pictures taken can be altered
(c) pictures you take can be altered
(d) can be altered your pictures

SOLUTION

디지털 사진의 시대에는 당신이 찍는 사진을 컴퓨터 소프트웨어로 변형할 수 있다.

⊞ 기출 POINT

can be altered의 주어인 pictures를 수식하는 말이 맞게 쓰였는지 확인한다. 관계대명사 which는 목적격이므로 생략 가능하여 pictures you take가 맞다. 분사가 단독으로 명사를 수식할 때는 명사 앞에 와야 하므로 (b)는 오답이다. (a)는 taken by you처럼 분사 뒤에 따라오는 말이 있을 때는 분사가 명사 뒤에서 수식해야 한다.
take pictures 사진 찍다 **alter** 변형하다 정답_(c)

36

_____ in excessive quantities, caffeine may cause insomnia and headaches.

(a) Consume
(b) Consumed
(c) Consuming
(d) To consume

SOLUTION

과도한 양을 섭취하면 카페인은 불면증과 두통을 유발할 수 있다.

⊞ 기출 POINT

분사구문에서 주어는 주절과 같기 때문에 생략된 것이다. caffeine이 주어이며 동사 Consume과 수동 관계이기 때문에 과거분사인 Consumed가 온다. 접속사로는 내용상 If가 되겠지만 생략되고, 주어와 being도 생략되어 Consumed만 문장의 맨 앞에 남은 분사구문이다.
excessive 과도한 **caffeine** 카페인 **insomnia** 불면증 정답_(b)

37

The manager demanded that the current project _____ done by the end of the week.

(a) had been
(b) is being
(c) be
(d) is

SOLUTION

매니저는 현재 프로젝트를 이번 주까지 완료하라고 요구했다.

⊞ 기출 POINT

충고, 요구, 제안, 명령을 나타내는 동사(demand, suggest, insist, propose, request, order)의 목적어가 되는 that 절의 동사는 should가 생략된 동사원형을 쓴다. 따라서 빈칸에는 be가 적절하다.

demand 요구하다   current 현재의   정답 (c)

38

This website provides _____ on the causes of high blood pressure and treatment options.

(a) the informations
(b) an information
(c) informations
(d) information

SOLUTION

이 홈페이지는 고혈압의 원인과 치료 대안에 대한 정보를 제공한다.

⊞ 기출 POINT

information은 셀 수 없는 명사로 a/ an을 쓸 수 없고 복수형도 만들 수 없다. 셀 수 있기 위해서는 a piece of/ two pieces of와 같은 별도의 표현을 써야 한다.

provide 제공하다   cause 원인   high blood pressure 고혈압
treatment option 치료 대안   정답 (d)

39

The young mother _____ for only an hour when her baby's cries woke her.

(a) sleeps
(b) has slept
(c) will have slept
(d) had been sleeping

SOLUTION

그 젊은 어머니는 아이의 울음소리에 깨서 잠을 한 시간밖에 못 잤다.

⊞ 기출 POINT

'울음소리에 깼을 때 한 시간밖에 못 자고 있었다'는 내용이다. 깼을 때가 과거이므로 특정 과거를 기준으로 이전까지의 일을 나타내는 과거완료형 혹은 그 과거 전까지 행동이 지속되고 있었다는 것을 나타내는 과거완료 진행형이 적절하다.

cry 울음   wake 깨우다   정답 (d)

40

It was Audrey Hepburn's beauty, coupled with her vulnerability, that made her _____ presence.

(a) compelling such an on-screen
(b) such an on-screen compelling
(c) such a compelling on-screen
(d) on-screen compelling such a

SOLUTION

오드리 헵번이 그토록 흡인력 있는 은막의 존재가 될 수 있었던 것은 그녀의 연약한 모습과 더불어 그녀의 미모 때문이었다.

⊞ 기출 POINT

⟨such+a(n)+형용사+명사⟩의 어순을 알고 있어야 한다. 내용을 볼 때 '흡인력 있는 은막의 존재'라는 말이 되어야 하므로 compelling on-screen presence의 순서가 되어야 한다. It is … that 강조구문이 전체 구조를 이루는 문장이라는 것도 확인해 두자.

couple ~와 결합하다   vulnerability 연약함   presence 존재
compelling 흡인력 있는   정답 (c)

41

(a) A It seems like our experiment is a failure.

(b) B Yeah, it isn't producing the results we expected.

(c) A We must have done something wrong.

(d) B Well, it might work good if we try it again with some changes.

SOLUTION

(a) 우리 실험이 실패한 것 같아.

(b) 그러게. 우리가 기대했던 결과가 나오질 않네.

(c) 뭔가 잘못한 게 분명해.

(d) 음, 약간 변경해서 다시 시도해 보면 잘될지도 몰라.

⊞ 기출 POINT

실험 결과가 잘 나오지 않은 상황의 대화이다. '실험을 다시 해보면 잘될지도 모른다'는 내용이 적절하다. 따라서 '잘 풀리다, 잘되다'의 뜻으로 work well이나 work better를 써야 한다. 구어체에서 good은 well 대신 doing pretty good, listen to me good처럼 부사로 쓰기도 하지만 문법적으로 work good은 잘못된 표현이다.

experiment 실험   **failure** 실패   **result** 결과

정답_(d) work good → work well

42

(a) A Alison is moving to Halifax in April.

(b) B That's so sudden. Why did she decide to do that?

(c) A She is offered a really good job there.

(d) B I see. Well, we'll have to visit her sometime.

SOLUTION

(a) 앨리슨이 4월에 핼리팩스로 이사한대.

(b) 굉장히 갑작스럽네. 왜 그러기로 했대?

(c) 그곳에 있는 굉장히 좋은 일자리를 제안받았어.

(d) 그렇구나. 음, 언제 한번 앨리슨 보러 가야겠네.

⊞ 기출 POINT

앨리슨이 떠나기로 결심한 이유를 묻는 질문에 대한 답인데 시제가 맞지 않는다. 일자리를 제안받고 결심한 것이므로 현재시제를 쓸 수 없다. 과거나 현재완료형으로 was offered나 has been offered가 되어야 한다.

offer 제안하다   **sometime** 언젠가

정답_(c) is offered → was offered/ has been offered

43

(a) A Good evening. Do you have a reservation?

(b) B My husband made one. He should be here already.

(c) A What name is under his reservation?

(d) B His last name is Chilton, Alan Chilton.

SOLUTION

(a) 안녕하세요. 예약하셨습니까?

(b) 제 남편이 예약했어요. 그이가 아마 벌써 와 있을 거예요.

(c) 예약자 성함이 어떻게 되십니까?

(d) 성이 칠튼이에요. 앨런 칠튼이요.

🎴 기출 POINT

예약을 확인하는 대화이다. 예약자 이름을 말할 때 〈under+이름〉을 쓴다. 전치사 under의 목적어가 의문사 What name인 의문문에서 전치사는 문장의 맨 앞이나 맨 뒤에 쓰기 때문에 What name is his reservation under?나 Under what name is his reservation?으로 써야 하므로 정답은 (c)이다.

reservation 예약

정답_(c) What name is under his reservation?
→ What name is his reservation under?
Under what name is his reservation?

44

(a) A I'm a bit nervous about going to the dentist this afternoon.

(b) B Don't be. The dentist will make sure it's virtually painless.

(c) A I guess you're right. Anyway, having a tooth pulled is a common procedure.

(d) B That's right, but there's no sense in worrying about it.

SOLUTION

(a) 오늘 오후에 치과에 가는 것 때문에 좀 긴장돼.

(b) 그러지 마. 치과 의사가 전혀 아프지 않게 해줄 거야.

(c) 네 말이 맞아. 아무튼 이를 뽑는 건 흔한 처치니까.

(d) 그래. 그리고 걱정해 봐야 아무 소용 없으니까.

🎴 기출 POINT

(d)에서 That's right과 there's no sense in worrying about it이 어떤 관계인지 알아야 접속사를 맞게 쓸 수 있다. 아프지 않을 것이라는 말에 동조하며 That's right이라고 하고 있다. 따라서 문맥상 자연스러우려면 접속사 but을 and나 so로 고쳐야 한다.

a bit 약간 **virtually** 사실상 **painless** 아프지 않은 **procedure** 절차; 순서

정답_(d) but → and/ so

45

(a) A Who was the man you were talking to outside the library?

(b) B He's the professor for which class I couldn't buy a textbook.

(c) A What did he say you should do?

(d) B He just said I could copy the relevant chapters from his book.

SOLUTION

(a) 도서관 밖에서 너랑 얘기하던 남자 누구야?

(b) 교수님인데 그분 수업에서 쓸 교재를 살 수가 없어서.

(c) 너한테 어떻게 하라고 하시든?

(d) 교수님 책에서 관련 챕터를 복사해도 된다고 하시던데.

⊞ 기출 POINT

(b)에서 선행사는 사람(the professor)이므로 소유격 관계대명사절에서는 which class가 아니라 whose class가 되어야 한다.

outside 밖에서 **textbook** 교재 **relevant** 관련된

정답 (b) which → whose

46

(a) Behaviorists believe that the basis of all learning in animals is reinforcement. (b) Reinforcement occurs when an animal associates a behavior with a reward. (c) For example, if a hungry rat gets a food pellet after pushing a lever, it is likely to push the lever again. (d) Thus, having learned correctly what to do, food is then given to the rat as a reward.

SOLUTION

(a) 행동주의자들은 동물의 모든 학습 기초는 강화라고 믿는다. (b) 강화는 동물이 행동과 보상을 연관지을 때 일어난다. (c) 예를 들면, 배고픈 쥐가 지렛대를 누른 후 먹이 덩어리를 얻는다면, 쥐는 아마도 그 지렛대를 다시 누를 것이다. (d) 따라서 해야 할 일을 제대로 학습하고 나면 먹이가 쥐에게 보상으로 주어진다.

⊞ 기출 POINT

(d)에서 having learned 이하는 분사구문을 이룬다. having learned의 주어는 a rat인데 주절의 주어인 food와 다르기 때문에 주어를 생략하려면 주절 food is then given to the rat as a reward를 the rat is given food as a reward로 바꿔야 한다.

behaviorist 행동주의자 **reinforcement** 강화 **associate** 연관짓다

reward 보상 **pellet** 작은 알 **lever** 지렛대

정답 (d) food is then given to the rat as a reward
→ the rat is given food as a reward

47

(a) Dab Away is part of Ellen Lange's daily maintenance system designed to cleanse and balance the skin. (b) It works to remove dirt, excess oil, makeup and dead skin cells, keeping your skin clean and healthy. (c) You can also use Dab Away as a fast-acted spot treatment to reduce oily skin and clear clogged pores. (d) It comes with our patented hygienic applicator that allows for extra precision spot treatment.

SOLUTION

(a) 댑 어웨이는 피부 청결과 균형을 위해 고안된 엘렌 레인지의 일일 유지 시스템의 일환입니다. (b) 댑 어웨이는 먼지와 과도한 피지, 화장과 죽은 피부세포를 제거하여 당신의 피부를 깨끗하고 건강하게 지켜 드립니다. (c) 또한 댑 어웨이는 피지를 줄이고 막힌 모공을 청소하기 위한 즉효성 스팟 트리트먼트로도 사용할 수 있습니다. (d) 댑 어웨이에는 더 정밀한 스팟 트리트먼트를 위해 특허받은 위생 도포기가 포함되어 있습니다.

기출 POINT

명사를 꾸며주는 분사의 형태에 대한 문제이다. 현재분사는 능동 또는 진행의 의미를 나타내고, 과거분사는 완료 또는 수동의 의미를 나타낸다. (c)에서 fast-acted는 spot treatment를 꾸며주는 말이므로 '빠르게 효과를 내는'이라는 능동의 의미를 가져야 하므로 fast-acting이 알맞다.

maintenance 유지 **cleanse** 청소하다 **dirt** 더러움 **excess** 과도한 **clogged pore** 막힌 모공 **patented** 특허받은 **hygienic applicator** 위생 도포기 **precision** 정밀한

정답 (c) fast-acted → fast-acting

48

(a) The main entrance to the ancient city of Babylon was called the Ishtar Gate. (b) It was constructed on the north side of the city in 575 BC by order of King Nebuchadnezzar Ⅱ. (c) Dedicated to the goddess Ishtar, the great Ishtar Gate was made of beautiful blue tiles. (d) This gate also decorated with golden bulls and lions, considered to be the favorite animals of Ishtar.

SOLUTION

(a) 고대 도시 바빌론의 정문은 이쉬타르 문이라고 불렸다. (b) 이 문은 느부갓네살 2세의 명령으로 기원전 575년 바빌론의 북쪽에 세워졌다. (c) 이쉬타르 여신에게 헌납한 이 거대한 이쉬타르 문은 아름다운 청색 타일로 만들어졌다. (d) 이 문은 이쉬타르가 가장 좋아하는 동물로 여겨지는 황금 황소와 사자로 장식되어 있다.

기출 POINT

(d)의 also에 주목하여 보면 (c) 문장에 덧붙여지는 설명임을 알 수 있다. 그래서 수동태 문장으로 This gate was also decorated with가 되어야 하므로 was가 적절하다. considered는 golden bulls and lions를 수식하는 말이다.

main entrance 정문 **construct** 건설하다 **dedicate** 헌납하다 **goddess** 여신 **decorate** 장식하다 **bull** 황소

정답 (d) also decorated → was also decorated

49

(a) By the early 1900s, astronomical standards for measuring time came to be regarded as problematic because of fluctuations in the Earth's rotation. (b) Scientists agreed that a new time standard was needed that would be independent of these fluctuations. (c) Because atoms of cesium emits a regular frequency, eventually cesium came to be used in the development of atomic clocks. (d) Eventually, in 1967, an international agreement confirmed that the cesium atomic clock would be the time standard for the world.

SOLUTION

(a) 1900년대 초반에 이르러 지구 자전의 변동으로 인해 시간을 측정하는 천문학적 표준에 문제가 있는 것으로 여겨지게 되었다. (b) 과학자들은 이 같은 변동에 좌우되지 않는 새로운 표준 시간이 필요하다는 데 동의했다. (c) 세슘 원자는 일정한 주파수를 내기 때문에 결국 세슘이 원자 시계 개발에 사용되기에 이르렀다. (d) 결국 1967년에 세슘 원자 시계가 세계 표준 시간이 될 것임을 국제적 합의에서 확인했다.

🔲 기출 POINT

(c)에서 Because절의 주어는 atoms of cesium이고 동사는 emits이므로 수의 일치가 되지 않는다. atoms는 복수이므로 동사는 emit가 되어야 한다. 종속절의 내용이 과학적인 사실을 나타낼 때 그 사실은 현재에도 유효한 것이므로 보통 현재시제를 쓰며 이는 시제 일치의 예외에 해당한다.

astronomical 천문학적인 **problematic** 문제가 있는 **fluctuation** 변동 **rotation** 회전 **cesium** 세슘 **frequency** 주파수 **emit** 방사하다, 내뿜다 **atomic** 원자의 　　정답_(c) emits → emit

50

(a) Anthropologists say that rituals play a major role in societies around the world. (b) These rituals are primarily of two kinds—rites of passage and rites of affliction. (c) Rites of passage take place at important moments in a person's life, such as when a boy enters into a manhood. (d) Rites of affliction arise in times of crisis such as during an illness or a disaster.

SOLUTION

(a) 인류학자들은 의식이 전세계 사회에서 중요한 역할을 한다고 말한다. (b) 이들 의식에는 크게 두 가지가 있으며, 통과 의례와 고통 의례가 그것이다. (c) 통과 의례는 소년이 남자가 될 때와 같이 한 사람의 인생에서 중요한 순간에 치러진다. (d) 고통 의례는 질병이나 재난과 같은 위기 시점에 일어난다.

🔲 기출 POINT

(c)에서 manhood는 셀 수 없는 명사이기 때문에 a를 붙이거나 복수형으로 사용할 수 없으므로 관사 a를 빼고 enters into manhood로 바꿔야 한다.

anthropologist 인류학자 **ritual** 의식 **play a major role** 중요한 역할을 하다 **primarily** 주로 **rite** 의례 **manhood** 성년 **affliction** 고통 **disaster** 재난 　　정답_(c) a manhood → manhood

1

A My son didn't get into the university he wanted to.
B Really? What a _____!

(a) fail
(b) pity
(c) luck
(d) grief

SOLUTION

A 우리 아들이 원하던 대학에 들어가지 못했어요.
B 정말요? 애석해서 어쩌지요.

🎫 기출 POINT

유감스러운 일, 애석한 일에 대한 위로의 표현으로 What a pity!를 쓴다. 다른 표현으로 I'm sorry to hear that/ That's too bad/ What a shame 등을 쓸 수 있다.

get into ~에 들어가다 **pity** 애석한 일 **grief** 슬픔   정답_(b)

2

A Hey, Iris! It's great to see you!
B Yeah, it's been _____ since I saw you last.

(a) ages
(b) dates
(c) times
(d) periods

SOLUTION

A 이봐, 아이리스! 만나서 반갑다!
B 그러게, 우리 마지막으로 본 지 한참 됐네.

🎫 기출 POINT

'본 지가 오래 되었어, 오랜만이야'라는 말을 쓸 때 '오랜 기간'은 관용적으로 ages를 쓴다. 오랜만이야: It's been ages since I saw you last./ I haven't seen you for ages.

since ~이래로 **period** 기간   정답_(a)

3

A Let's have dinner together tonight.
B I'd love to, but I already have _____.

(a) fixes
(b) plans
(c) things
(d) schemes

SOLUTION

A 오늘 저녁에 같이 저녁 식사하시죠.
B 그러고 싶은데, 이미 선약이 있어요.

🎫 기출 POINT

초대를 정중하게 거절하는 표현으로 기억해 두어야 할 문장이다. have 대신 have got도 쓸 수 있다. '선약'이라는 말로 plan을 쓴다.

fix 곤경 **scheme** 계획, 음모   정답_(b)

4

A I didn't understand the lecturer's main point. Did you?
B No, I had no idea what he was trying to _____.

(a) get across
(b) make out
(c) speak up
(d) push in

SOLUTION

A 나는 그 강사가 말하는 요점을 모르겠더라. 너는 알겠든?
B 아니, 그 사람이 무슨 이야기를 하고 싶었던 건지 당최 모르겠는데.

🎫 기출 POINT

'강연을 알아듣기 힘들었다'는 내용이다. '그가 강연을 통해 청중들에게 이해시키려고 했던 것이 무엇인지 모른다'는 말이므로 '이해시키다, 뜻을 전달하다'에 해당하는 get across가 들어가야 한다.

get across 이해시키다/ figure out, make out 이해하다

lecturer 강연자 **main point** 요점 **speak up** 크게 말하다
push in 억지로 밀고 들어오다   정답_(a)

5

A May I speak to Bill, please?

B Sure, please _____ the line for a minute.

(a) place

(b) hang

(c) hold

(d) rest

SOLUTION

A 빌과 통화할 수 있을까요?

B 그럼요. 잠시만 기다려주세요.

⊞ 기출 POINT

전화 통화 표현이다. Sure로 시작하므로 바꿔 줄 테니 기다리라는 말이 되어야 한다. '끊지 말고 기다리세요'는 hold the line을 쓴다. hold on/ hang on도 같은 의미이다. hang up 전화를 끊다/ put through 전화를 연결하다 ex) Don't hang up./ I'll put you through to him. **for a minute** 잠시만   **정답_(c)**

6

A Professor Lyndon is very opinionated.

B Yeah, and he doesn't like students with _____ views.

(a) relating

(b) differing

(c) assuming

(d) comparing

SOLUTION

A 린든 교수님은 굉장히 독선적이야.

B 맞아. 그리고 자신과 생각이 다른 학생들을 좋아하지 않으셔.

⊞ 기출 POINT

opinionated는 '자기 생각을 고집하는'의 뜻이므로 '의견이 다른 학생을 싫어한다'는 것이 알맞은 내용이 된다. '다른'이라는 말로 differing을 쓴다.

opinionated 독선적인 **relating** 관련이 있는 **assuming** 거만한   **정답_(b)**

7

A Oh, I forgot to bring my pen.

B Here, you can _____ mine.

(a) borrow

(b) handle

(c) write

(d) lend

SOLUTION

A 앗, 펜을 깜빡 잊고 안 가지고 왔네.

B 여기, 내 펜 빌려 써.

⊞ 기출 POINT

'내 펜을 빌려 써도 된다'는 말을 할 때 '빌리다'라는 단어로 borrow를 사용한다. lend 빌려주다/ rent 돈을 내고 빌리다 ex) Can you lend me your pen? 나에게 펜 좀 빌려줄 수 있니?/ rent a car 렌트카를 빌리다

forget to ~할 것을 잊다 **bring** 가져오다 **handle** 다루다 **lend** 빌려주다   **정답_(a)**

8

A Why don't you stop working on your essay and watch some football?

B No, it'll only be another half an hour before I _____.

(a) halt

(b) finish

(c) complete

(d) terminate

SOLUTION

A 에세이 그만 쓰고 축구 좀 보지 그래?

B 아니야, 30분만 더 하면 끝날 거야.

⊞ 기출 POINT

'끝내다'라는 의미를 가진 여러 단어의 쓰임을 묻는 문제이다. '30분 더 하면 끝날 거야'라는 말이므로 일반적으로 일을 '끝내다, 마치다'의 뜻인 finish가 알맞다. complete는 긴 과정을 끝내거나 불완전했던 것을 '완성하다'는 뜻이고 terminate는 '종결시키다'로 주로 문어체에 쓴다.

Why don't you...? ~하는 게 어때? **halt** 멈추다 **complete** 완결하다 **terminate** 종결시키다   **정답_(b)**

9

A Is this stream very deep?
B No. You can _____ to the other side.

(a) splash
(b) wade
(c) glide
(d) pace

SOLUTION

A 이 개천은 굉장히 깊은가요?
B 아니요. 걸어서 반대편까지 건널 수 있어요.

⊞ 기출 POINT
깊지 않다는 말과 잘 연결되는 것은 '반대편까지 걸어서 건널 수 있다'는 내용이다.
splash (물을) 튀기다 **wade** 걸어서 건너다 **glide** 미끄러지다 **pace** 걷다
                                                정답_(b)

10

A I'm so glad to finally have my diploma in my hand.
B Now you're _____ a college graduate!

(a) officially
(b) seemingly
(c) indefinitely
(d) consistently

SOLUTION

A 드디어 졸업장을 손에 쥐게 돼서 너무 기뻐.
B 이제 너도 공식적으로 대학 졸업생이 되었구나!

⊞ 기출 POINT
'졸업장을 받았으니 공식적인 의미에서 대학 졸업생이 되었다'는 내용이 잘 어울린다. seemingly는 '외관상으로'라는 뜻이다.
diploma 졸업장 **graduate** 졸업생 **officially** 공식적으로
indefinitely 불명확하게 **consistently** 꾸준히   정답_(a)

11

A Why don't you buy this bag?
B Because I want one with a shoulder _____.

(a) strap
(b) slack
(c) string
(d) strand

SOLUTION

A 이 가방 왜 안 사는 거야?
B 나는 어깨끈이 있는 가방을 원하거든.

⊞ 기출 POINT
가방 끈은 '가죽끈'을 의미하는 strap이란 단어를 사용한다. 소포를 포장하는 끈과 같이 여러 줄이 꼬인 모양의 끈은 string, 전선이나 머리카락은 strand를 사용한다.
strap 가죽끈 **slack** 느슨함 **string** 끈, 줄 **strand** 머리카락, 전선 가닥
                                                정답_(a)

12

A Anthony will turn out to be a great teacher.
B Absolutely. He's well _____ for the job.

(a) cared
(b) suited
(c) affected
(d) exposed

SOLUTION

A 앤서니는 훌륭한 교사가 될 겁니다.
B 물론이죠. 그는 그 일에 적임자예요.

⊞ 기출 POINT
훌륭한 교사가 될 거라는 말에 동의하려면 그 일에 적임자라는 응답이 와야 한다. 즉 '그 일에 딱 맞는'이라는 표현으로 well suited for the job을 쓴다. be suited for[to]는 '~에 잘 맞다'라는 뜻이다.
turn out ~임이 드러나다 **absolutely** 물론 **affect** 영향을 주다
expose 드러내다   정답_(b)

13

A Doug says this poem is satirical.
B No, he has _____ it incorrectly.

(a) impressed
(b) speculated
(c) conformed
(d) interpreted

A 더그는 이 시가 풍자적이라고 하네.
B 아니야, 더그가 이 시를 잘못 해석한 거야.

⊞ 기출 POINT

시를 풍자적이라고 한 것은 시를 해석한 것에 해당하므로 '해석하다'라는 의미의 interpret이 들어가야 한다. impress는 '~에게 (깊은) 인상을 주다, 감동시키다'라는 뜻이고 speculate은 '추측하다'라는 뜻이다.
poem 시 **satirical** 풍자적인 **speculate** 생각하다 **conform** 따르다 **interpret** 해석하다   정답_(d)

14

A Honey, is the baby asleep yet?
B Yes, she just _____ to sleep.

(a) caught on
(b) looked up
(c) threw away
(d) dropped off

SOLUTION

A 여보, 아기는 이제 잠들었어요?
B 네, 방금 잠들었어요.

⊞ 기출 POINT

'잠이 들다'는 뜻으로 drop off를 쓴다. '막 잠이 들었어요'는 just dropped off to sleep으로 나타낸다.
asleep 잠이 든 **catch on** 이해하다; 유행하다 **look up** 조사하다; 존경하다 **throw away** 버리다 **drop off** 잠이 들다   정답_(d)

15

A Excuse me, is this the administration office?
B No, that's at the other _____ of the hall.

(a) point
(b) limit
(c) end
(d) site

SOLUTION

A 죄송하지만, 여기가 총무과 사무실인가요?
B 아니요, 거긴 복도 반대 끝입니다.

⊞ 기출 POINT

사무실을 찾고 있는 것이므로 '복도 반대 끝'이라는 대답이 적절하다. '(면을 가진 물건의) 가장자리, 끝'을 의미하는 단어로 end를 쓰며 the end of a road/ the east end of a city 등으로 쓴다. site는 '대지, 장소, 현장'의 뜻이다.
administration office 총무과 사무실 **limit** 한계   정답_(c)

16

A Have you heard from Jim lately?
B No, he's been _____ these past few days.

(a) passive
(b) indistinct
(c) accessible
(d) unreachable

SOLUTION

A 짐한테 최근에 연락 받은 적 있니?
B 아니, 요 며칠 동안 연락 두절이었어.

⊞ 기출 POINT

No라고 답했으므로 '연락이 없다'는 답이 되어야 하므로 '연락이 되지 않는'의 뜻인 unreachable이 들어가야 한다. accessible은 '접근하기 쉬운, 손에 넣기 쉬운'이라는 뜻이다.
passive 수동적인 **indistinct** 뚜렷하지 않은   정답_(d)

17

A Tim is making a big mistake joining the police force.

B Well, let him be the _____ of that.

(a) judge
(b) umpire
(c) director
(d) authority

SOLUTION

A 팀이 경찰에 합류하는 건 엄청난 실수야.
B 음, 그건 그가 판단할 문제지.

⊞ 기출 POINT

다른 사람의 일에 대한 의견을 말하자 그건 그 사람이 알아서 할 일이라고 대답하는 내용이다. let … be the judge of that은 '~가 판단할 문제이다'라는 뜻의 관용 표현이다. umpire는 스포츠에서의 '심판'을 의미하는 단어이다.

make a mistake 실수하다   **join** 합류하다   **umpire** 심판
authority 권한   정답_(a)

18

A I hear today's meeting was cancelled.

B Yes, it's been _____ until next week.

(a) belated
(b) reissued
(c) updated
(d) postponed

SOLUTION

A 오늘 회의가 취소됐다는 이야기가 들리네요.
B 네, 다음 주로 미뤄졌습니다.

⊞ 기출 POINT

'오늘 회의가 취소되었고 다음 주로 연기되었다'는 내용이 적절하다. 과거의 특정 시점에서 현재까지 이어지므로 현재완료 시제가 사용되어야 한다. 또한 회의는 연기되는 것이기 때문에 수동태로 it's been postponed가 된다. belated는 '뒤늦은'이라는 뜻의 형용사로 a belated birthday present/ a belated apology 등으로 쓴다.

cancel 취소하다   **reissue** 재발행하다   **update** 최신의 것으로 하다
postpone 연기하다   정답_(d)

19

A The radio said the main highway is backed up.

B I'll look for an alternate _____, then.

(a) route
(b) track
(c) curb
(d) lane

SOLUTION

A 라디오에서 주요 고속도로가 정체됐다고 했어.
B 그럼 다른 길을 찾아볼게.

⊞ 기출 POINT

'주요 고속도로가 정체되고 있으니 다른 길을 찾아보겠다'는 내용이 되어야 한다. 대신할 만한 길은 '경로'의 뜻을 가진 route가 알맞다. track은 '자취', lane은 도로의 '차선'을 의미하는 단어이다.

be backed up 밀리다   **alternate** 대신하는   **route** 길, 경로   **track**
자취   **curb** (인도와 차도 사이의) 연석   **lane** (도로의) 차선   정답_(a)

20

A What did you do to make that dog you adopted less aggressive?

B Nothing. She's just become _____.

(a) sorer
(b) tamer
(c) looser
(d) brasher

SOLUTION

A 네가 입양한 개의 공격성을 줄이려고 어떻게 했니?
B 아무것도 안 했어. 그냥 더 얌전해졌어.

⊞ 기출 POINT

〈make+목적어+목적보어〉의 형태이다. '개를 덜 공격적으로 만들려고 어떻게 했느냐'는 말이므로 빈칸에는 less aggressive(덜 공격적인)와 같은 의미의 표현이 들어가야 한다. become 다음에 비교급(tamer)을 써서 좀 더 얌전한 상태가 되었다는 말이 적절하다. brasher는 '더 건방진'이라는 뜻이다.

aggressive 공격적인   **sore** 아픈   **tame** 순한   **loose** 느슨한
brash 건방진   정답_(b)

21

A I recently had knee surgery, so I'll need some special provisions on the flight.

B Certainly. We'll do all we can to _____ you.

(a) preclude
(b) encounter
(c) contravene
(d) accommodate

SOLUTION

A 저는 최근에 무릎 수술을 받았기 때문에 기내에서 특별 기내식이 필요할 겁니다.

B 알겠습니다. 배려할 수 있도록 최선을 다하겠습니다.

기출 POINT

항공편을 예약하는 상황에서 특별 기내식을 요청하는 고객의 말에 '최선을 다하겠다'고 답하는 상황이다. accommodate는 최선을 다해 '배려하다'는 의미로 사용될 수 있으므로 정답은 (d)이다.

surgery 수술 **provisions** 식량, 양식 **preclude** 방해하다
encounter 만나다 **contravene** 위반하다 **accommodate** 배려하다

정답_(d)

22

A Was the test hard?

B No, it was _____.

(a) a piece of cake
(b) a stitch in time
(c) like getting a raw deal
(d) like a bull in a china shop

SOLUTION

A 그 시험 어려웠니?

B 아니, 누워서 떡먹기였어.

기출 POINT

'아주 쉬운 일'은 a piece of cake이라는 표현을 쓴다. 다른 표현들의 뜻도 알아 두자. a stitch in time 적시에 하는 일/ get a raw deal 부당한 대우를 받다/ a bull in a china shop 마구 때려부수는 난폭자

a piece of cake 쉬운 일 **raw deal** 부당한 대우

정답_(a)

23

A Hello. Can one of your staff here at the hotel organize a tour for me?

B Yes, please see the _____ at that counter over there.

(a) server
(b) patron
(c) hotelier
(d) concierge

SOLUTION

A 안녕하세요. 여기 호텔 직원이 저를 위해 투어를 편성해 줄 수 있나요?

B 네, 저쪽 카운터에 있는 호텔 안내인에게 가보세요.

기출 POINT

'호텔 서비스를 안내하고 담당하여 투숙객들을 돕는 사람'을 뜻하는 단어는 concierge이다. hotelier는 hotelkeeper와 같은 말로 '호텔을 소유하거나 경영하는 사람'을 뜻한다.

staff 직원 **patron** 단골손님 **hotelier** 호텔 경영자 **concierge** (호텔의) 접수계, 안내인

정답_(d)

24

A Take two of these pills every four hours, and you should feel better in no time.

B Thanks, Dr. Zee. I hope they can help me _____ my cold.

(a) cut
(b) beat
(c) avert
(d) undo

SOLUTION

A 4시간마다 이 알약을 두 개씩 드시면 금세 좋아질 겁니다.

B 감사합니다, 지 선생님. 이 약을 먹고 감기가 나을 수 있으면 좋겠네요.

기출 POINT

감기약을 먹고 감기를 '이기다, 제압하다'라는 말이 되어야 하므로 beat을 쓴다. avert는 '피하다'의 뜻이므로 문맥상 맞지 않는다.

beat 이기다 **avert** 피하다 **undo** 원상태로 돌리다

정답_(b)

25

A I'd like to settle my bill and check out, please.
B Sure. Just give me a moment to _____ your expenses.

(a) tally
(b) charge
(c) submit
(d) proclaim

SOLUTION

A 제 계산서를 정산하고 체크아웃하고 싶습니다.
B 알겠습니다. 비용을 합산하는 동안 잠시만 기다려 주십시오.

기출 POINT
호텔에서 체크아웃하는 상황이므로 비용을 '합산하다, 총액을 계산하다'는 뜻의 tally를 쓴다. charge ~에게 부과하다 ex) charge him $100/ charge the bill to me
settle one's bill 계산하다 **expense** 비용 **tally** 합산하다
submit 제출하다 **proclaim** 선포하다   정답_(a)

26

The famous violinist Yehudi Menuhin _____ his first violin lesson at the age of three.

(a) took
(b) struck
(c) packed
(d) brought

SOLUTION

유명한 바이올리니스트 예후디 메뉴인은 세 살 때 첫 바이올린 레슨을 받았다.

기출 POINT
'첫 바이올린 수업을 받았다'는 내용이 되어야 하므로 '수업이나 강습을 받다'의 take a lesson을 쓴다.
strike 때리다 **pack** 짐을 꾸리다   정답_(a)

27

In most kingdoms throughout history, a king's first-born son was the natural _____ to the throne.

(a) kin
(b) heir
(c) royalty
(d) attendant

SOLUTION

역사상 대부분 왕국에서는 왕의 장남이 자연스럽게 왕위를 물려받았다.

기출 POINT
'왕의 장자가 왕위의 후계자가 된다'는 내용이 되어야 하므로 heir가 적절하다. heir는 '후계자', '법정 상속인' 등의 뜻으로 쓰인다.
throne 왕위 **kin** 친척 **heir** 상속인, 후계자 **royalty** 왕위
attendant 수행원   정답_(b)

28

Since the singer always looked calm and poised, no one ever guessed that she got _____ before every performance.

(a) mad
(b) tired
(c) bored
(d) nervous

SOLUTION

그 가수는 항상 차분하고 자신만만해 보였기 때문에 매 공연 전마다 그녀가 긴장한다는 것을 아무도 몰랐다.

기출 POINT
Since는 이유를 나타내는 접속사로 쓰였다. 빈칸에는 looked calm and poised와 반대 내용이 들어가야 하며 공연 전이라는 상황이 있으므로 '긴장한'이라는 뜻의 nervous가 알맞다.
calm 평온한 **poised** 자신만만한 **performance** 공연 **bored** 지루한   정답_(d)

29

To _____ the privacy of our customers, our company does not share any customer information.

(a) avoid
(b) protect
(c) resume
(d) determine

고객들의 개인정보 보호를 위해 저희 회사에서는 어떠한 고객 정보도 공유하지 않습니다.

⊞ 기출 POINT

회사가 고객의 정보를 공유하지 않는 목적이 들어가야 한다. privacy 는 '사생활'이라는 뜻이므로 고객의 사생활을 보호하는 것이 적절한 목적이다. 따라서 정답은 (b).

privacy 사생활   **share** 공유하다   **resume** 다시 시작하다
determine 결정하다   정답_(b)

30

Fashion magazines _____ the unrealistic idea that a woman has to be skinny to be beautiful.

(a) notice
(b) extract
(c) promote
(d) compensate

패션 잡지들은 여성이 아름다우려면 말라야 한다는 비현실적인 생각을 조장한다.

⊞ 기출 POINT

'여성이 아름다우려면 말라야 한다는 비현실적인 생각을 조장한다'는 내용이 되어야 한다. promote는 '설득하여 어떤 생각을 따르도록 한다' 는 뜻으로 쓸 수 있는 단어이다. extract는 '(글귀를) 인용하다; 발췌하다' 는 뜻이다.

skinny 마른, 앙상한   **promote** 조장하다   **compensate** 보상하다
                               정답_(c)

31

Prices have been increasing quickly because of the high _____ of inflation.

(a) rate
(b) cost
(c) quality
(d) budget

높은 인플레이션율 때문에 물가는 빠르게 상승 중이다.

⊞ 기출 POINT

inflation은 %로 표시하는 지수이므로 '비율'이라는 단어를 써서 rate of inflation으로 쓴다. cost는 '비용, 대가'라는 뜻이다.

inflation 인플레이션   **rate** 비율   **budget** 예산   정답_(a)

32

The novelist traveled all his life, _____ 25 times to live in various cities around the world.

(a) settling
(b) turning
(c) moving
(d) housing

그 소설가는 이사를 25번 하면서 전세계 여러 도시에서 생활하는 등 평생 떠돌아다녔다.

⊞ 기출 POINT

25 times에 유의하면 빈칸에 '이사하다'의 뜻인 move가 들어가서 '세계 여러 도시로 25번이나 이사했다'는 내용이 되어야 맞다는 것을 알 수 있다. settle은 '정착하다'라는 뜻으로 내용에 맞지 않고, house도 '살다'라는 뜻이므로 25번이라는 말과 맞지 않는다.

novelist 소설가   **settle** 정착하다   정답_(c)

33

Car-seat manufacturer Safe-Co has announced that a new form of car seat will be _____ for toddlers.

(a) developed
(b) increased
(c) guided
(d) solved

SOLUTION

카시트 제조업체 세이프 사는 신형 유아용 카시트가 개발될 것이라고 발표했다.

⊞ 기출 POINT

새로운 형태의 카시트에 대한 발표이므로 빈칸에는 '개발하다'라는 내용이 적절하다. 문맥상 미래이고 수동태이므로 will be developed가 된다.

manufacturer 제조업체 **announce** 발표하다 **toddler** 유아

정답_(a)

34

A top Chinese space official stated that China's exploration plans will include a robotic moon _____ within the year.

(a) lift
(b) duty
(c) action
(d) mission

SOLUTION

중국 최고위급 우주관료는 중국의 탐사 계획 중 연내에 로봇을 활용한 달탐사가 포함될 것이라고 말했다.

⊞ 기출 POINT

mission은 주로 '중요한 임무로 파견되는 일'을 의미하며 여기에서는 '우주 탐사 비행(space flight)'이라는 뜻으로 쓰이고 있다. action은 '조치, 전투' 등의 뜻으로 쓸 수 있다.

state 표명하다 **exploration** 탐사 **robotic** 로봇의 **mission** 우주 (탐사) 비행

정답_(d)

35

Instead of trying to solve the problems in her marriage, Judy took the _____ action of filing for divorce.

(a) drastic
(b) neutral
(c) dilatory
(d) amicable

SOLUTION

결혼 생활의 문제를 해결하려고 노력하는 대신 주디는 이혼 소송을 제기하는 극단적인 행동을 취했다.

⊞ 기출 POINT

instead of는 '~하는 대신에'라는 뜻이므로 반대의 내용이 와야 한다는 것을 알 수 있다. 문제를 해결하려고 노력하는 것과 반대 행동으로 이혼 소송을 하는 것이므로 '극단적인' 조치라는 말이 알맞다.

file for ~을 신청하다 **divorce** 이혼 **drastic** 극적인 **neutral** 중립적인 **dilatory** 행동이 느린 **amicable** 우호적인

정답_(a)

36

In order to enjoy the delicate taste of fine wine, one must _____ it slowly.

(a) indulge
(b) permeate
(c) expend
(d) savor

SOLUTION

고급 와인의 섬세한 맛을 즐기기 위해서는 천천히 음미해야 한다.

⊞ 기출 POINT

와인의 섬세한 맛을 즐기기 위해서 할 일에 대한 내용이다. '천천히 음미하다'는 말로 savor가 들어가야 가장 자연스러운 문장이 된다. indulge는 '빠져서 탐닉하다'라는 뜻이고, expend는 돈을 '소비하다'는 의미로 사용된다.

delicate 섬세한 **indulge** 빠지다, 탐닉하다 **permeate** 스며들다 **expend** 소비하다 **savor** 음미하다

정답_(d)

37

Rooftop solar panels _____ sunlight and turn it into electricity that can be used to heat water or cool homes.

(a) install
(b) absorb
(c) radiate
(d) exercise

SOLUTION

지붕용 태양열 집열판은 햇빛을 흡수해 이것으로 용수를 데우고 집을 냉방하는 데 쓸 수 있는 전기로 변환시킨다.

기출 POINT

'태양열 집열판은 햇빛을 흡수하여 전기로 변환시킨다'는 내용이 되어야 한다. '빨아들이다'라는 뜻인 absorb가 알맞다. radiate은 반대로 '방출하다'라는 뜻이다.

rooftop 지붕 **solar panel** 태양열 집열판 **install** 설치하다
absorb 흡수하다 **radiate** 방출하다, 방사하다   정답_(b)

38

At the restaurant, a tank of lobsters was wheeled to our table and we were asked to _____ which of them we would like to eat.

(a) point
(b) select
(c) instruct
(d) promise

SOLUTION

식당에서는 가재가 든 수조를 우리 테이블로 밀고 와서 그중에서 먹고 싶은 가재를 고를 수 있게 해주었다.

기출 POINT

which of them의 them은 lobsters이고 이것을 수식하는 말이 we would like to eat이므로 '우리가 먹고 싶은 가재'라는 뜻임을 알 수 있다. 먹고 싶은 바닷가재를 '선택하도록 해주었다'는 내용이 되어야 하므로 select가 알맞다. point는 '지적하다', instruct는 '지시하다'는 뜻이다.

lobster 바닷가재 **wheel** 밀다 **select** 선택하다 **instruct** 가르치다, 지시하다   정답_(b)

39

Graduates with degrees in English language and literature often _____ careers in teaching or in writing.

(a) pursue
(b) engage
(c) recognize
(d) apprehend

SOLUTION

영어 및 영문학 학위를 취득한 졸업생들은 종종 교직이나 집필 분야에 종사한다.

기출 POINT

'어떤 직업[분야]에 종사하다'라는 표현은 pursue careers in으로 나타낸다. engage는 똑같이 '종사하다'라는 뜻이지만 engage in business/engage himself in business 등으로 사용한다.

degree 학위 **literature** 문학 **career** 직업 **pursue** 종사하다; 추구하다 **engage** 종사하다 **apprehend** 파악하다   정답_(a)

40

Eating too much salty food may _____ to high blood pressure.

(a) react
(b) adjust
(c) proceed
(d) contribute

SOLUTION

짠 음식을 너무 많이 먹으면 고혈압을 일으킬 수 있다.

기출 POINT

contribute to는 좋은 의미로 '도움이 되다, 공헌하다'라는 뜻도 있지만, '~의 원인이 되다'라는 말로 질병과 같이 쓰이기도 한다. proceed to는 '다음 단계로 나아가다'는 뜻이므로 원인과 결과의 의미를 나타낼 수 없다.

high blood pressure 고혈압 **react** 반작용하다; 반응하다 **adjust** 조정하다 **proceed** 나아가다 **contribute** 기여하다   정답_(d)

41

The judge decided to _____ the contract between the two parties, canceling all commitments.

(a) annex
(b) dictate
(c) rescind
(d) mediate

SOLUTION

판사는 양자간의 계약을 무효화하고 모든 의무를 취소했다.

⊞ 기출 POINT

'계약의 모든 책임, 의무 사항을 취소한다'는 내용을 통해 판사의 결정을 추론해 볼 수 있다. '계약을 무효화하다'는 뜻이 되도록 rescind를 써야 한다. mediate은 '양자를 중재한다'는 뜻이므로 어울리지 않는다. **contract** 계약 **party** 당사자 **commitment** 의무, 책임 **annex** 첨가하다 **dictate** 명령하다 **rescind** 무효화하다 **mediate** 중재하다, 조정하다 　　　　　　　　　　　　　　　　　**정답** (c)

42

After World War II, the United States and the Soviet Union _____ as the world's superpowers.

(a) upheld
(b) interned
(c) emerged
(d) witnessed

SOLUTION

제2차 세계대전 이후 미국과 소련은 세계 초강대국으로 등장했다.

⊞ 기출 POINT

'미국과 소련이 세계의 초강대국으로 등장했다'는 내용이 적절하다. 빈칸 다음에 as가 나오므로 자동사로 쓰인 동사가 나와야 함을 알 수 있다. '~로 등장하다'는 말로 emerge as라는 표현을 쓴다. **Soviet Union** 소련, 소비에트 사회주의 연방 공화국 **superpower** 초강대국 **uphold** ~을 떠받치다 **intern** 억류하다 **emerge** 등장하다 **witness** 증거가 되다 　　　　　　　　　**정답** (c)

43

The company can continue to expand as long as we remain in _____ contact with industry leaders.

(a) delicate
(b) constant
(c) excessive
(d) redundant

SOLUTION

우리가 업계 지도자들과 지속적으로 접촉하는 한 회사는 계속 규모가 커질 수 있다.

⊞ 기출 POINT

continue to expand as long as라는 부분에 유의해서 빈칸에 들어갈 뜻을 생각해 본다. '업계 지도자들과 지속적인 접촉이 있는 한 확장할 수 있다'는 내용이 되어야 한다. 긍정적인 의미의 형용사가 들어가야 하므로 excessive나 redundant는 오답이다. **expand** 확장하다 **in contact with** ~와 접촉하여 **delicate** 민감한 **excessive** 과도한 **redundant** 과다한, 남아도는 　　　**정답** (b)

44

An action or gesture considered rude in one culture might _____ perfectly acceptable behavior in another.

(a) accuse
(b) extend
(c) divulge
(d) constitute

SOLUTION

한 문화에서 무례하다고 여겨지는 행동이나 몸짓이 다른 문화에서는 완전히 수용 가능한 행동이 될 수도 있다.

⊞ 기출 POINT

'한 문화에서는 무례한 것이 다른 문화에서는 수용될 수 있다'는 내용이므로 be considered as와 같은 의미의 단어가 빈칸에 들어가야 한다. constitute는 '~로 여겨지다'라는 뜻으로 사용된다. 쓰임의 형태가 우리말과 다르므로 주의하여 기억해 둘 표현이다. **acceptable** 수용 가능한 **accuse** 비난하다 **extend** 연장하다 **divulge** 폭로하다 **constitute** ~로 여겨지다 　　　　　　　**정답** (d)

45

Some panel monitors are _____ specifically for computer gaming.

(a) enlisted
(b) pictured
(c) designed
(d) compiled

SOLUTION

일부 패널 모니터는 특별히 컴퓨터 게임용으로 설계된다.

⊞ 기출 POINT

'일부는 컴퓨터 게임용으로 특별히 설계된다'는 내용이 적절하므로 '설계하다'라는 뜻으로 design이 알맞다. compile은 '책을 편집하다, 편찬하다'라는 뜻으로 쓴다.

specifically 특히   **enlist** 입대하다; 참여하다   **compile** 편집하다

정답_(c)

46

The 14th Dalai Lama fled to India when the Chinese brutally _____ an uprising of the Tibetan people in 1959.

(a) expedited
(b) fraternized
(c) anticipated
(d) suppressed

SOLUTION

14대 달라이 라마는 중국이 1959년 티벳인들의 반란을 잔인하게 진압했을 때 인도로 피신했다.

⊞ 기출 POINT

역사적인 내용을 잘 모른다고 하더라도 문장에서 힌트를 찾아내야 한다. brutally라는 부사에 이어질 수 있는 동사가 있어야 한다는 것이 힌트가 된다. '반란을 잔인하게 진압했다'는 내용이 되어 suppressed가 들어간다.

flee 도망가다   **brutally** 잔인하게   **uprising** 반란   **expedite** 진척시키다   **fraternize** 친화하다   **suppress** 진압하다

정답_(d)

47

In order to help protect the environment, many US states have _____ laws which forbid citizens from burning trash.

(a) enacted
(b) reneged
(c) depicted
(d) undermined

SOLUTION

환경 보호를 돕기 위해 미국 여러 주에서 쓰레기 소각을 금지하는 법을 제정했다.

⊞ 기출 POINT

선택지를 보면 빈칸에는 동사가 들어가야 하고 그 행동의 목적은 제시되어 있듯이 환경을 보호하기 위한 것이다. 미국 여러 주는 쓰레기 소각을 금하는 법을 '제정했다'는 내용이 되도록 enacted라는 단어를 쓴다.

forbid A from -ing A가 ~하는 것을 금하다   **enact** 제정하다   **renege** 약속을 어기다   **depict** 묘사하다   **undermine** 손상시키다

정답_(a)

48

Users can download a program to fix the _____ in their new "OfficeSpace Software" package.

(a) maneuver
(b) seizure
(c) glitch
(d) hack

SOLUTION

사용자들은 새 '오피스스페이스 소프트웨어' 패키지의 결함을 수정해주는 프로그램을 다운로드할 수 있다.

⊞ 기출 POINT

컴퓨터 소프트웨어를 발매한 이후 발견되는 결함이나 문제점들을 바로 잡아주는 프로그램을 다운로드할 수 있다는 내용이므로 '기계적인 결함'을 의미하는 glitch라는 단어가 적절하다.

maneuver 책략, 조치   **seizure** 발작   **glitch** 결함   **hack** 해커; 프로그램 조작

정답_(c)

49

Corruption was _____ under the country's former prime minister, and unfortunately, little has changed under the new government.

(a) scanty
(b) rampant
(c) glutinous
(d) miscreant

그 국가는 이전 국무총리 하에서 부패가 성행했고, 불행하게도 새 정부 하에서도 달라진 것은 거의 없었다.

⊞ 기출 POINT

힌트가 되는 말은 unfortunately, little has changed이다. '이전 국무총리 하에서 부패가 만연했다'는 뜻이 되어야 하므로 '성행하는'이라는 뜻의 rampant를 쓴다. scanty는 반대로 '아주 적은, 미미한'의 뜻이고 miscreant는 '사악한'이라는 뜻이다.

corruption 부패 **prime minister** 국무총리 **scanty** 적은
glutinous 접착성의 **miscreant** 사악한　　　　　**정답**_(b)

50

Due to the overuse of antibiotics, bacteria are becoming _____ to many of the drugs designed to fight them.

(a) susceptible
(b) infectious
(c) malleable
(d) resistant

항생제 남용으로 인해 박테리아와 싸우도록 고안된 많은 의약품에 대해 박테리아의 내성이 강해지고 있다.

⊞ 기출 POINT

them은 bacteria를 가리키고, the drugs designed to fight them은 antibiotics와 동격이다. '항생제를 남용함으로써 박테리아는 항생제를 견뎌내는 내성이 강해진다'는 내용이다. '내성이 있는'의 뜻으로 resistant는 자주 출제되는 어휘이다. susceptible과 malleable은 '영향받기 쉬운'이라는 반대의 뜻이다.

overuse 남용 **antibiotic** 항생물질 **susceptible** 영향받기 쉬운
infectious 전염성의 **malleable** 유순한, 영향받기 쉬운 **resistant**
내성이 있는　　　　　**정답**_(d)

Reading Comprehension

1

Have you heard about the new Ultrabody Fitness Center? No more hustle and bustle, no more hassles, and best of all, no more waiting! We offer a most convenient location, which is open 24 hours a day. At our gym, you'll find all the weight-training and aerobic-exercise equipment that meets your needs. Our professional trainers are also standing by round the clock to help you plan your workout regimen and offer nutritional advice. So, _____.

(a) sign up and start improving your health
(b) renew your membership before it expires
(c) stop by for great discounts on our products
(d) call to find out more about this new method

SOLUTION

새 울트라바디 헬스 클럽에 대해 들어보셨습니까? 더 이상 야단법석도, 골칫거리도, 그리고 무엇보다도 대기 시간이 없습니다! 저희는 하루 24시간 개방하며 매우 편리한 장소에 위치해 있습니다. 저희 헬스 클럽에서는 여러분의 필요에 맞는 웨이트 트레이닝과 유산소 운동용 기구를 찾으실 수 있습니다. 저희 전문 트레이너들 또한 여러분이 운동 계획을 세우는 데 도움을 드리고 영양학적 조언을 드리기 위해 항상 대기하고 있습니다. 그러니 등록하시고 여러분의 건강 개선을 시작하십시오.

⊞ 기출 POINT

헬스 클럽을 알리기 위한 광고문이다. 새로운 회원에게 센터의 특징과 위치, 서비스에 대해 소개하고 있다. 광고의 끝에서 So로 문장이 시작되고 있으므로 선택을 권유하는 내용이 들어가는 것이 적절하다. 등록을 하고 건강을 개선하라는 (a)가 답이 된다.

hustle and bustle 야단법석 **hassle** 골칫거리 **gym** 헬스 클럽 **aerobic-exercise** 유산소 운동 **equipment** 기구 **round the clock** 계속해서, 끊임없이 **regimen** 계획 **nutritional** 영양학적인

정답 _(a)

2

Gentle and polite people sometimes become quite the opposite when they go online, where they can be confrontational and aggressive. This is because they feel untouchable or protected through the anonymity the Internet provides. Anonymity gives them the sense that they can get away with things. It makes them bold. Thus, they _____ when they go online.

(a) say things they usually would not dare to
(b) are outgoing and friendly with everyone
(c) prefer to remain anonymous instead
(d) remain as shy as they are in real life

SOLUTION

온화하고 예의 바른 사람들이 온라인 상에서 때론 정반대가 되는데, 그들은 대립적이고 공격적이 된다. 이것은 인터넷이 제공하는 익명성 때문에 누구도 자신들을 건드릴 수 없거나 자신들이 보호받고 있다고 생각하기 때문이다. 익명성은 이들이 무슨 일을 해도 괜찮다고 생각하게 한다. 이 때문에 이들은 과감해진다. 그래서 이들은 평소에는 감히 할 수 없는 말들을 온라인 상에서는 하게 된다.

⊞ 기출 POINT

온화한 사람들이 온라인 환경에서 다른 모습이 될 수 있는 것은 인터넷이 주는 익명성 때문이라는 내용이다. 익명이기 때문에 어떤 일을 하든 보호받고 숨을 수 있다는 생각 때문에 과감해진다는 설명이다. 마지막 문장에 빈칸이 있을 때, 시작하는 접속사에 유의하자. 접속사는 앞뒤 문장을 연결하는 것이므로 중요한 힌트가 된다. Thus(그래서) 즉, 과감해져서 온화하고 예의 바른 사람들이 평소에는 할 수 없던 말을 한다는 내용이 와야 알맞다.

opposite 정반대의 **confrontational** 대립적인 **aggressive** 공격적인 **anonymity** 익명성 **get away with** 벌받지 않고 벗어나다 **outgoing** 외향적인

정답 _(a)

3

People lost in darkness or heavy fog, with only an inner sense of direction to guide them, will often walk in circles and sometimes return to the spot where they first became lost. This happens because no human body is perfectly balanced and individuals tend to favor either their right or left side. That favoritism then affects the direction of movement when they cannot see where they are going. Invariably, they will _____.

(a) rely on memory to find the way
(b) instinctively try to avoid the fog
(c) compensate for a lack of balance
(d) be unable to keep a straight path

SOLUTION

어둠이나 짙은 안개 속에서 길을 잃고, 자신들을 안내해 줄 것은 오직 내적 방향 감각뿐인 사람들은 종종 원을 그리며 걷고 때로는 처음 길을 잃었던 지점으로 돌아오기도 한다. 이것은 완벽하게 균형 잡힌 인체는 없으며 사람들은 자신의 오른쪽과 왼쪽 중 어느 한쪽을 더 선호하는 경향이 있기 때문에 발생한다. 이러한 선호도는 자신들이 어디로 가고 있는지 알 수 없을 때 이동 방향에 영향을 준다. 결코 사람들은 직선 경로를 계속 유지하지 못한다.

⊞ 기출 POINT
사람이 어둠 속에서 내적 방향 감각에만 의존하면 길을 헤매게 되는 이유에 대한 내용이다. 인체가 완벽하게 균형 잡혀 있지 않아서 어느 한쪽을 선호하고 이 선호도가 방향 감각에 영향을 준다는 설명이므로 (d)가 정답이다. 기억에 의존한다는 (a)는 언급되지 않은 것이므로 오답이다.
sense of direction 방향 감각   **spot** 장소   **favoritism** 선호도
invariably 반드시   **rely on** ～에 의지하다   **instinctively** 본능적으로
compensate for ～을 보상하다   정답_(d)

4

Since laws have been enacted to protect children from questionable TV advertising, marketers have turned their attention to the Internet. The versatility of this new medium offers ample opportunities to influence the buying habits of children. One online advertising tool they use is the "bot-buddy." A bot-buddy is a computer-generated talking character designed to _____.

(a) protect children from online strangers
(b) teach children about using the Internet
(c) get children interested in certain products
(d) inform parents of the dangers of advertising

SOLUTION

문제가 되는 TV 광고로부터 어린이들을 보호하기 위한 법이 제정된 이후로 마케터들은 인터넷으로 관심을 돌렸다. 이 새로운 매체의 다양성은 아이들의 구매 습관에 영향을 줄 수 있는 충분한 기회를 제공한다. 이들이 사용하는 한 가지 온라인 광고 도구는 '봇 버디'이다. 봇 버디는 아이들이 특정 상품에 관심을 가지게 하도록 고안된, 컴퓨터로 생성된 말하는 캐릭터이다.

⊞ 기출 POINT
유해한 TV 광고를 금하는 법을 피해서 마케터들은 인터넷이라는 자유로운 환경에서 광고를 만들고 이를 아이들에게 제공하려 한다는 내용이다. 그 예로 온라인 광고 도구인 봇 버디라는 캐릭터를 소개하고 있다. 상품을 광고하기 위한 도구이므로 아이들의 관심을 끌게 하는 캐릭터라는 설명이 알맞다.
enact 제정하다   **questionable** 문제가 되는   **versatility** 다양성
ample 충분한   **generated** 생성된   정답_(c)

5

It was clear from the 1920s on that Hollywood studios _____. In fact, there were so many avid moviegoers in America, the studios could expect to retrieve their production expenses and turn a profit solely on US soil. With a domestic market larger than that of any other country, studios had large enough budgets for every aspect of filmmaking, thus creating what was then the world's biggest movie industry.

(a) were focusing on their global success
(b) did not pay their stars enough money
(c) benefited from a huge domestic market
(d) saw color movies as the future of cinema

SOLUTION

1920년대 이후로 할리우드 영화 촬영소들이 대규모 내수 시장의 득을 봤다는 것은 분명하다. 사실 미국에는 열렬한 영화팬들이 많아서 영화 촬영소는 미국 시장만으로도 제작 비용을 회수하고 수익을 올릴 것을 기대할 수 있었다. 다른 어떤 국가보다도 내수 시장이 크기 때문에 영화 촬영소는 영화 제작의 모든 방면에 걸쳐 예산이 충분했고, 이로써 당시 세계 최대의 영화 산업을 창출해 냈다.

⊞ 기출 POINT

In fact 이하의 문장으로 보면 미국 영화는 내수 시장의 규모가 커서 미국 내에서만도 충분히 수입을 낼 수 있었고, 영화 제작에 충분한 예산이 할당되었으므로 세계 최대 영화 산업을 창출했다는 내용이다. 따라서 (c)가 도입문으로 적절하다. 나머지 선택지는 지문과 무관한 내용의 오답이다.

avid 열렬한 **moviegoer** 영화팬 **retrieve** 회수하다 **solely** 단지 **domestic market** 내수 시장 **filmmaking** 영화 제작 **create** 창출하다
정답_(c)

6

Recent studies show that parental involvement with homework can help a child succeed in school. However, in a survey carried out in 2006, many parents said they were surprised by the difficulty of their child's homework. It required skills they did not have, and so they lacked the confidence to help out as much as they would have liked to. Surveyed parents said they would spend more time helping their children _____.

(a) if their children wanted them to
(b) if the homework was not so difficult
(c) if teachers assigned more homework
(d) if they did not have to work long hours

SOLUTION

최근 연구에 따르면 부모가 숙제에 개입하는 것이 아이들로 하여금 좋은 학업 성취를 이루는 데 도움이 될 수 있다고 한다. 그러나 2006년 행해진 설문 조사에서 많은 학부모들은 자녀들의 숙제 난이도에 놀랐다고 말했다. 숙제를 하기 위해서는 부모들이 가지고 있지 않은 기술이 필요했고, 그래서 학부모들은 원하는 것만큼 충분히 도움을 줄 자신이 없었다. 설문에 응한 학부모들은 숙제가 그다지 어렵지 않다면 자녀들을 돕는 데 더 많은 시간을 할애하겠다고 말했다.

⊞ 기출 POINT

부모가 아이들의 숙제를 도와주면 학업에 도움이 되지만 숙제가 어렵기 때문에 부모들이 충분한 도움을 줄 자신이 없다는 내용이다. 따라서 결론에는 아이들의 숙제가 어렵지 않다면 더 많이 도울 것이라는 내용이 와야 한다. 현재 사실과 반대되는 내용을 가정할 때 주절에는 would+동사원형(spend)을 if절에는 동사의 과거형(was)을 쓴다는 점 알아두자.

involvement 개입 **survey** 설문조사 **confidence** 자신감 **assign** 할당하다
정답_(b)

7

_____ can be an exciting challenge, as you'll see in this month's *Do-It-Yourself* magazine. From re-plumbing pre-Civil War mansions to safely removing lead-based paint from late 19th-century brownstones, our experts in this month's issue will show you how. In addition, be sure to check out the special section entitled "Protecting a Historic Home" for information on products and tips on guarding your home against the elements.

(a) Updating your drab living space
(b) Choosing the right home security
(c) Restoring an old building or house
(d) Building a new house on your own

SOLUTION

오래된 건물이나 집을 복원하는 것은 여러분들이 이번 달 〈두 잇 유어 셀프〉 잡지에서 보게 될 것처럼 흥미로운 도전이 될 수 있습니다. 미국 남북전쟁 이전에 지어진 저택의 배관 설비를 바꾸는 것에서부터 19세기 말 갈색 사암 주택에서 납이 함유된 도료를 안전하게 제거하는 것까지 저희 전문가들은 이번 호를 통해 그 방법을 보여드릴 것입니다. 또한, 폭풍우로부터 여러분들의 집을 보호하는 제품의 정보와 팁을 담은 특별 섹션인 '유서 깊은 집 보호하기'도 꼭 확인하세요.

기출 POINT
잡지의 특별 섹션에 대해 홍보하는 글이다. 19세기 말에 지어진 오래된 집을 복원하고 보호하는 방법에 대한 정보를 주고 있으므로 도입 문장으로 (c)가 알맞다. 남북전쟁 이전 저택, 19세기 갈색 사암 주택, 유서 깊은 집 등을 통해 보통 집이 아니라 아주 오래된 집을 수리하고 보존하는 방법임을 확인할 수 있다. 따라서 단순히 집안을 바꾼다는 내용인 (a)는 오답이다.

re-plumb 배관 설비를 바꾸다 **lead-based** 납 성분이 함유된 **brownstone** 갈색 사암 주택(미국 19세기 말 건축, 갈색 사암으로 만든 주택) **issue** 발행물, ~호 **entitle** ~라는 제목을 붙이다 **guard against** ~로부터 보호하다 **the elements** 폭풍우 **drab** 칙칙한

정답_(c)

8

_____ in West Indian plantation colonies of the 18th century. Though up to 90% of the residents of these islands were black, the European minority owned most of the land and human resources. Some government officials and a handful of small farmers were not under European control; however, they depended just as much as everyone else upon the oppressive and exploitative plantation system. In short, everything revolved around the plantations and those who controlled them.

(a) Power was in the hands of the few
(b) Slave labor was the key to great wealth
(c) Racial segregation was the general rule
(d) High-level government corruption was rife

SOLUTION

18세기 서인도 농장 식민지에서 권력은 소수의 손에 쥐어져 있었다. 비록 이들 섬의 주민 90%가 흑인들이었지만, 소수 유럽인들이 대부분의 토지와 인력을 소유하고 있었다. 일부 정부 관료들과 몇몇 소규모 농부들은 유럽인의 통제를 받지 않았다. 하지만 이들도 억압적이고 착취적인 농장 체제에 의존하고 있기는 마찬가지였다. 즉, 모든 것은 농장과 농장을 통제하는 사람들 위주로 돌아갔다.

기출 POINT
18세기 서인도 농장 식민지 시대에는 소수의 유럽인들이 다수의 흑인을 통제할 수 있는 권력을 가지고 있었다는 내용이다. 빈칸 바로 뒷문장이 접속사 Though로 시작되므로 상반되는 내용이 나와야 하므로 (a)가 도입문으로 알맞다. (b)와 (c)는 노예 노동이나 인종 차별이 부의 요인이거나 일반적 법칙이었다는 내용 때문에 답이 될 수 없다.

plantation colony 농장 식민지 **resident** 거주민 **minority** 소수 **human resource** 인력 자원 **oppressive** 억압적인 **exploitative** 착취적인 **revolve** 돌아가다 **segregation** 인종 차별 **rife** 수없이 많은, 유포되어 있는

정답_(a)

9

Dear Customer,

This year marks BTC's 20th anniversary, and we would like to thank all of our customers for their support. We've come a long way in the boat building industry since 1988 with our Core-Bond, Poly-Bond and Core-Cell foam products. The demand for our foams has increased rapidly over the years. In fact, it looks like our products are set to become an industry standard. We have you to thank in helping to make us _____. We will continue to produce high-quality products, and we hope to enjoy your continued support.

Yours sincerely,

Thomas J. Brown, CEO

(a) the foam that we required for our boats
(b) the top custom-boat builder in the industry
(c) a leader in the manufacture of boating foam
(d) a regulator of industry standard specifications

SOLUTION

친애하는 고객님께,

올해는 BTC의 창사 20주년이며, 저희는 고객님들이 보내주신 성원에 감사드리고 싶습니다. 저희는 1988년 이래 코어본드, 폴리본드, 코어셀 발포 제품과 함께 선박 건조 업계에서 큰 발전을 이루었습니다. 저희 발포 제품에 대한 수요는 지난 몇 년간 빠르게 증가했습니다. 실로 저희 제품이 업계의 표준이 될 것으로 보입니다. 저희가 선박용 발포 제품 제조 부문에서 선도자가 될 수 있도록 도와주셔서 감사드립니다. 저희는 계속해서 고품질 제품을 생산할 것이니 여러분의 지속적인 성원을 바랍니다.

CEO 토마스 J. 브라운 드림

🔲 기출 POINT

창사 20주년을 맞아 고객들에게 지속적인 성원을 부탁하는 글이다. 빈칸에는 이 회사가 이룬 업적이 들어가야 한다. 이 회사는 선박 건조 업계에서 여러 종류의 본드와 발포 제품을 생산했고 발포 제품이 업계 표준이 될 정도로 성공적이었다는 설명이므로 (c)가 답이 된다. the top custom-boat builder(최고의 맞춤식 선박 건조업자)라는 (b)는 세부사항을 확인하지 않으면 고르기 쉬운 오답이다.

anniversary 기념일 **foam** 발포제 **rapidly** 신속히 **continued support** 계속적인 성원 **manufacture** 제조 **regulator** 규정자 **specifications** 설계서 　　　　　　정답_(c)

10

Ion Talzan's lifelong fascination with extraterrestrials and outer space has influenced his bizarre drawings, paintings and sculptures. Black holes, stars, UFOs—these are just a few of his intergalactic subjects. However, his pieces are not mere flights of fancy: Talzan aims for realism. His UFO diagrams, for example, combine art with technical precision, even including notes on the mechanics of spacecraft and electromagnetic propulsion. His work, as he sees it, is _____.

(a) a means of describing all of his fantasies
(b) a combination of the scientific and artistic
(c) a step towards debunking the myth of UFOs
(d) a way of showing kids the benefits of science

SOLUTION

이온 탈잔은 평생 외계인과 우주 공간에 매력을 느꼈고 이것은 그의 기묘한 스케치, 그림과 조각에 영향을 주었다. 블랙홀, 별, UFO와 같은 것들은 그의 우주적 소재의 몇 가지에 불과하다. 하지만 그의 작품들이 단순한 상상의 비약은 아니다. 탈잔은 현실주의를 겨냥한다. 예를 들면, 그의 UFO 그림은 예술과 기술적 정확성을 결합시키고 있으며, 심지어 우주선의 제작 기술과 전자기 추진에 대한 메모도 포함하고 있다. 그가 보는 그의 작품은 과학과 예술의 결합이다.

🔲 기출 POINT

이온 탈잔은 외계라는 주제로 미술 활동을 한 사람이며 상상만을 통해서가 아니라 사실주의에 기초를 두고 과학적인 정확성을 통해서 예술 작품을 만들어냈다는 설명에서 그의 작품은 (b) '과학적인 것과 예술적인 것의 결합'이라는 결론이 나올 수 있다.

extraterrestrial 외계인 **outer space** 외계 **bizarre** 기묘한 **intergalactic** 우주적인 **flight of fancy** 상상의 비약 **diagram** 도표 **precision** 정확성 **electromagnetic** 전자기의 **propulsion** 추진 **debunk** 폭로하다 **myth** 신화, 미신 　　　정답_(b)

11

Many couples in this country, like my wife and me, have what is called secondary infertility. That is when a couple has one child but cannot conceive another. Although the causes of this are almost identical to those of primary infertility, the emotional experience of secondary infertility can be very different. If we share our anguish with others, they often make us feel we are greedy and ungrateful. We cannot conceive a second child, but we are made to feel we have no right to complain. The fact is we _____.

(a) have looked into other child care services
(b) may be worse off than many others think
(c) are lucky enough to have no complaints
(d) should really try to have another child

SOLUTION

우리나라의 많은 부부들은 저와 제 아내처럼 소위 속발성 불임을 겪고 있습니다. 이것은 부부 사이에 아이가 한 명 태어났지만 둘째 아이를 가지지 못하는 경우를 말합니다. 비록 그 원인은 원발성 불임과 거의 동일하지만 속발성 불임의 정서적인 경험은 매우 다를 수 있습니다. 우리가 남들과 고충을 공유하면 이는 우리가 욕심이 많으며 고마워할 줄 모르는 것처럼 느끼게 만드는 경우가 종종 있습니다. 우리는 둘째 아이를 가질 수 없지만 불평할 권리는 없는 것처럼 느끼도록 강요받습니다. 사실 우리는 다른 많은 사람들이 생각하는 것보다 훨씬 더 힘들 수도 있습니다.

🎟 기출 POINT
속발성 불임 문제를 가지고 있는 사람이 고충을 호소하는 내용인데 그 고충이 다른 사람들의 생각 때문이라는 데 힌트가 있다. 두 번째 아이를 가지지 못하는 고통을 나누려 하면 사람들은 이들에게는 불평할 권리가 없는 것처럼 대한다는 것이 힘들다는 내용이다. 따라서 빈칸에 올 수 있는 내용은 (b)가 적절하다.

secondary infertility 속발성 불임 **conceive** 임신하다 **primary infertility** 원발성 불임 **anguish** 고충 **greedy** 욕심 많은 **ungrateful** 고마움을 모르는 정답_(b)

12

Perhaps more than any other alcoholic drink except wine, absinthe has had a reputation for being _____. Known as the "Green Fairy" for its emerald color, it was consumed in great quantities by them in the late 19th and early 20th century. Edgar Degas, Vincent van Gogh, Paul Gauguin and Pablo Picasso were all fans of the drink and its inspirational properties. Needless to say, absinthe also became synonymous with decadence, modernism and a bohemian lifestyle.

(a) a big part of the lives of the rich and famous
(b) associated with artists and artistic inspiration
(c) responsible for turning men into violent alcoholics
(d) the ruin of people who could have been great artists

SOLUTION

압생트는 아마 와인을 제외한 다른 어떤 주류보다도 예술가와 예술적 영감과 연관이 있다는 평판을 받아왔을 것이다. 에메랄드 빛깔로 인해 '녹색 요정'으로 알려진 압생트는 19세기 말과 20세기 초에 예술가들이 많이 마셨다. 에드가 드가, 빈센트 반 고흐, 폴 고갱과 파블로 피카소는 모두 압생트와 압생트가 주는 영감적인 특성에 팬이었다. 물론 압생트는 퇴폐, 모더니즘, 그리고 자유분방한 생활 양식과 동일시되기도 했다.

🎟 기출 POINT
압생트라는 술이 어떤 이유로 명성을 얻었는지를 묻는 문제이다. 그 술은 19세기 말과 20세기 초에 드가, 고흐, 고갱 같은 화가들이 좋아했고 당시의 예술 사조인 모더니즘과 자유분방함을 나타내는 생활 양식이었다는 설명이다. 이것을 바탕으로 볼 때 이 술은 예술가와 예술적인 영감을 연관시키는 것으로 명성을 얻었다는 (b)가 답이 된다.

alcoholic drink 주류 **reputation** 명성 **fairy** 요정 **inspirational** 영감을 주는 **synonymous** 동일한 **decadence** 퇴폐 **bohemian** 자유분방한 **associate** 결합시키다 **ruin** 멸망, 파멸 정답_(b)

13

Like Florence during the Renaissance, London in the 1800s or New York in the early 20th century, Shanghai has emerged as a global business hub. The tens of billions of dollars the Chinese government has poured into this city of 18 million residents have created one of the world's most business-friendly environments. The once rundown financial district, for example, is now an energetic strip of financial institutions, hip nightclubs, chic boutiques and trendy restaurants. Indeed, Shanghai has become _____.

(a) a hot destination for budget travelers
(b) the center for the latest fashion trends
(c) the new capital of business journalism
(d) a business-savvy and cosmopolitan city

SOLUTION

르네상스 시대의 피렌체, 1800년대의 런던이나 20세기 초반의 뉴욕처럼 상하이는 국제 비즈니스 중심지로 부상했다. 중국 정부가 인구 1,800만의 도시에 쏟아부은 수백 억 달러의 돈은 세계에서 가장 기업 친화적인 환경을 일궈냈다. 일례로 한때 황폐했던 금융 지구는 현재 금융 기관, 세련된 나이트클럽, 멋진 부티크, 그리고 최신 식당이 들어찬 활기찬 길이다. 실로 상하이는 비즈니스에 정통한 국제적인 도시가 되었다.

📋 기출 POINT

상하이가 어떤 도시로 변모했는지 결론짓는 문장을 찾는 문제이다. a global business hub, business-friendly environments, an energetic strip 등을 통해 비즈니스가 활발한 최신 유행의 도시가 되었음을 알 수 있다. 패션 유행의 중심지라는 (b)는 세부 정보에만 집중한 오답이고, (c)도 정확하게 정보를 확인하지 않으면 고를 수 있는 오답이다.

emerge 부상하다 **pour** 쏟아붓다 **once rundown** 한때 황폐했던 **financial district** 금융 지구 **strip** 거리 **hip** 앞서 있는 **chic** 멋진 **trendy** 최신 유행의 **business-savvy** 사업에 정통한 정답 _(d)

14

In fiction, a doppelganger is a double of a character, most often of the protagonist. This double or "evil twin" is sometimes employed by novelists as the representative of the dark side of a protagonist's personality or a sin they have committed, which they cannot escape from and inevitably have to confront. For instance, in Edgar Allan Poe's short story "William Wilson," the protagonist of questionable moral character is dogged by his doppelganger most tenaciously when his morals fail. When a doppelganger is around, then, it is often a moment when a protagonist _____.

(a) finds a new kind of inner strength
(b) admits to the limitations of human reason
(c) has to face an impure side of himself or herself
(d) sees the effects of having been double-crossed

SOLUTION

소설에서 분신이란 등장인물, 대부분의 경우는 주인공의 유령이다. 소설가들은 종종 이 유령 혹은 '사악한 쌍둥이'를 주인공 인격의 어두운 면, 혹은 그들이 저지른 죄로부터 벗어날 수 없으며 필연적으로 맞서야 하는 것을 나타내기 위해 사용한다. 예를 들면, 에드가 앨런 포우의 단편 소설 〈윌리엄 윌슨〉에서 의심스러운 도덕성을 지닌 주인공은 그의 도덕성이 무너졌을 때 자신의 분신으로부터 가장 끈질긴 미행을 당한다. 분신이 나타나면, 이는 종종 주인공이 자기 자신의 순수하지 못한 면을 직면해야 하는 순간을 뜻한다.

📋 기출 POINT

소설에 등장하는 도플갱어는 주인공의 악한 분신인데 이는 어두운 내면을 상징한다. 결론으로 알맞은 내용은 소설 속에서 도플갱어가 나타나는 순간은 자기 자신의 타락하고 불순한 모습을 직면하게 되는 순간이라는 (c)이다.

doppelganger 분신 **double** 꼭 닮은 사람 **protagonist** 주인공 **representative** 대표 **commit** 저지르다 **inevitably** 필연적으로 **confront** 맞서다 **moral** 도덕적인 **dog** 따라다니다, 미행당하다 **tenaciously** 끈질기게 **double-cross** 속이다 **impure** 불순한 정답 _(c)

15

At Sun Microsystems, we help businesses build, manage and profit from enterprise network computing. So it's no surprise that we offer a broad portfolio of support and network services. _____, through our Professional Services Organization, we help clients around the world manage their UNIX networks for maximum efficiency. With Sun, you can rest assured, knowing you've signed with a company dedicated to its clients' long-term success.

(a) Instead
(b) However
(c) Despite that
(d) For example

SOLUTION

썬 마이크로시스템즈에서는 기업들의 전산망을 구축, 관리하고 이로부터 수익을 올릴 수 있도록 도와드립니다. 그래서 저희가 광범위한 지원과 네트워크 서비스의 포트폴리오를 제공한다는 것은 놀라운 일이 아닙니다. 예를 들면, 저희는 전문 서비스 조직을 통해 전세계 클라이언트들이 최대한 효율적으로 유닉스 네트워크를 관리할 수 있게 도와드립니다. 썬과 함께라면 클라이언트의 장기적 성공에 헌신하는 기업과 손잡았다는 것을 알고 안심하실 수 있습니다.

기출 POINT

접속사인 연결어를 찾는 문제이다. 다양한 지원과 네트워크 서비스를 해왔다는 내용이 연결어 앞에 나온다. 연결어 뒤에는 전문 서비스 조직을 통해서 유닉스 네트워크를 관리할 수 있도록 클라이언트를 돕고 있다는 내용이 나온다. 따라서 일반적인 설명과 그 예의 관계이므로 For example이 적절하다.

profit 수익을 얻다 **enterprise** 기업 **maximum** 최대의
efficiency 효율성 **assure** 안심시키다 **dedicate** 헌신하다 **정답** _(d)

16

Last month's meeting of the International Monetary Fund in Singapore was held amid worry about the strain put on the Fund by two economic giants, China and the US. The strain is the result of the US borrowing approximately $3 billion a day coupled with China creating trade deficits and imbalances because of its artificially low currency. Neither country is willing to accept responsibility for the problem. _____, the US is criticizing China's undervalued currency for creating global economic concerns while China is blaming the US for habitually operating in the red.

(a) Hence
(b) Rather
(c) Likewise
(d) Meanwhile

SOLUTION

지난달 싱가포르에서 열린 국제통화기금 회의는 두 경제 대국인 중국과 미국으로 인해 국제통화기금이 받고 있는 부담에 대한 걱정 속에서 개최되었다. 이 부담은 매일 약 30억 달러에 달하는 미국의 차입과 중국의 인위적으로 낮은 환율로 인해 초래되고 있는 무역적자 및 불균형이 어우러진 것이다. 양국 어느 쪽도 이 문제에 대한 책임을 인정하려 하지 않는다. 오히려 미국은 중국의 평가절하된 통화가 국제적인 경제 우려를 조장하고 있다고 비난하는 반면 중국은 미국의 고질적인 적자를 탓하고 있다.

기출 POINT

지난달 열린 국제통화기금 회의에서의 쟁점에 관한 내용이다. 빈칸에 들어갈 단어는 접속사이므로 빈칸의 앞뒤 내용을 중점적으로 살핀다. 두 나라 모두 문제의 책임을 인정하지 않는다는 사실과 두 나라가 서로에게 책임을 전가하고 있다는 사실이 앞뒤에 있으므로 '오히려'라는 뜻의 Rather가 알맞다.

strain 부담 **couple with** ~와 결부되다 **trade deficit** 무역 적자
imbalance 불균형 **artificially** 인위적으로 **undervalued**
currency 평가절하된 통화 **habitually** 고질적으로 **in the red**
적자로 **정답** _(b)

17

For years health experts have told the public to eat more fruits and vegetables because of their ability to prevent disease. The latest research in Europe once again supports this recommendation. It shows that people from Mediterranean nations, where a large percentage of daily caloric intake comes from vegetables, have lower rates of cancer and heart disease than do people in Western Europe, where fewer vegetables are eaten.

Q What is the best title for the passage?
(a) Health Experts Urge a Change of Diet
(b) Fruits and Vegetables Help Reduce Disease
(c) Cancer Not Linked to Fruits and Vegetables
(d) Mediterranean Diets Are the World's Healthiest

SOLUTION

수년 동안 의료 전문가들은 과일과 채소가 질병을 예방하는 기능이 있으니 대중들에게 이들의 섭취를 늘리라고 이야기해 왔다. 유럽에서의 최근 연구는 다시 한번 이러한 권장을 지지한다. 연구에 따르면 일일 열량 섭취의 많은 부분을 채소에서 얻는 지중해 연안국 사람들은 채소를 더 적게 섭취하는 서구 유럽인들보다 암과 심장병 발병률이 더 낮다.

Q 지문의 가장 적합한 제목은?
(a) 의료 전문가들의 식단 변경 촉구
(b) 과일과 채소의 질병 발생 억제
(c) 채소, 과일과 무관하게 발생하는 암
(d) 세계에서 가장 건강에 좋은 지중해식 식단

⊞ 기출 POINT

과일과 채소가 질병을 예방하기 때문에 권장되었는데 이것이 최근 연구를 통해 또 다시 입증되었다는 내용이다. 그러므로 (b)가 제목으로 가장 적절하다. 전부터 알려진 사실이 바뀌지 않고 입증된 것이므로 (a)는 오답이고, (c)는 지문과 반대되는 내용이다. (d) 또한 내용의 비약이므로 답이 될 수 없다.

prevent 예방하다 **recommendation** 권장 **Mediterranean** 지중해의
intake 섭취 **urge** 촉구   **정답**_(b)

18

The states of New Hampshire and Vermont are a paradise for nature enthusiasts. As a matter of fact, they were voted the nation's top two vacation destinations, abundant in colorful mountain retreats, scenic lakes and picturesque local villages. Both states are ideal for water skiing, fishing, golf, tennis and hiking. Sailing the lakes and canoeing the rivers are also fun pastimes. So why not visit one of these entrancing states for your next vacation? For more information, check out our website at tours.org.

Q What is mainly being advertised about New Hampshire and Vermont in the advertisement?
(a) Their popular summer sports
(b) Their growing tourism industry
(c) Their attractions as vacation spots
(d) Their popularity for picturesque sightseeing

SOLUTION

뉴햄프셔 주와 버몬트 주는 자연을 사랑하는 사람들에게는 천국입니다. 사실 이 두 주는 형형색색의 많은 산장들과 아름다운 호수, 그림 같은 마을이 많아 미국 내 상위 두 곳의 휴양지로 선정되었습니다. 두 주는 수상 스키, 낚시, 골프, 테니스와 등산에 이상적입니다. 호수를 세일링하고 강에서 카누를 젓는 것도 재미있는 여가 활동입니다. 그러니 다음 휴가는 매혹적인 이 두 주 중 한 곳을 방문하는 것이 어떨까요? 더 많은 정보를 원하시면 저희 홈페이지 tours.org에서 확인하십시오.

Q 뉴햄프셔와 버몬트의 무엇에 대해 광고하고 있는가?
(a) 두 주의 인기 있는 여름 스포츠
(b) 두 주의 성장하는 관광업
(c) 휴가지로서 두 주의 매력
(d) 그림같이 아름다운 관광에 있어서 두 주의 인기

⊞ 기출 POINT

미국 내 최고의 휴양지로 선정된 두 주에 관한 내용이다. 아름다운 자연 경관을 자랑하고 여러 가지 야외 여가 활동을 즐길 곳으로 적당해서 휴가를 보내기 최적의 장소임을 광고하고 있으므로 (c)가 정답이다. 관광 산업이나 관광의 인기는 광고의 초점이 아니므로 (b)와 (d)는 오답이다.

enthusiast 열광자 **vacation destination** 휴양지 **abundant** 풍부한 **mountain retreat** 산장 **scenic** 아름다운 **picturesque** 그림 같은 **pastime** 여가 활동 **entrancing** 매혹적인 **sightseeing** 관광   **정답**_(c)

19

What is "good taste?" For most people, it is an adamantly subjective and highly changeable notion, yet somehow self-evident. This course explores "taste" as an abstract aesthetic sensibility and examines how it functions in the world of art and literature. We will investigate notions of aesthetics in readings ranging from the 18th-century Age of Reason through to modern critical thought. Writers to be observed include Jane Austen, David Hume, John Ruskin, Oscar Wilde and Harold Bloom.

Q   What is the passage mainly about?
(a) A course on aesthetics and literature
(b) A critical examination of famous authors
(c) A study of fiction during the 18th century
(d) A course on artworks throughout the ages

SOLUTION

'훌륭한 심미안'이란 무엇인가? 대부분 사람들에게 이것은 철저히 주관적이며 매우 가변적인 개념이지만, 어쨌든 자명한 것이다. 이 수업에서는 추상적인 심미감으로서의 '심미안'을 탐구하고, 이것이 예술과 문학의 세계에서 어떻게 기능하는지 살펴본다. 우리는 18세기 이성의 시대부터 근대 비판적 사고에 걸친 작품 속에서 미학의 개념을 알아볼 것이다. 살펴볼 작가들에는 제인 오스틴, 데이비드 흄, 존 러스킨, 오스카 와일드와 해럴드 블룸이 포함된다.

Q 지문의 주된 내용은?
(a) 미학과 문학에 관한 수업
(b) 유명한 작가들에 대한 비판적인 고찰
(c) 18세기 소설에 대한 연구
(d) 시대별 예술 작품 수업

기출 POINT

수업에 대한 소개이다. This course explores 이하에서 밝히듯이 심미안의 개념과 예술과 문학에서 심미안의 기능을 살펴보는 것이 이 수업의 목표이므로 (a)가 정답이다. 지문의 뒷부분에 나오는 작가들의 나열에만 집중하면 (b)나 (c)로 잘못 답할 수 있다.

adamantly 철저히 **subjective** 주관적인 **self-evident** 자명한
abstract 추상적인 **aesthetic sensibility** 심미감 **Age of Reason** 이성의 시대 **critical** 비판적인   정답_(a)

20

The Greenlake Outpatient & Acute Care Clinic will be celebrating its third birthday by holding a Children's Safety Fair on Saturday, March 15. There will be lots of fun activities and helpful demonstrations for the entire family from 10 a.m. to 1 p.m. Participants will be able to climb aboard a Greenlake Fire Department fire engine, see two police rescue simulations and watch an acute-care nurse demonstrate first aid for kids. Our clinic is located at 1475 Belvedere Road in Greenlake. Hope to see you there!

Q   What is the announcement mainly about?
(a) Fun activities for families
(b) A Safety fair at the clinic
(c) A day for firefighters' families
(d) Demonstrations by the fire department

SOLUTION

그린레이크 외래 및 급성 환자 진료소에서는 3월 15일 토요일 어린이들을 위한 안전 박람회 개최를 통해 3주년을 기념합니다. 오전 10시부터 오후 1시까지는 온 가족을 위한 여러 가지 재미있는 활동과 유용한 시연이 있을 예정입니다. 참가자들은 그린레이크 소방서의 소방차에 탑승할 수 있고, 두 개의 경찰 구조 시뮬레이션과 급성 환자를 치료하는 간호사가 아이들에게 응급 처치를 시연하는 것을 볼 수 있습니다. 우리 진료소는 그린레이크 벨브디어 가 1475번지에 위치해 있습니다. 그럼 박람회에서 뵐 수 있기를 바랍니다!

Q 공고문의 주된 내용은?
(a) 가족들을 위한 재미있는 활동
(b) 진료소에서 열리는 안전 박람회
(c) 소방관 가족들을 위한 하루
(d) 소방서에서의 시연

기출 POINT

공고문의 주된 내용을 찾는 문제는 첫 번째 문장을 정확하게 파악하고 넘어가는 것이 중요하다. 이 진료소에서 개최되는 3주년 기념 행사인 안전 박람회에서 있을 여러 활동과 프로그램에 대해 소개하고 있으므로 정답은 (b)이다.

outpatient 외래 환자 **acute** 급성의 **demonstration** 시연
participant 참가자 **rescue simulation** 구조 시뮬레이션
first aid 응급 처치 **be located at** ~에 위치하다   정답_(b)

21

As other countries have reached productivity levels similar to or greater than those of the United States over the past couple of decades, concern about the ability of US companies and their employees to keep up has increased. Some have found fault with the US education system for failing to equip students with the knowledge and experience they need to succeed in today's labor market. However, elements other than education also impact productivity, such as the low rate of investment in industrial plants and equipment, which in turn slows labor productivity.

Q What is the passage mainly about?
(a) Reasons for the US losing competitiveness in productivity
(b) Countries that have surpassed US productivity levels
(c) Areas where more investments need to be made
(d) Links between US education and the economy

SOLUTION

다른 국가들이 지난 20년간 미국과 비슷하거나 그보다 더 높은 생산성 수준을 달성하면서 미국 기업과 그 직원들이 그들에게 뒤지지 않을까에 대한 우려가 커졌다. 일부는 학생들이 오늘날의 노동시장에서 성공하는 데 필요한 지식과 경험을 갖추지 못하도록 한 미국 교육제도를 탓했다. 하지만 교육 이외에도 공장이나 산업 장비에 대한 낮은 투자율과 같이 결과적으로 노동 생산성을 둔화시키는 요소들도 생산성에 영향을 미친다.

Q 지문의 주된 내용은?
(a) 미국이 생산성에서 경쟁력을 잃고 있는 원인
(b) 미국의 생산성 수준을 추월한 국가들
(c) 더 많은 투자가 이뤄져야 할 분야들
(d) 미국 교육과 경제 간의 관계

기출 POINT

지난 20년간 다른 국가들이 미국과 비슷한 생산성 수준을 달성함에 따라 미국은 교육제도와 산업 설비 투자 미비 등으로 인해 우려할 만한 상태에 놓여 있다. 미국이 생산성에서 경쟁력을 잃은 이유가 지문의 주된 내용이므로 (a)가 정답이다.

productivity level 생산성 수준 **concern** 우려 **keep up** 유지하다 **find fault with** ~을 비난하다 **labor market** 노동시장 **impact** 영향을 주다 **investment** 투자 **competitiveness** 경쟁력 **surpass** 추월하다
정답_(a)

22

During the 1930s and 40s, the Nazis attempted to substantiate "Aryan" superiority through spurious interpretations of archaeology and biased archaeological theories. Nazi scholars conceived of a prehistory that located Germany as the origin of civilization, even to the point of suggesting that the ancient Greeks were Germanic. By using such pseudo-archaeology, the Nazi propaganda machine sought to prove that Germans were a superior race, which in turn was used to justify German domination of the world as something both desirable and inevitable.

Q What is the best title for the passage?
(a) Nazi Distortions of History to Justify Tyranny
(b) Nazi-era Contributions to Historical Research
(c) German Superiority Disproved by Archaeology
(d) Using Archaeology to Refute Historical Inevitability

SOLUTION

1930년대와 40년대에 나치 당원들은 위조된 고고학 해석과 편견이 개입된 고고학적 이론을 통해 아리아인의 우월성을 입증하려 했다. 나치 당원 학자들은 독일이 문명의 기원이 되는 선사 시대이고, 심지어는 고대 그리스인들이 독일인이었다고 했다. 이런 의사 고고학을 활용함으로써 나치의 선전 기관은 독일인들이 우월한 인종임을 증명하려 노력했고, 결국 이것이 독일의 세계 지배를 바람직하고 필연적인 것으로 정당화하는 데 쓰였던 것이다.

Q 지문의 가장 적합한 제목은?
(a) 독재 정당화를 위한 나치의 역사 왜곡
(b) 역사 연구에 대한 나치 시대의 공헌
(c) 고고학에 의해 반증된 독일의 우월성
(d) 역사적 필연성을 논박하기 위한 고고학 활용

기출 POINT

나치는 위조된 고고학 해석을 통해 선사 시대와 고대의 역사적 사실까지 왜곡했고 독일인이 우월한 인종임을 선전하여 세계 지배를 정당화하려 했다고 주장하는 내용이므로 (a)가 제목으로 가장 적절하다.

substantiate 입증하다 **spurious** 위조의 **archaeology** 고고학 **conceive** 생각하다 **prehistory** 선사 시대 **pseudo-archaeology** 의사 고고학 **propaganda** 선전 **seek to** 노력하다 **desirable** 바람직한 **inevitable** 필연적인 **distortion** 왜곡 **tyranny** 독재 **refute** 반박하다
정답_(a)

23

Noah Webster was born in 1758 in Connecticut to a family descended from Puritan governors. At the age of 16, he was admitted to Yale, and after his graduation he worked as a teacher. While teaching, he noticed numerous problems in the American school system, and he concluded that one solution was for Americans to learn from American textbooks. Hence, he compiled a grammar book, a reader and a spelling primer. As history now testifies, these represented the beginning of the standardization of American English.

Q Which of the following is correct about Noah Webster?
(a) He taught while studying at Yale.
(b) His ancestry included Puritan governors.
(c) He returned to university after he quit his job.
(d) He wrote a book on the American school system.

SOLUTION

노아 웹스터는 1758년 코네티컷에서 청교도 통치가의 후손으로 태어났다. 16세에 그는 예일대에 입학했고 졸업 후 교사로 일했다. 교사로 일하는 동안 그는 미국 학교 체계에서 수많은 문제를 발견했고, 한 가지 해결책은 미국인들이 미국 교과서를 통해 배우는 것이라고 결론지었다. 그래서 그는 문법책, 독본, 그리고 철자법 입문서를 집필했다. 역사가 이제 입증해 주듯이 이것들은 미국 영어 표준화의 시작이었다.

Q 노아 웹스터에 대해 옳은 것은?
(a) 그는 예일대 재학 중에 교사로 일했다.
(b) 그의 조상들 중에는 청교도 통치가들도 있었다.
(c) 그는 일을 그만두고 대학으로 돌아왔다.
(d) 그는 미국 학교 체계에 관한 책을 썼다.

⊞ 기출 POINT
노아 웹스터는 청교도 통치가의 후손이고, 예일대 졸업 후 교사로 일했다. 일을 그만두고 학업을 다시 시작했다는 내용은 없으며 미국 학교 체계에 관한 책이 아니라 문법책, 독본, 철자법 입문서를 썼으므로 정답은 (b)이다.

be descended from ~의 자손이다 **Puritan** 청교도 **governor** 통치가 **compile** 집필하다 **spelling primer** 철자법 입문서 **testify** 입증하다 **standardization** 표준화 **ancestry** 조상   정답_(b)

24

The WWBF World Championship, sponsored by the World Wide Basketball Federation, is an international basketball tournament for men's national teams held every other year. A parallel event for women, the WWBF World Championship for Women, is also held biannually, concurrently with the men's tournament but in a different country. All participant teams contend for the Dolmen Trophy, the first of which was awarded in the 1967 men's games. The tournaments' structure is similar but not identical to that of the FIFA World Cup.

Q Which of the following is correct about the men's WWBF World Championship according to the passage?
(a) It is no longer held once every two years.
(b) Its teams are mixed with players from different countries.
(c) It takes place at the same location as the women's tournament.
(d) Its tournament structure is similar to that of the FIFA World Cup.

SOLUTION

세계 농구 연맹이 후원하는 WWBF 세계 선수권 대회는 2년마다 열리는 남자 국가 대표팀의 국제 농구 토너먼트이다. 여자팀의 대응 행사인 WWBF 여자 세계 선수권 대회 역시 2년마다 남자 토너먼트와 함께 열리지만 다른 국가에서 열린다. 모든 참가팀은 고인돌 트로피를 따내기 위해 겨루며 첫 번째 고인돌 트로피가 수여된 것은 1967년 남자 경기에서였다. 토너먼트의 체계는 FIFA 월드컵의 토너먼트 체계와 유사하나 동일하지는 않다.

Q 지문에 따르면 남자 WWBF 세계 선수권 대회에 대해 옳은 것은?
(a) 더 이상 2년에 한 번씩 열리지 않는다.
(b) 팀에는 여러 나라 선수들이 섞여 있다.
(c) 여자 토너먼트와 같은 장소에서 열린다.
(d) 토너먼트 체계는 FIFA 월드컵의 체계와 유사하다.

⊞ 기출 POINT
남자 WWBF 세계 선수권 대회에 대해 맞는 내용을 찾는 문제이다. 이 대회는 2년마다 한 번씩 열리고, 국제적인 행사이지만 팀에 여러 국가의 선수가 섞여 있다는 언급은 없었다. 여자 선수권 대회와 같은 시기에 다른 장소에서 열리며, 토너먼트의 체계가 FIFA 월드컵과 비슷하다는 내용이다. 따라서 지문과 일치하는 것은 (d)이다.

sponsor 후원하다 **federation** 연맹 **parallel** 대응하는 **biannually** 2년마다 **concurrently** 동시에 **contend** 겨루다 **dolmen** 고인돌 **identical to** ~와 동일한   정답_(d)

25

The 1990s saw Paula Cole emerge from a supporting artist on Peter Gabriel's 1992-93 world tour to a pop sensation in her own right. Cole's first major breakthrough came with the success of her self-produced 1997 album *This Fire*, which included hit singles *"Where Have All the Cowboys Gone?"* and *"I Don't Want to Wait."* Cole went on to win the Grammy for Best New Artist in 1998. This was followed by her surprising eight-year hiatus from recording to raise her daughter. But Cole now finds herself in the spotlight again, thanks to her latest album *Courage* and an upcoming national tour.

Q Which of the following is correct about Paula Cole according to the passage?
(a) The album *This Fire* was successful.
(b) She toured with Peter Gabriel in 1998.
(c) She took a long break from recording in 1996.
(d) A Grammy was awarded to her for her album *Courage*.

SOLUTION

1990년대에 폴라 콜은 피터 가브리엘의 1992~1993년 세계 투어의 조역 아티스트에서 벗어나 혼자 힘으로 대중 인기스타가 되었다. 콜의 첫 번째 큰 발전은 그녀의 1997년 자작 앨범 〈디스 파이어〉의 성공으로 시작되었는데, 이 앨범에는 〈카우보이들은 모두 어디로 갔나?〉와 〈기다리고 싶지 않아〉 등 히트 싱글이 수록되어 있었다. 콜은 그 길로 1998년 그래미의 최고 신인 아티스트상을 거머쥐기에 이른다. 그 이후 그녀는 놀랍게도 음반업계를 떠나 8년간의 공백 기간 동안 딸을 양육하는 데 전념했다. 하지만 콜은 최신 앨범 〈용기〉와 곧 다가올 전국 투어로 세상의 이목을 끌고 있다.

Q 지문에 따르면 폴라 콜에 대해 옳은 것은?
(a) 음반 〈디스 파이어〉는 성공적이었다.
(b) 그녀는 1998년 피터 가브리엘과 함께 투어에 참여했다.
(c) 1996년 음반업계를 떠나 긴 공백기를 가졌다.
(d) 그녀는 음반 〈용기〉로 그래미 상을 거머쥐었다.

기출 POINT
폴라 콜에 대해 맞는 내용을 고르는 문제이다. 연도와 앨범명, 인명 등 다양한 세부 정보를 확인해야 하는 문제에 해당된다. 〈디스 파이어〉라는 앨범으로 성공이 시작되었다고 했으므로 정답은 (a).
emerge from A to B A에서 B로 등극하다 **supporting artist** 조역 아티스트 **pop sensation** 대중 인기스타 **breakthrough** 발전 **hiatus** 공백기 **in the spotlight** 세상의 이목을 끌어   정답_(a)

26

Canterbury Kennels specializes in breeding Chinese Shar Pei. Since 1979, we have been successfully breeding, raising and finding homes for these wonderful dogs. We have also run a carefully planned breeding program to produce healthy dogs with significantly minimized eye and breathing problems and with great dispositions. Whether you are looking for a good-natured family dog or a show dog to enter into competitions, we have the perfect puppy for you.

Q Which of the following is correct about Canterbury Kennels according to the advertisement?
(a) They specialize in various Asian breeds.
(b) They are a newly established company.
(c) Their breeding program minimizes physical problems.
(d) Their kennel produces only prize-winning show dogs.

SOLUTION

캔터베리 애견상은 중국산 샤페이 번식을 전문으로 합니다. 1979년부터 저희는 이 훌륭한 개들을 성공적으로 번식, 사육해 왔으며 이들에게 보금자리를 찾아 주었습니다. 저희는 또한 시력 및 호흡 문제를 상당히 최소화하고 기질이 좋은 건강한 개를 낳기 위해 신중히 만들어진 번식 프로그램을 운영하였습니다. 귀가 온순한 가족용 강아지를 찾고 있든, 아니면 대회에 출전할 출품견을 찾고 있든 저희는 귀하에게 꼭 맞는 개들을 보유하고 있습니다.

Q 광고에 따르면 캔터베리 애견상에 대해 옳은 것은?
(a) 이들은 다양한 아시아견 품종을 전문으로 다룬다.
(b) 이들은 신생 기업이다.
(c) 이들의 번식 프로그램은 신체적 문제를 최소화해 준다.
(d) 이 애견상은 대회 수상견만 내놓는다.

기출 POINT
중국산 샤페이 번식을 전문으로 하는 애견상의 광고 글이다. 중국산 샤페이 외에 다른 아시아 견종을 다룬다는 말은 없었고, 1979년부터 이 일을 해왔다고 했으므로 (a)와 (b)는 오답이다. 이곳의 번식 프로그램은 눈이나 호흡기의 문제점을 최소화해 준다고 했으므로 정답은 (c). 가정용 강아지와 대회에 나가는 강아지 모두를 살 수 있는 곳이라고 했으므로 (d)도 오답이다.
kennel 애견상 **specialize in** ~을 전문으로 하다 **breeding** 번식 **significantly** 상당히 **disposition** 기질   정답_(c)

27

The region of Angkor was once at the center of the Khmer civilization, which flourished from the 9th century to the 15th century. It was from there that ruling Khmer god-kings once controlled a vast territory extending south to the Mekong Delta in Vietnam, north into Laos and west over large tracts of what is now Thailand. Angkor had a population exceeding 1 million and was home to over 1,000 temples, including the famous Angkor Wat, the world's largest single religious monument. However, in 1431, the Angkor region was invaded and conquered by the Thais, bringing the Khmer civilization to an abrupt end.

Q Which of the following is correct according to the passage?
(a) Khmer territory once extended into present-day Thailand.
(b) The Khmer population exceeded 10 million at its peak.
(c) Khmer kings lived at the largest Angkor Wat temple.
(d) The Khmer people attacked the Thais in 1431.

SOLUTION

앙코르 지역은 한때 9세기부터 15세기까지 번창했던 크메르 문명의 중심이었다. 크메르를 통치한 신왕이 한때 남쪽으로는 베트남의 메콩 삼각주, 북쪽으로는 라오스, 서쪽으로는 오늘날의 태국인 커다란 지대에 이르는 광대한 영토를 지배했던 것도 바로 이곳이었다. 앙코르의 인구는 백만이 넘었고, 세계에서 단일 종교 건조물로는 최대 규모인 유명한 앙코르 와트를 포함, 천 개가 넘는 사원이 자리하고 있었다. 그러나 1431년 앙코르 지역은 태국인의 침략을 받아 정복당했고 크메르 문명은 갑작스러운 종말을 맞았다.

Q 지문에 따르면 옳은 것은?
(a) 크메르 영토는 한때 오늘날의 태국까지 뻗어 있었다.
(b) 크메르 인구는 최고로 많았을 때 천만 명이 넘었다.
(c) 크메르 왕들은 가장 규모가 큰 앙코르 와트 사원에서 살았다.
(d) 크메르인들은 1431년 태국인들을 공격했다.

기출 POINT
크메르 문명의 중심지였던 앙코르에 대한 내용이다. 한때 크메르의 영토는 현재의 태국까지 뻗어 있었고, 앙코르의 인구가 백만 명이었으며 천 개가 넘는 사원이 있었다. 그중 가장 큰 것이 앙코르 와트였는데, 이것은 1431년에 태국인의 침략을 받았다는 내용이다. (d)는 본문과 반대의 내용이고 크메르 전체 인구에 대한 언급은 없으므로 (b)도 오답이다.

flourish 번창하다 **extend** 이르다 **tract** 지대 **exceed** 넘다 **monument** 기념물 **invade** 침략하다 **conquer** 정복하다 **abrupt** 갑작스러운 **peak** 절정, 최고점   정답 _(a)

28

In California, 100,000 reports of elder abuse have so far been filed, accounting for 20% of the 500,000 reports nationwide. It is an alarming situation for the state, but professionals argue that these numbers do not even accurately represent the extent of the problem. A 2005 study concluded that only one in 14 cases of physical abuse and neglect is likely to be reported to authorities. If this statistic holds true today, California is assuredly in the grip of a crisis that needs immediate attention.

Q Which of the following is correct according to the passage?
(a) Today 20% of reported cases of elder abuse occur in California.
(b) One out of every 14 cases of elder abuse goes unreported.
(c) Elder abuse is in sharp decline according to a 2005 study.
(d) Physical abuse is reported less in California.

SOLUTION

캘리포니아에서는 이제까지 10만 건에 이르는 노인 학대 신고가 접수되어 전국 50만 건의 신고 중 20%를 차지했다. 이것은 캘리포니아 주로서는 놀라운 상황이지만 전문가들은 이 수치가 전혀 문제의 심각성을 정확하게 대변하지 못한다고 주장한다. 2005년 한 연구에서는 신체 학대와 방임 14건 중 한 건만이 당국에 신고되는 것으로 결론지었다. 이 통계치가 오늘날도 사실이라면 캘리포니아는 즉시 관심을 기울여야 할 위기에 처해 있는 것이 틀림없다.

Q 지문에 따르면 옳은 것은?
(a) 오늘날 신고되는 노인 학대 사건의 20%는 캘리포니아에서 발생한다.
(b) 노인 학대 사건 14건당 한 건은 신고되지 않는다.
(c) 2005년 한 연구에 의하면 노인 학대는 가파른 하락세를 보이고 있다.
(d) 캘리포니아에서의 신체 학대 신고는 다른 곳에 비해 적다.

기출 POINT
캘리포니아의 노인 학대 실태에 대한 내용이다. 전국에 신고된 노인 학대 사건의 20%가 캘리포니아에서 발생하고 있고, 2005년 한 연구 결과에 따르면 14건 중 한 건만이 당국에 신고된다고 했다. 따라서 지문의 내용과 일치하는 것은 (a)이다. (b)는 신고되지 않는 것이 아니라 신고되는 비율이므로 틀린 내용이다.

elder abuse 노인 학대 **file** 신고하다 **account for** ~만큼 차지하다 **accurately** 정확히 **represent** 대변하다 **extent** 정도, 범위 **neglect** 방임 **authorities** 당국 **statistic** 통계 **assuredly** 확실히 **in the grip of** ~에 휘말려 있는   정답 _(a)

29

Van Gogh loved vivid colors and exaggerated texture because they helped him show what he felt when he looked at a landscape. Take, for example, his painting called *The Starry Night,* painted at Saint-Remy in the south of France in 1889. The colors used—purples, blues, whites, yellows and black—are brighter than those of a usual night sky, done with strong lines and applied with varying thicknesses. Sometimes the paint is so thick that it resembles layers of clay. To gain this kind of effect, Van Gogh would paint with a knife and even apply paint directly from a tube.

Q Which of the following is correct about Van Gogh according to the passage?
(a) His *The Starry Night* was created with four colors.
(b) He used a knife to create texture in his paintings.
(c) He painted *The Starry Night* only with a brush.
(d) He favored purple, brown and yellow paints.

SOLUTION

반 고흐는 강렬한 색채와 과장된 질감이 자신이 풍경을 볼 때 느끼는 감정을 보여주는 데 유용했기 때문에 이것들을 매우 좋아했다. 예를 들어 1889년 프랑스 남부 생 레미에서 그렸던 그의 그림 〈별이 빛나는 밤〉을 살펴보자. 보라색, 푸른색, 흰색, 노란색, 검정색과 같이 그림에 사용된 색채는 일상적인 밤하늘의 색깔보다 더 밝고, 강한 선과 다양한 농도를 만들어냈다. 때로는 물감의 농도가 너무 짙어서 진흙층처럼 느껴질 정도이다. 이런 효과를 얻기 위해 반 고흐는 칼로 그림을 그렸고, 심지어 튜브로부터 직접 물감을 바르기도 했다.

Q 지문에 따르면 반 고흐에 대해 옳은 것은?
(a) 그의 〈별이 빛나는 밤〉은 네 가지 색상이 사용되었다.
(b) 그는 그림에서 질감을 만들어 내려고 칼을 사용했다.
(c) 그는 붓만 사용하여 〈별이 빛나는 밤〉을 그렸다.
(d) 그는 보라색, 갈색, 그리고 노란색 물감을 선호했다.

⊞ 기출 POINT

반 고흐의 화법에 대해 작품 〈별이 빛나는 밤〉을 예로 설명하는 내용이다. 그의 작품 〈별이 빛나는 밤〉은 5가지 색상을 사용했고, 강한 선과 다양한 농도를 보여주고 있다. 또한 과장된 질감을 나타내기 위해서 붓만 사용한 것이 아니라 칼로 그리기도 하고 튜브로 물감을 직접 바르기도 했으므로 (b)가 정답이다.

vivid 강렬한 **exaggerated** 과장된 **texture** 질감 **apply with** ~로 칠하다 **thickness** 농도 **layer** 층 **clay** 진흙 　　정답_(b)

30

Dear Householder,

Congratulations! You have been selected by our Awards Promotion Committee as the winner of a free two-day vacation at Holly Branch Resort in the beautiful Pocono Mountains. Upon confirmation of acceptance, you earn the right stay in one of our extravagant condominiums where you can enjoy swimming, horseback riding and wilderness hiking. All we ask is for you to attend one informational meeting on time-share plans. There is no obligation to buy, and the meeting will last only 30 minutes. To claim your prize, please call (734) 323-6446 and proceed with your reservation.

All the best,
Jim Crock/ Manager

Q Which of the following is correct according to the notice?
(a) Holly Branch Resort is offering a rebate on all its vacations.
(b) The householder has won a no-strings-attached vacation.
(c) The householder must attend a meeting to get the prize.
(d) Jim Crock will soon contact the householder by phone.

SOLUTION

주택 보유자 귀하.

축하드립니다! 귀하는 저희 상품 홍보 위원회에 의해 아름다운 포코노 산의 홀리 브랜치 리조트에서의 이틀간 무료 휴가 당첨자로 선정되었습니다. 수락 여부를 확인해 주시는 즉시 저희의 화려한 콘도에서 묵을 수 있는 자격을 얻게 됩니다. 이곳에서 귀하는 수영과 승마, 야생 등반을 즐길 수 있습니다. 저희 쪽에서 요청하는 것은 귀하께서 콘도 상품에 관한 한 차례 설명회에 참여하는 것뿐입니다. 반드시 구매해야 할 의무는 없으며 회의는 30분밖에 소요되지 않습니다. 경품을 수취하려면 (734) 323-6446으로 전화하셔서 예약을 진행하시기 바랍니다.

매니저 짐 크록 드림

Q 공지 내용에 따르면 옳은 것은?
(a) 홀리 브랜치 리조트는 모든 휴가 상품에 대해 환급을 제공하고 있다.
(b) 이 주택 보유자는 아무 조건이 붙지 않은 휴가에 당첨되었다.
(c) 이 주택 보유자는 상품을 받기 위해서 회의에 참여해야만 한다.
(d) 짐 크록은 곧 전화로 이 주택 보유자에게 연락을 취할 것이다.

⊞ 기출 POINT

편지글은 우선 보낸 사람과 받는 사람을 확인하는 것이 내용을 빠르게 이해하는 데 도움이 된다. 편지를 받은 사람은 콘도 상품에 대한 설명회에 한 번 참가하는 조건으로 무료 휴가 경품을 받을 수 있다고 했으므로 정답은 (c)이다.

confirmation 확인 **extravagant** 화려한 **wilderness hiking** 야생 등반 **claim** 수취하다 **proceed** 진행하다 **rebate** 환급, 리베이트 **no-strings-attached** 조건이 붙지 않은 　　정답_(c)

31

Research shows that one in three people will be diagnosed with cancer at some point. Older people are statistically more likely to get it, but cancer can strike at any age. Some cancers, such as breast cancer, are becoming more common, while instances of lung cancer have declined due to a drop in the number of smokers. Excluding certain skin cancers and lung cancer, the rate of cancer appears to be increasing by about 1% a year. However, the good news is that nowadays treatments for common types of cancer are proving more successful.

Q Which of the following is correct according to the passage?
(a) Cancer rates in older people are decreasing steadily.
(b) One in four people is likely to end up with cancer.
(c) Cases of skin cancer are rising by about 1% a year.
(d) Breast cancer rates have been increasing steadily.

SOLUTION

연구에 따르면 세 명 중 한 명은 언젠가는 암 진단을 받게 될 것이라고 한다. 통계적으로 봤을 때 노령자가 암에 걸릴 확률이 더 높지만, 암에 걸리는 데는 나이가 따로 없다. 유방암 등 일부 암은 점점 더 일반화되는 반면, 폐암 사례는 흡연자 수의 하락으로 줄어들고 있다. 특정 피부암과 폐암을 제외하면 암 발병률은 연간 약 1% 가량 증가하고 있는 것으로 보인다. 그러나 좋은 소식은 최근 흔한 종류의 암에 대한 치료가 점점 더 성공인 것으로 판명되고 있다는 점이다.

Q 지문에 따르면 옳은 것은?
(a) 노령자의 암 발병률은 꾸준히 하락하고 있다.
(b) 네 명 중 한 명은 암에 걸릴 것이다.
(c) 피부암 사례는 연간 약 1%씩 증가하고 있다.
(d) 유방암 발병률은 꾸준히 증가해 왔다.

⊞ 기출 POINT
암에 관련된 연구 결과에 대한 내용이다. 노령자들이 암에 걸릴 확률이 더 높다고 했고, 세 명 중 한 명꼴로 암 진단을 받게 되고 피부암과 폐암을 제외한 암은 매년 1%씩 증가하고 있으며 유방암의 발병은 더 흔한 일이 되어가고 있다고 했으므로 정답은 (d).
diagnose 진단하다   **strike** 갑자기 덮치다   **exclude** 제외하다
prove ~임이 알려지다   정답 (d)

32

In a study done on newborn infants, it was found that they are able to distinguish the human voice from other sounds. They also prefer to hear the human voice over other sounds. Female voices were what they liked most, and they preferred their mothers' voices to those of other women. However, they had no preference for their fathers' voices over those of other men. The infants tested responded equally well to live voices as they did to recorded ones, but they were much less responsive to non-speech sounds or instrumental music.

Q Which of the following is correct according to the passage?
(a) Infants have trouble distinguishing different sounds.
(b) Infants prefer instrumental sounds over the human voice.
(c) Infants like female voices more than male voices in general.
(d) Infants like their fathers' voices more than those of other men.

SOLUTION

신생아에 대한 연구에서, 신생아들이 사람 목소리와 다른 소리를 구별할 수 있음이 드러났다. 이들은 또한 다른 소리보다도 사람 목소리 듣는 것을 더 좋아한다. 신생아들은 여자 목소리를 가장 좋아했으며, 다른 여자들 목소리보다도 어머니 목소리를 선호했다. 그러나 다른 남자들 목소리보다 아버지 목소리를 선호하지는 않았다. 실험 대상 아기들은 녹음된 목소리와 실제 목소리에 똑같이 잘 반응했지만 비음성 소리와 악기 연주곡에 대해서는 훨씬 반응도가 낮았다.

Q 지문에 따르면 옳은 것은?
(a) 아기들은 서로 다른 소리를 구분하는 데 어려움을 겪는다.
(b) 아기들은 사람의 음성보다 악기 소리를 더 좋아한다.
(c) 아기들은 일반적으로 남자 목소리보다는 여자 목소리를 더 좋아한다.
(d) 아기들은 다른 남자들 목소리보다 아버지 목소리를 더 좋아한다.

⊞ 기출 POINT
신생아가 선호하는 소리에 대한 연구 결과이다. 신생아들은 목소리와 다른 소리를 구별하는 능력이 있고 다른 소리보다 사람 목소리를 더 듣기 좋아한다. 또한 여자 목소리를 가장 좋아하고 그중 엄마 목소리를 더 좋아하지만, 다른 남자와 아버지 목소리 중에 선호의 차이는 없다는 내용이다. 여성 목소리를 가장 좋아한다고 했으므로 (c)의 내용이 지문과 일치한다.
newborn infant 신생아   **distinguish A from B** A와 B를 구별하다
preference 선호   **live voice** 실제 목소리   **responsive** 반응하는
instrumental music 악기 연주곡   정답 (c)

33

To the Editor,

The excellent article in your February edition entitled "A Land Free from Intrusion" reflected only too clearly the fragile nature of the delicately balanced Arctic ecosystem. I work with an NGO that is petitioning the United Nations to designate the entire Arctic region a zone free of any kind of oil exploration and military activity. With the aid of publications like yours, we are positive that we can make progress in this campaign and realize our goal. Thank you.

Sincerely,
Robert S. Moore

Q What can be inferred about the writer?
(a) He supports environmental causes.
(b) He works for the United Nations.
(c) He was once an Arctic explorer.
(d) He works as an industrialist.

SOLUTION

편집장님께,

귀사의 2월 호에 실린 '침략 없는 땅'이라는 제목의 훌륭한 기사는 미묘한 균형을 이루고 있는 북극 생태계의 취약성에 대해 너무 분명하게 지적해 주었습니다. 저는 유엔에 전 북극권역을 어떠한 석유 탐사나 군사 활동도 없는 지역으로 지정해 줄 것을 탄원 중인 한 비정부기관에서 일하고 있습니다. 귀사의 글과 같은 간행물의 도움 덕택에 저희는 이 활동에서 진전을 이루고 저희의 목표를 이룰 수 있을 것으로 확신합니다. 감사합니다.

로버트 S. 무어 드림

Q 글을 쓴 사람에 대해 유추할 수 있는 것은?
(a) 환경 친화적인 명분을 지지한다.
(b) 유엔에서 일한다.
(c) 한때 북극 탐사원이었다.
(d) 기업가로 일한다.

⊞ 기출 POINT

로버트 무어라는 사람이 기사를 읽고 그 잡지사에 보낸 편지글이다. 그는 북극 생태계의 문제를 다룬 기사를 훌륭하다고 평하면서 자신은 북극 생태계를 지키는 운동을 하는 단체에서 일한다고 했다. 이 정보들을 통해 (a)를 유추할 수 있다.

intrusion 침략 **fragile** 취약한 **Arctic ecosystem** 북극 생태계 **petition** 탄원하다 **designate** 지정하다 **exploration** 탐사 **with the aid of** ～의 도움으로 **make progress** 진전을 이루다   정답_(a)

34

Nobody can perfect an organization overnight. If you happen to be an extremely charismatic and competent leader, your arrival may boost the morale of the group quickly and allow previously discouraged managers to confront problems they may have avoided under a different supervisor. However, such improvements are only immediate and temporary gains, much in the same way that an initial dose of drugs may have a short-term effect on a sick patient.

Q What can be inferred from the passage?
(a) Charisma is critical for getting business ideas off the ground.
(b) Ineffective organizations typically lack charismatic leaders.
(c) Dispirited managers are often advocates of radical change.
(d) Leaders should take a long-term view on problem-solving.

SOLUTION

하룻밤 사이에 조직을 완벽하게 만들 수 있는 사람은 아무도 없다. 당신이 매우 카리스마가 강하고 능력 있는 지도자라면, 당신이 조직에 투입되었을 때 집단의 사기를 빠르게 끌어올리고 이전에 의욕을 상실했던 관리자들이 다른 상사 밑에서라면 회피했을 문제들에 맞서게 할 수 있을지도 모른다. 그러나 이런 진전은 마치 최초 약물 투약이 아픈 환자에게 단기적으로 효과를 보이는 것과 마찬가지로 즉각적이고 일시적인 진전에 불과하다.

Q 지문에서 유추할 수 있는 것은?
(a) 카리스마는 비즈니스 아이디어를 실행에 옮기는 데 핵심적이다.
(b) 일반적으로 비효율적인 조직에는 카리스마 있는 지도자가 없다.
(c) 의기소침한 관리자들은 급진적인 변화를 지지하는 경우가 종종 있다.
(d) 지도자들은 문제 해결에 있어 장기적인 관점을 견지해야 한다.

⊞ 기출 POINT

지문의 첫 문장에 유의한다. 아무도 짧은 기간에 조직을 완벽하게 만들 수 없다는 내용이다. 카리스마 있는 지도자가 해낼 수 있는 성과들이 열거되다가 접속사 However 뒤에 그런 성과들은 순간적이고 단기적인 효과에 불과하다고 반박한다. 그러므로 (d)를 유추할 수 있다.

charismatic 카리스마 있는 **boost** 돋우다 **morale** 사기 **confront** 맞서다 **temporary** 일시적인 **initial** 최초의 **dose** 투약 **critical** 결정적인 **off the ground** 행동으로 옮겨져서 **advocate** 옹호자 **radical** 급진적인   정답_(d)

35

The claim that America owes a debt for the enslavement and segregation of African-Americans has been debated for over 150 years. In recent times, a new movement has been attempting to receive monetary compensation by suing the US government for wrongs against their ancestors. However, this has attracted opposition even from African-American scholars, who say that while the government should acknowledge guilt, those in the movement would be unjustly enriched if compensated, since they never suffered the dire consequences of slavery.

Q What can be inferred from the passage?
(a) Modern African-American scholars embrace the new movement.
(b) The US government can justly deny all the wrongdoings of slavery.
(c) Those suing for compensation are viewed by some as opportunistic.
(d) African-Americans will have a stronger say in government in the future.

SOLUTION

미국이 흑인 노예제와 인종 차별에 대한 빚을 지고 있다는 주장은 150년 이상 논란이 되어 왔다. 최근 선조가 저지른 과실에 대해 미국 정부를 상대로 소송을 제기함으로써 금전적인 보상을 받고자 하는 새로운 운동이 일어나고 있다. 그러나 심지어 흑인 학자들마저도 이에 대해 반대했다. 이 학자들은 정부가 과오를 인정해야 하는 것은 맞지만 이 운동을 벌이는 사람들은 노예제의 비참한 결과로 고통받은 적이 없기 때문에 보상이 지급된다면 이들은 부당한 이득을 취하는 셈이라고 말한다.

Q 지문에서 유추할 수 있는 것은?
(a) 근대 흑인 학자들은 그 새로운 운동을 받아들인다.
(b) 미국 정부에서는 노예제의 모든 죄를 정당하게 부인할 수 있다.
(c) 일부에서는 보상 목적으로 소송을 제기하는 사람들을 기회주의자라고 생각한다.
(d) 흑인들은 향후 정부에서 더 강한 발언권을 가지게 될 것이다.

기출 POINT
미국 흑인 노예제와 인종 차별 논란에 대한 내용이다. 정부를 상대로 소송을 해서 금전적인 보상을 받고자 하는 운동에 대해서 일부 학자들은 노예제의 고통을 받지 않은 사람들이 보상을 받는 것은 부당한 이득을 얻는 것이라고 비판한다. 따라서 정답은 (c)가 된다.

enslavement 노예제 **segregation** 인종 차별 **monetary compensation** 금전적 보상 **guilt** 과오 **enrich** 부유하게 하다 **dire** 비참한 **embrace** 받아들이다 **opportunistic** 기회주의적인 **say** 발언권 　　　　　　　　　　정답_(c)

36

The extinction rate for the world's 10,000 known bird species has been assessed at approximately one species every four years. However, according to Dr. Peter Lofton of Yale University, this rate falls short of taking into consideration elements such as the continual discovery of extinct bird species from fossil remains and the numerous "missing" species that scientists are hesitant to classify as extinct. Considering these factors, Dr. Lofton asserts that the extinction rate is currently approaching one bird species per year.

Q What can be inferred from the passage?
(a) The extinction rate would be more accurate if fossil findings were ignored.
(b) The identification of all missing bird species is relatively easy.
(c) The extinction rate of bird species will most likely increase with time.
(d) The extinction rate of bird species has been underestimated.

SOLUTION

세계에 알려진 10,000종의 조류는 대략 4년마다 한 종씩 멸종하고 있는 것으로 평가되었다. 그러나 예일대학교의 피터 로프튼 박사에 따르면 이 비율은 화석 잔해에서 발견된 멸종 조류종에 대한 계속적인 발견과 과학자들이 멸종으로 분류하기를 망설이는 수많은 '사라진' 종과 같은 요인들은 고려하지 않았다고 한다. 로프튼 박사는 이런 요인들을 감안하면 멸종률은 현재 매년 한 종에 육박하고 있다고 주장한다.

Q 지문에서 유추할 수 있는 것은?
(a) 화석 발견물을 무시하면 멸종률이 더 정확할 것이다.
(b) 사라진 모든 조류종에 대한 확인은 상대적으로 쉽다.
(c) 조류종의 멸종률은 시간이 지나면서 필시 더 증가할 것이다.
(d) 조류종의 멸종률은 과소평가되어 왔다.

기출 POINT
조류의 멸종 비율에 대한 글이다. 4년에 한 종씩 멸종한다고 알려져 있지만 화석 잔해에서 계속 발견되는 종들과 사라진 종들까지 감안하면 실질적으로 매년 한 종 정도라는 의견이므로 (d)의 내용을 유추할 수 있다. 지문의 내용은 실제 멸종률에 대한 주장이고 멸종률의 시간에 따른 변화는 추론할 수 없으므로 (c)는 오답이다.

extinction 멸종 **assess** 평가하다 **fall short of** ~이 부족하다 **take into consideration** 고려하다 **fossil remains** 화석 잔해 **hesitant** 주저하는 **classify** 분류하다 **assert** 주장하다 **accurate** 정확한 **identification** 확인 **underestimate** 과소평가하다 　　정답_(d)

37

Politicians are far more sophisticated now than they used to be in swaying public opinion and gaining votes. Now they target specific audiences, using complicated polling methods in order to address the right issues at the right time to the right people. They have speechwriters who can tailor speeches for any selected demographic. They have detailed knowledge of what kind of broadcasts particular voters listen to and when. It is a far cry from past political tactics, when speeches were given to everyone on broad issues affecting the nation as a whole.

Q What can be inferred about today's politicians from the passage?
(a) They are focusing efforts primarily on attracting wealthy voters.
(b) They are more sensitive to the concerns of diverse voter groups.
(c) They are not as sincere in what they say as politicians of the past.
(d) They are less aware of broad national issues than their predecessors.

SOLUTION

현재의 정치인들은 여론을 움직이고 표를 얻는 데 있어 과거보다 훨씬 더 능란하다. 요즘 정치인들은 적시에 적절한 사람들에게 적절한 이슈에 대해 연설하기 위해 복잡한 여론 조사 기법을 활용, 특정 청중을 공략한다. 이들은 특정 인구 집단을 위한 연설을 맞춤화할 수 있는 연설 원고 작성가를 두고 있다. 이들 작성가들은 특정 유권자들이 언제 어떤 방송을 듣는지 자세하게 알고 있다. 이것은 국가 전체에 영향을 주는 광범위한 이슈에 대해 모든 사람을 대상으로 연설을 했던 과거 정치 전술과 비교하면 매우 판이하다.

Q 지문에서 오늘날의 정치인들에 대해 유추할 수 있는 것은?
(a) 부유한 유권자들을 끌어들이는 데 주로 총력을 기울이고 있다.
(b) 다양한 유권자 집단의 관심사에 더 신경을 쓰고 있다.
(c) 자신들이 말하는 것에 대해 과거 정치인들만큼 진솔하지 못하다.
(d) 과거 정치인들만큼 광범위한 국가 이슈에 대해 잘 알고 있지 못하다.

⊞ 기출 POINT
요즘 정치인들의 여론과 표심을 얻는 방법에 대한 내용이다. 과거에는 국가 전체에 영향을 주는 이슈에 대해 모든 사람을 대상으로 연설을 했지만, 현재는 다양한 집단의 관심사에 맞는 맞춤 연설을 전략으로 삼고 있다는 내용에서 (b)를 유추할 수 있다.

sophisticated 능란한 **sway** 움직이다, 좌우하다 **target** 목표로 하다 **complicated** 복잡한 **polling method** 여론 조사 기법 **tailor** 맞춤화하다 **demographic** 인구학의 **a far cry from** ～와 전혀 다른 **tactic** 전법 정답_(b)

38

Most of us are aware of the dangers of skin cancer. (a) Recent studies suggest that up to one out of seven children will develop skin cancer as an adult. (b) This can be the result of a lifestyle with too much exposure to the sun or as little as just one incident of severe sunburn as a child. (c) Repeatedly apply sunscreen every two hours; more often if you get in the water. (d) So it is imperative to sun-proof your child every time he or she is out in the sun.

SOLUTION

우리들 대부분은 피부암의 위험에 대해 알고 있다. (a) 최근 연구에 의하면 어린이 7명 중 1명은 성인이 되었을 때 피부암에 걸린다고 한다. (b) 이것은 태양에 대한 지나친 노출을 하는 생활 양식이나 어렸을 때 단 한 번이라도 심각한 햇볕 화상을 입은 경험 때문일 수 있다. (c) 매 두 시간마다 자외선 차단제를 반복적으로 바르고 물에 들어가는 경우에는 더 자주 바르라. (d) 그래서 자녀들이 양지에 나와 있을 때마다 햇볕을 차단해 주어야만 한다.

⊞ 기출 POINT
어린이 7명 중 1명은 성인이 되면 피부암에 걸리는데 그 원인과 예방법에 대한 내용이다. (a), (b), (d)는 어렸을 때의 일과 관련된 피부암의 원인을 서술하고 있는데 (c)는 자주 자외선 차단제를 바르라는 일반적인 지시의 내용이므로 흐름에 맞지 않는다.

be aware of ～을 알고 있다 **skin cancer** 피부암 **exposure** 노출 **incident** 일, 사건 **severe** 심각한 **sunburn** 햇볕에 탐 **imperative** 필수적인 정답_(c)

39

Fall foliage had little competition when I drove through the panoramic Blue Ridge Parkway. (a) There were no billboards or convenience stores to distract me from faraway mountains and neighboring valleys. (b) Nothing dampened the beauty of the greenery everywhere—the golden poplars, scarlet sourwoods and orange sassafras. (c) A few cluttered stretches notwithstanding, travelers can go for hours without passing anything more obtrusive than the occasionally emerging farmhouses. (d) Numerous hiking trails that are well worth following are detailed on free trail maps available at parkway headquarters.

SOLUTION

수평으로 펼쳐진 블루 리지 파크웨이를 운전해 지났을 때 가을 낙엽과 경쟁하는 것은 거의 없었다. (a) 먼 산과 이웃한 계곡으로부터 내 주의를 분산시키는 광고판이나 편의점은 없었다. (b) 황금빛 백양나무, 선홍빛 철쭉나무와 주홍빛 사사프라스 등 푸른 잎의 아름다움을 무디게 하는 것은 그 어디에도 없었다. (c) 몇 군데 복잡한 구간이 있기는 하지만, 여행객들은 가끔씩 나타나는 농가 외에 눈에 들어오는 것이라고는 없는 길을 몇 시간이고 달릴 수 있다. (d) 가볼만한 수많은 등산로는 파크웨이 본부에 비치된 무료 등산로 지도에 자세하게 나와 있다.

⊞ 기출 POINT

블루 리지 파크웨이의 풍경에 대한 내용이다. 자연만 펼쳐진 도로의 모습을 묘사하는데 산과 계곡, 푸르른 나무들이 있고 가끔씩 나타나는 농가 말고는 아무것도 없는 길을 달릴 수 있다는 내용이다. 마지막 (d)는 등산로에 대한 것이므로 전체 흐름과 맞지 않는 내용이다.

fall foliage 가을 낙엽 **panoramic** 수평으로 펼쳐진 **distract** 주의를 분산하다 **dampen** 무디게 하다 **poplar** 백양나무 **sourwood** 철쭉나무 **sassafras** 사사프라스(나무) **cluttered** 어수선한 **stretch** 길 **notwithstanding** 그래도, 아무튼 **obtrusive** 눈에 띄는 **trail** 등산로 **정답**_(d)

40

It has become clear that Generation Xers are rejecting the distinction between Democrats and Republicans. (a) Even those who are actively engaged in national politics see partisan boundaries blurring into irrelevance. (b) Surveys suggest that no more than a third of the nation's population identifies with either political party. (c) This generation is focusing not on differences but on similarities between the two parties, seeing them both as corrupt and childish. (d) Not surprisingly, this group is least likely to favor the current two-party system and most likely to support independents.

SOLUTION

X세대들은 민주당과 공화당 간의 구분을 인정하지 않는다는 것이 분명해졌다. (a) 국내 정치에 활발하게 참여하고 있는 X세대들조차도 양당 간의 경계가 흐려져 부적절하다고 보고 있다. (b) 설문 조사에 따르면 국내 인구의 겨우 1/3만이 양당 중 어느 한 정당에 동조한다고 한다. (c) 이 세대는 양당 모두 부패했고 유치하다고 보는 등 양당 간의 차이점이 아니라 유사점에 주목하고 있다. (d) 이 집단이 현행 양당제에 찬성할 확률이 가장 낮고 무소속을 지지할 확률이 가장 높다는 것은 놀랄 일이 아니다.

⊞ 기출 POINT

X세대들의 양당제에 대한 의견을 다루는 글이다. 이들은 양당 모두 비슷하며 부패했고 유치하다고 평가하며 무소속을 지지하는 성향을 보인다는 흐름이다. 그런데 국민의 1/3만이 어느 한 정당에 동조한다는 (b)는 X세대들의 양당제에 대한 의견을 다루는 내용의 흐름에 맞지 않다.

Generation Xer X세대 **distinction** 구분 **Democrat** 민주당 **Republican** 공화당 **partisan** 당파적인 **blur** 흐려지다 **irrelevance** 부적절함 **identify with** ~와 동일시하다, ~에 동조하다 **least likely to** 가장 ~하지 않을 것 같은 **independent** 무소속자 **정답**_(b)

Answer Keys

🎧 Listening Comprehension

1	(a)	2	(b)	3	(d)	4	(c)	5	(b)	6	(a)	7	(c)	8	(c)	9	(d)	10	(c)
11	(d)	12	(a)	13	(d)	14	(c)	15	(b)	16	(c)	17	(a)	18	(b)	19	(b)	20	(c)
21	(a)	22	(d)	23	(a)	24	(c)	25	(d)	26	(b)	27	(a)	28	(b)	29	(a)	30	(c)
31	(c)	32	(a)	33	(a)	34	(c)	35	(b)	36	(b)	37	(b)	38	(d)	39	(c)	40	(a)
41	(b)	42	(d)	43	(a)	44	(d)	45	(d)	46	(a)	47	(b)	48	(c)	49	(d)	50	(b)
51	(d)	52	(c)	53	(d)	54	(c)	55	(b)	56	(c)	57	(d)	58	(d)	59	(a)	60	(d)

🦠 Grammar

1	(b)	2	(a)	3	(b)	4	(d)	5	(a)	6	(d)	7	(c)	8	(c)	9	(b)	10	(b)
11	(b)	12	(d)	13	(c)	14	(d)	15	(c)	16	(c)	17	(b)	18	(d)	19	(c)	20	(c)
21	(a)	22	(a)	23	(a)	24	(b)	25	(a)	26	(c)	27	(b)	28	(d)	29	(b)	30	(a)
31	(d)	32	(d)	33	(c)	34	(c)	35	(c)	36	(b)	37	(c)	38	(d)	39	(d)	40	(c)
41	(d)	42	(c)	43	(c)	44	(d)	45	(b)	46	(d)	47	(c)	48	(d)	49	(c)	50	(c)

🪟 Vocabulary

1	(b)	2	(a)	3	(b)	4	(a)	5	(c)	6	(b)	7	(a)	8	(b)	9	(b)	10	(a)
11	(a)	12	(b)	13	(d)	14	(d)	15	(c)	16	(d)	17	(a)	18	(d)	19	(a)	20	(b)
21	(d)	22	(a)	23	(d)	24	(b)	25	(a)	26	(a)	27	(b)	28	(d)	29	(b)	30	(c)
31	(a)	32	(c)	33	(a)	34	(d)	35	(a)	36	(d)	37	(b)	38	(b)	39	(a)	40	(d)
41	(c)	42	(c)	43	(b)	44	(d)	45	(c)	46	(d)	47	(a)	48	(c)	49	(b)	50	(d)

📑 Reading Comprehension

1	(a)	2	(a)	3	(d)	4	(c)	5	(c)	6	(b)	7	(c)	8	(a)	9	(c)	10	(b)
11	(b)	12	(b)	13	(d)	14	(c)	15	(d)	16	(b)	17	(b)	18	(c)	19	(a)	20	(b)
21	(a)	22	(a)	23	(b)	24	(d)	25	(a)	26	(c)	27	(a)	28	(a)	29	(b)	30	(c)
31	(d)	32	(c)	33	(a)	34	(d)	35	(c)	36	(d)	37	(b)	38	(c)	39	(d)	40	(b)

1

M　What're you so excited about?

W　_____

(a) I can't think straight.
(b) I knew you'd be happy.
(c) I passed my driving test.
(d) I don't want to hear about it.

SOLUTION

M　무슨 일로 그렇게 기분이 들떴니?
W　나 운전면허 시험 통과했어.

⊞ **기출 POINT**
What으로 시작하지만 이유를 묻는 질문이다. 의문사에만 집중하면 틀리기 쉬운 문제 유형이다. 이런 의문문으로 What are you so afraid of?/ What are you so busy about?/ What are you so worried about? 등이 있다. 기분이 들뜬 이유로 운전면허 시험 통과를 든 (c)가 알맞다.

straight 똑바로　**pass** 합격하다　　　　　　　정답_(c)

2

W　They say a table will be available in 20 minutes.

M　_____

(a) You can sit here.
(b) We'll just wait, then.
(c) These are reserved seats.
(d) We arrived 10 minutes ago.

SOLUTION

W　20분이면 자리가 날 거야.
M　그럼 그냥 기다리자.

⊞ **기출 POINT**
음식점에 온 두 사람의 대화이다. available은 '사용할 수 있는'의 뜻으로 회화에서 많이 쓰는 어휘이므로 정확히 알아둘 필요가 있다. 자리가 날 거라는 말에 기다리자는 응답이 적절하다. (c)의 reserved seats는 예약된 자리를 말한다.

available 유의어: usable, ready, unoccupied, vacant, obtainable, accessible

available 사용 가능한　**reserved** 예약된　　　　정답_(b)

3

M　Are these all your CDs?

W　_____

(a) I'll put them back for you.
(b) Actually, I don't like music.
(c) We're having a sale on old CDs.
(d) Yeah. I've been collecting them for years.

SOLUTION

M　이게 다 네 CD야?
W　응. 여러 해 동안 수집하고 있어.

⊞ **기출 POINT**
여러 해 동안 수집한 것들이라는 말이 가장 적절하다. 계속 모아 오고 있다는 뜻을 나타내기 위해 현재완료 진행 시제를 써서 I've been collecting이라고 답하고 있다. (a)의 put back은 '되돌리다'라는 뜻의 동사구이다. (c)의 having a sale on은 '할인 판매하고 있다'라는 뜻임에 유의한다.

actually 사실　**have a sale on** ~를 할인 판매 중이다　　정답_(d)

4

W Can I rent a bicycle in this park?

M _____

(a) That's not my bicycle.
(b) You should take the subway.
(c) They're available over there.
(d) Sure, you can park anywhere.

SOLUTION

W 이 공원에서 자전거를 대여할 수 있나요?
M 저쪽에 가면 이용할 수 있어요.

기출 POINT

rent는 사용료를 내고 '임대하다, 대여하다'라는 뜻으로 쓰인다.
(c) They're available over there는 '저쪽에서 이용할 수 있다'는 말
이므로 가장 알맞다. 질문의 Can I의 쓰임과 맞아 떨어지는 (d) Sure,
you can이 혼동을 줄 수 있지만 내용이 맞지 않는다.
rent 임대하다   **park** 공원; 주차하다   정답 _(c)

5

M I wish I could draw well, like you.

W _____

(a) That's okay. I don't mind.
(b) Thanks for the compliment.
(c) I can show you my paintings.
(d) No problem. I can finish in time.

SOLUTION

M 나도 너처럼 그림을 잘 그리면 좋을 텐데.
W 칭찬 고마워.

기출 POINT

I wish I could...는 가정법 문장이다. '너처럼 잘 그리면 좋을 텐데'라는
말에 대해 '칭찬해줘서 고맙다'는 말이 잘 어울린다. (a) That's okay.
I don't mind는 상대방의 사과에 대해 괜찮다고 답하는 말에 해당한다.
I wish I could+동사원형: 현재 사실과 반대되는 소망을 나타냄.
I wish ~라면 좋겠다   **compliment** 칭찬   **No problem.** 문제 없어.
정답 _(b)

6

W Do we have to finish the report by tomorrow?

M _____

(a) I'll have to do one, too.
(b) That's what I heard.
(c) Let's report it now.
(d) See you tomorrow.

SOLUTION

W 우리 내일까지 보고서 끝내야 되니?
M 나는 그렇게 들었어.

기출 POINT

Do we have to로 묻는 의문문이지만 응답은 '나는 그렇게 들었어'가
된다. 직접적인 응답이 아니므로 내용에 집중해야 답을 골라낼 수 있다.
질문의 have to를 똑같이 사용했다고 해서 (a)를 고르지 않도록 주의
한다.
by tomorrow 내일까지   **That's what I heard.** 나는 그렇게 들었어.
정답 _(b)

7

M   I'm sorry I lost my temper yesterday.

W   _____

(a) You should've told me so.
(b) But you had it this morning.
(c) That's all right. I understand.
(d) You're right. I think we're lost.

SOLUTION

M   어제 화내서 미안해.
W   괜찮아. 이해해.

⊞ 기출 POINT

사과에 대한 응답으로 (c) That's all right. I understand를 사용한다. lose one's temper는 '화를 내다'라는 관용표현이다. (a) You should've told me so에는 〈should+have p.p.〉 '~했어야 했는데'라는 형태가 쓰였다. 사과에 대한 응답: That's all right./ It doesn't matter. Never mind./ Okay, I accept your apology./ Don't blame yourself. I understand.

lose one's temper 화를 내다   **We're lost.** 길을 잃다.   정답 _(c)

8

W   What are the last four digits of your credit card number?

M   _____

(a) They're 7823.
(b) I carry it with me.
(c) I only have one card.
(d) Here are the other six.

SOLUTION

W   신용카드 번호 끝의 4자리가 무엇입니까?
M   7823입니다.

⊞ 기출 POINT

last four digits은 끝자리 숫자 네 개를 말한다. 대답은 (a) They're 7823가 적절하며 복수형인 They're임에 유의한다. 카드를 지니고 다닌다고 할 때 (b)처럼 말한다. (d)는 '여기 나머지 6개 숫자예요'라는 뜻이다.

digit 숫자   정답 (a)

9

M   How's the new professor doing?

W   _____

(a) She might be in class.
(b) I didn't catch her name.
(c) She seems to get along well.
(d) She majored in biochemistry.

SOLUTION

M   새 교수님은 어떻게 지내시니?
W   잘 지내고 계시는 것 같아.

⊞ 기출 POINT

How's the new professor doing?은 새 교수님의 안부를 묻는 말이다. 다른 사람의 안부를 묻는 질문에 대한 답으로 (c)의 잘 지내는 것 같다는 말이 적절하다. How를 놓치면 '수업 중일지도 몰라'라는 (a)를 답으로 하기 쉽다. 안부를 묻는 표현: How are you doing?/ How's it going?/ How's your family doing?/ How's everything?

professor 교수   **might be** ~일지도 모른다   **get along well** 잘 지내다
major in ~을 전공하다   **biochemistry** 생화학   정답 _(c)

10

W How did Vicky get so fluent in Japanese?

M _____

(a) I think she can speak Japanese.
(b) Actually she isn't Japanese.
(c) She once lived in Japan.
(d) I visited Japan twice.

SOLUTION

W 비키는 어떻게 그렇게 일본어가 유창해?
M 한때 일본에서 살았어.

🏵 **기출 POINT**

직접적인 응답이 아니어서 주의가 필요한 문제 유형이다. 비키가 일본어에 유창한 이유를 묻는 말에 그녀가 한때 일본에 살았다는 답이 가장 알맞다. (a)는 이유나 방법에 대한 내용이 아니다.

fluent 유창한 **Japanese** 일본어 **once** 한때   정답 _(c)

11

M Hi, Janice. What have you been up to these days?

W _____

(a) I'm not sure what I'll do.
(b) Tomorrow sounds better.
(c) I managed to do that yesterday.
(d) Not much, just staying warm indoors.

SOLUTION

M 안녕, 재니스. 요즘 뭐 하고 지냈어?
W 별로 한 것 없었고, 그냥 따뜻하게 집안에서 보냈어.

🏵 **기출 POINT**

What have you been up to these days?는 안부를 묻는 질문이다. Not much는 '별로 한 일 없어'라는 응답이고, stay indoors는 '실내에서 지내다'라는 표현이다. (b)는 오늘이나 내일 어떤 일을 하자는 제안에 대한 응답이 될 수 있다.

sound better 더 좋을 것 같다 **manage to** ~을 해내다
indoors 실내에   정답 _(d)

12

W Oh, no! Judy hasn't shown up for the audition yet!

M _____

(a) I can help her with the audition.
(b) I'm sure she's on her way here.
(c) I can't think of any other way.
(d) She's the best I've seen.

SOLUTION

W 앗, 이런! 주디가 아직 오디션에 안 나타났어!
M 오는 중일 거야.

🏵 **기출 POINT**

현재완료형 문장이면서 부정문이라서 놓치기 쉬운 문장이므로 주의가 필요하다. 주디가 아직 나타나지 않았다고 했으므로 여기로 오는 중일 거라는 (b)의 응답이 적절하다.

show up 나타나다 **audition** 오디션 **on one's way** 오는 중인
정답 _(b)

13

M You should get your brakes checked. They're squeaking.

W _____

(a) I should've asked you first.
(b) You should've said something.
(c) I'll take it to the garage tomorrow.
(d) It's too bad the car's been damaged.

SOLUTION

M 너 브레이크 검사해 봐야겠다. 끽끽 소리가 나는데.
W 내일 정비소에 가볼게.

기출 POINT

〈get+목적어+p.p.〉의 형태로 '브레이크 체크를 받다'는 뜻을 나타낸다. 질문의 should가 똑같이 사용되어 (a)나 (b)를 답으로 고르기 쉽지만 내일 정비소에 가져갈 거라는 (c)가 알맞다. 이처럼 Part 1에서는 질문에서 언급한 단어나 표현을 반복한 선택지는 오답일 가능성이 높다. (d)는 손상된 차를 보면서 할 수 있는 말이지 점검을 받으라는 제안에 대한 응답이 될 수 없다.

brake 브레이크 squeak 끽끽 소리가 나다 garage 정비소
It's too bad. 참 유감이다.   정답_(c)

14

W I'd like a room with an ocean view, please.

M _____

(a) We have a great view.
(b) I'm afraid they're all occupied.
(c) If there's room, we'll try to fit it in.
(d) The view is pretty this time of year.

SOLUTION

W 바다가 보이는 객실로 주세요.
M 죄송하지만 다 찼습니다.

기출 POINT

호텔을 예약하는 상황의 대화이다. I'm afraid they're all occupied (예약이 다 찼다)가 응답으로 적절하다. 호텔 관련 대화에서 구체적인 숙박 정보가 오는 선택지가 정답일 경우도 있지만, 여기서처럼 No 유형으로 대답한 대화도 자주 출제된다. occupied 대신에 booked up도 쓰인다. (c)는 room이라는 단어가 나와 혼동을 주기 쉬운데 '공간이 있으면 그것을 끼워넣도록 하겠다'는 말이므로 내용상 무관하다.

room with an ocean view 바다가 보이는 객실 occupied 자리가
찬 fit in 끼워넣다   정답_(b)

15

M Just be yourself, and you'll do fine in the interview.

W _____

(a) But you know I can't take stress well.
(b) I'd feel much better if I had done well.
(c) I've never felt comfortable with my looks.
(d) I never thought the interview would go that way.

SOLUTION

M 평소대로 하면 면접에서 잘할 거야.
W 하지만 내가 스트레스에 약한 거, 너도 알잖아.

기출 POINT

Just be yourself는 '평소대로 하라'는 말로 어떤 일을 앞두고 긴장하고 걱정하는 사람에게 해주는 말이다. (b)는 인터뷰가 끝난 후에 할 수 있는 말이다. (c)는 항상 외모 때문에 마음이 불편하다는 말이다.

Just be yourself. 평소대로 해. take stress well 스트레스에 강하다
comfortable 편안한   정답_(a)

16

W Can I give you a ride home?
M That would be great.
W How do you usually get home?
M _____

(a) I live in an apartment.
(b) I must be home by 11.
(c) It takes an hour by bus.
(d) I take the subway and then a bus.

SOLUTION

W 집까지 태워줄까?
M 그럼 좋지.
W 보통 집에 어떻게 가니?
M 지하철 탄 다음에 버스를 타.

기출 POINT

That would be great는 상대방의 제안을 허락, 동의하는 표현이다. How do you usually get home?은 일상적으로 반복되는 일이므로 현재시제가 사용된 문장이다. 보통 이런 문장은 usually, always, every day 등의 빈도 부사를 동반한다. 지하철을 타고 나서 버스도 탄다는 말은 take the subway and then a bus라고 표현한다.

give A a ride home A를 집까지 태워주다　**get home** 집에 가다

정답_(d)

17

M Are you busy?
W No. Why?
M Let's step out for some fresh air.
W _____

(a) I'd love that.
(b) I thought so.
(c) I tried it, too.
(d) I didn't mean it.

SOLUTION

M 바쁘니?
W 아니. 왜?
M 바람 좀 쐬러 밖에 나가자.
W 좋은 생각이야.

기출 POINT

step out for some fresh air는 '바람 좀 쐬러 나가다'라는 말이다. 제안에 대해 찬성하는 말은 (a) I'd love that이다. 다른 표현으로는 I'd like that/ That would be great/ That sounds good 등이 있다. (d)는 안 좋은 일을 했을 때 '그렇게 할 의도는 아니었다'는 말이다.

step out 나가다

정답_(a)

18

W Excuse me. Do downtown buses stop here?
M Yes, a couple of them do.
W Which one is quickest?
M _____

(a) About 20 minutes.
(b) It's far from here.
(c) Downtown is that way.
(d) That would be number 33.

SOLUTION

W 실례합니다. 시내로 가는 버스가 여기에 정차하나요?
M 네, 두 대 정차합니다.
W 어느 버스가 더 빨리 가나요?
M 33번 버스일 거예요.

기출 POINT

Which one이라는 의문사에 유의하면 답을 빨리 찾을 수 있는 문제이다. a couple of buses 중에서 어느 것이냐는 질문이므로 That would be number 33가 적절하다. '~일 거예요'라는 뜻인 That would be는 알아두어야 할 필수 표현이다.

downtown 시내　**a couple of** 두 개의; 두서넛의　**quickest** 가장 빠른

정답_(d)

19

M Miller & Coleman. How may I direct your call?

W May I speak to Mr. Coleman, please?

M He's gone to lunch. May I have him return your call?

W _____

(a) Yes, I'd appreciate it.
(b) No, I'm not returning.
(c) That isn't a problem.
(d) I'll let him know.

SOLUTION

M 밀러 앤 콜먼입니다. 어디로 연결해 드릴까요?

W 콜먼 씨와 통화할 수 있을까요?

M 점심식사 하러 가셨습니다. 다시 전화 드리라고 할까요?

W 네, 그래 주시면 감사하겠습니다.

田 기출 POINT

He's gone to lunch는 현재완료형이 쓰였다는 것을 기억해 둘 문장이다. May I have him return your call? 역시 중요 표현이다. have him return your call(그가 다시 전화 걸도록 한다)는 사역동사 have가 쓰인 말로 Shall I have him call you back?과 같은 말이다. I'd appreciate it은 보통 뒤에 if절이 와서 '~해 주시면 감사하겠습니다'를 의미한다.

direct the call 전화를 연결하다   **return the call** 다시 전화를 걸다

정답 (a)

20

W It's a nice picnic, isn't it?

M It sure is. But my son seems bored.

W That's a shame. Doesn't he like picnics?

M _____

(a) No, he doesn't eat much.
(b) Many parents brought kids.
(c) Not really. He likes to play alone.
(d) The weather isn't that nice today.

SOLUTION

W 즐거운 소풍이네요, 그렇죠?

M 그러게요. 그런데 우리 아들은 좀 지루한가 봐요.

W 유감이네요. 아드님이 소풍을 안 좋아하나요?

M 별로요. 혼자 노는 걸 좋아해요.

田 기출 POINT

'그렇죠?'로 다시 묻는 것은 부가의문문이다. 그에 대한 동감의 답은 It sure is(그러게요)이다. That's a shame은 That's too bad와 같은 말로 유감을 표시하는 말이다. Doesn't he like picnics?가 부정의문문이므로 주의가 필요하다. 부정문에 대한 동의이므로 부정으로, 즉 '별로 그렇지 않다'는 Not really로 답한 (c)가 정답이다.

bored 지루한   **That's a shame.** 유감이네요.

정답 (c)

21

M Could I see the doctor this week?

W I'm sorry. She's booked up until next Tuesday.

M Then how about Friday next week?

W _____

(a) Let me check her schedule.
(b) Next Friday is the 14th.
(c) It'll be my second visit.
(d) I can see you now.

SOLUTION

M 이번 주에 의사 선생님을 뵐 수 있을까요?

W 죄송하지만 다음 주 화요일까지는 예약이 다 차 있습니다.

M 그럼 다음 주 금요일은 어떤가요?

W 선생님 일정을 확인해 보죠.

田 기출 POINT

병원 예약 상황이다. 의사의 진료 예약이 찼다는 것을 She's booked up으로 쓴 것에 유의한다. 다음 주 금요일이 어떠냐는 질문에 대해 Let me check her schedule이라는 응답이 적절하다.

see the doctor 병원에 가다   **booked up** 예약이 찬

정답 (a)

22

W What is the most serious problem in this country?

M I'd say air pollution.

W Isn't that just an urban problem?

M _____

(a) It's not as bad as it seems.
(b) Actually, it's a nationwide problem.
(c) Yes, it has attracted much attention.
(d) The population is growing in this country.

SOLUTION

W 우리나라에서 가장 심각한 문제가 뭐니?
M 대기 오염이겠지.
W 그건 그냥 도시 문제 아니니?
M 사실 전국적인 문제야.

기출 POINT

urban problem이 아니냐고 묻는 질문에 nationwide problem이라고 답한 (b)가 정답이다. 문장 맨 앞의 Actually는 이야기하고 있는 화제에 새 정보를 추가하거나, 의견을 제시하거나 혹은 새로운 대화를 시작하기 위해 쓴다.

serious 심각한 **air pollution** 대기 오염 **urban** 도시의
nationwide 전국적인   정답_(b)

23

M How would you like your hair done?

W I'd like a trim.

M No perm or coloring?

W _____

(a) No, I disagree.
(b) Nothing too fancy.
(c) Maybe I should keep it long.
(d) No. I'm not a good painter.

SOLUTION

M 머리를 어떻게 해드릴까요?
W 살짝 다듬어 주세요.
M 펌이나 염색은 안 하고요?
W 너무 화려한 건 안 하려고요.

기출 POINT

How would you like...?는 주문받을 때 많이 나오는 문장이다. How would you like your steak (done)[your coffee]? 등으로 쓰인다. trim(다듬기), perm(펌머), coloring(염색), bang(앞머리) 등은 미용실 대화에서 많이 나오는 용어들이다. Nothing too fancy는 '너무 요란하지 않게요'라는 말이다. fancy는 장식이 많거나 디자인이 요란한 (decorative, complicated) 것을 나타내는 형용사이다.

trim 다듬기 **perm** 펌머 **coloring** 염색 **fancy** 요란한, 화려한
                                                     정답_(b)

24

W How was the Little League baseball game?

M Awful! A terrible thunderstorm spoiled everything.

W Oh, no. What did you do?

W _____

(a) We'll go again next weekend.
(b) We took the early bus to the park.
(c) We came down with food poisoning.
(d) We ran for cover and waited till it stopped.

SOLUTION

W 어린이 야구 리그 경기는 어땠어?
M 끔찍했어! 엄청난 폭우 때문에 모든 걸 망쳤어.
W 어머 저런. 너는 어떻게 했니?
W 급히 비를 피하고 나서 비가 멎을 때까지 기다렸어.

기출 POINT

How was...?는 '~가 어땠니?'라는 물음이다. 폭우가 와서 비가 멎을 때까지 기다렸다는 (d)가 가장 잘 어울린다. (a)는 내용상 답이 될 것 같지만 과거시제 질문인 What did you do?에 맞지 않는다. Part 2에서 내용상 흐름이 자연스럽더라도 시제가 어색한 오답 함정에 유의해야 한다.

awful 끔찍한 **thunderstorm** 폭우 **spoil** 망치다
come down with ~로 병이 나다 **food poisoning** 식중독
                                                     정답_(d)

25

M Where is our group going to go hiking?
W It was cancelled. Didn't you know that?
M I didn't get a call.
W _____

(a) I can give you a call.
(b) I'll find out where they went.
(c) You can still make a reservation.
(d) They sent out the notice by email.

SOLUTION

M 우리 조는 어디로 등산을 가는 거야?
W 그거 취소됐어. 몰랐니?
M 전화 못 받았는데.
W 이메일로 통지했어.

기출 POINT
취소 전화를 못 받았다는 말에 적절한 응답은 (d)의 '이메일로 통지했다'
이다. (b)는 Where is our group going to go hiking?이라는 질문
과 연결되는 것 같지만 where they went 부분이 다른 내용이다.
'전화를 받다'는 get a call, '네게 전화를 하다'는 give you a call로 쓴다.
go hiking 등산 가다 cancel 취소하다 get a call 전화를 받다
notice 통지   정답_(d)

26

W Could you check my car?
M What seems to be the problem?
W I can't get the engine to start.
M _____

(a) I can't start now.
(b) Okay, I'll have a look.
(c) It's easy to change the oil.
(d) Your car gets good mileage.

SOLUTION

W 제 차 좀 검사해 주시겠어요?
M 어디에 문제가 있는 것 같아요?
W 시동이 안 걸리네요.
M 알겠습니다. 제가 살펴보죠.

기출 POINT
문제점이 can't get the engine to start이므로 이에 대해 살펴보겠
다는 답이 자연스럽다. get은 목적어(the engine) 다음에 목적보어로
to+동사원형을 써서 '~하게 만들다'의 뜻이다. (c)는 엔진과 무관한 내
용이다.
have a look 살펴보다 get good mileage 연비가 높다   정답_(b)

27

M How are the job applicants this time?
W Not as good as we'd like them to be.
M You aren't thinking of rejecting them all, are
   you?
W _____

(a) I'll definitely work harder next time.
(b) I'll go through their résumés when I have time.
(c) I can't do that. We're shorthanded at the moment.
(d) Don't worry. I can always apply next time.

SOLUTION

M 이번 지원자들은 어때?
W 우리가 원하는 만큼 훌륭하지는 않아.
M 지원자들을 다 퇴짜 놓을 생각은 아니겠지?
W 그렇게는 못하지. 지금 일손이 모자라는데.

기출 POINT
Not as good as는 '~만큼 훌륭하지 않다'는 뜻의 비교 구문이다.
we'd like them to be는 '그들이 ~했으면 좋겠다'의 뜻으로 쓰였는데,
듣고 이해하기 쉽지 않으니 잘 익혀두어야 할 표현이다. think of -ing
는 '~을 생각 중이다'라는 뜻이고, we're shorthanded는 '일손이 부
족하다'는 말이다.
applicant 지원자 reject 거절하다 definitely 분명히
go through ~을 검토하다 shorthanded 일손이 모자라는 정답_(c)

28

W Do you want to go out tonight?

M Sure. We could go to our favorite restaurant.

W Actually, I'd like to do something different.

M _____

(a) I suppose that'd be difficult.
(b) I'll squeeze it into my schedule.
(c) I'm up for whatever you suggest.
(d) It's the new restaurant downtown.

SOLUTION

W 오늘 밤에 외출할래?

M 좋아. 우리가 제일 좋아하는 식당에 가면 되겠다.

W 실은 뭔가 다른 걸 해보고 싶어.

M 네가 제안하는 거라면 난 뭐든 좋아.

⊞ 기출 POINT

Actually는 화제에 새 정보를 추가하거나, 의견을 제시하거나, 새로운 대화를 시작하기 위해 쓴다. I'm up for whatever you suggest는 '네가 제안하는 것은 무엇이든 하고 싶다'는 말로 뭔가 다른 것을 원하는 여자의 말에 적절한 응답이다. '~을 기꺼이 하고 싶다'는 뜻으로 구어체에서 be up for라는 표현을 쓴다.

go out 외출하다, 데이트하다 **suppose** 생각하다 **squeeze into one's schedule** 일정에 끼워 넣다 **be up for** ~을 하고 싶다, 흥미가 있다

정답_(c)

29

M You look different today.

W You've noticed. I've had my hair colored.

M Oh, yes. It makes you look much younger.

W _____

(a) You can tell easily.
(b) That's nice to hear.
(c) I got it done recently.
(d) All I needed was a cut.

SOLUTION

M 오늘 달라 보이네요.

W 알아보시네요. 머리를 염색했어요.

M 아, 그래요. 훨씬 더 어려 보여요.

W 듣기 좋네요.

⊞ 기출 POINT

청해에서 현재완료 문장은 이해하기가 쉽지 않다. You've noticed/ I've had my hair colored와 같이 현재와 관련된 일을 말할 때 현재완료를 써서 말한 두 문장을 유의해서 익혀 둘 필요가 있다. 머리를 하는 일에 〈사역동사+목적어+p.p.〉 문형이 많이 쓰인다. 칭찬에 대한 응답으로 That's nice to hear가 알맞다. (c)는 머리를 언제했는지 물을 때 가능한 응답이다.

notice 알아보다 **have one's hair colored** 머리 염색을 하다 **recently** 최근에

정답_(b)

30

W Guess what? Rumor has it that I might be relocated to Paris.

M Really? Has your boss said anything?

W Not yet, but I want to start apartment hunting anyway.

M _____

(a) That's true. Rumors have been bad lately.
(b) If I were you, I would wait until it's definite.
(c) I heard it's a really nice apartment, anyway.
(d) That's what your boss said, so it must be true.

SOLUTION

W 있잖아, 내가 파리로 전근 갈지도 모른다는 소문이 있어.

M 정말? 너희 상사한테서 무슨 이야기 없었어?

W 아직. 그런데 어쨌든 아파트 구하는 일은 시작하고 싶어.

M 나라면 확정될 때까지 기다리겠어.

⊞ 기출 POINT

상사의 지시를 듣기 전에 아파트를 구하려는 사람에게 해주는 말로 적당한 것은 나라면 기다리겠다는 말이므로, 가정법 과거를 쓴 (b)가 알맞다. Rumor has it that은 'that 이하라는 소문이 있다'는 관용어구이다. (a), (c), (d)는 대화 중의 단어가 쓰여 혼동을 주는 선택지이다. Guess what?은 You know what?과 같이 의문문이 아니라 '저기 있잖아'라는 의미로 화제를 도입할 때 쓴다.

Guess what? 저기 있잖아. **Rumor has it that** ~라는 소문이 있다 **relocate** 전근시키다 **definite** 분명한 **must be** ~임에 틀림없다

정답_(b)

31

W Excuse me, can you help me get a book?

M Of course. Which one?

W The big green one there on the top shelf.

M The one called *Home and Gardening*?

W Yes, that's it. Thank you so much.

Q What is the man doing in the conversation?
(a) Getting a book from a shelf.
(b) Recommending a book to read.
(c) Showing the woman gardening books.
(d) Carrying heavy books for the woman.

SOLUTION

W 실례지만, 책 꺼내는 것 좀 도와주실 수 있으세요?

M 그럼요. 어떤 책이죠?

W 제일 꼭대기 선반에 있는 큰 초록색 책이요.

M 〈홈 앤 가드닝〉 말인가요?

W 네, 그거요. 감사합니다.

Q 대화에서 남자가 하고 있는 것은?
(a) 선반에서 책 꺼내기.
(b) 읽을 책 추천.
(c) 여자에게 원예 서적 보여주기.
(d) 여자의 무거운 책 운반.

⊞ 기출 POINT

대화의 첫 문장은 반드시 집중해서 들어야 한다. 여자의 부탁은 help me get a book이다. 〈help+목적어+(to)+동사원형〉의 문형은 필수적으로 알아 두어야 한다. 앞에서 말한 명사 book을 대신하는 대명사 one의 쓰임도 중요하다. The big green one, The one called 등으로 쓰였다.

recommend 추천하다   정답 _(a)

32

M Alicia's birthday is coming up soon.

W Any ideas for a present?

M No. She seems to have everything she needs.

W Well, let's treat her to a spa, then.

M That's a great idea!

W Yeah. We can share the cost.

Q What are the speakers discussing?
(a) Which spa to go to.
(b) When to have a party.
(c) Who will pay for a meal.
(d) What birthday gift to get.

SOLUTION

M 곧 얼리셔의 생일이야.

W 선물에 대한 아이디어 뭐 없니?

M 없어. 얼리셔는 필요한 건 다 있는 것 같아.

W 음. 그럼 스파에 보내주자.

M 그거 좋은 생각이다!

W 응. 비용은 우리가 분담하면 돼.

Q 화자들이 의논하고 있는 것은?
(a) 어느 스파에 갈 것인지.
(b) 언제 파티를 할 것인지.
(c) 식사비를 누가 낼 것인지.
(d) 어떤 생일 선물을 할 것인지.

⊞ 기출 POINT

얼리셔의 생일 선물에 대한 대화이다. 사줄 만한 것이 없다고 생각해서 treat her to a spa를 언급한다. treat A to B는 'A에게 B를 사주다, 한턱내다'의 뜻이다. 선물로 물건 대신 스파에 보내주자는 내용이다. treat은 명사로도 쓰여 '한턱내기, 대접'의 뜻을 나타낸다.

come up 다가오다   **treat A to B** A에게 B로 한턱내다   정답 _(d)

33

W Hey, Jim. What's wrong? You look upset.

M I am. It's because my roommate's brother is staying with us for a while.

W So, what's the problem?

M He eats all the food and never cleans up.

W Did you talk to him about it?

M I did, but it didn't help.

Q What is the man complaining about?
(a) A thoughtless house guest.
(b) His disrespectful brother.
(c) His messy roommate.
(d) A talkative friend.

SOLUTION

W 이봐, 짐. 무슨 일이야? 화난 것 같은데.

M 화났어. 내 룸메이트의 남동생이 한동안 우리랑 같이 지내고 있거든.

W 그런데 뭐가 문제야?

M 걔가 음식을 다 먹어치우고 청소도 절대 안 해.

W 거기에 대해 얘기해 봤어?

M 그랬는데, 별 효과가 없었어.

Q 남자가 불평하고 있는 것은?
(a) 집에서 머물고 있는 생각이 모자라는 손님.
(b) 자신의 무례한 남자 형제.
(c) 자신의 지저분한 룸메이트.
(d) 수다스러운 친구.

🎯 기출 POINT

무엇에 대해 불평하는지 묻고 있다. It's because 다음에 이유가 제시된다. 룸메이트의 형제가 머물고 있는데 음식을 먹어치우고 청소도 하지 않아서 문제라고 한다. (a) A thoughtless house guest가 적절한 답이다. disrespectful은 '무례한'이라는 뜻이고, messy는 '지저분한'이라는 뜻이라서 혼동을 일으킬 수 있다. 대명사 His에 유의하여 실수하지 않도록 한다.

upset 화난 **clean up** 치우다   정답_(a)

34

M I'm looking forward to staying at a beach cabin.

W Yeah. I'm glad we chose an island holiday.

M Me, too. It'll be a great vacation.

W We can just relax and swim all day.

M Or we can go fishing on a boat.

W I can't wait to get on the plane tomorrow.

Q What are the speakers mainly discussing?
(a) Where their cabin is.
(b) How good their beach cabin is.
(c) How nice their vacation will be.
(d) What time they will go swimming.

SOLUTION

M 해변 오두막에 묵을 게 기대된다.

W 응. 섬에서 휴가를 보내기로 해서 기뻐.

M 나도, 멋진 휴가가 될 거야.

W 온종일 편하게 쉬면서 수영할 수 있어.

M 아니면 배 타고 낚시하러 가든지.

W 내일 비행기 탈 때까지 못 기다리겠어.

Q 화자들이 주로 논의하고 있는 것은?
(a) 오두막이 어디에 있는지.
(b) 해변 오두막이 얼마나 좋은지.
(c) 휴가가 얼마나 좋을지.
(d) 언제 수영하러 갈지.

🎯 기출 POINT

섬에서 보낼 휴가에 대한 이야기가 주된 것이다. 느긋하게 수영하고 낚시하는 멋진 휴가가 될 것이라는 내용이므로 How nice their vacation will be가 알맞다. beach cabin은 숙소이므로 상세 내용이다. look forward to -ing는 '~을 기대하다'라는 뜻이고, I can't wait to는 '빨리 ~하고 싶다'는 표현으로 자주 등장한다.

look forward to -ing ~을 기대하다 **cabin** 통나무집
I can't wait to 빨리 ~하고 싶다   정답_(c)

35

W So, did you find a summer job yet?

M Yes. I'm working as a sales assistant at the new Grady's.

W The new Grady's? Where?

M It's up on 5th street, next to Sports Mart.

W What's the workload like?

M It's not too hard.

Q What are the speakers mainly talking about?
(a) The man's summer job.
(b) The man's plan for summer.
(c) The amount of work at Grady's.
(d) The location of Sports Mart.

SOLUTION

W 그래서 여름 동안 일할 곳은 찾은 거야?

M 응. 새로 생긴 그레이디스에서 판매 보조원으로 일하고 있어.

W 새로 생긴 그레이디스라고? 어딘데?

M 5번 가에 있는 스포츠 마트 옆에 있어.

W 업무량은 어때?

M 아주 힘들지는 않아.

Q 대화의 주된 내용은?
(a) 남자의 여름 일자리.
(b) 남자의 여름 계획.
(c) 그레이디스에서의 업무량.
(d) 스포츠 마트의 위치.

기출 POINT

남자의 summer job에 대한 질문으로 시작하는 대화이다. 상점에서 하는 일, 상점의 위치, 업무량 등 남자의 summer job에 대한 전반적인 내용이다. (c)는 상세 정보에 해당되고 (b)는 너무 광범위한 말이다. Part 3의 대의파악 문제에서 너무 자세하거나 너무 광범위한 선택지는 오답일 가능성이 높다.

sales assistant 판매 보조원 **next to** ~의 옆에 **workload** 업무량

정답_(a)

36

M Kathy, do you know much about database programs?

W I've had some experience with them. Why?

M I want to set up a customized database on my computer.

W Well, I can show you a good program and help set it up.

M Oh, good. Is it hard to change the settings?

W No, it's pretty easy once you know how.

Q What does the man mainly want to do?
(a) Get help to fix his database problems.
(b) Learn how to put data into a database.
(c) Install a database program on his computer.
(d) Update a software program to a new version.

SOLUTION

M 캐시, 데이터베이스 프로그램에 대해 잘 아니?

W 다뤄본 적 있어. 왜?

M 내 컴퓨터에 맞춤화된 데이터베이스를 설정하고 싶어서.

W 음, 좋은 프로그램이 있는데 내가 설치하는 걸 도와줄게.

M 와, 잘됐다. 설정을 변경하는 게 어렵니?

W 아니, 일단 방법을 알면 꽤 쉬워.

Q 남자가 하고 싶어 하는 일은?
(a) 데이터베이스 문제를 해결하는 데 도움을 받는 것.
(b) 데이터를 데이터베이스에 입력하는 방법을 배우는 것.
(c) 컴퓨터에 데이터베이스 프로그램을 설치하는 것.
(d) 소프트웨어 프로그램을 새 버전으로 업데이트하는 것.

기출 POINT

첫 질문에서 데이터베이스 프로그램에 대해 묻는다. 남자가 하고 싶은 것은 I want to set up a customized database on my computer라는 말에 드러나 있다. once you know how는 '일단 방법을 알게 되면'의 뜻이다. '설정하다, 설치하다'는 뜻의 set up을 install로 바꾸어 표현한 (c)가 정답이다. 대화 내용을 그대로 말하지 않고 바꿔 표현한 선택지를 잘 이해하면 Part 3 정답을 쉽게 고를 수 있다.

customized 맞춤화된 **set up** 설치하다 **setting** 설정 **install** 설치하다 **update** 업데이트하다

정답_(c)

37

M Hello, Sarah Boggins? It's George.

W Oh, George from my indoor soccer team?

M Yes, I'm calling about a team meeting we're having tomorrow.

W Why so soon? The start of the season is weeks away.

M We'll just be introducing new players—that sort of thing.

W Okay, what time and where is it?

M We're meeting at the gym tomorrow night, around 7.

W Okay, then. I'll be there.

Q What is the main topic of the conversation?
(a) Asking people to join an indoor soccer team.
(b) Introducing the captain to a new team member.
(c) Giving team members the latest soccer results.
(d) Organizing a pre-season sports team gathering.

SOLUTION

M 여보세요. 새라 보긴스 씨? 저 조지예요.

W 아, 실내 축구팀의 조지요?

M 네. 내일 있을 팀 회의 때문에 전화하는 거예요.

W 왜 이렇게 빨라요? 시즌이 시작되려면 몇 주 남았는데.

M 신입 선수들 소개도 하고… 그런 것 때문이에요.

W 알겠어요. 시간과 장소는요?

M 내일 밤 7시경에 체육관에서 모입니다.

W 좋아요, 그럼. 나갈게요.

Q 대화의 주요 화제는?
(a) 사람들에게 실내 축구팀에 입단할 것을 요구하는 것.
(b) 팀장을 새 팀원에게 소개하는 것.
(c) 팀원들에게 최신 축구 경기 결과를 알려주는 것.
(d) 시즌 전 스포츠팀 모임을 준비하는 것.

기출 POINT

전화 대화에서는 I'm/ You're 대신에 This is/ It's를 쓰고 전화를 건 목적은 I'm calling about으로 표현한다. 용건은 I'm calling about a team meeting we're having tomorrow에 나타나 있다. 또 시즌의 시작은 몇 주가 남았다고 했으므로 pre-season sports team gathering에 대한 대화임을 알 수 있다. 새로운 팀 선수를 소개한다는 내용에 집중해서 (b)를 답으로 고르지 않도록 주의한다.

indoor 실내의 **that sort of thing** 그런 일 **gym** 체육관 **정답**_(d)

38

M Hi, Susan. I haven't seen you for a while. What's new?

W Well, I started dating that guy I told you about last time.

M The guy you met online?

W Yeah, we've met a few times.

M Wow. So, has he turned out as you expected?

W Actually, we get on really well.

Q Who is the woman dating?
(a) Someone she met online.
(b) Someone she met at a party.
(c) Someone the man introduced.
(d) Someone she knew as a friend.

SOLUTION

M 안녕, 수잔. 못 본 지 한참 됐다. 뭐 새로운 일 없니?

W 저, 나 지난번에 너한테 얘기했던 그 남자랑 만나기 시작했어.

M 인터넷에서 만났다는 그 남자?

W 응. 몇 번 만났어.

M 우와, 네가 기대했던 대로든?

W 실은 우리 정말 잘되고 있어.

Q 여자는 누구와 만나고 있는가?
(a) 인터넷에서 만난 사람.
(b) 파티에서 만난 사람.
(c) 남자가 소개해 준 사람.
(d) 친구로 알고 지내던 사람.

기출 POINT

안부를 묻는 표현으로 What's new?(뭐 새로운 일 없니?)가 쓰였다. dating하는 사람이 누구인지 묻는 질문이므로 dating이라는 말이 나오는 부분에 유의한다. The guy you met online에서 답을 찾을 수 있다.

I haven't seen you for a while. 오랜만이야. **turn out** ~임이 드러나다 **get on well** 잘되다 **정답**_(a)

39

M I wonder if I'm making the right choice.
W You mean quitting your job to become a teacher?
M Yes. It's a bit of a risk to leave my current job.
W I think you should do it. What are you worried about?
M Well, the future is always uncertain.
W Don't worry. There are always jobs for teachers.

Q What does the woman advise the man to do?
(a) Become a teacher.
(b) Do not take a risk.
(c) Do not leave his job.
(d) Find a better-paying job.

SOLUTION

M 내가 옳은 선택을 하는 건지 모르겠어.
W 직장을 그만두고 교사가 되기로 한 거 말이니?
M 응. 현재의 직장을 그만두는 건 모험이잖아.
W 나는 네가 그래야 한다고 생각하는데. 뭐가 걱정되는 거야?
M 음. 미래는 항상 불확실하잖아.
W 걱정 마. 교사 일자리는 항상 있으니까.

Q 여자가 남자에게 조언하는 것은?
(a) 교사가 될 것.
(b) 모험을 하지 말 것.
(c) 일자리를 그만두지 말 것.
(d) 수입이 더 좋은 일자리를 찾을 것.

🏁 기출 POINT

I wonder if는 if 이하인지 아닌지 잘 모르겠다는 말이다. 여자는 고민하는 남자에게 교사가 되라고 말하고 있다. I think you should do it과 There are always jobs for teachers에서 교사가 되라는 여자의 조언을 찾아볼 수 있다. (b)와 (c)는 같은 내용으로 여자의 조언과 정반대의 내용이다.

I wonder if ~인지 궁금하다   quit one's job 직장을 그만두다   risk 위험   current 현재의   uncertain 불확실한   정답_(a)

40

M Hi, I have a question about the security check.
W What would you like to know?
M Do I have to put all luggage through the X-ray machine?
W All your carry-on luggage has to go through, yes.
M But I'm worried about damaging my laptop.
W Oh, it's safe. The X-ray doesn't affect laptops.

Q Which is correct according to the conversation?
(a) The woman X-rayed the man's carry-on bags.
(b) The woman wants the man to show her his laptop.
(c) The man does not need to have his laptop X-rayed.
(d) The man is concerned that his laptop might be damaged.

SOLUTION

M 안녕하세요. 보안 검사에 대해 질문이 있는데요.
W 무엇을 알고 싶은가요?
M 제 여행 가방을 전부 X선 기기에 통과시켜야 하나요?
W 네. 기내 반입 수하물은 전부 통과시키셔야 합니다.
M 하지만 제 노트북이 손상될까 봐 걱정돼서요.
W 아. 안전해요. X선은 노트북에 영향을 미치지 않습니다.

Q 대화에 따르면 옳은 것은?
(a) 여자는 남자의 기내 반입용 가방들을 X선에 투과시켰다.
(b) 여자는 남자가 노트북을 보여주기를 원한다.
(c) 남자는 노트북을 X선에 투과시킬 필요가 없다.
(d) 남자는 노트북이 망가질까 봐 걱정하고 있다.

🏁 기출 POINT

공항의 보안 검사와 관련된 대화이다. carry-on luggage는 '기내 반입 수하물'을 말한다. 남자는 노트북이 손상될까 봐 X선 투과를 걱정하고 있으므로 (d)가 맞는 내용이다. 보안 검사를 하기 전에 묻는 것이므로 (a)의 투과시켰다(X-rayed)는 오답이다.

security check 보안 검사   luggage 짐   carry-on luggage 기내 반입용 수하물   go through 통과하다   laptop 노트북   정답_(d)

41

W Daniel, you own a blue SUV, don't you?

M Yes, it's in the office parking lot, why?

W Well, when I came back from lunch, I noticed the lights were on.

M Oh! I must have left them on this morning. I hope the battery's okay.

W Could be, but the lights were a bit dim.

M Thanks, I'll go and check things out.

Q Which is correct according to the conversation?

(a) The woman just had lunch with the man.

(b) The man parked his car in the wrong spot.

(c) The man forgot to turn off his car headlights.

(d) The woman had an accident with the man's car.

SOLUTION

W 대니얼, 네 차가 파란색 SUV 맞지?

M 응, 사무실 주차장에 있는데, 왜?

W 음, 점심 먹고 돌아오다가 보니까 등이 켜져 있더라.

M 아! 아침에 켜 놓고 내린 모양이네. 배터리가 괜찮아야 할 텐데.

W 그럴 거야. 그런데 불빛이 좀 어둡기는 하더라.

M 고마워. 가서 확인해 볼게.

Q 대화에 따르면 옳은 것은?

(a) 여자는 방금 남자와 점심을 같이 했다.

(b) 남자는 차를 잘못된 장소에 주차했다.

(c) 남자는 깜빡 잊고 차의 전조등을 끄지 않았다.

(d) 여자는 남자의 차와 사고가 났었다.

기출 POINT

남자의 차에 불이 켜 있는 것을 여자가 보았다고 했으므로 남자는 전조등을 끄지 않고 내렸음을 알 수 있다. 〈must+have p.p.〉는 과거에 '~했음에 틀림없다'는 표현이다. 여자와 남자는 같이 점심을 먹은 것이 아니며 주차는 회사 주차장에 했다는 내용이 옳은 내용이다.

own 소유하다 **SUV** 스포츠 범용차(sport utility vehicle) **parking lot** 주차장 **dim** 흐릿한　　　　　　　　　　　　　정답_(c)

42

M Have you been following the scandal at PostCom?

W Well, I've heard the CEO's been indicted for fraud.

M Yeah, he's scheduled to go on trial next month.

W Good thing. People lost their life savings in that collapse.

M I know. My uncle lost $20,000. He's devastated.

W Really? I didn't know that. I hope he can get some of it back.

Q Which is correct according to the conversation?

(a) The man's uncle was indicted for losing $20,000.

(b) The CEO of PostCom is going to be tried for fraud.

(c) The two people hope they can get their money back.

(d) The woman had not heard about the financial scandal.

SOLUTION

M 포스트컴 스캔들 잘 알고 있니?

W 음. CEO가 사기로 기소되었다고 들었어.

M 응, 그 사람이 다음 달에 법정에 서기로 되어 있어.

W 잘됐네. 그 회사가 무너지면서 사람들이 평생 저축한 돈을 잃었잖아.

M 그러게. 우리 삼촌도 2만 달러를 손해보셨어. 마음이 많이 지치셨지.

W 정말? 그건 몰랐어. 조금이나마 돈을 되찾기를 바랄게.

Q 대화에 따르면 옳은 것은?

(a) 남자의 삼촌은 2만 달러를 손해본 것에 대해 기소당했다.

(b) 포스트컴의 CEO는 사기로 법정에 서게 된다.

(c) 두 사람은 자신들의 돈을 되찾기를 바란다.

(d) 여자는 그 금융 스캔들에 대해 들어보지 못했다.

기출 POINT

Have you been following the scandal?은 스캔들에 대한 소식을 계속 주시하고 있었냐는 말이다. be indicted for는 '~로 기소되다'의 뜻이므로 'PostCom의 CEO가 사기로 법정에 서게 된다'는 (b)가 맞는 내용이다. 남자의 삼촌이 2만 달러를 사기당하고 힘들어 했으므로 (a)와 (c)는 오답이다.

scandal 스캔들 **indict** 기소하다 **fraud** 사기 **go on trial** 법정에 서다 **savings** 예금 **collapse** 무너지다 **devastate** 황폐화시키다 **financial** 금융의　　　　　　　　　　　　　　정답_(b)

43

M Clare, can I have a word with you?

W Sure. Is there a problem?

M Well, you've been late for work every day this week.

W Oh, my kids started at a new school, and I've been driving them there.

M Will you have to do that every day from now on?

W No, just this week. The school bus starts operating next week.

Q What can be inferred about the woman's kids?

(a) They do not like their new school.

(b) They take extra lessons before school.

(c) They will take a bus to school after this week.

(d) They have been late to school every day this week.

SOLUTION

M 클레어, 잠깐 이야기 좀 할 수 있을까요?

W 그럼요. 무슨 문제 있나요?

M 저, 클레어 씨가 이번 주에 매일 회사에 늦었어요.

W 아, 아이들이 새 학교에 다니기 시작했는데, 차로 학교까지 데려다 주느라고요.

M 그럼 지금부터 매일 그렇게 해야 하는 겁니까?

W 아니요, 이번 주만요. 다음 주부터는 학교 버스가 운행을 시작합니다.

Q 여자의 아이들에 대해 추론할 수 있는 것은?

(a) 새 학교를 좋아하지 않는다.

(b) 학교 수업 전 추가 수업을 듣는다.

(c) 다음 주부터는 버스를 타고 학교에 갈 것이다.

(d) 아이들은 이번 주 내내 학교에 지각했다.

기출 POINT

대화를 청하는 말로 Can I have a word with you?(얘기 좀 할 수 있을까요?)가 사용되었다. 이번 주 내내 출근이 늦었다는 것을 강조하기 위해 현재완료로 you've been late for work every day this week라고 말하고 있다. 마지막 문장을 통해 여자의 아이들이 다음 주부터 학교 버스로 등교할 것을 알 수 있다.

have a word with ~와 이야기를 하다 **from now on** 지금부터 **operate** 운행하다

정답_(c)

44

M What are you doing?

W I'm working on a paper.

M Why do you have these CDs? Is it for your music class?

W Right. I'm doing a paper on the Beatles.

M Wow, the Beatles! What will you focus on?

W I'm writing about the influences in their music.

Q What can be inferred from the conversation?

(a) The man does not like the Beatles.

(b) The woman will finish her paper soon.

(c) The woman wants the man to help her.

(d) The man finds the woman's topic interesting.

SOLUTION

M 뭐 하고 있어?

W 리포트 쓰는 중이야.

M 이 CD들은 왜 가지고 있는 거야? 음악수업 리포트니?

W 맞아. 비틀즈에 대한 리포트를 쓰고 있어.

M 우와, 비틀즈구나! 어디에 중점을 둬서 쓸 거야?

W 그들 음악의 영향력에 대해 쓰고 있어.

Q 대화에서 추론할 수 있는 것은?

(a) 남자는 비틀즈를 좋아하지 않는다.

(b) 여자는 곧 리포트를 끝낼 것이다.

(c) 여자는 남자가 자신을 도와주기를 원한다.

(d) 남자는 여자의 주제가 흥미롭다고 생각한다.

기출 POINT

여자가 비틀즈에 대한 리포트를 쓰고 있다고 하자 남자가 감탄하며 Wow, the Beatles!라고 한 것으로 보아 흥미롭게 생각한다는 추론이 가능하다. 리포트를 쓰는 중이라는 말을 I'm working on a paper/ I'm doing a paper on the Beatles의 두 문장에서 찾아 볼 수 있다.

work on ~을 작업 중이다 **do a paper** 리포트를 쓰다 **focus on** ~을 중점적으로 다루다

정답_(d)

45

M I can't believe the guy in that movie.

W Why not? Wouldn't you risk your life for a woman?

M Not like that guy. He didn't have a chance of succeeding.

W You don't have a romantic bone in your body.

M Hey, it's not that. I'm just being realistic!

W He risked his life for love. That's realistic to me.

Q What can be inferred about the speakers?

(a) They like to see romantic movies together.

(b) They have different interpretations of the character's actions.

(c) They will see another movie together soon.

(d) They both dislike movies that are unrealistic.

SOLUTION

M 그 영화 속 남자 정말 믿을 수 없어.

W 왜? 너는 한 여자를 위해서 네 인생을 걸지 않을 거니?

M 저 남자처럼은 아니지. 저 남자는 성공할 확률이 없었잖아.

W 너는 로맨틱한 구석이라고는 없는 애구나.

M 야, 그게 아니잖아. 난 그저 현실적인 거라고!

W 저 남자는 사랑을 위해 인생을 걸었어. 나한테는 그게 현실적이야.

Q 화자들에 대해 추론할 수 있는 것은?

(a) 함께 로맨틱한 영화를 보는 것을 좋아한다.

(b) 등장인물의 행동을 서로 다르게 해석한다.

(c) 곧 함께 다른 영화를 보러 갈 것이다.

(d) 둘 다 비현실적인 영화를 싫어한다.

기출 POINT

영화 주인공에 대한 대화이다. 여자는 여자를 위해 목숨을 거는 주인공이 현실적이라고 생각하지만 남자는 성공할 가능성이 없는 일을 하는 비현실적인 인물로 본다. '너는 ~하지 않을 거니?'라는 말로 쓰인 Wouldn't you...? 문장은 알아듣기 쉽지 않으므로 익혀둘 필요가 있다.

risk one's life for ~을 위해 목숨을 걸다 **have a chance of -ing** ~할 가능성이 있다 **romantic bone** 로맨틱한 면 **realistic** 현실적인

정답_(b)

46

Welcome to all parents. As you know, one of the most defining characteristics of Cardston High School is its commitment to community service through a wide range of volunteer and service activities. In keeping with its reputation, we have begun a new initiative to upgrade the school's facilities, increasing accessibility for children with physical disabilities.

Q What is the speaker mainly talking about?

(a) The students' commitment to education.

(b) The good reputation of Cardston High School.

(c) The problems that children with physical disabilities face at school.

(d) The school's plan to improve the facilities for handicapped children.

SOLUTION

모든 학부형들께 환영의 말씀을 드립니다. 아시다시피 카드스턴 고등학교의 가장 뚜렷한 특징 중 하나는 다양한 자원 봉사 활동을 통해 지역 사회 봉사에 헌신하고 있다는 것입니다. 그 명성을 지켜나가고자 저희는 신체적 장애가 있는 어린이의 접근성을 높이는 등 학교 시설을 개선하는 새로운 구상에 착수했습니다.

Q 화자가 주로 이야기하고 있는 것은?

(a) 학생들의 교육에 대한 헌신.

(b) 카드스턴 고등학교의 훌륭한 명성.

(c) 신체적 장애가 있는 어린이들이 학교에서 당면하는 문제들.

(d) 장애 아동들을 위한 시설을 개선하기로 한 학교의 계획.

기출 POINT

이 학교의 특징은 지역 사회의 봉사 활동에 헌신하는 것이며 이번에는 장애를 가진 학생들이 이용할 수 있도록 학교의 시설을 개선하겠다는 구상에 대한 내용이다. 신체적 장애 어린이들이 학교에서 겪는 문제에 대한 언급은 없으므로 (c)는 맞지 않는다.

defining 뚜렷한 **characteristics** 특징 **disability** 장애 **commitment to** ~에의 헌신 **community service** 지역 봉사 **volunteer** 자원 봉사자 **reputation** 명성 **initiative** 구상 **accessibility** 접근성 **handicapped** 장애의

정답_(d)

Actual Test 2

47

As I have stated many times, high blood pressure is a silent killer because it has no symptoms; many people don't even know they have it until it's too late. Unfortunately, these people are often the victims of stroke, heart attack, heart failure or kidney failure. So it's very important that you get your blood pressure checked regularly.

Q What is the main point of the talk?
(a) The primary symptoms of high blood pressure.
(b) The different treatments for high blood pressure.
(c) The kind of people affected by high blood pressure.
(d) The importance of regular blood pressure checkups.

SOLUTION

제가 수차례 언급했듯이, 고혈압은 증상이 없기 때문에 소리 없는 살인자입니다. 많은 사람들이 손쓰기에 너무 늦을 때까지 자신이 고혈압이라는 것조차 모르죠. 불행하게도 이 사람들이 종종 뇌졸중, 심장마비, 심부전이나 신부전의 희생자가 됩니다. 그래서 정기적으로 혈압을 검사하는 것이 매우 중요하죠.

Q 담화문의 요점은?
(a) 고혈압의 주요 증상.
(b) 고혈압에 대한 여러 가지 치료법.
(c) 고혈압에 걸리는 사람들의 유형.
(d) 정기적인 혈압 검사의 중요성.

▦ 기출 POINT
고혈압은 증상이 없어서 오랫동안 자각하지 못하며 합병증까지 생기게 되기 때문에 정기적인 혈압 검사가 중요하다는 내용이다. 당위성을 의미하는 형용사 다음에 〈(should)+동사원형〉이 It's very important that you get your blood pressure checked regularly에 쓰였다. 〈get+목적어+p.p.〉 형태의 사역동사 쓰임도 유의한다.
state 언급하다 **high blood pressure** 고혈압 **symptom** 증상
unfortunately 불행히도 **victim** 희생자 **stroke** 뇌졸중
heart attack 심장마비 **heart failure** 심부전 **kidney** 신장
정답_(d)

48

Friends and family gathered here today, I would like to express my sympathies to you on behalf of the Solomon Foundation. We are all deeply saddened by the loss of Anne Brooks on December 1. Anne was one of the founders of the Solomon Foundation and a Lifetime Honorary Member. She was greatly respected and admired by all of us. To her husband, Gil Brooks and to their son, Marcus, please accept our condolences.

Q What is the main purpose of the speech?
(a) To honor the memory of Mrs. Brooks.
(b) To request help for a charity foundation.
(c) To say prayers for Gil and Marcus Brooks.
(d) To thank Mrs. Brooks for the work she has done.

SOLUTION

솔로몬 재단을 대신해 오늘 이 자리에 모인 친구와 가족들 여러분께 애도의 말씀을 전합니다. 우리 모두는 12월 1일 앤 브룩스가 유명을 달리한 것에 대해 깊은 슬픔을 느끼고 있습니다. 앤은 솔로몬 재단의 창립자들 중 일원이자 평생 명예회원이었습니다. 앤은 우리 모두의 깊은 경의와 존경을 받았습니다. 앤의 남편 되는 길 브룩스와 아들인 마커스에 조의를 표합니다.

Q 연설의 주요 목적은?
(a) 브룩스 여사를 추모하기 위해.
(b) 자선재단을 위한 도움을 요청하기 위해.
(c) 길 브룩스와 마커스 브룩스를 위한 기도를 하기 위해.
(d) 브룩스 여사의 업적에 대해 감사하기 위해.

▦ 기출 POINT
수동태 문장이 많이 사용된 연설로 격식을 갖춘 말하기의 예를 보여주는 문제이다. I would like to express my sympathies to you에서 연설의 목적을 찾아 볼 수 있다. 그리고 saddened by the loss of Anne Brooks에서 추모하려는 의도를 알 수 있다. 고인이 된 사람을 기리는 것은 to honor the memory of 로 표현하므로 답은 (a)이다.
gather 모이다 **sympathy** 애도 **on behalf of** ~을 대신해서
sadden 슬퍼지다 **condolence** 조의 **charity foundation** 자선재단 **prayer** 기도
정답_(a)

49

All women deserve the right to fully participate in the social and political lives of their countries if freedom and democracy are to thrive and endure. Yet many women who wished to participate in this forum have not been able to attend, or have been prohibited from speaking publicly. I call on those who have been accorded these basic rights to speak out on behalf of repressed women.

Q What is the main topic of the talk?
(a) The abuse against women around the world.
(b) The reasons why women are still repressed.
(c) The right of women everywhere to free speech.
(d) The need for women to attend political conferences.

SOLUTION

자유와 민주주의가 번창하고 지속되려면 모든 여성들이 국가의 사회 및 정치 생활에 온전히 참여할 권리를 받아야 마땅합니다. 하지만 이 같은 장에 참여하기를 원했던 많은 여성들은 참여할 수 없었거나, 대중들을 상대로 연설하는 것이 금지됐습니다. 저는 이러한 기본권을 부여받은 사람들이 억압받는 여성들을 대신해 기탄없이 말해 줄 것을 요청합니다.

Q 담화문의 요점은?
(a) 전세계 여성들에 대한 학대.
(b) 여성들이 아직도 억압받는 이유.
(c) 여성들이 어디서나 언론의 자유를 가질 권리.
(d) 여성들이 정치 회담에 참여할 필요성.

기출 POINT

to participate in this forum, speaking publicly, to speak out on behalf of repressed women 등에서 글의 요점이 나타나 있다. 모든 여성들이 사회 및 정치 생활에 참여해야 하고 공개적인 연설이나 토론에 참여할 권리가 있다는 것이 요점이다. (d)는 일부분에 불과한 내용이므로 답이 될 수 없다.

deserve ~을 받아 마땅하다 **democracy** 민주주의 **thrive** 번영하다 **forum** 공개 토론의 장 **prohibit A from B** A를 B하지 못하게 막다 **call on** 청하다 **accord** ~을 주다 **repressed** 억압받는 **abuse** 학대   **정답** (c)

50

Yesterday I focused on the foreign policies of the American National Security Council, but today I want to talk about the President's influence on them. Each President introduces his own administrative approach that affects council policy-making for successive generations, whether through the style of leadership or the direction of national policy. We can still see the effects of President Nixon's decisions on today's foreign policy processes.

Q What is the lecture mainly about?
(a) The influence of President Nixon on foreign policy decisions.
(b) How each President's foreign policy actions affect the future.
(c) The role of the National Security Council in foreign policy affairs.
(d) What methods are used by the President to influence national policy.

SOLUTION

어제는 미국 국가 안전 보장회의의 외교정책에 초점을 맞췄지만, 오늘은 이에 대한 대통령의 영향력에 대해 이야기해 보겠습니다. 각 대통령은 통치 스타일을 통해서든 아니면 국가 정책 방향을 통해서든 수세대에 걸쳐 국가 안전 보장회의 정책 입안에 영향을 주는 자신만의 행정 접근법을 도입합니다. 우리는 닉슨 대통령의 결정이 오늘날 외교정책 과정에 미치는 영향을 여전히 볼 수 있습니다.

Q 강의의 주된 내용은?
(a) 외교정책 결정에 대한 닉슨 대통령의 영향력.
(b) 각 대통령의 외교정책 행동이 미래에 미치는 영향.
(c) 외교정책 부문에서 국가 안전 보장회의의 역할.
(d) 대통령이 국가 정책에 영향을 주기 위해 사용하는 방법들.

기출 POINT

Yesterday I focused on.... but today I want to talk about은 강의 시작을 나타내는 표현들이다. 강의의 요지는 첫 문장에서 찾을 수 있다. American National Security Council의 외교정책에 대한 대통령의 영향력, 각 대통령이 자신만의 행정 접근법을 가지고 영향력을 행사할 수 있다는 내용을 통해 답을 찾아낼 수 있다. 닉슨은 이러한 영향력의 한 예에 불과하므로 (a)는 오답이다.

foreign policy 외교정책 **National Security Council** 국가 안전 보장회의 **administrative** 행정적인 **policy-making** 정책 결정 **successive** 계승되는   **정답** (b)

51

A project team evolves and changes markedly during its lifetime. Working as a project manager, I've witnessed the process many times. It has three stages: forming, storming and normalizing. Our team has just completed the forming stage of being brought together. Next, we will experience the storming phase in which everyone is unsure of each other and things are unsettled. With my guidance, that will pass into the normalizing stage, when everyone knows their place and knows what to do.

Q What is the speaker mainly talking about?
(a) The efficiency of his team under his leadership.
(b) The reorganization of his team's key personnel.
(c) The progressive stages of his team's new project.
(d) The phases of his team's growth and development.

SOLUTION

프로젝트 팀은 그 주기 속에서 현저하게 진화하고 변화합니다. 프로젝트 관리자로 일하면서 나는 이 과정을 여러 차례 보았습니다. 프로젝트 팀에는 형성, 격동, 그리고 정상화의 세 단계가 있습니다. 우리 팀은 조직이 되는 형성 단계를 이제 막 끝냈죠. 다음으로 우리는 격동 단계를 경험할 텐데, 이 단계에서는 모두가 서로에 대해 확신을 가지지 못하고 상황은 불안정합니다. 내 지침을 따르면 이 단계는 정상화 단계로 넘어가게 되고, 이 단계에서는 모두가 자신이 있어야 할 곳을 알고 무엇을 해야 하는지 알게 됩니다.

Q 화자가 주로 이야기하고 있는 것은?
(a) 자신의 통솔 하에서 팀의 효율성.
(b) 팀의 핵심 인력 재편성.
(c) 자신의 팀의 새 프로젝트 진행 단계.
(d) 자신의 팀의 성장 및 발달 단계들.

기출 POINT
첫 번째 문장은 반드시 집중해서 들어야 한다. 프로젝트 팀이 주기 속에서 진화하고 변화한다는 것이다. 그리고 그 단계를 형성, 격동, 정상화의 세 단계로 나누어 설명하는 내용이다. 화자가 자신의 팀의 성장과 발달의 단계에 대해 이야기한다는 (d)가 답이다. 프로젝트의 진행 단계를 설명한 것이 아니므로 (c)는 오답이다.

evolve 진화하다 **markedly** 현저하게 **witness** 목격하다
normalize 정상화하다 **complete** 완성하다 **phase** 단계 **정답_(d)**

52

Inertia is one of the fundamental laws of physics. It is the force by which objects tend to stay at rest or uniformly in motion unless they are acted upon by some outside force. For example, imagine you are standing on a school bus. As long as the bus is not moving, you can stand still. This is your state of inertia. But if the driver accelerates suddenly, you will be jolted backwards. That is when your inertia is changed.

Q What is the main purpose of the lecture?
(a) To explain what inertia is by giving an example.
(b) To summarize the physics involved in bus travel.
(c) To introduce students to basic concepts in physics.
(d) To describe the effects of inertia on a human body.

SOLUTION

관성은 물리학의 근본 법칙 중 하나입니다. 이것은 물체가 어떤 외부의 힘이 작용하지 않으면 멈춰 있으려고 하거나 한결같이 움직이고자 하는 성향을 띄게 만드는 힘이죠. 예를 들어 여러분이 학교 버스 안에 서 있다고 생각해 보세요. 버스가 움직이고 있지 않는 한, 여러분은 가만히 서 있을 수 있습니다. 이것이 여러분의 관성 상태죠. 하지만 기사가 갑자기 가속을 하면 여러분은 몸이 뒤로 쏠릴 겁니다. 이때 바로 여러분의 관성이 변화된 겁니다.

Q 강의의 주요 목적은?
(a) 예시를 통한 관성 설명.
(b) 버스 여행과 관련된 물리학 요약.
(c) 학생들에게 물리학 기본 개념 소개.
(d) 관성이 인체에 미치는 영향 기술.

기출 POINT
물리학의 법칙인 관성의 개념을 설명하는 강의이다. 관성에 대해 정의하고 버스 안에서 급출발할 때의 예시를 통해 관성의 개념을 설명하는 것이지 인체에 끼치는 영향을 설명하는 것이 아니므로 (d)는 오답이다.

inertia 관성 **fundamental** 근본적인 **physics** 물리학 **tend to** ~하는 경향이 있다 **accelerate** 가속하다 **jolt** 세게 흔들다
concept 개념   **정답_(a)**

53

Our art history class today begins with the great Vincent van Gogh. He began painting at the age of 30 around 1880, and though he studied briefly in Antwerp and Paris, he was largely self-taught. After his brother Theo introduced Vincent to famous artists in Paris in 1888, he really began to grow as an artist. Influenced by Degas, Gauguin, Seurat and Toulouse-Lautrec, Van Gogh began experimenting with different brush techniques and the use of brighter and more vivid colors.

Q Which is correct according to the lecture?
(a) Van Gogh grew up in Antwerp.
(b) Van Gogh experimented with dark colors.
(c) Van Gogh's brother Theo taught him to paint.
(d) Van Gogh's style was influenced by many painters.

SOLUTION

오늘 우리 예술사 수업은 그 위대한 빈센트 반 고흐로 시작합니다. 고흐는 1880년경 서른의 나이에 그림을 그리기 시작했고, 앤트워프와 파리에서 잠깐 공부하기는 했지만 거의 독학을 했죠. 그의 동생인 테오가 1888년 빈센트를 파리의 유명 예술가들에게 소개시킨 후에 빈센트는 진정한 예술가로서 성장하기 시작했습니다. 드가, 고갱, 쇠라와 툴루즈 로트렉의 영향을 받은 반 고흐는 다양한 붓놀림과 더 밝고 강렬한 색채로 실험을 하기 시작했죠.

Q 강의에 따르면 옳은 것은?
(a) 반 고흐는 앤트워프에서 자랐다.
(b) 반 고흐는 어두운 색깔로 실험했다.
(c) 반 고흐의 동생 테오가 그에게 그림 그리는 것을 가르쳤다.
(d) 반 고흐의 양식은 여러 화가들로부터 영향을 받았다.

기출 POINT

화가 반 고흐에 대한 강의이다. 강의에 따르면 반 고흐는 앤트워프에서 잠깐 그림을 공부했고, 밝은 색을 가지고 실험했으며, 동생 테오가 그를 파리의 유명 화가들에게 소개했다. 또한 여러 화가들의 영향을 받았으므로 정답은 (d)이다.

though 비록 **briefly** 잠깐 **self-taught** 독학한 **experiment** 실험하다 **brush technique** 붓놀림 기법 **vivid** 강렬한 정답_(d)

54

The Victoria Festival, produced by the Victoria Foundation for the Humanities, welcomes you to its annual celebration of books, reading, writing and the printed word. Come and share in the latest on how we tell stories and share our lives; hear visiting authors and participate in writing workshops. The Victoria Festival runs from January 10 to February 20. See your local paper for festival details.

Q Which is correct about the Victoria Festival?
(a) It focuses on new types of media.
(b) It celebrates the medium of written language.
(c) It holds demonstrations of old printing methods.
(d) It emphasizes the need for more writing workshops.

SOLUTION

빅토리아 인문 재단이 준비한 빅토리아 축제는 책과 독서, 글쓰기와 인쇄물에 대한 연례 제전을 찾아주신 여러분을 환영합니다. 이야기를 하고 삶을 공유하는 방식에 대한 최신 정보를 함께 공유하십시오. 객원 작가의 이야기를 듣고, 작문 워크숍에 참여하세요. 빅토리아 축제는 1월 10일부터 2월 20일까지 열립니다. 축제에 대한 자세한 사항은 지방 신문을 참고하세요.

Q 빅토리아 축제에 대해 옳은 것은?
(a) 새로운 형태의 매체에 중점을 둔다.
(b) 문자언어 매체에 대한 제전이다.
(c) 구식 인쇄술을 시연한다.
(d) 더 많은 작문 워크숍의 필요성을 강조한다.

기출 POINT

빅토리아 축제는 출판물 관련 매체를 다루고 있으므로 문자언어라는 매체에 중점을 두고 있고, 작가들의 강연과 창작 워크숍 등의 행사로 구성되어 있다. 새로운 매체나 구식 인쇄 기법의 시연은 언급되지 않았고, 워크숍의 필요성을 강조하지 않으므로 (b)가 정답이다.

annual 연례의 **celebration** 제전 **visiting author** 객원 작가

정답_(b)

55

In this fashion studies lecture, we'll cover a period in which almost all women wore corsets, from 1820 to 1910. This historical peak for the corset was influenced by social perceptions. Women still wore corsets for the traditional reason, to shape the figure, but the perception of the day was that women had weak minds and bodies, and therefore, they also needed to wear corsets for moral and medical support as well. In hindsight, tight corsets were a direct reflection of the constraints imposed on women by society.

Q Which is correct about the corset in the 1800s?
(a) It was proven to provide women with medical benefits.
(b) It was widely used in line with strict social conventions.
(c) It was a fashion that most women regarded as a burden.
(d) It was socially unacceptable for some women to wear one.

SOLUTION

이 패션학 강의에서는 거의 모든 여성들이 코르셋을 착용했던 1820년부터 1910년까지의 기간을 다룰 겁니다. 코르셋의 역사적 정점은 사회적 인식에 영향을 받았어요. 여성들은 여전히 전통적인 이유, 즉 몸매를 바로 잡기 위해 코르셋을 착용했지만, 여자는 신체적으로 또 정신적으로 약하기 때문에 도덕적 및 의학적 도움을 받기 위해서도 코르셋을 입어야 한다는 게 당시의 인식이었어요. 돌아보면 꽉 끼는 코르셋은 사회가 여성에게 부과한 제약을 직접적으로 반영한 것이었죠.

Q 1800년대 코르셋에 대해 옳은 것은?
(a) 여성들에게 의학적 혜택을 주는 것으로 입증되었다.
(b) 엄격한 사회적 관습과 조화를 이루며 널리 사용되었다.
(c) 많은 여성들이 부담스럽게 생각한 패션이었다.
(d) 일부 여성이 코르셋을 착용하는 것은 사회적으로 용납되지 않았다.

기출 POINT
코르셋이 가장 유행한 1800년대와 현재의 사용 목적이 다르다는 것에 유의하면서 들어야 한다. 코르셋은 당시의 사회적 인식의 영향이다. 여성은 심신이 약하기 때문에 도덕적이고 의학적인 도움을 받기 위해 코르셋을 입어야 한다는 엄격한 사회적 인식 때문에 1800년대에 널리 사용되었다는 것이다. 의학적인 혜택을 받는 것은 언급되어 있지 않고 부담스럽게 생각되었다는 설명도 없었다.

cover 다루다 period 기간 peak 정점 perception 인식
in hindsight 돌아보면 reflection 반영 constraint 제약
impose on ~에게 부과하다   정답 (b)

56

Ethical concerns have been raised concerning the world's first partial face transplant on a 38-year-old woman who had transplant surgery to replace her nose, lips and chin after being mauled by a dog. A medical ethics panel has criticized the surgeons who performed the surgery, saying they should have first attempted standard reconstructive surgery. The panel has recommended disciplinary action for what it sees as a violation of medical ethics.

Q Which is correct according to the passage?
(a) Surgeons' choice of a transplant was criticized.
(b) The face transplant triggered a medical lawsuit.
(c) Face surgery was performed without the patient's consent.
(d) An ethics panel advised against an operation on a woman's face.

SOLUTION

개에게 물린 후 코, 입술과 턱을 복원하는 이식 수술을 받은 38세 여성에 대한 세계 최초의 부분 안면 이식 수술에 대해 윤리적 우려가 제기되었다. 의학 윤리 전문 위원회는 이 수술을 실시한 외과의사들은 우선 표준적인 재건 수술을 시도했어야 했다며 이들을 비난했다. 전문 위원회는 이것을 의학 윤리 위반으로 보고 징계 조치를 권고했다.

Q 지문의 내용으로 옳은 것은?
(a) 이식 수술에 대한 외과의들의 선택이 비판을 받았다.
(b) 안면 이식 수술은 의료소송을 촉발시켰다.
(c) 안면 수술은 환자의 동의 없이 이루어졌다.
(d) 윤리 전문 위원회에서는 여성의 안면 수술에 반대 의견을 제시했다.

기출 POINT
세계 최초로 실시된 부분 안면 이식 수술에 대한 내용이다. 외과의사들에 대한 의학 윤리 전문 위원회의 태도에 유의하여 들어야 하는 문제이다. criticized, has recommended disciplinary action에 두 가지 대응이 나타나 있다. 표준적인 재건 수술을 했어야 했다는 비난과 의학 윤리 위반으로 징계 조치를 권고한 것이다. 따라서 비난을 받았다는 (a)가 내용과 일치한다.

ethical 윤리적인 concern 우려 concerning 관련된 partial 부분적인 transplant 이식하다 surgery 수술 maul 할퀴어 상처내다 surgeon 외과의사 reconstructive 재건의 disciplinary 징계의 violation 위반 trigger 유발하다 consent 동의   정답 (a)

57

The New York Housing Authority has implemented a new guideline to deter public misuse of apartment subsidies. City building supervisor Tom Whitman announced today that the Housing Authority would reassess some 50,000 households that currently collect state rental support. It will then determine their qualifications, considering a surge in employment. Whitman expressed his desire to work with the families to make sure the reassessment is fair and equitable for everyone.

Q Which is correct according to the news report?
(a) Nearly 50,000 families are misusing subsidies.
(b) Abuse of public funding has increased recently.
(c) The current subsidy system is unfair to families.
(d) The new policy will reduce abuse of public funds.

SOLUTION

뉴욕 주택공사에서는 대중들의 아파트 보조금 악용을 방지하기 위한 새로운 지침을 이행했다. 톰 위트먼 뉴욕시 건물 감독관은 주택공사는 현재 주로부터 월세 지원을 받고 있는 5만여 가구에 대한 재평가를 실시하겠다고 오늘 발표했다. 이에 따라 취업의 급증을 고려해 주택공사에서는 이들의 자격 요건을 결정할 것이다. 위트먼은 재평가가 모두에게 공정하고 형평성을 가질 수 있도록 하기 위해 해당 가구들과 협력하고자 하는 뜻을 내비쳤다.

Q 뉴스 보도에 따르면 옳은 것은?
(a) 거의 5만 가구가 보조금을 악용하고 있다.
(b) 공적 자금 남용이 최근 증가했다.
(c) 현 보조금 체계는 가구들에게 불공평하다.
(d) 새 정책은 공적 자금의 악용을 줄일 것이다.

🏛 기출 POINT

뉴욕 주택공사의 새 지침에 대한 뉴스 보도이다. 아파트 보조금 악용을 막기 위해 현재 지원 받는 가구에 대한 재평가를 통해 공정하고 형평성 있는 보조금 지원을 이루겠다는 내용이다. 새 정책이 공적 자금의 악용을 줄일 것이라는 (d)가 내용과 일치한다.

implement 이행하다 **deter** 방지하다 **misuse** 악용 **subsidy** 보조금 **supervisor** 감독관 **qualification** 자격요건 **surge** 급증 **reassessment** 재평가 **equitable** 형평성 있는　　　　정답_(d)

58

In this part of my lecture, I'd like to focus on the difficulties of essay writing instruction. Essay writing is never the easiest discipline to teach. Instructors often experience strong resistance on the part of students to being told that there is a right or wrong way to express what they see as their own ideas, and they often question or even resent seeing a grade on a written assignment. But invariably, they need to be taught how to write an essay well because most of them simply do not know how.

Q What can be inferred from the lecture?
(a) There is no right way to teach essay writing.
(b) Students should not be given grades on their writing.
(c) Students often fail to be objective about their writing skills.
(d) Most essay writing instruction is ineffective.

SOLUTION

이번 강의에서는 에세이 작문 교육의 어려움에 초점을 두려고 합니다. 에세이 작문은 절대 쉽게 가르칠 수 있는 과목이 아니에요. 강사들은 학생들이 자신의 생각을 표현하는 데 옳고 그른 방법이 있다는 이야기를 듣는 것에 대해 종종 강하게 반발하거나, 또 학생들이 작문 과제에 학점이 매겨진다는 데 대해 이의를 제기하거나 심지어 기분 나쁘게 생각하는 경우도 많이 경험합니다. 하지만 많은 학생들이 기본적으로 에세이 쓰는 법을 모르기 때문에 이에 대해 배울 필요가 있다는 데는 예외가 없어요.

Q 강의에서 추론할 수 있는 것은?
(a) 에세이 작문을 가르치는 데 정답은 없다.
(b) 학생들은 작문에 대해 학점을 받아서는 안 된다.
(c) 학생들은 자신의 작문 실력에 대해 객관적이지 못한 경우가 많다.
(d) 대부분의 에세이 작문 교육은 효과가 없다.

🏛 기출 POINT

에세이 작문 교육이 어려운 이유는 학생들의 반응 때문인데 학생들은 자신의 생각을 표현하는 데 옳고 그른 방법이 있다는 것과 학점이 매겨진다는 것을 수긍하지 못한다는 것이다. 따라서 학생들이 자신의 작문 실력에 대해 객관적인 관점을 갖기가 힘들다는 (c)를 추론할 수 있다.

instruction 교육 **discipline** 훈련 **resistance** 저항 **resent** 화내다 **assignment** 과제 **invariably** 예외 없이 **fail to** ~하지 못하다 **objective** 객관적인　　　　정답_(c)

59

Even as we're gathered at this meeting, thieves around the world are destroying mankind's history in various spots. With axes, shovels and crowbars, they are stealing inestimably precious objects from sites in the mountains of Peru to the coasts of Sicily and the deserts of Iraq. These criminals are causing incalculable damage in terms of valuable information about the past. And we see no signs of improvement.

Q What will the speaker most likely talk about next?
(a) Some recent, startling discoveries of past civilizations.
(b) Important sites that archaeologists and historians study.
(c) The need for a renewed effort to control artifact looters.
(d) Recent cases of robberies at famous international museums.

SOLUTION

우리가 회의에 모여 있는 지금 이 순간에도 전세계 도둑들은 여러 장소에서 인류의 역사를 파괴하고 있습니다. 도끼, 삽과 쇠지레를 사용해 이들은 페루의 산속에서부터 시칠리아 해안과 이라크의 사막에서까지 아주 귀중한 물건들을 훔치고 있습니다. 이들 범죄자들은 과거의 귀중한 정보에 대해 막대한 피해를 유발하고 있습니다. 그리고 우리는 이에 대한 어떠한 개선의 기미도 보지 못하고 있습니다.

Q 화자가 앞으로 이야기할 것 같은 내용은?
(a) 과거 문명에 대한 최근의 일부 놀랄 만한 발견들.
(b) 고고학자와 사학자들이 연구하는 주요 유적지.
(c) 유물 약탈자들을 통제하기 위한 노력을 새로이 할 필요성.
(d) 유명 국제 박물관에서의 최근 강도 사건들.

🎫 기출 POINT

다음에 이어질 내용을 추측하는 문제이다. 마지막 문장은 개선의 징조가 없다는 문제점을 제기하는 내용이다. 그러므로 (c)의 유물 약탈자들을 통제하기 위한 새로운 노력이 필요하다는 주장이 이어져야 자연스럽다. 페루의 산과 시칠리아 해안 등을 예로 들어 유물 현장의 약탈 사건을 말하는 것이므로 (d)의 최근 박물관 강도 사건은 관점이 다른 예가 되어 오답이다.

axe 도끼 shovel 삽 crowbar 쇠지레 inestimably 평가할수없이
incalculable 셀 수 없는 in terms of ~에 대해 startling 놀랍게 하는 archaeologist 고고학자 artifact looter 유물 약탈자

정답_(c)

60

If you find that your car payments have become a bigger financial drain than you had anticipated, don't risk having your car repossessed or ruining your credit rating by missing payments. Instead, refinance your auto loan at a lower interest rate. It works in the same way as refinancing a mortgage. You simply search for a new lender who can take over your existing loan with better payment terms and perhaps a better rate.

Q What can be inferred from the instructions?
(a) Your credit rating affects the kind of car loan you can get.
(b) Refinancing a car loan is easier than refinancing a mortgage.
(c) Downsizing your car is a good way to avoid expensive payments.
(d) Restructuring finances can save you from having to sell your car.

SOLUTION

귀하의 자동차 할부금이 생각했던 것보다 재정적 부담이 더 크다는 것을 깨달으셨다면, 할부금을 내지 못해 자동차를 회수당하거나 신용등급을 망칠 수도 있는 위험을 감수하지 마십시오. 그 대신 더 낮은 금리로 자동차 대출을 재융자하십시오. 그 방식은 주택을 재융자받는 것과 마찬가지입니다. 귀하는 그저 현재 대출을 더 나은 납부 조건과 더 나은 금리로 받을 수 있는 새 대출기관을 찾기만 하면 됩니다.

Q 설명에서 유추할 수 있는 것은?
(a) 신용등급은 자동차 대출 형태에 영향을 준다.
(b) 자동차 대출을 재융자하는 것은 모기지를 재융자하는 것보다 쉽다.
(c) 자동차를 소형으로 바꾸는 것은 값비싼 할부금을 피할 수 있는 좋은 방법이다.
(d) 재정 구조를 재편하면 차를 팔아야 하는 상황을 면할 수 있다.

🎫 기출 POINT

자동차 할부대금 부담이 클 때의 대응 방법을 알려주는 내용이다. 할부금을 내지 못해서 차를 회수당하거나 신용등급이 낮아지지 않도록 자동차 대출을 재융자받으라는 지침을 준다. 주택 융자금과 마찬가지로 자동차 대출도 다른 대출로 재융자를 받으면 된다는 것이다. 재정 구조의 개편을 통해 차를 회수당하는 상황을 면할 수 있다는 (d)가 추론 가능하다.

drain 부담 repossess 회수하다 ruin 망치다 credit rating 신용등급 refinance 재융자하다 auto loan 자동차 대출 mortgage 모기지, 융자

정답_(d)

Grammar

1

A Is there something special you want for your birthday?

B As long as it's _____, anything will be okay.

(a) expensive not so
(b) so expensive not
(c) too expensive not
(d) not too expensive

SOLUTION

A 생일에 뭐 특별히 원하는 게 있니?
B 너무 비싸지만 않으면 아무거나 좋아.

⊞ 기출 POINT

'별로 ~하지 않다'라는 표현으로 not too를 써서 not too expensive 가 된다. not too는 not very와 같은 뜻으로 구어체에서 주로 쓴다. something special은 something, nothing, anything 등 -thing 으로 끝나는 명사를 형용사가 뒤에서 수식하는 경우이다.

not too 별로 ~않다 **as long as** ~하는 한   정답_(d)

2

A Did anyone call while I was away?

B Yes, there _____ a call from your insurance company.

(a) is
(b) was
(c) will be
(d) is to be

SOLUTION

A 내가 없는 동안 전화한 사람이 있었나요?
B 네. 보험회사에서 전화가 왔었습니다.

⊞ 기출 POINT

〈There+be동사〉로 존재를 나타내는 구문이다. 질문이 Did anyone call...?로 과거시제인 것에 맞게 과거로 답하여 There was가 된다.
유도부사인 There/ Here 다음에 올 수 있는 동사: be, come, go, seem, appear, remain, happen, live 등 ex) There seems to be a dog in the room./ There goes our bus!

while ~동안 **insurance** 보험   정답_(b)

3

A You seem _____ talented at singing.

B Thanks for the compliment.

(a) very
(b) well
(c) such
(d) that

SOLUTION

A 너는 노래하는 데 굉장히 재능이 뛰어난 것 같아.
B 칭찬 고마워.

⊞ 기출 POINT

부사 very는 형용사, 부사, 현재분사형 형용사를 수식한다. 형태는 과 거분사지만 이미 하나의 형용사로 굳어져 쓰이는 talented와 같은 형 용사도 수식한다. 감정, 상태를 나타내는 형용사인 tired, interested, excited, pleased 등도 very로 수식.

talented 재능 있는 **compliment** 칭찬   정답_(a)

4

A May I speak to Dr. Wilson, please?

B I'm sorry, _____ he isn't in.

(a) so
(b) yet
(c) but
(d) and

SOLUTION

A 윌슨 박사님과 통화할 수 있을까요?
B 죄송하지만 안 계시는데요.

⊞ 기출 POINT

유감스러운 말을 전할 때 I'm sorry를 앞에 붙여서 안타까움을 표시하 는데 접속사 but이 들어가서 I'm sorry, but...의 형태가 된다.

정답_(c)

5

A I have to pay my phone bill by tomorrow, but I've got no money.

B I hope you don't expect me _____.

(a) of anything to do
(b) to do anything about it
(c) doing for that anything
(d) doing anything about it

SOLUTION

A 내일까지 전화요금을 내야 하는데, 돈이 없어.
B 내가 뭘 어떻게 해주길 바라는 건 아니었음 좋겠다.

⊞ 기출 POINT

I hope 다음에 that이 생략된 절이 온 형태로 동사 expect의 용법 문제이다. '누가 ~하기를 기대하다'는 뜻으로 〈expect+목적어+to+동사원형〉의 형태를 쓴다. expect의 용법: I expect to succeed. 나는 성공할 것이다./ I expect him to succeed, I expect that he will succeed. 나는 그가 성공할 거라 기대한다.

phone bill 전화요금 청구서 **have got** 가지고 있다   정답_(b)

6

A I couldn't keep my eyes open throughout the lecture.

B _____ I. It was really boring.

(a) Could either
(b) Either could
(c) Could neither
(d) Neither could

SOLUTION

A 강의 내내 눈이 감겨서 혼났어.
B 나도 마찬가지였어. 정말 지루하더라.

⊞ 기출 POINT

부정문에서 '마찬가지로 ~이다'는 either를 사용하고 부정은 not either를 줄여 neither로 쓴다. 부정어가 문장 앞에 오면 주어와 동사는 도치되는데, be동사나 조동사가 쓰인 경우는 그대로 쓰고 일반동사의 경우는 do동사로 대신한다. 〈keep+목적어+목적보어(형용사)〉는 '~를 …하게 두다'라는 뜻이다.

throughout 내내 **lecture** 강의   정답_(d)

7

A Isn't it time you _____ your homework?
B Can't I do it after this TV show?

(a) started
(b) will start
(c) have started
(d) will be starting

SOLUTION

A 숙제 시작해야 하는 시간 아니니?
B 이 TV 프로그램 끝나고 하면 안 될까요?

⊞ 기출 POINT

벌써 했어야 하는데 아직도 하지 않았다는 뜻으로 It is time (that)이라는 표현을 쓴다. 현재 사실에 대한 반대를 가정하는 것이므로 that절에서 동사를 가정법 과거 형태로 쓴다는 것에 유의해야 한다.

It is about time/ It is high time 등도 같은 뜻으로 가정법 과거 형태로 사용한다.

It is time (that) 이미 ~했어야 하는 시간이다   정답_(a)

8

A Excuse me. Can I get my camera _____ here?

B Yes, what seems to be the problem?

(a) repair
(b) to repair
(c) repaired
(d) repairing

SOLUTION

A 실례합니다. 제 카메라를 고쳐주실 수 있나요?
B 네, 어디가 문제인 것 같으세요?

⊞ 기출 POINT

사역동사 〈get+목적어+목적보어(to+동사원형/ p.p.)〉 형태를 묻는 문제이다. 목적어와 목적보어의 관계가 능동이면 to+동사원형을 쓰고, 수동이면 과거분사를 쓴다. my camera와 repair를 볼 때 카메라는 수리되는 수동의 관계이므로 repaired가 답이 된다. get은 사역동사지만 have, make, let처럼 목적어와 목적보어의 관계가 능동일 때 동사원형을 쓰지 않고 to+동사원형을 쓴다.

seem to ~인 것 같다 **repair** 수리하다   정답_(c)

9

A Would you like us _____ your new computer?

B No, I'll take it with me now.

(a) deliver
(b) to deliver
(c) delivering
(d) to delivering

SOLUTION

A 새 컴퓨터를 배달해 드릴까요?

B 아니요. 제가 그냥 들고 가겠습니다.

⊞ 기출 POINT

Would you like us[me] to...?는 '~해 드릴까요?'라는 뜻으로 정중한 제안의 표현이다. 남이 '~해 주기를 바란다'고 할 때 〈like+목적어+to+동사원형〉을 쓴다. I would like you to deliver it과 같은 문장으로 쓰인다.

Would you like us to+동사원형...? ~해 드릴까요? **deliver 배달하다**

정답_(b)

10

A May I have tomorrow off?

B Sure. Tomorrow probably won't be _____.

(a) busy day
(b) a busy day
(c) the busy day
(d) any busy day

SOLUTION

A 내일 휴가를 써도 될까요?

B 그러세요. 내일은 아마 바쁘지 않을 것 같으니까.

⊞ 기출 POINT

관사의 쓰임에 대한 문제이다. have tomorrow off는 '내일 휴가를 쓰다'라는 뜻이다. 이 문장에서 busy day는 특정한 날을 말하는 것이 아니라 불특정한 어떤 바쁜 하루를 의미하므로 부정관사 a를 써서 a busy day가 되어야 한다.

have (a day) off (하루) 휴가를 얻다 **probably** 아마도

정답_(b)

11

A Are you a graduate student here?

B Yes, I'm working on my PhD _____ biology.

(a) in
(b) to
(c) on
(d) for

SOLUTION

A 이곳 대학원생이세요?

B 네, 생물학 박사과정을 밟고 있습니다.

⊞ 기출 POINT

문맥에 알맞은 전치사를 고르는 문제이다. 생물학이라는 전공에서의 박사이므로 전치사 in이 알맞다. 전치사 in은 어떤 분야나 활동 영역을 나타내는 전치사로 사용된다. ex) She is an expert in math./ I major in biology.

graduate student 대학원생 **PhD** 박사(Doctor of Philosophy)

정답_(a)

12

A I think I deserve a higher salary.

B Why don't you _____?

(a) ask a raise to your boss
(b) your boss ask for a raise
(c) ask your boss for a raise
(d) for a raise ask your boss

SOLUTION

A 나는 더 많은 급여를 받을 자격이 있다고 생각해.

B 급여를 인상해 달라고 상사에게 말하지 그래?

⊞ 기출 POINT

〈ask+사람+for+일〉은 '~에게 …을 요구하다'라는 뜻이다. ask for help[money]는 전치사 for를 써서 '도움[돈]을 바라고 요구하다'는 뜻이고 동사 demand를 써도 된다. 〈ask+일+of+사람〉: ~에게 …을 부탁하다 ex) I ask nothing of you. 난 너에게 아무 것도 부탁하지 않아.

deserve ~할[받을] 만하다 **salary** 급여 **raise** 인상

정답_(c)

Actual Test 2

13

A Do you have to leave so soon?
B Yes, I _____ be going. I have another appointment.

(a) can
(b) may
(c) must
(d) would

SOLUTION

A 이렇게 금방 가야 돼?
B 응, 가봐야 돼. 또 다른 약속이 있어.

⊞ 기출 POINT
'가봐야 한다'는 말로 must be going을 쓴다. '~해야만 한다'는 의무의 조동사 must나 have to로 어쩔 수 없이 가야만 한다는 뜻을 나타낸다. 현재형을 써도 되지만 구어체에서는 이처럼 진행형을 써서 표현한다. 같은 표현으로 I must be leaving now/ I have to leave now/ I'm sorry, but I should go now 등을 쓴다.
leave 떠나다 **appointment** 약속   정답_(c)

14

A Billy left a big mess in the kitchen this morning.
B I've _____, and he said it wouldn't happen again.

(a) been speaking it to him
(b) to him spoken about it
(c) about it spoken to him
(d) spoken to him about it

SOLUTION

A 오늘 아침에 빌리가 부엌을 엉망으로 만들어 놨어.
B 빌리한테 얘기를 했는데, 다시는 그런 일 없을 거라고 하더라.

⊞ 기출 POINT
현재완료 형태이므로 빈칸에는 동사 spoken이 먼저 온다. speak to는 동사+전치사로 쓰이기 때문에 speak to him을 먼저 쓰고 뒤에 전치사+목적어인 about it이 온다.
mess 엉망인 상태 **speak to** ~에게 말하다   정답_(d)

15

A Why did you miss art class yesterday?
B I didn't _____, but my friends made me do it.

(a) plan
(b) plan to
(c) plan do
(d) plan to it

SOLUTION

A 어제 미술 수업에 왜 결석했니?
B 계획했던 건 아닌데, 친구들 때문에.

⊞ 기출 POINT
동사 plan은 목적어로 to+동사원형이나 -ing형을 다 취할 수 있지만 여기서는 to+동사원형을 썼다. I didn't plan to의 to는 부정사의 반복을 피하기 위하여 줄여서 to만을 쓴 대부정사이다. 즉, to 다음에는 miss art class가 생략되어 있다. ex) You can leave here if you want to (leave)./ She didn't pass the test, but she still hopes to (pass the test).
miss (수업 등에) 출석하지 않다   정답_(b)

16

A Do you want _____?
B Sure, I'd like that very much.

(a) me going to a football game
(b) to go a football game with me
(c) with me go to a football game
(d) to go to a football game with me

SOLUTION

A 나랑 풋볼 경기에 같이 갈래?
B 그럼. 아주 좋지.

⊞ 기출 POINT
want 다음에 to부정사를 쓰면 '~하고 싶다'의 뜻이다. I'd like that very much는 제안에 대해 찬성하는 말이다.
• I want to do… 나는 ~하고 싶다
• I want … to do it. ~가 …해주기를 바라다
• I want … done right now. 지금 ~가 되기를 바라다
• I want … ready by tomorrow. ~가 내일까지 되기를 바라다
I'd like that. 그거 좋네.   정답_(d)

17

A How did the conference go?
B Great. One of the good things _____ that no speaker went over their time.

(a) is
(b) are
(c) was
(d) were

SOLUTION

A 회의는 어땠니?
B 좋았어. 좋은 일 중 하나는 어떤 연사도 시간을 초과하지 않았다는 거야.

기출 POINT

One of the(~중의 하나) 다음에는 복수형태가 나온다. 그러나 주어는 One이므로 단수이고 of the good things는 One을 꾸며주는 말임을 주의해야 한다. 과거의 일에 대해 How did...?로 물었으므로 응답 역시 과거시제 was를 써야 한다.
How did ... go? ~은 어땠니?   **conference** 회의   **go over time** 시간을 초과하다   정답_(c)

18

A Are you doing anything special tonight?
B I'm _____ a play.

(a) thinking to go to
(b) going thinking of
(c) about to go I think
(d) thinking of going to

SOLUTION

A 오늘 밤에 특별히 계획한 게 있니?
B 연극 보러 가려고 생각 중이야.

기출 POINT

A는 미래의 일을 현재진행형으로 묻고 있다. 이처럼 미래의 계획을 말할 때 현재진행형을 쓴다.
I'm thinking of는 '~을 할까 생각 중이다'는 뜻이며 앞으로의 계획에 대해 말할 때 주로 사용한다. think of의 목적어는 -ing형을 취하고 consider -ing도 같은 뜻으로 쓴다.
think of ~에 대해 생각하다   **go to a play** 연극 보러 가다   정답_(d)

19

A Thank you for coming to my concert on such short notice.
B If I had known about it sooner, I _____ have brought my wife.

(a) shall
(b) must
(c) could
(d) should

SOLUTION

A 그렇게 급하게 연락을 받고도 제 콘서트에 와주셔서 감사해요.
B 더 일찍 알았더라면 집사람도 함께 왔을 겁니다.

기출 POINT

〈If+주어+had+p.p., 주어+조동사의 과거형+have+p.p.〉로 나타내는 가정법 과거완료 문장이다. 빈칸에는 조동사의 과거형이 들어가야 하는데 내용상 '데리고 올 수 있었다'는 뜻이 되므로 could가 적절하다.
on such short notice 그렇게 급한 연락에   **bring** 데리고 오다   정답_(c)

20

A Who would you recommend as our new chairperson?
B John is the person _____ I believe is capable of getting the job done.

(a) who
(b) what
(c) which
(d) where

SOLUTION

A 새 의장으로 너는 누구를 추천할 거니?
B 존이 그 일을 해낼 능력이 있는 사람인 것 같아.

기출 POINT

the person이라는 선행사를 꾸며 주는 절을 이끄는 관계대명사를 고르는 문제이다. the person은 뒤의 형용사절에서 believe의 목적어가 되므로 사람 목적격인 whom이 답인데, 사람 목적격에는 whom을 대신해서 who를 많이 쓴다.
recommend 추천하다   **chairperson** 의장   **be capable of** ~을 할 수 있다   정답_(a)

21

Students found guilty of _____ inappropriate behavior as fighting or throwing things will be punished.

(a) so
(b) too
(c) such
(d) much

SOLUTION

싸움을 한다거나 물건을 던지는 등의 부적절한 행동을 범한 학생들은 처벌을 받을 것이다.

⊞ 기출 POINT

such ... as는 '~와 같은'의 뜻으로 구체적인 예를 들 때 사용하는 표현이다. inappropriate behavior의 예로 fighting과 throwing things를 들었다.

find guilty of ~의 죄로 판결되다   **inappropriate** 부적절한   **fight** 싸우다   **punish** 처벌하다   정답_(c)

22

Our current CEO _____ by the company's Board of Directors last year.

(a) appoints
(b) appointed
(c) is appointed
(d) was appointed

SOLUTION

우리의 현 CEO는 작년에 회사 이사회에서 임명되었다.

⊞ 기출 POINT

appoint는 '임명하다'라는 뜻의 타동사이다. 주어인 Our current CEO는 임명되는 것이므로 수동태 문장이 되어야 한다. last year라는 명확한 과거 시점이 있으므로 과거시제 was appointed가 적절하다.

current 지금의   **CEO** 최고경영책임자(chief executive officer)   **Board of Directors** 이사회   **appoint** 임명하다   정답_(d)

23

_____ west in 1892, Gerald Clemens made sure all his prize possessions rode with him in the wagon.

(a) While having traveled
(b) To have traveled
(c) While traveling
(d) Traveled

SOLUTION

1892년 서부를 여행하는 동안 제럴드 클레멘스는 반드시 자신의 모든 소유물을 마차에 실어 함께 이동하도록 했다.

⊞ 기출 POINT

빈칸에는 내용을 보충하는 분사구문이 와야 한다. 접속사는 '~동안'의 While이 오고, 주어는 주절의 Gerald Clemens와 같아서 생략되고, 주절과 같은 때이므로 완료가 아닌 traveling이 쓰인다. 주절의 rode 는 made sure와 시제 일치 때문에 과거형으로 쓰였다.

make sure 반드시 ~하다   **prize possession** 소유물   **ride** (말을) 타다   **wagon** 마차   정답_(c)

24

_____ a balanced diet is one way to prevent tooth decay and gum disease.

(a) Eat
(b) Eating
(c) To be eating
(d) Having eaten

SOLUTION

균형 잡힌 식사를 하는 것은 충치와 잇몸 질환을 예방하는 한 가지 방법이다.

⊞ 기출 POINT

동사가 주어 자리에 오기 위해서는 -ing형이나 to+동사원형의 형태가 되어야 한다. 일반적인 진술의 경우에는 완료시제가 아닌 단순시제를 사용한다.

balanced diet 균형 잡힌 식단   **prevent** 예방하다   **tooth decay** 충치   **gum** 잇몸   정답_(b)

25

Many of the new policewomen _____ to take part in important assignments.

(a) not being allowed resented
(b) resented not being allowed
(c) being not allowed resented
(d) resented not to being allowed

SOLUTION

많은 신임 여경들은 중요한 임무에 참여하지 못하는 것을 불쾌하게 생각했다.

⊞ 기출 POINT

'참여를 허락받지 못한 것에 분개하다'는 뜻이 되어야 하며 동사 resent 는 동명사를 목적어로 취한다. allow는 〈allow+목적어+to+동사원형〉의 형태로 '~을 허락하다'로 쓰므로 여기서는 수동태인 〈be allowed to+동사원형〉이 되어야 한다. 동명사를 부정하는 not이 동명사 앞에 위치하는 것에 유의한다.

policewoman 여경 **take part in** ~에 참여하다 **assignment** 임무 **resent** 분개하다   정답_(b)

26

_____ her work aside, the grandmother began to tell the story of her past to her grandchildren.

(a) Put
(b) To put
(c) Putting
(d) Being put

SOLUTION

하던 일을 제쳐놓고 할머니는 자신의 과거 이야기를 손자들에게 하기 시작했다.

⊞ 기출 POINT

빈칸 뒤에 완벽한 문장이 왔으므로 빈칸에 들어갈 동사 put의 형태는 문맥에 따라 결정해야 하는데 '~하면서(동시상황)'의 경우에는 현재분사를, '~하기 위해서(목적)'는 to+동사원형을 쓴다. 하던 일을 제쳐놓고 이야기를 시작했다는 내용이므로 동시 상황에 해당한다.

put aside 제쳐놓다   정답_(c)

27

Blood _____ to the heart from the body is low in oxygen and high in carbon dioxide.

(a) returns
(b) to return
(c) returning
(d) to be returning

SOLUTION

몸에서 다시 심장으로 돌아오는 혈액은 산소 함량이 낮고 이산화탄소 함량은 높다.

⊞ 기출 POINT

문장의 서술어는 is이므로 빈칸에 들어갈 동사 return을 분사형태인 returning으로 써서 형용사처럼 명사 blood를 뒤에서 수식하는 구조의 문장이다. 관계대명사절처럼 생각해서 Blood (which is) returning에서 〈관계대명사+be동사〉가 생략된 것으로 이해하면 쉽다.

blood 혈액 **oxygen** 산소 **carbon dioxide** 이산화탄소   정답_(c)

28

Wars leave painful memories _____ many veterans would rather forget.

(a) that
(b) what
(c) of whom
(d) by which

SOLUTION

전쟁은 많은 퇴역 군인들이 차라리 잊고 싶은 고통스러운 기억들을 남긴다.

⊞ 기출 POINT

적절한 관계대명사를 찾는 문제이다. 선행사는 painful memories이고 뒤의 형용사절에 있는 forget의 목적어가 되므로 that이나 which가 알맞다.

leave 남기다 **painful** 아픈 **veteran** 퇴역 군인 **would rather** 차라리 ~하고 싶다   정답_(a)

29

The increasing use of _____ has led to a reduction in the types of jobs people can perform.

(a) machinery
(b) machineries
(c) a machinery
(d) the machineries

SOLUTION

기계 사용의 증가로 사람들이 할 수 있는 일의 종류가 감소했다.

⊞ 기출 POINT

명사 machinery는 셀 수 없는 집합적인 물질 명사이므로 부정관사와 함께 쓰이지 않으며 복수형도 불가능하다.

집합적인 물질 명사: machinery, equipment, luggage, baggage

increasing 증가하는 **reduction** 감소 **perform** 행하다
machinery 기계   정답_(a)

30

As you progress through this course, you _____ all the skills needed to become a systems administrator.

(a) developed
(b) will develop
(c) have developed
(d) are about to develop

SOLUTION

이 과정을 들으면서 시스템 관리자가 되기 위해 필요한 모든 기술을 개발하게 될 것이다.

⊞ 기출 POINT

내용상 미래의 일이므로 빈칸에는 미래시제가 들어간다. As가 이끄는 부사절에는 미래를 대신하는 현재시제가 사용되었다. 시간이나 조건을 나타내는 부사절(when, after, before, as, if)에서는 내용상 미래의 일도 현재시제로 표현한다.

progress 나아가다 **systems administrator** 시스템 관리자
develop 발달시키다   정답_(b)

31

Jack can barely replace a fuse, _____ repair a broken TV set.

(a) yet
(b) while
(c) even so
(d) much less

SOLUTION

잭은 고장난 TV 수상기를 수리하는 것은 고사하고 퓨즈도 간신히 교체한다.

⊞ 기출 POINT

much less는 부정문에서 더 심한 것을 말할 때 쓰는 '하물며 ~도 아니다'의 표현이다. barely는 hardly, seldom 등과 같이 '거의 ~가 아니다'로 부정의 의미를 갖는다. much less 다음에는 명사(구)를 쓸 수 있지만 while이나 even so는 절을 써야 한다.

barely 거의 ~않다 **replace** 교체하다 **even so** 그렇다 하더라도
much less 하물며 ~도 아니다   정답_(d)

32

The eye focuses light on the retina through an opening _____ size adjusts in order to change the amount of entering light.

(a) that
(b) what
(c) which
(d) whose

SOLUTION

눈은 한 틈을 통해 망막상에 빛의 초점을 맞추는데, 이 틈의 크기가 유입되는 빛의 양을 조절하기 위해 변한다.

⊞ 기출 POINT

적절한 관계대명사를 고르는 문제이다. 선행사인 an opening과 size의 관계를 보면 '틈의 크기'가 되어야 하므로 소유격이 와야 한다. 선행사가 사물이므로 of which나 whose가 가능하다.

retina 망막 **adjust** 조정하다 **in order to** ~하기 위해서 **amount** 양
                                      정답_(d)

33

Steve hand-washed and rinsed his T-shirt and jeans thoroughly before hanging _____.

(a) up to dry them
(b) them up to dry
(c) to dry them up
(d) up them to dry

SOLUTION

스티브는 자신의 티셔츠와 청바지를 널어 말리려고 손으로 빨고 헹구었다.

기출 POINT

2어동사(동사+부사)의 목적어가 대명사일 때 목적어의 위치에 대한 문제이다. 대명사인 목적어는 동사와 부사 사이. 즉 hang과 up 사이에 hang them up의 형태로 사용된다. hang up them은 불가능하다. 대명사가 아닌 명사 목적어는 동사와 부사 사이와 부사 뒤 모두 쓰일 수 있다.

hand-wash 손빨래하다　**rinse** 헹구다　**thoroughly** 철저히
hang up 널다　　　　　　　　　　　　　　　　정답_(b)

34

The manager's job was allocating work to _____ employee fairly.

(a) all
(b) both
(c) each
(d) some

SOLUTION

관리자의 업무는 각 직원들에게 공정하게 업무를 할당하는 것이었다.

기출 POINT

employee가 단수 명사임에 유의한다. 한정사인 each는 단수 명사를 수식하여 '각각의'란 뜻으로 쓰이고 대명사로도 쓰인다. Each of us has a dog에서 each는 단수 취급하여 단수에 맞는 동사 has를 쓴다.

allocate 할당하다　**employee** 직원　**fairly** 공정하게　정답_(c)

35

It is incorrect to say that we are the only species _____.

(a) that culture we depend to survive on
(b) that depends on culture for survival
(c) depend on culture for that survival
(d) that survival depends on culture

SOLUTION

우리가 생존을 위해 문화에 의존하는 유일한 종족이라고 말하는 것은 옳지 않다.

기출 POINT

only는 '유일한'의 뜻으로 단수명사 앞에 쓰고. 정관사 the가 붙어 the only로 쓴다. species는 단수와 복수 형태가 같은 명사인데 여기서는 단수이므로 that절의 동사는 depends가 되어야 한다.

incorrect 틀린　**species** 종　**depend on** ~에 의존하다　**survival** 생존　　　　　　　　　　　　　　　　　　　　　　　정답_(b)

36

Parents _____ not purchase the new uniforms this year if they do not wish to do so.

(a) need
(b) must
(c) could
(d) would

SOLUTION

학부형들은 원하지 않으면 올해 새 교복을 구매하지 않아도 된다.

기출 POINT

내용으로 볼 때 적절한 조동사를 고르는 문제이다. if절이 '원하지 않으면'이므로 빈칸에는 '굳이 ~할 필요가 없다'는 내용이 보충되어야 한다. '~할 필요가 없다'는 조동사 need not이 알맞은 답이다.

purchase 구매하다　**uniform** 교복　　　　　　　　　　정답_(a)

37

Her experience in prison was so traumatic for the young woman that she had a hard time _____.

(a) describing it to anyone
(b) for anyone describing it
(c) to describe it for anyone
(d) to be describing it to anyone

SOLUTION

그녀의 수감 경험은 젊은 여성으로서는 너무나 정신적인 충격이어서 누구에게든 그것에 대해 설명하는 데 어려움을 겪었다.

기출 POINT
동명사가 쓰인 관용적 표현에 대한 문제이다. have a hard time 다음에는 전치사 in이 생략되어 목적어로 동명사 형태인 describing이 사용된다. have a difficulty[trouble] in -ing/ spend time (in) -ing/ be busy (in) -ing 등도 많이 출제되는 표현이다.
traumatic 충격적인 **have a hard time -ing** ~하는 데 어려움을 겪다 **describe** 설명하다   정답_(a)

38

By January 15, we _____ over 100 applications for the technician position.

(a) will process
(b) have processed
(c) have been processing
(d) will have processed

SOLUTION

1월 15일까지 우리는 기술직에 대해 100여 개가 넘는 지원서를 처리하게 될 것이다.

기출 POINT
미래의 시점을 나타내는 부사구와 함께 쓰여 '미래 어느 시점이 되면 ~한 셈이 된다'는 뜻으로 쓰는 것이 미래완료 시제이다. By January 15가 미래의 특정 시점이므로 미래완료 시제가 적절하다.
application 지원서 **technician** 기술자 **process** 처리하다   정답_(d)

39

No significant changes in the levels of hormone _____ in the patients.

(a) observe
(b) observes
(c) was observed
(d) were observed

SOLUTION

환자들에게 어떠한 주목할 만한 호르몬 수치의 변화도 관찰되지 않았다.

기출 POINT
주어와의 관계를 살펴보면 동사 observe의 형태를 결정할 수 있다. 주어는 significant changes이므로 복수이며 변화는 '관찰하는' 것이 아니라 '관찰되는' 것이므로 수동의 관계이다. 따라서 적절한 답은 were observed이다.
significant 주목할 만한 **hormone** 호르몬 **patient** 환자   정답_(d)

40

_____ without passing the exam in this country.

(a) Can a single teacher not be tenured
(b) Not a single teacher can be tenured
(c) A single teacher can be not tenured
(d) No single teacher cannot be tenured

SOLUTION

이 나라에서는 시험을 통과하지 않으면 어떤 교사도 재임 자격이 주어지지 않는다.

기출 POINT
'하나도 ~아니다'라는 뜻으로 no+명사, not a+명사, not any+명사의 형태가 사용된다. 뒤의 without 역시 부정을 표현하는 것에 유의하면 Not a single teacher can be를 찾을 수 있다. (d)는 부정이 두 번 나와서 다른 내용이 된다.
tenure (종신적 지위로) 재임권을 주다   정답_(b)

41

(a) A So, tell me how your date went last night.

(b) B It was horrible. I don't want to talk about it.

(c) A But you want to meet her for a long time.

(d) B Well, she was very different from what I had expected.

(a) 그래서, 어젯밤 데이트는 어땠는지 말해 봐.

(b) 끔찍했어. 이야기하고 싶지 않아.

(c) 하지만 오랫동안 그 여자를 만나고 싶어 했잖아.

(d) 음, 내가 기대했던 것과는 아주 달랐어.

⊞ 기출 POINT

내용상 오랫동안 그 여자를 만나고 싶어 했던 것을 알 수 있다. for a long time은 현재완료 시제와 함께 쓰인다. 따라서 (c)의 want를 have wanted로 고쳐야 한다.

horrible 끔찍한 **different from** ~와 다른

정답_(c) want → have wanted

42

(a) A We must take care of this financial problem right away.

(b) B Yes, I have a team working on a solution as we speak.

(c) A The board members wants it sorted out by tomorrow morning.

(d) B Don't worry. We'll fix the problem by this afternoon.

(a) 우리는 이 재정 문제를 당장 해결해야 합니다.

(b) 네. 현재 한 팀에게 우리가 이야기를 나누고 있는 것에 대한 해결책을 찾도록 해두었습니다.

(c) 이사회 위원들은 내일 아침까지 이 문제를 해결하고 싶어 합니다.

(d) 걱정 마십시오. 오늘 오후까지 문제를 해결할 겁니다.

⊞ 기출 POINT

(c)에서 board는 '위원회'라는 뜻으로 집합적인 의미를 담고 있지만 셀 수 있는 명사로 단수 취급한다. 따라서 the board of directors 다음에는 단수 동사를 쓴다. 하지만 여기에서는 board members라는 복수로 표현되었으므로 동사는 wants가 아니라 want가 알맞다.

financial 재정적인 **solution** 해결책 **board member** 이사회 위원

sort out 해결하다 **fix** 해결하다

정답_(c) wants → want

43

(a) A My head is throbbing with pain.

(b) B Another headache? Did you take some aspirin?

(c) A I did half an hour ago, but it's not working.

(d) B Relaxing quietly helps usually my headaches.

SOLUTION

(a) 머리가 지끈지끈 아프다.

(b) 또 두통이니? 아스피린 먹었어?

(c) 30분 전에 먹었는데, 듣지를 않네.

(d) 나는 두통이 있을 때 조용히 휴식을 취하는 게 도움이 되더라.

🎛 기출 POINT

빈도부사의 위치는 be동사나 조동사 뒤, 일반동사 앞이다. 따라서 (d)는 usually helps의 어순이 되어야 한다. 빈도부사: always, often, usually, sometimes, hardly, never

throb (머리가) 지끈지끈 쑤시다 **aspirin** 아스피린 **half an hour** 30분 **relax** 편히 쉬다 **정답** (d) helps usually → usually helps

44

(a) A Hello. Is there anything in the reference section you need help with?

(b) B It'd be grateful if you could help me find some old news articles about cloning.

(c) A Are you interested in back issues of magazines or newspapers?

(d) B I think I need to search through both.

SOLUTION

(a) 안녕하세요. 참고문헌 섹션에서 도움이 필요하신가요?

(b) 복제에 대한 이전 기사 찾는 것을 도와주시면 감사하겠는데요.

(c) 과월호 잡지나 신문에 관심 있으세요?

(d) 둘 다 검색해 봐야 할 것 같네요.

🎛 기출 POINT

형용사 grateful은 '감사하는, 고맙게 여기는'이라는 뜻이므로 사람이 주어가 되어야 한다. 따라서 (b)는 I'd be grateful이 적절하다. 〈help+목적어+(to)+동사원형〉의 형태도 많이 출제되는 표현이다.

reference 참고 **grateful** 감사하는 **news article** 뉴스 기사 **cloning** 복제 **back issue** 과월호 **search through** 검색하다

정답 (b) It'd be grateful → I'd be grateful

45

(a) A Hey, can't you drive more carefully?
Now I have lipstick all over my face.

(b) B Well, it's not my fault that your face got
messy with lipstick.

(c) A Not your fault? It's because you made
sudden stop at the corner.

(d) B Don't blame my driving. You should've put
on your makeup at home.

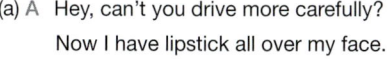

SOLUTION

(a) 야, 운전 좀 더 조심스럽게 못하겠니? 얼굴이 립스틱 범벅이 됐잖아.
(b) 음, 립스틱 때문에 네 얼굴이 지저분하게 된 게 내 잘못은 아니지.
(c) 네 잘못이 아니라고? 네가 코너에서 급정거해서 그런 거잖아.
(d) 내 운전 탓하지 마라. 화장은 집에서 했어야지.

⊞ 기출 POINT

'급정거하다'는 make a sudden stop이라는 표현을 쓰므로 (c)의
made sudden stop에서 stop 앞에 부정관사 a를 써야 알맞다.
fault 잘못 **messy** 엉망인 **sudden** 급작스런 **blame** 탓하다
put on one's makeup 화장하다   정답_(c) made sudden stop
→ made a sudden stop

46

(a) Of all its accomplishments, the West is
perhaps most proud of its scientific progress.
(b) But this did not happen in isolation; its early
progress was influenced by the Arab world.
(c) Important discoveries made by Arab scholars
published in texts that eventually made their way
to Europe. (d) Medieval monks and scribes then
made these discoveries accessible to Western
scientists by translating the texts into Latin.

SOLUTION

(a) 모든 업적 중에서 서구는 아마도 과학적 진보를 가장 자랑스러워할
것이다. (b) 하지만 이것이 고립적으로 발생한 것은 아니다. 초기 진보는
아랍권의 영향을 받았다. (c) 아랍 학자들의 중요한 발견은 글로 쓰여졌
는데, 이것이 결국 유럽으로 유입되었다. (d) 중세 수도승과 필경사들은
그 글을 라틴어로 번역함으로써 서구 과학자들이 이 발견을 접할 수 있
게 해주었다.

⊞ 기출 POINT

주어가 긴 문장의 구조를 파악하는 문제이다. (c)의 주어는 Important
discoveries made by Arab scholars이고 서술어는 published이
다. 발견에 대한 글은 출판되는 것이므로 수동태로 were published가
되어야 한다.

accomplishment 업적 **isolation** 고립 **eventually** 결국 **make
one's way to** ~로 나아가다 **medieval** 중세의 **scribe** 필경사
accessible 접근하기 쉬운 **translate** 번역하다

정답_(c) published → were published

47

(a) On behalf of the school board, I would like to thank you for playing the piano at our reception. (b) Had it not been for your performance, I don't think our reception were half as successful. (c) You kept everybody entertained, and people simply did not want to leave. (d) I will certainly call you again for our next reception if you are available.

SOLUTION

(a) 학교 이사회를 대신해서 저는 여러분들이 저희 환영회에서 피아노를 연주해 주신 것에 대해 감사 말씀을 드리고 싶습니다. (b) 여러분들의 연주가 없었다면 저희 환영회는 절반 만큼의 성공도 거두지 못했을 것입니다. (c) 여러분들은 모든 사람들을 즐겁게 해줬고, 사람들은 자리를 떠나고 싶어 하지 않았죠. (d) 시간이 괜찮으시다면 저희의 다음 환영회에도 여러분들께 꼭 부탁을 드리겠습니다.

⊞ 기출 POINT

If절에 '~이 아니었더라면'이라는 뜻의 Had it not been for가 나와서 가정법 과거완료 문장임을 알 수 있다. 환영회는 과거의 일이므로 가정법 과거완료 주절의 형태로 〈조동사+have p.p.〉가 되어야 한다. 따라서 our reception would have been이 적절하다.

on behalf of ~를 대신해서   school board 학교 이사회
reception 환영회   performance 연주   entertain 즐겁게 하다
available 시간이 되는   정답_(b) our reception were
→ our reception would have been

48

(a) Unlike other cancers, pancreatic tumors typically produce symptoms only after spreading throughout the body. (b) By then, drugs do not provide many relief, and patients die after a few pain-filled months. (c) Patients die so quickly that sometimes doctors do not even have time to examine their tumors properly. (d) Because it is difficult to diagnose early, pancreatic cancer is the fourth leading cause of cancer death.

SOLUTION

(a) 다른 암과는 달리 췌장 종양은 일반적으로 몸 전체로 퍼진 후에야 증상이 나타난다. (b) 그때가 되면 약이 큰 도움이 되지 못하고, 환자들은 몇 달 동안 고통만 잔뜩 느끼고 나서 사망하게 된다. (c) 환자들이 너무나 빨리 사망하기 때문에 의사들은 종양을 제대로 검사할 시간조차 없는 경우도 있다. (d) 초기 진단이 어렵기 때문에 췌장암은 암으로 인한 네 번째 주요 사망 원인이다.

⊞ 기출 POINT

(b)에서 명사 relief는 셀 수 없는 명사이므로 many로 수식할 수 없고 much를 쓴다.

cancer 암   pancreatic tumor 췌장 종양   symptom 증상
spread 퍼지다   relief 경감   diagnose 진단하다   leading 주요한
                          정답_(b) many relief → much relief

49

(a) Baby hamsters are born blind, deaf and totally dependent on their mothers. (b) But they mature very quickly, reach full maturity in a little over a month. (c) Within seven days, they are covered in fur and begin to look more like their parents. (d) By day seventeen, they are old enough to leave the burrow and search for their own food.

SOLUTION

(a) 새끼 햄스터들은 눈이 보이지 않고 귀가 들리지 않는 상태로 태어나고, 어미에게 완전히 의존한다. (b) 하지만 이들은 매우 빠르게 성숙해서, 한 달이 조금 지나면 완전히 성숙하게 된다. (c) 7일 내에 이들은 몸이 털로 뒤덮이고 부모와 더욱 비슷한 모습을 띄기 시작한다. (d) 17일째가 되면 이들은 굴을 떠나 스스로 먹이를 찾을 만큼 성숙하게 된다.

⊞ 기출 POINT

(b)의 서술어인 mature와 reach가 연결어 없이 나열될 수 없다. 내용상 성장해서 한 달 조금 지나면 완전히 성숙하게 된다는 뜻이므로 연속적으로 일어나는 일을 나타내는 부사구의 형태가 알맞다. 따라서 reach를 reaching으로 바꿔 분사구문으로 표현해야 한다.

mature 성숙한 **maturity** 완숙기 **fur** 털 **burrow** 굴

정답 _(b) reach → reaching

50

(a) Over the last decade, scientists have saved at least 16 species from disappearing to captive breeding programs. (b) A number of these have been so successful that other programs are being launched around the globe. (c) Twenty more species are currently being seriously considered for breeding programs. (d) But conservationists and zoologists worldwide are working together to increase this number to 30.

SOLUTION

(a) 지난 10년간 과학자들은 포획 사육 프로그램을 통해 적어도 16개 종을 사멸에서 구했다. (b) 많은 포획 사육 프로그램들이 너무나 성공적이어서 다른 프로그램들이 전세계적으로 시작되고 있다. (c) 현재 20개 이상의 종이 사육 프로그램용으로 진지하게 고려 중이다. (d) 하지만 전 세계 자연 보호론자와 동물학자들은 이 수치를 30종으로 높이기 위해 함께 힘쓰고 있다.

⊞ 기출 POINT

(a)에서 save A from B의 형태로 16종을 멸종으로부터 구했다는 내용이 되어야 한다. 그런데 포획 사육 프로그램을 통해서 이 일을 이룬 것이므로 전치사는 to가 아니라 through가 적절하다.

decade 10년 **captive breeding** 포획 사육 **launch** 시작하다 **conservationist** 보호론자 **zoologist** 동물학자

정답 _(a) to → through

Actual Test 2

1

A Do you still have those books on finance that I _____ you?

B They're at home. I'll return them to you tomorrow.

(a) let
(b) lent
(c) sold
(d) owed

SOLUTION

A 아직도 내가 빌려줬던 그 재무 관련 서적들 가지고 있니?
B 집에 있어. 내일 돌려줄게.

⊞ 기출 POINT

B가 돌려주겠다고 한 것으로 볼 때 책은 A의 것이고 A가 B에게 빌려준 것임을 알 수 있다. 따라서 빈칸에는 '빌려주다'의 뜻인 lend가 들어가야 한다. 반대로 '빌리다'는 borrow이고, let은 부동산을 '세놓다'는 의미로 쓴다.

finance 재무 **let** (집 등을) 세놓다 **lend** 빌려주다 **owe** 빚지다

정답_(b)

2

A Excuse me, what's the best way to get downtown from here?

B It's best to _____ bus number 602.

(a) pay
(b) take
(c) lead
(d) view

SOLUTION

A 실례지만, 여기에서 시내로 가는 가장 좋은 방법이 뭔가요?
B 602번 버스를 타는 게 제일 좋아요.

⊞ 기출 POINT

길 찾기와 관련된 대화이다. 어떤 장소로 가는 가장 좋은 방법을 물을 때 What's the best way to...?를 쓴다. 버스나 지하철, 택시 등 교통수단을 '타다'라고 표현할 때 take를 쓴다.

take 타다 **lead** 이끌다 **view** 보다

정답_(b)

3

A Do you know when Caroline will be back?

B Sorry, I have no _____.

(a) idea
(b) goal
(c) mind
(d) sense

SOLUTION

A 캐롤라인이 언제 돌아오는지 아세요?
B 죄송하지만 모르겠습니다.

⊞ 기출 POINT

아는지를 물었는데 응답이 Sorry로 시작하고 있으므로 '모르겠다'는 말이 적절하다. 명사 idea를 써서 I have no idea라고 표현한다. sense는 I have no sense of direction(나는 방향감각이 없다)처럼 감각을 의미할 때 쓴다.

goal 목표 **mind** 정신 **sense** 감각

정답_(a)

4

A Did you get some sleep?

B Yes. I had plenty of _____.

(a) rest
(b) snore
(c) amount
(d) moment

SOLUTION

A 잠 좀 잤니?
B 응. 푹 쉬었어.

⊞ 기출 POINT

잠을 좀 잤느냐는 질문에는 많이 쉬었다는 답이 적절하다. plenty of는 셀 수 없는 명사 앞에서 많은 양을 나타내는 표현이다.

잠을 자다: get some[much/ any] sleep

plenty of 풍부한 **rest** 휴식 **snore** 코골기 **amount** 양 정답_(a)

5

A _____ me a call as soon as you arrive in Paris.

B Sure. I'll call you when I get there.

(a) Give
(b) Drop
(c) Send
(d) Fire

SOLUTION

A 파리에 도착하자마자 나한테 전화해.
B 그럼. 거기 도착하면 전화할게.

기출 POINT

'~에게 전화하다'는 말로 give ... a call을 쓴다. I'll call you라는 응답으로 보아 나에게 전화해 달라는 말이 되어야 하므로 빈칸에 give가 적절하다. drop A a line은 'A에게 몇 자 적어 보내다'는 뜻이다.
전화 관련 표현: return a call 전화한 사람에게 전화해 주다/ take[answer] a call 전화를 받다/ make a call 전화를 걸다
arrive 도착하다 **get** 도착하다 **send** 보내다 정답_(a)

6

A Good morning, Service Department. Can I help you?

B Yes, my Internet _____ is down. I can't get online.

(a) station
(b) detection
(c) admission
(d) connection

SOLUTION

A 안녕하세요, 고객 센터입니다. 도와드릴까요?
B 네, 인터넷 접속이 끊어졌어요. 온라인 접속이 안 됩니다.

기출 POINT

온라인에 접속이 안 된다는 말로 볼 때 인터넷 '접속, 연결'을 의미하는 명사 connection이 들어가야 한다.
department 부서 **down** 접속이 끊어진 **get online** 온라인 접속하다
station 방송국 **detection** 탐지 **admission** 입장 **connection** 연결 정답_(d)

7

A Shall we meet at noon?

B That's _____ with me.

(a) fine
(b) neat
(c) sure
(d) right

SOLUTION

A 정오에 만날까?
B 나는 좋아.

기출 POINT

약속을 정하는 대화이다. Shall we...?는 제안하는 말이고 이에 동의할 때 '나는 괜찮아, 좋아'라는 말로 That's fine with me를 쓴다.
비슷한 표현으로 That's okay with me/ No problem/ That sounds great 등이 있다.
noon 정오 **neat** 깔끔한; 멋진 정답_(a)

8

A Do you have enough money to go to Europe this summer?

B Yes, I've been _____ for this trip for the past three years.

(a) saving up
(b) holding off
(c) starting over
(d) waiting around

SOLUTION

A 올여름 유럽에 갈 만큼 충분한 돈이 있나요?
B 네, 지난 3년간 이 여행을 가려고 돈을 모았거든요.

기출 POINT

money라는 말과 관련해서 여행을 위해 돈을 모아왔다는 내용이 알맞다. '돈을 모으다'는 save up이라는 표현을 쓴다. hold off는 '미루다'는 뜻이고, start over는 '다시 시작하다'라는 뜻이다.
save up (돈을) 모으다 **hold off** 미루다 **start over** 다시 시작하다
wait around 근처를 거닐며 기다리다 정답_(a)

9

A We can't finish this report by five.

B No, there's no way it can be _____ by then.

(a) ended
(b) rounded
(c) completed
(d) terminated

SOLUTION

A 이 보고서는 5시까지 못 끝내.

B 그럼, 그때까지는 무슨 수를 써도 못 끝내지.

⊞ 기출 POINT

부정문에 대해 No로 동의하는 내용이다. There's no way는 '~할 방법이 없다'는 뜻으로 can't와 같고 빈칸에는 '완성하다'라는 complete이 적절하다. terminate은 공식적인 말로 '종결되다'라는 뜻이다. round는 round off의 형태로 '(행사 등을) 마무리하다'는 뜻이며 They rounded off the meal with some cheese처럼 쓰인다.

complete 완성하다 **terminate** 종결하다 정답_(c)

10

A How was your vacation in Rome?

B Great, except for being awakened every Sunday by the _____ of church bells.

(a) hitting
(b) ringing
(c) banging
(d) roaring

SOLUTION

A 로마에서의 휴가는 어땠어?

B 좋았어. 일요일마다 교회 종소리 때문에 잠이 깼던 것만 빼면.

⊞ 기출 POINT

교회 종이 '울리다'는 동사는 ring을 써야 한다. 종소리가 울리는 것 때문에 시끄러웠다는 내용이므로 종을 치는 hitting이나 banging은 답이 될 수 없다.

except for ~을 제외하고 **bang** 세게 치다 **roar** 으르렁거리다 정답_(b)

11

A Could you take me for driving practice before my driving test?

B I'd rather not. You and I will probably _____fighting.

(a) end up
(b) go after
(c) run into
(d) count on

SOLUTION

A 운전면허 시험 전에 운전 연습 시켜줄 수 있니?

B 안 하는 게 좋겠어. 아마 결국 싸우게 될 거야.

⊞ 기출 POINT

I'd rather not(그렇게 안 하는 게 좋겠다)이라고 거절하며 그 이유를 말하는 문장이다. '결국에는 ~상황에 이르다'라는 뜻으로 end up+장소/ -ing를 쓴다. 싸우고 말게 될 것이라는 말은 end up fighting이 되어야 알맞다. run into는 '곤란 따위에 부딪히다'는 의미이다.

end up -ing 결국 ~에 이르다 **go after** ~을 뒤쫓다 **run into** ~에 부딪히다 **count on** ~을 의지하다 정답_(a)

12

A It's a problem to have a busy road so close to the school.

B Well, the town council plans to _____ safety measures soon.

(a) remit
(b) transmit
(c) implement
(d) supplement

SOLUTION

A 학교랑 그렇게 가까운 도로가 번잡하다는 건 문제야.

B 음, 시 위원회에서 곧 안전 대책을 시행할 계획이야.

⊞ 기출 POINT

문제점에 대한 시 위원회의 해결책을 알려주는 내용이다. safety measures(안전 대책)에 맞는 동사로 약속, 계획 등을 '시행하다'는 뜻의 implement가 적절하다.

council 위원회 **safety** 안전 **remit** 송금하다 **implement** 시행하다 **supplement** 보충하다 정답_(c)

13

A This soup doesn't have much taste.

B I know. It really is quite _____.

(a) soft
(b) salty
(c) bland
(d) smooth

SOLUTION

A 이 수프는 별 맛이 없다.
B 그러게. 꽤 싱거워.

⊞ 기출 POINT

doesn't have much taste와 같은 뜻이 되는 형용사를 고르는 문제이다. '맛이 밍밍한, 맛없는'의 뜻으로 bland를 써야 한다. 영영 정의를 참고하면 having little or no distinctive flavor라는 설명이다.
taste 맛 **bland** 밍밍한   정답 _(c)

14

A Oh, no. I got three Cs this semester.

B Just _____ about it and move on.

(a) forget
(b) doubt
(c) think
(d) tell

SOLUTION

A 아, 안 돼. 이번 학기에 C학점이 세 개야.
B 그냥 잊어버리고 다음에 잘해.

⊞ 기출 POINT

나쁜 성적을 받아서 좌절하는 사람을 격려하는 말이다. move on은 과거의 실패를 뒤로하고 앞으로 나아가자는 뜻이다. 앞으로 잘할 생각을 하자는 내용이 되어야 하므로 빈칸에 forget이 적절하다.
semester 학기 **move on** 계속 나아가다 **doubt** 의심하다 정답 _(a)

15

A They say the hotel shuttle bus won't arrive for at least 15 minutes.

B In that case, let's _____ a taxi.
I'm too tired to wait.

(a) elect
(b) trace
(c) catch
(d) chase

SOLUTION

A 호텔 셔틀버스가 15분 후에 올 거래.
B 그럼 택시를 타자. 기다리기에 너무 피곤해.

⊞ 기출 POINT

기다리기 힘들다는 말로 볼 때 빈칸에는 택시를 '잡자'는 말이 적절하다. '택시를 타다'로 catch a taxi, take a taxi, get a taxi 등을 쓰고 '택시를 부르다'로는 hail a taxi를 쓴다.
shuttle bus 셔틀버스 **at least** 적어도 **elect** 선거하다 **trace** 더듬다 **chase** 추격하다   정답 _(c)

16

A Dr. Lewis said she hasn't seen a Northern Red Wolf for 20 years.

B I'm afraid they may now be _____.

(a) extinct
(b) hidden
(c) sporadic
(d) dormant

SOLUTION

A 루이스 박사님 말씀이 북부 붉은 늑대를 20년 동안 한 마리도 못 보셨답니다.
B 이제 멸종한 게 아닐까 싶네요.

⊞ 기출 POINT

I'm afraid는 유감스러운 내용을 말할 때 쓰는 표현이므로 '멸종한'의 뜻인 extinct가 가장 알맞다. sporadic은 '드문, 산재하는'의 뜻이고 dormant는 '휴면하는'의 뜻이다.
extinct 멸종된 **sporadic** 산재하는 **dormant** 잠자는   정답 _(a)

17

A Can I have vegetarian meals on the flight?
B Certainly. There's no extra _____.

(a) fare
(b) price
(c) ticket
(d) charge

SOLUTION

A 기내에서 채식주의자용 식사를 할 수 있나요?
B 물론입니다. 추가 비용은 없습니다.

⊞ 기출 POINT
추가 요금이 없다는 말의 '요금'은 charge를 쓴다. charge는 일을 하는 데 드는 시간, 노력에 대한 지불 요금이다. fare는 운임, 교통요금 등에 쓰는 말이다.
요금 관련 단어: fee 교육, 의료, 법률 서비스 비용/ price 가게, 식당에서의 비용/ cost 물건을 사거나 만들 때 드는 총액 ex) wholesale price 도매가/ cut costs 비용을 절감하다
vegetarian 채식주의의 **meal** 식사 **extra** 여분의 **정답_(d)**

18

A Would you like coffee or tea, sir?
B I'll have tea, please. No, on second
_____, make it coffee.

(a) choice
(b) thought
(c) decision
(d) selection

SOLUTION

A 선생님, 커피로 하시겠습니까, 차로 하시겠습니까?
B 차로 주십시오. 아니, 다시 생각해 봤는데 커피로 주십시오.

⊞ 기출 POINT
이미 한 결정을 바꾸는 말로 '다시 생각해 봤는데'라는 뜻의 on second thought을 쓴다. 보통 앞의 결정과 반대 내용이 나오게 된다.
decision 결정 **selection** 선택 **정답_(b)**

19

A Did you reserve a table at the restaurant?
B I couldn't. They were all _____.

(a) sat down
(b) filled out
(c) phoned in
(d) booked up

SOLUTION

A 식당에 예약은 했니?
B 못했어. 예약이 다 찼더라.

⊞ 기출 POINT
reserve a table at은 '~식당에 예약하다'는 뜻이다. 못했다는 말로 보아 예약이 찼다는 말이 알맞다. book은 '예약하다'라는 뜻이고, booked up은 '예약이 다 찬'의 뜻이다.
reserve 예약하다 **fill out** 양식을 작성하다 **booked up** 예약이 찬
정답_(d)

20

A I usually don't have time to eat in the morning.
B But it's really bad for your health to
_____ breakfast.

(a) reject
(b) jump
(c) pass
(d) skip

SOLUTION

A 나는 보통 아침 식사를 할 시간이 없어.
B 그렇지만 아침을 거르는 건 건강에 정말 나빠.

⊞ 기출 POINT
아침을 거르는 것은 건강에 아주 나쁘다는 말이 되어야 한다. skip은 '뛰어넘다, 생략하다'라는 뜻인데 끼니나 음식 등을 '먹지 않고 지나치다, 거르다'라는 말로 쓴다.
health 건강 **reject** 거절하다 **pass** 통과하다 **skip** 거르다 **정답_(d)**

21

A Why do you leave the car _____ for so long?

B Because it takes a long time to warm up.

(a) idling
(b) turning
(c) steering
(d) wheeling

A 왜 그렇게 오랫동안 차를 공회전시키는 거야?
B 엔진을 데우는 데 시간이 오래 걸려서.

⊞ 기출 POINT

추운 날씨에 시동을 켜고 발진하면 엔진에 무리가 가므로 일정시간 공회전을 시켜 엔진의 온도를 높여주는 것에 대한 대화이다. leave는 보어를 동반하여 '~한 상태로 두다'로 쓴다. '공회전하다'는 동사 idle이다.
warm up 준비하다 **idle** 공회전하다 **steer** 향하다 **wheel** 미끄러지 듯 달리다   정답_(a)

22

A What did your grandfather do during World War II?

B He _____ in the British Royal Navy.

(a) served
(b) existed
(c) appeared
(d) maintained

A 너희 할아버지께서는 2차 세계대전 기간에 뭘 하셨니?
B 영국 해군에 복무하셨어.

⊞ 기출 POINT

serve는 '임기 동안 일하다'는 뜻인데 군에 '복무하다'는 의미로도 사용한다. '군복무'는 military service로, '육군에서 복무하다'는 serve in the army로 나타낸다.
navy 해군 **serve** 복무하다 **exist** 존재하다 **maintain** 유지하다
정답_(a)

23

A I checked all of my computer settings, but it still isn't working properly.

B Maybe you have _____ something.

(a) overseen
(b) overcome
(c) overlooked
(d) overpowered

A 컴퓨터 설정을 모두 확인해 봤는데 여전히 제대로 작동하지 않아.
B 아마 뭔가 빠뜨리고 못 봤을 거야.

⊞ 기출 POINT

컴퓨터 설정을 확인한 후이므로 뭔가 빠뜨리고 못 봤을 거라는 말이 알맞다. 동사 overlook은 '빠뜨리고 지나다'라는 의미로 사용한다. 형태가 비슷해서 혼동을 주는 나머지 선택지에 유의하자.
setting 설정 **properly** 제대로 **oversee** 감시하다 **overcome** 극복하다 **overlook** 못 보고 지나치다 **overpower** 제압하다 정답_(c)

24

A I'm delighted to present you with this teaching award.

B It was a(n) _____ to have been a part of the competition. Thank you.

(a) glory
(b) virtue
(c) award
(d) privilege

A 이 강의 상을 귀하께 드리게 되어 기쁩니다.
B 이 대회에 참여할 수 있어 영광이었습니다. 감사합니다.

⊞ 기출 POINT

시상식에서 이루어지는 대화이다. 상을 수여해서 기쁘다는 말에 대해 It was a privilege to라는 관용적 표현을 써서 참가한 것이 '영광, 영예'였다고 답하는 것이 알맞다. '이 상을 수여하다'는 말로 present you with this award라는 표현을 사용한다.
delighted 기쁜 **present** 주다 **award** 상 **competition** 대회
virtue 미덕 **privilege** 특권, 명예   정답_(d)

25

A I decided to shave off my _____.
   What do you think?
B You look great. Now I can finally see your cute
   chin.

(a) goatee
(b) tresses
(c) whiskers
(d) mustache

SOLUTION

A 내 턱밑 수염을 밀어버렸어. 어때?
B 멋져. 이제야 네 귀여운 턱을 볼 수 있구나.

⊞ 기출 POINT

턱을 볼 수 있게 되었다는 말로 볼 때, 턱에 난 수염을 밀었다는 말이 적
절하다. goatee는 턱밑에 난 염소 수염을 말하고, whisker는 얼굴 옆
면에 난 수염을, mustache는 코 아래에 난 수염을 의미한다.

shave off (수염을) 밀어버리다 **goatee** 아래턱 수염 **tress** 땋은 머리
whisker 구레나룻 **mustache** 콧수염   정답_(a)

26

After a ten-minute _____, the meeting
continued for another two hours.

(a) stop
(b) time
(c) break
(d) gap

SOLUTION

10분간 휴식 후 회의는 또 다시 두 시간 동안 계속됐다.

⊞ 기출 POINT

일이나 수업 등에서 잠깐의 휴식을 의미하는 단어로 break를 쓴다.
coffee break(휴식시간), spring break(봄 방학), take a ten-
minute break(10분간 휴식을 하다) 등으로 표현한다. gap은 '틈, 간격,
격차'의 뜻이므로 부적절하다.

continue 계속되다 **break** 휴식 **gap** 틈, 간격, 격차   정답_(c)

27

Feeding the farm animals was not as easy as it
_____ at first.

(a) meant
(b) looked
(c) expected
(d) previewed

SOLUTION

농장 동물에게 먹이를 주는 것은 처음에 봤던 것처럼 쉽지 않았다.

⊞ 기출 POINT

not as ... as 구문으로 비교하는 내용이다. 처음 봤을 때보다 어렵다는
내용이므로 looked가 적절하다. expected나 previewed는 주어
it에 이어지는 동사로 부적절하다.

feed 먹이를 주다 **preview** 미리 보다   정답_(b)

28

The French Foreign Minister hoped to _____
the crisis in trade negotiations with the US.

(a) vanish
(b) resolve
(c) formalize
(d) undermine

SOLUTION

프랑스 외무장관은 미국과의 교역 협상 위기를 해결하기를 희망했다.

⊞ 기출 POINT

명사 crisis와 연결될 동사로 '해결하다'라는 뜻의 resolve가 가장 적절
하다. solve와 같은 뜻으로 resolve a problem[conflict] 등의 표현
을 쓴다. undermine은 '손상시키다'라는 뜻으로 내용에 맞지 않는다.

foreign minister 외무장관 **crisis** 위기 **negotiation** 협상
vanish 사라지다 **resolve** 해결하다 **formalize** 형식을 갖추다
undermine 해치다, 손상시키다   정답_(b)

29

To prolong their life, _____ unused batteries in a cool, dry place away from heat or flame.

(a) fix
(b) add
(c) store
(d) prepare

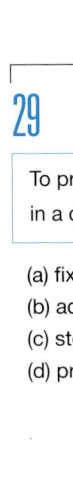

SOLUTION

건전지 수명을 연장하려면 사용하지 않은 건전지는 열이나 불꽃에서 떨어진 시원하고 건조한 장소에 보관하십시오.

기출 POINT
장소를 나타내는 전치사 in과 연결하여 의미가 적절한 동사는 '보관하다'는 뜻의 store이다. fix는 '수리하다'는 뜻이다.
prolong 연장하다 **unused** 사용하지 않은 **battery** 건전지, 충전기
flame 불길 **fix** 수리하다 **store** 보관하다   정답_(c)

30

Fashion magazines are now encouraging women over 40 to _____ a more feminine and youthful dress style.

(a) meet
(b) force
(c) adopt
(d) inhabit

SOLUTION

이제 패션 잡지들은 40세 이상 여성들에게 더 여성스럽고 젊은 스타일로 옷을 입도록 북돋우고 있다.

기출 POINT
빈칸에 들어갈 동사를 하도록 잡지가 권하고 있다는 내용이다. dress style과 연결되는 동사로 '택하다, 고르다'라는 뜻의 adopt를 쓴다. force는 '강요하다'의 뜻이므로 encourage to force로 연결될 수 없으므로 부적절하다.
encourage 북돋우다 **feminine** 여성스러운 **youthful** 젊은
force 강요하다 **adopt** 취하다, 선택하다   정답_(c)

31

Biologists often _____ different types of life forms based on their DNA.

(a) inspire
(b) classify
(c) recollect
(d) entertain

SOLUTION

생물학자들은 종종 DNA를 기준으로 서로 다른 형태의 생명체를 분류한다.

기출 POINT
'~을 기준으로 하여'라는 뜻의 based on과 의미가 통하는 동사를 고른다. 기준에 따라 '분류하다'는 classify가 알맞다. recollect는 '생각해내다, 회상하다'는 뜻이므로 부적절하다.
biologist 생물학자 **life form** 생명체 **inspire** 고무하다 **classify** 분류하다 **recollect** 회상하다 **entertain** 즐겁게 하다   정답_(b)

32

The old man was filled with _____ after he learned that he had won the lottery.

(a) joy
(b) deceit
(c) victory
(d) attitude

SOLUTION

그 노인은 자신이 복권에 당첨되었다는 사실을 알고 뛸 듯이 기뻤다.

기출 POINT
복권 당첨 소식을 알고 아주 기뻤다는 내용이 자연스럽다. be filled with 다음에는 감정이 나오는 것이 가장 적절하므로 joy가 알맞다.
be filled with ~로 가득 차다 **win the lottery** 복권에 당첨되다
deceit 사기, 속임수 **attitude** 태도   정답_(a)

33

There are several ATMs inside the park that _____ major credit cards.

(a) proceed
(b) deposit
(c) accept
(d) utilize

SOLUTION

주요 신용카드를 취급하는 현금 자동인출기 몇 대가 공원 안에 있다.

⊞ 기출 POINT

that절 이하에는 ATM이 하는 일에 대한 내용이다. 주요 신용카드를 '취급한다'는 뜻으로 동사 accept가 적절하다. Do you accept credit cards?(신용카드로 계산되나요?)처럼 쓴다. utilize는 '효율적으로 이용하다'는 뜻이다. utilize waste products, utilize the vitamins 등으로 표현한다.

ATM 현금 자동인출기 **proceed** 나아가다 **deposit** 예금하다
utilize 활용하다   정답_(c)

34

Public buildings are often _____ with decorations that reflect their usage.

(a) barred
(b) tainted
(c) granted
(d) adorned

SOLUTION

공공 건물은 용도를 반영하는 장식으로 꾸며진 경우가 많다.

⊞ 기출 POINT

with decorations와 호응하여 문맥에 어울리는 동사는 adorned이다. be adorned with는 '~으로 꾸며지다'라는 뜻으로 쓴다.

decoration 장식 **reflect** 반영하다 **usage** 용도 **bar** 막다, 방해하다 **taint** 더럽히다 **grant** 주다 **adorn** 꾸미다   정답_(d)

35

Even though crime may never be completely _____ from our community, it can be reduced.

(a) deducted
(b) dismissed
(c) eliminated
(d) subtracted

SOLUTION

우리 지역사회에서 범죄를 완전히 근절할 수는 없더라도 줄일 수는 있다.

⊞ 기출 POINT

내용상 빈칸에는 전치사 from과 호응하고 reduce보다 정도가 더 강한 뜻의 동사가 적절하다는 것을 알 수 있다. 범죄가 줄어드는 것보다 강한 의미로 완전히 소멸된다는 내용이 되도록 '제거하다'라는 뜻의 eliminate를 쓰는 것이 알맞다.

even though 비록 ~일지라도 **completely** 완전히 **community** 지역사회 **reduce** 줄이다 **deduct** 빼다 **dismiss** 해산시키다
eliminate 제거하다 **subtract** 빼다   정답_(c)

36

The recent revival of interest in Jane Austen owes a great deal to the successful film _____ of her novels.

(a) adaptations
(b) conversions
(c) modifications
(d) transformations

SOLUTION

제인 오스틴에 대한 관심이 최근 되살아난 것은 그녀의 소설이 성공적인 영화로 각색되었다는 것이 큰 작용을 했다.

⊞ 기출 POINT

형태를 바꾸는 것과 관련된 단어들이 선택지를 구성하고 있다. 장르에 맞도록 '각색'하는 것은 adaptation을 쓴다. 제도나 계획 수정은 modification을, 목표나 체계를 전환하는 것은 conversion을 쓴다.

revival 재생 **owe A to B** A는 B의 덕택이다 **adaptation** 각색
conversion 전환 **modification** 변경 **transformation** 변형
                                                        정답_(a)

37

This new thermos is _____ to keep liquids cold for up to three hours.

(a) engaged
(b) designed
(c) suggested
(d) composed

SOLUTION

이 새 보온병은 3시간까지 액체를 차갑게 보관할 수 있도록 설계되었다.

⊞ 기출 POINT

'~할 수 있도록 설계되었다'는 뜻이 되어야 하므로 design이 적절하다. compose는 '구성하다'의 뜻이므로 문맥에 맞지 않는다. up to 다음에 시간을 써서 '~까지'를 나타냈다.

thermos 보온병 **liquid** 액체 **design** 설계하다 **compose** 구성하다
정답_(b)

38

The high cost of AIDS medication is a significant _____ on Britain's healthcare system.

(a) burden
(b) residue
(c) inflation
(d) depression

SOLUTION

AIDS 치료약의 높은 비용은 영국 의료보험 체계에 상당한 부담이다.

⊞ 기출 POINT

치료약의 높은 비용이 영국 의료 체계에 상당한 '부담'이 된다는 내용이 알맞다. 전치사 on과 호응하여 적절한 단어는 burden이다. inflation 이나 depression은 내용상 맞지 않는다.

medication 치료약 **significant** 상당한 **healthcare system** 의료 체계 **residue** 나머지 **inflation** 팽창 **depression** 침체
정답_(a)

39

Cancellations of hotel reservations without 24 hours' notice are _____ to a penalty.

(a) prior
(b) subject
(c) common
(d) standard

SOLUTION

24시간 전 고지 없이 호텔 예약을 취소하면 위약금이 부과된다.

⊞ 기출 POINT

24시간 전에 알리지 않고 예약을 취소하는 것은 위약금을 '내는 수밖에 없다'는 내용이 되어야 한다. 제시된 be와 to 사이에 적절한 형용사로 subject가 알맞다. prior to는 '~전에'라는 뜻이고, be common to 는 '~에 공통이다'라는 뜻이다.

cancellation 취소 **notice** 고지 **penalty** 벌금 **prior to** ~전에 **be subject to** ~을 받다 **common** 공통의
정답_(b)

40

The process of evaporation creates a cooling effect when it dries _____ on your skin.

(a) irritation
(b) alteration
(c) perspiration
(d) condensation

SOLUTION

증발 작용을 통해 피부에서 땀이 마르면서 냉각 효과가 생긴다.

⊞ 기출 POINT

증발 작용으로 냉각 효과가 생기는 것은 피부 위의 땀이 마르기 때문이다. 빈칸 앞의 dries와 어울리는 명사는 perspiration뿐이다.

evaporation 증발 **create** 생기다 **irritation** 염증 **alteration** 변경 **perspiration** 땀 **condensation** 응축
정답_(c)

41

The meaning of the poem was so vague that few students _____ it at first.

(a) grasped
(b) clutched
(c) swallowed
(d) established

SOLUTION

그 시의 의미는 너무 모호해서 처음에 그것을 이해한 학생들이 거의 없었다.

기출 POINT

few students가 주어이므로 처음에 시의 의미를 이해한 학생들이 거의 없다는 내용이 알맞다. 의미를 '파악하다, 이해하다'의 뜻으로 동사 grasp를 쓴다. grasp은 '움켜잡다'라는 의미로도 사용되고, (b)의 clutch 역시 같은 뜻이다.

vague 애매한   **grasp** 이해하다   **clutch** 붙잡다   **swallow** 삼키다

정답_(a)

42

Hollywood movies _____ unrealistic images of Western culture that are accepted as accurate throughout the world.

(a) assume
(b) project
(c) scatter
(d) install

SOLUTION

할리우드 영화는 전세계에서 정확하다고 받아들여지는 서구 문화에 대한 비현실적인 이미지를 보여준다.

기출 POINT

할리우드 영화가 비현실적인 이미지를 보여준다는 의미이다. '투영하다, 투사하다'라는 의미로 project가 적절하다. scatter는 '흩뿌리다'라는 뜻으로 공간적으로 퍼뜨리는 의미를 내포한다.

accurate 정확한   **assume** 가정하다   **project** 비추다. 표현하다   **scatter** 퍼뜨리다   **install** 설치하다

정답_(b)

43

Internships at Sandern University are _____ to full-time students.

(a) arranged
(b) enclosed
(c) attached
(d) limited

SOLUTION

샌던 대학의 인턴 기회는 정규 학생들에게 제한되어 있다.

기출 POINT

전치사 to에 이어지는 어구의 뜻을 고려해 볼 때, be limited to가 '~에 제한되다'의 뜻을 나타낼 수 있다. be enclosed는 with나 by를 동반하여 '~에 에워싸이다'라는 뜻으로 쓰인다.

internship 인턴(기간)   **enclose** 에워싸다   **attach** 붙이다   **limit** 제한하다

정답_(d)

44

Visitors to Vacaville should be warned that the area is sometimes affected by a _____ odor coming from oil refineries.

(a) cruel
(b) base
(c) foul
(d) thin

SOLUTION

이 지역이 때로는 정유공장에서 나오는 악취에 영향을 받는다는 것을 배커빌 방문객들에게 알려 주어야 한다.

기출 POINT

be affected by는 '~에 의해 영향을 받다'라는 뜻이다. 정유공장에서 나는 냄새에 대해 경고해 주어야 한다는 것으로 보아 '악취가 나는'이 가장 적절하다. foul은 '더러운'이라는 뜻도 있지만 구체적으로 '악취의'라는 뜻이 있다.

warn 경고하다   **affect** 영향을 주다   **odor** 냄새   **oil refinery** 정유공장   **cruel** 잔인한   **foul** 악취가 나는   **thin** 희박한

정답_(c)

45

Even though the filmmakers proclaimed a commitment to _____, their film is seriously flawed with historical inaccuracies.

(a) authority
(b) objectivity
(c) spontaneity
(d) authenticity

SOLUTION

영화 제작자들이 진실성에 대한 헌신을 주장했지만, 그들의 영화는 역사적 부정확성이라는 심각한 결함을 안고 있다.

기출 POINT
Even though라는 접속사를 볼 때 두 절의 내용이 상반되는 것임을 알 수 있다. 역사적 사실에 정확히 맞지 않는다는 내용에 반대가 되는 것은 '진실성'에 전념했다는 것이 된다. 진실성을 나타내는 명사는 authenticity이다.
proclaim 주장하다 **commitment** 헌신 **flaw** 흠이 가게 하다
inaccuracy 부정확성 **authority** 권위 **objectivity** 객관성
spontaneity 자발성 **authenticity** 진실성 　　　　정답_(d)

46

The caste system, the traditional method of stratifying Hindu society, shapes nearly every _____ of life in India.

(a) facet
(b) class
(c) status
(d) vector

SOLUTION

힌두교 사회의 계층을 나누는 전통적 방식인 카스트 제도는 인도에서의 삶 거의 모든 측면을 형성한다.

기출 POINT
힌두 사회를 서열화하는 카스트 제도는 인도에서의 삶 거의 모든 '측면'을 형성한다는 내용이다. 동사 shapes와 잘 연결될 수 있는 명사를 고르는 것이 힌트가 되므로 '측면'이라는 뜻의 facet이 알맞다.
caste system 카스트 제도 **stratify** 계층을 나누다 **facet** 측면
status 지위 **vector** 벡터, 방향량 　　　　정답_(a)

47

Tests show that ginger may enhance cancer treatment by _____ resistance to chemotherapy.

(a) vacillating
(b) brandishing
(c) circumventing
(d) substantiating

SOLUTION

실험에 따르면 생강은 화학요법에 대한 내성을 방해함으로써 암 치료를 향상시킬 수 있음을 보여준다.

기출 POINT
비교하는 내용이 생강과 화학요법임에 유의한다. 생강이 화학요법에 대한 내성이 생기는 것을 피하도록 해준다는 의미가 되려면 내성을 '피하다, 우회하다'라는 뜻의 circumvent를 써야 한다. substantiate는 어떤 사실이 진실임을 '실증하다'라는 의미이다.
ginger 생강 **enhance** 향상시키다 **resistance** 내성
chemotherapy 화학요법 **vacillate** 흔들다 **brandish** 휘두르다
circumvent 피하다, 우회하다 **substantiate** 실증하다 　　정답_(c)

48

With a population made up of people from many different countries, New York City is one of the most _____ cities in the world.

(a) infusive
(b) enigmatic
(c) provincial
(d) cosmopolitan

SOLUTION

다양한 국가 출신의 사람들로 구성된, 뉴욕시는 전세계에서 가장 국제적인 도시 중 하나이다.

기출 POINT
여러 다른 나라에서 온 사람들로 구성된 도시라는 설명을 볼 때 빈칸에는 '국제적인, 전세계적인' 도시라는 뜻의 cosmopolitan이 적절하다.
population 사람들 **infusive** 고취시키는 **enigmatic** 불가사의한
provincial 지방의 **cosmopolitan** 국제적인 　　　　정답_(d)

Actual Test 2

49

Unfortunately, the results of the research cannot
be accepted without considerable _____ .

(a) sobriety
(b) symmetry
(c) altercation
(d) qualification

SOLUTION

불행하게도 그 연구 결과는 충분한 조건 없이는 수용될 수 없다.

기출 POINT

연구 결과가 그대로는 수용되기 어렵고 충분한 조건이 있어야 수용될
수 있다는 내용이다. 즉, 조건부로 수용 가능하다는 말이 되어야 하므로
qualification이 적절하다.

unfortunately 불행히도 **considerable** 상당한 **sobriety** 절제
symmetry 대칭 **altercation** 언쟁 **qualification** 조건   **정답**_(d)

50

Many people regard capital punishment as a(n)
_____ of the most fundamental human
right.

(a) salutation
(b) retribution
(c) infringement
(d) embezzlement

SOLUTION

많은 사람들은 사형을 가장 기본적인 인권침해로 간주한다.

기출 POINT

사형제도를 기본적인 인권의 '침해'라고 생각한다는 내용이 되어야 한다.
retribution은 죄에 대한 '응보, 보복'의 뜻이고, infringement는 법규
의 '위반'이나 권리의 '침해'의 뜻으로 쓰인다.

capital punishment 사형 **fundamental** 기본적인 **salutation**
인사 **retribution** 보복 **infringement** 침해 **embezzlement**
횡령   **정답**_(c)

1

Although you probably know that certain bacteria can cause harm, you might not be fully aware of the huge benefits bacteria can also provide. For instance, bacteria are crucial for a healthy balance in nutrition, since they produce essential elements such as nitrogen and sulfur for plants, which in turn are consumed by animals and humans. Bacteria are also instrumental in the manufacture of life-saving medicines. Thus, the presence of bacteria is _____.

(a) likely to cause us harm
(b) linked to poor nutrition
(c) helpful for growing plants
(d) necessary in our daily lives

SOLUTION

특정 박테리아가 해를 끼칠 수 있다는 것은 여러분들도 아마 알겠지만, 박테리아가 제공할 수 있는 엄청난 혜택에 대해서는 제대로 모르고 있을 수도 있습니다. 예를 들면 박테리아는 질소나 황과 같이 식물에 필수적인 원소들을 생산하고, 이것이 다시 동물과 인간에 의해 소비되기 때문에 적절한 양분 균형에 있어 중요합니다. 박테리아는 또한 생명을 구하는 의약품 제조에 도움이 됩니다. 이와 같이 박테리아의 존재는 우리의 일상 생활에 필요하죠.

⊞ 기출 POINT

마지막 문장을 고르는 문제이다. 첫 문장은 반드시 집중해서 읽고 넘어가야 한다. 첫 문장에서 주제가 제시되고 마지막 문장에서 결론으로 주제가 반복되는 경우가 많기 때문이다. 박테리아가 큰 혜택을 준다는 언급 다음으로 박테리아가 영양분을 만들고 의약품 제조에도 쓰이는 예를 나열하고 있다. 빈칸이 있는 마지막 문장은 접속사 Thus로 시작하므로 전체 내용에 대한 결론임을 예측할 수 있으므로 (d)가 가장 적절하다.

be aware of ~을 알다 **benefit** 혜택 **provide** 공급하다 **crucial** 중요한 **nutrition** 영양 **nitrogen** 질소 **sulfur** 황 **consume** 소비하다 **instrumental** 도움이 되는 **manufacture** 제조 **presence** 존재 **정답** (d)

2

Dear Editor,

My husband and I moved to this community last year. One day, while running some errands in Hooverville, we decided to have lunch at what we now consider one of our community's best tourist attractions, Bob Green's Bar & Grill. We have never tasted such good food—especially, their seafood dishes—and nothing beats the kind of service they offer. On top of this, Bob and the staff are very good-humored as well. We _____ this restaurant and hope you can find a spot in your magazine to publish this letter.

Sincerely,
Elaine E. Wilson
Parksville

(a) would like to visit
(b) highly recommend
(c) can hardly tolerate
(d) really advise against

SOLUTION

편집장 귀하.

남편과 저는 작년에 이 지역으로 이사해 왔습니다. 하루는 후버빌에서 볼일을 보다가 우리 지역 최고의 관광 명소 중 하나인 밥 그린스 바 & 그릴에서 점심을 먹기로 했습니다. 우리는 그렇게 맛있는 음식을 먹어 본 적이 없었고, 특히 그곳의 해산물 요리가 맛있었습니다. 그리고 그곳의 서비스는 그야말로 최고였습니다. 게다가 밥과 그 스탭들은 아주 상냥합니다. 저희는 이 식당을 강력 추천하며 이 편지를 귀사의 잡지에 실어 주실 수 있기를 기대합니다.

파크스빌의
일레인 E. 윌슨 드림

⊞ 기출 POINT

편지글의 끝부분에 들어갈 내용을 고르는 문제는 편지를 쓴 목적과 관련된 경우가 많다. 우선 편지의 수신자와 발신자를 확인하고 빠르게 내용을 확인해야 한다. 세부 정보를 모두 확인하지 않아도 식당에 갔었고 좋았다는 내용을 통해 편지를 쓰는 목적으로 highly recommend가 빈칸에 알맞은 것을 알 수 있다. hardly tolerate이나 advise against는 정반대의 의도일 때 적절한 표현이다.

community 지역사회 **run an errand** 볼일을 보다
tourist attraction 관광 명소 **nothing beats A** A가 최고이다
good-humored 상냥한 **highly recommend** 적극적으로 추천하다
tolerate 참다 **advise against** ~에 반대 의견을 제시하다 **정답** (b)

3

_____ remains a major problem for the company. This is mainly because of an unexpected rise in resignations and retirements. The problem has been made worse because none of the company's existing employees have the experience or qualifications necessary to fill vacant positions. To prevent this from happening in the future, the company will provide training programs so that existing employees can advance where and when necessary. In the meantime, new staff will need to be sourced outside of the company.

(a) The training of new staff
(b) The government's new policy
(c) A reduction in company profits
(d) A lack of staff in key departments

SOLUTION

핵심 부서의 인원 부족은 아직도 회사의 주요 문제가 되고 있습니다. 주 원인은 예상치 못한 사직과 퇴직의 증가입니다. 회사의 현 직원 중 공석을 메우는 데 필요한 경험이나 자격 요건을 갖춘 직원이 없다는 것 때문에 문제는 더 심각해졌습니다. 이런 일이 향후 발생하는 것을 막기 위해 회사에서는 연수 프로그램을 제공함으로써 현 직원들이 필요한 자리와 시점에 승진할 수 있도록 할 것입니다. 그 동안은 새 직원을 사외에서 조달해야 할 것입니다.

기출 POINT

직원 부족의 실태와 대응 방안에 대한 글이다. 도입 문장의 일부를 찾는 문제이므로 제시된 부분과 이어지는 문장에 유의한다. 예상치 못한 사직과 퇴직, 그리고 그 공석을 메울 경력과 자격 요건을 갖춘 인력이 부족하다는 내용이므로 회사의 주요 문제는 (d) 핵심 부서의 인력 부족임을 알 수 있다. (a)는 문제점에 대한 앞으로의 대응 방식에 해당된다.

resignation 사직 **retirement** 퇴직 **qualification** 자격요건 **advance** 승진하다 **where and when necessary** 필요한 장소와 때 **in the meantime** 그 동안에 **source** 조달하다 **profit** 수익

정답 (d)

4

Writing in Egypt goes back to about 3000 BC. Some historians speculate that the Egyptians learned how to write from the Sumerians, who had a flourishing civilization at the time. However, the Egyptian form of writing, hieroglyphs, does not look the same or work the same way as the Sumerian form of writing, cuneiform. So, it is possible that _____.

(a) Egyptians must have copied them
(b) Egyptians invented their own writing
(c) Sumerians built schools and libraries
(d) Egyptians and Sumerians were at war

SOLUTION

이집트의 글쓰기는 기원전 3000년 경으로 거슬러 올라간다. 일부 사학자들은 이집트인들이 당시 번영하는 문명을 누리던 수메르인들로부터 글 쓰는 법을 배웠을 것으로 추정한다. 그러나 이집트의 문자 형태인 상형 문자는 수메르 문자 형태인 설형 문자와 그 형태와 작용 원리가 다르다. 그래서 이집트인들이 자신들만의 집필법을 발명할 수 있었다.

기출 POINT

이집트인의 집필법에 대해 상반된 견해를 다루는 글이다. 이집트 문자가 수메르 문명에서 영향을 받은 것이라는 의견과 반대로 이집트의 상형 문자가 수메르의 설형 문자와 다르다는 의견을 제시한다. 빈칸의 내용은 이 두 번째 의견에 이어지는 결론임에 유의해야 한다. 따라서 이집트인들이 고유의 집필법을 발명했을 가능성이 있다는 (b)가 적절하다.

speculate 추정하다 **Sumerian** 수메르 사람, 수메르의 **flourishing** 번영하는 **hieroglyph** 상형 문자 **cuneiform** 설형 문자

정답 (b)

5

The Austin Air HE-3 was the best of the air purifiers we tested in terms of value for money. This model uses a true HEPA (High-Energy Particulate Air) filter, with a capacity to trap 99.97% of contaminants in a 700-square-foot room. While the Austin Air HE-3 is not as quiet as other models reviewed, it is half the cost. The warranty is also especially impressive, and with proper maintenance, you won't need to change the HEPA filter for five years. Our conclusion is that the Austin Air HE-3 is _____.

(a) an excellent air purifier for the elderly
(b) the cheapest air purifier on the market
(c) the best model available in all categories
(d) an efficient and cost-effective air purifier

SOLUTION

오스틴 에어 HE-3은 가격 대비 우리가 실험한 공기 정화기들 중 최고였다. 이 모델은 진정한 HEPA (고효율 입자 공기) 필터를 사용하며, 이 필터는 700제곱피트 크기의 방에 있는 오염물질의 99.97%를 걸러낼 수 있는 용량을 보유하고 있다. 검토한 다른 모델들에 비해 오스틴 에어 HE-3은 소음도가 낮지는 않지만 비용은 절반이다. 보증 역시 매우 인상적이며, 적절하게 관리해 주면 HEPA 필터는 5년간 교체할 필요가 없다. 우리는 오스틴 에어 HE-3이 효율적이고 비용 효율이 높은 공기 정화기라고 결론지었다.

⊞ 기출 POINT

공기 정화기의 성능에 대한 글이다. 첫 문장에서 가격 대비 성능이 최고라는 특징을 제시하고 있다. 다음으로 오염물질을 걸러내는 필터의 용량과 소음도, 비용, 보증, 그리고 교체가 5년간 불필요하다는 설명이 이어진다. 따라서 이 제품이 효율적이고 비용 효율이 높다는 내용이 가장 적절하므로 (d)가 정답이다.

purifier 정화기 **in terms of** ~의 관점에서 **filter** 필터 **capacity** 용량 **contaminant** 오염물질 **warranty** 보증 **maintenance** 관리 **conclusion** 결론 **cost-effective** 비용 효율이 높은 **정답_(d)**

6

How can traditional art and culture _____? That's the idea behind the latest exhibit at Stokes Gallery, where traditional folk art is seen combined with 21st-century technology. One artist uses digital tapestries to simulate a loom; another combines a photo process with computer technology to make images inspired by her Mexican roots; while another uses recycled computer parts to create sculptures of cultural icons. You will find it surprising how a computer can be used to express traditional cultural ideas.

(a) be effectively promoted online
(b) change the way we view our future
(c) withstand the influence of globalized culture
(d) incorporate computers or modern technology

SOLUTION

전통 예술과 문화가 어떻게 컴퓨터나 현대 기술과 결합될 수 있을까? 이것이 스톡스 갤러리에서 열리는 최근 전시회의 배경 개념으로, 이 전시회에서는 전통 민속 예술이 21세기 기술과 융합되어 보여집니다. 한 예술가는 디지털 태피스트리를 사용하여 베틀을 흉내내고, 사진술과 컴퓨터 기술을 결합시켜 멕시코인이라는 자신의 뿌리에서 영감을 받은 이미지를 만드는 예술가도 있습니다. 또 다른 예술가는 재활용된 컴퓨터 부품을 사용해 문화적 아이콘 조각을 창조하기도 합니다. 여러분은 컴퓨터가 전통적인 문화적 관념을 표현하는 데 어떻게 사용될 수 있는지에 대해 놀라게 될 것입니다.

⊞ 기출 POINT

최근 미술 전시에 대한 소개글이다. 도입 문장에 빈칸이 들어간 문제는 도입문과 이어지는 다음 문장에 집중해야 한다. 첫 번째 문장이 전시의 주제이며 두 번째 문장의 combined with 21st-century technology가 빈칸을 찾는 단서가 된다. 전통 베틀을 구현한 디지털 태피스트리, 재활용한 컴퓨터로 만든 조각 작품 등을 예로 들었다. 전통 예술과 문화가 컴퓨터나 현대 기술과 어떻게 융합할 수 있느냐가 도입문으로 적절하다.

exhibit 전시 **folk art** 민속 예술 **tapestry** 태피스트리, 벽걸이 융단 **simulate** 흉내내다 **loom** 베틀 **sculpture** 조각 **icon** 아이콘, 기호 **promote** 증진하다 **withstand** 견뎌내다 **incorporate** 결합하다

정답_(d)

7

Korea's King Sejong was _____.
He established the *Jibhyeonjeon* or "Hall of Worthies," early in his reign, where the Chosun Dynasty's best scholars flocked to pursue and conduct research. Simultaneously, he also demonstrated a keen interest in day-to-day government affairs, tenaciously seeking ways to improve the lives of the public by reforming the tax system and refining a wide range of government affairs. Consequently, during his rule, major progress was made in virtually every field: agriculture, astronomy, defense, diplomacy, geography, medicine, printing and science.

(a) a clever man who became famous for scholarship
(b) a great king who was admired in Asian countries
(c) the ruler who invented and widely spread Hangul
(d) an innovator who cared about social improvements

SOLUTION

한국의 세종대왕은 사회 개선에 관심을 가졌던 혁신가였다. 그는 집권 초에 집현전, 즉 현인들의 전당을 설립하였고, 이곳에서는 조선왕조 최고의 학자들이 모여 연구를 추구하고 수행했다. 동시에 세종대왕은 일상적인 정부 업무에도 높은 관심을 보여 세제를 개혁하고 다양한 정부 업무를 가다듬어 대중의 삶을 개선하는 방법을 끈질기게 탐구했다. 그 결과 세종대왕 집권 당시 농업, 천문학, 국방, 외교, 지리, 의학, 인쇄술 및 과학 등 사실상 모든 분야에서 큰 진전이 있었다.

⊞ 기출 POINT

세종대왕의 업적에 대한 글이다. 도입 문장이지만 전체적인 내용을 정리하는 문장이다. 세종대왕에 대한 평가가 먼저 나오고 이어 그의 여러 업적이 병렬적으로 나열되고 있어 결론까지 확인하는 풀이 방법이 요구된다. 학자들의 연구와 병행하여 대중의 삶을 개선할 수 있는 여러 개혁을 수행했다는 내용이므로 사회 개선에 관심을 가진 혁신가였다는 (d)가 가장 알맞다. 아는 내용의 익숙한 지문이라도 상식 선에서 답을 고르지 않고, 문맥의 흐름을 통해 답을 찾는 것이 TEPS 독해 Part 1의 문제 풀이 요령이다.

worthies 훌륭한 사람, 양반 **reign** 집권 **flock** 모이다 **pursue** 추구하다 **conduct** 수행하다 **simultaneously** 동시에 **demonstrate** 보여주다 **day-to-day** 일상의 **tenaciously** 끈질기게 **reform** 개혁하다 **refine** 정제하다 **consequently** 결과적으로 **agriculture** 농업 **astronomy** 천문학 **defense** 국방 **diplomacy** 외교 **printing** 인쇄술   정답_(d)

8

Obstetricians are looking to the government to intervene in their industry. Skyrocketing malpractice insurance costs have forced thousands of obstetricians to close their businesses, leaving many expectant women with nowhere to turn for medical care. However, legislation now being debated at state and national levels could deliver a much-needed solution. The new legislation is expected to _____.

(a) finance new hospitals throughout the district
(b) speed the process of getting licensed in obstetrics
(c) improve the quality of medical care for expectant women
(d) totally reform malpractice insurance practices in obstetrics

SOLUTION

산부인과 의사들은 정부가 산과업계에 개입해 줄 것을 기대하고 있다. 천정부지로 치솟는 의료 과실 배상 보험금으로 인해 수천 명의 산부인과 의사가 병원문을 닫았고, 많은 임신부들이 갈 병원을 잃게 되었다. 그러나 현재 주정부 및 국가 차원에서 토론 중인 법안은 절실하게 필요한 해결책을 내놓을 수 있을지도 모른다. 새 법안은 산부인과에서의 의료 과실 배상 보험 관행을 완전히 개혁할 것으로 기대된다.

⊞ 기출 POINT

마지막 문장을 먼저 확인하고 중점적으로 볼 내용을 추측한 후 지문을 읽는다. 빈칸에는 새로운 법안이 할 역할로 기대되는 내용이 적절하다는 것을 알 수 있다. 산부인과 의사들은 의료 과실 배상 보험금이 너무 높아 병원문을 닫아야 하는 현실에 대한 해결책을 요구하고 있다는 내용이다. 두 번째 문장에 나오는 Skyrocketing malpractice insurance costs가 문제이므로 이것을 총체적으로 개혁할 것이라는 (d)의 내용이 알맞다.

obstetrician 산부인과 의사 **intervene** 개입하다 **skyrocketing** 치솟는 **malpractice** 의료 과실 **expectant** 임신한 **with nowhere to turn** 갈 곳이 없는 상태로 **legislation** 법안 **much-needed** 절실히 필요한 **district** 지역 **obstetrics** 산부인과   정답_(d)

9

Mistaken notions—such as the idea that blood-letting cures the sick or that some races are inferior to others—have often been taken for fact and then rejected with fresh insights. Toward the end of the 20th century, science and government assured us that neither pesticides nor buried toxic wastes would harm human beings. Such false notions remind us that what we call facts _____.

(a) had an unexpected effect on scientific progress
(b) cannot be changed simply by what people say
(c) are the creations of human minds and fallible
(d) are valid if we have scientific proof

SOLUTION

피를 뽑는 것이 병든 사람들을 치료한다거나 일부 인종이 다른 인종에 비해 열등하다거나 하는 잘못된 관념들은 종종 사실로 받아들여졌다가 새로운 식견에 의해 폐기되었다. 20세기 말경 과학과 정부는 살충제와 땅속에 묻힌 독성 폐기물 그 어느 것도 인간에게 해를 끼치지 않는다며 우리를 안심시켰다. 우리가 사실이라고 부르는 이러한 잘못된 관념은 인간 마음의 산물이며 틀리기 쉬운 것임을 상기시킨다.

기출 POINT

잘못된 관념과 사실이란 말에 유의하며 전체 지문을 읽어야 한다. 피를 뽑는 것이 치료라거나 인종 간에 우열이 있다는 것, 살충제나 독성 폐기물이 해가 없다는 것과 같은 잘못된 관념들이 한때는 사실로 받아들여졌고, 이것은 인간 정신의 산물이며 틀리기 쉽다는 것을 알게 해준다는 (c)의 결론에 이르게 한다.

notion 관념 **blood-letting** 피를 뽑는 것 **inferior to** ~보다 열등한 **be taken for** ~로 받아들여지다 **insight** 식견 **assure** 안심시키다 **pesticide** 살충제 **buried** 매립된 **toxic waste** 독성 폐기물 **fallible** 틀리기 쉬운 것 **정답_**(c)

10

The Vision Award is an annual award recognizing _____. The award includes a crystal plaque, a special banquet honoring the recipient and a $10,000 cash donation toward furthering the winner's charity work. We are currently looking for nominees who are actively involved in any kind of service for the disadvantaged. They should work with minimal means and have a good record of helping those in need. Nominations will be accepted until January 31.

(a) significant volunteer work for the underprivileged
(b) substantial contributions toward curing blindness
(c) outstanding achievement in visual arts and design
(d) excellence in community planning and development

SOLUTION

비전 상은 혜택받지 못하는 사람들을 위한 중요한 자원봉사를 연례적으로 표창하는 상입니다. 이 상에는 수정 상패, 수상자를 축하하기 위한 특별 연회와 수상자의 자선 업무를 촉진하기 위한 현금 만 달러의 상금이 포함됩니다. 저희는 현재 불우한 사람들을 위해 이 같은 봉사에 활발히 참여하고 있는 후보자들을 찾고 있습니다. 후보자는 최소한의 자금으로 일을 해야 하며, 어려운 이들을 도운 훌륭한 기록이 있어야 합니다. 후보자 추천은 1월 31일까지입니다.

기출 POINT

도입문은 비전 상의 취지에 대한 문장이다. 이어지는 문장의 furthering the winner's charity work라는 부분과 후보자의 요건으로 actively involved in any kind of service for the disadvantaged라고 제시한 부분에서 답을 찾을 수 있다. 혜택받지 못한 사람들을 위한 중요한 자원봉사를 표창하는 상이라는 (a)가 도입문의 내용으로 적절하다.

annual 연례의 **crystal plaque** 수정 상패 **banquet** 연회 **recipient** 수상자 **donation** 기부금 **further** 촉진하다 **charity** 봉사 **nominee** 후보자 **the disadvantaged** 어려운 사람들 **minimal** 최소한의 **means** 자금 **nomination** 후보자 추천 **the underprivileged** 혜택받지 못한 사람들 **substantial** 상당한 **contribution** 공헌 **outstanding** 뛰어난 **정답_**(a)

11

Archaeologists reported yesterday that they have finished uncovering a masterpiece of Mayan art that _____. This artifact, a 30-by-3-foot mural in vivid colors depicting the ancient culture's mythology of creation and kingship, is the centerpiece of a larger mural that, until recently, archaeologists dated to the culture's classical period. However, new tests have revealed that the centerpiece and larger mural are older than originally estimated, dating to about 100 BC. This indicates that the Mayan classical period, which was thought to have begun after AD 250, probably began much earlier.

(a) shows how authentic their use of color and shape was
(b) reveals an unusual use of symbols and writing methods
(c) suggests a surprisingly early flowering of the civilization
(d) proves that the Mayans knew their civilization was in decline

SOLUTION

어제 고고학자들은 마야 문명이 놀라울 만큼 일찍 꽃피웠음을 암시하는 마야 예술 걸작에 대한 발굴 작업을 마쳤다고 보고했다. 이 유물은 고대 마야 문화의 창조 신화와 왕권을 표현한 화려한 색채의 가로 30피트, 세로 3피트 크기 벽화로, 최근까지 고고학자들이 마야 문화의 고전기로 그 연대를 추정했던 큰 벽화의 중심부이다. 그러나 새로운 실험에서 이 중심부와 큰 벽화는 약 기원전 100년으로 거슬러 올라가 원래 추정했던 것보다 더 오래된 것으로 밝혀졌다. 이는 기원 250년 이후에 시작된 것으로 생각되었던 마야 고전기가 아마 훨씬 더 일찍 시작되었을 것임을 암시한다.

⊞ 기출 POINT
마야 예술 걸작을 수식하는 문장이 that 다음의 빈칸에 들어가야 한다. 새로운 실험을 통해 밝혀진 바에 따르면 이 벽화의 중심부와 큰 벽화는 추정보다 더 오래되었고, 이는 마야 문명의 고전기가 더 오래 전이라는 것을 암시한다는 내용이다. 그러므로 문명이 매우 일찍 꽃피웠다는 것을 암시한다는 (c)가 가장 알맞다.

archaeologist 고고학자 **masterpiece** 걸작 **artifact** 유물 **mural** 벽화 **depict** 표현하다 **mythology** 신화 **kingship** 왕권 **centerpiece** 중심부 **reveal** 드러내다 **estimate** 추정하다 **indicate** 암시하다 **authentic** 진짜의 **decline** 쇠퇴 정답_(c)

12

Ezra Pound played a large part in renewing English poetry in the Modernist era of the early 20th century. Yet he _____. He has been condemned as an elitist, an obscurantist and a charlatan—a man deficient in self-knowledge, with no real understanding of the modern world despite his Modernist posturing. And his fascist sympathies will forever taint his lofty conception of the artist and civilization.

(a) remains a flawed and controversial figure
(b) captured the spirit of his age like no other
(c) did not single-handedly revolutionize poetics
(d) defied the expectations of his literary colleagues

SOLUTION

에즈라 파운드는 20세기 초 모더니즘 시대 영시를 쇄신하는 데 큰 공헌을 했다. 그러나 그는 결함이 있고 논란이 있는 인물로 남아 있다. 그는 엘리트주의자이자 반계몽주의자이며 허풍선이로, 또한 모더니스트인 척하는 태도에도 불구하고 근대 세계에 대한 어떠한 실질적 이해도 하지 못한, 자기 인식이 부족한 인물이라는 비판을 받아왔다. 그리고 파시즘에 대한 그의 동조는 예술가와 문명에 관한 그의 고매한 관념에 영원한 오점으로 남을 것이다.

⊞ 기출 POINT
빈칸 앞에 나오는 Yet에 유의해야 하는 문제이다. 도입문과 반대 문장이 되어야 한다는 힌트를 가지고 풀이를 시작할 수 있다. 에즈라 파운드는 영시의 역사에서 중요한 인물이라는 것과 상반되는 내용이 빈칸에 들어간다. 문제가 있는 그의 여러 성향에 대한 나열이 이어지므로 그는 결점이 있고 논란이 있는 인물로 남아 있다는 (a)가 문맥상 적절하다.

Modernist era 모더니즘 시기 **elitist** 엘리트주의자 **obscurantist** 반계몽주의자 **charlatan** 허풍선이 **deficient** 부족한 **posturing** 가식적인 태도 **fascist sympathies** 파시즘 동조 **taint** 더럽히다 **lofty** 고매한 **conception** 관념 **flawed** 결함이 있는 **controversial** 논란이 있는 **single-handedly** 단독으로 **defy** 도전하다 정답_(a)

13

Early biologists who studied reflexes regarded these basic reactions to be inherited and common to all members of any given species. They also viewed instinct and learning as two separate aspects of automatic behavior. However, in some ingenious experiments, Josh Kalahan of the Milton University has demonstrated that certain automatic behaviors actually demand subtle forms of experience. In other words, _____.

(a) some instinctive behaviors are partially learned
(b) instinctive behavior can lead to violent situations
(c) learned behaviors are not always taught by parents
(d) human behavior can be explained by genetics alone

SOLUTION

반사신경을 연구했던 초기 생물학자들은 이 기본적인 반응은 모든 종의 전 개체들에게 유전되며 공통으로 발견되는 것이라고 여겼다. 그들은 또한 본능과 학습을 자동 행위라는 측면에서 별개의 것으로 보았다. 그러나 몇몇 독창적인 실험을 통해 밀턴 대학의 조쉬 캘러핸은 특정 자동 행위에는 실제로 미묘한 형태의 경험이 필요하다는 것을 보여주었다. 즉, 일부 본능적 행위는 부분적으로 학습된다는 것이다.

⊞ 기출 POINT

반사신경에 대한 생물학적인 연구이다. 빈칸 앞에 주어진 연결어는 In other words로 바로 앞의 내용을 다시 한번 설명하는 문장이 빈칸에 들어간다는 힌트를 얻을 수 있다. 본능과 학습은 자동적인 반사 반응에 있어서 별개의 측면으로 보았으나, 새로운 실험을 통해 어떤 자동적인 반사는 미묘한 형태의 경험이 필요하다는 것이 밝혀졌다. 즉 본능과 학습이 별개가 아니라 일부 본능적인 행동은 부분적으로 학습된다는 (a)가 정답이다.

biologist 생물학자 **reflex** 반사신경 **reaction** 반응 **inherit** 유전되다 **instinct** 본능 **separate** 이질적인 **ingenious** 독창적인 **subtle** 미묘한 **genetics** 유전학   **정답**_(a)

14

In 1865 the sculptor Rodin submitted his bronze head called *Man with a Broken Nose* to the Salon, an art gallery in Paris. The piece demonstrated all the rugged strength and realism that is characteristic of Rodin's style, but the Salon's jury rejected it. Rodin was not deterred, and years later in 1877, he submitted his life-size sculpture of a man, called the *Age of Bronze*, to the Salon. It was accepted, yet it caused an immediate controversy, for it was so lifelike that people thought it to have been cast from the living model. People found _____.

(a) Rodin's realistic sculptures to be better than those of other artists
(b) Rodin too preoccupied with the evil side of human nature
(c) Rodin's kind of realism too confronting and radical
(d) Rodin to be a persistent and determined man

SOLUTION

1865년 조각가 로댕은 〈코가 부러진 남자〉라는 그의 청동 두상을 파리의 한 아트 갤러리인 살롱에 출품했다. 그 작품은 로댕 스타일의 특징인 거친 힘과 사실주의를 여실히 보여주었지만, 살롱의 심사위원들은 이 작품에 퇴짜를 놓았다. 로댕은 이에 굴하지 않았고, 수년이 흐른 뒤인 1877년, 〈청동 시대〉라는 남자 실물 크기 조각을 살롱에 출품했다. 이 작품은 받아들여지기는 했지만, 너무나 실물 같아서 사람들이 이것을 살아 있는 모델 몸에 틀을 떠서 만든 것으로 생각했기 때문에 즉각적인 논란을 불러일으켰다. 사람들은 로댕의 사실주의가 너무 대립적이며 급진적이라고 생각했다.

⊞ 기출 POINT

마지막 문장은 People found라는 말이 있으므로 사람들이 빈칸의 내용처럼 생각했다는 의미가 되어야 한다. 로댕의 조각 작품에 대한 내용이므로 그에 대한 사람들의 생각을 중심으로 지문을 읽어야 한다. 너무나 실물 같아서 살아 있는 모델 몸에 틀을 떠서 만들었다고 생각하게 한 그의 작품을 통해 사람들은 로댕의 사실주의가 대립적이고 급진적인 것이라고 생각했다는 것을 추론할 수 있다.

sculptor 조각가 **submit** 출품하다 **bronze** 청동 **demonstrate** 보여주다 **rugged** 거친 **characteristic** 특징 **jury** 심사위원 **deter** 단념시키다 **controversy** 논란 **lifelike** 실물 같은 **cast** 상을 뜨다 **preoccupy** 사로잡다 **confronting** 대립적인 **radical** 급진적인 **persistent** 완고한   **정답**_(c)

Actual Test 2

15

The English Language Institute at Whitford College caters to international applicants seeking admittance to graduate programs at American postsecondary schools. Through an intensive 25-hour-a-week curriculum, students enrolled are given the opportunity to prepare for the challenges in language and communication inside American classrooms. The objective of the Institute, _____, is to equip its ESL students with the necessary language skills to achieve academic success in any degree program at an American university.

(a) however
(b) therefore
(c) additionally
(d) nevertheless

SOLUTION

휘트퍼드 대학의 영어 어학원은 미국의 중등 교육과정 이후 대학원 프로그램에 입학을 희망하는 국제 지원자들에게 적합합니다. 주당 25시간의 집중적인 교과과정을 통해 등록한 학생들은 미국 교실 내 언어 및 의사소통의 어려움에 대비할 기회를 가지게 됩니다. 그러므로 어학원의 목표는 ESL 학생들에게 미국 대학의 어떤 학위 과정에서라도 학업의 성공을 달성하는 데 필요한 언어 능력을 배양해 주는 것입니다.

기출 POINT
연결어를 찾는 문제는 빈칸 앞뒤의 맥락을 중점적으로 살펴야 한다.
어학원의 목표는 미국 교실에서의 원활한 언어 소통을 위한 교육과 미국 대학의 학위 과정을 해낼 수 있는 언어 능력을 길러주는 것이다. 마지막 문장에서 두 내용을 연결해 주면서 결론적으로 정리하고 있으므로 빈칸에는 therefore가 알맞다.

applicant 지원자 **admittance** 입학 **postsecondary** 중등 교육 이후의 **intensive** 집중적인 **curriculum** 교과과정 **enroll** 등록하다 **objective** 목표 **equip** 배양하다 **degree** 학위   정답_(b)

16

Acid rain is primarily the result of the release of sulfur oxides into the atmosphere. The main sources of such emissions are most likely electrical plants, industrial boilers and large smelters. Gases that are vented into the air by tall industrial chimneys get caught up in prevailing winds where they are converted into dilute solutions of sulfuric and nitric acids. _____, the acid rain problem partially comes from earlier attempts to clear air pollution by raising the heights of smokestacks.

(a) However
(b) Ironically
(c) Particularly
(d) Consequently

SOLUTION

산성비는 주로 황산화물이 대기 중으로 배출되기 때문에 생긴다. 이러한 배출물의 주요 배출원은 전력 발전소, 공업용 보일러와 대형 제련소일 가능성이 크다. 높은 공업용 굴뚝을 통해 대기 중으로 배출된 기체는 탁월풍에 휩쓸리고, 이 안에서 황산 및 질산 희석용액으로 전환된다. 아이러니하게도 산성비 문제는 부분적으로 굴뚝을 더 높게 만들어 대기 오염을 없애고자 했던 이전의 노력 때문이다.

기출 POINT
산성비에 대한 내용이다. 산성비는 높은 공업용 굴뚝에서 나오는 배출원들이 탁월풍에 끌려 황산 질산 용액으로 바뀌게 되어 생기는 것이다. 부분적으로 산성비 문제는 굴뚝 높이를 높여서 대기오염 문제를 해결하려고 했던 것 때문이다. 오염을 해결하려던 것이 오히려 오염을 만들어 내는 결과가 되었으므로 연결어로 적절한 것은 Ironically이다.

acid rain 산성비 **primarily** 주로 **release** 배출 **sulfur oxide** 황산화물 **emission** 배출 **electrical plant** 전력 발전소 **smelter** 제련소 **vent** 새어나오다 **prevailing wind** 탁월풍 **convert** 전환하다 **dilute solution** 희석용액 **sulfuric acid** 황산 **nitric acid** 질산 **smokestack** 굴뚝   정답_(b)

17

In the past, the value of money was determined by the value of the material from which it was made, such as silver or gold. However, carrying around a lot of precious metal was cumbersome and often dangerous. As an alternative, banknotes were introduced. These were originally a kind of promissory note for an amount of precious metal stored in a vault somewhere. But eventually, as banknotes became more widely used, they were accepted as equivalent to precious metal and given the status of paper money.

Q What is the passage about?
(a) What banknotes were once made of
(b) Why banks stored precious metals
(c) When cash became widely used
(d) How paper money originated

SOLUTION

과거에는 돈의 가치가 은이나 금과 같이 돈의 재료가 된 물질의 가치에 의해 결정됐다. 그러나 다량의 귀금속을 소지하고 다니는 것은 번거롭기도 하고 종종 위험하기도 했다. 대안으로 은행권이 도입되었다. 이것은 원래 어딘가에 있는 금고에 저장된 귀금속의 양에 대한 일종의 약속어음이었다. 하지만 결국 은행권이 더 널리 사용되면서 이것이 귀금속과 동일하게 취급되었고 지폐의 위상을 가지게 되었다.

Q 지문은 무엇에 관한 것인가?
(a) 한때 은행권의 재료가 되었던 것
(b) 은행이 귀금속을 보관해 두었던 이유
(c) 현금이 널리 사용되게 되었던 때
(d) 지폐의 기원

🏛 기출 POINT
처음에는 돈의 가치가 귀금속으로 결정되었지만 휴대의 불편과 위험 때문에 은행권이 생겼다. 이는 초기에는 약속어음 형식이었으나 현재의 은행권이 통용되면서 지폐로서의 위상을 갖게 되었다는 내용이다. 지폐가 처음 생기게 된 배경에 대한 설명이므로 정답은 (d).

precious metal 귀금속 **cumbersome** 번거로운 **alternative** 대안 **promissory note** 약속어음 **store** 저장하다 **vault** 금고 **banknote** 은행권 **equivalent** 동일한
정답_(d)

18

Preparing balanced, healthy snacks for children can be time-consuming, but a helpful tip is to get them used to eating cheese. Bread or crackers with cheese and an apple is a healthy snack which only takes 30 seconds to prepare. Moreover, your kids do not have to sit down to eat it; they can take it with them outside.

Q What is the main idea of the passage?
(a) Children should eat at regular intervals.
(b) Making snacks can be time-consuming.
(c) Eating between meals makes children fat.
(d) Cheese is one of the best snacks for children.

SOLUTION

아이들을 위해 균형 잡히고 건강에 좋은 간식을 만들어 주는 데는 시간이 많이 들 수 있는데, 한 가지 유용한 팁은 아이들이 치즈를 먹는 데 익숙해지도록 만들라는 것이다. 치즈를 얹은 빵 혹은 크래커와 사과 한 개는 건강에 좋은 간식이고, 만드는 데 30초밖에 걸리지 않는다. 게다가 아이들은 이것을 꼭 앉아서 먹을 필요없이 밖에 들고 나갈 수도 있다.

Q 지문의 주제는?
(a) 아이들은 일정한 간격을 두고 먹어야 한다.
(b) 간식을 만드는 것은 시간이 많이 걸릴 수 있다.
(c) 간식을 먹으면 아이들이 뚱뚱해진다.
(d) 치즈는 아이들에게 가장 좋은 간식 중 하나이다.

🏛 기출 POINT
첫 번째 문장에 주제가 나타나 있는 글이다. helpful tip으로 제시한 방법은 아이들을 치즈에 익숙해지도록 만들라는 것이다. 치즈가 들어간 빵이나 크래커와 사과는 준비하는 시간이 짧으면서 건강에 좋은 간식이라고 언급한다. 마지막 문장은 이런 간식의 이점에 대해 설명하는 내용이다. 따라서 정답은 (d).

time-consuming 시간이 드는 **healthy snack** 건강에 좋은 간식 **moreover** 게다가 **interval** 간격 **eating between meals** 간식
정답_(d)

19

Now, for the first time ever at the Apollo Museum, you can see the most accurately built representations of the famous machines envisaged by Leonardo da Vinci. The Apollo Museum is exhibiting over one hundred models of some of Leonardo da Vinci's unrealized machines and inventions created by artists and scientists from around the world. All models have been painstakingly based on Leonardo's original sketches. This amazing exhibition is at the Apollo from January 20 to March 10.

Q What type of exhibit is the museum announcement about?
(a) Da Vinci's machine models
(b) Da Vinci's original sketches
(c) Models based on Da Vinci's designs
(d) The evolution of Da Vinci's machines

SOLUTION

이제 아폴로 박물관에서 사상 최초로 레오나르도 다 빈치가 머릿속에 그렸던 유명한 기계들의 가장 정확한 구현물들을 보실 수 있습니다. 아폴로 박물관에서는 세상의 빛을 보지 못했던 레오나르도 다 빈치의 일부 기계와 발명품 중 전세계 예술가와 과학자들이 만들어낸 백여 개의 모델을 전시 중입니다. 전 모델은 레오나르도의 원본 스케치를 공들여 따랐습니다. 이 놀라운 전시회는 1월 20일부터 3월 10일까지 아폴로 박물관에서 열립니다.

Q 박물관 안내문은 어떤 종류의 전시회에 대한 것인가?
(a) 다 빈치의 기계 모델
(b) 다 빈치의 원본 스케치
(c) 다 빈치의 스케치에 기반한 모델들
(d) 다 빈치 기계들의 진화

⊞ 기출 POINT
박물관의 전시를 공고하는 글이다. 다 빈치가 상상했던 기계와 발명품들을 구현하여 만든 모델들을 전시하는 행사이다. 다 빈치의 원본 스케치에 기반하여 여러 예술가와 과학자들이 함께 만들어낸 작품들이라는 내용이므로 (c)가 적절하다.
accurately 정확히 **representation** 구현물 **envisage** 상상하다
exhibit 전시하다 **painstakingly** 공들여   정답_(c)

20

It is hard to believe that 19 computers can solve the problems of Dipichi, a tiny community in Haiti, where people battle daily against poverty, illiteracy and hunger. Yet that is exactly what US computer giant Hewlett-Packard (HP) and the Haitian government hope to achieve with a new IT lab being launched this month. The IT lab will provide information, education and training for Dipichi locals testing the theory that technology can tackle poverty. If successful, HP will introduce the lab concept to other destitute communities around the world.

Q What is the best title for the passage?
(a) Heavy Cost of Bridging Digital Divide in Haiti
(b) Computer Literacy Guarantees Quality of Life
(c) Delivering Low-Cost Technology to the World ↘
(d) Using Computer Technology to Combat Poverty

SOLUTION

19대의 컴퓨터가 사람들이 매일 가난과 문맹, 배고픔과 싸우는 아이티의 작은 마을 디피치의 문제를 해결할 수 있다는 것은 믿기 어렵다. 하지만 이것이 바로 이번 달 새로운 IT 실습실을 시작함으로써 미국 컴퓨터 대기업인 휴렛—팩커드(HP)와 아이티 정부가 달성하고자 기대하는 것이다. 이 IT 실습실에서는 기술이 빈곤을 해결할 수 있다는 이론을 실험하면서 디피치 주민들에게 정보와 교육, 훈련을 제공하게 될 것이다. 성공한다면 HP는 전세계의 다른 궁핍한 지역에도 이 실습실 개념을 도입할 것이다.

Q 지문의 가장 적합한 제목은?
(a) 아이티에서 기술 격차를 줄이는 데 드는 많은 비용
(b) 컴퓨터 활용 능력이 삶의 질 보장
(c) 세상에 저비용 기술 제공
(d) 가난을 이겨내기 위한 컴퓨터 기술 활용

⊞ 기출 POINT
디피치라는 마을에 19대의 컴퓨터가 있는 실습실을 만들어 마을의 변화를 일으키겠다는 프로젝트의 내용이다. 디피치 마을의 문제는 where 이하에 제시되어 있는 바와 같이 가난, 문맹과 배고픔인데, HP는 컴퓨터를 통해 정보와 교육과 훈련을 제공하여 기술이 가난을 해결할 수 있다는 전례를 보이겠다는 의도이다. 따라서 정답은 (d)이다.
community 지역 **battle against** ~에 맞서 싸우다 **poverty** 가난
illiteracy 문맹 **IT lab** IT(information technology) 실험실
launch 시작하다 **tackle** 다루다 **destitute** 궁핍한 **bridge** 격차를 줄이다   정답_(d)

21

Dear Sir,

I purchased a metal detector from your company for the amount of $225 and with a 30-day money-back guarantee. However, this product did not perform satisfactorily, so I decided to return it under the conditions of the guarantee. When returning the item, I opted to have the price of the product credited to my account. That was three weeks ago. Still, no credit has been applied to my account. Please look into this issue so that I do not need to take further action.

Q What is the writer's main point in the letter?
(a) He has been planning to buy a metal detector for weeks.
(b) He wants to know when his purchase will be delivered.
(c) He has not been given a refund for a returned product.
(d) He is going to take action if his money is not returned.

SOLUTION

담당자 귀하,

저는 귀사의 225달러짜리 금속 탐지기를 구매했고 30일 내 환불 보증을 받았습니다. 하지만 제품 성능이 만족스럽지 않아서 보증 조건 하에 제품을 반품하기로 결정했습니다. 제품을 반품하면서 저는 제품 가격을 제 계좌로 환급해 주는 쪽을 택했습니다. 이것이 3주 전입니다. 그러나 아직까지 제 계좌로 환불이 되지 않았습니다. 이 문제를 살펴보시고 제가 추가적인 행동을 취할 필요가 없도록 해주시기 바랍니다.

Q 편지를 쓴 사람의 요점은?
(a) 몇 주 동안 금속 탐지기를 사려고 계획해 왔다.
(b) 구매한 제품이 언제 배달되는지 알고 싶어 한다.
(c) 반품한 제품에 대한 환불을 받지 못했다.
(d) 돈이 환불되지 않으면 조치를 취할 것이다.

⊞ 기출 POINT

편지를 쓴 사람의 요점은 마지막 부분에 제시되어 있다. 금속 탐지기를 샀지만 작동이 만족스럽지 않아 환불받는 절차를 밟았는데, 3주가 지나도록 환급이 되지 않고 있다는 내용이므로 (c)가 정답이다. 3주 전 이후로 현재까지 계속되는 일이므로 현재완료를 사용하고 있다.

purchase 구매하다 **metal detector** 금속 탐지기 **money-back guarantee** 환불보증 **satisfactorily** 만족스럽게 **item** 제품 **opt** 선택하다 **account** 계좌 **issue** 문제   정답_(c)

22

The revolutionary sentiments of the 60s gave rise to a new kind of politician in the West, and nowhere is this better exemplified than in Canada's Prime Minister, Pierre Elliott Trudeau. A charismatic individual who came to power in 1968 with tremendous public support, he served as a stark contrast to the older, more conservative generation of politicians who had been ruling Canada. Trudeau refused to be encumbered by conventional party policies, but rather left everything open to question and welcomed change, especially in policies concerning foreign affairs and national defense.

Q What is the writer's main point about Pierre Trudeau?
(a) He represented a fresh and innovative approach to politics.
(b) He was passionate in his devotion to traditional party ideals.
(c) He focused his political strategy on foreign affairs and defense.
(d) He refused to let revolutionary attitudes influence his leadership.

SOLUTION

60년대 혁명적 정서는 서구에서 새로운 부류의 정치가들을 낳았고, 이의 가장 좋은 사례가 바로 캐나다의 총리인 피에르 엘리엇 트뤼도이다. 그는 1968년 엄청난 대중적 지지와 함께 정권을 잡은 카리스마를 갖춘 인물로 이전에 캐나다를 다스려왔던 더 보수적이고 늙은 정치 세대들과는 극명한 대비를 이뤘다. 트뤼도는 보수적인 정당 정책에 방해를 받는 것을 거부했고 모든 일에 쟁점의 여지를 남겨두었으며, 특히 외교 및 국방 관련 정책에서의 변화를 환영했다.

Q 피에르 트뤼도에 관한 요지는?
(a) 정치에 대해 신선하고 혁신적인 접근 방식의 표본이었다.
(b) 전통적인 정당 이념에 열정적으로 헌신했다.
(c) 그의 정치적 전략을 외교와 국방에 집중했다.
(d) 혁명적인 태도가 그의 통솔력에 영향을 미치는 것을 거부했다.

⊞ 기출 POINT

피에르 트뤼도에 대한 기술을 찾는 문제이다. 그의 성향에 대한 묘사나 설명 부분을 찾으면서 지문을 읽는다. 60년대의 혁명적 정서, 이전 정치인들과 대비, 변화에 수용적이라는 지문의 내용을 볼 때, (a)가 트뤼도를 가장 잘 묘사했다.

revolutionary 혁명적인 **sentiment** 정서 **give rise to** ~을 일으키다 **politician** 정치가 **exemplify** 예시하다 **charismatic** 카리스마 있는 **tremendous** 엄청난 **stark** 극명한 **conservative** 보수적인 **refuse to** ~을 거부하다 **encumber** 방해하다 **conventional** 전통적인 **foreign affair** 외교 정책 **passionate** 열정적인 **devotion** 헌신   정답_(a)

23

An old people's home in Sibbhult, southern Sweden found itself under siege from two drunken elks Friday night. The elks had become drunk on fermented apples they found near the old people's home and had threatened residents. Police arrived at the scene quickly, but their attempts to chase the elks away proved unsuccessful until a police dog was brought in to help. The dog scared the elks back into a nearby forest.

Q What scared off the elks?
(a) A police dog
(b) A police officer
(c) A drunken man
(d) Some neighbors

SOLUTION

스웨덴 남부 시불트에 있는 한 노령자들의 가택이 금요일 밤 술 취한 엘크 두 마리에 의해 포위당했다. 엘크들은 노령자들의 가택 부근에서 발견한 발효 사과를 먹고 취해 주민들을 위협했다. 경찰이 현장에 신속하게 도착했지만, 지원을 위한 경찰견이 투입되고 나서야 엘크들을 쫓아낼 수 있었다. 경찰견은 엘크들을 겁주어 부근 숲으로 다시 쫓아 보냈다.

Q 엘크들을 겁주어 쫓은 것은?
(a) 경찰견
(b) 경찰관
(c) 남자 취객
(d) 몇몇 이웃들

▦ 기출 POINT
세부 정보에 대한 문제 유형이다. 문제를 먼저 읽고 나서 지문을 읽으면 많은 시간을 절약할 수 있다. 지문의 중간 부분부터 엘크를 쫓아내기 위한 방법에 대해 언급하고 있다. 경찰이 시도했지만 성공하지 못했고 경찰견이 가까운 숲으로 겁주어 쫓아 보냈다는 내용이므로 정답은 (a).
siege 포위, 공격   **drunken** 술 취한   **elk** 엘크(북유럽의 큰 사슴) **fermented** 발효된   **threaten** 위협하다   **resident** 주민   **attempt** 시도   **chase away** 쫓아내다   **prove** ~임이 판명나다   **scare off** 겁주어 쫓다
정답_(a)

24

From ancient times, the Hawaiian island of Molokai was worshiped and feared as a center of mysticism and witchcraft. Then, starting in 1866, Hawaiians with Hansen's disease (leprosy) were abandoned on Molokai's Kalaupapa Peninsula to face death. The isolated settlement persisted in horrific circumstances until the arrival of Father Damien, a Catholic priest from Belgium, in 1873. He treated the settlers with dignity and gave them a sense of hope.

Q Which of the following is correct according to the passage?
(a) Hansen's disease originated in Belgium.
(b) Father Damien contracted leprosy in Hawaii.
(c) Molokai used to have a large leprosy hospital.
(d) Molokai lepers were helped by Father Damien.

SOLUTION

고대부터 하와이 섬인 몰로카이는 신비주의와 마법의 중심지로 경외의 대상이었다. 그러다가 1866년부터 한센병(나병)을 앓았던 하와이인들은 몰로카이의 칼라우파파 반도에 버려져 죽음을 맞았다. 이 고립된 부락은 끔찍한 환경 속에서도 1873년 벨기에의 천주교 신부인 다미엔 신부가 도착할 때까지 살아남았다. 다미엔 신부는 존엄성을 가지고 부락민들을 대했으며 이들에게 희망을 심어주었다.

Q 지문에 따르면 옳은 것은?
(a) 한센병은 벨기에에서 유래했다.
(b) 다미엔 신부는 하와이에서 나병에 걸렸다.
(c) 몰로카이에는 대규모 나병 병원이 있었다.
(d) 몰로카이 나병 환자들은 다미엔 신부의 도움을 받았다.

▦ 기출 POINT
하와이 섬인 몰로카이 반도에 한센병 환자들이 버려져 죽어가고 있었는데 여기에 벨기에의 다미엔 신부가 와서 이들을 돌보았다는 내용이므로 (d)가 지문과 일치한다. 나머지 선택지는 언급되지 않은 내용이므로 오답이다.
worship 숭배하다   **mysticism** 신비주의   **witchcraft** 마법 **Hansen disease** 한센병   **leprosy** 나병   **abandon** 버리다 **isolated** 고립된   **persist** 지속하다   **horrific** 끔찍한   **circumstance** 상황   **dignity** 존엄성   **contract** (병에) 걸리다   **leper** 한센병 환자
정답_(d)

25

The Detroit Zoo is to hold its fourth annual Earth Day Festival this weekend. The festival promotes the importance of worldwide conservation and environmental education through Earth-friendly activities. Children can participate in crafts, face painting and even wall climbing, all while learning about the importance of preserving our natural world. "Smokey the Bear" will also be on hand to give children and adults tips about the environment. All proceeds from the festival go to the zoo's conservation program.

Q Which of the following is correct about the Earth Day Festival?
(a) Its aim is to teach children the importance of education.
(b) It gives children information about the environment.
(c) It sells crafts that have been made by children.
(d) Its purpose is to promote the Detroit Zoo.

SOLUTION

디트로이트 동물원에서는 이번 주말 제4회 연례 지구의 날 축제를 개최합니다. 본 축제는 지구 친화적인 활동을 통해 세계 보호와 환경 교육의 중요성을 홍보합니다. 어린이들은 공예, 페이스 페인팅과 암벽 등반에 참여할 수 있으며, 그 과정에서 우리 자연계를 보존하는 것의 중요성에 대해 배우게 됩니다. '스모키 곰'도 출연해서 어린이와 성인들에게 환경에 대한 정보를 알려줄 것입니다. 축제의 수익금 전액은 동물원의 보존 프로그램에 쓰입니다.

Q 지구의 날 축제에 대해 옳은 것은?
(a) 어린이들에게 교육의 중요성을 가르치기 위한 것이다.
(b) 어린이들에게 환경에 대한 정보를 준다.
(c) 어린이들이 만든 공예품을 판매한다.
(d) 디트로이트 동물원을 홍보하기 위한 것이다.

🎫 기출 POINT

지구의 날 축제는 아이들에게 환경에 대한 정보를 주고 공예, 페이스 페인팅, 암벽 등반 등 환경 보존의 중요성에 대해 배울 수 있는 여러 프로그램이 준비되어 있다. 따라서 정답은 (b)이다.

annual 연례의 **conservation** 보호 **Earth-friendly** 지구 친화적인 **craft** 공예 **wall climbing** 암벽 등반 **preserve** 보존하다 **on hand** 출연하여 **proceeds** 수익 **aim** 목적 　　　　　　정답_(b)

26

Ardente presents Immortelle, our newest winter coat. It has a sophisticated single-button wrap styling, with pockets to complement its clean lines. But this coat isn't just for show. It's as comfortable as it looks and also practical. Our Italian mill created a special blend of wools to bring you a coat that's soft, warm and elegant, yet durable enough to be worn as part of your daily wardrobe. Look for the Immortelle, available at all Ardente boutiques across Europe.

Q Which of the following is correct about the Immortelle?
(a) It is suitable for everyday wear.
(b) It is made of polyester material.
(c) It is made by an Italian designer.
(d) It is designed for formal occasions.

SOLUTION

아르덩트에서는 최신 겨울 코트인 임모르텔을 선보입니다. 이 코트는 고급스러운 싱글 버튼 랩 스타일이며, 주머니가 있어 깔끔한 라인을 보완해 줍니다. 하지만 이 코트는 단지 보기에만 좋은 것이 아닙니다. 이 코트는 보이는 것 만큼 편안하며 또한 실용적입니다. 저희 이탈리아 공장은 부드럽고 포근하면서 우아한, 그러나 내구성이 뛰어나 일상생활에서 입을 수 있는 코트를 위한 특수 울 혼방을 만들었습니다. 임모르텔을 찾으세요. 임모르텔은 유럽 전역의 모든 아르덩트 부티크에 입점되어 있습니다.

Q 임모르텔에 대해 옳은 것은?
(a) 매일 입기에 적당하다.
(b) 폴리에스터 소재로 만들어졌다.
(c) 이탈리아 디자이너가 만들었다.
(d) 공식석상용으로 디자인되었다.

🎫 기출 POINT

최신 겨울 코트 제품에 대한 홍보이다. 임모르텔은 durable enough to be worn as part of your daily wardrobe이라는 부분에서 일상복으로 적당한 옷임을 알 수 있다. 울 혼방으로 만들어진 이 소재는 이탈리아 공장에서 제작되었으므로 지문과 일치하는 내용은 (a)이다.

present 선보이다 **sophisticated** 세련된 **complement** 보완하다 **mill** 공장 **blend** 혼방 **elegant** 우아한 **durable** 내구성 있는 **wardrobe** 의상 **boutique** 부티크 　　　　정답 (a)

27

There are two basic types of strengthening exercises: isotonic and isometric. Isotonic exercises are a type of resistance training that involves motion, expanding and contracting muscles in order to make them bigger and firmer. Weight lifting is the most common form of isotonic exercise. In isometric exercises, by contrast, there is little or no motion involved. You push as hard as you can against an immovable object or else tense your muscles for ten seconds. These exercises are usually used in physical rehabilitation for people who do not have the full range of motion.

Q Which of the following is correct according to the passage?

(a) Isotonic exercises are less active than isometric exercises.

(b) Isotonic exercises are not effective for people who are active.

(c) Isometric exercises are most suitable for physically fit people.

(d) Isometric exercises are good for people with physical limitations.

SOLUTION

근력 강화 운동에는 기본적으로 등장성 운동과 등척성 운동 두 가지 형태가 있다. 등장성 운동은 근육을 더 크고 단단하게 만들기 위해 근육을 이완하고 수축하는 움직임으로 구성된 저항 훈련의 일종이다. 웨이트 리프팅은 등장성 운동의 가장 일반적인 형태이다. 등척성 운동은 반대로 움직임이 거의 없거나 아예 없다. 움직이지 않는 물체를 최대한 세게 밀거나 혹은 10초 동안 근육을 긴장시킨다. 이런 운동은 몸을 자유자재로 움직일 수 없는 사람들의 물리적 재활에 일반적으로 사용된다.

Q 지문에 따르면 옳은 것은?
(a) 등장성 운동은 등척성 운동보다 움직임이 덜하다.
(b) 등장성 운동은 활동적인 사람들에게는 효과적이지 못하다.
(c) 등척성 운동은 신체적으로 건강한 사람들에게 가장 적절하다.
(d) 등척성 운동은 신체적으로 제약이 있는 사람들에게 좋다.

⊞ 기출 POINT
두 가지 근력 강화 운동 방식에 대한 비교 설명이다. 등장성 운동은 근육을 움직이는 운동이므로 활동적인 사람에게 맞는 운동 방식이고, 등척성 운동은 움직이지 않는 물체를 미는 방식이라서 움직임이 덜하고 신체적으로 제약이 있는 사람들에게 맞는 운동 방식이다. 따라서 (d)가 일치하는 내용이다.

isotonic 등장성의 **isometric** 등척성의 **resistance** 저항
expand 이완하다 **contract** 수축하다 **immovable** 움직일 수 없는
rehabilitation 재활 **range** 범위   정답_(d)

28

The US Treasury Department has integrated several new anti-counterfeiting measures to combat increased counterfeiting with home computers and printers. One method is the use of special color-shifting ink that alters its hue when viewed at an angle. Another method is to randomly embed very small pieces of reflective plastic into the linen paper already used. The Department also incorporates a thin, metallic line that runs from the top to the bottom of the bills. None of these methods can be reproduced on home computers.

Q Which of the following is correct according to the passage?

(a) Special paper with plastic implants can deter counterfeiting.

(b) Anti-counterfeiting methods have not changed significantly.

(c) Special ink is being used by counterfeiters on home computers.

(d) Home computers are now able to counterfeit any kind of bank note.

SOLUTION

미국 재무부는 가정용 컴퓨터와 프린터를 활용한 위폐 제조 증가에 맞서기 위해 몇 가지 새로운 위조 방지 대책을 통합했다. 한 가지 방법은 특정 각도에서 보면 그 색이 변하는 특수 색 변환 잉크를 사용하는 것이다. 또 다른 방법은 이미 사용 중인 리넨지 속에 매우 작은 반사 플라스틱 조각들을 무작위로 심어두는 것이다. 재무부는 또한 지폐의 위쪽 끝부터 아래쪽 끝까지 이어진 얇은 금속선도 집어넣는다. 이들 방법 중 그 어느 것도 가정용 컴퓨터로는 재현할 수 없다.

Q 지문에 따르면 옳은 것은?
(a) 플라스틱 이식물이 있는 특수 종이는 위조를 방지할 수 있다.
(b) 위조 방지 대책에는 크게 변화가 없었다.
(c) 특수 잉크가 위폐 제조업자들의 가정용 컴퓨터에서 사용되고 있다.
(d) 이제 가정용 컴퓨터로 어떤 종류의 은행권이라도 위조할 수 있다.

⊞ 기출 POINT
위폐 방지를 위한 방법에 대한 글이다. 컴퓨터와 프린터를 이용한 위폐 제작을 방지하기 위해 색 변환 잉크를 쓰거나, 종이 속에 반사 플라스틱 조각을 심어두거나, 위에서 아래쪽까지 이어지는 금속선을 넣는 방법을 이용하므로 (a)가 적절하다.

US Treasury Department 미국 재무부 **integrate** 통합하다
anti-counterfeiting 위조 방지의 **color-shifting** 색 변환 **alter** 바꾸다 **hue** 색조 **randomly** 무작위로 **embed** 파묻다 **reflective** 반사하는 **incorporate** 통합하다 **metallic** 금속의 **implant** 이식물 **deter** 막다. 그만두게 하다 **significantly** 상당히   정답_(a)

29

UN predictions paint a stunning picture of urban life in Asia in 2010. If current population growth and urban migration trends continue, 30 cities in Asia will have populations greater than 5 million (compared with 11 European cities and only two US cities). The largest will be Shanghai and Bombay, each with 20 million people. Beijing, Dhaka, Jakarta, Manila, Tianjin, Calcutta and Delhi will have more than 15 million people each. These figures will be the result of a shift from rural to urban living that is even now dramatically changing the face of Asia.

Q Which of the following is correct about UN predictions for Asia in 2010?
(a) Asia's population will grow partly because of immigration.
(b) More than 5 million people will live in each of 30 Asian cities.
(c) New cities will be created because of Asia's growing population.
(d) The current number of people moving to urban areas will double.

SOLUTION

UN의 예측은 2010년 아시아에서의 도시 생활에 대한 놀라운 모습을 보여준다. 현재의 인구 증가와 도시 이주 추세가 지속된다면, 아시아 30개 도시에서 인구가 5백만 이상이 될 것이다 (유럽 도시의 경우는 11개이고 미국 도시는 겨우 2개이다). 가장 인구가 많은 도시는 상하이와 봄베이로, 각각 2천 만의 인구를 보유하게 된다. 북경, 다카, 자카르타, 마닐라, 천진, 캘커타와 델리에는 각각 1천 5백만 이상의 인구가 살게 될 것이다. 이들 수치는 지금도 극적으로 아시아를 변모시키고 있는 이촌향도의 결과가 될 것이다.

Q 2010년 아시아에 대한 UN 예측에 대해 옳은 것은?
(a) 아시아의 인구는 이민 때문에 부분적으로 늘어날 것이다.
(b) 5백만 이상의 인구가 30개 아시아 도시 각각에 거주하게 될 것이다.
(c) 아시아의 늘어나는 인구로 인해 신도시가 생겨날 것이다.
(d) 도시로 이주하는 사람들의 수치는 배가 될 것이다.

🔠 기출 POINT

숫자와 지명 등이 나오는 이런 유형의 지문은 세부 정보를 정확하게 확인하는 과정이 필요하다. 2010년 아시아의 인구에 대한 UN의 예측은 아시아 30개 도시의 인구가 5백만 이상이 될 것이라는 내용이므로 일치하는 것은 (b)이다. 도시로 이주하는 인구의 증가는 언급되었지만 2배가 될 것이라는 예측은 없으므로 (d)는 오답이다.

prediction 예측 stunning 놀라운 urban 도시의 migration 이주 trend 추세 figure 수치 shift 이동 dramatically 극적으로

정답_(b)

30

Dear Sara,

I was sorry to hear you couldn't make it to our high school reunion. It's unbelievable to hear that you're living in Perth, of all places. As you may know, I remained near our hometown after graduating, so I have always been curious about what it would be like to live abroad. I'm not sure whether you know, but Jim Frobish also lives in Australia, though I think he's in Brisbane working as a machinist. On the other hand, Anne Singer moved to Singapore, where she is a manager at an international export company. I can email you their contact information or other people's, so let me know if you're interested.

Best wishes,
Allison

Q Which of the following is correct according to the letter?
(a) Jim is employed as a machinist.
(b) Sara manages an export company.
(c) Anne is currently living in Brisbane.
(d) Allison did not go to the school reunion.

SOLUTION

새라에게,

고등학교 동창회 모임에 올 수 없다는 이야기를 듣고 유감스럽게 생각했단다. 네가 퍼스에 살고 있다는 이야기를 듣고 믿기 힘들었어. 알겠지만, 나는 졸업 후에도 고향 부근에 남았고 그래서 항상 해외에서 사는 건 어떤 걸까 궁금했었거든. 네가 아는지 모르겠지만, 짐 프로비쉬도 호주에 살고 있어. 그런데 짐은 브리즈번에서 기계 수리공으로 일하고 있는 것 같아. 반면에 앤 싱어는 싱가폴로 이주했고, 그곳에서 국제 수출 회사의 매니저로 있어. 내가 너한테 짐과 싱어의 연락처나 다른 사람들 연락처를 이메일로 보내줄 수 있으니까 관심 있으면 알려주렴.

안부를 전하며,
앨리슨

Q 편지 내용에 따르면 옳은 것은?
(a) 짐은 기계 수리공으로 일한다.
(b) 새라는 수출 회사를 운영한다.
(c) 앤은 현재 브리즈번에 살고 있다.
(d) 앨리슨은 학교 동창회에 참석하지 않았다.

🔠 기출 POINT

동창회에 참석하지 못한 친구 새라에게 친구들의 소식을 전하기 위한 앨리슨의 편지이다. 짐은 호주에 살면서 기계 수리공으로 일하고 있고, 앤은 싱가폴로 이사해서 수출 회사의 매니저로 일하고 있다. 따라서 정답은 (a)이다.

school reunion 동창회 모임 live abroad 해외에서 살다 machinist 기계 수리공 contact information 연락처

정답_(a)

31

Robert Schumann was a Romantic composer whose most notable masterpieces were in the areas of choral music, Lieder (German art songs) and piano music. He usually composed at the keyboard, and he included the piano in almost every single piece of work. In many of his Lieder, voice and piano go side by side, with the vocal line adding yet another layer of tone to the piano score. However, Schumann made the piano partake fully in the expression of emotions in such tunes, and his most characteristic music often came after the vocal parts had finished.

Q Which of the following is correct according to the passage?
(a) Schumann's singing ability was one of his many talents.
(b) Piano played a crucial role in Schumann's compositions.
(c) Vocal components overrode the piano in Schumann's music.
(d) Piano pieces by Schumann are complex and difficult to play.

SOLUTION

로베르트 슈만은 가장 주목할 만한 걸작들이 합창 음악인 리트(독일 예술 가곡)와 피아노 음악 분야에 속하는 낭만파 작곡가였다. 슈만은 보통 건반에서 작곡을 했고, 거의 모든 작품에 피아노를 포함시켰다. 그의 여러 리트 곡에서 성부와 피아노가 나란히 진행되고, 성악부가 피아노 악보에 또 한 층의 음색을 더해 준다. 그러나 슈만은 그런 곡조들 속에서 피아노가 감정 표현에 온전히 한몫을 하도록 했으며, 그의 가장 특징적인 음악은 성악부가 끝난 후 시작되는 경우가 많았다.

Q 지문에 따르면 옳은 것은?
(a) 슈만의 성악 능력은 그의 여러 재능 중 하나였다.
(b) 피아노는 슈만의 작곡에서 중대한 역할을 했다.
(c) 슈만의 음악에서는 성악 요소가 피아노에 우선한다.
(d) 슈만의 피아노 곡들은 복잡하며 연주하기 어렵다.

🏳 기출 POINT

슈만의 음악적 특징에 대한 글이다. 그는 피아노를 거의 모든 작품에 포함시켰고 성악 파트가 들어가기 하지만 피아노가 중요한 감정 표현이나 특징이 되는 파트를 맡도록 작곡했다는 내용이므로 (b)가 정답이다.

composer 작곡가 **notable** 주목할 만한 **masterpiece** 걸작
choral music 합창 음악 **Lied** 리트 (복수형은 Lieder, 독일 예술 가곡)
keyboard 건반 **side by side** 나란히 **vocal** 성악의 **layer** 층
tone 음색 **score** 악보 **partake** 참가하다 **tune** 곡조 **crucial**
중대한 **component** 요소 **override** 우선하다   정답 _(b)

32

While most people think the fax machine is a modern invention, it was actually invented before the telephone. Scottish mechanic Alexander Bain patented his "electric printing and signal telegraph" in 1843, more than 30 years before the first phone was invented in 1876. Bain proposed using a scanning needle that could create an electrical signal when it touched a raised metal surface. The needle would be attached to a pendulum synchronized with another pendulum and needle on a receiving machine. Bain never built his machine, but Giovanni Caselli used much the same principle for a fax service between Paris and Lyon in 1863.

Q Which of the following is correct according to the passage?
(a) Bain's fax machine was forgotten until the last century.
(b) A fax service existed before the phone was invented.
(c) The first fax machine was first patented by Caselli.
(d) Bain started the first fax machine company.

SOLUTION

대부분 사람들은 팩스가 근대 발명품이라고 생각하지만, 실제로 팩스는 전화보다 먼저 발명되었다. 스코틀랜드의 기계공이었던 알렉산더 베인은 1843년 그의 '전자 인쇄 및 신호 전신'에 대해 특허를 얻었는데, 이것은 1876년 최초의 전화가 발명되기 30여 년 전이었다. 베인은 양각의 금속 표면에 닿으면 전자 신호를 만들어낼 수 있는 스캐닝 바늘의 사용을 제안했다. 이 바늘은 바늘과 같이 움직이는 또 하나의 추와 수신기에 있는 추에 부착되었다. 베인은 이 기계를 만들지는 않았지만, 지오반니 카셀리가 1863년 파리와 리옹 간 팩스 서비스에 거의 동일한 원리를 사용했다.

Q 지문에 따르면 옳은 것은?
(a) 베인의 팩스는 지난 세기까지 잊혔다.
(b) 팩스 서비스는 전화가 발명되기 전에 존재했다.
(c) 최초의 팩스는 카셀리가 처음으로 특허를 얻었다.
(d) 베인은 최초의 팩스 회사를 창업했다.

🏳 기출 POINT

팩스는 전화보다 30여 년 전에 알렉산더 베인에 의해 발명되었다. 베인은 1843년에 특허를 받았으나 실제로 기계를 만든 것은 카셀리였다. 본문에 베인이 팩스 회사를 시작했다는 언급은 없으므로 지문과 일치하는 것은 (b)이다.

patent 특허를 얻다 **signal** 신호의 **telegraph** 전신, 전보 **scanning**
스캔을 하는 **needle** 바늘 **raised** 양각의 **attach to** ~에 부착하다
pendulum 추 **synchronize** 동시에 일어나다 **principle** 원리

정답 _(b)

33

Conflict among siblings isn't unique to humans; it happens in every animal species that raises several young simultaneously. In most species, this rivalry is an important means of survival in the struggle for resources. However, that is not the case for human children who usually do not have to compete with each other for food and shelter. But other effects of sibling rivalry may prove crucial to their survival. For example, learning to cope with disagreements and disputes with siblings helps to promote important social skills, such as valuing another person's perspective, compromise and negotiation, and controlling anti-social behavior.

Q What can be inferred from the passage?
(a) A child without siblings will often have violent tendencies.
(b) Sibling conflict can have a beneficial effect upon children.
(c) Wealthy families are much more prone to sibling conflicts.
(d) Sibling conflict originates from a lack of basic resources.

SOLUTION

형제간 대립은 인간에게서만 볼 수 있는 것은 아니다. 이것은 몇몇 새끼들을 동시에 양육하는 동물 종 모두에서 볼 수 있다. 대부분 종에서 이 경쟁 행위는 자원을 위한 투쟁에서 중요한 생존 수단이다. 그러나, 이것은 일반적으로 식량과 보금자리를 위해 서로 경쟁할 필요가 없는 인간의 자식들에게는 해당되지 않는다. 하지만 형제 경쟁 행위의 다른 효과는 인간 생존에 중요한 것으로 밝혀질 수도 있다. 예를 들면, 형제와의 불화와 분쟁 해결법을 배우는 것은 다른 사람의 관점을 존중하고 타협하고 협상하는 등의 중요한 사회적 기술을 장려하고 반사회적인 행동을 통제하는 데 도움이 된다.

Q 지문에서 유추할 수 있는 것은?
(a) 형제가 없는 아이는 폭력적인 성향을 띠는 경우가 많을 것이다.
(b) 형제간 대립이 아이들에게 유익한 영향을 줄 수 있다.
(c) 형제간 대립은 부유한 가정에서 더 쉽게 일어난다.
(d) 형제간 대립은 기본적인 자원의 부족에서 생겨난다.

田 기출 POINT
인간의 형제간 경쟁 행위는 형제와의 불화와 분쟁을 처리하고 남과 타협하는 사회적 성격을 만들어가는 수단이 된다. 따라서 형제간 대립이 아이들에게 유익한 영향을 줄 수 있다는 (b)를 추론할 수 있다.
conflict 대립 **sibling** 형제 **simultaneously** 동시에 **rivalry** 경쟁 **resource** 자원 **crucial** 중대한 **cope with** ~을 처리하다 **dispute** 논쟁하다 **value** 존중하다 **perspective** 관점 **compromise** 타협하다 **prone to** ~하기 쉬운 **originate from** ~에서 기원하다 　정답 _(b)

34

Having gone through application forms and witnessed firsthand what young adults have to bear in order to get admitted to university, I have to say, something is seriously wrong with our university entrance system. As it stands, youngsters desiring to attend university must accomplish more than what their parents had to in their days. As Dean of Admissions, I see young people who run their own businesses, own patents and do PhD-level research, just to get accepted. Their whole world is centered around studying, and they don't seem to know about anything else in life.

Q Which statement would the writer most likely agree with?
(a) Youths are so focused on entering university that they lack other experience.
(b) It is difficult to select students among many equally qualified applicants.
(c) Teenagers waste too much time on things not associated with school.
(d) Exceptional achievements do not guarantee entrance to university.

SOLUTION

지원서 양식을 검토하고 십대 후반의 청소년들이 대학에 입학하기 위해서 어떤 일들을 감수해야 하는지 직접 보고 나니 나는 우리 대학 입시 제도에 무언가 심각한 오류가 있다고밖에 말할 수 없습니다. 지금 현 상태로는 대학에 다니고 싶어 하는 젊은이들이 이들의 부모들이 그 나이에 성취해야 했던 것보다 더 많은 것을 이뤄야 합니다. 입학 사정관으로서 저는 단지 입학을 위해 직접 사업을 운영하고 특허를 취득하며 박사 학위 수준의 연구활동을 하는 젊은이들을 봅니다. 이들의 세상은 공부 위주로 돌아가고, 이들은 삶에서 다른 어떤 것도 알고 있지 못한 것 같습니다.

Q 필자가 동의할 가능성이 가장 높은 진술은?
(a) 젊은이들은 대학에 들어가는 데 너무 집중한 나머지 다른 경험이 부족하다.
(b) 자격 요건이 동등한 많은 지원자들 중에서 학생들을 선발하는 것은 어렵다.
(c) 십대들은 학교와 관련 없는 것들에 너무 많은 시간을 낭비한다.
(d) 우수한 성적이 대학 입학을 보장해 주지는 않는다.

田 기출 POINT
필자의 전체적인 주장을 이해하고 그의 생각에 맞는 진술을 찾는 문제이다. 필자는 현 대학 입학 제도가 입학을 위한 활동에만 집중하고 다른 이외의 것은 알지 못하는 젊은이들을 만들어 내는 제도라고 비판한다. 따라서 정답은 (a)이다.
go through 검토하다 **application form** 지원서 양식 **firsthand** 직접적으로 **as it stands** 현 상태로는 **accomplish** 성취하다 **associated with** ~와 관련된 **exceptional** 우수한 　정답 _(a)

Reading Comprehension

35

The Tower of London, one of the most famous historical buildings in the world, was begun by the Norman King, William the Conqueror, who defeated Anglo-Saxon England in 1066. He built the Tower's central fortress not only to protect the city from invaders, but also to protect the conquering Normans from the people of London. It was begun in 1078 and was the most impressive structure most Anglo-Saxons had ever seen. It created a sense of fear and wonder for them that was intensified a century later when the tower was used to keep, torture and execute prisoners.

Q What can be inferred from the passage?
(a) The tower gave Londoners a sense of pride in their city.
(b) The tower served the Normans as a symbol of their power.
(c) Londoners fiercely resisted the rule of the Norman conquerors.
(d) William the Conqueror eventually converted the tower to a prison.

SOLUTION

전세계에서 가장 유명한 역사적 건축물 중 하나인 런던 타워는 1066년 앵글로 색슨 영국을 무찌른 노르만 왕, 정복자 윌리엄에 의해 공사가 시작되었다. 그는 단지 침략자들로부터 런던을 보호하는 것뿐 아니라 노르만 정복자들을 런던 주민들로부터 보호할 목적으로 런던 타워의 중앙 요새를 축조했다. 공사는 1078년에 시작되었고, 이 건물은 대부분의 앵글로 색슨인들이 보았던 구조물 중 가장 인상적인 구조물이었다. 런던 타워는 이들로 하여금 두려움과 경외심을 갖게 했으며, 100년 후 런던 타워가 죄수들을 가두고 고문하며 처형하는 데 사용되면서 이런 감정은 더 커졌다.

Q 지문에서 유추할 수 있는 것은?
(a) 런던 타워는 런던 주민들에게 런던에 대한 자긍심을 심어주었다.
(b) 런던 타워는 노르만인들에게 이들 권력의 상징으로서 역할을 했다.
(c) 런던 주민들은 노르만 정복자들의 통치에 격렬하게 저항했다.
(d) 정복자 윌리엄은 결국 런던 타워를 감옥으로 개조했다.

기출 POINT
런던 타워의 역사적 배경에 대한 내용이다. 앵글로 색슨인을 무찌른 노르만 왕, 정복자 윌리엄에 의해 공사가 시작되었으며 앵글로 색슨인들에게 두려움과 경외의 대상이었다. 또한 나중에는 죄수들을 처형하는 장소로 쓰였으므로 (b)의 내용을 추론할 수 있다.
defeat 물리치다 **fortress** 요새 **invader** 침략자 **conquer** 정복하다 **intensify** 강화하다 **torture** 고문하다 **execute** 처형하다 **sense of pride** 자긍심 **resist** 저항하다 **convert** 개조하다
정답_(b)

36

In the past, it has been difficult to show a direct causal link between exposure to violence and violent behavior. However, a new study by US researchers claims to have isolated the independent contribution to violence. They compared 1,500 teenagers from a variety of socio-economic backgrounds with a similar likelihood of being exposed to violence. The results seem to confirm people's suspicions: exposure to violence in turn breeds violent behavior among youth.

Q What can be inferred from the report?
(a) Acts of violence may be entirely justified in some cases.
(b) Watching violence and doing violence have no direct link.
(c) Teenage violence is an endemic problem throughout the United States.
(d) Ordinary individuals may commit violence if they are exposed to violence.

SOLUTION

과거에는 폭력에 대한 노출과 폭력적인 행동 간의 직접적 연관 관계를 보여주기가 어려웠다. 하지만 미국 연구원들의 새로운 연구는 폭력에 대한 독립적 기여를 분리해 냈다고 주장하고 있다. 이들은 다양한 사회·경제적 배경을 가졌으며, 폭력에 노출되었을 확률이 유사한 1,500명의 십대들을 비교했다. 그 결과는 사람들의 의심, 즉 폭력에 대한 노출이 결국 젊은이들 사이에서 폭력적인 행동을 조장한다는 것을 확인해 주는 듯하다.

Q 보고서에서 유추할 수 있는 것은?
(a) 폭력 행위는 일부 경우에 있어서 완전히 정당화될 수도 있다.
(b) 폭력을 보는 것과 행하는 것 사이에는 직접적 관련이 없다.
(c) 십대 폭력은 미국 전역에 만연한 문제이다.
(d) 평범한 사람들도 폭력에 노출되면 폭력을 자행할 수도 있다.

기출 POINT
폭력에 대한 노출과 폭력적인 행동 사이의 연관성에 대한 내용이다. 이 둘의 직접적인 연관 관계를 보여주는 한 새로운 연구는 폭력에 노출되는 것이 폭력적인 행동을 조장한다는 주장을 확증했다. 이것을 통해 (d)를 유추할 수 있으며, (b)는 반대의 내용이고 십대 폭력이 심각하다는 (c)는 언급되지 않았다.
exposure 노출 **violence** 폭력 **claim** 주장하다 **isolate** 분리하다 **independent** 독립적인 **contribution** 기여 **socio-economic** 사회 경제적인 **likelihood** 유사함 **confirm** 확인하다 **suspicion** 의심 **breed** 조장하다 **entirely** 전적으로 **justify** 정당화하다 **endemic** 만연한 **commit** 저지르다
정답_(d)

37

The government's failure to provide more funding for public housing is adversely affecting the working poor—those who are employed full-time but remain near or below the poverty line. And statistics back this up by clearly showing a direct correlation between affordable public housing and the ability to maintain employment. So the government needs to act quickly in resolving this public housing issue; otherwise, large scale, costly social problems associated with homelessness and unemployment are likely to emerge in cities across the country.

Q What can be inferred from the passage?
(a) The government should increase the wages of the working poor.
(b) Increased funding for public housing now will save money later.
(c) The economy is suffering as a result of the government's policies.
(d) Better employment opportunities should be available for the poor.

SOLUTION

정부가 공공 주택에 대해 더 많은 기금을 제공하지 못함으로써 가난한 노동자 계층, 즉 정규직으로 고용은 되어 있으나 빈곤선 부근, 혹은 빈곤선 이하의 생활을 하고 있는 사람들에게 부정적인 영향을 끼치고 있다. 그리고 통계치는 적정가의 공공 주택과 고용을 유지할 수 있는 능력 간에 직접적인 상관관계가 있음을 분명히 보여주며 이를 뒷받침한다. 따라서 정부는 공공 주택 문제를 해결하기 위해 발 빠르게 움직여야 한다. 그렇지 않으면 대규모의 높은 비용을 치르게 될, 무주택자와 실업과 연관된 사회 문제가 전국 여러 도시에서 나타날 수 있다.

Q 지문에서 유추할 수 있는 것은?
(a) 정부는 가난한 노동자들의 임금을 인상해야 한다.
(b) 지금 공공 주택에 대한 기금을 늘리면 향후 돈을 절약할 수 있게 될 것이다.
(c) 정부 정책의 결과로 경제가 고통받고 있다.
(d) 빈곤층에게 더 나은 고용 기회가 주어져야 한다.

기출 POINT

정부가 공공 주택에 기금을 충분히 제공하지 못해서 빈곤층에게 나쁜 영향을 주고 있다는 지적으로 시작한다. 통계를 볼 때 공공 주택 문제와 고용 유지의 관계가 밀접하기 때문에 빨리 이 문제를 해결하지 못하면 더 큰 규모와 비용의 사회 문제들을 떠맡게 될 것이라는 내용이다. 따라서 필자는 (b)를 암시하고 있다.

funding 자금 **public housing** 공공 주택 **adversely affect** 부정적인 영향을 주다 **statistics** 통계 **back up** 뒷받침하다 **correlation** 상관관계 **affordable** (가격이) 알맞은 **resolve** 해결하다 **costly** 비용이 많이 드는 **emerge** 나타나다 　　　　　**정답** (b)

38

Noisy lawnmowers disturbing the peace of a Sunday afternoon are not a problem in Japan. (a) Nor are Japanese homeowners bothered by neighborhood children kicking a ball into their backyard. (b) Japanese society is known for its politeness. (c) It is simply because hardly anyone in Japan has enough lawn to need a lawnmower. (d) Houses with backyards and lawns are rare in this crowded country.

SOLUTION

일요일 오후의 평화를 깨는 시끄러운 잔디 깎는 기계 소리는 일본에서 문제가 되지 않는다. (a) 이웃집 어린이들이 자기 집 뒤뜰로 공을 차는 일 때문에 성가셔 하는 일본 주택 소유자들도 문제가 되지 않는다. (b) 일본 사회는 공손함으로 유명하다. (c) 이것은 바로 일본에서는 잔디 깎는 기계가 있어야 할 만큼 넓은 잔디밭을 소유하고 있는 사람이 거의 없기 때문이다. (d) 뒤뜰과 잔디밭이 딸린 주택은 이 혼잡한 나라에서는 드물다.

기출 POINT

이웃의 잔디 깎는 소리나 공 차는 아이들의 시끄러운 소리가 문제되지 않는 곳이 일본이며, 그 이유는 일본에는 넓은 잔디밭이 있는 주택이 드물기 때문이라는 내용이다. (b)는 지문에서 제시된 이웃의 소음이 없는 이유와 무관하므로 글의 흐름에 맞지 않는 문장이다.

lawnmower 잔디 깎는 기계 **disturb** 방해하다 **bother** 성가시게 하다 **backyard** 뒤뜰 **politeness** 공손함 　　　　　**정답** (b)

Actual Test 2

39

No one knows when alcohol was first produced by humans. (a) Early hominids could have begun making it after experiencing the effects of eating fermented fruit. (b) This theory is supported by the way monkeys have been observed piling fruit in rock crevices and waiting for it to rot so they could drink fermented juice. (c) Giraffes have not been observed to get drunk by eating fermented fruit. (d) In any case, throughout history, wherever humans have had access to fruit, they have tried to make fermented beverages.

SOLUTION

언제 처음으로 인간이 알코올을 생산했는지 아무도 모른다. (a) 일찍이 원시 인류는 발효된 과일을 먹었을 때의 효과를 경험하고 나서 알코올을 만들기 시작했을 수도 있다. (b) 이 이론은 원숭이들이 바위 틈 사이에 과일을 쌓아둔 후 발효된 과즙을 마실 수 있도록 이것이 상할 때까지 기다리는 것이 관측되었다는 사실에 의해 뒷받침된다. (c) 기린은 발효된 과일을 먹고 취한 모습이 관찰된 바 없다. (d) 여하튼 역사를 통틀어 과일을 구할 수 있었던 곳에서라면 어디에서나 인간은 발효된 음료를 만들고자 시도해 왔다.

기출 POINT

술의 기원에 대한 추측을 다루는 글이다. 원시 인류가 발효된 과일을 먹은 효과를 경험하고 만들었을 거라는 생각, 원숭이들이 과일을 저장해두고 발효되면 먹었다는 증거, 인간은 과일이 있던 곳이라면 어디에서든 알코올을 만들려고 했다는 내용들이 제시된다. 하지만 (c)는 전체 흐름에 맞지 않는 내용이다.

hominid 원시 인류 **fermented** 발효된 **pile** 쌓다 **crevice** (바위의) 틈, 균열 **rot** 상하다 **have access to** ~에 접근할 수 있다 **beverage** 음료   정답_(c)

40

Modeo's Supreme Single-Serve coffeemaker boasts a line of improvements that enable you to fully personalize your home coffee experience. (a) Unlike our previous Modeo coffeemaker, this new model allows you to select from various serving capacities. (b) Aesthetic improvements include a new chrome silver body and an LCD display. (c) We have also added the refinement of an adjustable nozzle to accommodate different size mugs. (d) And it has a 33% larger water reservoir, enough to brew coffee for family and friends without refilling.

SOLUTION

모데오 사의 수프림 한 잔용 커피메이커는 여러분이 가정에서 커피 경험을 완전히 맞춤화할 수 있는 여러 개선 사항을 자랑으로 삼고 있습니다. (a) 모데오 커피메이커 구모델과 달리, 신모델은 다양한 서빙 용량을 선택할 수 있습니다. (b) 새로운 크롬 은색 몸체와 LCD 표시창으로 미학적 개선을 꾀했습니다. (c) 또한 조절 노즐을 더 세련되게 다듬어 여러 크기의 머그컵을 사용할 수 있도록 했습니다. (d) 그리고 물 넣는 곳이 33% 더 커져서 물을 다시 채우지 않고도 가족과 친구들에게 커피를 끓여줄 수 있습니다.

기출 POINT

커피메이커 신모델에 대한 내용이다. 새로 추가된 개선 사항으로 다양한 서빙 용량 선택, 여러 크기의 머그컵 사용 가능, 저수통이 커서 많은 양을 한 번에 만들 수 있는 기능이 있다. 크롬 은색 몸체와 LCD 표시창은 맞춤화하는 개선 사항과는 거리가 먼 요소이므로 흐름에 맞지 않는 것은 (b)이다.

boast 자랑하다 **personalize** 맞춤화하다 **capacity** 용량 **aesthetic** 미학적인 **refinement** 세련화 **adjustable** 조절할 수 있는 **nozzle** 노즐 **accommodate** 수용하다 **water reservoir** 저수통 **brew** (차를) 끓이다 **refill** 다시 채우다   정답_(b)

Answer Keys

🎧 Listening Comprehension

1	(c)	2	(b)	3	(d)	4	(c)	5	(b)	6	(b)	7	(c)	8	(a)	9	(c)	10	(c)
11	(d)	12	(b)	13	(c)	14	(b)	15	(a)	16	(d)	17	(a)	18	(d)	19	(a)	20	(c)
21	(a)	22	(b)	23	(b)	24	(d)	25	(d)	26	(b)	27	(c)	28	(c)	29	(b)	30	(b)
31	(a)	32	(d)	33	(a)	34	(c)	35	(a)	36	(c)	37	(d)	38	(a)	39	(a)	40	(d)
41	(c)	42	(b)	43	(c)	44	(d)	45	(b)	46	(d)	47	(d)	48	(a)	49	(c)	50	(b)
51	(d)	52	(a)	53	(d)	54	(b)	55	(b)	56	(a)	57	(d)	58	(c)	59	(c)	60	(d)

✏️ Grammar

1	(d)	2	(b)	3	(a)	4	(c)	5	(b)	6	(d)	7	(a)	8	(c)	9	(b)	10	(b)
11	(a)	12	(c)	13	(c)	14	(d)	15	(b)	16	(d)	17	(c)	18	(d)	19	(c)	20	(a)
21	(c)	22	(d)	23	(c)	24	(b)	25	(b)	26	(c)	27	(c)	28	(a)	29	(a)	30	(b)
31	(d)	32	(d)	33	(b)	34	(c)	35	(b)	36	(a)	37	(a)	38	(d)	39	(d)	40	(b)
41	(c)	42	(c)	43	(d)	44	(b)	45	(c)	46	(c)	47	(b)	48	(b)	49	(b)	50	(a)

📖 Vocabulary

1	(b)	2	(b)	3	(a)	4	(a)	5	(a)	6	(d)	7	(a)	8	(a)	9	(c)	10	(b)
11	(a)	12	(c)	13	(c)	14	(a)	15	(c)	16	(a)	17	(d)	18	(b)	19	(d)	20	(d)
21	(a)	22	(a)	23	(c)	24	(d)	25	(a)	26	(c)	27	(b)	28	(b)	29	(c)	30	(c)
31	(b)	32	(a)	33	(c)	34	(d)	35	(c)	36	(a)	37	(b)	38	(a)	39	(b)	40	(c)
41	(a)	42	(b)	43	(d)	44	(c)	45	(d)	46	(a)	47	(c)	48	(d)	49	(d)	50	(c)

📑 Reading Comprehension

1	(d)	2	(b)	3	(d)	4	(b)	5	(d)	6	(d)	7	(d)	8	(d)	9	(c)	10	(a)
11	(c)	12	(a)	13	(a)	14	(c)	15	(b)	16	(b)	17	(d)	18	(d)	19	(c)	20	(d)
21	(c)	22	(a)	23	(a)	24	(d)	25	(b)	26	(a)	27	(d)	28	(a)	29	(b)	30	(a)
31	(b)	32	(b)	33	(b)	34	(a)	35	(b)	36	(d)	37	(b)	38	(b)	39	(c)	40	(b)

1

M Where is the director's office, please?

W _____

(a) It's on the 6th floor.
(b) You just missed him.
(c) I keep it on my desk.
(d) I'm in my office now.

SOLUTION

M 소장님 사무실이 어디죠?
W 6층에 있습니다.

⊞ 기출 POINT

문장 처음에 나오는 의문사는 중요하므로 반드시 집중해서 들어야 한다. 장소를 묻고 있으므로 on the 6th floor라는 응답이 알맞다. 건물의 floor(층)는 서수로 쓰고 앞에 전치사 on을 쓴다. ex) on the top floor/ on the second floor

director 소장, 이사 **miss** 놓치다   정답_(a)

2

W When does the next flight for Paris leave?

M _____

(a) It'll take about six hours.
(b) That's where I'm going.
(c) It departs at 2:30 p.m.
(d) I'd like to visit there.

SOLUTION

W 다음 파리행 비행기는 언제 출발합니까?
M 오후 2시 30분에 출발합니다.

⊞ 기출 POINT

'출발하다'라는 뜻의 동사 leave와 동의어는 depart이다. 미래의 일이지만 예정된 출발이나 도착은 현재시제로 말한다는 것에 유의한다. 출발 시각을 알려주는 (c)가 정답이다. (a)는 '약 6시간이 걸린다'는 말이므로 때를 묻는 말에 알맞은 응답이 아니다.

flight 항공편 **leave** 출발하다 **depart** 출발하다   정답_(c)

3

M I don't feel like having lunch with Robert tomorrow.

W _____

(a) Robert can cook lunch.
(b) Let's make it tomorrow.
(c) You should cancel it, then.
(d) But you didn't eat that much.

SOLUTION

M 내일 로버트랑 점심 먹고 싶지 않아.
W 그럼 그 약속 취소해야겠다.

⊞ 기출 POINT

feel like -ing는 '~하고 싶다'는 표현이다. '내일 로버트와 점심을 먹고 싶지 않다'는 말에 대해 그럼 취소하라는 대답이 가장 알맞다. 약속이라는 단어가 언급되지 않았으므로 전체 내용에 집중해야 틀리지 않는 문제이다. (b) Let's make it tomorrow(내일로 하자)는 마지막의 tomorrow를 놓치면 답으로 하기 쉽다.

feel like -ing ~하고 싶다 **make it** (서로) 만나기로 하다 **cancel** 취소하다   정답_(c)

4

W How was your vacation?

M _____

(a) In Japan for a week.
(b) That's exactly what I did.
(c) Everything's planned out.
(d) I had a very relaxing time.

SOLUTION

W 휴가는 어땠어?
M 굉장히 느긋한 시간을 보냈어.

기출 POINT

How was your vacation?은 휴가가 어땠냐는 질문이다. How was...?라는 질문에는 한 일이나 느낀 것을 응답으로 말한다. relaxing time을 보냈다는 말이 가장 적절하다. (a)는 장소와 기간을 말하고 있으므로 오답이다.

exactly 정확히 **plan out** 계획하다 **relaxing** 느긋한 　　정답_(d)

5

M Thanks for treating me to a great dinner.

W _____

(a) I'm glad you liked it.
(b) It's my treat this time.
(c) You're welcome to join me.
(d) That sounds like a good idea.

SOLUTION

M 멋진 저녁 대접해 줘서 고마워.
W 마음에 들었다니 다행이야.

기출 POINT

treat A to B는 'A에게 B를 대접하다'라는 표현이다. 저녁 접대에 대해 감사를 표하고 있으므로 (a) '마음에 들어서 기쁘다'는 응답이 알맞다. (b)는 '이번엔 내가 내겠다'는 뜻이고, (c)는 '나와 함께 해도 좋다'는 의미이므로 상황에 맞지 않는다.

treat 대접하다 **sound like** ~인 것 같다 　　정답_(a)

6

W I'm out of printer paper. Do you have any?

M _____

(a) No, just a small one.
(b) I'm printing it out now.
(c) Wait. I'll get you some.
(d) That printer is very old.

SOLUTION

W 프린터 용지가 떨어졌는데, 너 혹시 있니?
M 기다려. 내가 좀 가져다 줄게.

기출 POINT

any는 앞의 명사 printer paper를 대신하는 말이다. (c) I'll get you some의 some 역시 printer paper를 대신하는 대명사로 쓰였다. printer paper는 셀 수 없는 명사이고 (a)의 one은 셀 수 있는 명사를 가리키므로 (a)는 오답이다.

out of ~이 떨어진, 다 쓴 **print out** 출력하다 　　정답_(c)

Actual Test 3

7

M Hey, Jennifer! I haven't seen you in a while.

W _____

(a) I met an acquaintance.
(b) Yeah. It's been months.
(c) I'll touch base with you shortly.
(d) Right, you haven't changed a bit, either.

SOLUTION

M 이봐, 제니퍼! 못 본 지 꽤 됐다.
W 응. 몇 달 됐지.

⊞ **기출 POINT**

인사말로 쓰는 I haven't seen you in a while은 '꽤 오랜만이다'라는 뜻이다. 응답으로는 (b) '몇 달 되었다'가 적당하다. 더 오랜만에 만났을 때에는 in a while 대신에 in years, for ages 등을 쓰거나 It's been years라는 표현을 사용한다. (c)는 '곧 연락하겠다'는 말이다.

in a while 한동안   **acquaintance** 아는 사람   **touch base with** ~와 연락하다   **정답_(b)**

8

W You're late again. What's your excuse this time?

M _____

(a) It's just not possible.
(b) I'm sorry about yesterday.
(c) I'm certain it wasn't me.
(d) My car broke down on the way.

SOLUTION

W 또 늦었구나. 이번 변명거리는 뭐니?
M 오는 길에 차가 고장났어.

⊞ **기출 POINT**

excuse가 '변명거리, 핑계'라는 뜻임을 알아야 풀 수 있는 문제이다. 늦은 사람에게 What's your excuse this time?이라고 하는 것으로 보아 상대가 자주 늦는 사람임을 알 수 있다. 변명으로 적절한 것은 (d)이다. break down은 '고장나다', on the way는 '오는 길에'라는 뜻이다.

excuse 변명거리, 핑계   **certain** 확실한   **정답_(d)**

9

M Hi, I'm calling to speak to Stacy.

W _____

(a) I'll give you my number.
(b) No problem. I'll go get her.
(c) You should speak to her about it.
(d) Sure. You can call her at any time.

SOLUTION

M 여보세요, 스테이시와 통화하려고 하는데요.
W 네. 바꿔 드리겠습니다.

⊞ **기출 POINT**

전화를 건 용건을 말하는 표현으로 〈I'm callling to+동사원형〉을 쓴다. Can I speak to Stacy?와 같은 말로 I'm calling to speak to Stacy를 쓴 것이다. 전화 관련 표현: I'll go get her. Will you hold the line please? 바꿔 줄게요. 잠시만 기다리시겠어요?

I'm calling to+동사원형 ~때문에 전화했어요   **정답_(b)**

10

W I wish I had studied harder this semester.

M _____

(a) I didn't think it'd be so hard.
(b) Your teachers must be proud.
(c) Review your notes once more.
(d) It's not too late to make up for it.

SOLUTION

W 이번 학기에 공부를 더 열심히 했더라면 좋았을 텐데.
M 만회하기에 아주 늦은 건 아니야.

기출 POINT

I wish 다음에는 가정법을 쓴다. 가정법 과거완료(had studied)이므로 과거의 일에 대한 것이며, '이번 학기에 열심히 공부하지 못했다'는 말이 된다. make up for는 '(부족한 것을) 보충하다, 만회하다'라는 뜻이다. 과거의 일에 대한 후회를 나타내므로 복습을 하라는 (c)는 적절한 응답이 아니다.

I wish ~라면 좋겠다   semester 학기   review 복습하다
make up for ~을 만회하다   정답_(d)

11

M It's a shame Bob injured his leg. He'll miss weeks of football.

W _____

(a) It's been tough missing a game.
(b) Yes, indeed. He made the finals.
(c) It's not too serious, so he may not.
(d) You're right. I'll pass on your advice.

SOLUTION

M 밥이 다리를 다쳤다니 유감이다. 몇 주 동안 축구를 못할 거야.
W 아주 심각하지는 않으니까 그렇지 않을지도 몰라.

기출 POINT

It's a shame (that)은 유감을 표시하는 말로 that 이하에 유감스러운 내용을 말한다. (c)는 may not 뒤에 miss weeks of football이 생략된 것으로 '상태가 심각하지 않으니 경기에 빠지지 않을 수도 있다'는 의미로 정답이다. (a)의 It's been tough는 현재완료로 쓰여서 '지금까지 빠지고 있었다'는 뜻이므로 부적절하다. (d)는 상대방이 적절한 충고를 했을 때 받아들이겠다는 내용이다.

It's a shame that ~이 유감이다   injure 다치다   final 결승
pass on ~을 전하다   정답_(c)

12

W How can I contact you at your office?

M _____

(a) I should be at the office soon.
(b) I'll do it after I check my schedule.
(c) You can reach me at extension 201.
(d) Please get back to me with the details.

SOLUTION

W 사무실에서 너한테 어떻게 연락하면 돼?
M 내선번호 201로 연락할 수 있어.

기출 POINT

How can I...?는 방법을 묻는 질문으로 여기서는 사무실로 연락할 방법을 묻고 있다. '연락하다'는 의미로 contact나 reach를 쓸 수 있다. ex) You can contact me./ You can reach me. extension 201은 내선번호가 201이라는 뜻으로 (c)가 정답이다. (d)는 다시 연락해서 자세한 정보를 달라는 말이다.

contact 연락하다   reach ~에 닿다. 연락하다   extension 내선
detail 세부 정보   정답_(c)

Actual Test 3

13

M Judy, what have you done with my trophy?

W _____

(a) No need to blame yourself.
(b) I moved it to polish the shelf.
(c) I agree you were sure to win it.
(d) Don't worry. I'll win the next one.

SOLUTION

M 주디, 내 트로피 어쨌어?
W 선반 닦으려고 내가 치워놨어.

⊞ 기출 POINT

What have you done with...?는 '~을 가지고 어쨌니?'라는 뜻으로 물건을 찾을 때 하는 말이다. 트로피가 놓여 있던 선반을 닦으려고 치워 놨다는 (b)가 가장 적절하다. (a)는 자책하는 사람에게 해줄 수 있는 말이고, (c)는 '네가 상을 타는 게 너무나 확실했다'는 데 동의한다는 의미이다.
trophy 트로피 **blame** ~를 탓하다 **polish** 닦다 　정답_(b)

14

W What's the best way to get downtown?

M _____

(a) I wanted to help, but I wasn't aware.
(b) I usually take a bus from downtown.
(c) You can, but the subway is better.
(d) You're better off grabbing a cab.

SOLUTION

W 시내로 가는 가장 좋은 방법이 뭐죠?
M 택시를 타는 편이 나을 거예요.

⊞ 기출 POINT

be better off -ing는 제안하거나 충고할 때 쓰는 표현으로 You're better off -ing/ You'd be better off -ing는 '네가 ~하는 게 나을 거야'라는 뜻이다. (a)는 과거시제라서 어울리지 않고 (b)는 downtown을 이용해 혼동을 주지만 적절하지 않다.
downtown 시내 중심가 **be aware** 알다 **better off** 더 나은, 더 행복한 **grab a cab** 택시를 타다 　정답_(d)

15

M It's a pity we have to work on such a sunny day.

W _____

(a) I couldn't agree more.
(b) Yes, it's looking really shiny.
(c) Thank you for making the offer.
(d) The work will surely be done today.

SOLUTION

M 이렇게 화창한 날 일을 해야 하다니 애석하군.
W 내 말이 바로 그 말이야.

⊞ 기출 POINT

It's a pity 다음에는 좋지 않은 일을 나타내서 '~해서 애석하다'는 뜻으로 쓰인다. 이 말에 대한 응답으로 동감을 표시하는 I couldn't agree more(전적으로 동감이다)가 적절하다. 부정문의 형태이므로 혼동하기 쉬운 표현이다. _상대방의 말에 동의할 때: I absolutely agree with you./ You can say that again./ That makes two of us._
It's a pity (that) ~이어서 유감이다 **make an offer** 제안하다
　정답_(a)

16

W This year's winter isn't very cold.

M It's because of global warming.

W Really? Will it be like this every winter?

M _____

(a) Whatever you say.

(b) I've noticed that, too.

(c) That's what I've heard.

(d) I didn't expect it to be so.

SOLUTION

W 올 겨울은 그다지 춥지 않네.

M 지구 온난화 때문이야.

W 정말? 겨울마다 이럴까?

M 그렇다고 들었어.

🏛 기출 POINT

지구 온난화에 대한 대화이다. 겨울마다 이럴 것인지 묻는 말에 대한 대답으로 가능한 것은 '그렇게 들었다'는 (c)가 적절하다. (a)는 '뭐든 말만 해'이고, 질문이 미래에 대한 예측이므로 과거로 답한 (d)는 오답이다.

global warming 지구 온난화 **Whatever you say.** 뭐든 말만 해.

정답 _(c)

Actual Test 3

17

M What's that awful smell?

W It's a durian, a kind of fruit.

M Wow, it smells bad for a fruit.

W _____

(a) But it tastes great.

(b) I like all fruits.

(c) I hope not.

(d) I'll peel it.

SOLUTION

M 이 고약한 냄새는 뭐야?

W 두리안이라고, 과일의 일종이야.

M 우와, 과일치고 냄새가 정말 고약하다.

W 그렇지만 맛은 좋아.

🏛 기출 POINT

It smells bad for a fruit은 '과일치고 냄새가 나쁘다'는 말에 대해 '맛은 훌륭하다'는 응답이 알맞다. Is Jenny still sick?과 같은 질문에 대해 '그렇지 않기를 바란다'는 응답으로 (c) I hope not을 쓴다.

awful 고약한 **durian** 두리안 (과일의 일종) **peel** 껍질을 벗기다

정답 _(a)

18

W Brad, can this jacket go in the washing machine?

M No, it's made of delicate fabric.

W What should I do, then?

M _____

(a) Take it to the dry cleaners.

(b) Put the temperature on low.

(c) There is nothing you can do.

(d) It should be washed regularly.

SOLUTION

W 브래드, 이 재킷 세탁기에 넣어도 될까?

M 아니, 그건 조심스럽게 다뤄야 하는 옷감이야.

W 그럼 어떻게 해야 되는데?

M 세탁소에 맡겨야지.

🏛 기출 POINT

delicate fabric이라는 말을 놓치지 않아야 풀 수 있는 문제이다. 섬세한 옷감으로 만들어졌으니 세탁기로는 안 되고 세탁소에 가져가라는 (a)가 정답이다. 온도를 낮게 맞추라는 (b)의 내용은 다림질과 관련된 말로 쓸 수 있다.

washing machine 세탁기 **be made of** ~으로 만들어지다

delicate 섬세한 **fabric** 섬유 **dry cleaners** 세탁소

temperature 온도 **regularly** 규칙적으로

정답 _(a)

19

M How long have you been here in New York?
W Umm, nearly a week.
M And are you enjoying it?
W _____

(a) This is my second visit.
(b) It's been fantastic so far.
(c) That's the part I enjoyed.
(d) Just for a couple of weeks.

SOLUTION

M 여기 뉴욕에는 얼마나 오래 있었어?
W 음, 거의 일주일.
M 좋은 시간 보내고 있어?
W 지금까지는 환상적이었어.

⊞ 기출 POINT
기간을 묻는 질문으로 How long have you p.p....?를 쓴다. Are you enjoying it?은 좋은 시간을 보내고 있느냐는 질문이다. 일주일 전부터 지금까지 이어지는 내용이므로 현재완료 시제가 사용된 (b)가 적절하다.

nearly 거의 **fantastic** 환상적인   정답_(b)

20

W Hi, Mark, how have you been?
M Very well. What about you?
W Oh, work has been keeping me busy.
M _____

(a) I'm glad to meet you.
(b) It's been the same with me.
(c) I'm heading off to my office.
(d) I just started my own business.

SOLUTION

W 안녕 마크, 어떻게 지냈니?
M 아주 잘 지냈어. 넌 어때?
W 아, 회사 때문에 바빴어.
M 나도 마찬가지였어.

⊞ 기출 POINT
안부를 묻는 How have you been?과 그 응답인 Very well. What about you?가 사용되었다. '회사 일로 바빴다'는 말에 (b)의 응답이 적절하다. '회사 때문에 바빴다'는 말을 무생물 주어인 work를 사용하여 work has been keeping me busy로 나타낼 수 있다는 것에 유의한다.

What about you? 너는 어때? **head off to** ~로 향해 떠나다
          정답_(b)

21

M Good morning. Can I help you?
W Yes, I want to post this package to Japan.
M How would you like to send it?
W _____

(a) Whichever way is quickest.
(b) I need to purchase a stamp.
(c) I'll mail it by this afternoon.
(d) The mail hasn't arrived yet.

SOLUTION

M 안녕하세요. 도와드릴까요?
W 네. 이 소포를 일본으로 부치고 싶습니다.
M 어떻게 보내시겠습니까?
W 제일 빠른 걸로요.

⊞ 기출 POINT
우체국에서 소포를 부치는 상황이다. How would you like to...?는 주문을 할 때 많이 듣는 말로 여기서는 우편물을 어떤 방식으로 보내겠냐는 질문이 된다. 가장 빠른 방법으로 하겠다는 (a)가 알맞다. 우체국 관련 용어: regular[express] mail 보통[빠른] 우편/ registered mail 등기/ express delivery 속달/ money order 우편환

package 소포 **purchase** 구매하다 **mail** 우송하다   정답_(a)

22

W Autumn is lovely in Korea.

M Yes, I love the colors of the leaves.

W And the weather is perfect.

M _____

(a) I prefer spring flowers.

(b) But it looks fine to me.

(c) It depends on the time of year.

(d) Right, not too hot and not too cold.

SOLUTION

W 한국은 가을이 아름다워요.

M 네, 저는 단풍을 아주 좋아합니다.

W 그리고 날씨도 완벽하죠.

M 맞아요. 너무 덥지도 않고 너무 춥지도 않아요.

⊞ 기출 POINT

한국의 가을에 대한 대화로 가을의 아름다움, 좋은 날씨를 언급한다. 이에 대해 (d)가 동감하는 부연 내용이므로 정답이다. (c)는 '연중 어느 때냐에 달렸다'는 뜻이다.

prefer ~을 선호하다   **depend on** ~에 달려 있다   정답_(d)

23

M That was a wonderful meal!

W It sure was. What did you like best?

M The smoked salmon.

W _____

(a) Mine was satisfactory.

(b) In that case, have two.

(c) I'll prepare it that way.

(d) Me, too. It was delicious.

SOLUTION

M 훌륭한 식사였어요!

W 정말 그랬어요. 제일 맛있는 음식이 뭐였어요?

M 훈제 연어요.

W 저도 훈제 연어가 맛있었어요.

⊞ 기출 POINT

It sure was는 상대의 말에 동조하는 표현이다. 음식 중에서 무엇이 가장 좋았냐는 질문에 대해 훈제 연어라고 답했다. 이 말에 동의하는 말이 (d)이다. (b)는 '그렇다면 두 개를 드세요'란 말이므로 식사 중이라면 가능한 답이 될 수도 있다. (c)는 '그런 식으로 준비할게요'라는 말이다.

It sure was. 정말 그랬어요.   **smoked salmon** 훈제 연어

satisfactory 만족스러운   **delicious** 맛있는   정답_(d)

24

W Hello. Can I speak to Evan Daley, please?

M Sorry, he's moved to the personnel department.

W Oh, then, please put me through to that department.

M _____

(a) Of course, I'll take you there personally.

(b) You can't go in at the moment.

(c) I'll let him know you called.

(d) Certainly. Please hold.

SOLUTION

W 여보세요. 에반 데일리와 통화할 수 있을까요?

M 죄송합니다만 에반 데일리는 인사부로 부서가 바뀌었습니다.

W 아, 그러면 그 부서로 제 전화를 돌려주세요.

M 알겠습니다. 끊지 말고 기다리세요.

⊞ 기출 POINT

전화를 다른 사람이나 부서로 '연결해 주다'는 표현은 put through이다. Please hold는 끊지 말고 기다리라는 말로 (d)가 정답이다. (c)의 I'll let him know you called는 '전화 온 것을 전하겠다'는 표현이다.

personnel department 인사부   **personally** 직접   **I'll let him know you called.** 전화했다고 전해 드릴게요.   **Please hold.** 기다리세요.   정답_(d)

25

M What are your career plans for after college?

W I want to get a job in a large corporation.

M Do you have any specific one in mind?

W _____

(a) I might go abroad or continue studying.

(b) No, I'm planning to apply to several.

(c) I'll be graduating next year.

(d) No, I don't mind it at all.

SOLUTION

M 대학 졸업 후 진로 계획이 어떻게 되니?

W 대기업에 일자리를 얻고 싶어.

M 구체적으로 마음에 두고 있는 곳이 있어?

W 아니, 몇 군데 지원해 볼 계획이야.

기출 POINT

career plan은 '직업 진로에 대한 계획'을 말한다. one은 앞에서 말한 large corporation을 가리킨다. 구체적으로 마음에 두고 있는 특정 대기업이 있냐는 질문에 하나를 정해두지 않았고 몇 군데 지원할 계획이라는 내용이 자연스럽다. 계획을 말하는 표현으로 〈I'm planning to+동사원형〉을 사용한다. 미래의 계획에 대해 I'll be graduating next year처럼 미래진행 시제를 쓰는 것도 기억해 두어야 한다.

career 직업 **corporation** 기업 **I don't mind it at all.** 정말 괜찮아요. 정답_(b)

26

W Tony! You still haven't changed the bathroom light bulb.

M Don't worry. I'll do it.

W But why didn't you do it this morning when I asked?

M _____

(a) I'll be ready in five minutes.

(b) I hope you don't mind the wait.

(c) It took me all morning to change it.

(d) There was an important game on TV.

SOLUTION

W 토니! 아직 화장실 전구 안 갈았구나.

M 걱정 마. 내가 할 거야.

W 하지만 왜 오늘 아침에 내가 부탁했을 때 안 했어?

M TV에서 중요한 경기를 방영하고 있었어.

기출 POINT

과거부터 현재까지 계속되는 일이니까 현재완료 시제로 still haven't changed라고 말하고 있다. this morning when I asked라는 과거 시점이 나오면 why didn't you do처럼 과거시제로 쓴다는 것에 유의한다. 부탁받은 대로 하지 않은 이유로 (d)가 타당하다.

light bulb 전구 **wait** 기다림, 지연 정답_(d)

27

M Are you going to try out for the school play?

W No, I don't think so.

M Why not? You'll surely get a role.

W _____

(a) The odds are in our favor.

(b) I doubt it. It's very competitive.

(c) I guess I'm a pretty good player.

(d) No, I'm not going to the play tonight.

SOLUTION

M 학교 연극에 나가볼 거니?

W 아니, 안 할 것 같아.

M 왜? 너라면 분명 배역을 받을 텐데.

W 글쎄. 경쟁이 굉장히 치열해서 말이야.

기출 POINT

학교 연극 선발 시험에 나가볼 거냐고 묻는 질문에 I don't think so라고 대답한다. 분명히 배역을 따낼 것이라는 말에 의구심을 표현하는 말로 (b)가 적절하다. (a)는 '우리 편이 유리하다'는 말이다.

try out for ~을 위한 적격 시험을 보다 **odds** 유리한 조건 **doubt** 의심하다 **competitive** 경쟁이 치열한 정답_(b)

28

W　Would you like to go out for a movie after work?

M　Sure, that'd be great.

W　What if we meet around 6 in the lobby?

M　_____

(a) All right, but don't let it delay you.

(b) That's a bit early. Make it 6:30.

(c) I'll buy the ticket first.

(d) I'll be ready for you.

SOLUTION

W　퇴근하고 같이 영화보러 갈래?

M　좋아. 그거 좋겠다.

W　로비에서 6시경에 만나면 어떨까?

M　그건 좀 이른데. 6시 반으로 하자.

기출 POINT

What if...?는 '~라면 어떨까?'라는 제안의 말로 쓰인다. 제안한 시각이 너무 이르니 좀 더 늦은 시각으로 하자는 (b)가 적절한 응답이다. (b)에서 Make it은 '만나기로 하다'는 뜻으로 사용되었다. (a)는 그것 때문에 늦지 않도록 하라는 말이므로 문맥상 맞지 않다.

What if...? ~하면 어떨까?　**lobby** 로비　**delay** 지연시키다　정답_(b)

29

M　I wouldn't talk to John about his job.

W　Why? What happened?

M　He got laid off, and he's very sensitive about it.

W　_____

(a) I won't bring it up, then.

(b) Yeah, he can be very picky.

(c) It saddens me to see him go.

(d) Okay, I'll help him look for one.

SOLUTION

M　나라면 존에게 그의 일에 대해서는 언급하지 않을 거야.

W　왜? 무슨 일 있었어?

M　해고당했고, 거기에 대해서 굉장히 예민해.

W　그럼 그 이야기는 꺼내지 않을게.

기출 POINT

⟨I wouldn't+동사원형⟩은 가정법 형태의 문장으로 '나라면 ~하지 않을 거야'라는 표현이다. 존이 해고를 당해서 예민하다는 말에 그 이야기를 꺼내지 않을 것이라는 (a)가 정답이다.

get laid off 해고당하다　**sensitive** 예민한　**picky** 까다로운

sadden 슬프게 하다　정답_(a)

30

W　The presentation you prepared looks great.

M　Thanks. I hope it helps in getting our proposal accepted.

W　Well, it'll definitely boost our chances.

M　_____

(a) I promise I'll try harder next time.

(b) I suppose that depends on the proposal.

(c) A lot went into it, so I hope you're right.

(d) Come on, let's not start apportioning blame.

SOLUTION

W　네가 준비한 프레젠테이션 훌륭해 보인다.

M　고마워. 우리 제안이 받아들여지는 데 도움이 되면 좋겠어.

W　분명 가능성을 높여줄 거야.

M　거기에 많은 걸 투자했으니까 네 말대로 됐으면 좋겠어.

기출 POINT

it helps in -ing는 '~하는 데 도움이 되다'라는 뜻이고, boost our chances는 '가능성을 높이다'라는 표현이다. 남자의 프레젠테이션이 도움이 될 것이라는 여자의 말에 대한 응답으로 (c)가 적절하다. (d)는 남의 탓으로 돌리려는 사람에게 해줄 수 있는 말이다.

presentation 프레젠테이션, 발표　**proposal** 제안　**definitely** 분명히

boost 높이다　**chance** 가능성　**apportion** 할당하다　정답_(c)

31

W   I can't decide what to order.
M   Well, I'm going to have spaghetti.
W   Hmm. That sounds good.
M   Yes, I'll get the seafood one.
W   Actually, I'll have that as well.
M   Okay, I'll order two of these, then.

Q   What is the conversation mainly about?
(a) Cooking a spaghetti dish.
(b) Choosing a good restaurant.
(c) Deciding which meal to have.
(d) Taking orders from customers.

SOLUTION

W   뭘 주문할지 결정을 못하겠어.
M   나는 스파게티를 시킬 거야.
W   음. 그거 괜찮은데.
M   응. 난 해물 스파게티로 하려고.
W   그럼 말이야. 나도 그걸 주문할게.
M   좋아. 그럼 이걸로 두 개 주문할게.
Q   대화의 주된 내용은?
(a) 스파게티 요리하기.
(b) 좋은 식당 선택하기.
(c) 식사 메뉴 결정하기.
(d) 주문받기.

⊞ 기출 POINT

첫 번째 말에 주제가 나오는 경우가 많으니 반드시 집중해서 들어야 한다. what to order에 대해 서로의 의견을 나누는 내용이 주가 되므로 (c)가 답이다. '~을 먹겠다'는 말로 I'm going to have/ I'll get/ I'll have 등의 표현을 쓰고 있다.
order 주문하다   **actually** 사실   정답_(c)

32

W   Ed, we missed you at bingo night.
M   I know. I wasn't feeling very well.
W   You'll come to the next one, won't you?
M   It depends on whether I have the time.
W   Well, I hope you can come.
M   Yeah, I'll try to.

Q   What is mainly being discussed in the conversation?
(a) The man's luck at bingo.
(b) The man's interest in going out.
(c) The man's participation in bingo night.
(d) The man's excuse for not playing bingo.

SOLUTION

W   에드, 너 어젯밤 빙고 파티에 안 왔더라.
M   그래. 몸이 별로 안 좋았어.
W   다음번 빙고에는 올 거지?
M   시간 되면 가겠지.
W   음. 네가 올 수 있으면 좋겠다.
M   응. 노력해 볼게.
Q   대화에서 주로 논의되고 있는 것은?
(a) 남자의 빙고 운.
(b) 남자의 외출에 대한 관심.
(c) 남자의 빙고 파티 참여.
(d) 남자가 빙고를 하지 않는 핑계.

⊞ 기출 POINT

bingo night은 '밤에 모여서 빙고를 하는 모임'이다. 이런 문화에 대해 잘 모른다고 하더라도 missed나 come to the next one, hope you can come에서 bingo night이 정기적으로 모이는 행사임을 알 수 있다. 남자의 참여에 대한 논의가 주된 것이므로 정답은 (c)이다.
I wasn't feeling very well. 몸이 좋지 않았어.   **It depends on...**
~에 달려 있다   **participation** 참여   **excuse** 핑계   정답_(c)

33

M So, when do we arrive in Frankfurt?

W Our flight lands around one in the morning.

M How will we find a hotel that early in the morning?

W I guess there will be some near the airport.

M They'll be expensive, though.

W But it's only for one night.

Q What are the man and woman mainly discussing?

(a) Finding accommodation in Frankfurt.

(b) Staying in Frankfurt for a vacation.

(c) Landing in Frankfurt late at night.

(d) Booking seats on a flight.

SOLUTION

M 그래서, 프랑크푸르트에는 언제 도착해?

W 우리 비행기는 새벽 한 시쯤 착륙해.

M 그 새벽에 호텔은 어떻게 잡지?

W 공항 근처에 호텔이 좀 있을 거야.

M 하지만 비쌀 텐데.

W 그래도 1박만 하는 거니까.

Q 남자와 여자가 논의하는 내용은?

(a) 프랑크푸르트에서 숙소를 찾는 것.

(b) 휴가로 프랑크푸르트에 머무는 것.

(c) 밤늦게 프랑크푸르트에 착륙하는 것.

(d) 비행기 좌석을 예약하는 것.

⊞ 기출 POINT

새벽에 프랑크푸르트에 도착하여 호텔을 찾는 일에 대해 논의하고 있다. 비싸지만 하루니까 공항 근처로 구하자는 의견을 나누는 내용이다. hotel 대신에 accommodation이라는 단어를 알면 쉽게 풀 수 있는 문제이다. (c)는 대화의 앞부분에 국한된 주제이다. 이렇게 Part 3의 대의 파악 문제에서는 지엽적인 사실을 진술한 오답 함정에 주의해야 한다.

land 착륙하다   **accommodation** 숙소   **book** ~을 예약하다

정답_(a)

34

M Professor Marcus, could I audit your class?

W Yes, you're welcome to sit in on my class on one condition.

M Oh, what might that be?

W Well, I expect auditing students to attend class regularly.

M Oh, don't worry. I'll turn up for every class.

W Good. Then I'll see you in my next class.

Q What is the man mainly doing in the conversation?

(a) Promising to come to class on time.

(b) Obtaining permission to audit a class.

(c) Getting advice on improving his grade.

(d) Inquiring about getting private lessons.

SOLUTION

M 마커스 교수님. 교수님 강의를 청강해도 될까요?

W 그럼. 내 수업에 들어오는 건 좋은데 한 가지 조건이 있어.

M 아, 그게 뭘까요?

W 음. 청강생들은 강의에 빠지지 않고 출석해 주길 바란다.

M 아, 걱정 마세요. 저는 모든 수업에 출석할 겁니다.

W 좋아. 그럼. 다음번 내 수업 시간에 보자꾸나.

Q 남자가 대화에서 하고 있는 일은?

(a) 수업에 정시에 오겠다고 약속하는 것.

(b) 청강에 대한 허가를 얻는 것.

(c) 학점을 높이기 위한 조언을 구하는 것.

(d) 개인 교습을 받기 위해 문의하는 것.

⊞ 기출 POINT

강의를 청강해도 좋을지 묻는 질문으로 시작되는 대화이다. you're welcome to sit in on my class와 I'll see you in my next class에서 청강 허락을 받은 것임을 알 수 있다. 청강생은 auditing student라고 한다. 〈expect+목적어+to+동사원형〉은 '목적어가 ~하기를 기대하다'라는 표현이다.

auditing student 청강생   **turn up** 나타나다   **private lesson** 개인교습

정답_(b)

Actual Test 3

35

W Paul, you bought a new camera recently, didn't you?
M Yeah, I got a good digital one.
W I want to buy a camera too, but I don't know what to get.
M Well, you could search online for something you like.
W Is that what you did?
M Yeah, that way I could compare models easily.

Q What is the main topic of the conversation?
(a) How to shop for a camera.
(b) Where to buy cameras online.
(c) Where to buy the best digital cameras.
(d) How to compare the prices of cameras.

SOLUTION

W 폴, 너 최근에 새 카메라 사지 않았니?
M 응, 좋은 디지털 카메라를 샀지.
W 나도 카메라를 사고 싶은데, 뭘 사야 할지 모르겠어.
M 음, 네가 좋아하는 걸 인터넷으로 검색할 수 있을 거야.
W 너도 그렇게 했어?
M 응, 그렇게 해서 모델들을 쉽게 비교할 수 있었어.

Q 대화의 주된 화제는?
(a) 카메라 쇼핑법.
(b) 인터넷에서 카메라를 살 수 있는 곳.
(c) 최고의 디지털 카메라를 살 수 있는 곳.
(d) 카메라 가격 비교법.

기출 POINT
최근 카메라를 산 사람이 사려고 하는 사람에게 인터넷 검색을 통한 쇼핑을 제안하는 내용이므로 정답은 (a)이다. 인터넷에서 카메라를 사라고 조언한 것은 아니므로 (b)는 오답이다.
recently 최근에 **search online** 인터넷을 검색하다   정답_(a)

36

M Thanks for helping me clean out my dad's attic.
W Oh, it's interesting—all of the stuff here.
M Yeah. He never liked to throw anything out.
W I wonder what we'll find.
M Well, let's focus on moving everything downstairs first.
W Okay. Where should we begin?
M We'll start with these boxes.

Q What is the conversation mainly about?
(a) The cleaning out of the attic.
(b) The amount of things in the attic.
(c) The things the man's father found.
(d) The personality of the man's father.

SOLUTION

M 우리 아버지 다락방 청소하는 걸 도와줘서 고마워.
W 아, 재미있는데 뭘. 여기 있는 물건들이 전부 다 흥미로워.
M 응. 아버지는 물건 버리는 걸 좋아하지 않으셨거든.
W 뭘 찾아낼지 궁금한데.
M 음, 우선 전부 아래층으로 옮기는 것부터 하자.
W 좋아. 뭐부터 시작할까?
M 이 상자들부터 시작할 거야.

Q 대화의 주된 내용은?
(a) 다락방을 청소하는 것.
(b) 다락방에 있는 물건의 양.
(c) 남자의 아버지가 찾아낸 물건들.
(d) 남자 아버지의 성격.

기출 POINT
아버지의 다락방을 청소하는 일에 대한 대화이다. He never liked to throw anything out을 통해 아버지가 버리는 걸 좋아하지 않아서 물건이 많이 쌓여 있다는 것을 알 수 있다. 박스부터 시작해서 물건을 아래층으로 옮기자는 말도 청소하는 것에 대한 것이므로 (a)가 정답이다.
attic 다락방 **stuff** 물건 **throw out** 버리다 **downstairs** 아래층으로
personality 성격   정답_(a)

37

M I'm not sure starting my own business was a good move.

W Why not? You said it would do well.

M I know, but it's not covering the loan I took out to finance it.

W I'm sure you'll get on top of things eventually.

M I hope so, but business is slow at the moment.

W Don't worry. Things are bound to pick up.

Q What is the woman doing in the conversation?
(a) Advising the man to take risks.
(b) Encouraging the man to work harder.
(c) Telling the man how to finance a business.
(d) Reassuring the man of his business venture.

SOLUTION

M 내 사업을 시작하는 게 잘한 일인지 모르겠어.

W 왜? 잘될 거라고 말했잖아.

M 알아. 그런데 사업 자금을 조달하느라 받은 대출을 감당하지 못하는 상황이야.

W 넌 결국 다 극복해 낼 거라고 확신해.

M 나도 그랬으면 좋겠어. 그런데 지금 사업이 침체기라서.

W 걱정 마. 상황은 좋아지기 마련이니까.

Q 대화에서 여자가 하고 있는 일은?
(a) 남자에게 모험을 하라고 조언하는 것.
(b) 남자에게 더 열심히 일하라고 격려하는 것.
(c) 남자에게 사업 자금을 조달하는 방법에 대해 이야기하는 것.
(d) 남자에게 그의 사업 시도에 대해 남자를 안심시키는 것.

⊞ 기출 POINT

I'm not sure..., business is slow at the moment 등에서 사업에 대해 우려하고 있는 남자의 심정이 드러나 있다. 여자는 이에 대해 I'm sure you'll get on top of things, Things are bound to pick up 등의 말로 격려하고 있으므로 (d)가 답이다. move는 명사로 '결정, 행동'의 뜻이고 a good move/ next move 등으로 사용된다.

move 행동; 결정 **loan** 대출 **finance** 자금을 대다 **eventually** 결국 **be bound to** ∼하게 되다 **get on top of** ∼을 이겨내다

정답_(d)

38

W Oh, my god! It's almost 4 o'clock.

M What's the matter?

W I'm supposed to meet Jenny at 4.

M Really? Where?

W At the Hawthorn Mall, and it usually takes 15 minutes to get there.

M Then hurry! If the traffic isn't bad, you won't be too late.

Q Which is correct according to the conversation?
(a) The woman is late for an appointment.
(b) The man offered to give the woman a ride.
(c) The woman forgot to tell Jenny to meet later.
(d) The man reminded the woman of her appointment.

SOLUTION

W 어, 큰일났다! 4시가 다 됐어.

M 무슨 일인데?

W 4시에 제니랑 만나기로 했거든.

M 정말? 어디서?

W 호손 쇼핑몰에서. 보통 거기까지 가려면 15분은 걸려.

M 그럼 서둘러! 교통 상황이 나쁘지 않으면 많이 늦지는 않을 거야.

Q 대화에 따르면 옳은 것은?
(a) 여자는 약속에 늦었다.
(b) 남자는 여자에게 차를 태워주겠다며 제안했다.
(c) 여자는 제니에게 나중에 만나자고 이야기하는 것을 잊었다.
(d) 남자는 여자에게 약속을 상기시켜 주었다.

⊞ 기출 POINT

4시가 다 되었는데 15분 정도 거리에 있는 장소에 가야 하므로 약속에 늦었다는 (a)가 사실이다. be supposed to는 '∼하기로 되어 있다'는 뜻으로 예정된 일을 말할 때 사용하는데 보통 일어나지 않은 일을 의미할 때가 많다. remind A of B는 'A에게 B를 상기시키다'라는 어구로 reminded the woman of her appointment는 '그녀에게 약속을 상기시켜 주었다'라는 뜻이다. be supposed to+동사원형: ∼할 예정이다 ex) The movie was supposed to start at 7./ You're supposed to come here./ I was supposed to meet him for lunch.

offer to+동사원형 ∼을 제안하다 **give A a ride** A를 차로 데려다 주다 **remind A of B** A에게 B를 일깨워 주다

정답_(a)

Actual Test 3

163

39

W How is your new director at the company?

M Well, he's a lot different from our previous one.

W So, do you think he'll do a better job?

M I'm not sure yet. He wants to make significant changes.

W That might work out for the better.

M Maybe. It's a wait-and-see situation.

Q Which is correct according to the conversation?
(a) The previous director was like the new one.
(b) The new director plans to make big changes.
(c) The man thinks the new director will do well.
(d) The man expects the new director to do a better job.

SOLUTION

W 회사의 새 이사님은 어때?

M 그게 말이야. 이전 이사님과는 굉장히 달라.

W 그래서, 새 이사님이 일을 더 잘할 거라고 생각해?

M 아직은 잘 모르겠어. 상당한 변화를 일으키고 싶어 해.

W 더 나아질 수도 있겠네.

M 그럴지도. 지켜봐야지.

Q 대화에 따르면 옳은 것은?
(a) 이전 이사는 새 이사와 비슷했다.
(b) 새 이사는 큰 변화를 일으키려고 계획한다.
(c) 남자는 새 이사가 잘할 것이라고 생각한다.
(d) 남자는 새 이사가 일을 더 잘해 주기를 기대한다.

기출 POINT
회사의 새 이사에 대한 대화이다. 비교하는 대상이 있을 때 정보를 구분하여 듣는 연습이 필요하다. 이전 이사와는 다르고 많은 변화를 일으키려 하고 있다고 했으므로 일치하는 내용은 (b)이다. wait-and-see situation은 '두고 볼 상황'이라는 뜻으로 남자는 새 이사에 대해 어떤 판단이나 평가를 내리지 않고 있으므로 (c)는 오답이다.

director 이사   previous 이전의   significant 중대한   wait-and-see 일의 진행을 지켜봐야 하는, 두고 볼   정답_(b)

40

M What did you think of the Trio Band's new album?

W It wasn't nearly as good as their last one.

M Yeah, it's more mainstream.

W Definitely. It's more like pop than rock music.

M They'll lose fans because of that.

W Yeah, I won't be buying their next album if it's the same.

Q Which is correct about the Trio Band's new album according to the conversation?
(a) It is equally as good as their last one.
(b) It has a pop rather than a rock orientation.
(c) It has lived up to the woman's expectations.
(d) It will increase the number of the band's fans.

SOLUTION

M 트리오 밴드의 새 음반 어땠어?

W 지난번 음반에 비하면 형편없었어.

M 맞아. 이번 음반은 더 주류 음악이야.

W 확실히 그래. 그건 록음악이라기보다는 대중음악이지.

M 그 밴드 그것 때문에 팬들을 잃을 거야.

W 맞아. 다음에도 이러면 다음번 음반은 안 살 거야.

Q 대화에 따르면 트리오 밴드의 새 음반에 대해 옳은 것은?
(a) 지난번 음반만큼 훌륭하다.
(b) 록 성향보다는 대중음악적 성향이 강하다.
(c) 여자의 기대에 부합했다.
(d) 밴드의 팬 수가 늘어날 것이다.

기출 POINT
What did you think of...?는 느낌이나 의견을 묻는 질문이다. 비교해보니 별로 좋지 않았다는 말은 wasn't nearly as good as라고 표현했다. 그들의 음악은 과거의 것보다 좋지 않고 대중음악적 성향이 강하다는 의견이다. I won't be buying their next album if it's the same은 미래에 대한 일을 미래진행 시제로 나타낸 문장이다.

mainstream 주류의   definitely 당연하지   정답_(b)

41

W I'd like to register for Italian 201 at 7:30, please.
M I'm sorry, but that class is full.
W Oh, but I need that class to graduate this June.
M That class is also taught at 9:30. You could take that.
W I can't because of my schedule. What can I do?
M You should probably see the Italian course supervisor for help.

Q Which is correct according to the conversation?
(a) The woman wants to cancel her registration.
(b) The woman asks to see the man's supervisor.
(c) The man advises the woman to graduate early.
(d) The man suggests the woman take another class.

SOLUTION

W 7시 30분 이탈리아어 201 강의에 등록하고 싶습니다.
M 죄송하지만 그 수업은 인원이 다 찼어요.
W 아, 하지만 이번 6월에 졸업하려면 그 수업을 들어야 해요.
M 그 수업은 9시 30분에도 있습니다. 그걸 들으면 될 텐데요.
W 제 일정 때문에 그럴 수가 없거든요. 어떻게 하면 될까요?
M 이탈리아어 강의 관리하시는 분을 만나 도움을 구해야 할 것 같네요.

Q 대화에 따르면 옳은 것은?
(a) 여자는 등록을 취소하고 싶어 한다.
(b) 여자는 남자의 상사를 만나게 해달라고 요청한다.
(c) 남자는 여자에게 일찍 졸업하라고 조언한다.
(d) 남자는 여자에게 다른 수업을 들으라고 제안한다.

기출 POINT
수강 신청을 하는 대화이다. 여자는 7시 30분 이탈리아어 201 강의를 꼭 들어야 하고 남자는 다른 시간대 강의를 제안하는 내용이다. 수강 신청을 하는 것은 register for라는 표현을 쓰고 강의를 '선택하다'라는 뜻의 동사는 take를 쓴다.

register 등록하다   supervisor 상사; 관리자   정답_(d)

42

M Hi, what are you reading?
W Oh, it's an Agatha Christie book.
M Let me see. *Death on the Nile*. I've seen the movie.
W Oh, you must know the whole story, then.
M Yes, but I wouldn't mind reading the book. Can I borrow it later?
W Even though you know what happens at the end?
M Yeah. I would still like to read it.

Q Which is correct about the man according to the conversation?
(a) He has read all of Agatha Christie's books.
(b) He is going to take the woman to a movie.
(c) He wants to give the woman a book.
(d) He knows the story of the book.

SOLUTION

M 안녕, 뭘 읽고 있어?
W 아, 아가사 크리스티의 책이야.
M 어디 보자. 〈나일강의 죽음〉이구나. 나는 영화로 봤어.
W 아, 그럼 너 줄거리를 다 알고 있겠구나.
M 응. 하지만 책을 읽는 것도 좋을 것 같아. 나중에 빌려도 될까?
W 결말이 어떻다는 걸 알고 있는데도 말이야?
M 응. 그래도 읽어보고 싶어.

Q 대화에 따르면 남자에 대해 옳은 것은?
(a) 아가사 크리스티의 책을 모두 읽었다.
(b) 여자를 영화관에 데리고 갈 것이다.
(c) 여자에게 책을 주고 싶어 한다.
(d) 책 줄거리를 알고 있다.

기출 POINT
아가사 크리스티의 책에 관한 대화이다. 남자는 여자가 읽고 있는 책을 이미 영화로 봐서 내용을 알고 있지만 다시 책으로 읽어보고 싶다면서 빌려 달라고 하는 내용이다. I wouldn't mind reading the book은 '책을 읽는 것도 좋을 것 같다는 뜻으로 정답은 (d)이다.

Let me see. 어디 보자.   mind -ing ~을 꺼리다   even though 비록 ~지만   at the end 결말에는   정답_(d)

43

W Are you almost done with the computer?

M Why? Do you need to use it?

W No, it's just that you spend too much time on it.

M Just a few hours a day isn't too much time.

W But you spend at least 3 hours a day on that thing after you come home from work.

M Well, it helps me to relax.

Q What can be inferred from the conversation?

(a) The man is unlikely to change his habits.

(b) The man is not willing to share his computer.

(c) The woman does not like waiting for the computer.

(d) The woman does not know how to use the computer.

SOLUTION

W 컴퓨터 거의 다 썼니?

M 왜? 컴퓨터 써야 돼?

W 아니. 그냥 네가 컴퓨터를 너무 오래 해서.

M 하루에 몇 시간이 그렇게 긴 시간은 아니잖아.

W 하지만 넌 퇴근하고 돌아와서 하루에 적어도 3시간은 컴퓨터를 하잖아.

M 음, 긴장을 푸는 데 도움이 되거든.

Q 대화에서 유추할 수 있는 것은?

(a) 남자는 자신의 습관을 고칠 것 같지 않다.

(b) 남자는 자신의 컴퓨터를 같이 쓰려고 하지 않는다.

(c) 여자는 컴퓨터를 쓰기 위해 기다리는 것을 좋아하지 않는다.

(d) 여자는 컴퓨터 사용법을 모른다.

🖽 기출 POINT

여자는 남자가 너무 오랫동안 컴퓨터를 한다고 생각하나 남자는 그렇게 생각하지 않는다는 내용으로 의견이 대립되고 있다. spend time on 은 '~에 시간을 쓰다'라는 표현이다. it's just that은 '그냥 ~라서 그래'라는 말로 특별한 이유를 대지 않을 때 쓴다. 많은 시간이 아니라는 말과 긴장을 푸는 데 도움이 된다는 말을 볼 때 (a)를 유추할 수 있다.

be done with ~을 끝내다 **spend time on** ~에 시간을 소비하다
help A (to)+동사원형 A가 ~하는 것을 돕다 **be unlikely to** ~할 것 같지 않다 **be willing to** 기꺼이 ~하다   **정답_(a)**

44

M Hello. I'm here to speak to Mr. Bellows. I'm his attorney.

W I'm sorry, but he's at a company meeting.

M But I need to talk to him urgently.

W I understand, sir, but he can't be interrupted right now.

M Then, when do you expect him to be finished?

W Perhaps in half an hour.

M Okay. Thank you.

Q What can be inferred from the conversation?

(a) The attorney will phone Mr. Bellows immediately.

(b) Mr. Bellows is presently hiring another attorney.

(c) Mr. Bellows' company meeting will be cut short.

(d) The attorney will wait until Mr. Bellows is free.

SOLUTION

M 안녕하세요. 벨로우즈 씨께 드릴 말씀이 있어 왔습니다. 저는 벨로우즈 씨의 변호사입니다.

W 죄송하지만, 회의 중이십니다.

M 하지만 급하게 말씀을 드려야 하는데요.

W 선생님. 이해는 합니다만 지금 당장은 벨로우즈 씨를 방해할 수 없습니다.

M 그럼 언제쯤 끝날 것 같나요?

W 아마도 30분 후에요.

M 알겠습니다. 감사합니다.

Q 대화에서 유추할 수 있는 것은?

(a) 변호사는 벨로우즈 씨에게 바로 전화할 것이다.

(b) 벨로우즈 씨는 현재 또 다른 변호사를 채용하는 중이다.

(c) 벨로우즈 씨의 회의가 단축될 것이다.

(d) 변호사는 벨로우즈 씨가 시간이 날 때까지 기다릴 것이다.

🖽 기출 POINT

방문 목적을 말하는 표현은 〈I'm here to+동사원형〉이다. 여자의 대답이 he can't be interrupted right now이므로 '만나게 해줄 수 없다'는 것을 알 수 있다. 끝나는 예상 시간을 묻고 있으므로 그때까지 기다릴 것임을 추측할 수 있다.

attorney 변호사 **urgently** 급하게 **interrupt** 방해하다 **presently** 현재는 **hire** 고용하다 **cut short** 단축하다   **정답_(d)**

45

W This burger place is too crowded. Let's go somewhere else.

M But we just got here.

W Yes, but you know I don't like standing in lines.

M Okay, then where do you want to go?

W What about a pizza place?

M I don't think there's one around here.

W What about Mexican? I saw a Taco Casa down the street.

M Okay, we can have lunch there.

Q What can be inferred from the conversation?
(a) The woman does not enjoy fast food.
(b) The woman's favorite fast food is pizza.
(c) The man does not mind what he eats for lunch.
(d) The man is irritated by the woman's fickleness.

SOLUTION

W 이 햄버거 집 너무 붐빈다. 어디 다른 데 가자.

M 하지만 지금 막 도착했잖아.

W 그래. 하지만 줄 서서 기다리는 걸 안 좋아하는 건 너도 알잖아.

M 좋아, 그럼 어딜 가고 싶은데?

W 피자집은 어때?

M 이 근처에 피자집은 없는 것 같은데.

W 멕시코 식당은 어때? 길 저쪽에 타코 카사가 있던데.

M 좋아. 거기서 점심 먹으면 되겠다.

Q 대화에서 유추할 수 있는 것은?
(a) 여자는 패스트푸드를 즐기지 않는다.
(b) 여자가 가장 좋아하는 패스트푸드는 피자이다.
(c) 남자는 점심으로 무엇을 먹든 괜찮다.
(d) 남자는 여자의 까다로움에 짜증이 난다.

📖 기출 POINT

여자는 버거를 파는 음식점에 사람이 많아서 다른 곳으로 가길 원한다. 남자는 여자가 제안하는 모든 음식에 반대하지 않는 것으로 보아 (c)를 추론할 수 있다. '~은 어때?'라는 제안의 말로 What about...?을 사용한다. 남자의 대답을 어느 정도 기억하고 있어야 쉽게 풀 수 있는 문제 유형이다.

crowded 붐비는   stand in line 줄 서다   be irritated by ~때문에 짜증이 나다   fickleness 까다로움, 변덕   정답_(c)

46

Books don't cost much, if you think about it. In New York, movies cost $10; Broadway shows cost $75; and concerts or sports events cost $50. But all of these only give you around 2 hours of entertainment. A book, if it's good, can give 10 times that much, and you can lend it or even sell it later. So around $15 for a book seems quite reasonable.

Q What is the main idea of the talk?
(a) Books are usually better than the movies based on them.
(b) Seeing a movie is less expensive than attending a play.
(c) Books are not overpriced for the enjoyment you get.
(d) People today can enjoy many forms of entertainment.

SOLUTION

생각해 보면, 책이 그다지 비싼 게 아닙니다. 뉴욕에서는 영화를 보는 데 10달러가 듭니다. 브로드웨이 뮤지컬을 보려면 75달러가 들고, 콘서트나 스포츠 경기를 관람하려면 50달러가 들죠. 하지만 이 모든 것은 여러분에게 두 시간 정도의 오락만을 제공할 뿐입니다. 책은, 좋은 책이라면 그 10배의 오락을 제공해 줄 수 있고, 나중에 빌려주거나 심지어 팔 수도 있죠. 그러니까 책 한 권에 15달러 정도를 지불하는 것은 꽤 적정하다고 생각됩니다.

Q 담화문의 주제는?
(a) 책은 일반적으로 책을 각색한 영화보다 더 낫다.
(b) 영화를 보는 것은 연극을 관람하는 것보다 덜 비싸다.
(c) 책이 주는 기쁨을 생각하면 책 가격이 너무 비싼 것은 아니다.
(d) 현대인들은 여러 형태의 오락을 향유할 수 있다.

📖 기출 POINT

책값에 대한 이야기를 듣고 주제를 파악하는 문제이다. 이런 유형의 문제에서 주제는 첫 부분에 언급되는 일이 많으므로 첫 문장에 집중해야 한다. 책이 주는 즐거움을 영화와 뮤지컬, 콘서트나 경기에 비교하면서 15달러 정도인 책값이 많이 비싼 것은 아니라는 결론을 내리고 있다.

cost 비용이 들다   entertainment 오락   reasonable 적정한   overpriced 너무 비싼   정답_(c)

47

Guests at the Ice Hotel can select from a series of fun activities. If you are an outdoor person, you can participate in cross-country skiing or snowshoeing excursions. We also offer plenty of snowmobiles for rent. But if you are into something more relaxing, try our ice-carving classes, or even ice-lake fishing. Who knows? Maybe you'll catch some fish to put on your own dinner table! For more information, ask our receptionists about recreational activities for guests.

Q What is the main topic of the announcement?
(a) Winter activities for hotel guests.
(b) Procedures for attending hotel classes.
(c) Sporting events organized by the hotel.
(d) Indoor attractions hotel guests can enjoy.

SOLUTION

아이스 호텔 숙박객들은 여러 가지 신나는 활동을 선택할 수 있습니다. 야외 활동을 즐기는 분이라면 크로스 컨트리 스키나 스노우슈잉 유람에 참여하실 수 있습니다. 또한 대여용 설상차도 충분히 구비해 두고 있습니다. 하지만 좀 더 느긋한 무언가를 좋아하신다면 저희의 얼음 조각 수업을 듣거나 호수에서 얼음 낚시를 해보십시오. 누가 알겠습니까? 여러분의 저녁상에 올릴 고기를 낚게 될지도 모르는 일이니까요! 더 많은 정보를 원하시면 숙박객을 위한 휴양 활동에 대해 저희 접수원에게 문의하십시오.

Q 공지사항의 주제는?
(a) 호텔 숙박객을 위한 겨울 활동.
(b) 호텔 강습에 참여하기 위한 절차.
(c) 호텔에서 조직한 스포츠 행사.
(d) 호텔 숙박객들이 즐길 수 있는 실내 명소.

기출 POINT
주로 첫 문장에 주제가 제시된다. 아이스 호텔의 숙박객들은 여러 활동을 즐길 수 있다는 내용의 공고이다. 뒤에 자세한 정보를 주고 있는 skiing, snowshoeing excursions, ice-carving classes 등을 볼 때 겨울 휴양 활동에 대한 안내이므로 (a)가 주제가 된다. be into는 '~을 아주 좋아하다'라는 뜻이다.

a series of 여러 가지의 **participate in** ~에 참가하다 **excursion** 유람 **receptionist** 접수원 **recreational activity** 휴양 활동 **procedure** 절차 **indoor attraction** 실내 명소   정답_(a)

48

Here's some American history you may not know. In 1812, a man named Sam Wilson started supplying meat to the American army in barrels, on which were stamped the letters "US." In those days, the term "United States" wasn't often used, so people wondered what US stood for. As a joke, someone said that US stood for "Uncle Sam," referring to Sam Wilson. As time went on, the expression "Uncle Sam" became associated solely with the US government.

Q What is the lecture mainly about?
(a) How the term "Uncle Sam" originated.
(b) Who first coined the phrase "Uncle Sam."
(c) What the expression "Uncle Sam" refers to.
(d) Why "Uncle Sam" is a commonly used expression.

SOLUTION

여러분이 모를 수도 있는 미국 역사를 하나 알려드리죠. 1812년, 샘 윌슨이라는 남자가 통에 고기를 담아 미군에 공급하기 시작했는데, 이 통에 'US'라는 글자가 찍혀 있었어요. 그 당시 '합중국'이라는 용어가 그다지 자주 사용되지 않았기 때문에 사람들은 US가 무엇을 나타내는지 궁금해했습니다. 농담으로 누군가가 US는 '샘 아저씨' 즉 샘 윌슨을 일컫는 것이라고 말했습니다. 시간이 흐르면서 '샘 아저씨'라는 표현은 미국 정부와 연관해서만 쓰이게 되었습니다.

Q 강의의 주제는?
(a) '샘 아저씨'라는 용어의 기원.
(b) '샘 아저씨'라는 문구를 처음 만든 사람.
(c) '샘 아저씨'라는 표현이 가리키는 것.
(d) '샘 아저씨'라는 표현이 일상적으로 사용된 이유.

기출 POINT
United States를 나타내는 US가 샘 아저씨와 연관되게 된 배경에 대한 이야기이다. 누군가가 농담으로 US가 샘 윌슨의 준말이라고 말한 후, 'Uncle Sam'이란 표현은 US 정부와 관련되어 사용되었다는 내용이다. 이 강의는 미국 정부를 나타내는 표현인 Uncle Sam이라는 용어의 기원에 대해 다루고 있다.

barrel 배럴, 통 **stand for** ~을 상징하다 **refer to** ~을 지칭하다 **become associated with** ~와 연관하게 되다 **solely** 단독으로 **term** 용어 **originate** 기원하다 **coin** (신어 등을) 만들어내다

정답_(a)

49

Nationwide efforts are being made for a new, less stressful primary school test for seven-year-olds in England, which could put an end to "high-stakes" examinations for that age group starting next year. The government hopes to create a more flexible approach to testing and to lessen pressure on children by placing greater weight on the evaluation of teachers.

Q   What is the main idea of the news report?
(a) English teachers will be given more responsibility.
(b) Standards have been lowered in English primary schools.
(c) Changes have been implemented in English primary school testing.
(d) Students have been allowed more flexibility in English primary schools.

SOLUTION

영국의 7세 아동들에게 새롭고 스트레스가 덜한 학교 시험을 제공하기 위한 거국적인 노력이 진행 중이며, 이로써 내년부터 7세 아동들에 대해 '큰 중압감을 야기하는' 시험이 막을 내릴 수도 있게 되었습니다. 정부는 교사들의 평가에 더 많은 비중을 둠으로써 시험 방식에 대해 좀 더 유연하게 접근하고 아이들이 받는 부담을 줄이기를 바라고 있습니다.

Q   뉴스 보도의 주된 내용은?
(a) 영국 교사들은 더 많은 책임을 부여받게 될 것이다.
(b) 영국 초등학교에 대한 표준이 낮아졌다.
(c) 영국의 초등학교 시험에 대한 변화가 시행되었다.
(d) 영국 초등학교에서 학생들에게 더 많은 유연성을 허용했다.

기출 POINT

요점을 묻는 문제는 처음 부분에 집중해야 한다. less stressful primary school test를 만들기 위한 노력에 대한 내용이므로 (c)가 정답이다. 교사들의 평가에 비중을 두겠다는 내용에 집중하면 (a)를 답으로 혼동할 수 있다.

nationwide 전국적인   **stressful** 스트레스를 주는   **put an end to** ~을 끝내다   **high-stakes** 큰 중압감을 주는   **flexible** 유연한   **evaluation** 평가   **responsibility** 책임감   **implement** 시행하다

정답_(c)

50

All architecture students here would have heard of Brasilia, the capital of Brazil, with its reputation as a failed experiment in urban planning. Conceived just over 50 years ago and built from the ground up, the capital has been criticized for its cold and desolate design. It's true that it's seen growth and an influx of residents, and that it's admired by architects for its modernist and futuristic structures, but on the whole, the city is just not people-friendly.

Q   What is the main topic of the lecture?
(a) Brazil's contributions to architecture.
(b) The significance of Brasilia to Brazilians.
(c) The bad reputation of the city of Brasilia.
(d) The way Brasilia came back from near-failure.

SOLUTION

이 자리에 있는 건축학도들이라면 모두 브라질의 수도인 브라질리아에 대해 들어봤을 겁니다. 브라질리아는 도시 계획의 실패 사례라는 평판을 받고 있죠. 단 50여 년 전에 착상되어 허허벌판 위에 지어진 이 수도는 그 차갑고 황량한 디자인으로 비판을 받아왔습니다. 브라질리아가 성장했고 주민들의 유입이 늘어났으며, 그 근대적이며 미래적인 건물들이 건축가들의 감탄을 받고 있는 것도 사실이지만, 전체적으로 브라질리아는 전혀 인간 친화적이지 못합니다.

Q   강의의 주된 내용은?
(a) 건축에 대한 브라질의 기여도.
(b) 브라질 사람들에게 있어 브라질리아의 중요성.
(c) 브라질리아라는 도시에 대한 좋지 않은 평판.
(d) 브라질리아가 실패 직전에서 재기할 수 있었던 방법.

기출 POINT

요점은 첫 문장에 제시되어 있다. 브라질리아가 도시 계획에 실패한 사례로 알려진 사실을 언급하며 비난받는 이유를 제시하고 있다. 이후에 평판에 대한 변화의 요소가 있지만 전체적으로 인간 친화적이지 못한 것으로 결론짓고 있으므로 정답은 (c)이다.

architecture 건축학   **reputation** 명성   **experiment** 실험   **conceive** 구상하다   **criticize** 비난하다   **desolate** 황량한   **influx** 유입   **resident** 주민   **futuristic** 미래주의적인   **people-friendly** 인간 친화적인

정답_(c)

51

I am delighted to inform you that Rwanda's mountain gorillas have returned from the brink of extinction. Our study shows that over the last 15 years, this gorilla population has been on the rise by 10 percent. This has occurred despite the Rwandan genocide, armed insurgents in the area, human-spread sicknesses, poaching and constant pressure from land-hungry peasants. Today, 354 gorillas inhabit the misty rainforest below Rwanda's Virunga volcanoes, and prospects for their survival are quite bright.

Q What is the main idea of the talk?
(a) Rwandan gorillas have suffered over many years.
(b) Gorillas have returned to Rwanda in recent years.
(c) Human beings are again causing the deaths of gorillas.
(d) Rwandan gorillas are no longer threatened with extinction.

SOLUTION

르완다의 마운틴 고릴라들이 멸종 위기에서 회생했음을 여러분께 알리게 되어 기쁩니다. 우리 연구에 따르면 지난 15년간 이들 고릴라 개체군의 수는 10% 증가했습니다. 르완다의 인종학살, 지역의 무장 반군 세력, 인간 전염병, 밀렵, 그리고 토지에 굶주린 소작인들로부터의 끊임없는 압력에도 불구하고 이 같은 증가가 이루어진 것입니다. 현재 고릴라 354마리가 르완다의 비룽가 화산 아래 안개 낀 열대 우림 속에 서식하고 있으며, 이들의 생존 전망은 꽤 밝습니다.

Q 담화문의 주제는?
(a) 르완다의 고릴라들은 여러 해 동안 고통받았다.
(b) 고릴라들은 최근 르완다로 다시 돌아왔다.
(c) 인간들은 다시 고릴라들의 죽음을 유발하고 있다.
(d) 르완다 고릴라들은 더 이상 멸종 위험을 받고 있지 않다.

기출 POINT

르완다의 고릴라들이 멸종 위기에서 벗어났다는 내용이다. 고릴라 개체 수가 지난 15년 동안 10% 증가했고, 여러 어려운 상황 속에서도 생존 전망이 밝다고 결론짓고 있다. 고릴라들이 이제 멸종의 위협에서 벗어나 증가하는 추세에 있으므로 (d)가 적절하다.

be delighted to ~해서 기쁘다 **brink** 직전, 가장자리 **extinction** 멸종 **genocide** 인종학살 **insurgent** 반란군 **poach** 밀렵하다 **peasant** 소작인 **prospect** 전망 **threaten** 위협하다 정답_(d)

52

Now I'd like to discuss the common cinematic device known as the flashback. It is used when the linear progress of a film narrative is stopped to present information on past events. This technique gives filmmakers more flexibility in telling their story. They can add depth to character, provide background, or create new perspectives on events in the film. Sometimes, films are made that almost entirely consist of a flashback, such as Spielberg's *Saving Private Ryan*.

Q What is the main point about flashbacks in the lecture?
(a) They interrupt a narrative that provides background.
(b) They are used to enhance an audience's expectations.
(c) They are employed to broaden the scope of a narrative.
(d) They can show a character's wishes for a different past.

SOLUTION

이제 그럼 플래시백(회상)이라고 알려진 영화적 흔한 장치에 대해 논의하도록 하겠습니다. 이것은 영화 스토리의 선형적 진행이 과거 사건들에 대한 정보를 주기 위해 중지될 때 사용됩니다. 이 기법은 영화 제작자들이 이야기를 풀어나가는 데 더 많은 유연성을 제공합니다. 제작자들은 등장인물에 깊이를 더하고, 배경 설명을 하거나 혹은 영화 속 사건들에 대해 새로운 관점을 창출해 낼 수 있죠. 때로는 스필버그의 〈라이언 일병 구하기〉처럼 영화의 거의 전부가 플래시백(회상)으로 구성되기도 합니다.

Q 강의에서 플래시백(회상)에 대한 요점은?
(a) 배경 설명을 하는 스토리를 방해한다.
(b) 관객의 기대를 높이기 위해 사용된다.
(c) 스토리의 범위를 확장하기 위해 활용된다.
(d) 다른 과거를 바라는 등장인물의 소원을 보여줄 수 있다.

기출 POINT

플래시백(회상) 기법에 대해 말한 세 번째 문장에서 요점이 제시되고 있다. 부연 설명으로 플래시백(회상) 기법은 인물에 깊이를 더하고, 배경을 제공하며, 사건에 새로운 관점을 창출해 내는 역할을 한다고 했으므로 스토리의 범위를 넓히는 데 활용된다는 것이 요점이다.

cinematic 영화적인 **flashback** 회상 **linear** 선형적인 **perspective** 관점 **consist of** ~로 구성되다 **interrupt** 방해하다 **enhance** 높이다 정답_(c)

53

Good morning. Today's weather forecast calls for overcast skies with snow flurries in the central parts of the nation, where the high is expected to reach two degrees Celsius later in the day. Southern areas can expect showers accompanied by thunderstorms and a high of four degrees. Lows will range from eight to five degrees below zero Celsius across the nation.

Q What weather conditions can southern areas expect?
(a) Clear and sunny skies.
(b) Rain with thunderstorms.
(c) Flurries and cloudy conditions.
(d) Temperatures over five degrees.

SOLUTION

안녕하십니까. 오늘의 일기 예보에 따르면 우리나라 중부에 진눈깨비가 흩날리는 찌푸린 하늘이 예상되고, 중부 지방의 최고 기온은 오후에 섭씨 2도에 달할 것으로 예상됩니다. 남부 지방에서는 뇌우를 동반한 소나기가 내릴 수 있으며, 최고 기온은 4도가 되겠습니다. 최저 기온은 전국적으로 영하 8도에서 5도까지 분포하겠습니다.

Q 남부 지방에서 기대할 수 있는 날씨는?
(a) 맑고 화창한 하늘.
(b) 뇌우를 동반한 비.
(c) 진눈깨비와 구름 낀 하늘.
(d) 5도 이상의 기온.

⊞ 기출 POINT

southern area의 날씨 예보를 집중해서 듣는다. 방송의 앞 부분에는 central parts에 대한 예보가 나오고 중간 이후에 남부 지방에서 showers accompanied by thunderstorm이 예상된다는 내용이 나오므로 정답은 (b)이다.

weather forecast 일기 예보 **overcast** 찌푸린 **snow flurry** 진눈깨비 **Celsius** 섭씨 **accompany** 동반하다 **thunderstorm** 뇌우 **range** ~에 분포하다   정답 (b)

54

Don't miss the 10th Annual Prescott Home & Garden Festival that will be held on Sunday, February 24, from 11 a.m. until 5 p.m. You can browse or purchase merchandise from over 150 stalls. You also have a chance of winning a $1000 gift certificate for furniture and garden supplies. Just pick up an entry form at participating restaurants and shops in Prescott and hand it in at the main entrance for the Prescott Home & Garden Festival. Don't miss it!

Q Which is correct according to the announcement?
(a) The festival is held every Sunday during the month of February.
(b) Merchandise can be purchased from the Festival's website.
(c) All restaurants and shops have gift certificate entry forms.
(d) People may submit entry forms when entering the festival.

SOLUTION

2월 24일 일요일 오전 11시부터 오후 5시까지 열리는 제10회 연례 프리스캇 주택·정원 축제를 놓치지 마십시오. 150여 개의 매대에서 상품을 둘러보거나 구매하실 수 있습니다. 또한 1,000달러 상당의 가구 및 정원 용품용 상품권을 탈 수 있는 기회도 있습니다. 프리스캇 내 참여 식당과 상점에 비치된 응모 양식을 구한 후 프리스캇 주택·정원 축제 정문에서 제출하세요. 이 기회를 놓치지 마세요!

Q 공고에 따르면 옳은 것은?
(a) 전시회는 2월 동안 매주 일요일마다 열린다.
(b) 상품은 축제 홈페이지에서 구매할 수 있다.
(c) 모든 식당과 상점에는 상품권 응모 양식이 비치되어 있다.
(d) 사람들은 축제에 입장할 때 응모 양식을 제출할 수 있다.

⊞ 기출 POINT

이 축제는 연례 행사라고 했으므로 1년에 한 번 하루 동안 열리는 행사이다. 행사 장소에서 물건을 구매할 수 있고, 모든 식당은 아니고 행사에 참여하는 음식점과 상점에서 상품권을 응모할 수 있는 양식을 구할 수 있다. hand it in at the main entrance라는 부분에서 입장할 때 응모 양식을 제출할 수 있음을 알 수 있으므로 정답은 (d)이다.

annual 연례의 **browse** 둘러보다 **purchase** 구매하다 **merchandise** 상품 **stall** 매대 **gift certificate** 상품권 **submit** 제출하다   정답 (d)

55

On tonight's program, we'll talk about choosing an easy-to-maintain kitchen. The main thing is to select a kitchen with surfaces that are easy to clean. Sure, natural wood looks wonderful, but it requires a great deal of maintenance. A laminated surface, on the other hand, doesn't. Also, you want kitchen walls made of a material that will resist grease, oil vapor and moisture from your cooking.

Q Which is correct according to the radio program?
(a) Laminated surfaces require little maintenance.
(b) Kitchen walls must absorb moisture properly.
(c) Natural wood surfaces are best in kitchens.
(d) Mess is unavoidable in a busy kitchen.

SOLUTION

오늘 밤 프로그램에서는 관리하기 쉬운 부엌을 선택하는 것에 대해 이야기하도록 하겠습니다. 핵심은 청소하기 쉬운 바닥으로 된 부엌을 선택하는 겁니다. 물론 자연 목재는 보기에 멋지지만, 엄청난 유지 보수를 요구합니다. 반면에 합판 바닥은 그렇지 않습니다. 또한 여러분은 요리 시 발생하는 기름때, 기름 입자와 습기에 견딜 수 있는 자재로 시공되어 있는 부엌 벽면을 원합니다.

Q 라디오 프로그램에 따르면 옳은 것은?
(a) 합판 바닥은 유지 보수가 거의 필요 없다.
(b) 부엌 벽면은 습기를 제대로 흡수해야 한다.
(c) 자연산 나무 바닥은 부엌에 최상이다.
(d) 분주한 부엌에서 혼잡은 불가피하다.

기출 POINT

kitchen surface에 대한 방송 내용이다. 부엌 바닥 자재로서 자연 목재와 합판을 비교하면서 합판의 장점을 제시하고 있다. 합판은 오염에 강하기 때문에 유지 보수가 거의 필요 없다는 (a)가 방송과 일치하는 내용이다.

easy-to-maintain 관리하기 쉬운 **maintenance** 유지 보수
laminated surface 합판 바닥 **material** 자재 **grease** 기름때 **vapor**
수증기 **moisture** 습기   정답_(a)

56

I'd like to remind students that the Media for Democracy in Africa (MFDA) forum is on this week. For those who don't know, the MFDA originated at a conference of journalist organizations in Harare in 1993 for the purpose of promoting independent journalism, human rights and democracy in Africa. The MFDA believes that obstacles to media freedom in Africa prevent the development of democracy. I hope you can all attend this worthy forum.

Q Which is correct according to the announcement?
(a) Support for the MFDA in Africa is lacking.
(b) Journalist organizations established the MFDA.
(c) The MFDA is a newspaper published in Harare.
(d) The MFDA forum is restricted to members only.

SOLUTION

아프리카 내 민주주의를 위한 매체(MFDA) 포럼이 이번 주에 열린다는 것을 학생들에게 상기시켜 주고 싶어요. 모르는 학생들을 위해, MFDA는 아프리카 내 언론의 독립, 인권과 민주주의를 촉진할 목적으로 1993년 하라레에서 열린 언론인 기구들의 회의에서 시작되었습니다. MFDA는 아프리카에서의 매체 자유의 걸림돌이 민주주의 발전을 저해하고 있다고 생각합니다. 여러분들이 이 가치 있는 포럼에 참여할 수 있길 바랍니다.

Q 공지사항에 따르면 옳은 것은?
(a) 아프리카에서 MFDA에 대한 지지가 부족하다.
(b) 언론인 기구들이 MFDA를 창설했다.
(c) MFDA는 하라레에서 발간되는 신문이다.
(d) MFDA 포럼은 철저하게 회원제로 운영된다.

기출 POINT

공고에 따르면 MFDA는 언론인 기구들이 하라레에서 창설한 조직이며 아프리카 민주주의 발전을 위해 언론의 독립을 목표로 하는 포럼이므로 정답은 (b)이다. 이 포럼에 대한 국내의 지지가 부족하다는 언급은 없고 MFDA는 신문이 아닌 포럼이며 일부에게 제한된 것이 아니라 학생들이 참가할 수 있는 공개된 행사이다.

remind 상기시키다 **forum** 포럼 **conference** 회의 **journalist**
언론인 **democracy** 민주주의 **obstacle** 걸림돌 **worthy** 가치 있는
establish 설립하다 **be restricted to** ~에 국한되다   정답_(b)

57

First, I must remind everyone here that everything that takes place at this union meeting is strictly confidential. It would greatly jeopardize our position if the press got wind of our strategy. As you know, contract negotiations have stalled and we're getting the same old run-around from company bosses. Therefore, I propose we vote to go out on strike the day after tomorrow. All those in favor, please give me a show of hands.

Q Which is correct according to the speech?
(a) Company bosses have not been cooperative.
(b) The press has jeopardized the union's tactics.
(c) The union will hold a vote the day after tomorrow.
(d) Negotiations were completed in favor of the union.

SOLUTION

우선, 저는 이 자리의 모든 분들께 이번 조합 회의에서 일어나는 모든 일들은 극비라는 사실을 상기시켜 드려야 할 것 같습니다. 만약 언론에서 우리 전략을 눈치채게 되면 우리의 입지가 아주 위태롭게 될 것입니다. 여러분도 아시다시피, 계약 협상이 교착 상태에 빠졌고, 회사 사주들은 매번 그래왔던 것처럼 우리들에게 발뺌만 하고 있죠. 그래서 저는 내일 모레 파업에 돌입하는 것에 대한 투표를 실시할 것을 제안합니다. 찬성하시는 모든 분들은 손을 들어 주십시오.

Q 연설에 따르면 옳은 것은?
(a) 회사 사주들은 협조적이지 않았다.
(b) 언론에서 조합의 전술을 위험에 빠뜨렸다.
(c) 조합은 내일 모레 투표를 실시할 것이다.
(d) 협상은 조합 측에 유리하게 이루어졌다.

기출 POINT

협상은 교착 상태에 있고 회사 중역들은 늘 그랬듯이 발뺌만 하고 있다는 내용으로 볼 때 회사 사주들이 비협조적이라는 (a)가 일치하는 내용임을 알 수 있다. 언론이 조합의 전술을 위험하게 하는 것이 아니라 언론에 의해 전술이 노출되는 것이 위험하다는 내용이므로 (b)는 오답이다.
strictly 엄격하게　**confidential** 비밀의　**jeopardize** 위태롭게 하다　**get wind of** 낌새를 채다　**strategy** 전략　**negotiation** 협상　**stall** 꼼짝 못하다　**run-around** 발뺌　**go out on strike** 파업에 돌입하다　**cooperative** 협조적인　**tactics** 전술　**complete** 완결짓다

정답_(a)

58

Hello, Spark's Computer Supplies? This is Angelina Stanford from ErgoTech in Phoenix. I'm calling to leave a message concerning a mistake in an order. Our invoice number is 2908. I've noticed that you have invoiced us for 50 LCD monitor filters, but we only made an order for 30. I've also checked with our warehouse staff, and they confirmed we only received 30, as requested. I'd appreciate it if you could get back to me first thing in the morning so we can sort things out.

Q What can be inferred from the recorded message?
(a) Spark's Computer Supplies will receive a call next morning.
(b) Spark's Computer Supplies is a new company.
(c) The caller received an erroneous invoice.
(d) The caller wants to change her order.

SOLUTION

여보세요, 스파크 컴퓨터 용품점이죠? 저는 피닉스에 있는 어고테크의 안젤리나 스탠퍼드라고 합니다. 주문 오류가 있어 이렇게 메시지를 남깁니다. 저희의 송장번호는 2908입니다. 저희 측에 LCD 모니터 필터 50개에 대해 송장을 보낸 것을 봤는데, 저희는 30개만 주문했습니다. 저희 쪽 창고 직원에게 확인해 봤는데, 우리가 요청한 대로 30개만 수령했다고 합니다. 문제를 해결할 수 있도록 내일 아침 출근하자마자 전화 주시면 감사하겠습니다.

Q 녹음 메시지에서 유추할 수 있는 것은?
(a) 스파크 컴퓨터 용품점은 내일 아침 전화를 한 통 받을 것이다.
(b) 스파크 컴퓨터 용품점은 신규 회사이다.
(c) 전화를 건 사람은 잘못된 송장을 받았다.
(d) 전화를 건 사람은 주문을 변경하고 싶어 한다.

기출 POINT

전화를 건 용건에 대한 표현은 〈I'm calling to+동사원형〉으로 나타내므로 이 부분에 집중한다. concerning a mistake in an order 때문에 전화해서 메시지를 남긴다는 내용이다. 처음에 30개를 주문했는데 50개를 신청하는 송장을 보낸 것을 정정하기 위한 통화 메시지이다.
I'm calling to+동사원형 ~하기 위해 전화하다　**concerning** ~와 관련하여　**invoice** 송장을 보내다　**warehouse** 창고　**confirm** 확인하다　**sort out** 해결하다　**erroneous** 잘못된

정답_(c)

59

Today's lecture focuses on subatomic particles called neutrinos, which come from the cosmos and can help us learn about the universe. Neutrinos are created during nuclear fusion when stars are born, and they are the most numerous particles in the universe. Although hard to detect, billions of neutrinos pass through every square inch of space every second. They are a fundamental component of the universe, and studying them can help us know more about its destiny, such as whether it will expand forever or collapse.

Q What can be inferred from the lecture?
(a) Neutrinos prove that the universe is expanding.
(b) Under certain conditions neutrinos produce light.
(c) Neutrinos are emitted by the Earth out into space.
(d) Scientists are undecided on the fate of the universe.

SOLUTION

오늘의 강의는 중성미자라고 불리는 아원자 입자에 중점을 둘 것입니다. 이 입자는 우주에서 생성되며 우리가 우주를 배우는 데 도움이 될 것입니다. 중성미자는 별들이 생성될 때 핵융합 과정에서 생기며, 이들은 우주에서 그 수가 가장 많습니다. 탐지하기는 어렵지만 수십 억 개의 중성미자가 매 초 우주 공간 구석구석을 모두 지나갑니다. 이들은 우주의 근본적 요소이고, 이들을 연구함으로써 우주가 영원히 팽창할 것인지 아니면 붕괴될 것인지와 같은 우주의 운명을 더 많이 알아내는 데 도움이 될 것입니다.

Q 강의에서 유추할 수 있는 것은?
(a) 중성미자는 우주가 팽창하고 있음을 입증한다.
(b) 특정 조건에서 중성미자는 빛을 발한다.
(c) 중성미자는 지구에 의해 우주로 발산된다.
(d) 과학자들은 우주의 운명에 대해 확신을 가지지 못하고 있다.

기출 POINT

중성미자에 대한 강의이다. 이 중성미자는 별들이 생성될 때 만들어지고 우주 공간 전체에 퍼져 있어서 그것을 연구하면 우주가 계속 팽창할 것인지 붕괴할 것인지 알 수 있다는 내용이다. 이 말을 통해 현재까지의 과학적인 연구 결과 우주가 팽창되는지 붕괴되는지, 미래에 정해진 예측이 없다는 사실을 알 수 있으므로 (d)가 정답이다.

subatomic particle 아원자 입자   neutrino 중성미자   cosmos 우주   nuclear fusion 핵융합   detect 찾다   component 요소   destiny 운명   expand 확장하다   collapse 붕괴하다   emit 방출하다   fate 운명   정답_(d)

60

While working as a business educator, I've seen business education dramatically change over the last ten years. We've incorporated online business courses into our curriculum, and we're teaching students trendy new business models and corporate practices. We also teach ethics courses now, but they don't seem to have sunk in. If what we hear in the news is anything to go by, I suspect business graduates are more interested in attaining course credits than in acquiring a moral conscience.

Q What will the speaker probably talk about next?
(a) The concept of leadership among business students.
(b) Recent examples of unethical conduct in businesses.
(c) The problem of falling grades in business education.
(d) Graduates who have successful Internet businesses.

SOLUTION

경영학 교육자로 일하면서 나는 지난 10년간 경영학 교육이 극적으로 변화하는 것을 보았습니다. 우리는 우리 교육과정에 온라인 비즈니스 과정을 편입시켰고, 학생들에게 첨단 신규 비즈니스 모델과 기업 관행에 대해 가르치고 있습니다. 우리는 또한 현재 윤리 과정도 가르치고 있지만, 이 과정에 대한 인식이 아직 제대로 되지 않은 것 같습니다. 우리가 뉴스에서 듣는 것들이 판단의 근거가 될 수 있다면, 나는 경영대학원 졸업생들은 도덕적 양심을 얻는 것보다는 학과 학점을 따는 데 더 관심이 있지 않나 생각합니다.

Q 화자가 앞으로 말할 내용은?
(a) 경영학과 학생들 사이에서 리더십의 개념.
(b) 기업들의 비윤리적 행위에 대한 최근 사례들.
(c) 경영학 교육에서 학점이 낮아지는 문제.
(d) 성공적으로 인터넷 사업을 하는 졸업생들.

기출 POINT

이어지는 내용을 찾는 문제는 마지막 부분에 집중해야 한다. 마지막에 경영학을 전공한 졸업생들이 도덕적 양심보다 학점에만 관심이 있다는 우려를 제시하고 있으므로 이러한 우려의 배경이 될 만한 내용이 나와야 할 것이다. 실제적으로 비윤리적인 행위 사례를 든 (b)가 알맞은 답이다.

educator 교육자   dramatically 극적으로   incorporate 편입하다   curriculum 교육과정   ethics 윤리   sink in 서서히 이해되다   credit 학점   moral conscience 도덕적 양심   정답_(b)

Grammar

25 minutes

1

A What do students think of the library's new facilities?

B Most students I know _____ them useful.

(a) find
(b) finds
(c) is found
(d) are found

SOLUTION

A 학생들이 도서관의 새 시설에 대해 어떻게 생각하나요?
B 제가 아는 대부분의 학생들은 유용하다고 생각해요.

기출 POINT

What do you think of...?는 느낌이나 의견을 묻는 말이다. 동사 find는 〈find+목적어+(to be)+형용사/명사〉의 형태로 '…가 ～라고 생각하다, 느끼다'라는 뜻을 나타낸다. 주어가 복수이므로 find가 정답이다. 〈목적어+(to be)+형용사/명사〉를 취하는 동사: think, find, feel, believe, suppose

think of ～라고 생각하다, 느끼다   **facility** 시설   정답_(a)

2

A Did you buy some French bread?

B No, there was _____ left.

(a) any
(b) none
(c) some
(d) neither

SOLUTION

A 프랑스 빵 좀 샀니?
B 아니. 하나도 안 남았더라.

기출 POINT

〈there+be동사+주어〉는 '～이 있다'를 나타내는 표현으로 빈칸에는 주어가 들어가야 한다. French bread를 대신하는 대명사가 와야 하는데 문맥상 남아 있지 않다는 말이 되어야 하므로 none과 neither가 가능하다. neither는 대상이 두 개일 경우에 사용하므로 none이 정답이다.
left 남겨진   정답_(b)

3

A Did you get that computer game?

B No. By the time I got to the store, every copy _____.

(a) is sold
(b) will be sold
(c) has been sold
(d) had been sold

SOLUTION

A 그 컴퓨터 게임 구했니?
B 아니. 내가 가게에 도착했을 때 게임이 다 팔렸어.

기출 POINT

By the time은 '～할 때까지, 할 때쯤에'라는 뜻으로 주절에는 완료시제가 많이 나온다. 가게에 도착한 때가 과거이고 게임이 팔린 것은 더 이전이므로 과거완료 시제로 표현해야 한다.
get 구하다   **by the time** ～할 때까지   **copy** 한 부, 한 본   정답_(d)

4

A Why were you at the supermarket for so long?

B There was _____ a long line at the counter that I was delayed.

(a) so
(b) too
(c) such
(d) much

SOLUTION

A 슈퍼마켓에서 왜 그렇게 오래 있었어?
B 카운터에 줄이 너무 길어서 늦어졌어.

기출 POINT

'～할 정도로'라는 뜻인 such[so] ... that 구문은 '너무 ～해서 …가 되다'는 결과를 표현한다. such 다음에는 a(n)같은 관사, 형용사, 명사의 어순이 된다. 어순에 유의할 표현: such[quite]+a(n)+형용사+명사, so[too]+형용사+a(n)+명사 ex) such a funny character/too difficult a problem
for so long 그렇게 오랫동안   정답_(c)

175

5

A Let me pay for the dinner.
B Absolutely not. _____ for it this time.

(a) I'll pay
(b) I had paid
(c) I was paying
(d) I'll have paid

SOLUTION

A 저녁은 내가 낼게.
B 절대 안 돼. 이번에는 내가 낼 거야.

⊞ 기출 POINT

Let me는 '내가 ~할게'라는 말이고 Absolutely not은 '절대 안 돼'라는 말로 쓰였다. '이번에는 내가 내겠다'는 뜻으로 의지를 표현하는 미래 시제가 되어야 하므로 (a)가 정답이다.

let me 내가 ~할게 **absolutely** 절대

정답_(a)

6

A I'm tired of Jake's screw-ups at work.
B Calm down, honey. There is nobody _____ doesn't have faults.

(a) that
(b) which
(c) whom
(d) whose

SOLUTION

A 회사에서 제이크가 실수하는 게 지겨워.
B 진정해요, 여보. 흠 없는 사람이 어디 있나요.

⊞ 기출 POINT

nobody를 수식하는 관계대명사절 문제이다. 선행사 nobody가 관계대명사절의 주어이므로 주격 관계대명사 who나 that이 와야 한다. 그러나 -thing이나 -body로 끝나는 something, nothing, anybody, nobody와 같은 부정대명사가 선행사로 오면 that을 사용해야 한다.

be tired of ~이 지긋지긋하다, 싫다 **screw-up** 중대한 실수 **calm down** 진정하다 **fault** 결점

정답_(a)

7

A Alex is very knowledgeable about this town's history.
B He should be. He _____ here for years.

(a) lives
(b) was lived
(c) is being lived
(d) has been living

SOLUTION

A 알렉스는 이 마을 역사에 대해 굉장히 박식해.
B 그럴 만도 하지. 여기 몇 년째 살고 있으니까.

⊞ 기출 POINT

should가 강한 추측을 나타내는 조동사로 쓰인 경우이다. 그가 몇 년째 여기에 살고 있어서 그럴 것이라는 내용이 알맞다. 과거부터 현재에도 계속 살고 있는 것이므로 현재완료진행 시제를 사용한 (d)가 정답이다.

knowledgeable 지식이 있는 **should** ~일 것이다(강한 추측)

정답_(d)

8

A Is the coach worried about the team?
B Yes, their poor fitness is _____ concerns him most.

(a) that
(b) what
(c) where
(d) which

SOLUTION

A 코치가 팀에 대해 걱정하고 있나요?
B 네, 팀의 건강 상태가 좋지 않은 게 코치가 가장 우려하는 점이죠.

⊞ 기출 POINT

관계대명사를 고르는 문제이다. concerns는 관계대명사절의 동사이므로 주격 관계대명사가 와야 하고, 선행사가 없으니 선행사를 포함하는 관계대명사 what이 적절하다. concern이 명사 이외에도 동사로 쓰여서 '~를 걱정하게 만들다'의 뜻으로 쓰인다는 것을 알면 쉽게 풀 수 있는 문제이다.

be worried about ~에 대해 걱정하다 **fitness** 건강 상태 **concern** ~을 걱정하게 하다

정답_(b)

9

A What's the rate for a double room?
B A hundred dollars _____.

(a) night
(b) a night
(c) the night
(d) any night

SOLUTION

A 2인실 숙박료가 얼마죠?
B 1박에 100달러입니다.

⊞ 기출 POINT

단위를 나타내는 말 앞에 쓰이는 부정관사인 a(n)는 '~당, ~에'의 뜻으로 사용되어 100 dollars a night은 '1박에 100달러'라는 표현이다. 참고로 rate는 기준에 따라 매겨지는 요금을 나타낼 때 쓰는 단어로 우편, 화물, 전화, 호텔 등의 요금에 사용한다. ex) interest rate/ postal rate/ insurance rate/ higher rate of tax 등

rate 요금　　　　　　　　　　　　　　　　　　　　정답_(b)

10

A What do you think of Mrs. Davis as a teacher?
B She is _____ as anyone I've met.

(a) as a patient teacher
(b) as patient a teacher
(c) a very patient teacher
(d) a teacher that is patient

SOLUTION

A 데이비스 씨를 교사로서 어떻게 생각하세요?
B 그분은 제가 만난 사람들 중 가장 인내심이 많은 교사예요.

⊞ 기출 POINT

as ... as구문이다. '…만큼 ~한'이라는 동등 비교의 형태이지만, as anyone I've met (만나본 그 누구 만큼)은 내용상 최상급을 나타내고 있다. 이때 〈as+형용사+a(n)+명사〉의 어순을 따르는 것에 주의해야 한다.
think of A as B A를 B로 생각하다　**patient** 인내심이 많은　정답_(b)

11

A You should bring an umbrella in case it rains.
B Good idea. It _____.

(a) looks it might
(b) looks like might
(c) might look like it
(d) looks like it might

SOLUTION

A 비가 올 때를 대비해서 우산을 가지고 와야 할 거야.
B 좋은 생각이야. 비가 올 것처럼 보이네.

⊞ 기출 POINT

look like는 '~할 것처럼 보이다'는 뜻으로 뒤에 명사나 절(주어+동사)이 올 수 있다. 따라서 looks like it might rain이 적절한데, rain은 앞에서 언급한 동사이므로 생략하여 정답은 (d)가 된다.
in case ~를 대비해서　　　　　　　　　　　　　　정답_(d)

12

A What will you do _____ the park?
B I'll just walk around for a while.

(a) at
(b) on
(c) for
(d) about

SOLUTION

A 공원에서 뭘 할 거니?
B 잠깐 산책하려고.

⊞ 기출 POINT

산책을 할 것이라는 대답으로 보아 '공원에서 무엇을 할 것이냐'는 질문이 되어야 하므로 장소를 나타내는 전치사 at이 알맞다.
walk around 산책하다　**for a while** 잠시 동안　정답_(a)

13

A I want a handheld PC.
B I'd like one, too, or something of _____.

(a) kind
(b) a kind
(c) the kind
(d) each kind

SOLUTION

A 포켓용 PC를 갖고 싶어.
B 나도 포켓용 PC나 아니면 그런 비슷한 것 하나 가지고 싶더라.

⊞ 기출 POINT
something of the kind는 대화 중에서 말하고 있는 대상, '그것과 같은 것'이라는 뜻으로 쓰는 말이다. 앞의 one은 handheld PC를 말한다.
a kind 표현: a kind of gray color 회색 비슷한 색/ You and your wife are two of a kind. 너와 부인은 똑같아.
handheld 포켓용의   정답_(c)

14

A What does that article say men's average life expectancy is?
B It says _____.

(a) it's about 78 years
(b) about 78 old years
(c) about 78 age of years
(d) it's age of about 78 years

SOLUTION

A 기사에서 남자들의 평균 수명이 얼마라고 하니?
B 78세 정도 된대.

⊞ 기출 POINT
It says는 책, 기사, 표지판 등에 쓰여 있는 내용을 전할 때 사용하는 말이다. It says 뒤에는 절이 나와 'that 이하라고 쓰여 있다, 말하고 있다'라고 해석한다. 수명이 78세라는 말이므로 (a)가 정답이다.
article 기사 **average** 평균의 **life expectancy** 수명   정답_(a)

15

A Tell Sue I found her phone.
B _____ her, I bet she has already bought a new one.

(a) To know
(b) Knowing
(c) Having known
(d) To have known

SOLUTION

A 수한테 내가 그녀의 전화기를 찾았다고 말해줘.
B 걔를 알아서 하는 말이지만, 틀림없이 벌써 새 전화기를 샀을 거야.

⊞ 기출 POINT
빈칸에 들어갈 수 있는 부사구는 to부정사구나 분사구문인데 내용상 '그녀를 알기 위해서'라는 뜻이 될 수 없으므로 이유를 말하는 분사구문이 들어가는 것이 알맞다. I bet 절보다 이전에 일어난 일이 아니므로 〈동사원형+-ing〉 형태인 Knowing이 답이 된다.
I bet (that) ~라고 장담하다   정답_(b)

16

A The concert tickets have sold out. We'll never get to see it now.
B No, I _____.

(a) think it not suppose
(b) suppose we'll not so
(c) don't think I suppose
(d) don't suppose we will

SOLUTION

A 콘서트 입장권이 매진이야. 이제 그 콘서트는 절대 못 보겠구나.
B 그래, 나도 못 볼 거라고 생각해.

⊞ 기출 POINT
get to는 '~하게 되다'의 뜻으로 never get to see는 '절대 못 보게 되다'는 말이다. 부정문에 No로 답했으므로 빈칸에는 부정문 형태의 동조하는 말이 들어가야 한다. 단, suppose, think 등의 동사가 들어가는 부정문은 I suppose we won't가 아니라 I don't suppose we will과 같이 suppose에 부정어를 붙인다.
sell out (상품을) 다 팔다, 매진되다 **suppose** 생각하다, 추측하다
정답_(d)

17

A Is it true Susan expanded her business?
B Yes. _____ that she opened another.

(a) So successful her first store was
(b) Successful was her first store so
(c) Her first store was so successful
(d) Her first store was successful so

SOLUTION

A 수잔이 사업을 확장했다는 게 정말이에요?
B 네. 첫 상점이 성공적이어서 한 곳 더 열었어요.

⊞ 기출 POINT

so that은 in order that이라는 뜻이므로 목적의 의미가 담겨 있다. 따라서 '첫 상점이 성공적이라서 상점을 한 곳 더 열었다네요'가 되려면 '너무 ~해서 …하다'의 뜻인 so ... that을 써야 한다.
expand 확장하다 **successful** 성공적인 **so ... that** 너무 ~해서 …하다
정답_(c)

18

A What do you think of the newcomer?
B There is _____.

(a) about him no single thing I like
(b) no single thing I about him like
(c) a single thing that I don't like him
(d) not a single thing about him that I like

SOLUTION

A 새로 온 사람에 대해서 어떻게 생각해?
B 내가 좋아하는 구석이라고는 눈 씻고 봐도 없어.

⊞ 기출 POINT

not a single은 not even one. 즉 '한 명도, 하나도 ~아니다'의 뜻으로 사람이나 사물 명사 앞에 사용된다. There is 다음에는 주어인 not a single thing이 와야 하고, 수식어인 about him이 이어지고, not a single thing을 수식하는 관계대명사절 that I like는 마지막에 와야 한다.
newcomer 새로 온 사람
정답_(d)

19

A Why didn't you tell me you were going back to school?
B I _____ you if you had been willing to listen.

(a) had told
(b) was telling
(c) will have told
(d) would have told

SOLUTION

A 학교로 다시 돌아간다고 왜 나한테 말하지 않았어?
B 네가 기꺼이 들어주려고 했더라면 너한테 이야기했을 거야.

⊞ 기출 POINT

if you had been willing to를 통해 '~했더라면'이라는 뜻의 가정법 과거완료 문장임을 알 수 있다. 빈칸은 주절이므로, 〈조동사 과거형+have+p.p.〉 형태의 (d)가 정답이다.
be willing to 기꺼이 ~하다
정답_(d)

20

A It's so hot! Let's get out of this heat.
B Yeah, we shouldn't _____.

(a) jog in the hottest part of the day
(b) in the hottest part of the day jog
(c) be jogging it's the day's hottest part
(d) the hottest part of the day be jogging

SOLUTION

A 너무 덥다! 이 뙤약볕을 피하자.
B 그래, 하루 중 제일 뜨거운 시간에 조깅하면 안 되지.

⊞ 기출 POINT

shouldn't는 '~하지 말아야 한다'는 뜻의 조동사이므로 동사원형이 와야 한다. jog와 be jogging이 가능하지만 '하루 중 가장 더운 때'를 in the hottest part of the day로 나타내므로 (a)가 정답이다. (c)처럼 연결어 없이 동사 뒤에 바로 절(it's the day's)이 올 수 없다.
get out of ~을 피하다
정답_(a)

21

Ink _____ for drawing as well as writing throughout history.

(a) used
(b) will use
(c) has been used
(d) was being used

SOLUTION

잉크는 역사를 통틀어 집필뿐만 아니라 그림에도 사용되었다.

⊞ 기출 POINT

throughout history를 볼 때 '과거 역사부터 지금까지 내내 사용되었다'는 내용이 되어야 하므로 현재완료 시제가 적절하다. Ink는 사용되는 것이므로 수동태인 has been used가 와야 한다.

drawing 그림   **A as well as B** B뿐만 아니라 A도   **정답_(c)**

22

After a half hour of rowing, the man stopped _____.

(a) eat
(b) to eat
(c) eating
(d) of eating

SOLUTION

반 시간 동안 노를 젓고 나서 남자는 음식을 먹기 위해 멈췄다.

⊞ 기출 POINT

동사 stop의 목적어로 to부정사와 -ing형이 모두 올 수 있으나 의미가 다르다는 것을 알아야 풀 수 있는 문제이다. 내용상 '노를 젓고 나서 음식을 먹기 위해 멈췄다'는 뜻이 되어야 하므로 stopped to eat이 정답이다. stopped eating은 '먹는 것을 멈췄다'는 뜻이다.

a half hour 반 시간   **row** 노를 젓다   **정답_(b)**

23

For most people, London is _____ an expensive city to live in.

(a) so
(b) very
(c) even
(d) quite

SOLUTION

대부분 사람들에게 런던은 생활하기에 물가가 꽤 비싼 곳이다.

⊞ 기출 POINT

어순 문제이다. 일반적인 어순은 〈관사+부사+형용사+명사〉이지만, 부사로 쓰인 quite는 〈quite+a(n)+(형용사)+명사〉의 어순을 따른다. so는 〈so+형용사+a(n)+명사〉의 어순이 된다.

expensive 비싼   **even** 심지어   **quite** 꽤   **정답_(d)**

24

News sources state that there _____ have been a radiation leak at the nuclear power plant.

(a) can
(b) dare
(c) need
(d) might

SOLUTION

취재원은 그 핵발전소에서 방사선 누출이 있었을 수도 있다고 보도했다.

⊞ 기출 POINT

조동사 문제이다. 〈조동사+have+p.p.〉는 과거의 일을 표현할 때 사용한다. '~했을지도 모른다'는 추측의 의미를 나타내는 might have p.p.가 가능하다. might 대신 may를 사용하여 약한 추측을 나타낼 수도 있다.

과거 일에 대한 추측: must have p.p. ~했음에 틀림없다/ might[may] have p.p. ~했을지도 모른다/ can't have p.p. ~했을 리가 없다

news source 취재원   **state** 진술하다   **radiation leak** 방사선 누출
nuclear 핵의   **power plant** 발전소   **정답_(d)**

25

The writer's latest novel _____ very differently from his earlier work.

(a) has been reading
(b) will be reading
(c) is reading
(d) reads

SOLUTION

그 작가의 최근 소설은 그의 이전 작품과는 상당히 다른 느낌을 준다.

⊞ 기출 POINT

동사 read는 자동사로 사용될 때 보어를 동반하여 '읽어서 ～한 느낌을 주다'라는 뜻이다. read very differently는 '매우 다른 느낌으로 읽힌다'는 의미이다. 책의 성격에 대한 진술이므로 시제는 단순 현재시제가 알맞다. 수동의 의미를 나타내는 동사 : 사물 주어+sell, read, wash, cook ex) This car sells badly./ The tablecloth washes very well.

latest 최근의 **differently** 판이하게 **earlier** 이전의   정답_(d)

26

A girl _____ in the choir amazed the audience with her voice.

(a) sings
(b) to sing
(c) singing
(d) to be singing

SOLUTION

합창단에서 노래하는 소녀의 목소리는 관객들을 깜짝 놀라게 했다.

⊞ 기출 POINT

문장의 서술어는 amazed이므로 빈칸에 들어갈 동사(sing)는 현재분사형(singing)으로 써서 형용사처럼 명사 girl을 수식하는 구조가 되어야 한다. A girl who was singing에서 〈관계대명사+be동사〉가 생략된 것으로 보면 이해가 쉽다.

choir 합창단 **amaze** 놀라게 하다 **audience** 관객   정답_(c)

27

Children under 8 are not allowed to use the swimming pool _____ they are with an adult.

(a) for
(b) yet
(c) unless
(d) whereas

SOLUTION

8세 미만의 어린이들은 성인을 동반하지 않으면 수영장을 이용할 수 없다.

⊞ 기출 POINT

'성인을 동반하지 않으면'이라는 뜻이 되어야 하므로 빈칸에는 if not에 해당하는 말인 unless가 들어가야 한다. 〈allow+목적어+to+동사원형〉의 형태로 '～하게 허락하다'의 구문이 수동태인 〈be allowed to+동사원형〉으로 사용되었다. whereas는 '～에 반하여, 그러나'의 뜻이다.

be allowed to+동사원형 ～하도록 허락되다   정답_(c)

28

The values of the Shinto belief system _____ many Japanese traditions.

(a) characterize
(b) characterizes
(c) is characterizing
(d) are characterizing

SOLUTION

신도 신념 체계의 가치관은 수많은 일본 전통의 특징을 갖는다.

⊞ 기출 POINT

characterize는 타동사로 '～의 특징을 갖다'는 말로 쓰인다. 우리말 해석과 직접 연결되지 않는 이런 류의 동사는 쓰임을 잘 익혀두어야 한다. values는 '가치관, 가치 기준'이라는 뜻으로 복수 취급하며 moral values/ traditional values 등으로 사용된다.

values 가치관 **belief system** 신념 체계 **tradition** 전통
characterize 특징을 갖다   정답_(a)

29

Grouping words _____ similar meanings may help language learners build vocabulary.

(a) to
(b) for
(c) with
(d) about

SOLUTION

유사한 의미를 지닌 단어들을 하나로 묶는 것은 언어 학습자들이 어휘력을 높이는 데 도움이 될 수 있다.

⊞ 기출 POINT

전치사 with는 '~을 가지고 있는'의 뜻으로 쓰인다. '유사한 의미를 지닌 단어들'이라는 뜻이 되어야 적절하므로 words with similar meanings가 되어야 한다.

similar 유사한 **vocabulary** 어휘   정답_(c)

30

_____ for over 20 years, Bill and Angie know each other inside and out.

(a) To be married
(b) They are married
(c) Having been married
(d) They are being married

SOLUTION

결혼한 지 20년이 넘은 빌과 앤지는 서로를 속속들이 다 알고 있다.

⊞ 기출 POINT

이유를 나타내는 분사구문이 들어가야 한다. 주어는 Bill and Angie로 주절과 같으므로 생략하고, 접속사도 생략한다. 문맥상 주절은 현재의 일이지만 분사구문은 이보다 더 앞선 시제에 일어난 일이므로 〈Having+p.p.〉 형태의 완료분사 구문이 와야 한다. 또한 '~와 결혼하다'는 be married와 같이 수동태로 쓰므로 완료분사 구문의 수동형인 (c) Having been married가 정답이다.

inside and out 속속들이   정답_(c)

31

US political parties conduct national nominating conventions, _____ are held every four years.

(a) that
(b) what
(c) which
(d) where

SOLUTION

미국 정당들은 전당 지명 대회를 실시하며, 이는 4년에 한 번 개최된다.

⊞ 기출 POINT

관계대명사의 계속적 용법에서는 that을 쓸 수 없고 which만 쓸 수 있다. 여기에서 which는 national nominating conventions를 선행사로 받는 주격 관계대명사이다.

political party 정당 **conduct** 실시하다 **national nominating convention** 전당 지명 대회   정답_(c)

32

A Wisconsin soda fountain owner _____ the first ice cream sundae in 1881.

(a) reputed to invent
(b) invented to be reputed
(c) is reputed to have invented
(d) has invented it being reputed

SOLUTION

위스콘신의 한 탄산 음료 기계 소유주가 1881년 선데이 아이스크림을 처음으로 발명한 것으로 일컬어지고 있다.

⊞ 기출 POINT

be reputed to는 '~라고 일컬어지다'는 뜻이다. be reputed 다음에는 to부정사가 오는데 발명을 한 것은 과거시제인 1881년이므로 현재시제(is reputed) 보다 이전임을 알 수 있다. 따라서 to부정사의 완료형인 to have p.p.가 와야 하므로, 정답은 (c)이다.

soda fountain 탄산 음료 기계 **ice cream sundae** 선데이 아이스크림 **reputed** ~이라 일컬어지는   정답_(c)

33

The need for mathematical and problem-solving skills _____ in many fields.

(a) has increased
(b) was increased
(c) have increased
(d) were increased

SOLUTION

여러 분야에서 수학 및 문제 해결 능력의 필요성이 증가하고 있다.

기출 POINT

주어는 The need이고 for mathematical and problem-solving skills는 수식어구이므로 단수형인 has increased가 정답이다. **mathematical** 수학적인 **problem-solving skill** 문제 해결 능력 **field** 분야

정답_(a)

34

In 1878, an area which _____, was settled by Manoah Stevens and his family.

(a) Jacobston would be known as later
(b) later known as Jacobston would be
(c) would later be known as Jacobston
(d) later Jacobston would be known as

SOLUTION

1878년에 제이콥스턴으로 알려진 지역에 마노아 스티븐스와 그의 가족들이 정착했다.

기출 POINT

which에 이어지는 빈칸은 선행사 an area를 수식하는 관계대명사절이다. an area가 주어이므로 동사인 would later be known이 오고 수식어인 as Jacobson이 이어지는 것이 알맞으므로 정답은 (c)이다. **settle** 정착하다 **be known as** ～로 알려지다

정답_(c)

35

During the American Revolutionary War, _____ thousand British Loyalists returned to England.

(a) few
(b) every
(c) much
(d) several

SOLUTION

미국 독립전쟁 당시 수천 명의 영국 정부 지지자들은 영국으로 귀환했다.

기출 POINT

thousand 앞에는 수를 나타내는 한정사가 와야 한다. a, two, several, a few 등이 올 수 있다. thousands of처럼 복수형으로 쓰면 '수많은'이라는 의미이다.
American Revolutionary War 미국 독립전쟁 **British Loyalist** 영국 정부 지지자

정답_(d)

36

Chinese law makes _____ his pregnant wife until well after her delivery.

(a) a man illegal to divorce
(b) illegal for a man to divorce
(c) to divorce illegal for a man
(d) it illegal for a man to divorce

SOLUTION

중국 법에서는 임신한 부인이 출산을 한 후 상당한 시간이 흐르기 전까지 남자가 그 부인과 이혼하는 것은 불법이다.

기출 POINT

〈make+목적어+목적보어〉로 '～을 …하게 만들다'라는 뜻을 나타낸다. 목적어가 to divorce 이하와 같이 긴 경우에는 이것을 가목적어인 it으로 대신하여 앞에 두고 긴 목적어를 뒤에 쓴다. to divorce의 주어는 a man이므로 for a man의 형태로 to부정사 앞에 위치하도록 한다. **pregnant** 임신한 **delivery** 출산 **illegal** 불법인 **divorce** 이혼하다

정답_(d)

37

_____ the archaeologists had located the ancient site, they organized its excavation.

(a) If
(b) Till
(c) That
(d) Once

SOLUTION

일단 고대 유적지를 찾은 후, 고고학자들은 그에 대한 발굴을 준비했다.

⊞ 기출 POINT

시제에 유의해서 보면 앞은 had located이고 뒤는 organized로 시간상 차이가 있다. 의미상 '일단 ∼하고 나자, ∼하자마자'의 뜻이 적절하므로 접속사 Once가 정답이다.

archaeologist 고고학자 **site** 장소 **excavation** 발굴   정답_(d)

38

The research has provided conclusive results, _____ in the table at the end of this document.

(a) details summarizing it are
(b) of which summarized are details
(c) the details of which summarizing it
(d) the details of which are summarized

SOLUTION

연구는 결정적인 결과를 제공해 주었으며, 세부사항은 이 문건 끝에 있는 표에 요약되어 있다.

⊞ 기출 POINT

선행사 뒤에 comma가 오는 관계대명사의 계속적 용법이다. 선행사는 conclusive results인데 이것의 세부사항이므로 소유격 관계대명사가 와야 한다. 수식어구가 있는 소유격 관계대명사는 수식어를 앞에 써서 the details of which가 되고 서술어인 are summarized가 그 다음에 와야 한다.

research 연구 **conclusive** 결정적인 **document** 문서 **summarize** 요약하다   정답_(d)

39

Scarcely _____ the table when the doorbell rang.

(a) did he set
(b) had he set
(c) was he setting
(d) has he been setting

SOLUTION

그가 상을 차리자마자 초인종이 울렸다.

⊞ 기출 POINT

Scarcely ... when[before]는 '∼하자마자 …하다'로 거의 동시에 일어나는 일을 나타낼 때 쓰는 어구이다. 주의할 것은 시제로 주절에는 〈had+p.p.〉를 쓰고 when절에는 과거시제를 쓴다는 것이다. 또, 부정어 Scarcely가 문두에 오기 때문에 주어와 동사가 도치되어 Scarcely had he set이 된다.

scarcely 거의 ∼않다 **set the table** 상을 차리다   정답_(b)

40

_____ Stalin's communist government, and those who did were sent off to labor camps.

(a) Few dared to speak out against
(b) Speaking out few dared against
(c) To speak against it were few daring
(d) Against were to speak few who dared

SOLUTION

감히 스탈린의 공산 정부에 반하는 말을 입 밖에 내는 사람은 거의 없었고, 그런 사람들은 노동 수용소로 쫓겨났다.

⊞ 기출 POINT

those who did에 해당하는 내용이 빈칸에 들어가야 한다. 주어는 사람을 나타내는 Few이다. dare는 '감히 ∼하다'는 뜻의 일반동사로 종종 to부정사가 따라온다. speak out은 '솔직히 말하다', against는 '∼에 반하여'의 뜻을 나타낸다.

communist government 공산 정부 **send off** 쫓아 버리다
labor camp 노동 수용소   정답_(a)

41

(a) A Did you go on a vacation last year?

(b) B No, I didn't. I couldn't afford to do.

(c) A How about this year? Do you have any vacation plans?

(d) B Yes, I'm thinking of going to Spain.

SOLUTION

(a) 작년에 휴가 갔었니?

(b) 아니, 안 갔어. 갈 형편이 아니었거든.

(c) 올해는 어때? 휴가 계획 세웠어?

(d) 응, 스페인으로 가려고 생각 중이야.

⊞ 기출 POINT

이미 사용한 동사의 반복을 피하기 위하여 to부정사에서 동사원형을 생략하고 to만 사용할 경우 이를 대부정사라 한다. 따라서 (b)에서 afford to do 대신에 afford to가 되어야 한다.

정답_(b) afford to do → afford to

42

(a) A Hello. This is Jim from Citiplex. Could I speak to Tom in sales, please?

(b) B I'm afraid his line is busy right now. Can I take a message?

(c) A Yes, I just want to request that he'll send me the list of this week's sales items.

(d) B No problem. I'll tell him as soon as he's free.

SOLUTION

(a) 여보세요, 씨티플렉스의 짐입니다. 영업부의 톰과 통화할 수 있을까요?

(b) 죄송하지만 톰이 지금 통화 중이네요. 용건을 남겨주시겠어요?

(c) 네, 톰에게 이번 주 세일 품목 목록을 보내 달라고 요청하고 싶어서요.

(d) 알겠습니다. 톰과 통화가 되는 대로 바로 이야기하겠습니다.

⊞ 기출 POINT

request는 '요청하다, 요구하다'의 뜻으로 demand, insist, suggest, recommend 등과 마찬가지로 that절에서 가정법 현재, 즉 《(should)+동사원형》만을 쓴다. 따라서 (c)는 인칭이나 시제와 상관없이 request that he (should) send me로 바꾸어야 한다.

I'm afraid (that) ~라서 유감이다 **request** 요청하다 **sales item** 판매 품목

정답_(c) he'll send → he send

43

(a) A Why do we have to get up so early tomorrow morning?

(b) B Because the traffic would be bad if we don't get an early start.

(c) A As long as we have good music, I don't mind being stuck in traffic.

(d) B You wouldn't say that if you had to do the driving.

SOLUTION

(a) 내일 아침에 왜 그렇게 일찍 일어나야 되는 거야?

(b) 일찍 출발하지 않으면 차가 막힐 테니까 그렇지.

(c) 좋은 음악만 있다면 차가 막혀도 난 상관없는데.

(d) 네가 운전을 해야 한다면 그렇게 말 못할걸.

⊞ 기출 POINT

(b)의 if we don't get은 동사가 현재시제로 사용된 것으로 보아 단순히 조건을 나타내는 부사절이다. 가정법이 아니므로 주절의 동사는 will be bad가 알맞다.

mind -ing ~을 꺼리다   **be stuck in** ~에 묶이다   **do the driving** 운전을 하다

정답_(b) would → will

44

(a) A For how long did you study French?

(b) B I studied it in high school for three years.

(c) A Did you continue with French when you went to college?

(d) B Yes, but I stopped to take French in my second year.

SOLUTION

(a) 불어를 얼마나 공부했어요?

(b) 고등학교에서 3년간 공부했어요.

(c) 대학에 가서도 계속 불어 공부를 했었나요?

(d) 네, 하지만 2학년 때 불어 수업 수강을 중단했어요.

⊞ 기출 POINT

동사 stop은 to부정사와 -ing를 모두 목적어로 사용할 수 있지만 뜻이 다르므로 구별해야 한다. (d)의 stopped to take French는 '불어를 배우기 위해 중단했다'의 뜻이므로 stopped taking으로 바꿔야 한다. continue with French는 '불어를 계속하다'라는 뜻이다.

continue 계속하다

정답_(d) to take → taking

45

(a) A Hey, Jerry, do you think you can give me a hand on the weekend?

(b) B I'm not sure whether I'll have the time or not. What do you need help with?

(c) A I just need help rearranging some furnitures in my apartment.

(d) B That shouldn't take long. I could come over Sunday afternoon.

SOLUTION

(a) 이봐, 제리, 주말에 나 좀 도와줄 수 있을 것 같아?
(b) 시간이 있을지 모르겠다. 무슨 일로 도움이 필요한데?
(c) 아파트에 가구 배치를 다시 하는 데 도움이 필요해서.
(d) 그리 오래 걸리지 않을 거야. 일요일 오후에 갈 수 있어.

기출 POINT

(c)에서 명사 furniture는 셀 수 없는 명사로 관사를 쓸 수 없고 복수형이 될 수도 없다. 따라서 수량을 표시할 때에는 a piece of furniture/ two pieces of furniture의 형태로 나타낸다.
give ... a hand ~에게 도움을 주다   **whether** ~인지 아닌지

정답_(c) furnitures → furniture

46

(a) In the past, many food dyes were made from plants, animals or insects. (b) Some of these traditional dyes are being still used instead of synthetic dyes. (c) One example is cochineal, which is a crimson-colored dye made from tiny insects. (d) These cochineal insects, which live on cactus plants, are gathered by hand to make the dye.

SOLUTION

(a) 과거에는 식물이나 동물, 곤충으로 식용 착색료를 많이 만들었다. (b) 이들 전통적인 염료의 일부는 합성 염료 대신 아직 사용되고 있다. (c) 일례가 코치닐인데, 이것은 작은 곤충으로 만드는 심홍색 염료이다. (d) 이 코치닐의 원료가 되는 곤충은 선인장에 살고, 염료를 만들고자 손으로 채집한다.

기출 POINT

부사 still은 주로 일반동사 앞에, be동사나 조동사 뒤에 쓰인다. 따라서 (b)에서는 be동사 뒤에 와서 are still being used의 어순이 되어야 한다.
food dye 식용 착색료 **insect** 곤충 **synthetic** 합성의 **cochineal** 코치닐 **crimson** 심홍색 **cactus** 선인장

정답_(b) are being still → are still being

47

(a) Cape Town and its surrounding areas once teemed with millions of workers. (b) They come to the region to earn a modest income by doing manual laboring jobs. (c) Often they worked under extreme conditions, with little prospect of getting anything better. (d) However, they kept working because they were supporting families hundreds of miles away.

SOLUTION

(a) 케이프 타운과 그 주변 일대는 한때 수백만 명의 노동자들로 붐볐다. (b) 그들은 육체 노동일을 해서 적은 보수라도 벌어보려고 이 지역으로 온다. (c) 그들은 종종 극단적인 조건에서 상황이 나아질 전망이 거의 없이 일을 했다. (d) 그러나 그들은 수백 마일 떨어진 곳의 가족들을 부양하고 있었기 때문에 일을 계속했다.

기출 POINT

전체 내용이 모두 과거의 일이므로 (b) 역시 과거시제가 되어야 한다. modest는 '대단하지 않은', '값이 적은'의 뜻으로 사용된다.

surrounding 주변의 **teem with** ~로 붐비다 **region** 지역 **modest** 적은 **manual laboring** 육체 노동 **extreme** 극단적인 **prospect** 전망

정답_(b) come → came

48

(a) Daycare centers in this community are run by local authorities or by volunteer organizations. (b) Centers range from informal community-based groups setting up by parents to large-scale businesses. (c) The problem is that all of them are usually overfilled because people are in such desperate need of daycare. (d) So the government needs to expand existing centers or make new ones.

SOLUTION

(a) 이 지역 보육원들은 지역 당국이나 자원봉사 조직에 의해 운영된다. (b) 보육원들은 부모들이 세운 비공식 지역사회 기반 단체에서부터 대규모 사업체에 이르기까지 다양하다. (c) 문제는 사람들의 보육 수요가 너무 절실하다 보니 이들 보육원들이 전부 인원 과잉 상태라는 것이다. (d) 따라서 정부는 기존의 보육원들을 확장하거나 새로이 보육원을 확충해야 한다.

기출 POINT

(b)에서 setting up by parents는 informal community-based groups를 수식하는 어구이다. 비공식 지역사회 기반 단체는 부모들에 의해 세워지는 것이므로 setting이 아니라 과거분사 set으로 써야 한다.

daycare center 보육원 **community** 지역단체 **authorities** 당국 **volunteer** 자원봉사의 **range from A to B** A에서 B까지 이르다 **large-scale** 대규모의 **overfilled** 과잉의 **desperate** 절박한 **expand** 확충하다

정답_(b) setting → set

49

(a) The eyes of the chameleon are unique because they are not dependent on each other. (b) The eyes are not in sockets like ours but exist as slightly raised turrets on either side of a chameleon's head. (c) Chameleons can thus aim their eyes so that one eye can look ahead while the other looks back. (d) Moving independently, the world can be seen by a chameleon in almost 360-degree vision.

SOLUTION

(a) 카멜레온의 눈은 독특하게도 두 눈이 서로에게 예속되어 있지 않다.
(b) 이들의 눈은 인간의 눈처럼 안와에 있지 않고 카멜레온의 머리 양쪽에 살짝 튀어나온 돌출부로 존재한다. (c) 그래서 카멜레온은 한쪽 눈이 앞을 볼 때 다른 쪽 눈은 뒤를 보도록 눈을 조준할 수 있다. (d) 독립적으로 움직이기 때문에 카멜레온은 360도의 시각으로 세상을 볼 수 있다.

⊞ 기출 POINT

(d)에서 주절의 주어(the world)와 Moving의 주어는 일치하지 않으므로 현재와 같은 형태의 분사구문은 어색하다. Moving의 주체를 살려서 콤마 이하를 the eyes of a chameleon can see the world로 고치면 자연스럽다.

chameleon 카멜레온 **unique** 독특한 **be dependent on** ~에 예속되다 **socket** (눈)구멍 **slightly** 약간 **turret** 돌출부 **independently** 독립적으로

> 정답_(d) the world can be seen by a chameleon
> → the eyes of a chameleon can see the world

50

(a) During the 19th century, the focus of geographical exploration and mapping turned to the Arctic. (b) Many of the explorers who sailed to the Arctic sought a fabled Northwest Passage between Asia and Europe. (c) One of the most famous of them was British sailor called William Perry who made numerous voyages to the Arctic. (d) His trip to the Arctic Archipelago is considered to be one of the most important in the history of Arctic exploration.

SOLUTION

(a) 19세기 동안 지리적 탐사와 지도 제작의 초점은 북극권에 맞춰졌다.
(b) 북극 항해를 떠난 많은 탐험가들은 아시아와 유럽 간 전설적인 북서 항로로 향했다. (c) 가장 유명한 사람 중 하나인 윌리엄 페리는 영국 선원으로 북극을 수차례 항해했던 사람이다. (d) 그의 북극해 제도 항해는 북극 탐사 사상 가장 중요한 탐사 중 하나로 간주된다.

⊞ 기출 POINT

(c)의 British sailor 앞에 관사가 필요한데 이미 언급된 대상이 아니므로 부정관사인 a가 와서 a British sailor called William Perry가 되어야 한다.

focus 초점 **geographical** 지리적인 **exploration** 탐사 **Arctic** 북극 **seek** 향하다 **fabled** 전설적인 **numerous** 수많은 **voyage** 항해

> 정답_(c) British sailor → a British sailor

1

A Hi, Amanda. I'm so glad you could come to my party.

B Oh, hi Tim. Thanks for _____ me.

(a) noting
(b) placing
(c) inviting
(d) showing

SOLUTION

A 안녕, 아만다. 파티에 와줘서 정말 기뻐.
B 아, 안녕 팀. 초대해 줘서 고마워.

⊞ **기출 POINT**

I'm so glad you could come to my party는 파티에 와줘서 감사해하는 말이다. 그에 대한 응답으로 '초대해 줘서 감사하다'는 말이 되어야 하므로 inviting이 알맞다.

Thanks for ~해서 고마워   **notice** 알아보다   **place** 앉히다

정답_(c)

2

A Excuse me, but how do I dial outside from this office phone?

B Just press zero for an outside _____.

(a) line
(b) talk
(c) ring
(d) voice

SOLUTION

A 죄송하지만, 이 사무실 전화로 외부 전화를 어떻게 거나요?
B 외부 회선은 0번을 누르시면 됩니다.

⊞ **기출 POINT**

'외부 전화, 외부 회선 통화'를 나타내는 표현은 outside line을 쓴다.
전화 관련 표현: How can I get an outside line? 외부 전화를 어떻게 거나요?/ Dial 9 to get an outside call. 외부 통화는 9번을 누르세요/ Press 0 to make an outgoing call. 외부 통화를 하려면 0번을 누르세요.

dial outside from ~의 외부로 전화 걸다

정답_(a)

3

A Please turn down your music. I can hear it even in the other room.

B Oh, I didn't think it was that _____.

(a) full
(b) loud
(c) huge
(d) strong

SOLUTION

A 음악 소리 좀 줄여줘. 다른 방에서도 들려.
B 아, 소리가 그렇게 큰 줄 몰랐어.

⊞ **기출 POINT**

'소리가 크다'는 뜻을 나타내는 말로 loud를 쓴다. that은 부사로 쓰여 '그만큼, 그렇게'의 뜻이며 that much/ that far/ that bad 등의 표현을 사용한다.

turn down 소리를 줄이다   **full** 최대의   **loud** 소리가 큰   정답_(b)

4

A Hello. I have an appointment with Dr. Robins.

B Certainly. Please _____ a seat.

(a) take
(b) wait
(c) hold
(d) bring

SOLUTION

A 안녕하세요. 로빈스 박사님과 약속이 있습니다.
B 알겠습니다. 자리에 앉으시죠.

⊞ **기출 POINT**

사무실에 찾아와서 방문 목적을 얘기하는 상대방에게 자리에 앉으라는 응답이 알맞다. '자리에 앉다'로 take a seat/ have a seat을 쓴다.

appointment 약속   **certainly** 물론   정답_(a)

5

A Kevin has shown amazing improvement in his music lessons.
B Yes, he's very _____ in music.

(a) played
(b) talented
(c) oriented
(d) expressed

SOLUTION

A 케빈은 음악 수업에서 놀라운 발전을 보여줬어요.
B 네, 그 아이는 음악에 뛰어난 소질이 있어요.

기출 POINT

소질이나 재능이 있을 때 talented를 쓴다. 유사한 말로 gifted도 쓸 수 있다. oriented는 '지대한 관심을 가지고 있는, ~지향의'라는 의미이며 family-oriented[youth-oriented] culture 등으로 쓰인다.
amazing 놀라운 **improvement** 발전 **talented** 재능이 있는
oriented ~지향의   정답_(b)

6

A I really appreciate the pay raise the company gave me.
B Well, you _____ it.

(a) deserved
(b) afforded
(c) charged
(d) claimed

SOLUTION

A 회사에서 급여를 인상해 준 것을 정말 감사하게 생각합니다.
B 음, 자네는 자격이 있었네.

기출 POINT

동사 deserve는 '~할 만하다'는 말로 뒤에 명사가 와서 deserve attention/ deserve the punishment/ deserve a holiday 등으로 쓰인다. deserve 다음에 to부정사가 오는 deserve to win/ deserve to succeed 등의 표현도 알아두자.
appreciate 감사하다 **pay raise** 급여 인상 **deserve** ~할 만하다
afford ~할 여유가 있다 **charge** 부가하다 **claim** 주장하다 정답_(a)

7

A Hello, I'm calling for Mr. Stone, please.
B Yes, I'll _____ you to him now.

(a) deter
(b) usher
(c) locate
(d) transfer

SOLUTION

A 여보세요, 스톤 씨와 통화하고 싶습니다.
B 네, 그쪽으로 전화를 돌려 드리겠습니다.

기출 POINT

전화상에서 '~에게 돌려주겠다'는 말로 transfer ... to를 쓴다. transfer you to Mr. Kim/ transfer you to the sales department와 같이 to 다음에 사람, 부서 등이 온다. put ... through to도 같은 뜻으로 쓰는 표현이다.
I'm calling for ~와 통화하려고 한다 **deter** 막다 **usher** 안내하다
locate ~에 두다   정답_(d)

8

A Did you get Jennifer to join our gym?
B No. She wasn't _____.

(a) included
(b) occupied
(c) interested
(d) concerned

SOLUTION

A 제니퍼가 우리 헬스 클럽에 가입하도록 했니?
B 아니. 그 애는 관심이 없었어.

기출 POINT

get Jennifer to join our gym은 '제니퍼가 우리 헬스 클럽에 가입하도록 하다'라는 말이고, No라고 했으므로 그 애가 '관심이 없다'는 말이 들어가야 적절하다. '흥미가 있는, 관심을 보이는'이라는 뜻의 interested가 정답이다. occupied는 '사용 중인'의 뜻이고, concerned는 '걱정하는, 관계가 있는'의 뜻이다.
gym 헬스 클럽 **occupied** 사용 중인 **concerned** 걱정스러운; 관계된
정답_(c)

9

A I'm planning to live and work overseas. I think it'll be fun.
B Good idea. I wouldn't mind living _____, either.

(a) abroad
(b) beyond
(c) outwards
(d) worldwide

SOLUTION

A 해외에 살면서 일하려고 계획 중이야. 재미있을 것 같아.
B 좋은 생각이다. 나도 해외에 사는 건 상관없을 것 같아.

⊞ 기출 POINT
overseas는 부사로 '해외에서'라는 뜻이며 같은 말로 abroad를 쓸 수 있다. study abroad/ travel abroad 등의 표현으로 쓰인다. outwards 또는 outward는 '바깥쪽으로'라는 뜻이다.
ex) The door opens outwards. 문이 밖으로 열린다.
overseas 해외에서 **mind -ing** ~을 꺼리다 **abroad** 해외에서
beyond ~너머에 **outward(s)** 바깥쪽으로   정답_(a)

10

A John and Mark are twin brothers, aren't they?
B No, but they do look very much _____.

(a) alike
(b) copied
(c) parallel
(d) matched

SOLUTION

A 존과 마크는 쌍둥이 형제 아니니?
B 아니. 그런데 개네들 정말 많이 닮았어.

⊞ 기출 POINT
'사람이 서로 닮아 보인다'는 말로 적절한 것은 look alike이다. alike 는 '서로 같은'이라는 뜻의 형용사이다. alike는 명사를 수식하는 형태로 는 쓰이지 않고 be동사나 look, seem과 같은 동사 다음에 보어로 오며 서술적 용법으로만 사용된다.
twin brother 쌍둥이 형제 **alike** 서로 같은 **copied** 모방한
parallel 평행의, 비슷한   정답_(a)

11

A Was your cat all right after her ten-story fall?
B Yes. She _____ survived it.

(a) tenderly
(b) suddenly
(c) reasonably
(d) miraculously

SOLUTION

A 네 고양이 10층에서 떨어지고 나서 괜찮았니?
B 네. 기적적으로 살았어요.

⊞ 기출 POINT
survive는 '~을 견디고 죽지 않다'는 뜻으로 목적어를 써서 survive the accident/ survive the war 등으로 사용한다. 여기서는 10층에 서 떨어지고 나서 죽지 않은 것이므로 miraculously가 알맞다.
ten-story 10층의 **fall** 낙하 **tenderly** 부드럽게 **reasonably**
타당하게 **miraculously** 기적적으로   정답_(d)

12

A Frank graduated from this school.
B Really? I didn't know he was a Hope College _____!

(a) faculty
(b) prodigy
(c) alumnus
(d) associate

SOLUTION

A 프랭크가 이 학교를 졸업했어요.
B 그래요? 프랭크가 호프 대학 동문인 건 몰랐습니다!

⊞ 기출 POINT
같은 학교 졸업생인 '동문'을 가리키는 단어로 alumnus를 쓴다.
faculty 교수단; 교직원 **prodigy** 천재 **alumnus** (남자) 동문, 졸업
생 **associate** 동료   정답_(c)

13

A Sorry I forgot to pick up your suits from the dry cleaner.

B That's okay. I should've _____ you.

(a) reminded
(b) persuaded
(c) advertised
(d) memorized

SOLUTION

A 미안. 세탁소에서 네 정장 찾아오는 걸 잊었어.
B 괜찮아. 내가 너한테 다시 알려줬어야 했는데.

⊞ 기출 POINT

동사 remind는 사람을 목적어로 동반하여 그 사람이 할 일에 대해서 '알려주다, 기억하도록 하다'의 뜻으로 쓰인다. remind Jenny about the party on Sunday/ remind me what to do 등과 같이 사용한다.
forget to ~할 것을 잊다 **suit** 정장 **dry cleaner** 세탁소 **remind** ~을 상기시키다 **persuade** 설득하다 **advertise** 광고하다
memorize 암기하다   정답_(a)

14

A Do you want to meet at the mall at 4?

B That's too early, but I can _____ it by 5.

(a) see
(b) meet
(c) make
(d) reach

SOLUTION

A 쇼핑몰에서 4시에 만날래?
B 그건 너무 이르고, 5시간에는 갈 수 있어.

⊞ 기출 POINT

만날 약속 시간을 정하는 대화이다. 몇 시까지 '갈 수 있다'는 말로 make it을 쓴다. make it의 여러 가지 의미: ~에서 성공하다 She made it as an actress./ 제시간에 도착하다 The bus leaves in five minutes. We can't make it.
make it (시간 내에) 갈 수 있다; ~을 이루다, 성공하다 **reach** 도착하다   정답_(c)

15

A I don't know what to do about the misplaced order.

B You need to at least try to _____ the problem.

(a) sort out
(b) stick up
(c) switch off
(d) saw down

SOLUTION

A 주문을 잘못했는데 어떻게 해야 할지 모르겠어.
B 적어도 문제를 해결해 보려고 노력은 해야지.

⊞ 기출 POINT

misplaced order는 '실수로 주문을 잘못한 것'을 말한다. 문제를 해결하려고 노력하라는 충고를 하는 것이 적절하므로 '해결하다'는 의미의 sort out이 정답이다.
misplaced 잘못된 **sort out** 해결하다 **stick up** 튀어나오다
switch off 스위치를 끄다; 흥미를 잃다   정답_(a)

16

A Excuse me. Can you direct me to the Rand Hospital?

B I'm sorry, but I don't have a(n) _____ where that is.

(a) opinion
(b) locality
(c) mind
(d) clue

SOLUTION

A 실례합니다. 랜드 병원으로 가는 길을 알려주시겠어요?
B 죄송합니다만, 어디 있는지 모르겠네요.

⊞ 기출 POINT

길을 묻는 사람에게 '미안하지만 잘 모른다'고 답하는 내용이다. clue는 '실마리, 단서'이고 '전혀 모르겠다'는 말로 don't have a clue라는 표현을 사용한다.
direct 길을 알려주다 **locality** 장소 **clue** 단서   정답_(d)

17

A Should I tip taxi drivers here?

B No, it's not _____ to tip drivers in this country.

(a) optional
(b) customary
(c) fundamental
(d) rudimentary

SOLUTION

A 여기서는 택시 기사들한테 팁을 줘야 하니?

B 아니, 이 나라에서는 운전 기사들에게 팁을 주는 건 관례가 아니야.

⊞ 기출 POINT

문화에 대해서 묻는 질문이다. No라고 답했으므로 택시 운전기사에게 팁을 주는 것이 관례적이지 않다는 말이 적절하다. custom은 '관례'라는 명사이고 이것의 형용사형이 customary이다. '팁을 주다'라는 tip은 타동사로 사람을 목적어로 해서 tip taxi drivers와 같이 사용된다.

optional 선택적인 **customary** 관례적인 **fundamental** 기본적인 **rudimentary** 기초적인   정답 _(b)

18

A Sandra is sad about her breakup.

B I know, but she'll _____.

(a) pass it on
(b) get over it
(c) settle on it
(d) slip it through

SOLUTION

A 샌드라는 실연 때문에 슬퍼하고 있어.

B 그러게, 하지만 극복할 거야.

⊞ 기출 POINT

breakup은 '실연'이라는 뜻이므로 빈칸에는 '극복하다'는 의미의 get over가 적절하다. get over the shock/ get over the disease 등과 같이 사용한다. 관용적으로 get over it을 쓰며 get it over는 단순히 '끝내다, 마치다'이므로 구분해서 알아두자.

breakup 실연 **pass on** ~을 넘기다 **get over** ~을 극복하다. 벗어나다 **settle on** ~에 정착하다 **slip through** ~을 지나가다. 통과하다   정답 (b)

19

A So, how has our business been performing since January?

B Not bad. Our sales _____ has increased by 15%.

(a) addition
(b) volume
(c) depth
(d) spot

SOLUTION

A 그래서, 1월 이후로 우리 사업 실적이 어땠습니까?

B 나쁘지 않았습니다. 저희 판매량은 15% 증가했습니다.

⊞ 기출 POINT

많은 양의 '총량, 총계'를 나타내는 단어로 volume을 쓴다. sales volume/ volume of traffic/ total volume of business/ volume of trade 등으로 사용한다.

perform 수행하다 **addition** 부가, 증가 **volume** 양, 분량 **depth** 깊이 **spot** 장소   정답 _(b)

20

A Your statistics are extensive.

B Yes, they were _____ over many years.

(a) inverted
(b) compiled
(c) fabricated
(d) assembled

SOLUTION

A 통계치가 방대하군요.

B 네, 여러 해 동안 수집한 자료거든요.

⊞ 기출 POINT

extensive는 '방대한'이라는 뜻이므로 빈칸에는 '여러 곳으로부터 정보를 수집하여 리스트를 만들다'는 의미의 compile이 알맞다. assemble은 '많은 사람이나 물건을 한 자리에 모이게 하다'는 의미이므로 적절하지 않다.

statistics 통계치 **extensive** 방대한 **invert** 역전하다 **fabricate** 조작하다 **assemble** 모으다. 소집하다   정답 (b)

21

A May I bring my baby's bottle on the plane?
B Yes, but it must pass through security in a(n)
_____ bag to ensure it is safe.

(a) takeout
(b) well-being
(c) airsickness
(d) tamper-proof

SOLUTION

A 아기 젖병을 가지고 비행기에 탑승해도 될까요?
B 네, 하지만 젖병을 변조 방지 봉투에 넣어서 안전하게 하신 후에 보안 검색대를 통과시켜야 합니다.

⊞ 기출 POINT

항공 안전을 위해 액체나 젤류는 tamper-proof bag 또는 tamper-evident bag에 넣도록 하는 규정에 대한 내용이다. 열면 표시가 나도록 해서 개봉하지 못하도록 봉인 포장하는 것이 tamper-proof이다.
security 보안 검색대 **ensure** 확실하게 하다 **airsickness** 비행기 멀미 **tamper-proof** 개봉 방지의, 봉인 포장의   정답_(d)

22

A So, your thesis is about the oppression of women in the Third World?
B Yes, that's the _____ of it.

(a) gist
(b) hub
(c) tally
(d) aspect

SOLUTION

A 그래서, 네 논문은 제3세계의 여성 억압에 관한 내용이니?
B 네, 요점을 말하자면 그렇죠.

⊞ 기출 POINT

'글이나 말의 요지'를 말하는 단어는 gist이다. gist of his speech/gist of the argument 등으로 사용한다.
oppression 억압 **Third World** 제3세계 **gist** 요점 **hub** 중추 **tally** 득점 **aspect** 관점   정답_(a)

23

A That doctor seems nice.
B Yes. He always treats patients _____.

(a) timidly
(b) cynically
(c) ruggedly
(d) courteously

SOLUTION

A 그 의사 선생님 좋아 보이더라.
B 네. 선생님은 환자를 항상 자상하게 대해 주세요.

⊞ 기출 POINT

좋은 의사라고 했으므로 긍정적인 의미의 어휘를 찾으면 된다.
courteous는 예의가 바르고 다른 사람을 존중하는 태도를 가리키는 단어이다. timidly는 '소심하게, 용기 없이'라는 뜻이므로 적절하지 않다.
treat 대하다 **timidly** 소심하게 **cynically** 냉소적으로 **ruggedly** 거칠게 **courteously** 정중하게   정답_(d)

24

A I heard your blind date didn't work out.
B No, she _____.

(a) pushed me through
(b) dropped me down
(c) turned me over
(d) stood me up

SOLUTION

A 소개팅이 잘 안 됐다고 들었어.
B 응, 여자쪽에서 나를 바람맞혔지.

⊞ 기출 POINT

'소개팅이 잘되지 않았다'고 했으므로 '그 애가 나를 바람맞혔다'는 내용이 가장 적절하다. stand A up은 'A를 바람맞히다'의 뜻으로 사용된다. '어떤 일이 잘되지 않았다'는 말은 didn't work out을 쓴다.
blind date 소개팅 **work out** ~가 잘되다 **push ... through** ~를 억지로 시키다 **turn over** 뒤집다 **stand A up** A를 바람맞히다
          정답_(d)

25

A The heat and humidity is so stifling that I don't feel like moving.

B Yeah, it makes me feel _____, too.

(a) guileless
(b) lethargic
(c) distraught
(d) overwrought

SOLUTION

A 열기와 습기 때문에 숨이 막힐 것 같아서 꼼짝도 하기 싫어.
B 응, 나도 무기력해져.

⊞ 기출 POINT

don't feel like moving과 내용이 연결되는 형용사가 들어가야 한다. 따라서 '느리고 무기력한'이라는 뜻의 lethargic이 알맞다. distraught 는 화가 나거나 걱정으로 인해 '제정신이 아닌'이라는 뜻이고 overwrought는 overwork의 과거분사로 '너무 긴장한'이라는 뜻이다.
humidity 습도 **stifling** 숨이 막히는 **guileless** 교활하지 않은
lethargic 무기력한 **distraught** 정신이 혼란스러운 **정답_(b)**

26

Jane looks so young that people make the _____ of thinking she is a teenager.

(a) sum
(b) fault
(c) mistake
(d) memory

SOLUTION

제인은 너무 어려 보여서 사람들은 그녀를 십대로 생각하는 실수를 범한다.

⊞ 기출 POINT

'그녀가 십대라고 생각하는 실수를 저지르다'는 내용이 되어야 한다. '실수, 잘못'으로 mistake과 fault를 쓸 수 있지만 make the mistake of -ing의 형태로 사용하는 mistake이 정답이다.
teenager 십대 **sum** 개요, 요약 **fault** 잘못 **정답_(c)**

27

It is crucial that documents are carefully proofread and errors are _____.

(a) corrected
(b) accessed
(c) rubbed
(d) exited

SOLUTION

신중하게 문서들을 교정하고 오류를 수정하는 것이 중요하다.

⊞ 기출 POINT

'문서를 교정하고 오류를 수정한다'는 내용이 가장 잘 어울리므로 errors are corrected가 되어야 한다. correct는 '바로 잡다, 수정하다' 의 뜻이다.
crucial 중요한 **document** 문서 **proofread** 교정하다 **access** 입수하다 **rub** 문지르다 **정답_(a)**

28

We apologize for any inconvenience _____ by the train's late arrival.

(a) caused
(b) resulted
(c) bothered
(d) suspected

SOLUTION

기차의 연착으로 불편을 드려 죄송합니다.

⊞ 기출 POINT

'기차의 연착으로 인해 일어난 불편함'이라는 내용이 되어야 하므로 caused가 알맞다. result는 전치사 in을 동반하여 be resulted in (~의 결과를 가져오다)으로 사용된다.
apologize for ~에 대해 사과하다 **inconvenience** 불편 **bother** 괴롭히다 **suspect** 의심하다 **정답_(a)**

29

Our telescopes' mounts are capable of vertical and horizontal movement so that the telescope can be _____ in any direction.

(a) pointed
(b) viewed
(c) slipped
(d) framed

SOLUTION

저희 망원경 거치대는 망원경이 어떤 방향이라도 가리킬 수 있도록 수직 및 수평 조정이 가능합니다.

▦ 기출 POINT

망원경 거치대에 대한 설명이다. '이 거치대는 수직, 수평 조정이 가능하다'고 했으므로 '망원경이 어떤 방향이든 가리킬 수 있다'는 내용이 되어야 한다. '방향을 가리키다'는 뜻의 pointed가 정답이다. viewed가 들어가면 can be viewed in any direction이 되어 '망원경이 어떤 방향에서든 보인다'는 다른 뜻이 된다.

telescope 망원경 **mount** 거치대 **vertical** 수직의 **horizontal** 수평의 **slip** 미끄러지다 **frame** ∼의 틀을 잡다   **정답_(a)**

30

Education News is _____ six times a year and is aimed at teachers and parents.

(a) reviewed
(b) contained
(c) published
(d) subscribed

SOLUTION

〈교육 소식〉은 1년에 여섯 번 출간되며 교사와 학부모들을 대상으로 한다.

▦ 기출 POINT

잡지의 특성에 대한 내용이다. '대상은 교사와 학부모이고 1년에 여섯 번 출간된다'는 내용이 적절하므로 published가 정답이다. subscribe는 '정기구독을 하다'이다.

be aimed at ∼을 겨냥하다 **contain** 포함하다 **publish** 출판하다 **subscribe** 정기구독하다   **정답_(c)**

31

A leader's central responsibility is to _____ the conditions necessary for a society's growth and success.

(a) equip
(b) create
(c) handle
(d) donate

SOLUTION

지도자의 주된 책임은 사회의 성장과 발전에 필요한 환경을 조성하는 것이다.

▦ 기출 POINT

환경 조건을 '조성한다'는 뜻으로 create이 적절하다. equip은 '기계 설비 등을 갖추다, 장비를 구비하다'는 뜻으로 문맥상 적절하지 않다.

central 주된 **responsibility** 책임 **equip** 갖추다, 장비하다 **create** 창조하다 **handle** 다루다 **donate** 기부하다   **정답_(b)**

32

Acquiring insights into other countries' cultures is an essential _____ of a well-rounded education.

(a) component
(b) strategy
(c) layout
(d) tactic

SOLUTION

다른 국가들의 문화에 대한 통찰을 얻는 것은 균형 잡힌 교육의 필수적인 요소이다.

▦ 기출 POINT

타국 문화에 대한 통찰력을 얻는 것이 균형 잡힌 교육의 '전략'이나 '전술'이라는 말은 어울리지 않으므로 '요소'라는 뜻의 component가 알맞다.

acquire 얻다, 습득하다 **insight** 통찰 **well-rounded** 균형 잡힌 **component** 요소 **strategy** 전략 **layout** 배치, 설계 **tactic** 전술   **정답_(a)**

Actual Test 3

33

Cut your caffeine intake by _____ non-caffeinated drinks for caffeinated ones.

(a) changing
(b) replacing
(c) purchasing
(d) substituting

SOLUTION

카페인 음료를 무카페인 음료로 대체함으로써 카페인 섭취를 줄이시오.

기출 POINT

전치사 for를 동반하여 '~을 대신하다, 대체하다'의 뜻으로 쓰는 어구를 찾는 문제이다. substitute는 substitute A for B의 형태로 써서 'B 대신 A를 사용하다'의 뜻이다. replace는 by나 with를 동반하여 replace A with[by] B의 형태로 사용한다.

intake 섭취   **replace** 대체하다   **purchase** 구매하다   **substitute** 대신하다   정답_(d)

34

The first half of the 20th century saw the world _____ in two global wars.

(a) broiled
(b) engaged
(c) mounted
(d) committed

SOLUTION

20세기 전반에 세계는 두 차례의 세계 전쟁에 휘말렸다.

기출 POINT

세계 전쟁에 휘말린 것, 관여한 것에 대한 내용이므로 in[on]을 동반하여 '~에 연관되다'의 뜻으로 사용되는 engage가 정답이다. 무생물(The first half of the 20th century)이 문장의 주어로 쓰였음에 유의하며, saw 대신 witnessed를 쓸 수 있다는 것도 알아두자.

broil 굽다   **engage** 관여하다   **mount** 오르다   **commit** 저지르다   정답_(b)

35

Economic growth has increased in _____ contrast to the decline experienced last year.

(a) random
(b) morbid
(c) sharp
(d) lined

SOLUTION

지난해 겪었던 경기 침체와는 극명한 대조를 이루며 경제 성장이 증가했다.

기출 POINT

대조를 이루는 것이 Economic growth has increased와 decline experienced last year이다. 형용사 sharp는 차이를 나타내는 말과 함께 쓰여서 차이가 '매우 크고 뚜렷한'이라는 뜻이다. sharp difference/ sharp contrast/ sharp distinction 등으로 쓰인다. random은 '무작위의'라는 뜻이고, lined는 '줄을 그은'이라는 뜻이다.

contrast 대조   **decline** 침체   **random** 무작위의   **morbid** 병적인   **sharp** 뚜렷한   정답_(c)

36

The minimum wage ensures that all entry-level workers _____ a fair base wage.

(a) obtain
(b) request
(c) bargain
(d) establish

SOLUTION

최저 임금은 모든 하급직 근로자들이 공정한 기본급을 받을 수 있도록 보장한다.

기출 POINT

동사 ensure는 뒤에 명사구나 절이 와서 '~을 확실하게 하다, 보장하다'의 뜻으로 쓰인다. '최저 임금이라는 제도는 공정한 급여를 받을 수 있도록 보장한다'는 내용이 되어야 하므로 obtain이 정답이다.

minimum 최소의   **ensure** 보장하다   **entry-level** 하급직의   **fair** 공정한   **base** 기초; 바닥   **bargain** 흥정하다   정답_(a)

37

The girl slept so _____ that the thunder did not wake her up.

(a) firmly
(b) wholly
(c) entirely
(d) soundly

SOLUTION

소녀는 너무 곤히 자서 천둥 소리에도 깨지 않았다.

⊞ 기출 POINT

soundly는 '온전하게'라는 뜻이 있지만 sleep soundly는 '잠을 푹, 곤히 자다'라는 뜻이다.

wake up ~를 깨우다 firmly 확고하게 wholly 전적으로 entirely 완전히, 아주 soundly 곤히   정답_(d)

38

The film is a reflection of the violence that _____ American culture.

(a) exudes
(b) spreads
(c) pervades
(d) subsumes

SOLUTION

그 영화는 미국 문화에 팽배해 있는 폭력에 대한 고찰이다.

⊞ 기출 POINT

American culture를 목적어로 삼아 '미국 문화에 퍼져 있다'는 뜻을 나타낼 수 있는 동사를 고르는 것이 핵심이다. pervade는 어떤 장소에 '널리 퍼지다, 고루 미치다'의 뜻으로 pervade the air/ pervade the country/ pervade the American culture 등으로 사용한다.

reflection 고찰 violence 폭력 exude 스며 나오다 spread 퍼지다 pervade 팽배하다 subsume 포함하다   정답_(c)

39

Industrialized nations should take the _____ and reduce greenhouse gas emissions.

(a) operation
(b) initiative
(c) example
(d) position

SOLUTION

선진국들이 자발적으로 나서서 온실가스 배출을 줄여야 한다.

⊞ 기출 POINT

take the initiative는 '자발적으로 나서다, 주도권을 잡다'라는 뜻이다.

industrialized 산업화된 reduce 감소시키다 greenhouse gas 온실가스 emission 배출 operation 운영 initiative 주도권   정답_(b)

40

Some people say even friends can betray you and that you can only _____ on yourself in the end.

(a) check
(b) focus
(c) insist
(d) rely

SOLUTION

어떤 사람들은 친구들조차도 당신을 배신할 수 있고 결국 의지할 수 있는 건 자기 자신뿐이라고 말한다.

⊞ 기출 POINT

'친구조차 배신할 수 있다'는 내용에 이어지는 말로 적절한 것은 '결국 자신만을 의지할 수 있다'는 내용이므로 전치사 on과 함께 쓰일 수 있는 rely가 정답이다. rely on your judgment/ rely on your sister 등으로 사용되며 focus on은 '~에 집중하다'라는 뜻이다.

betray 배신하다 in the end 결국에는 focus 집중하다 insist 주장하다 rely 의지하다   정답_(d)

41

The author dwells on _____ matters rather than on the essentials of medieval history.

(a) trivial
(b) relevant
(c) elemental
(d) invaluable

SOLUTION

작가는 중세사의 핵심보다는 사소한 문제에 대해 자세히 쓰고 있다.

⊞ 기출 POINT

rather than을 통해 두 가지 대상이 대조되고 있음을 알 수 있다. essentials of medieval history와 대조되는 내용으로 나올 수 있는 것이 trivial matters이다. dwell on은 '~에 대해 길게 얘기하거나 쓰다'는 표현이다.

author 작가 **medieval** 중세의 **trivial** 사소한 **relevant** 적절한 **elemental** 기본적인 **invaluable** 매우 귀중한 　　　　정답_(a)

42

Berbers residing near the Mediterranean Sea make a(n) _____ as farmers.

(a) living
(b) existing
(c) provision
(d) occupation

SOLUTION

지중해 부근에 거주하는 베르베르인들은 농부로서 생계를 꾸려간다.

⊞ 기출 POINT

make a(n)와 함께 쓰여 '직업으로 하다, 생계를 꾸리다'로 사용할 수 있는 단어는 living이다. make a living as farmers는 '농부로 먹고 산다'는 뜻이다.

reside 살다 **Mediterranean Sea** 지중해 **provision** 준비 **occupation** 직업 　　　　정답_(a)

43

Orangutans are closely _____ to humans genetically.

(a) placed
(b) related
(c) referred
(d) attributed

SOLUTION

오랑우탄은 유전적으로 인간과 매우 비슷하다.

⊞ 기출 POINT

'유전적으로 인간과 관련이 있다'는 내용이 되어야 한다. be placed to 는 '~로 보내지다, 회부되다'라는 뜻이다. be related to가 '~와 관련이 있다'라는 의미이고 be referred to as는 '~라고 불려지다'는 뜻이다. be attributed to는 작품 등을 '~의 것이라고 하다'는 뜻이다.

orangutan 오랑우탄 **genetically** 유전적으로 　　　　정답_(b)

44

Research shows that there is a(n) _____ difference between the way problems are solved by experts and by novices.

(a) stark
(b) crass
(c) obtuse
(d) rotund

SOLUTION

연구는 전문가와 초심자 간에 문제를 해결하는 방법에 뚜렷한 차이가 있음을 보여준다.

⊞ 기출 POINT

expert와 novice가 문제를 해결하는 방식에 분명한 차이가 있다는 내용이 되어야 한다. difference를 수식하는 '뚜렷한'이라는 의미의 단어는 stark이다.

expert 전문가 **novice** 초심자 **stark** 뚜렷한 **crass** 우둔한 **obtuse** 무딘 **rotund** 둥근 　　　　정답_(a)

45

The government will _____ anyone hunting elephants illegally.

(a) prosecute
(b) institute
(c) legislate
(d) refute

정부는 불법으로 코끼리를 사냥하는 사람을 모두 기소할 것이다.

⊞ 기출 POINT

불법적인 일을 하는 사람, 즉 anyone을 목적어로 취하는 동사를 묻고 있다. prosecute anyone이 되어야 '~하는 사람은 누구든지 기소한다'는 내용이 된다. refute는 다른 사람의 의견에 '반박하다'는 뜻이다.

illegally 불법으로 **prosecute** 기소하다 **institute** 설립하다
legislate 법률로 제정하다 **refute** 반박하다 　　　정답_(a)

46

Teaching disabled children is laborious yet rewarding, requiring determination, _____ and hard work.

(a) rendition
(b) distraction
(c) pertinacity
(d) infrastructure

장애아를 가르치는 일은 고되지만 보람 있는 일로, 결단력과 끈기 그리고 열심히 일할 것을 요구한다.

⊞ 기출 POINT

determination, hard work와 비슷한 의미의 단어가 와야 하므로 매우 굳건한 태도로 어떤 일을 믿거나 하는 것을 의미하는 pertinacity가 정답이다.

disabled 장애의 **laborious** 고된 **rewarding** 보람이 있는
determination 결단력 **rendition** 번역 **distraction** 주의 산만
pertinacity 끈기 **infrastructure** 기반 시설 　　　정답_(c)

47

From the remarks of the woman he was questioning, the detective _____ that she must have committed the crime.

(a) plied
(b) reduced
(c) deduced
(d) conferred

형사는 자신이 심문하던 여성의 말에서 그녀가 범행을 저질렀음이 틀림없다고 추론했다.

⊞ 기출 POINT

must have p.p는 '~했음에 틀림없다'는 말이므로 that 이하의 내용을 추론했다는 말이 들어가야 한다. deduce는 that절을 목적어로 취해 '~라고 추론하다'는 뜻이다.

remark 말 **question** 심문하다 **detective** 형사 **commit** 저지르다 **crime** 범죄 **ply** 캐묻다 **deduce** 추론하다 **confer** 수여하다 　　　정답_(c)

48

The president felt _____ when he was accused unfairly by many reporters at the press conference.

(a) piqued
(b) felicitous
(c) appeased
(d) exonerated

사장은 기자 회견에서 여러 기자들로부터 부당하게 비난을 받자 화가 났다.

⊞ 기출 POINT

부당하게 비난을 받았을 때 느꼈을 기분에 대한 내용이 나와야 한다. piqued는 놀림이나 무시를 받았을 때 '기분이 상하거나 화가 나는'이라는 의미를 담고 있으므로 정답이다. appeased는 '진정된, 평안을 찾은'이란 뜻이다.

accuse 비난하다 **unfairly** 부당하게 **press conference** 기자 회견 **piqued** 화나는 **felicitous** 적절한, 타당한 **appeased** 진정된 **exonerated** 면제된 　　　정답_(a)

Actual Test 3

49

Most of the damage caused by an earthquake results from seismic waves that _____ out from a fault line at 8,000 or more miles per hour.

(a) exhale
(b) expunge
(c) prolapse
(d) propagate

SOLUTION

지진에 의한 피해의 대부분은 단층선에서부터 시속 8,000마일 이상의 속도로 퍼져 나가는 지진파 때문이다.

기출 POINT

보통 '번식하다'의 뜻으로 사용되는 propagate는 음향이나 전파가 '퍼져 나가다'의 뜻도 가지고 있다. 따라서 단층선에서부터 지진파가 '퍼져 나간다'는 의미가 되어야 하므로 정답은 (d)이다.

seismic wave 진동파   **fault line** 단층선   **exhale** 내쉬다
expunge 삭제하다   **prolapse** 탈수하다   **propagate** 전파하다

정답_(d)

50

A(n) _____ administration should be set up until a permanent governing body is established in the country.

(a) interim
(b) panoptic
(c) subsistent
(d) centrifugal

SOLUTION

나라에 영구 통치 기관이 설립될 때까지 임시 행정부를 수립해야 한다.

기출 POINT

내용상 '영구 통치 기관'인 permanent governing body와 대조되는 어구가 앞에 나와야 하므로 '임시적인 통치 기관'인 an interim administration이 알맞다. 형용사 interim은 interim measure/ interim payment/ interim report 등으로 사용된다.

administration 행정부   **permanent** 영구적인   **interim** 임시의
panoptic 모든 것이 한눈에 보이는   **subsistent** 존재하는   **centrifugal** 원심력의

정답_(a)

1

A good résumé can only get you to the interview stage. In order to finally get a job, it is important to do well in the interview, beginning with a strong first impression. First impressions are critical because recruiters often make decisions based on them. So if you think your résumé is all that counts, think again. Right or wrong, final judgments _____.

(a) can be affected by your work
(b) can depend on who you know
(c) are made based on your résumé
(d) are influenced by initial meetings

SOLUTION

이력서가 괜찮을 때 면접 단계까지는 올라갈 수 있다. 최종적으로 일자리를 얻으려면 강한 첫인상으로 시작해서 면접을 잘하는 것이 중요하다. 채용자들은 첫인상에 근거해 의사 결정을 내리는 경우가 많기 때문에 첫인상은 매우 중요하다. 그래서 이력서가 전부라고 생각한다면 생각을 바꿔라. 옳건 그르건 최종 판단은 최초의 만남에 영향을 받는다.

⊞ 기출 POINT

취업을 하기 위해서는 이력서보다 면접에서의 인상이 중요함을 설명하는 글이다. 마지막 부분에서, 이력서가 전부라고 생각했다면 다시 생각해 보라고 했으므로 빈칸에는 채용자들의 최종 결정은 '최초의 만남에 영향을 받는다'는 (d)가 적절하다.

résumé 이력서 **first impression** 첫인상 **critical** 매우 중요한
recruiter 채용자 **count** 중요하다 **initial** 최초의   정답_(d)

2

Around 2000 BC, during the Shang Dynasty, people in China _____. There were gods that represented nature, such as weather and sky gods. There was also a higher god called Shang-Ti who ruled over all others. The ancient Chinese even believed that their ancestors became like gods when they died. Gods were clearly a very important part of their lives.

(a) were fearful of God's wrath
(b) worshipped many different gods
(c) constantly disagreed over religion
(d) praised some gods more than others

SOLUTION

기원전 2000년경 상 왕조 동안 중국 사람들은 여러 다른 신을 숭배했다. 날씨와 같이 자연을 나타내는 신도 있었고 하늘 신도 있었다. 또한 다른 모든 신들 위에 군림했던 상제라는 신도 있었다. 고대 중국인들은 심지어 자신들의 조상은 죽어서 신과 같이 된다고 믿었다. 신들은 분명 그들 삶의 매우 중요한 일부였다.

⊞ 기출 POINT

도입부이면서 요지가 되는 내용을 찾아야 하는 문제이다. 자연을 나타내는 신들, 그보다 상위 수준의 신 등 다양한 신들이 있었고 조상들이 죽어서 신과 같이 된다고 믿었다는 내용이 이어지므로 (b)가 적절하다.

dynasty 왕조 **represent** 나타내다 **ancestor** 조상 **be fearful of** ~을 두려워하다 **wrath** 분노 **worship** 숭배하다 **constantly** 지속적으로 **praise** 칭찬하다   정답_(b)

3

One of the sites I visited in Paris was the Alma Bridge over the Seine River, which is famous for a large statue of an infantry soldier that stands next to it. The statue is the only surviving part of the original Alma Bridge built in 1854, and Parisians used to use it as a gauge of river water levels. If the statue's toes got wet, Paris would be on flood alert. If his ankles went under water, riverside roads would be closed. If his hips were wet, that would mean _____.

(a) the river water had lowered
(b) the city might soon be flooded
(c) the bridge was in need of repair
(d) the statue would need to be moved

SOLUTION

내가 파리에서 방문했던 곳 중 하나는 센 강 위의 알마교였는데, 이곳은 그 옆에 있는 대형 보병상으로 유명하다. 이 상은 1854년 지어진 본래의 알마교 중에서 유일하게 보존된 것인데, 파리 사람들은 과거에 이것을 강의 수위 측정계로 사용했다. 상의 발가락이 젖으면 파리에는 홍수 경보가 내려졌다. 상의 발목이 물에 잠기면, 강변 도로가 폐쇄됐다. 상의 엉덩이가 젖으면 파리가 곧 범람할 것을 뜻했다.

⊞ 기출 POINT
알마교에 있는 보병상이 강의 수위 측정계로 사용되었다는 내용이다. 발가락에서 발목이 잠긴 후 엉덩이까지 물이 차오르면 앞선 상황보다 더욱 심각한 상태라는 것을 암시하므로 도시가 범람한다는 (b)가 정답이다.

statue 상, 동상 **infantry soldier** 보병 **Parisian** 파리인 **gauge** 측정계 **water level** 수위 **alert** 경보 정답_(b)

4

Welcome to Hermitage National Park. Visitors to the park are welcome to camp by the beautiful Lake Piron. However, please take caution not to harm the environment. Littering, cutting down trees and building unauthorized bonfires are strictly illegal, and those caught engaging in such activities face severe fines and penalties. A full list of prohibited activities is available at each ranger station or on our website. Please help us _____.

(a) stop people fishing in the lake
(b) keep the new facilities clean
(c) preserve the environment
(d) stop all of the wastage

SOLUTION

허미티지 국립공원에 오신 것을 환영합니다. 이 공원을 찾는 방문객들은 아름다운 파이런 호숫가에서 야영을 해도 됩니다. 하지만 환경을 해치지 않도록 주의해 주십시오. 쓰레기 투기, 나무를 베거나 허가 없이 모닥불을 피우는 것은 절대 불법이며, 이같은 행동을 하다가 적발된 사람들은 상당한 벌금과 과태료를 물게 됩니다. 금지된 활동 목록은 각 공원 관리소나 저희 홈페이지에서 보실 수 있습니다. 환경을 보존할 수 있도록 협조해 주십시오.

⊞ 기출 POINT
공원 방문객들에게 당부하는 글로 주의 사항을 요약하는 내용이 빈칸에 들어가야 한다. 두 번째 문장에서 환경을 해치지 말아 달라는 주제가 제시되어 있고 세부적인 지침에 대한 설명이 나오므로 정답은 환경보존에 대한 협조를 구하는 (c)이다.

litter 쓰레기를 투기하다 **unauthorized** 허가받지 않은 **bonfire** 모닥불 **fine** 벌금 **penalty** 과태료 **prohibited** 금지된 **available** 이용 가능한 **ranger station** 관리소 **wastage** 낭비 정답_(c)

5

Disgraced journalist Lewis Landow has apologized today after a scandal concerning a falsified report. Last week Landow's column for *Life Today* magazine included a brief account of the Republican National Convention. The problem was that the convention had not taken place at the time. Landow's account was fictional, a fact exposed when *Life Today* magazines arrived in subscribers' mailboxes before the convention, earlier than he had thought they would. Landow was visibly upset _____.

(a) by *Life Today*'s account of his life
(b) about the false reports against him
(c) at not becoming a Republican candidate
(d) when admitting that his report was fake

불명예를 입은 기자인 루이스 랜도우는 왜곡 보도와 관련한 물의 후 오늘 사과했다. 지난주 〈오늘의 삶〉 잡지 내 랜도우의 컬럼에는 공화당 전국 전당 대회의 짤막한 보도가 실렸다. 문제는 전당 대회가 그 당시 아직 열리지 않았다는 것이다. 랜도우의 설명은 지어낸 것이었으며, 랜도우가 생각했던 것보다 빨리, 전당 대회에 앞서 잡지 구독자들의 우편함에 〈오늘의 삶〉 잡지가 배달되면서 이 같은 사실이 발각되었다. 랜도우는 그의 보도가 가짜였음을 인정했을 때 당황하는 기색이 역력했다.

⊞ 기출 POINT
루이스 랜도우라는 기자가 열리지 않은 전당 대회에 대해 지어서 쓴 기사가 잡지 구독자들에게 일찍 배포되면서 사실이 밝혀진 사건이다. 랜도우가 자신의 보도가 가짜였다는 것을 인정할 때 당황한 얼굴이었다는 내용이 가장 적절하다.

disgraced 불명예를 입은   **scandal** 물의, 추문   **falsified** 왜곡된, 위조된   **account** 설명   **convention** 전당 대회   **fictional** 지어낸   **expose** 노출하다   정답_(d)

6

Carter carburetors were used on most GMC passenger trucks from 1941 to 1948. They were hardy contraptions, but they sometimes made trucks idle roughly. However, that was easily fixed. The float lever could be easily bent slightly upwards to lower the float level, or downwards to raise it. Nothing more was needed than a pair of nose pliers and a gentle touch. This same method is still used by owners and collectors of these old trucks today. It just goes to show that Carter carburetors _____.

(a) sell for a high price among collectors
(b) are still durable and easy to maintain
(c) perform as well as modern carburetors
(d) can easily be replaced with newer ones

카터 카뷰레터는 1941년부터 1948년까지 대부분의 GMC 승용 트럭에 사용되었다. 이것은 내구성이 높은 고안물이었으나, 때로는 이것 때문에 트럭의 공회전 시 소음이 높아지기도 했다. 그러나 문제는 쉽게 해결됐다. 손쉽게 플로트 레버를 살짝 위로 구부려 플로트 레벨을 낮추거나, 아래로 구부려 플로트 레벨을 높일 수 있었다. 노즈 플라이어(펜치) 한 개로 약간 손보는 것 외에는 다른 아무것도 필요 없었다. 이 똑같은 방법은 이 구형 트럭의 소유주와 수집가들에 의해 오늘날도 여전히 사용되고 있다. 이것은 카터 카뷰레터가 여전히 튼튼하고 유지 보수가 쉽다는 것을 보여주는 것이다.

⊞ 기출 POINT
카뷰레터는 문제점이 있지만 내구성이 있고 조작 방법이 간단하다는 것을 알 수 있으므로 빈칸에는 튼튼하고 유지 보수가 쉽다는 (b)가 적절하다.

carburetor 카뷰레터   **hardy** 튼튼한   **contraption** 고안물   **idle** 공회전하다   **float lever** 플로트 레버   **slightly** 약간   **nose plier** 노즈 플라이어(펜치)   **durable** 내구성 있는   **replace** 대신하다   정답 (b)

7

Certain advocates of vegetarianism in the 1800s believed that _____. Consequently, their lifestyle was not just about physical health or the ethical treatment of animals. They saw carnivorism as something that transformed a person's behavior. It was deemed identical to cruelty and bad-temperedness; it was even regarded as leading to robbery, sycophancy and despotism. They went so far as to see meat eating as the source of all evil, blaming it for such abhorrences as the slave trade.

(a) cruelty to animals was uncivilized
(b) vegetables would guarantee a long life
(c) meat eating was against the word of God
(d) food formed character and affected the mind

SOLUTION

1800년대 일부 채식주의 주창자들은 음식이 성격을 형성하고 정신에 영향을 준다고 믿었다. 그 결과, 이들의 생활양식은 단순히 신체적 건강이나 동물에 대한 윤리적 처우에 대한 것만은 아니었다. 이들은 육식주의를 사람의 행동을 변화시키는 무언가로 보았다. 이것은 잔인함 및 나쁜 성격과 동일한 것으로 간주되었다. 심지어는 강도, 아첨과 횡포에까지 이르는 것으로 여겨지기도 했다. 이들은 육식을 모든 악의 근원으로 보아, 노예 매매와 같은 혐오 행위까지도 육식 때문이라고 주장하기도 했다.

🏛 기출 POINT

도입 문장 다음에 Consequently(그래서)라는 접속사가 이어지므로 전제가 빈칸에 들어가야 한다. 육식주의가 나쁜 성격과 흉악한 행위의 원인이 된다고 믿었다는 내용이 이어지므로 '음식이 성격을 만들고 정신에 영향을 준다'는 (d)가 전제로 들어가야 자연스러운 문맥이 된다.

ethical 윤리적인 **treatment** 대우 **carnivorism** 육식주의 **transform** 변형시키다 **deem** ~라고 여기다 **identical** 동일한 **cruelty** 잔인함 **bad-temperedness** 나쁜 성격 **sycophancy** 아첨 **despotism** 횡포 **abhorrence** 혐오 　　　정답_(d)

8

Repressing sneezes may be harmful to your health. Air escaping from your nose and mouth during a sneeze can reach a maximum speed of 100 mph. Therefore, sneezing while holding your breath or blocking your lips or nose builds up enormous pressure in the nose and throat. Such pressure may push bacteria from your nose into your sinuses or into your ears through the Eustachian tubes. When you sneeze, you should cover your nose and mouth with a tissue. But it is recommended that _____.

(a) you use more than one tissue at such times
(b) you refrain from any measure to stifle a sneeze
(c) you do not sneeze in the direction of other people
(d) you seek medical advice if you are sneezing too often

SOLUTION

재채기를 참는 것은 건강에 해로울 수 있다. 재채기를 하는 동안 코와 입으로부터 빠져나가는 공기는 그 속도가 최고 시속 100마일에 달한다. 따라서 숨을 참는 동안, 혹은 입술이나 코를 막은 상태에서 재채기를 하게 되면 코와 목구멍에 대한 압력이 엄청나게 증가하게 된다. 이 같은 압력은 박테리아를 코에서부터 비강으로 밀어넣거나 혹은 유스타키오관을 통해 귀로 밀어보낼 수 있다. 재채기를 할 때는 휴지로 코와 입을 가려야 한다. 하지만 재채기를 참으려는 행동은 절대 하지 않을 것을 권한다.

🏛 기출 POINT

첫 문장과 마지막 문장이 비슷한 내용으로 반복되는 경우가 많이 있다. 재채기를 참으면 엄청난 속도로 공기가 움직이면서 세균이 몸 안쪽으로 들어가버리고 몸을 상하게 할 수 있다는 설명이다. 그러므로 휴지로 가리기는 해야 하지만 참으려는 어떤 방법도 쓰지 말라는 (b)가 정답이다.

repress 억누르다 **enormous** 엄청난 **sinus** 비강 **Eustachian tubes** 유스타키오관, 이관 **recommend** 권하다 **refrain from** ~을 삼가다 **stifle** 참다, 억제하다 　　　정답_(b)

9

Dear Editor,

I'm very concerned about the rise in serious crimes being committed by youths. Many of these youths laugh at the justice system. That is because they get off lightly and receive sentences for children, which are often lenient, even though they have committed adult crimes. Since there are no serious consequences for their actions, the message sent to such juvenile criminals is that crime doesn't matter. At the moment, _____.

Yours sincerely,
Tony Bundy

(a) juvenile offenders are treated inhumanely
(b) court procedures are being reformed
(c) victims of crimes are being ignored
(d) punishments do not fit the crimes

SOLUTION

편집자 귀하.

젊은이들이 저지르고 있는 중범죄의 증가에 대해 매우 우려하고 있습니다. 이들 젊은이 중 많은 사람들은 사법 제도를 비웃습니다. 이것은 이들이 성인 범죄를 저질렀음에도 불구하고 큰 처벌을 받지 않고, 종종 관대한 어린이용 구형을 받기 때문입니다. 이들의 행동에 대한 심각한 결과가 없기 때문에, 범죄는 큰 문제가 아니라는 메시지가 이 같은 청소년 범죄자들에게 전달되는 것입니다. 현재는 처벌이 범죄에 적합하지 않습니다.

토니 번디 드림

기출 POINT
청소년의 심각한 범죄 증가에 대한 우려를 표시하는 편지이다. 필자는 현 사법 제도는 심각한 범죄를 저지르는 청소년들을 너무 약하게 처벌하고 있다고 주장한다. 결론적으로 현재 '처벌은 범죄에 적정하지 않다'는 말이 들어가야 하므로 정답은 (d)이다.
concerned 우려하는   **get off** (처벌에서) 벗어나다   **commit** 저지르다   **justice system** 사법 제도   **sentence** 처벌   **lenient** 관대한   **juvenile criminal** 청소년 범죄자   **offender** 범법자   **inhumanely** 비인간적으로   **court procedure** 법정 절차   **reform** 개정하다

정답_(d)

10

In ancient Egypt, a wide social rift separated the small group of rulers and the nobility from the majority of the populace at the bottom of the social ladder. To be more precise, pharaohs were at the top of the ladder and slaves and farmers were at the other end. This pyramid-like social stratification and top-down power structure governed every sphere of life. It meant that _____.

(a) society's rules were enforced by soldiers
(b) nobles were constantly fighting to gain power
(c) there were more slaves than there were farmers
(d) most wealth and power was in the hands of the few

SOLUTION

고대 이집트에서는 광범위한 사회 격차가 소수의 통치자들 및 귀족들을 사회 밑바닥 계층에 있는 대부분의 서민들과 분리했다. 더 정확히 말하자면, 파라오들이 최상위 계층에 있었고, 노예와 농부들은 그 반대편 끝에 있었다. 이 피라미드형 사회 계층과 상명하달식 권력 구조는 삶의 모든 측면을 지배했다. 이는 곧 대부분의 부와 권력은 소수의 손에 쥐어져 있었음을 뜻했다.

기출 POINT
고대 이집트의 사회구조는 소수의 지배층과 다수의 피지배층으로 분리되어 있다는 내용이다. 이러한 계층 구조는 삶의 모든 측면을 지배했다는 것으로 보아 '대부분의 부와 권력이 소수의 손에 있었다'는 (d)가 와야 한다.
rift 균열, 격차   **nobility** 귀족   **majority** 다수   **populace** 서민   **pharaoh** 파라오   **pyramid-like** 피라미드형의   **stratification** 계층   **top-down** 상명하달식(ant. bottom-up)   **sphere** 범위

정답_(d)

11

Overwhelming evidence suggests that _____ _____. Studies have shown that children subjected to such treatment are significantly more likely to subject other people to physical punishments, both as children and as adults. In addition, the more violently children are punished, the more aggressive and violent they become later. One study found that among a group of children, the ones spanked the most as 3- to 5-year-olds exhibited more anti-social behavior than other children when observed 2 years later.

(a) parents should not spare children from spanking
(b) some punishments are more effective than others
(c) children should not be pushed too hard by parents
(d) corporal punishment increases aggressive behavior

SOLUTION

압도적인 증거에 따르면 체벌이 공격적인 행동을 증가시킨다고 한다. 연구에서는 이러한 처우를 받은 어린 아이들은 어렸을 때도 그렇고 성인이 되어서도 다른 사람들에게 신체적 처벌을 가할 가능성이 훨씬 더 높음을 보여줬다. 또한, 아이들이 더 폭력적으로 체벌을 받을수록, 이들은 후에 더 공격적이고 난폭하게 변한다. 한 연구에서는 한 집단의 어린이들 중에서 3세에서 5세 사이에 엉덩이를 가장 많이 맞은 아이들은 2년 후 관찰했을 때 그렇지 않은 어린 아이들보다 반사회적인 행동을 더 많이 보이는 것으로 드러났다.

🎯 기출 POINT

such treatment를 받은 아이들이 타인에게 신체적 처벌을 가하기 쉽다고 했으므로 빈칸에는 체벌이 공격적인 행동을 증가시킨다는 내용이 알맞다. the more 주어+동사, the more 주어+동사: ~하면 할수록 더욱 ~하다

overwhelming 압도적인   **be subjected to** ~을 당하다
significantly 상당히   **physical punishment** 신체적 처벌
aggressive 공격적인   **spank** 엉덩이를 때리다   **exhibit** 보이다
anti-social 반사회적인   **corporal** 신체적인   정답 (d)

12

Melatonin, a hormone found in all living creatures, is produced according to the daily patterns of light and darkness experienced by an animal. The production variation of melatonin acts as an internal seasonal clock for many animals, scheduling their mating or hibernation behaviors. This has been demonstrated in a laboratory with Siberian hamsters. As long as the light patterns of their natural environment are mimicked, the hamsters continue to follow seasonal eating, sleeping and mating patterns despite being in a laboratory because melatonin works like _____.

(a) a crucial hormone for human reproduction
(b) an internal timer that regulates different events
(c) a mechanism that governs night-time behavior
(d) a vital component for a healthy immune system

SOLUTION

살아 있는 모든 생명체에서 발견되는 호르몬 멜라토닌은 동물이 경험하는 빛과 어둠의 일간 패턴에 따라 생성된다. 멜라토닌 생성의 변동은 여러 동물들에게 체내의 계절적 시계처럼 작용, 이들의 교미 및 동면 습성의 시점을 결정하기도 한다. 이는 시베리아 햄스터 실험에서도 보여졌다. 자연환경 속의 빛 패턴을 모방하기만 하면, 햄스터들은 실험실 안에 있음에도 불구하고 계속적으로 주기적인 식사, 취침 및 교미 패턴을 지켰다. 이것은 멜라토닌이 여러 사건을 조절하는 내부 타이머처럼 작용하기 때문이다.

🎯 기출 POINT

자연 환경을 모방한 실험실 환경에서도 멜라토닌의 작용으로 인해 계절에 맞는 생활 패턴을 보여준다는 것은 멜라토닌이 여러 사건을 통제하는 내부적인 타이머로 작용하기 때문이다.

melatonin 멜라토닌   **living creature** 생명체   **variation** 변동
mating 짝짓기   **hibernation** 동면   **demonstrate** 보여주다
mimic 흉내내다   **reproduction** 번식   **regulate** 통제하다
immune system 면역 체계   정답 (b)

13

Back when the Tudors ruled England, the district in London currently known as Soho used to be a hunting ground of open fields and duck ponds where Londoners hunted wild game. Later, it became well known as London's shabby red-light district. Today, Soho still remains a hunting ground, only now people stroll through its lively streets, posh stores, cafés and clubs in search of food, drink and dancing. Its name now is synonymous with _____.

(a) trendy attractions rather than raunchy entertainment
(b) disreputable and seedier sides of London night life
(c) exorbitantly high rents and high property prices
(d) one of the oldest traditions of English history

SOLUTION

튜더인들이 영국을 통치하던 시절, 현재 소호로 알려진 런던의 지역은 런던 주민들이 야생 짐승을 사냥했던 탁 트인 들판의 사냥터이자 오리 사냥 연못이었다. 이후 그곳은 런던의 허름한 홍등가로 유명해졌다. 오늘날, 소호는 여전히 사냥터이지만, 이제 사람들은 활기찬 거리, 고급 상점, 카페와 클럽을 누비며 음식과 술, 춤을 찾아 이곳을 거닌다. 이제 그 이름은 누추한 유흥보다는 유행의 첨단을 걷는 명소와 동일시되고 있다.

⊞ 기출 POINT

런던 소호 지역의 과거와 현재 모습을 비교하는 글로 그 지역은 과거 사냥터였다가 후에 홍등가로 알려지게 되었고, 현재는 유행의 첨단을 걷는 명소가 되었다는 내용이다. 따라서 과거와 대조되는 소호의 현재 모습을 잘 요약한 (a)가 정답이다.

district 지구 **shabby** 초라한 **stroll** 거닐다 **posh** 고급의, 호화로운 **synonymous** 동일한 **trendy** 최신의 **raunchy** 초라한 **seedy** 누추한 **exorbitantly** 턱없이 **property** 부동산

정답_(a)

14

Haza Mining is a budding Mexican-based mining and exploration firm focused on extracting and developing gold, copper and industrial mineral substances. The company owns the Summit silver-gold property in southwest Mexico, which contains 117 acres of patented and 600 acres of unpatented mining claims; mineral lease rights to the Olego gold property near Mexico City; and a high-quality mica mine and processing complex in the eastern Sonora State. Haza plans to continue to _____.

(a) develop its extensive real-estate holdings in Mexico
(b) build a diverse portfolio of high-quality mineral assets
(c) proceed with its acquisition of international mining interests
(d) maintain its long-held industry lead with further exploration

SOLUTION

하자 광업은 금, 구리 및 공업 광물질을 추출하고 개발하는 데 주력하고 있는 멕시코 기반의 신생 광업 및 탐사업체입니다. 이 기업은 전매 특허를 받은 광구 117에이커와 전매 특허를 받지 않은 광구 600에이커가 포함된 멕시코 남서부의 서밋 금은 대지, 멕시코 시티 근처 금 대지인 올레고에 대한 광물 임차권, 그리고 소노라 주 동부에 고급 운모 광산 및 처리 단지를 소유하고 있습니다. 하자 광업은 계속해서 고급 광물 자산의 다각화된 포트폴리오를 구축할 계획입니다.

⊞ 기출 POINT

하자 광업이라는 멕시코 회사의 광산 자산에 대한 내용이다. 하자 광업의 사업 계획을 요약하는 마지막 문장으로 (b)가 적절하다. (a)는 넓은 범위의 부동산 보유지를 개발한다는 내용이라서 부적절하다.

budding 신생의 **exploration** 탐사 **extract** 추출하다 **copper** 구리 **mineral substance** 광물질 **patented** 특허를 받은 **lease right** 임차권 **mica** 운모 **holdings** 보유지, 소유재산

정답_(b)

15

The traditional values of many Asian cultures share the strong belief that adult children are responsible for the care of their aging parents. Such filial commitment is taken for granted, so failing to take care of one's parents is viewed in a very negative light. Regardless of the expenses, support of elderly parents should always be a priority. _____, an adult would be obliged not to accept a great job offer if it entailed a move that would negatively affect the care of his or her aging parents.

(a) For instance
(b) In addition
(c) However
(d) Then

SOLUTION

많은 아시아 문화의 전통적인 가치관에서는 성인이 된 자식들은 고령의 부모를 돌볼 책임이 있다는 강한 믿음을 공유하고 있다. 이 같은 자식으로서의 도리는 당연한 것으로 여겨지기 때문에 자신의 부모를 보살피지 못하면 이는 매우 부정적으로 비춰진다. 비용에 상관없이 나이 든 부모를 부양하는 것은 항상 우선순위가 되어야 한다. 예를 들면, 좋은 직장 제안을 받더라도 이로 인해 고령의 부모를 돌보는 데 부정적인 영향을 미치게 된다면 이 제안을 받아들이지 않을 것이다.

田 기출 POINT

빈칸에는 연결어가 들어가므로 빈칸 앞뒤에 유의하여 답을 찾도록 한다. 연로한 부모를 모시는 것이 최우선 순위가 된다는 내용과 그 예로 좋은 직장 제안까지 포기할 수 있다는 문장이 뒤따른다. 앞의 전제에 대한 실제적인 예가 되므로 (a)가 정답이다.

filial commitment 자식의 도리   **be taken for granted** 당연하게 여겨지다   **priority** 우선순위   **be obliged to** 어쩔 수 없이 ~하다   **entail** 포함하다   **move** 변화   정답_(a)

16

English translations of literary classics can never match their originals. Nonetheless, translators strive to create definitive English versions out of the myriad of possible readings, which is why new translations of literary classics, such as Dante's *The Divine Comedy*, appear in every generation. These versions are always going to be provisional, limited and defined by the talents of translators. _____, in rare instances, translators do manage to produce a work of such excellence that it attains classic status itself.

(a) Yet
(b) Instead
(c) Furthermore
(d) Subsequently

SOLUTION

고전 문학 작품의 영어 번역은 원문에 절대 필적할 수 없다. 그럼에도 번역가들은 수많은 작품 가운데 완성된 영어 번역문을 만들어 내기 위해 노력하며, 그래서 단테의 〈신곡〉과 같은 고전 문학 작품에 대한 새로운 번역물들이 세대마다 발표되는 것이다. 이들 번역물은 항상 번역가의 재능에 의해 좌우되고 제한되며 정의된다. 그러나 드문 경우, 번역가들이 너무나도 훌륭한 작품을 내놓아서 번역물 자체가 고전으로서의 지위를 얻는 경우도 있기는 하다.

田 기출 POINT

빈칸 앞에는 하나의 고전 작품에 여러 번역물들이 있지만 번역가의 재능에 의해 영향을 받는다는 내용이고, 빈칸 뒤에는 간혹 번역 그 자체로 고전의 지위를 얻기도 한다는 내용이므로 이 두 가지 상반되는 내용의 연결어로 Yet이 적절하다.

literary classic 고전 문학   **nonetheless** 그럼에도 불구하고   **translator** 번역가   **strive to** ~하려고 노력하다   **definitive** 완성된   **a myriad of** 수많은   **provisional** 임시의, 일시적인   **subsequently** 그 결과로   정답_(a)

17

Our university's Teacher Training Program is an intensive eight-month program that enables liberal arts graduates to earn a teaching certificate at the elementary or secondary level. Teacher trainees gain field experiences in local schools, are paired up with teachers, attend classes and workshops, and go through 32 credit hours of practical coursework. Students in the program are eligible for student loans and are also awarded a stipend for their regular school work during the academic year.

Q What is the advertisement mainly about?
(a) The details of a teacher training course
(b) The jobs currently available for teachers
(c) The rules for teachers working at a college
(d) The amount of work an average teacher does

SOLUTION

우리 대학의 교사 연수 프로그램은 인문계 졸업생들이 초등 혹은 중등 교육 교사 자격증을 획득할 수 있도록 해주는 8개월 집중 프로그램입니다. 교생 실습자들은 지역 학교에서 현장 경험을 쌓고, 현직 교사들과 한 조가 되어 수업과 워크숍에 참여하며, 32학점의 실습 과정을 거치게 됩니다. 프로그램에 등록한 교생들은 학자금 대출 자격이 주어지며 학년도 동안 정규 학교 업무에 대한 수당을 지급받습니다.

Q 광고의 주된 내용은?
(a) 교생 실습 과정의 세부사항
(b) 교사들에게 현재 가용한 일자리들
(c) 대학에서 일하는 교사들에 대한 규칙
(d) 일반 교사들의 업무량

기출 POINT

첫 번째 문장에서 대학의 Teacher Training Program에 대한 광고임을 알 수 있다. 인문계 졸업생들이 집중 과정을 통해 초등, 중등 교사 자격증을 얻을 수 있도록 하는 프로그램의 세부사항에 대한 내용이므로 (a)가 정답이다.

intensive 집중적인 **liberal arts** 인문계 **teacher trainee** 교생 실습자 **field experience** 현장 경험 **credit** 학점 **eligible** 자격이 있는 **student loan** 학자금 대출 **stipend** 수당   정답 (a)

18

Medical scientists now admit that little kids are not exclusively responsible for spreading the flu from daycares and classrooms to the rest of the community every year, as was once believed. New research on seasonal flu patterns indicates that working adults are more likely the culprits for the dispersion of flu nationwide. This discovery, published in the journal *Science*, could have profound implications for regulating annual flu outbreaks and any potential influenza pandemics.

Q What is the main idea of the passage?
(a) Protecting children from flu is now more difficult.
(b) Seasonal flu patterns have changed dramatically.
(c) Flu pandemics will be more common in the future.
(d) Adults are spreading influenza more than children.

SOLUTION

의료 과학자들은 한때 믿었던 것처럼 어린 아이들에게만 매년 보육원이나 교실에서 지역사회 전체로 독감을 퍼뜨리는 데 책임이 있는 것은 아니라는 사실을 이제 인정한다. 주기적 독감 패턴에 대한 새 연구에서는 직장을 가진 성인들이 독감을 전국적으로 확산시키는 주범일 가능성이 더 높다는 것을 보여준다. 학술지 〈사이언스〉에 발표된 이 발견은 연간 독감 발병과 잠재적인 독감 유행을 통제하는 데 깊은 시사점이 있다.

Q 지문의 주제는?
(a) 아이들을 독감으로부터 보호하는 것이 이제는 더 어렵다.
(b) 주기적 독감 패턴은 극적으로 변했다.
(c) 독감 유행은 미래에 더 일반화될 것이다.
(d) 성인들이 아이들보다 독감을 더 많이 확산시킨다.

기출 POINT

통념을 깨는 새로운 정보를 제시하는 글로 새로운 연구 결과, 아이들보다 직장에서 일하는 어른들이 독감을 퍼뜨리는 주범이라고 밝히고 있으므로 정답은 (d)이다.

exclusively 독점적으로 **spread** 퍼뜨리다 **daycare** 보육원 **indicate** 가리키다 **culprit** 범인 **dispersion** 확산 **implication** 함축 **profound** 풍부한 **outbreak** 발생 **pandemic** 유행
정답 (d)

19

Toxic ammonia seeped from a cooling tube Wednesday as astronauts worked on mending the cooling system outside of the International Space Station. The astronauts, Mike Evans and Irvin Wilson, fortunately did not come in contact with the ammonia. The leak occurred towards the completion of an eight-hour spacewalk. Tests in the airlock afterward showed no sign of contamination. Ammonia is a big menace because it is highly poisonous and could cause respiratory problems if it makes its way into the space station.

Q   What is the best title for the passage?
(a) Leak Threatens Future of Space Station
(b) Spacewalkers Avert Collision in Outer Space
(c) Space Station in Danger Due to Cooling System
(d) Astronauts Avoid Toxic Substance Contamination

SOLUTION

수요일 우주 비행사들이 국제 우주 정거장 외부에서 냉각 시스템을 수리하던 중 독성 암모니아가 냉각 튜브에서 스며 나왔다. 우주 비행사 마이크 에반스와 어빈 윌슨은 다행히 이 암모니아와 접촉하지 않았다. 누출은 8시간의 우주 유영이 끝나가던 시점에 발생했다. 이후 기밀구역에서 실시한 시험에서 오염의 징후는 발견되지 않았다. 암모니아는 독성이 매우 높고, 우주 정거장 안으로 유입될 경우 호흡기 장애를 유발할 수 있어 큰 위협이다.

Q 지문에 가장 적절한 제목은?
(a) 우주 정거장 미래를 위협하는 누출
(b) 우주에서 유영 중 충돌을 피한 우주 비행사들
(c) 냉각 시스템 때문에 위험에 빠진 우주 정거장
(d) 독성 물질 오염을 피한 우주 비행사들

기출 POINT

냉각 튜브에서 스며 나온 독성 암모니아가 다행히 우주 비행사들과 접촉하지 않았다는 내용으로, 이 독성 암모니아가 우주 정거장 안으로 유입되면 호흡기 장애를 유발한다고 했으므로 제목은 (d)가 적절하다. 우주 정거장의 미래에 대한 언급은 없으므로 (a)는 오답이다. 냉각 시스템이 우주 정거장을 위험하게 만든 것이 아니므로 (c)도 제목이 될 수 없다.
ammonia 암모니아   **seep** 스며 나오다   **mend** 수리하다   **leak** 누수   **completion** 완성   **airlock** 기밀구역   **contamination** 오염   **menace** 위협   **poisonous** 독성이 있는   **respiratory problem** 호흡기 장애   **make one's way into** ~로 유입되다   **avert** 피하다   **collision** 충돌
정답_(d)

20

It has been known for some time that many animals learn by observation and imitation. In an early experiment that tested this idea, a cat was trained to obtain food by pressing a bar when a light went on. A second cat was then placed near the trained cat to watch how it obtained food. After a period, the second cat was placed alone near the bar and light. When the light went on, the second cat pressed the bar to get food. Apparently the cat had learned what to do from watching the trained cat.

Q   What is the passage mainly about?
(a) Ways that animals cooperate
(b) Training animals to get their own food
(c) Experimenting to change animal behavior
(d) Animals' ability to learn through observation

SOLUTION

많은 동물들이 관찰과 모방을 통해 학습한다는 것이 알려진 지는 꽤 됐다. 이 개념을 실험하기 위한 초기 실험에서 고양이는 전구가 켜질 때 막대를 누르면 먹이를 얻도록 훈련받았다. 그리고 나서 두 번째 고양이를 훈련된 고양이 옆에 두어 첫 번째 고양이가 어떻게 먹이를 얻는지 지켜보도록 했다. 얼마 후 두 번째 고양이는 혼자 막대와 전구 근처에 놓여졌다. 전구가 켜지면, 두 번째 고양이는 막대를 눌러 먹이를 얻었다. 분명 그 고양이는 훈련된 고양이를 보고 어떻게 해야 할지 터득했던 것이다.

Q 지문의 주된 내용은?
(a) 동물의 협력 방식
(b) 동물이 스스로 먹이를 얻도록 하는 훈련
(c) 동물 습성 변화를 위한 실험
(d) 관찰을 통해 학습하는 동물의 능력

기출 POINT

첫 번째 문장에서 많은 동물들이 관찰과 모방을 통해 배운다고 했다. 그 예로 고양이가 다른 고양이의 먹이 얻는 방식을 관찰하고 배우는 실험을 제시하고 있다. 따라서 주로 관찰을 통해 학습하는 동물들의 능력에 관한 내용이므로 정답은 (d)이다.
observation 관찰   **imitation** 모방   **trained** 훈련받은   **obtain** 얻다   **apparently** 분명히   **cooperate** 협력하다
정답_(d)

21

In times of famine, early intervention in the form of cash or vouchers with which food can be bought on the market can prevent the unintended ill effects of food aid. Food aid is detrimental when it is sent to a country for long periods because it can ruin local farmers. This in turn erodes a country's agricultural capacity. A case in point is Ethiopia, which received food aid equivalent to 15% of its annual cereal production in 2003, and today it has lower agricultural yields than it had prior to the famine. Cash or vouchers could have prevented this from happening.

Q What is the main idea of the passage?
(a) Early intervention is ultimately the best method of famine relief.
(b) Belated food aid can have adverse side effects on local agriculture.
(c) Food aid has been the source of agricultural setbacks in Ethiopia.
(d) Cash or vouchers are more effective against famine than food aid.

SOLUTION

기근 시에는 시장에서 식량을 살 수 있는 현금이나 상품권 형태의 조기 개입으로 식량 원조의 의도치 않은 악영향을 방지할 수 있다. 식량 원조가 한 국가에 장기간 제공되면 지역 영농업자들을 파산시킬 수 있으므로 해롭고 이는 다시 국가의 농업 역량을 좀먹는다. 그 적절한 사례가 에티오피아로, 에티오피아는 2003년 연간 곡물 생산량의 15%에 해당하는 식량 원조를 제공받았으며, 현재 기근 이전보다 농업 수확량이 더 낮다. 현금이나 상품권은 이런 현상이 발생하는 것을 막을 수 있었을 것이다.

Q 지문의 주제는?
(a) 조기 개입이 궁극적으로 기근 구호에 대한 최선의 방책이다.
(b) 뒤늦은 식량 원조는 지역 농업에 부정적인 부작용을 낳을 수 있다.
(c) 식량 원조는 에티오피아 내 농업 실패의 원천이었다.
(d) 현금이나 상품권은 기근에 대비하여 식량 원조보다 훨씬 효과적이다.

🎫 기출 POINT

주제는 첫 번째 문장에 드러나는 경우가 많다. 기근일 때 식량 원조보다는 음식을 사먹을 수 있는 현금이나 상품권이 그 나라에 더 효과적인 방법이라는 주장이므로 주제는 (d)이다.

famine 기근 **intervention** 개입 **voucher** 상품권 **ill effect** 악영향 **food aid** 식량 원조 **detrimental** 해로운 **erode** 좀먹다 **equivalent to** ~에 해당하는 **yield** 수확량 **prior to** ~전에 **ultimately** 궁극적으로 **belated** 때늦은 **adverse** 부정적인 **side effect** 부작용 **setback** 실패, 퇴보   정답_(d)

22

Dance history is more advanced as a discipline in comparison to dance criticism. It boasts an increasingly refined methodology, an expanding body of literature and a growing number of experts devoted to it. More and more dance historians hold professional positions in academia than do exponents of dance criticism, and, interestingly, none of the best active dance critics in the US today holds an academic position. These factors, together with the rather weak formal training required for dance criticism, mean that dance history will keep advancing as a discipline in contrast to dance criticism.

Q What is the passage mainly about?
(a) The benefits of scholars working in dance-related fields
(b) The opportunities available to dance experts in criticism
(c) The emerging growth of academic interest in the field of dance
(d) The academic prospects for dance history compared to dance criticism

SOLUTION

무용사는 무용 평론과 비교해서 학문으로서 더 발전되어 있다. 무용사는 점점 더 세련된 방법론, 늘어나는 문헌과 이에 헌신하는 전문가 수의 증가를 자랑한다. 무용 평론계보다 더 많은 무용사 학자들이 점점 더 학계에서 전문적인 입지를 구축하고 있지만, 재미있게도 오늘날 미국 내 현업 최고의 무용 평론가 중 그 누구도 학계에 몸담은 사람은 없다. 이들 요인은, 무용 평론에 필요한 정식 교육이 상대적으로 미약하다는 점과 함께 무용사가 무용 평론과는 대조적으로 학문으로서 계속 진보해 나갈 것임을 의미한다.

Q 지문의 주된 내용은?
(a) 무용 관련 분야에서 일하는 학자들의 이득
(b) 무용 평론 전문가들이 누릴 수 있는 기회
(c) 무용 분야에 대한 학계 관심의 증가
(d) 무용 평론과 비교한 무용사의 학문적 전망

🎫 기출 POINT

두 가지 학문 분야인 무용사와 무용 평론을 비교하는 내용이다. 무용사는 학문적으로 발전해 나가고 있지만 무용 평론은 정식 교육이 미약하다는 대조적인 상황을 다루고 있다. 따라서 정답은 (d)이다.

discipline 학문 **in comparison to** ~와 비교해서 **boast** 자랑하다 **methodology** 방법론 **expand** 확장하다 **exponent** 대표적 인물, 상징 **in contrast to** ~와 대조적으로   정답_(d)

Actual Test 3

23

A unique new book on art entitled *Inspired Children* focuses on the childhood art of great artists. Readers will gain a glimpse of budding talent from works such as a pencil drawing by a 4-year-old Keith Haring that has his signature polka dots, or the people and animals sketched by Vincent van Gogh at age 8. All drawings and paintings in this marvelous book are accompanied by excellent analyses and explanations by experts.

Q Which of the following is correct about *Inspired Children*?
(a) It presents art featuring children.
(b) It shows famous works for children.
(c) It focuses on Van Gogh's late works.
(d) It contains expert analyses on child art.

SOLUTION

〈영감받는 아이들〉이라는 제목의 독특한 예술 신간 서적은 예술 거장들의 어린 시절 예술에 초점을 둔다. 독자들은 특유의 물방울 무늬를 사용한 네 살배기 키스 해링의 연필 소묘나, 빈센트 반 고흐가 여덟 살에 그린 사람과 동물 스케치 등의 작품을 통해 싹트는 재능을 엿보게 될 것이다. 이 멋진 책에 수록된 스케치와 그림 하나하나에는 전문가들의 훌륭한 분석과 설명이 곁들여져 있다.

Q 〈영감받는 아이들〉에 대해 옳은 것은?
(a) 어린이를 소재로 한 예술을 보여준다.
(b) 어린이들을 위한 유명 작품들을 보여준다.
(c) 반 고흐의 후기 작품들에 집중한다.
(d) 아동 예술에 대한 전문가의 분석이 포함되어 있다.

⊞ 기출 POINT
〈영감받는 아이들〉이라는 새로운 책에 대한 소개의 내용이다. 고흐나 키스 해링 등 유명 화가들의 어릴 적 작품을 수록하고 전문가들의 분석과 설명을 담고 있는 책으로 지문과 일치하는 내용은 (d)이다. (a)는 '아이를 등장시키는, 아이를 소재로 하는 예술을 보여준다'는 말이므로 오답이다.

entitled 제목이 붙은 **glimpse** 흘끗 봄 **budding** 싹트는
signature 특유의 것, 대표적인 것 **polka dot** 물방울 무늬
marvelous 놀라운 **be accompanied by** ~가 동반되다
analysis 분석 **explanation** 설명 **expert** 전문가 　　　정답_(d)

24

In the 1800s, the high number of Irish, Polish and Italian immigrants settling in New York had a big impact on the social character of the city. Because they arrived in such great numbers, they changed the whole ethnic makeup of local populations. For example, hundreds of thousands of Irish immigrants led to one-third of New York's population born by 1855 being Irish.

Q Which of the following is correct according to the passage?
(a) Few 19th-century immigrants were Irish.
(b) Many Irish immigrants settled in New York.
(c) Most Irish immigrants settled in rural areas.
(d) Irish immigrants first arrived in America in 1855.

SOLUTION

1800년대에 뉴욕에 대거 정착한 아일랜드, 폴란드, 이탈리아 이민자들은 뉴욕의 사회적 특징에 큰 영향을 주었다. 너무 많은 수가 이주해서 이들은 지역 인구의 인종 구성 전체를 바꾸어 놓았다. 예를 들면, 수십만 명의 아일랜드 이민자들로 인해 1855년까지 출생한 뉴욕 인구의 3분의 1이 아일랜드인이었다.

Q 지문에 따르면 옳은 것은?
(a) 19세기 이민자 중 아일랜드인은 거의 없었다.
(b) 많은 아일랜드 이민자들이 뉴욕에 정착했다.
(c) 대부분 아일랜드 이민자들은 시골 지역에 정착했다.
(d) 아일랜드 이민자들은 1855년에 처음 미국에 도착했다.

⊞ 기출 POINT
19세기 뉴욕에 정착한 다수의 아일랜드, 폴란드, 이탈리아에서 온 이민자들은 뉴욕의 전체 인종 구성을 바꾸는 데 영향을 주었다. 1855년까지 태어난 뉴욕 인구의 1/3이 아일랜드인이었다고 했으므로 일치하는 내용은 (b)이다.

immigrant 이민자 **settle in** ~에 정착하다 **impact on** ~에 영향 **ethnic makeup** 인종 구성 **hundreds of thousands of** 수십만의 　　　정답_(b)

25

Join the Clifford Hotel for a fun night when you can try out wines from all of the award-winning wineries in the prestigious 2008 Orange County Commercial Wine Competition. You can also treat yourself to gourmet food from a selection of Orange County's finest restaurants, enjoy live music, participate in a raffle to win a free bottle of fine wine, or join a silent auction! It's only $50 per person if you register by February 27, or $60 at the door. See you there on Sunday, March 9, 2 p.m. to 10 p.m., at the Clifford Hotel. Call (714) 708-1636 to register.

Q Which of the following is correct about the advertised event?
(a) You get to vote in a wine competition.
(b) You can save money by pre-registering.
(c) You can taste food from around the world.
(d) You must register by March 9 for a discount.

SOLUTION

명성 높은 2008년 오렌지 카운티 상업 와인 상품 대회에서 수상한 모든 포도주 양조장의 와인을 시음해 볼 수 있는 클리퍼드 호텔에서의 신나는 밤에 동참하십시오. 엄선된 오렌지 카운티 최고급 식당들의 미식가들을 위한 음식을 맛보고 생음악도 즐기며, 무료 고급 와인 한 병이 경품으로 걸려 있는 추첨에 참여하시거나 입찰 경매에 참가하실 수도 있습니다! 2월 27일까지 등록하시면 1인당 단 50달러이며, 당일에는 60달러입니다. 3월 9일 일요일 오후 2시부터 10시까지 클리퍼드 호텔에서 여러분들을 뵙겠습니다. 등록하시려면 (714) 708-1636으로 전화하십시오.

Q 행사 광고에 대해 옳은 것은?
(a) 와인 대회에서 투표를 하게 된다.
(b) 사전 등록하면 돈을 절약할 수 있다.
(c) 세계 각지의 음식을 시식할 수 있다.
(d) 할인을 받으려면 3월 9일까지 등록해야 한다.

🌐 기출 POINT
클리퍼드 호텔에서 열리는 와인 행사 광고이다. 2월 27일까지 예약하면 할인을 해주고 있으므로 (b)가 지문과 일치하는 내용이다. 사전 등록은 pre-registering이라는 단어를 쓴다.
try out 해보다　**winery** 포도주 양조장　**prestigious** 고급의
competition 경연대회　**gourmet food** 미식가의[고급] 음식
raffle 추첨　**auction** 경매　**register** 등록하다　　정답 (b)

26

Dear Mom and Dad,

My sophomore year at college is off to a great start. I have finally found a better place to live! The two apartment mates I live with now share the same kind of lifestyle with me. They clean the apartment about once a month and do the dishes about once a week (or they wait until we run out of clean ones!). I get along with these guys much better than the guy in my old place who expected everything to be clean 24/7. It was simply unbearable! Anyway, I'll fill you in on more once I've settled in!

Love,
Matt

Q Which of the following is correct according to the letter?
(a) Matt's last place was too hard to clean.
(b) Matt's new apartment mates are dirtier than he is.
(c) Matt's old apartment mate liked things to be clean.
(d) Matt's new apartment is shared by five people.

SOLUTION

사랑하는 엄마 아빠,

2학년 대학 생활은 출발이 좋아요. 드디어 생활하기에 더 좋은 곳을 찾았어요! 지금 아파트에서 함께 살고 있는 친구들 두 명은 저랑 생활 방식이 같아요. 친구들은 한 달에 한 번 정도 아파트를 청소하고 일주일에 한 번 정도 설거지를 해요(아니면 닦아놓은 접시들이 떨어질 때까지 기다리거나요!). 항상 모든 것이 깨끗하기를 기대했던 이전 룸메이트보다 이 친구들이랑 훨씬 더 잘 지내요. 그때는 그야말로 참을 수가 없었어요! 어쨌든, 일단 좀 자리가 잡히면 좀 더 많이 이야기해 드릴게요.

맷 드림

Q 편지 내용에 따르면 옳은 것은?
(a) 맷의 지난번 집은 청소하기가 너무 힘들었다.
(b) 맷의 새 룸메이트들은 맷보다 더 지저분하다.
(c) 맷의 옛 룸메이트는 깨끗한 것을 좋아했다.
(d) 맷의 새 아파트에는 5명이 함께 생활하고 있다.

🌐 기출 POINT
is off to a great start, better place to live 등을 통해 새로운 룸메이트들과의 삶에 만족스러워하고 있음을 알 수 있다. 다섯 번째 문장 than 이하를 통해 옛 룸메이트는 (c)처럼 항상 깨끗하게 해두는 것을 좋아했음을 알 수 있다.
be off to a great start 멋지게 시작하다　**run out of** ~이 떨어지다
24/7 항시(하루 24시간 1주 7일 동안)　**unbearable** 참을 수 없는　**fill in** ~에게 알리다, 설명하다　　정답 (c)

27

New beverage policies for schools will go into effect starting this fall semester. Under these new guidelines, elementary and middle school students will have a wider range of nutritious low-calorie beverage options, which include fruit juices, low-fat milk and bottled water. At high schools, these beverages will be available in addition to diet sodas, sports drinks and low-calorie teas. This initiative is all part of a broader effort to educate children about the significance of a healthy lifestyle and a balanced diet.

Q Which of the following is correct about the new guidelines?
(a) Sodas are available in high schools.
(b) They have been in effect since last fall.
(c) Sports drinks are sold in middle schools.
(d) Some drinks are free of charge to students.

SOLUTION

이번 가을 학기부터 학교에서 새 음료수 방침이 실시될 것입니다. 이 새 지침 하에서 초등학생 및 중학생들은 다양한 종류의 영양가 높은 저열량 음료수를 선택할 수 있을 것이며, 여기에는 과일 주스, 저지방 우유와 생수가 포함됩니다. 고등학교에서는 이들 음료 외에도 다이어트 청량음료, 스포츠 음료 및 저열량 차도 접할 수 있을 것입니다. 이번 추진 계획은 모두 건강한 생활양식과 균형 잡힌 식사의 중요성에 대해 어린 이들을 교육하기 위한 더 광범위한 노력의 일환입니다.

Q 새 지침에 대해 옳은 것은?
(a) 고등학교에서는 청량음료를 접할 수 있다.
(b) 새 지침은 지난 가을부터 실시되고 있었다.
(c) 스포츠 음료는 중학교에서 판매된다.
(d) 일부 음료는 학생들에게 무료이다.

▦ 기출 POINT
학교의 새 음료수 방침에 대한 내용이다. 이번 가을 학기부터 실시될 방침이며 고등학교에서는 청량음료와 스포츠 음료가 판매될 것이라고 했으므로 일치하는 내용은 (a)이다.
go into effect 실시되다 **range** 범위 **nutritious** 영양가 높은
low-calorie 저칼로리의 **option** 선택 사양 **low-fat** 저지방의
bottled water 생수 **initiative** 추진계획 **significance** 중요성

정답_(a)

28

Huave is a language spoken by the native Huave people on the Pacific coast of Southern Oaxaca, Mexico. The language is used only in four villages in the Isthmus of Tehuantepec by some 18,000 residents. While still in use in the social life of these four villages, Huave is, nonetheless, a language in danger of extinction. Despite cultural fieldwork and linguistic revitalization projects sponsored and conducted by American universities in Huave communities, it is just a matter of time until only the elders will remember how to speak Huave.

Q Which of the following is correct about the Huave language?
(a) It has become endangered despite its continued use.
(b) It continues to be spoken in most regions of Mexico.
(c) It is only spoken by the aged Huave population.
(d) It is now simply used for special ceremonies.

SOLUTION

우아베는 멕시코 옥사카 남부 태평양 해안에 사는 토착 우아베인들이 사용하는 언어이다. 이 언어는 테우안테펙 지협의 4개 마을 1만 8천여 명의 주민들만이 사용하고 있다. 우아베는 이들 4개 마을의 사회 생활에서 여전히 사용되고 있기는 하지만 소멸 위기에 처한 언어이다. 우아베 지역사회의 미국 대학들이 후원하고 실시 중인 문화 현지 연구 및 언어 활성화 프로젝트에도 불구하고, 우아베어를 할 줄 아는 사람들로서 노령자들만 남는 것은 그저 시간 문제이다.

Q 우아베어에 대해 옳은 것은?
(a) 계속적인 사용에도 불구하고 소멸 위기에 처해 있다.
(b) 멕시코 대부분 지역에서 계속 사용되고 있다.
(c) 노령의 우아베인들만 사용하고 있다.
(d) 이제 특수 의식에만 사용된다.

▦ 기출 POINT
우아베어는 멕시코의 네 마을에서만 사용되는 언어이고, 활성화 노력에도 불구하고 사멸되어 나이 많은 사람들만이 기억하게 될 것은 시간 문제라는 내용이므로 지문과 일치하는 설명은 (a)뿐이다.
resident 주민 **nonetheless** ~에도 불구하고 **extinction** 소멸
linguistic 언어학적인 **revitalization** 활성화 **sponsor** 후원하다
conduct 실시하다 **endangered** 소멸 위기에 처한 **continued**
지속적인 **ceremony** 의식

정답_(a)

29

Lisa Turner has always had a problem with faces. As a child, she struggled to pick out her own face in school photos, and she has always been hard-pressed to describe her mother's features. Over the years, she has offended countless friends because she has passed them by as if they were strangers. "I lose friends because they think I'm ignoring them," says Turner. She is not ignoring them but has prosopagnosia or, more commonly, face-blindness. Once thought to be exceedingly rare and only the result of brain injury, a recent study has shown that prosopagnosia is inheritable and surprisingly common.

Q Which of the following is correct about Lisa Turner?
(a) She had a brain injury when young.
(b) She had no pictures taken in school.
(c) She has a disorder that can be inherited.
(d) She has trouble remembering people's names.

SOLUTION

리사 터너는 항상 사람들의 얼굴을 식별하는 데 어려움을 겪었다. 어려서 그녀는 학교 사진들 속에서 자기 자신의 얼굴도 겨우 골라냈으며, 자기 어머니의 특징을 묘사할 때 항상 난감해했다. 그간 그녀는 친구들을 마치 모르는 사람인양 지나치는 통에 수많은 친구들의 감정을 상하게 만들었다. "친구들은 내가 자기들을 무시한다고 생각하기 때문에 나는 친구들을 잃었어요"라고 터너는 말한다. 그녀는 그들을 무시하는 것이 아니라, 상모실인증 더 일반적으로는 말하자면 안면 인식 장애를 겪고 있는 것이다. 이는 한때는 극도로 드물고 뇌 손상의 결과로만 나타나는 것으로 생각되었으나, 최근 연구에서는 상모실인증이 유전될 수 있고 놀랄 만큼 흔하다는 것을 보여주었다.

Q 리사 터너에 대해 옳은 것은?
(a) 어려서 뇌를 다쳤다.
(b) 학교에서 사진을 찍지 않았다.
(c) 유전될 수 있는 장애를 가지고 있다.
(d) 사람들의 이름을 기억하는 데 어려움을 겪고 있다.

기출 POINT
리사 터너는 사람들의 얼굴을 식별하기 힘들어하는 안면 인식 장애를 가지고 있다. 최근 연구 결과에 따르면 이 장애는 유전될 수 있고 생각보다 흔한 것임을 알 수 있다. 그녀가 어릴 때 뇌를 다쳤다는 언급은 없었으므로 일치하는 것은 (c)이다.

struggle to ~하려고 애쓰다 **hard-pressed** 곤경에 빠진 **offend** 기분 나쁘게 하다 **prosopagnosia** 상모실인증 **exceedingly** 극도로 **brain injury** 뇌 손상 **inheritable** 유전되는 **disorder** 장애

정답_(c)

30

Dear Mr. Green,

I am writing to apply for the position of a full-time systems consultant posted in the *Times*. Please find attached my CV. Although I am a recent business school graduate, I have considerable work experience. While studying, I worked various part-time jobs involving software development. Also, the studies I undertook were practically oriented, so I have a good knowledge of current business systems and procedures. Should you require any further information, please do not hesitate to contact me.

Best Regards,
James Field

Q Which of the following is correct about the writer?
(a) He gained his job experience after graduation.
(b) He has worked in software development.
(c) He is applying for a part-time position.
(d) He sent in his CV earlier.

SOLUTION

그린 선생님 귀하.

〈타임즈〉에 게재된 시스템 컨설턴트직 정규직에 지원하기 위해 이렇게 편지 드립니다. 첨부된 제 이력서를 참고해 주십시오. 비록 저는 최근에 경영대학원을 졸업했으나, 상당한 업무 경력을 가지고 있습니다. 재학 중에 아르바이트로 소프트웨어 개발에 관한 다양한 일을 했습니다. 또한 연구 방향이 실용적이었기 때문에 현 비즈니스 시스템과 절차에 대해 충분한 지식을 갖추고 있습니다. 추가 정보가 더 필요하면, 주저하지 말고 저에게 연락 주십시오.

제임스 필드 드림

Q 필자에 대해 옳은 것은?
(a) 졸업 후 경력을 쌓았다.
(b) 소프트웨어 개발 분야에서 일한 경험이 있다.
(c) 아르바이트 자리에 지원하고 있다.
(d) 이전에 자신의 이력서를 보냈다.

기출 POINT
입사지원 편지 내용이다. 필자는 학생일 때부터 일과 관련된 경력을 쌓았고, 아르바이트로 소프트웨어 개발을 한 적이 있고, 정규직에 지원한 것이며, 이력서를 함께 첨부해서 보내고 있다. 따라서 일치하는 내용은 (b)이다.

apply for ~에 지원하다 **attach** 첨부하다 **CV** 이력서(curriculum vitae) **considerable** 상당한 **undertake** 맡다 **practically oriented** 실용성 지향 **have a good knowledge of** ~에 대해 잘 알다 **hesitate to** ~하는 것을 주저하다

정답_(b)

31

It took nearly a year and a half after renowned novelist, professor and Nobel laureate Saul Bellow died, in April, 2005, for the last of his documents to arrive at Regenstein Library of the University of Chicago. The documents— comprising letters, notes, typewritten drafts, galley proofs, unpublished speeches and essays— filled approximately 150 boxes. Among the papers are Bellow's correspondences to and from authors like John Cheever, Bernard Malamud and Allan Bloom. There are also revisions of five novels Bellow had published. The library is extremely grateful to acquire this prized collection.

Q Which of the following is correct about Saul Bellow according to the passage?
(a) He kept letters from other writers.
(b) He was writing a new novel when he died.
(c) He graduated from the University of Chicago.
(d) He left five unpublished novels among his papers.

SOLUTION

유명한 소설가이자 교수, 노벨상 수상자인 솔 벨로가 2005년 4월 세상을 떠난 후 거의 1년 반이 지나서야 그의 마지막 문서들이 시카고 대학 레겐슈타인 도서관에 도착했다. 서한, 메모, 타자기로 친 초안들, 교정쇄, 출판되지 않은 연설문과 에세이로 구성된 그 문서들은 대략 상자 150개를 채웠다. 문서들 중에는 벨로가 존 치버, 버나드 맬러머드와 앨런 블룸과 같은 작가들과 주고받은 서한들도 있다. 또한 벨로가 펴냈던 다섯 편의 소설에 대한 수정본도 있다. 레겐슈타인 도서관에서는 이 훌륭한 소장품을 얻게 되어 매우 감사해하고 있다.

Q 지문에 따르면 솔 벨로에 대해 옳은 것은?
(a) 다른 작가들과의 편지를 모아두었다.
(b) 사망 시에 새로운 소설을 집필 중이었다.
(c) 시카고 대학을 졸업했다.
(d) 문서들 중에 출간되지 않은 소설 다섯 편을 남겨두었다.

⊞ 기출 POINT
솔 벨로의 유품인 문서들에 관한 내용이다. 다른 작가들과 왕래한 편지를 가지고 있었고 자신이 펴낸 다섯 편의 소설에 대한 수정본도 있었다. 이 문서들은 시카고 대학 레겐슈타인 도서관에 기증되었다. 따라서 정답은 (a)이다.

renowned 유명한 Nobel laureate 노벨상 수상자 comprise ~로 이루어지다 draft 원고 galley proof 교정쇄 correspondence 편지, 서신 왕래 revision 수정본 prized 가치 있는, 중요한 collection 소장품   정답_(a)

32

At Shepherd's Menswear, we ship ordered items on the same business day if ordered by noon. Orders received in the afternoon are shipped the next business day. However, actual delivery time may vary. A delivery driver may decide not to leave a package at your door if you are not home. If you cannot wait for a delivery, we recommend that you leave us instructions as to where the delivery can be made instead.

Q Which of the following is correct according to the passage?
(a) Every item ordered before noon is shipped the next day.
(b) Customers should contact delivery drivers when ordering.
(c) A delivery driver may not deliver your package if you are not home.
(d) Delivery instructions must be given by customers for every shipment.

SOLUTION

셰퍼드 남성 의류점에서는 정오까지 주문하시면 주문 당일에 상품들을 배송해 드립니다. 오후에 접수된 주문들은 다음 영업일에 보내집니다. 그러나 실제 배송 시간에는 차이가 있을 수 있습니다. 배송 기사는 고객이 부재 중일 경우 문 앞에 소포를 놓아두지 않을 수도 있습니다. 배송을 기다릴 수 없으면, 대신 어느 주소로 배송하면 될지 저희들에게 알려 줄 것을 권합니다.

Q 지문에 따르면 옳은 것은?
(a) 정오 전에 주문한 모든 물품은 다음 날 배송된다.
(b) 고객들은 주문할 때 배송 기사들과 연락해야 한다.
(c) 배송 기사들은 고객이 부재 중일 경우 소포를 배달하지 않을 수도 있다.
(d) 모든 발송분에 대해 고객들은 배송 지침을 주어야 한다.

⊞ 기출 POINT
정오까지 주문하면 당일에 보내주고 정오 이후에 주문하면 다음 날 보내주며, 배송 기사들이 고객이 부재 중일 경우 소포를 놓고 가지 않을 수도 있다는 내용이므로 정답은 (c)이다. 다른 주소로 받기를 원하면 배송 지침을 남겨주어야 한다고 했으므로 (d)는 오답이다.

ship 배송하다 ordered item 주문한 물품 business day 영업일 delivery 배달 vary 다르다 package 소포 instruction 지침   정답_(c)

33

Before the discovery of vitamins, people naturally protected their bodies from diseases caused by vitamin deficiency simply by consuming a wide variety of vegetables and fruit. There were some people, however, such as explorers and sailors, who often did not have access to their usual range of food choices for long periods of time. As a result, they fell sick with illnesses such as scurvy, which is caused by lack of vitamin C.

Q What can be inferred from the passage?
(a) Sailors and explorers could not store fruit for long.
(b) Instances of scurvy never occur in today's world.
(c) There was no cure for scurvy in ancient times.
(d) Vitamin deficiency mainly affects children.

SOLUTION

비타민이 발견되기 전에 사람들은 그저 다양한 채소와 과일을 섭취함으로써 비타민 결핍으로 인한 질병으로부터 몸을 자연스럽게 보호했다. 그러나 탐험가나 선원들과 같이 장기간 일상적인 다양한 식품들을 섭취할 수 없는 경우가 많았던 사람들이 있었다. 그 결과 이들은 비타민 C 결핍으로 인해 생기는 괴혈병과 같은 병에 걸렸다.

Q 지문에서 유추할 수 있는 것은?
(a) 선원과 탐험가들은 장기간 과일을 보관할 수 없었다.
(b) 괴혈병 사례는 오늘날에는 절대 발생하지 않는다.
(c) 고대에는 괴혈병에 대한 치료법이 없었다.
(d) 비타민 결핍은 주로 어린이들에게 영향을 준다.

⊞ 기출 POINT
사람들은 채소나 과일을 섭취함으로써 비타민 결핍으로부터 오는 질병을 막았는데 장기간 여행하는 탐험가나 선원들은 다양한 식품을 섭취할 수가 없어서 비타민 C의 결핍증인 괴혈병과 같은 질병에 걸리게 되었다고 했으므로 (a)를 유추할 수 있다.

deficiency 부족 **explorer** 탐험가 **have access to** ~을 얻을 수 있다 **as a result** 결과적으로 **illness** 질병 **scurvy** 괴혈병

정답 _(a)

34

At Paramount High School, incoming teachers are required to spend some of their planning periods doubling as hall monitors. Desks are placed in the halls for teachers to use. All hall monitors will have an assigned partner, so they must check the schedule and coordinate with their partners on preferences for monitoring times. After two semesters, teachers will be exempt from hall monitoring duties unless special situations arise.

Q What can be inferred about the monitoring policy from the passage?
(a) Not all teachers have the duty of monitoring halls.
(b) Unruly students must take time out at desks in the halls.
(c) Extra pay will be given to teachers who do the monitoring.
(d) Teachers are encouraged to remain standing while monitoring.

SOLUTION

파라마운트 고등학교에서 신임 교사들은 기획 기간 중 일부 동안 복도 감시 근무도 겸해야 합니다. 교사들이 사용할 수 있는 책상이 복도에 배치됩니다. 모든 복도 감시 요원들에게는 파트너 한 명이 배정되므로, 선호하는 감시 시간과 관련해서 파트너들과 일정을 확인하고 조율해야 합니다. 두 학기가 지난 후 교사들은 특별한 상황이 발생하지 않는 한 복도 감시 직무에서 해제될 것입니다.

Q 감시 방침에 관해 지문에서 유추할 수 있는 것은?
(a) 모든 교사들이 다 복도 감시 의무를 지고 있는 것은 아니다.
(b) 버릇없는 학생들은 복도에 비치된 책상으로 쫓겨날 것이다.
(c) 감시 업무를 하는 교사들에게는 추가 급여가 지급될 것이다.
(d) 교사들은 감시 활동을 하는 동안 일어서 있도록 장려받는다.

⊞ 기출 POINT
신임 교사들은 복도 감시 활동을 하는데 특별한 일이 발생하지 않으면 두 학기 후에는 하지 않게 된다고 했으므로 학교의 모든 교사들이 복도 감시 활동을 하는 것은 아님을 유추할 수 있다. 감시 활동 중에 서 있어야 하거나 급여가 추가된다는 내용은 없었다.

incoming 신임의 **double** 겸하다 **monitor** 감시원 **assigned** 배정된 **coordinate with** ~와 조율하다 **preference** 선호도 **exempt from** ~에서 해제된 **unruly** 버릇없는

정답 _(a)

35

Zach Corporation has built its reputation for more than 30 years on an uncompromising commitment to sound systems. Now, Zach gives you even more lifelike sound in your own home with the new Zach 321 Home Entertainment System. This system can recreate full orchestral sound in your living room or the intricate arrangements of a jazz quartet in your den. Visit your local electronics store and hear the amazing Zach 321 for yourself. Also, order a Zach 321 before March 1 and save $75.

Q What can be inferred about the Zach sound system?
(a) It is sold exclusively at Zach retail outlets.
(b) It is designed to work best in outdoor settings.
(c) It is able to reproduce a highly authentic sound.
(d) It is at the low end of the market in terms of price.

SOLUTION

재크 기업은 음향 시스템에 대한 타협 없는 헌신으로 30여 년간 그 명성을 쌓아 왔습니다. 이제 재크는 신형 재크 321 홈 엔터테인먼트 시스템으로 여러분의 가정에 더욱 실감 나는 음향을 제공합니다. 본 시스템으로 여러분의 거실에 오케스트라가 연주하는 음악을, 혹은 여러분의 서재에 섬세한 재즈 사중주의 연주곡을 재현하는 것이 가능합니다. 지역 전자제품점을 방문하셔서 놀라운 재크 321의 음향을 직접 체험해 보십시오. 그리고 3월 1일 이전에 재크 321을 주문하시고 75달러의 할인 혜택도 누리십시오.

Q 재크 음향 시스템에 대해 유추할 수 있는 것은?
(a) 재크 소매점에서만 독점 판매된다.
(b) 야외에서 가장 잘 작동하도록 설계되었다.
(c) 고도로 원음에 가까운 음향을 재생할 수 있다.
(d) 가격은 저가에 속한다.

🎛 기출 POINT

재크 음향 시스템은 거실이나 서재, 즉 실내 환경에서 사용하는 시스템이며 가격에 대한 언급은 없으므로 저가인지 알 수 없다. lifelike sound는 다른 말로 authentic sound라고 할 수 있으므로 (c)를 유추할 수 있다.

reputation 명성 **uncompromising** 타협 없는 **commitment** 헌신 **lifelike** 실제의 **recreate** 재현하다 **intricate** 섬세한 **den** 별실 **exclusively** 독점적으로 **authentic** 실제 같은 **in terms of** ~의 측면에서   정답_(c)

36

Eureka, an Internet encyclopedia, is not the paradise of clear and accurate knowledge one would hope to find. As a repository of user-generated content, it has errors in it, and although it is considerably larger than offline counterparts, it is far from being complete. Some people have tried to vandalize it by erasing or falsifying entries; at one point, the entire staff of Congress was barred from Eureka for sabotaging one another's profiles. In a way, this online encyclopedia is as much a litmus test of human nature as it is a reference tool.

Q What can be inferred from the passage?
(a) User content sites are rarely consulted by professionals.
(b) Encyclopedias everywhere tend to have occasional errors.
(c) Workplace sabotage occurs more on the Internet than elsewhere.
(d) A certain level of skepticism is necessary with online information.

SOLUTION

인터넷 백과사전인 유레카는 사람들이 찾고자 하는 분명하고 정확한 지식의 천국은 아니다. 유레카는 사용자 제작 콘텐츠의 보고로서 오류도 있고 비록 백과사전 책들보다 상당히 더 크기는 하지만 전혀 완벽하지 않다. 일부 사람들은 입력 사항을 지우거나 왜곡함으로써 유레카를 파손하려고 시도하기도 했다. 의회 직원 전원이 서로의 프로필을 고의로 훼손한 혐의로 유레카 접속을 금지당했던 적도 있다. 어떻게 보면 이 온라인 백과사전은 참고 도구일 뿐 아니라 인간 본성에 대한 시금석이기도 하다.

Q 지문에서 유추할 수 있는 것은?
(a) 사용자 콘텐츠 홈페이지는 전문가들의 조언을 받는 경우가 드물다.
(b) 각지의 백과사전들은 때때로 오류를 범하는 경향이 있다.
(c) 업무의 고의적 파괴는 그 어디보다 인터넷에서 가장 많이 발생한다.
(d) 온라인 정보에 대해서는 어느 정도 의심해 봐야 한다.

🎛 기출 POINT

인터넷 백과사전인 유레카는 분명하고 정확한 지식을 주지 못하는 경우가 있다고 한다. 그 이유는 유레카가 UGC의 일종으로 사용자 조작이 가능하기 때문에 왜곡, 훼손되는 등의 문제가 생길 수 있기 때문이다. 따라서 (d)가 추론 가능하다.

repository 저장소 **user-generated content (UGC)** 사용자 제작 콘텐츠 **vandalize** 파손하다 **falsify entries** 입력 사항을 왜곡하다 **bar A from B** A를 B에서 막다 **sabotage** 사보타주, 일부러 파괴하다 **litmus test** 시금석 **skepticism** 의심   정답_(d)

37

Ken Kesey's landmark 1962 novel, *One Flew over the Cuckoo's Nest*, helped shape the attitude of America's youth toward authority. The plot develops in a mental institution in which Kesey's main character, McMurphy, one of the inmates, is pictured as saner than the hospital's authorities. Anti-establishment youths throughout the 60s identified themselves with the novel and McMurphy's fight against authorities. They saw the upside-down, oppressive logic of McMurphy's keepers as similar to the official US government rationales for the war in Vietnam at the time. They also maintained the view that America itself was a kind of mental ward.

Q What can be inferred about American youths in the 1960s according to the passage?
(a) They felt that mental patients should be released into society.
(b) They saw soldiers in Vietnam as equivalent to mental patients.
(c) They saw themselves as saner than those in charge of the country.
(d) They regarded everyday people as less enlightened than the insane.

SOLUTION

켄 케이시의 획기적인 1962년작 소설 〈빠꾸기 둥지 위로 날아간 새〉는 권위에 대한 미국 젊은이들의 태도를 형성하는 데 도움을 주었다. 줄거리는 케이시의 주인공인 맥머피라는 한 환자가 병원 당국보다 더 정상으로 그려지는 정신병원을 배경으로 전개된다. 60년대 내내 기성 체제에 반기를 들었던 젊은이들은 스스로를 이 소설, 그리고 맥머피의 권위에 대한 투쟁과 동일시했다. 그들은 맥머피의 감시원들의 전도된, 그리고 억압적인 논리를 당시 미국 정부의 베트남 전에 대한 공식 논거와 유사하다고 보았다. 그들은 또한 미국 그 자체가 일종의 정신병동이라는 관점을 내세우기도 했다.

Q 1960년대 미국 젊은이들에 대해 유추할 수 있는 것은?
(a) 정신병자들을 사회 속으로 풀어주어야 한다고 느꼈다.
(b) 베트남 전의 장병들이 정신병자와 같다고 보았다.
(c) 스스로를 미국을 책임지고 있는 사람들보다 더 정상이라고 보았다.
(d) 일상생활 속의 사람들이 정신병자보다 덜 개화되었다고 여겼다.

⊞ 기출 POINT
이 소설이 1960년대 젊은이들의 태도를 형성하는 데 영향을 주었다고 했으므로 반체제 운동, 권위에 대한 투쟁을 표방하는 것이라고 볼 수 있다. 따라서 국가를 맡고 있는 사람들, 즉, 정부 당국보다 자신들을 더 정상이라고 생각했다는 (c)를 유추할 수 있다.

landmark 획기적인 것 **mental institution** 정신병원 **inmate** 입원환자 **sane** 정상인, 멀쩡한 **anti-establishment** 반체제 운동의 **upside-down** 전도된 **oppressive** 억압적인 **rationale** 이론적 근거 **ward** 병동   정답_(c)

38

In my experience, the key to being productive as a writer is sticking to a regular schedule. (a) I make sure that I sit down to write by 10 a.m. each morning for five days a week. (b) Of course, some people feel that writing is not about being a slave to a schedule. (c) However, if you don't have that discipline, then maybe you're not cut out to be a writer. (d) I wrote my first book while seated at a small desk in the corner of my bedroom.

SOLUTION

내 경험으로 보면, 생산적인 작가가 되는 열쇠는 규칙적인 일과를 지키는 것이다. (a) 나는 꼭 일주일에 5일은 매일 아침 글을 쓰기 위해 10시에 자리에 앉는다. (b) 물론 어떤 사람들은 집필이 일정의 노예가 되는 것이 아니라고 생각한다. (c) 그러나 이 같은 규율이 없으면 작가가 될 자질이 없는 것인지도 모른다. (d) 나는 침실 구석의 작은 책상에 앉아서 내 첫 번째 책을 집필했다.

⊞ 기출 POINT
생산적인 작가가 되기 위해서는 규칙적인 일과를 지켜야 한다는 글이다. 일주일에 날과 시간을 정해 놓고 글을 써야 하는데 이것은 일정의 노예가 되는 것이 아니고 규율이 있어야 작가의 자질을 갖춘 것이라는 내용이다. (d)는 흐름과 무관한 문장이다.

productive 생산적인 **stick to** ~을 고수하다 **discipline** 규율 **cut out to+동사원형** ~하는 데 적임인   정답_(d)

39

William Shakespeare was born in 1564 in Stratford-upon-Avon, England. (a) He spent the first 20 years of his life there, where a modest schooling barely prepared him for the theater. (b) He eventually married a young woman named Anne Hathaway, with whom he later had three children. (c) No one really knows how Shakespeare began his drama career after his academic training, but he started acting sometime around 1585. (d) What is certain, however, is that by 1592 he had established himself as an actor and a playwright of note.

SOLUTION

윌리엄 셰익스피어는 1564년 영국 스트랫퍼드-어폰-에이번에서 태어났다. (a) 그는 태어난 후 20년을 그곳에서 보냈으나, 이곳에서의 정규 교육은 그가 연극을 위한 준비를 하기에는 부족했다. (b) 그는 결국 앤 해서웨이라는 이름의 젊은 여성과 결혼을 하게 되고, 이후 이 여성과의 사이에 세 명의 자녀를 두게 된다. (c) 셰익스피어가 학업을 마친 후 어떻게 연극의 길로 들어서게 되었는지 확실히 아는 사람은 아무도 없으나, 그는 1585년경에 연극배우로 일하기 시작했다. (d) 하지만 분명한 것은, 1592년에 이르러 그는 유명한 배우이자 극작가로 이미 그 이름을 알렸다는 것이다.

 기출 POINT

셰익스피어의 연극 경력과 관련된 내용이다. 학교 교육은 연극을 하기에는 부족한 준비에 불과했고 학업을 마친 후 연극의 길로 들어서 1592년에는 결국 유명한 배우이자 극작가가 되었다. (b)는 전기적인 사실이지만 연극과 관련된 경력을 서술하는 문맥에 맞지 않는 내용이다.

modest 부족한 **barely** 거의 ~못하다 **academic training** 학업
playwright 극작가 **of note** 명성, 유명한 　　　　정답 (b)

40

The demand for copies of Martin Luther's works in the early 1500s was huge throughout Europe. (a) Between 1518 and 1521, no fewer than 800 editions of a hundred of his works were published in several languages. (b) Luther's works were censored and his adherents persecuted in many parts of Europe by the Catholic Church. (c) Thanks to the invention of the printing press, copies of his sermons, edifying tracts and vigorous polemics were all available to the public. (d) Without mass production, the popularity and impact of Luther across Europe would not have been nearly as great.

SOLUTION

1500년대 초 마틴 루터의 작품 사본은 유럽 전역에서 그 수요가 엄청나게 높았다. (a) 1518년과 1521년 사이에 자그마치 그의 작품 100편의 800판이 여러 언어로 출간되었다. (b) 루터의 작품은 검열을 당했고 그의 신봉자들은 천주 교회에 의해 유럽 곳곳에서 박해를 받았다. (c) 인쇄기의 발명 덕택에 그의 설교 사본들, 교화용 소책자와 박력 있는 논증법을 대중들이 모두 접할 수 있게 되었다. (d) 대량 생산이 없었다면 유럽 전역에서 루터의 인기와 영향력은 그토록 대단하지 않았을 것이다.

⊞ 기출 POINT

마틴 루터의 작품에 대한 인기를 다루는 내용이다. 유럽 전역에서 수요가 엄청나게 높았고, 인쇄기 발명으로 대중들이 다양한 책자를 접할 수 있었으며 유럽 전역까지 루터의 인기와 영향력을 미칠 수 있었다. (b)의 내용은 인기와 영향력에 대한 주제와 맞지 않으므로 오답이다.

demand 수요 **edition** (초판·재판의) 판 **censor** 검열하다
adherent 신봉자 **persecute** 박해하다 **edifying tract** 교화용 소책자 **vigorous** 박력 있는 **polemic** 논쟁 **impact** 영향력
　　　　정답 (b)

Answer Keys

🎧 Listening Comprehension

1	(a)	2	(c)	3	(c)	4	(d)	5	(a)	6	(c)	7	(b)	8	(d)	9	(b)	10	(d)
11	(c)	12	(c)	13	(b)	14	(d)	15	(a)	16	(c)	17	(a)	18	(a)	19	(b)	20	(b)
21	(a)	22	(d)	23	(d)	24	(d)	25	(b)	26	(d)	27	(b)	28	(b)	29	(a)	30	(c)
31	(c)	32	(c)	33	(a)	34	(b)	35	(a)	36	(a)	37	(d)	38	(a)	39	(b)	40	(b)
41	(d)	42	(d)	43	(a)	44	(d)	45	(c)	46	(c)	47	(a)	48	(a)	49	(c)	50	(c)
51	(d)	52	(c)	53	(b)	54	(d)	55	(a)	56	(b)	57	(a)	58	(c)	59	(d)	60	(b)

🔬 Grammar

1	(a)	2	(b)	3	(d)	4	(c)	5	(a)	6	(a)	7	(d)	8	(b)	9	(b)	10	(b)
11	(d)	12	(a)	13	(c)	14	(a)	15	(b)	16	(d)	17	(c)	18	(d)	19	(d)	20	(a)
21	(c)	22	(b)	23	(d)	24	(d)	25	(d)	26	(c)	27	(c)	28	(a)	29	(c)	30	(c)
31	(c)	32	(c)	33	(a)	34	(c)	35	(d)	36	(d)	37	(d)	38	(d)	39	(b)	40	(a)
41	(b)	42	(c)	43	(b)	44	(d)	45	(c)	46	(b)	47	(b)	48	(b)	49	(d)	50	(c)

🗔 Vocabulary

1	(c)	2	(a)	3	(b)	4	(a)	5	(b)	6	(a)	7	(d)	8	(c)	9	(a)	10	(a)
11	(d)	12	(c)	13	(a)	14	(c)	15	(a)	16	(d)	17	(b)	18	(b)	19	(b)	20	(b)
21	(d)	22	(a)	23	(d)	24	(d)	25	(b)	26	(c)	27	(a)	28	(a)	29	(a)	30	(c)
31	(b)	32	(a)	33	(d)	34	(b)	35	(c)	36	(a)	37	(d)	38	(c)	39	(b)	40	(d)
41	(a)	42	(a)	43	(b)	44	(a)	45	(a)	46	(c)	47	(c)	48	(a)	49	(d)	50	(a)

📖 Reading Comprehension

1	(d)	2	(b)	3	(b)	4	(c)	5	(d)	6	(b)	7	(d)	8	(b)	9	(d)	10	(d)
11	(d)	12	(b)	13	(a)	14	(b)	15	(a)	16	(a)	17	(a)	18	(d)	19	(d)	20	(d)
21	(d)	22	(d)	23	(d)	24	(b)	25	(b)	26	(c)	27	(a)	28	(a)	29	(c)	30	(b)
31	(a)	32	(c)	33	(a)	34	(a)	35	(c)	36	(d)	37	(c)	38	(d)	39	(b)	40	(b)

1

> M Where's your car parked?
> W _____

(a) We rented a car.
(b) It can go in back.
(c) The traffic's bad.
(d) Around the corner.

SOLUTION

M 차 어디에 주차했니?
W 코너 돌아서.

⊞ 기출 POINT

질문에 나오는 의문사는 항상 집중해서 들어야 한다. Where로 시작하는 질문이므로 장소로 답하는 (d)가 적절한 응답이다. Where did you park your car?의 다른 말이 Where's your car parked?이며 (b)는 '뒤로 들어갈 수 있다'는 말이다.
park 주차하다 **rent** 렌트하다, 임대하다 **The traffic is bad.** 교통 상황이 안 좋다. **정답** (d)

2

> W Stormy weather was forecast. Maybe you shouldn't go out.
> M _____

(a) I'll call again soon.
(b) Don't walk out like that.
(c) That's okay, I'll be alone.
(d) Then I'd better stay in.

SOLUTION

W 폭풍이 칠 거라고 예고했어. 너 외출하면 안 될 것 같아.
M 그럼 그냥 안에 있어야겠다.

⊞ 기출 POINT

폭풍 예보가 있으니 나가지 말라는 충고에 대해 '그럼 안에 있는 게 낫겠다'는 응답이 적절하다. Maybe you shouldn't…는 '~하지 않아야 할 것 같다'는 약한 충고의 표현이다. 반대로 had better는 '~하는 것이 낫겠다'이다. 충고와 응답에 쓰이는 shouldn't와 had better에 유의하자.
stormy 폭풍우가 치는 **forecast** 예보하다 **I'd better** ~하는 게 낫다 **정답** (d)

3

> M I'm tired of driving. Would you mind taking the wheel?
> W _____

(a) Sure, I can take over.
(b) No, I wouldn't agree.
(c) I could use a break.
(d) Go right ahead.

SOLUTION

M 운전하는 거 지겹다. 네가 운전대 좀 잡아볼래?
W 그래. 내가 할게.

⊞ 기출 POINT

Would you mind -ing?는 '~해주시겠습니까?'라고 정중하게 부탁할 때 사용하는 표현이다. Would you mind if…?/ Mind if…?의 형태로도 쓰이며 승낙할 때는 Sure/ Okay/ All right 등을 쓴다. No, not at all/ Certainly not/ No, I don't mind 등도 승낙의 다른 표현이다. take over는 '~을 대신하다, 인계받다'의 뜻이므로 '내가 대신할게'라는 응답이 된다.
be tired of -ing ~하는 것이 지겹다 **mind -ing** ~을 꺼리다 **take the wheel** 운전대를 잡다 **정답** (a)

4

W Did you have trouble getting here?

M _____

(a) Actually, I don't get it.
(b) Yes, I believe we met here.
(c) No, your directions were clear.
(d) But I don't want to cause trouble.

SOLUTION

W 여기까지 오는 데 힘들지 않았나요?
M 아니요, 길 안내를 분명하게 해주셨어요.

⊞ 기출 POINT

Did you have trouble getting here?는 여기 오는 데 힘들지 않았느냐는 질문이다. 이에 대해 '길 안내를 분명하게 해주셔서 힘들지 않았다'는 말이 적절한 응답이 된다. '길 안내'는 directions라는 단어를 쓴다. (a)는 안내를 듣고 나서 잘 이해하지 못했을 때 할 수 있는 말이다.
have trouble -ing ~하는 데 문제가 있다   **directions** 길 안내
clear 분명한, 명확한   **cause trouble** 문제를 일으키다   정답_(c)

5

M When's John coming back from university?

W _____

(a) Yes, for the summer.
(b) It could be any day.
(c) No, he's not back.
(d) Two weeks ago.

SOLUTION

M 존은 언제 대학에서 돌아오는 거야?
W 곧 올 거야.

⊞ 기출 POINT

의문사와 시제에 집중해야 할 문제이다. When is John coming back은 미래에 예정된 일이므로 is coming이라는 진행형이 쓰일 수 있다. It could be any day는 날이 가까워서 언제든 될 수 있다는 말로, 결국 '곧 올 거다'라는 뜻이다. (a) '여름 동안'은 얼마 동안 머무를지에 대한 응답이다.
come back 돌아오다   정답_(b)

6

W Excuse me, but where can I catch the train for Boston?

M _____

(a) It's all right.
(b) Every 20 minutes.
(c) This isn't your train.
(d) At platform number 4.

SOLUTION

W 죄송하지만 보스턴으로 가는 기차는 어디서 타나요?
M 4번 승강장입니다.

⊞ 기출 POINT

의문사에 유의하자. 위치나 장소를 물을 때는 Where can I...?를 쓴다. 기차 타는 곳을 묻는 질문에 승강장 번호로 답하는 (d)가 정답이다. (b)는 '20분마다 온다'는 말이고, (c)는 '그것은 네가 탈 기차가 아니다'는 말이다.
catch the train 기차를 타다   **every 20 minutes** 20분마다
platform 승강장   정답_(d)

7

M If I buy this car, how much do I need for a
down payment?

W _____

(a) You should pay now.
(b) We charge by the hour.
(c) By credit card, preferably.
(d) We expect $5,000 up front.

SOLUTION

M 이 차를 산다면 계약금을 얼마나 내야 하죠?
W 선금 5천 달러를 내야 합니다.

⊞ 기출 POINT
생소한 단어나 표현이 나오더라도 전체적인 내용을 파악하면 얼마든지
풀 수 있다. how much do I need for는 '~에 얼마가 필요한지' 묻
는 말이므로 '할부금의 계약금, 첫 불입금'인 down payment라는 용
어를 모른다고 하더라도 (d)를 답으로 골라낼 수 있어야 한다. (c)는 '가
급적이면 신용카드로요'라는 말이다.
down payment 계약금, 첫 불입금   **charge** ~을 청구하다   **by the
hour** 시간당   **preferably** 가급적이면   **up front** 선금으로   **정답**_(d)

8

W Did you know that Sam got a university
scholarship?

M _____

(a) No, I didn't get one.
(b) No, he hasn't applied yet.
(c) Yes, I'm so happy for him.
(d) Yes, he got a bachelor's degree.

SOLUTION

W 샘이 대학 장학금을 받았다는 거 알고 있었니?
M 응. 너무 잘됐어.

⊞ 기출 POINT
다른 사람의 소식을 묻는 말과 그에 대한 응답이다. Did you know
that...?이므로 Yes나 No로 답해야 하며, 기쁜 소식을 들은 후 '그에
게 잘된 일이네'라고 한 (c)가 적절한 응답이다.
scholarship 장학금   **apply** 신청하다   **bachelor's degree** 학사
정답_(c)

9

M Look at the long line at the ticket booth.
W _____

(a) It's been a long time.
(b) I lost my ticket on the way.
(c) I won't wait for you any longer.
(d) Maybe we should come back another day.

SOLUTION

M 매표소에 저 긴 줄 좀 봐.
W 다른 날 다시 와야 할 것 같아.

⊞ 기출 POINT
긴 줄을 보라는 말에 (d) '다른 날 다시 와야 할 것 같다'는 제안을 하는
것이 적절하다. Maybe we should는 '~해야 할 것 같다'는 제안의
표현이다. (c)는 상대방을 오랫동안 기다리게 한 상황에서 할 수 있는
말이고, (a)는 질문의 long을 이용하여 혼동을 주기 위한 선택지이다.
ticket booth 매표소   **It's been a long time.** 오랜만이야.   **on the
way** 중간에, 오는 길에   **another day** 다른 날   **정답**_(d)

10

W Would you like to join me for tea sometime?

M _____

(a) Sounds great. Let's do that.
(b) Of course. Help yourself.
(c) Sure, I'd love some.
(d) Sorry, but I'm full.

SOLUTION

W 언제 저랑 차 한잔 하시겠어요?
M 좋죠. 그렇게 합시다.

⊞ 기출 POINT

Would you like to…?는 제안의 표현이고 제안에 동의하거나 제안을 수락하는 표현으로 Sounds great. Let's do that이 알맞다.
(c)는 상대방이 차나 음식을 권했을 때 가능한 응답이다. 제안을 수락할 때: That sounds wonderful./ Sure, I'd love to do./ That would be great./ That sounds good to me.

join me for 함께 ~하다 Help yourself. 마음껏 드세요. I'd love some. 저도 좀 먹어 볼게요. I'm full. 배가 부르다. 정답_(a)

11

M I'm really glad to have met you tonight.

W _____

(a) I'll meet you at seven.
(b) Right. I think we've met before.
(c) I'm sorry, but I'm really busy.
(d) Me, too. Let's get together again.

SOLUTION

M 오늘밤 만나서 정말 반가웠어.
W 나도. 또 보자.

⊞ 기출 POINT

헤어지면서 하는 대화이다. I'm really glad to meet you는 만났을 때 하는 말이지만, to 다음에 현재완료를 쓴 I'm really glad to have met you는 헤어질 때 '만나서 좋았다'는 인사이다. 동감하면서 '다음에 또 만나'고 답하는 (d)가 적절한 응답이다. 헤어질 때의 인사: It was nice seeing you./ It was nice meeting you./ Nice meeting you./ Nice talking to you.

I'm glad to ~해서 기쁘다 get together 만나다, 모이다 정답_(d)

12

W What do you think caused the drop in enrollment this year?

M _____

(a) There shouldn't be any.
(b) It's causing many problems.
(c) There are several likely factors.
(d) It's because students skip class.

SOLUTION

W 올해 입학률이 하락한 이유가 뭐라고 생각하세요?
M 몇 가지 그럴 법한 요인들이 있습니다.

⊞ 기출 POINT

What do you think caused…?는 ~의 원인에 대한 상대방의 의견을 묻는 질문이다. '몇 가지 그럴 법한 요인들이 있다'는 (c)가 의견의 도입부로 적절하다. (d)는 It's because로 시작하여 혼동을 주고 있으며 뒷부분 내용이 질문과 맞지 않아 오답이다.

drop 하락 enrollment 입학률 likely factor 그럴 법한 요인 skip 빠지다 정답_(c)

Actual Test 4

227

13

M Excuse me, waitress, but my food is cold.

W _____

(a) I'm afraid there's no way to eat it.
(b) I'm sorry, sir. I'll warm it up for you.
(c) Unfortunately, we're completely out.
(d) You should've asked before I cooked it.

SOLUTION

M 아가씨, 제 음식이 차갑네요.
W 죄송합니다, 손님. 다시 데워 드리겠습니다.

⊞ 기출 POINT
식당에서 '음식이 차갑다'고 불만을 표시하는 상황으로 '다시 데워 드리겠다'는 (b)가 적절한 응답이다. (a)는 손님이 할 수 있는 말이고, (c)는 '다 팔리고 없다'는 말로 내용에 맞지 않는다.
I'm afraid ~해서 유감이다   **warm up** 데우다   **completely** 완전히
정답_(b)

14

W Did you watch the soccer game yesterday?

M _____

(a) You bet.
(b) It depends.
(c) Yes, it was.
(d) Not tonight.

SOLUTION

W 어제 축구 경기 봤니?
M 당연하지.

⊞ 기출 POINT
상대방의 추측이나 제안에 대해 긍정의 답인 Yes의 강한 표현으로 You bet을 쓴다. 질문과 같이 과거의 일이나 Are you coming tomorrow?처럼 미래의 일, 혹은 Will you help me?처럼 제안에 응답하는 말로도 쓸 수 있다. It depends는 '때에 따라 다르다'는 말로 확실하지 않은 응답을 할 때 쓴다.
You bet. 당연하지.   **It depends.** 때에 따라 다르다.
정답_(a)

15

M We got the shipment. Would you fax us the invoice?

W _____

(a) Yes, I got your fax.
(b) No, it's not over yet.
(c) No, I'll pack it myself.
(d) Yes, that would be fastest.

SOLUTION

M 배송품은 받았습니다. 저희에게 송장을 팩스로 보내주시겠습니까?
W 네, 그게 제일 빠르겠네요.

⊞ 기출 POINT
배송품을 받은 후 송장을 받아 그 금액만큼 지급하는 과정에 대한 대화이다. invoice(송장)는 보낸 물건의 명세서로, 지불할 대금 내역을 기록한 거래 내역서이다. 물건을 받은 사람은 송장을 받고 대금을 지급하는 절차로 이루어진다는 것도 참고로 알아두자. 팩스로 보내주시겠냐는 말에 대한 응답으로 (d)가 적절하다.
shipment 배송   **invoice** 송장   **I'll pack it myself.** 제가 직접 포장할게요.
정답_(d)

16

W Why are you buying so many snacks?
M I have a weakness for junk food.
W But it's not healthy.
M _____

(a) I bought another one.
(b) No, they ran out of them.
(c) I know, but it's very tasty.
(d) I'm not as weak as you think.

SOLUTION

W 간식을 왜 그렇게 많이 사는 거야?
M 인스턴트 식품이라면 내가 사족을 못 써.
W 하지만 건강에 안 좋잖아.
M 아는데, 너무 맛있어.

기출 POINT

have a weakness for는 '~을 지나치게 좋아하다'라는 표현이다. '건
강에 좋지 않다'는 말에 대한 응답으로 (c)가 가장 적절하다. (d)는 앞에
서 말한 not healthy에 이어지는 말로 생각하기 쉬운 오답 함정이다.
have a weakness for ~을 지나치게 좋아하다 **junk food** 정크 푸드,
인스턴트 식품 **run out of** ~이 다 떨어지다 **tasty** 맛있는   **정답_(c)**

17

M I hate to leave the party, but it's getting late.
W Thanks for coming. It was good to see you.
M I had a good time, too.
W _____

(a) I'm glad you enjoyed yourself.
(b) You've been very generous.
(c) I'm sorry you had to miss it.
(d) We're looking forward to it.

SOLUTION

M 파티를 떠나기는 싫지만, 시간이 늦어서요.
W 와줘서 감사합니다. 뵙게 되어 반가웠습니다.
M 저도 좋은 시간 보냈습니다.
W 즐거웠다니 기쁘네요.

기출 POINT

모임을 끝내고 떠나면서 하는 대화이다. '좋은 시간을 보냈다'는 인사로
I had a good time, too라는 말을 했고, 이에 대한 응답으로 '즐거웠
다니 기쁘네요'라고 한 (a)가 적절하다. enjoy oneself는 '즐겁게 보내
다'라는 뜻이다.
leave 떠나다 **enjoy oneself** 즐겁게 보내다 **generous** 관대한
miss 놓치다 **look forward to** ~을 고대하다   **정답_(a)**

18

W Hi, this is Jennifer, Daniel's piano teacher.
M Oh, hi. Is everything okay?
W I'm afraid he hasn't been practicing enough at home.
M _____

(a) He's not home right now.
(b) He shouldn't play around too much.
(c) Sorry. I'll make sure he practices regularly.
(d) Yes, he plays well, though he doesn't practice.

SOLUTION

W 안녕하세요, 저는 대니얼의 피아노 선생님 제니퍼예요.
M 아, 안녕하세요. 별일 없으시죠?
W 대니얼이 집에서 충분히 연습을 해오지 않아서요.
M 죄송합니다. 제가 규칙적으로 연습하도록 시킬게요.

기출 POINT

Is everything okay?는 '별일 없으시죠?'라는 인사말이다. 유감스러운
내용을 말할 때는 I'm afraid로 시작한다. '계속 연습을 잘 해오지 않는
다'는 의미로 현재완료 진행형인 he hasn't been practicing을 썼다
는 것에 유의한다. I'll make sure는 '~을 확실히 하겠다'라는 표현이다.
I'm afraid ~해서 유감이다 **practice** 연습하다 **make sure** ~을
확실히 하다 **regularly** 규칙적으로   **정답_(c)**

19

M How are you enjoying business school?
W Well, the truth is, I'm not. It's really hard.
M I'm sure it is. But don't give up.
W _____

(a) I guess that's true.
(b) Don't worry. I won't.
(c) I'll be sure to try that.
(d) I haven't given anything.

SOLUTION

M 경영 대학원은 재미있니?
W 음, 그게 말이야. 실은 재미없어. 정말 힘들어.
M 물론 그렇겠지. 하지만 포기하지 마.
W 걱정 마. 포기 안 할 거야.

⊞ 기출 POINT
힘들지만 포기하지 말라는 권유에 대해 답하는 말이다. Don't give up 은 부정문이므로 I won't라는 응답이 적절하다. (c)는 '그걸 꼭 해보도록 할게'라는 말이므로 내용에 맞지 않는다. the truth is는 '사실은'이라는 말로 The truth is that의 형태로도 쓰지만 여기서처럼 문장 중간에 쓰기도 한다.
business school 경영 대학원 **the truth is** 사실은 **give up** 포기하다   정답_(b)

20

W I've decided to volunteer at the hospital.
M Why did you decide to do that?
W I wanted to give something back to the community.
M _____

(a) But you shouldn't have.
(b) That's very noble of you.
(c) I hardly ever give money.
(d) You should see a doctor about it.

SOLUTION

W 병원에서 자원 봉사하기로 했어.
M 왜 그러기로 한 거야?
W 지역 사회에 뭔가 되돌려주고 싶었어.
M 너 정말 훌륭하다.

⊞ 기출 POINT
상대방의 좋은 성품에 대해 칭찬하는 말은 It's noble of you이다. 상대방의 성품을 칭찬할 때는 That's[It's] nice[kind/ generous/ wise] of you to+동사원형의 형태를 쓴다.
volunteer 자원 봉사하다 **community** 지역 사회 **You shouldn't have.** 너는 하지 말았어야 했다. **noble** 숭고한, 훌륭한 **hardly ever** 거의 ~하지 않다   정답_(b)

21

M Did you hear about the forest fire?
W Yes, I saw the news. It's terrible.
M It'll take a long time for the forest to recover.
W _____

(a) It all started in the morning.
(b) Actually, I think they put it out.
(c) Yeah. It'll take years of replanting.
(d) You'll need to take care of the forest.

SOLUTION

M 산불 소식 들었니?
W 응, 뉴스 봤어. 끔찍해.
M 숲이 회복되려면 오랜 시간이 걸릴 거야.
W 그래. 몇 년 동안 나무를 다시 심어야겠지.

⊞ 기출 POINT
산불 때문에 숲이 타버린 뉴스에 대한 대화이다. It'll take a long time for the forest to recover는 〈It takes+시간+to+동사원형〉의 형태로 '~하는 데 …시간이 걸리다'는 표현이다. 상대방의 말에 동조하면서 같은 의견을 말하는 (c)가 정답이다. (d)는 비슷한 주제의 내용이지만 상대방에게 훈계하는 내용이므로 적절하지 않다.
forest fire 산불 **put out** 끄다 **replant** 다시 심다 **take care of** ~을 돌보다   정답_(c)

22

W Let's have barbeque for dinner.
M Didn't you hear that grilled meat can cause cancer?
W But grilled burgers taste really good.
M _____

(a) Okay, I'll turn off the stove.
(b) Let's get ready for the party.
(c) We can go grocery shopping now.
(d) I know, but I don't want to take a chance.

SOLUTION

W 저녁에 바비큐 해먹자.
M 구운 고기가 암을 유발할 수 있다는 것 못 들었어?
W 하지만 구운 햄버그 스테이크는 정말 맛있잖아.
M 아는데, 위험을 무릅쓰긴 싫어.

기출 POINT

Didn't you hear that...?은 들은 정보에 대해 묻는 말이다. 암을 유발한다고 믿는 사람의 대답으로는 (d) '위험을 무릅쓰긴 싫다'가 알맞다. take a chance는 '모험을 하다, 위험을 무릅쓰고 해보다'라는 뜻이다.
barbeque 바비큐 **grilled meat** 구운 고기 **cancer** 암 **turn off** 끄다 **grocery** 식료품 **take a chance** 위험을 무릅쓰다   정답 (d)

23

M Do you have plans for winter vacation?
W I'm thinking about going someplace warm.
M How about Phuket? The weather is nice, and it's not that expensive.
W _____

(a) There are cheap hotels near here.
(b) Yes, the weather has been nice lately.
(c) Sounds like the kind of place I'd enjoy.
(d) Our company gives extra vacation time.

SOLUTION

M 겨울 휴가 계획은 있으세요?
W 어디 따뜻한 곳으로 갈까 생각 중이에요.
M 푸켓은 어때요? 날씨도 좋고, 그렇게 비싸지도 않아요.
W 제가 좋아할 만한 장소 같네요.

기출 POINT

제안에 대한 응답을 묻는 문제이다. How about...?은 제안의 표현이므로 이에 동의하는 (c)가 정답이다. (a)는 expensive에 연결되는 내용처럼 보이지만 near here 때문에 오답이다.
I'm thinking about -ing ~할까 생각 중이다 **lately** 최근에 **extra** 추가의   정답 (c)

24

W You look lost. Can I help you?
M Yes. I'm looking for the Sunheim Building.
W It's a block back that way, on your right.
M _____

(a) Yes, I'll be all right.
(b) No, I couldn't go back.
(c) Sorry. I can't find the block.
(d) Really? I must've missed it somehow.

SOLUTION

W 길을 잃은 것 같은데, 제가 도와드릴까요?
M 네. 선하임 건물을 찾고 있어요.
W 저쪽으로 한 블록 다시 돌아가시면 오른쪽에 있어요.
M 그래요? 제가 어쩌다 지나친 모양이네요.

기출 POINT

가고자 하는 곳을 묻는 표현으로 I'm looking for가 쓰였다. a block back that way는 '저쪽으로 한 블록 돌아가라'는 안내인데 왔던 길을 돌아가라는 것이므로 어쩌다 지나친 모양이라고 한 (d)가 정답이다.
I must've missed it은 〈must+have+p.p.〉를 써서 과거의 일에 대한 추측을 말하는 표현이다.
lost 길을 잃은 **look for** ~을 찾다 **somehow** 어쩌다   정답 (d)

25

M Susan, would you fax this, please?
W The fax machine's broken.
M But this needs to be sent right away.
W _____

(a) I'll type it by tonight.
(b) I'll order more fax paper.
(c) We could scan and email it.
(d) The repairman won't know the way.

SOLUTION

M 수잔, 이것 좀 팩스로 보내주겠어요?
W 팩스기가 고장 났어요.
M 하지만 이건 당장 보내야 하는데.
W 스캔해서 이메일로 보낼 수 있어요.

⊞ 기출 POINT
팩스를 보내려는데 팩스기가 고장 난 상황이다. '당장 보내야 한다'는 말에 대해 적절한 응답은 다른 방법을 제시하는 (c)이다. (a)는 가능한 응답처럼 보이지만 남자가 '당장 보내야 한다'고 했으므로 적절하지 않다.
fax 팩스로 보내다   **broken** 고장 난   **send away** 보내다
repairman 수리공   정답_(c)

26

W Hello. May I speak to Jennifer, please?
M I'm sorry. Who did you wish to speak to?
W Jennifer. Jennifer Jones.
M _____

(a) She's been here for two years.
(b) She's busy at the moment.
(c) She didn't give her name.
(d) She'll see you soon.

SOLUTION

W 여보세요. 제니퍼와 통화할 수 있을까요?
M 미안하지만, 누구와 통화하고 싶다고요?
W 제니퍼요. 제니퍼 존스.
M 지금 다른 전화를 받고 있어요.

⊞ 기출 POINT
전화 상의 대화이다. I'm sorry. Who did you wish to speak to? 는 상대방의 말을 잘 알아듣지 못했을 때 할 수 있는 말이다. 그 사람이 지금 통화 중이라서 전화를 받을 수 없다는 (b)가 적절한 응답이다. (d)는 상대방을 직접 만나러 왔을 때 할 수 있는 말이다.
busy 통화 중인   **at the moment** 지금   **give one's name** 이름을 알려주다   정답_(b)

27

M Dinner was delicious. Thank you.
W Would you like some ice cream for dessert?
M I'd better not. I'm watching my weight.
W _____

(a) I don't think a little will hurt.
(b) It's okay, there's plenty more.
(c) We should watch what happens.
(d) Right. I've gained a few pounds.

SOLUTION

M 저녁 맛있었어. 고마워.
W 디저트로 아이스크림 먹을래?
M 안 먹는 게 좋겠어. 체중 조절 중이라서.
W 조금 먹는다고 별일 있겠니.

⊞ 기출 POINT
음식을 권할 때 쓰는 표현은 Would you like some...?이며 사양할 때 I'd better not이라고 답할 수 있다. watch my weight는 '체중을 조절하다'는 표현이다. (a) '조금 먹는 건 괜찮을 것 같다'는 말로 정답이고, (c)는 watch에 집중하면 속기 쉬운 선택지이다. (d)는 음식을 권유한 사람이 할 말로는 적절하지 않다.
I'd better not. 그러지 않는 게 좋겠어.   **gain a few pound** 살이 찌다   정답_(a)

28

W Didn't you say the report would be finished by today?
M I'm sorry. I was so busy that I didn't have time to finish it.
W But we need it for tomorrow's presentation.
M _____

(a) I'll definitely arrive early tomorrow.
(b) I didn't know the due date was today.
(c) Because I had to train new employees.
(d) I'll have it on your desk by the end of today.

SOLUTION

W 오늘까지 보고서가 완료될 거라고 하지 않았나요?
M 죄송합니다. 너무 바빠서 보고서를 끝낼 시간이 없었습니다.
W 하지만 내일 발표에 그 보고서가 필요합니다.
M 오늘 마감 때까지 책상에 두겠습니다.

⊞ 기출 POINT
'내일 아침 발표에 필요하다'는 말에 대한 응답으로 '오늘 마감 때까지는 끝내겠다'는 내용이 적절하다. '바빠서 못했다'고 말해놓고 '기한을 몰랐다'는 (b)는 앞뒤가 맞지 않는다.
presentation 발표 **definitely** 확실히 **due date** 마감일 **train** 훈련시키다 **employee** 직원 정답_(d)

29

M Congratulations on completing the project! It's a real achievement.
W Thanks, but I was only part of a team.
M Don't be modest. Your vision led the way.
W _____

(a) Yes, it was a modest design.
(b) I'm sorry. Have I offended you?
(c) You're right. My vision is better now.
(d) True, but many people made it a reality.

SOLUTION

M 프로젝트 완료한 것 축하해요! 정말 큰 성취네요.
W 고마워요, 하지만 저는 그저 팀의 일원이었을 뿐이에요.
M 겸손하긴요. 당신의 비전이 방향을 이끌었는데요.
W 그렇기는 하지만, 많은 사람들이 그걸 현실로 만든 거니까요.

⊞ 기출 POINT
축하와 감사 표현에 대한 문제이다. '~을 축하한다'는 말로 Congratulations on을 쓴다. '팀의 일원이었다'는 겸손의 말에 대해 당신의 비전 때문이라는 칭찬이 이어지므로 이 말에 동감하면서 다른 사람들의 노고를 치하하는 말이 나와야 자연스럽다. make it a reality는 '현실로 만들다'라는 뜻이다.
congratulation 축하 **complete** 완성하다 **achievement** 성취 **modest** 겸손한; 수수한 **vision** 비전 **offend** 감정을 상하게 하다 **reality** 현실 정답_(d)

30

W I'm thinking of buying a treadmill.
M Don't. You'll be wasting money.
W No, I won't. I'll use it every day.
M _____

(a) Good luck. You should enjoy it.
(b) I doubt it. You'll quit after a month.
(c) Sure. It saves time to exercise at home.
(d) Really? It's better than never exercising.

SOLUTION

W 러닝 머신을 살까 생각 중이야.
M 사지 마. 돈만 낭비할 거야.
W 아니, 낭비하지 않을 거야. 매일 사용할 건데.
M 글쎄, 한 달 후면 그만둘 거야.

⊞ 기출 POINT
treadmill이 '러닝 머신'임을 알면 이해가 쉬운 대화이다. I'm thinking of -ing는 '~할까 생각 중이다'라는 말로 상대방의 의견을 듣고자 할 때 쓰는 말이다. I doubt it은 그러지 않을 거라는 강한 의심을 표현하는 말로 정답은 (b)이다.
treadmill 러닝 머신 **waste** 낭비하다 **I doubt it.** 안 그럴 것 같은데. **quit** 그만두다 **save** 덜어주다; ~의 낭비를 막다 정답_(b)

31

M Hi, Jeanie. It's Greg calling. What are you up to?

W Just relaxing after a hard day at work.

M Well, how about going out to eat tonight?

W Okay. I could really use a quiet night out.

M Let's head out, say, in an hour?

W Sure, I'll see you then.

Q What does the man want Jeanie to do?
(a) Go out for dinner together.
(b) Come home in an hour.
(c) Order take-out food.
(d) Find him a new job.

SOLUTION

M 안녕, 지니. 나 그렉인데, 뭐 하고 있어?

W 그냥 회사에서 고된 하루를 마치고 와서 쉬고 있지.

M 음, 오늘 저녁 외식하는 거 어때?

W 좋아. 조용한 외출이 되었으면 좋겠다.

M 그럼, 한 시간쯤 있다가 나갈까?

W 좋아. 그럼 그때 보자.

Q 남자가 지니가 해주기를 바라는 것은?
(a) 함께 저녁 먹으러 나가는 것.
(b) 한 시간 후에 집에 돌아오는 것.
(c) 테이크 아웃 음식을 주문하는 것.
(d) 자신에게 새 일자리를 구해주는 것.

⊞ 기출 POINT

남자의 제안을 잘 들어야 하는 문제이다. going out to eat tonight 이라고 제안하고 있으므로 답은 (a)가 된다. head out은 '밖으로 나가다'는 말이다. 시간 앞에 전치사 in을 쓰면 '~후에'라는 말이고, take-out food는 '포장, 배달이 되는 음식'을 의미한다.

What are you up to? 뭐 하고 있어? **relax** 쉬다 **go out to eat** 외식하다 **could use** ~을 얻을 수 있으면 좋겠다 **head out** 밖으로 나가다 **order take-out food** 테이크 아웃 음식을 주문하다 **정답_(a)**

32

M I'd like to return this watch I bought last week.

W Could you tell me why?

M It suddenly stopped working.

W Let's see if it works with a new battery first.

M But it's a new watch! It shouldn't need a new battery.

W We usually check the battery before we do a return.

Q What does the man want to do?
(a) Return a watch.
(b) Get a free watch.
(c) Change batteries.
(d) Buy a new battery.

SOLUTION

M 지난주에 산 이 시계를 반품하고 싶습니다.

W 이유를 말씀해 주시겠습니까?

M 갑자기 작동이 멈췄어요.

W 우선 건전지를 새로 갈아 끼워서 작동이 되는지 보죠.

M 하지만 새 시계잖아요! 새 건전지가 필요할 리 없잖아요?

W 저희는 반품을 받기 전에 보통 건전지를 확인합니다.

Q 남자가 하기 원하는 것은?
(a) 시계 반품.
(b) 공짜 시계 받기.
(c) 건전지 교환.
(d) 새 건전지 구매.

⊞ 기출 POINT

첫 번째 말에서 남자는 I'd like to를 써서 원하는 바를 말하고 있다. return this watch는 '시계를 반품하다'의 뜻이고 do a return은 '반품을 해주다'라는 뜻이다. 반품의 이유가 suddenly stopped working이기 때문에 건전지를 확인하는 것이지 남자가 건전지를 바꾸기 위해 온 것은 아니다.

stop working 작동이 멈추다 **see if** ~인지 보다 **정답_(a)**

33

W I almost got hit by a motorcycle yesterday.
M Oh, no! How did that happen?
W I was about to cross a street when a motorcycle sped through a red light.
M Wow, you must've been really scared.
W Tell me about it. I was so shocked that I literally froze for a moment.
M Well, I'm glad nothing bad happened to you.

Q What is the main topic of the conversation?
(a) Where the woman was going earlier.
(b) How fast the motorcyclist passed by.
(c) Why the woman is scared of motorcycles.
(d) What happened at a crossing the day before.

SOLUTION

W 어제 오토바이에 치일 뻔했어요.
M 오, 저런! 어떻게 됐던 거야?
W 길을 건너려고 하는데 오토바이가 빨간 불을 무시하고 속력을 내서 지나갔어요.
M 우와, 정말 무서웠겠구나.
W 말도 마세요. 너무 충격을 받아서 말 그대로 잠시 얼어 붙었다니까요.
M 음, 아무 일도 없었으니 다행이다.

Q 대화의 주제는?
(a) 여자가 전에 갔던 장소.
(b) 오토바이 운전자의 운전 속도.
(c) 여자가 오토바이를 무서워하는 이유.
(d) 전날 건널목에서 생긴 일.

🏷 기출 POINT

대화의 첫 문장에 어제 오토바이에 치일 뻔했던 사건이 제시되어 있다. '길을 건너려는 중에 오토바이가 신호를 무시하고 속력을 냈다'는 얘기에 큰일나지 않아 다행이라는 말로 끝맺고 있다. 따라서 대화의 주제는 (d)이다. must've been scared는 '겁났겠다'라는 과거의 일에 대한 추측의 표현이다. freeze는 자동사로 '꼼짝 못하게 되다'라는 뜻으로 쓰였다.

get hit 치이다 **be about to** 막 ~하려던 참이다 **motorcycle** 오토바이 **speed** 질주하다 **literally** 말 그대로 **freeze** 꼼짝 못하게 되다; 얼어 붙다 **crossing** 건널목   정답_(d)

34

M I can't stand waiting at airports.
W I know. Flight delays are a pain.
M I'm going to grab something to read.
W That's a good idea.
M There's a bookstore over there.
W I hope it's got some decent books.

Q What are the speakers mainly doing?
(a) Looking for something to pass time.
(b) Transferring to a different plane.
(c) Trying to buy a plane ticket.
(d) Searching for a bookstore.

SOLUTION

M 공항에서 기다리는 건 참을 수가 없어.
W 그러게. 비행기 연착은 정말 진절머리 나.
M 난 뭐 좀 읽을래.
W 좋은 생각이야.
M 저쪽에 서점이 있는데.
W 괜찮은 책들이 좀 있으면 좋겠다.

Q 화자들이 하고 있는 일은?
(a) 시간을 보낼 무언가를 찾고 있다.
(b) 다른 비행기로 갈아타고 있다.
(c) 비행기표를 사려고 하고 있다.
(d) 서점을 찾고 있다.

🏷 기출 POINT

비행기가 연착된 상황에서 시간을 보낼 뭔가를 찾는 내용이다. I'm going to grab something to read는 '읽을거리를 찾아봐야겠다'는 말이다. grab: 간단히 ~을 하다 grab some sleep/ grab a bite/ grab a cup of coffee

stand 참다 **flight delay** 비행기 연착 **pain** 고통 **decent** 괜찮은 **pass time** 시간을 보내다 **transfer** 갈아타다   정답_(a)

35

M I don't know how to handle my assistant anymore.

W Why? What's wrong?

M She's always late and is often disrespectful to my clients.

W You need to talk to her about it.

M Actually, I've been dropping hints that I'm not happy with her.

W Maybe it's time to have a serious talk with her.

Q Why is the man complaining to the woman?
(a) He is losing many of his clients.
(b) He finds it hard to deal with clients.
(c) He wants to apply for a new position.
(d) He is having trouble with his assistant.

SOLUTION

M 내 보조를 더 이상 어째야 할지 모르겠어.

W 왜? 무슨 일이야?

M 항상 지각인데다가 내 의뢰인들한테도 무례하게 구는 경우가 많아서.

W 보조랑 이것에 관해서 이야기를 해야겠다.

M 실은 내가 못마땅해한다는 점을 넌지시 알리긴 했거든.

W 아마도 그 보조랑 진지하게 이야기를 나눌 시점이 된 것 같아.

Q 남자가 여자에게 불평하는 이유는?
(a) 자신의 의뢰인들을 잃고 있다.
(b) 의뢰인들을 상대하는 것이 어렵다.
(c) 새 자리에 지원하고 싶다.
(d) 자신의 보조와 문제가 있다.

🏦 기출 POINT

남자의 문제는 첫 문장에 제시되어 있다. how to handle my assistant에 대한 고민이다. '문제점에 대해 넌지시 말하고 있다'는 말에 여자는 '진지한 대화를 해봐야 할 때가 된 것 같다'고 충고한다. drop hints that은 '~라는 암시를 주다'라는 뜻이며 암시를 계속 주었다는 의미를 나타내기 위해 현재완료 진행을 사용하고 있다.

handle 다루다 **assistant** 보조, 조수 **disrespectful** 무례한 **client** 의뢰인 **drop hints** 넌지시 알리다 **it's time to+동사원형** ~해야 할 때다 **deal with** ~을 대하다
정답_(d)

36

W I didn't think crossing the border would take this long.

M The border guards are only doing their job.

W I know. But do they really need to check everyone?

M What do you mean?

W They should just focus on high-risk people.

Q What is the conversation mainly about?
(a) Inconveniences with crossing a border.
(b) Problems with illegal border crossings.
(c) Being respectful to border guards.
(d) The need for more border staff.

SOLUTION

W 국경을 통과하는 데 이렇게 시간이 오래 걸릴 줄 몰랐어.

M 국경 수비대는 그저 자기 일을 하는 거잖아.

W 알아. 하지만 정말 모든 사람을 일일이 확인해야 할까?

M 무슨 뜻이야?

W 위험성이 높은 사람들한테만 집중해야지.

Q 대화의 주된 내용은?
(a) 국경 통과의 불편함.
(b) 불법 국경 통과 문제.
(c) 국경 수비대에게 공손함.
(d) 국경 인력 충원의 필요성.

🏦 기출 POINT

첫 번째 문장에 화제가 제시되는데 '국경을 통과하는 것이 너무 오래 걸렸다'는 내용이다. take this long은 '이렇게 오래 걸리다'라는 말이며, this와 that은 형용사를 수식하는 부사로 각각 '이만큼이나', '그렇게까지'라는 뜻으로 사용된다.

cross the border 국경을 통과하다 **guard** 수비대 **focus on** ~에 집중하다 **high-risk** 위험성이 높은 **inconvenience** 불편함 **illegal** 불법의 **respectful** 공손한
정답_(a)

37

W Don't you think the recruiting process was very simple this time?

M Yes. I was surprised, since we had three times more applicants.

W What do you suppose made it easier?

M Probably the way we sorted through applicants' résumés on-screen first.

W Yeah, last time we had to print out all the applications, which was very time-consuming and a waste of paper.

M If we have to do it again, let's do it the way we did this time.

Q What is the conversation mainly about?
(a) How many more people applied for a position.
(b) How simple the recruiting process was this time.
(c) Why fewer applicants passed the screening process.
(d) Why so much time and paper was wasted in recruiting.

SOLUTION

W 이번 채용 절차는 아주 간단한 것 같지 않아요?

M 네. 저도 놀랐다니까요. 지원자가 세 배나 더 많았음에도 불구하고요.

W 왜 채용 절차가 더 쉬워졌다고 생각하세요?

M 아마 지원자들의 이력서를 먼저 모니터 상에서 분류했던 방식 때문일 거예요.

W 그래요, 지난번에는 지원서를 전부 출력했는데, 그게 굉장히 시간이 많이 들고 종이도 낭비였죠.

M 다시 채용을 해야 한다면 이번에 했던 방식으로 하죠.

Q 대화의 주된 내용은?
(a) 얼마나 더 많은 사람들이 지원했는지.
(b) 이번 채용 절차가 얼마나 간단했는지.
(c) 왜 선발 과정을 통과한 지원자가 더 적었는지.
(d) 왜 채용에서 그렇게 많은 시간과 종이가 낭비되었는지.

⊞ 기출 POINT

대화의 첫 번째 문장은 반드시 집중해서 들어야 한다. '이번 채용 절차가 간단해진 것 같다'고 하자 지원자가 많았지만 지원서를 출력하지 않고 모니터 상에서 분류하는 방식을 사용했기 때문이라고 하고 있다. 따라서 주된 내용은 (b)이다.

recruit 채용 process 절차 sort through 분류하다 applicant 지원자 résumé 이력서 print out 출력하다 time-consuming 시간이 걸리는 screening 심사하는 정답_(b)

38

M I've been really stressed lately.

W Have you been working too hard?

M Probably. I'm starting to feel run down.

W You should try doing yoga.

M Do you think it'll relax me?

W Sure. It's great for relieving tension.

Q Why does the woman recommend yoga to the man?
(a) Because he has been very tense.
(b) Because he has trouble sleeping.
(c) Because he needs it for work.
(d) Because he is out of shape.

SOLUTION

M 나 요즘 정말 스트레스받고 있어.

W 일을 너무 열심히 했니?

M 아마도, 지치기 시작하는 것 같아.

W 요가를 해봐야겠구나.

M 요가를 하면 긴장이 풀릴까?

W 그럼. 요가가 긴장을 푸는 데 아주 좋아.

Q 여자가 남자에게 요가를 권유하는 이유는?
(a) 남자가 매우 긴장해 있어서.
(b) 남자가 잠을 잘 못 자서.
(c) 남자의 업무에 필요해서.
(d) 남자의 체력이 떨어져서.

⊞ 기출 POINT

세부 정보와 전체의 내용을 다 참고해야 하는 문제이다. 남자가 '스트레스가 심해서 지치는 것 같다'고 하자 여자가 요가를 권하고 있다. 권유의 이유는 남자의 말 중 relax와 여자의 응답인 relieving tension에서 찾을 수 있다.

run down 지친 relieve tension 긴장을 풀다 tense 긴장한 out of shape 체력이 떨어진; 몸매가 엉망이 된 정답_(a)

39

M   How may I help you?
W   I need some material to make a piano cover.
M   I see. What kind of material do you have in mind?
W   I'd like something light that hangs nicely.
M   How about this chintz? It's very light and is often used for covers.
W   That looks nice. I like its floral print.

Q   Which is correct about the woman?
(a) She likes the material the man shows her.
(b) She wants to buy some material to make a dress.
(c) She wants to sell her old piano and buy a new one.
(d) She is planning to hang some floral prints in her home.

SOLUTION

M   어떻게 도와드릴까요?
W   피아노 덮개를 만들 재료가 필요해서요.
M   그렇군요. 어떤 소재를 생각하고 계신가요?
W   가볍고 걸어 놨을 때 멋진 거면 좋겠어요.
M   이 사라사 무명은 어떠세요? 아주 가볍고 덮개로도 많이 쓰여요.
W   좋아 보이네요. 꽃무늬가 마음에 듭니다.

Q   여자에 대해 옳은 것은?
(a) 남자가 보여준 소재를 좋아한다.
(b) 옷 만들 재료를 조금 사고 싶어 한다.
(c) 예전 피아노를 팔고 새 피아노를 사고 싶어 한다.
(d) 집에 꽃 그림을 걸 계획이다.

기출 POINT
옷감 상점에서의 대화이다. 여자는 피아노 덮개를 만들 재료를 사러 왔고 상점 점원이 보여준 소재를 마음에 들어 했으므로 대화와 일치하는 것은 (a)이다.
material 재료   **have in mind** 생각하고 있다   **chintz** 사라사 무명
floral print 꽃무늬   정답_(a)

40

M   If the play starts at 8 o'clock, then we should meet at 6 o'clock.
W   That's too early. The theater is nearby.
M   Aren't we having dinner first?
W   Yes, but it won't take long. How about 6:45?
M   Let's meet at 6:30, just to be safe.
W   Okay. And if I'm late, you can get a table.

Q What time is the woman going to meet the man?
(a) At 6 o'clock.
(b) At 6:30.
(c) At 6:45.
(d) At 8 o'clock.

SOLUTION

M   연극 시작이 8시면 우리는 6시에 만나야 돼.
W   너무 이르다. 극장이 이 근처인데.
M   우선 저녁부터 먹을 거 아니야?
W   맞아. 하지만 오래 걸리지 않을 거야. 6시 45분 어때?
M   안전하게 6시 30분에 만나자.
W   좋아. 그리고 만약 내가 늦으면 식당에 자리를 잡아둬.

Q   여자가 남자를 만날 시각은?
(a) 6시.
(b) 6시 30분.
(c) 6시 45분.
(d) 8시.

기출 POINT
시간 약속을 정하는 대화이며 대화 전체에서 약속 시각이 세 번 언급된다. 6시에 만나기를 제안했다가 상대방은 식사 시간이 그리 길지 않을 것이니 6시 45분에 만나자고 제안하고, 결국은 6시 30분에 만나는 것으로 결정하는 내용이다. 미래에 예정된 계획에 대해서 현재진행형을 쓴 Aren't we having dinner first?라는 표현에 유의하자.
theater 극장   **nearby** 가까운   **just to be safe** 안전하게
get a table 자리를 잡다   정답_(b)

41

M That's a lovely dress.

W Thanks. I made it myself.

M Where did you learn to sew?

W My mother taught me when I was young.

M Do you make all your clothes?

W Not all, but a lot of them.

Q Which is correct according to the conversation?

(a) The woman knows how to sew.

(b) The woman has many new dresses.

(c) The woman designs her mother's clothes.

(d) The woman was taught to sew by the man.

SOLUTION

M 그 옷 귀엽다.

W 고마워. 내가 직접 만들었어.

M 바느질하는 건 어디서 배웠니?

W 어렸을 때 우리 어머니가 가르쳐 주셨어.

M 옷은 전부 만들어 입니?

W 전부는 아니고 많이.

Q 대화 내용 중 옳은 것은?

(a) 여자는 바느질하는 법을 안다.

(b) 여자는 새 옷이 많다.

(c) 여자는 그녀의 어머니 옷을 디자인한다.

(d) 남자는 여자에게 바느질하는 법을 가르쳤다.

⊞ 기출 POINT

여자는 어렸을 때 어머니에게서 바느질을 배웠고, 많은 옷을 만들어 입는다는 내용이다. I made it myself에서 myself는 내가 직접 만들었다는 것을 강조하기 위해 사용되었다.

sew 바느질하다 how to+동사원형 ~하는 법   정답_(a)

42

W What's the fastest way to ship packages in the US?

M That would be express mail, which guarantees next-day delivery.

W Can this package be delivered by dinnertime tomorrow?

M Sure, express mail arrives by 3 p.m. to most US destinations.

W So, what happens if it doesn't get there on time?

M That's highly unlikely. But if it did happen, you'd get your money back.

Q Which is correct about express mail according to the conversation?

(a) Packages are delivered around dinnertime.

(b) Next-day delivery is guaranteed worldwide.

(c) The service is available for large packages only.

(d) Items generally arrive by 3 p.m. the next day in the US.

SOLUTION

W 미국에서 소포를 보내는 가장 빠른 방법이 뭐죠?

M 빠른 우편일 겁니다. 익일 배송을 보장하거든요.

W 이 소포가 내일 저녁 식사 시간까지 배달될 수 있을까요?

M 그럼요. 빠른 우편은 대부분의 미국 내 행선지에 오후 3시까지 도착합니다.

W 그럼, 제시간에 도착하지 못하면 어떻게 되나요?

M 그럴 확률은 매우 적습니다. 하지만, 그런 경우에는 환불을 받을 겁니다.

Q 대화에서 빠른 우편에 대해 옳은 것은?

(a) 소포는 저녁 식사 시간 무렵에 배달된다.

(b) 익일 배송이 전세계적으로 보장된다.

(c) 서비스는 대형 소포만 가능하다.

(d) 물건들은 일반적으로 미국 내에 익일 오후 3시까지 도착한다.

⊞ 기출 POINT

우체국 직원과 손님과의 대화이다. 처음 Question을 들은 후 두 번째 들을 때는 express mail에 대한 정보에 집중해야 한다는 것을 알 수 있다. 빠른 우편으로 소포를 보내면 미국 내에서는 다음날 오후 3시까지 도착한다고 했으므로 정답은 (d)이다.

package 소포 express mail 빠른 우편 guarantee 보장하다
next-day delivery 익일 배송 destination 행선지 unlikely 가능성이 적은   정답_(d)

43

M I'd like to exchange this shirt.
W Is there something wrong with it?
M There's a small hole in the sleeve.
W Would you like to exchange the shirt or get a refund?
M I'd prefer to exchange it for another shirt in the same style.
W All right. I'll get you one from the back.

Q What can be inferred about the man from the conversation?
(a) He tore a hole in the shirt.
(b) He likes the style of the shirt.
(c) He wants to buy another shirt.
(d) He will buy a shirt in another store.

SOLUTION

M 이 셔츠를 교환하고 싶습니다.
W 문제가 있나요?
M 소매에 작은 구멍이 있어요.
W 셔츠를 교환할래요, 아니면 환불 받을래요?
M 같은 스타일의 다른 셔츠로 교환하고 싶네요.
W 알겠습니다. 뒤쪽에서 가져다 드리겠습니다.

Q 대화에서 남자에 대해 추론할 수 있는 것은?
(a) 셔츠에 구멍을 냈다.
(b) 셔츠 스타일을 마음에 들어 한다.
(c) 셔츠를 하나 더 사고 싶어 한다.
(d) 다른 상점에서 셔츠를 한 벌 살 것이다.

기출 POINT
상점에서 상품을 교환하는 상황이다. 남자의 첫 번째 말에서 옷을 교환하려는 의도를 알 수 있다. 소매 쪽에 구멍이 있는데, 환불이 아니라 같은 옷으로 교환하기를 원하고 있으므로 (b)를 추론할 수 있다.
exchange 교환하다 **sleeve** 소매 **refund** 환불 **prefer to** ~ 하기를 선호하다 **tear a hole** 찢어서 구멍을 내다   정답_(b)

44

M The nurse said you're feeling pain. Where does it hurt?
W Mostly in my stomach.
M I see. When did you last eat?
W Before bed last night. I woke up feeling nauseous.
M Do you have any food allergies?
W Not that I know of. Do you think it's serious?
M Probably not. I suspect it's just indigestion, but we'd better make sure.

Q What will the doctor most likely do next?
(a) Examine another patient.
(b) Tell the woman to exercise.
(c) Run some tests on the woman.
(d) Give the woman something to eat.

SOLUTION

M 간호사가 그러던데 아프다면서요. 어디가 안 좋은가요?
W 주로 배가 아파요.
M 그렇군요. 마지막으로 음식을 먹은 게 언젠가요?
W 어젯밤 잠자리에 들기 전에요. 일어나니 속이 메스꺼웠어요.
M 음식 알레르기가 있나요?
W 제가 알기로는 없는데요. 심각한가요?
M 아마 아닐 거예요. 그냥 소화 불량인 것 같지만 확실히 하는 게 좋겠어요.

Q 의사가 앞으로 할 일은?
(a) 다른 환자를 검진한다.
(b) 여자에게 운동을 하라고 말한다.
(c) 여자에게 다른 테스트를 해본다.
(d) 여자에게 먹을 것을 준다.

기출 POINT
다음으로 할 일에 대한 추측의 문제는 마지막 말을 집중해서 들어야 한다. 소화 불량인 것 같지만 확실히 하자는 것이므로 다른 검사를 하게 될 것을 예측할 수 있다. '어디가 아프세요?'라는 말은 Where does it hurt?라고 표현한다. Not that I know of는 '내가 아는 한 없다'는 말이다.
stomach 위; 배, 복부 **nauseous** 메스껍게 하는 **food allergy** 음식 알레르기 **Not that I know of.** 내가 아는 한 없다. **indigestion** 소화 불량 **examine** 검사하다   정답_(c)

45

W I heard you sold your downtown apartment last month.

M I did, but I regret it now.

W How come?

M Apartment prices downtown soared right after I sold it.

W But you did buy another one soon after selling it, right?

M Yeah, a bigger one in the suburbs. But the price there hasn't increased much.

Q Which statement would the man most likely agree with?

(a) Moving requires too much money.

(b) He sold his old apartment too soon.

(c) He should have invested more money.

(d) It was a bad idea to buy a big apartment.

SOLUTION

W 지난달에 시내에 있는 네 아파트를 팔았다면서.

M 그랬지, 그런데 지금 후회해.

W 왜?

M 내가 아파트를 팔고 난 직후에 시내 아파트 가격이 급등했어.

W 하지만 그 아파트를 팔고 곧 다른 아파트를 샀잖아?

M 응, 교외에 더 큰 아파트를 샀어. 그런데 그쪽 시세는 크게 오르지 않았거든.

Q 남자가 동의할 것 같은 진술은?

(a) 이사에는 너무 돈이 많이 든다.

(b) 남자는 자신의 예전 아파트를 너무 일찍 팔았다.

(c) 남자는 더 많은 돈을 투자했어야 했다.

(d) 큰 아파트를 사는 것은 좋지 않은 생각이다.

🎟 기출 POINT

대화 내용과 연관된 진술을 찾는 문제로 전체적인 내용을 듣고 정리하는 능력이 필요하다. '아파트를 팔고 나니 아파트 가격이 바로 급등했다'는 것을 '그가 아파트를 너무 일찍 팔았다'는 진술로 정리할 수 있으므로 정답은 (b)이다. How come?은 Why?와 같은 표현이고 soar는 '급격하게 오르다'라는 뜻이다.

regret 후회하다 **soar** 폭등하다 **suburb** 교외 **invest** 투자하다

정답_(b)

46

Since its introduction in 1992, the Canyonero has revolutionized the sport-utility market. With best-in-class traction and power, the all-new Canyonero is built to master every imaginable day-to-day driving condition, whether on-road or off-road. Now, the third generation Canyonero gives you even better road handling and incorporates the latest technology. Call your nearest dealer now for a test drive.

Q What is mainly being advertised?

(a) Canyonero's off-road features.

(b) Different types of the Canyonero.

(c) The latest version of the Canyonero.

(d) Canyonero's practical driving capabilities.

SOLUTION

1992년 도입된 이후 캐녀네로는 SUV 시장에 혁명을 불러 일으켰습니다. 동급 최강의 구동력과 파워를 갖추고 있습니다. 완전히 새로워진 캐녀네로는 포장 도로이건 비포장 도로이건 상상할 수 있는 모든 운전 상황에 숙달되도록 제작되었습니다. 이제 제 3세대 캐녀네로는 도로 상황에 더 잘 대처할 수 있게 해주며 최신 기술도 추가되었습니다. 지금 가장 가까운 판매 대리점에 전화하셔서 시운전을 해보세요.

Q 주된 광고 대상은?

(a) 비포장 도로에서 캐녀네로의 특징.

(b) 여러 형태의 캐녀네로.

(c) 캐녀네로 최신 모델.

(d) 캐녀네로의 실용적인 운전 성능.

🎟 기출 POINT

캐녀네로라는 SUV 차량에 대한 광고이다. '최신 캐녀네로는 최강의 구동력과 힘을 가지고 최신 기술 또한 추가되었다'고 했으므로 주된 광고 대상은 all-new Canyonero이다. 참고로 SUV는 Sports Utility Vehicle의 약자로 험한 도로에서도 주행 능력이 뛰어나 각종 스포츠 활동에 적합한 스포츠형 다목적 차량을 말한다.

revolutionize 혁명을 일으키다 **sport-utility market** SUV 시장
best-in-class 동급 최강의 **traction** 구동력 **on-road** 포장 도로
incorporate 섞다, 짜 넣다 **dealer** 판매 대리점 **test drive** 시운전
feature 특징 **practical** 실용적인 **capability** 성능   정답_(c)

47

Today we'll explore the work of Edward Henry Weston, possibly the most influential photographer of the 20th century. He initially concentrated on photographing natural scenes. Then, in 1906, Weston worked in California as a door-to-door portrait photographer. Later he attended the Illinois College of Photography, where he experimented with light and the human form. This launched a career that culminated 20 years later in his famous nude portraits.

Q What is mainly discussed about Edward Henry Weston?
(a) His photographic career.
(b) His favorite subject matter.
(c) Where he found inspiration.
(d) How he became interested in photography.

SOLUTION

오늘은 20세기에서 가장 영향력이 큰 사진작가라 할 수 있는 에드워드 헨리 웨스턴의 작품을 살펴보겠습니다. 그는 처음에는 자연 풍경을 사진에 담는 데 주력했어요. 그러다가 1906년 웨스턴은 캘리포니아에서 방문 인물 사진작가로 일했습니다. 이후 그는 일리노이 사진대학에 다니면서 빛과 인간의 형상을 실험했죠. 이것이 20년 후 유명한 나체 인물 사진들로 절정에 달했던 그의 이력의 시작이었습니다.

Q 에드워드 헨리 웨스턴에 대해 주로 논의된 내용은?
(a) 사진작가로서의 이력.
(b) 가장 좋아하는 주제.
(c) 영감을 얻었던 곳.
(d) 사진에 관심을 가지게 된 배경.

🏛 기출 POINT
에드워드 헨리 웨스턴의 사진 작품 활동과 관련된 내용이다. 처음에는 자연 풍경을 담다가 인물 사진으로 옮겨가서 나체 사진으로 최고점에 올랐다는 시기별 작품 이력에 대한 설명이 나온다. 따라서 정답은 (a)이다.

explore 탐험하다 influential 영향력이 큰 initially 처음에는 concentrate on ~에 몰두하다 door-to-door 방문하는 portrait 인물 사진 experiment 실험하다 launch 시작하다 culminate 절정에 달하다 subject matter 주제 inspiration 영감   **정답_(a)**

48

Due to severe drought conditions, compulsory water restrictions are now in effect. Residents may not wash cars, and can water their lawns only once a week on designated days. Those of you residing on the northern part of town may water yards only on Tuesdays and Fridays, while those on the south side of town may do so Mondays and Thursdays. Anyone caught violating these regulations will face heavy penalties.

Q What is the main subject of the announcement?
(a) Home gardening tips for dry conditions.
(b) New water conservation rules.
(c) Penalties for using too much water.
(d) Instructions on washing cars.

SOLUTION

극심한 가뭄으로 인해 의무적 제한 급수가 시행 중입니다. 주민은 세차를 할 수 없으며, 잔디밭에 물을 주는 것은 일주일에 한 번 지정된 요일에만 가능합니다. 마을 북부에 거주하고 있는 주민들은 매주 화요일과 금요일에만 뜰에 물을 줄 수 있으며, 마을 남쪽에 거주하는 주민들은 매주 월요일과 목요일에만 가능합니다. 이 규정을 위반하다 적발된 사람에게는 상당한 벌금이 부과될 것입니다.

Q 공고의 주제는?
(a) 건조한 환경에서 집 정원을 가꾸는 비결.
(b) 새로운 물 절약 규정.
(c) 물을 너무 많이 사용하는 것에 대한 벌금.
(d) 세차 방법.

🏛 기출 POINT
의무적인 제한 급수제에 대한 내용으로 세차나 잔디밭 물 주기의 규칙에 대한 공고이다. 따라서 '새로운 물 절약 규정'이라는 (b)가 주제로 적절하다. (a)는 혼동을 주기 위해 본문의 drought conditions와 비슷한 dry conditions를 사용했으나 오답이다.

severe 극심한 drought 가뭄 compulsory 의무적인 restriction 제한 in effect 발효 중인 resident 거주자 designated 지정된 reside 거주하다 conservation 절약 violate 위반하다 regulation 규정 face 직면하다 penalty 벌금   **정답_(b)**

49

As computers make inroads in every phase of business, are people no longer important? Not necessarily so. Of course, many blue-collar workers and clerks have been replaced by computers due to the advance and spread of the efficient modern device. On the other hand, however, computer technology has also given birth to many new jobs that require expert thinking and complex communication.

Q What is the main topic of the talk?
(a) Which jobs use computers most.
(b) Why people were replaced by computers.
(c) How computers have changed the job market.
(d) When computers started to improve the quality of work.

SOLUTION

컴퓨터가 비즈니스의 전면에 파고 드는 가운데, 인간은 더 이상 중요하지 않은 걸까요? 꼭 그런 것은 아닙니다. 물론 많은 육체 노동자들과 점원들은 효율적인 근대 기기들의 발전과 확산으로 인하여 컴퓨터로 대체되었습니다. 그러나 반면 컴퓨터 기술은 전문가적 사고와 복잡한 커뮤니케이션을 요하는 여러 신규 직종을 낳기도 했습니다.

Q 담화문의 주제는?
(a) 컴퓨터를 가장 많이 사용하는 직종.
(b) 컴퓨터가 사람을 대체하는 이유.
(c) 컴퓨터가 채용 시장을 변화시킨 방법.
(d) 컴퓨터가 업무의 질을 향상시키기 시작한 시기.

🎫 기출 POINT

'컴퓨터는 많은 육체 근로자들과 점원들의 일자리를 빼앗았지만, 다른 한편으로는 새로운 직종을 창출해 내기도 한다'는 내용이다. 결국 컴퓨터 기술이 발전하면서 생긴 채용 시장의 변화가 이야기의 주제이다. be replaced by는 '~으로 대체되다'라는 말이며 give birth to는 '~을 낳다'라는 뜻이다.

make inroads in ~로 잠식하다, 침해하다 **phase** 면, 단계
blue-collar worker 육체 노동자 **replace** 대체하다 **advance** 진보 **spread** 확산 **efficient** 효율적인 **device** 기기 **give birth to** ~을 낳다 **expert** 전문가 정답_(c)

50

In an effort to avert a global bird flu pandemic, several Asian governments have adopted a novel strategy: vaccinating poultry workers and farmers with the conventional flu vaccine, which may reduce the risk of new virus strains forming. This came after scientists expressed fears that, if poultry workers catch both conventional and bird flu, the human and bird viruses could merge, creating a super-virus that would spread easily among humans.

Q According to the report, what is the goal of the new strategy?
(a) Developing a vaccine against bird flu.
(b) Vaccinating Asian workers against bird flu.
(c) Stopping the spread of the flu virus in Asia.
(d) Preventing the creation of a new bird flu virus.

SOLUTION

전세계적인 조류 독감 유행을 막기 위한 노력으로 몇몇 아시아 정부에서는 새로운 전략을 채택했습니다. 이것은 가금류를 다루는 노동자와 영농업자들에게 재래식 독감 백신을 접종하는 것으로, 이는 새로운 바이러스 종이 형성될 위험을 낮출 수 있습니다. 이것은 만약 가금류를 다루는 노동자들이 재래 독감과 조류 독감에 모두 걸릴 경우 인간 바이러스와 조류 바이러스가 결합해 인간들 사이에 쉽게 확산될 수퍼 바이러스를 만들어 낼 수 있다는 과학자들의 우려가 표명된 이후 취해진 조치였습니다.

Q 보도에 따르면 새 전략의 목표는?
(a) 조류 독감에 대한 백신 개발.
(b) 아시아 노동자들을 대상으로 한 조류 독감 백신 접종.
(c) 아시아에서의 독감 바이러스 확산 저지.
(d) 새로운 조류 독감 바이러스 생성 예방.

🎫 기출 POINT

새 전략의 목표를 전략의 내용이나 부차적인 정보와 혼동하지 않아야 한다. 첫 번째 말 which may reduce the new risk of new virus strains forming과 마지막 말 creating a super virus that would spread easily among humans에서 전략의 목표를 찾을 수 있다. 따라서 정답은 (d)이다.

avert 피하다 **bird flu** 조류 독감 **pandemic** 전국적 유행병 **adopt** 채택하다 **novel** 새로운 **strategy** 전략 **vaccinate** 백신을 접종하다 **poultry** 가금류 **conventional** 재래식의 **strain** 변형 **merge** 결합하다 정답_(d)

51

With television, a child can watch a fighter pilot shoot down a plane piloted by another human being. With video games, the child "becomes" the fighter pilot. While the child in both cases inhabits a world in which actions appear to have no consequences, the difference, I believe, is that video games are more harmful, since they actively teach dissociation between personal actions and their consequences.

Q What is the main idea of the talk?
(a) TV and video games are too violent.
(b) TV and video games make children passive.
(c) Video games are more detrimental than television.
(d) Video games encourage children to act aggressively.

SOLUTION

텔레비전을 통해 아이는 전투기 조종사가 다른 사람이 조종하고 있는 비행기를 격추시키는 것을 볼 수 있다. 비디오 게임을 통해 이 아이는 그 전투기 조종사가 된다. 두 경우 모두 아이는 행동이 어떠한 결과도 수반하지 않는 것처럼 보이는 세상에 살고 있지만, 내 생각에 차이점은 비디오 게임은 개인적 행동과 그 결과 사이의 분리를 적극적으로 가르치기 때문에 더 해롭다.

Q 담화문의 주제는?
(a) TV와 비디오 게임은 너무 폭력적이다.
(b) TV와 비디오 게임은 아이들을 수동적으로 만든다.
(c) 비디오 게임은 텔레비전보다 더 해롭다.
(d) 비디오 게임은 아이들이 공격적으로 행동하도록 조장한다.

田 기출 POINT

텔레비전과 비디오 게임의 비교를 통해 이것들이 개인의 행동에 어떤 영향을 미치는지를 설명하고 있다. 비디오 게임에서는 아이가 직접 전투기 조종사가 되기 때문에 행동과 그 결과가 무관해 보이는 세상을 접하게 되고, 결국 이것이 아이에게 더 해롭다는 내용이다. 따라서 정답은 (c).

fighter pilot 전투기 조종사 **shoot down** 격추시키다 **inhabit** 살다 **consequence** 결과 **dissociation** 분리 **passive** 수동적인 **detrimental** 해로운 **aggressively** 공격적으로   **정답_(c)**

52

HIV, the virus that causes AIDS, has proven to be a diabolical foe, hiding inside immune cells and mutating so fast that it is, effectively, a moving target. For example, over a decade, as many as 15 different viral forms can develop within one patient. Because of this rapid evolution, researchers have been unable to develop an effective vaccine, for by the time a new drug has been developed to stop one strain, new drug-resistant strains have already evolved.

Q What is the topic of the talk?
(a) How an AIDS vaccine will become a reality.
(b) How difficult it is to fight against HIV.
(c) How effective AIDS treatments are.
(d) How destructive HIV is.

SOLUTION

AIDS를 일으키는 바이러스인 HIV는 면역세포 안에 숨어서 너무나 빨리 돌연 변이를 하기 때문에 사실상 움직이는 표적과 같은 사악한 적수인 것으로 입증되었다. 예를 들면, 10년 동안 자그마치 15개의 다른 형태의 바이러스가 한 환자의 몸 안에서 발생할 수 있다. 이같이 빠른 진화로 인해 연구자들은 효과적인 백신을 개발할 수 없었다. 왜냐하면 하나의 종을 저지하기 위해 신약이 개발될 즈음이면 이미 약에 내성을 가진 새로운 종들이 생겨났기 때문이다.

Q 담화문의 소재는 ?
(a) AIDS 백신이 실현되는 방법.
(b) HIV와 싸우는 것의 어려움.
(c) AIDS 치료의 효율성.
(d) HIV의 파괴성.

田 기출 POINT

HIV의 빠른 진화 속도 때문에 효과적인 백신을 만들어 내기가 힘들다는 것이다. 즉 HIV에 대항하여 싸우는 일이 얼마나 어려운지가 담화문의 소재이다. (d)가 답이 되기 위해서는 바이러스가 일으키는 증상이나 피해자의 수 등의 내용이 나와야 할 것이다.

diabolical 사악한 **foe** 적 **immune cell** 면역세포 **mutate** 변이하다 **target** 표적 **decade** 10년 **viral** 바이러스의 **rapid** 빠른 **evolution** 진화 **strain** 변종 **drug-resistant** 약에 내성을 지닌   **정답_(b)**

53

Tonight, we'll look at the best times of year for a tropical vacation in Thailand. Most people visit between October and April. Less popular is the rainy season, from May to September, though the term "rainy season" can be misleading for potential tourists. While downpours can be drenching, they usually occur late in the afternoon and are short-lived. Moreover, because the skies darken before a storm, you may have as much as an hour's notice before a downpour hits.

Q When do most people visit Thailand?
(a) After May.
(b) Before September.
(c) Between October and April.
(d) Between May and September.

SOLUTION

오늘 밤, 우리는 태국에서 열대 휴가를 보내기에 연중 가장 좋은 시기를 살펴볼 겁니다. 대부분 사람들은 10월에서 4월 사이에 방문합니다. 그보다 인기가 덜한 시기는 우기인 5월부터 9월까지이지만, 우기라는 말을 잠재적인 관광객들은 오해할 수 있습니다. 폭우가 퍼부을 수는 있지만 이것은 주로 오후 늦게 발생하고 금세 그치죠. 게다가 폭풍우 전에는 하늘이 어두워지기 때문에 폭우가 내리기 한 시간 정도 전에 예측할 수도 있고요.

Q 가장 많은 사람들이 태국을 방문하는 시기는?
(a) 5월 이후.
(b) 9월 이전.
(c) 10월부터 4월 사이.
(d) 5월부터 9월 사이.

🏷 기출 POINT

세부 정보에 대한 문제이다. 가장 많은 사람들이 태국을 방문하는 시기는 두 번째 말에서 알 수 있듯이 (c)이다. 5월에서 9월까지의 우기에는 관광객이 적은데, 사실 심각한 날씨는 아니라고 설명하고 있다.

tropical 열대의 **rainy season** 우기 **mislead** 오도하다
potential 잠재적인 **downpour** 폭우 **drenching** 억수로 퍼붓는
short-lived 일시적인   정답_(c)

54

Learning from others is second nature to humans: we do it more readily than other species. Therefore, when a young chimpanzee is brought up with a human child, the direction of influence will more likely be from the chimp to the kid than vice versa. This was discovered by Martin and Ann Brown, who had to halt a co-rearing experiment when their son began to bark like the female ape with whom he was being raised.

Q Why did the Browns terminate the experiment?
(a) The chimpanzee was not well-behaved.
(b) Their son began to imitate the chimpanzee.
(c) The chimpanzee began making strange noises.
(d) The son became violent toward his parents.

SOLUTION

타인으로부터 배우는 것은 인간의 제 2의 천성이다. 인간은 다른 종들보다 남으로부터 훨씬 쉽게 배운다. 따라서 어린 침팬지가 어린 아이와 함께 사육될 경우, 영향력이 미치는 방향은 침팬지에서 아이에게 미칠 확률이 그 반대일 경우보다 더 높을 것이다. 이것을 발견한 사람은 마틴과 앤 브라운이었는데, 이들은 암컷 유인원과 함께 자라고 있던 그들의 아들이 암컷 유인원처럼 고함을 지르기 시작하자 공동 사육 실험을 중지해야 했다.

Q 브라운 부부가 실험을 종료해야 했던 이유는?
(a) 침팬지가 얌전하게 굴지 않았다.
(b) 자신들의 아들이 침팬지를 모방하기 시작했다.
(c) 침팬지가 이상한 소음을 내기 시작했다.
(d) 아들이 부모에게 폭력적으로 변했다.

🏷 기출 POINT

실험을 중지했다는 내용은 마지막 부분에 나오는데 had to halt 이하에서 그 이유를 말하고 있다. 아이와 침팬지를 함께 키웠더니 타인으로부터 학습하는 능력이 뛰어난 어린 아이가 침팬지를 모방하는 결과를 보였기 때문이다.

second nature 제 2의 천성 **readily** 선뜻, 쉽사리 **species** 종
chimp 침팬지 **vice versa** 거꾸로, 반대로 **halt** 중지하다 **co-rearing** 공동 양육의 **bark** 고함을 지르다 **ape** 유인원 **terminate** 종료하다
well-behaved 행실이 단정한 **imitate** 모방하다   정답_(b)

55

You are cordially invited to a workshop on Internet security to be held on Friday, February 9 from 3 p.m. to 5 p.m. Join Community Outreach Program Manager, Cheryl Owen, for online safety tips you can follow at home. Though this workshop is to benefit, primarily, teenagers, we strongly urge both teens and their guardians to participate together in this workshop. Don't miss this great opportunity to discuss online safety with a specialist.

Q Which is correct about the workshop?
(a) It will be a Friday morning session.
(b) It will focus on home safety measures.
(c) Guardians are encouraged to attend with their teens.
(d) Restrictions on the use of the Internet will be discussed.

SOLUTION

귀하를 2월 9일, 금요일 오후 3시부터 5시까지 열리는 인터넷 보안 워크숍에 정성껏 모시겠습니다. 지역사회 봉사 프로그램 매니저인 셰릴 오웬과 함께 집에서 실행할 수 있는 온라인 보안 팁을 알아보십시오. 이 워크숍은 주로 십대들에게 도움을 주기 위한 것이기는 하지만, 십대들과 보호자들이 워크숍에 함께 참여할 것을 적극 권유합니다. 전문가와 온라인 보안에 대해 토의할 수 있는 이 훌륭한 기회를 놓치지 마십시오.

Q 워크숍에 대해 옳은 것은?
(a) 워크숍은 금요일 오전 강의일 것이다.
(b) 워크숍은 가정 안전 대책에 초점을 둘 것이다.
(c) 보호자들에게 십대 자녀들과 함께 참여할 것을 장려하고 있다.
(d) 인터넷 사용의 제약에 대해 논의할 것이다.

⊞ 기출 POINT

워크숍은 금요일 오후 강의이고, 인터넷 보안에 대한 프로그램이며, 보호자들이 십대 자녀들과 함께 참가하기를 권유하고 있는 내용이다. 이 내용과 일치하는 것은 (c)이다. 〈urge A to+동사원형〉은 'A가 ~하기를 강력히 권유하다'는 뜻이다. Internet security, online safety라는 말들에서 워크숍의 주제를 찾을 수 있다.

cordially 정성껏 security 보안 outreach 봉사 활동 benefit 혜택을 주다 urge 권유하다 guardian 보호자 participate in ~에 참여하다 opportunity 기회 specialist 전문가 session 수업 restriction 제약   정답_(c)

56

Over this coming semester, you will have one midterm and one final exam. The midterm will cover assigned materials to date and comprise 25% of your grade. There are two parts to the midterm, the first being two essays based on the course materials to assess your ability to analyze them. The second part is six short-answer questions covering the issues discussed in class. The final exam will be cumulative, and comprise 30% of your grade. The format will be similar to the midterm, but there will be ten short-answer questions.

Q Which is correct according to the instructions?
(a) The midterm and final will be the same length.
(b) The final will not have short-answer questions.
(c) The midterm and final will not overlap in content.
(d) The midterm will include the analysis of course materials.

SOLUTION

다가오는 학기 중에 여러분들은 중간고사 한 번, 기말고사 한 번을 치르게 됩니다. 중간고사는 이제까지 내준 자료 중에서 출제될 것이고 학점의 25%를 차지할 겁니다. 중간고사는 두 부분으로 이루어지며, 첫 번째 부분은 여러분들의 자료 분석력을 평가하기 위해 수업 교재를 기반으로 두 편의 에세이를 작성하는 것입니다. 두 번째 부분은 수업 시간에 논의한 이슈들에 관한 6개의 단답형 문항입니다. 기말고사 범위는 처음부터이고, 학점의 30%를 차지할 것입니다. 형식은 중간고사와 유사하지만 단답형 문제가 10문항입니다.

Q 지시 사항에 대해 옳은 것은?
(a) 중간고사와 기말고사는 그 범위가 동일할 것이다.
(b) 기말고사에는 단답형 문항이 없을 것이다.
(c) 중간고사와 기말고사는 그 범위가 중복되지 않을 것이다.
(d) 중간고사에는 수업 교재의 분석이 포함된다.

⊞ 기출 POINT

중간고사와 기말고사에 대해 설명해 주는 내용이다. 중간고사는 내준 자료가 범위이고, 기말고사는 처음부터라고 했으므로 범위는 다르나 중복된다. 기말고사에는 단답형 문제가 4문항 더 많다는 차이가 있다. 중간고사의 첫 번째 부분은 교재를 분석하여 에세이를 작성하는 문제가 나온다고 했으므로 일치하는 설명은 (d)이다.

semester 학기 midterm 중간 고사 assign 배정하다 comprise 차지하다 assess 평가하다 analyze 분석하다 cumulative 누적되는 overlap 겹치다, 중복되다 content 범위   정답_(d)

57

The movie *Bad Vibrations* is a sophisticated blend of fantasy, romance, comedy and film noir featuring interwoven plots that span three decades. In other hands, this radical mix might have been impossibly bewildering, but director Mandover's skill as a storyteller prevents any confusion. The cinematography and music are as seductive as the script, as is an outstanding performance by Gael Bucchi, playing the femme fatale. *Bad Vibrations* is ultimately a "whodunnit" that keeps you guessing until the end.

Q Which is correct about *Bad Vibrations*?
(a) It is a thrilling story about forbidden love.
(b) Its many plot twists are impossible to follow.
(c) Its music is as enjoyable as its clever storyline.
(d) It is a comedy containing some supernatural elements.

SOLUTION

영화 〈나쁜 느낌〉은 판타지, 로맨스, 코미디와 누아르 영화를 세련되게 혼합한 작품으로 30년에 걸쳐 뒤섞인 줄거리가 그 특징이다. 한편 이 급진적인 조합은 매우 당혹스러웠을 수도 있었으나, 맨도버 감독의 이야기꾼으로서의 솜씨는 모든 혼란을 막아준다. 영화 촬영술과 음악도 대본만큼이나 유혹적이며, 팜므 파탈 역할의 게일 부키의 연기도 뛰어나다. 〈나쁜 느낌〉은 궁극적으로 당신을 끝까지 추측하게 만들 추리 영화이다.

Q 〈나쁜 느낌〉에 대해 옳은 것은?
(a) 금지된 사랑에 대한 스릴러이다.
(b) 영화의 뒤섞인 줄거리는 따라가기 불가능하다.
(c) 음악은 재치 있는 줄거리만큼이나 유쾌하다.
(d) 초자연적인 요소를 담고 있는 코미디이다.

기출 POINT

이 영화는 여러 장르가 혼합되어 있고, 복잡한 줄거리를 가지고 있으나 잘 혼합된 이야기만큼이나 영화 촬영술과 음악이 유혹적이라고 했으므로 (c)가 적절하다. 복잡한 줄거리지만 따라가기 힘든 것이 아니라 혼란을 주지 않도록 만드는 기술을 보여주고 있다고 했으므로 (b)는 오답이다.

vibrations 느낌, 분위기 **sophisticated** 세련된 **blend** 조합 **film noir** 누아르 영화 **interwoven plot** 복잡한 줄거리 **span** ~에 걸치다 **radical** 급진적인 **bewildering** 당혹스러운 **cinematography** 영화 촬영술 **seductive** 매혹적인 **outstanding** 뛰어난 **femme fatale** 팜므 파탈 **whodunnit** 추리 영화 **supernatural** 초자연적인 **정답** (c)

58

Last month, panicky astronomers debated warning ranking NASA officials and the White House about a space rock potentially on a collision course with the Earth in just hours' time. It was a Hollywood doomsday scenario that quickly fizzled out. Further observations indicated that the initial rough calculation of the asteroid's size and trajectory were way off. In fact, it passed by harmlessly and headed out into distant space.

Q What can be inferred about the incident in the report?
(a) NASA did not tell the public for fear of causing distress.
(b) Astronomers nearly created a global panic for nothing.
(c) Hollywood is planning a movie based on the scenario.
(d) Asteroids are not a serious threat to human civilization.

SOLUTION

지난달, 겁에 질린 천문학자들은 NASA 고위급 관계자와 백악관과 우주 암석이 몇 시간 내에 지구와 정면 충돌할 수도 있다고 경고하는 것을 놓고 논쟁을 벌였다. 그것은 영화 속에나 나올, 금세 수그러든 종말론적 시나리오였다. 추가적인 관측에 따르면 운석의 크기 및 궤적에 대한 최초의 개략적 계산은 너무나 빗나가 있었다. 사실 운석은 아무 피해도 주지 않고 지나쳐 먼 우주를 향해 갔다.

Q 보도된 사건에 대해 유추할 수 있는 것은?
(a) NASA는 대중들에게 근심을 유발할 것을 우려해 말하지 않았다.
(b) 천문학자들은 아무것도 아닌 일로 국제적인 공황을 일으킬 뻔했다.
(c) 할리우드는 이 시나리오를 기반으로 영화를 기획 중이다.
(d) 운석은 인간 문명에 매우 위협적인 것은 아니다.

기출 POINT

천문학자들은 우주 암석이 지구와 충돌하게 될 것이라고 경고했지만 잘못된 계산에 의한 것임이 밝혀지고 결국 운석은 멀리 비켜갔던 사건에 대한 내용이다. 천문학자들의 잘못된 계산으로 지구 종말이라는 국제적인 공황상태를 만들 뻔했다는 것을 유추할 수 있으므로 정답은 (b)이다.

panicky 겁에 질린 **astronomer** 천문학자 **ranking** 간부의 **collision** 충돌 **doomsday scenario** 종말론 시나리오 **fizzle out** 수그러들다 **initial** 최초의 **rough** 대충의 **calculation** 계산 **asteroid** 운석 **trajectory** 궤적 **way off** 완전히 틀린 **distress** 곤란 **정답** (b)

59

US companies spend more than $250 billion yearly on application development for approximately 175,000 Information Technology projects. The average cost per development project for a large company is $2,322,000; for a medium-sized company, $1,331,000; and for a small company, $434,000. Despite the tremendous cash investments, the majority of these projects will fail due to inadequate planning and foresight. And only methodical planning in early stages will prevent wasted money.

Q What can be inferred about the speaker's view of technology projects?
(a) Their failure rates will soon decrease.
(b) Too little money is invested in projects.
(c) Large companies have a higher failure rate.
(d) It is necessary to rethink project strategies.

SOLUTION

미국 기업들은 약 175,000건의 정보 기술 프로젝트를 응용 개발하는 데 연간 2천 5백 억 달러 이상을 지출합니다. 대기업의 개발 프로젝트당 평균 비용은 2,322,000달러이고, 중소기업은 1,331,000달러, 소기업은 434,000달러이죠. 이같이 엄청난 현금 투자에도 불구하고 이들 프로젝트 대부분은 부적절한 기획 및 선견지명으로 인해 실패합니다. 그래서 초기 단계의 조직적인 기획만이 자금 낭비를 막아줄 것입니다.

Q 기술 프로젝트에 대한 화자의 관점에서 유추할 수 있는 것은?
(a) 기술 프로젝트의 실패율은 곧 하락할 것이다.
(b) 프로젝트에 투자되는 돈이 너무 적다.
(c) 대기업들의 실패율이 더 높다.
(d) 프로젝트 전략 재고가 필요하다.

기출 POINT
화자는 기술 프로젝트의 투자 규모를 세부적으로 설명하고 이런 큰 규모에도 불구하고 기획이나 예측의 부적절함으로 인해 대부분이 실패하고 있다고 평가하고 있다. 마지막 말에서는 초기 단계에서 조직적인 기획이 있어야 낭비를 막을 수 있을 것이라고 했으므로 프로젝트 전략 재고가 필요하다는 (d)를 유추할 수 있다.

application development 응용 개발 **approximately** 대략 **tremendous** 엄청난 **investment** 투자 **inadequate** 부적절한 **foresight** 선견지명 **methodical** 조직적 방식의   **정답**_(d)

60

Good morning and welcome to the course preview for Sociology 351. The objective of this course is to cultivate greater sensitivity to gender issues and better understanding of males in society. We will begin by examining historical and socio-cultural perceptions of virility. We will investigate an array of topics to generate a more transparent picture of what it means to be born male, including the conditions of daily life that give men privileges, and their roles in the family, workplace and politics.

Q What can be inferred about the course?
(a) It is intended primarily for male students.
(b) It is critical of historical approaches to gender issues.
(c) It will help women receive equal treatment in society.
(d) It will offer sociological explanations for men's preferential treatment.

SOLUTION

안녕하세요. 사회학 351 강의 개관에 오신 것을 환영합니다. 이 과정의 목표는 성 문제에 대한 감수성을 높이고 남성 사회에 대한 보다 높은 이해를 배양하는 것입니다. 우선 남성성에 관한 역사적·사회 문화적 관념들에 대해 살펴보는 것으로 시작할 것입니다. 우리는 남성들에게 특권을 부여하는 일상생활의 환경들과, 가정과 직장 그리고 정치 속 남성의 역할을 포함, 남성으로 태어난다는 것이 어떤 의미인지에 대해 좀 더 투명한 그림을 그려줄 수 있는 일련의 주제들을 연구할 것입니다.

Q 수업에 대해 유추할 수 있는 것은?
(a) 주로 남학생들을 위한 강의이다.
(b) 성 문제에 대한 역사적 접근법에 대해 비판적이다.
(c) 여성들이 사회에서 평등한 대우를 받는 데 도움을 줄 것이다.
(d) 남성 우대를 사회학적으로 설명해 줄 것이다.

기출 POINT
강의 목표로 성 문제를 인식하는 감수성과 사회 속의 남성에 대한 이해를 높이는 것을 들고 있다. 남성성에 대한 역사적·사회 문화적 관념을 밝히고 남성의 특권과 역할에 대해 살펴보게 된다고 말하고 있으므로 이 강의는 남성 우대 문제에 대한 사회학적 설명을 제공할 것으로 유추해 볼 수 있다. 역사적 접근법에 대해 비판하는 것은 아니므로 (b)는 답이 될 수 없다.

preview 개관 **cultivate** 배양하다 **sensitivity** 감수성 **gender issue** 성 문제 **perception** 관념 **virility** 남성성 **investigate** 살펴보다 **an array of** 일련의 ~ **transparent** 투명한 **privilege** 특권 **critical of** ~에 대해 비판적인 **preferential treatment** 우대
정답_(d)

1

A Can you get this report done in two hours?

B I _____ do my best.

(a) will
(b) may
(c) need
(d) might

SOLUTION

A 이 보고서 2시간 내에는 마칠 수 있니?

B 최선을 다해 볼게.

⊞ **기출 POINT**

조동사 will은 주어의 의지로 기꺼이 하겠다는 뜻을 나타낸다. ex) I'll check your letter for you, if you want. I'll do my best는 '최선을 다하겠다'는 의지를 나타내는 말이므로 정답은 (a)이다.

get A done A를 끝내다 **do one's best** 최선을 다하다 **정답_(a)**

2

A Do you mind sharing your room with a guest for a few days?

B It won't bother me _____ much as long as she doesn't make a mess.

(a) far
(b) too
(c) well
(d) such

SOLUTION

A 며칠 동안 손님이랑 네 방을 같이 써도 괜찮겠니?

B 손님이 어지르지만 않는다면 별로 신경 쓰이지 않을 거야.

⊞ **기출 POINT**

Do you mind -ing?는 '~하기를 꺼리니?'라는 표현으로 이에 대한 응답이 부정이면 '괜찮다'는 말이 된다. 따라서, It won't bother me는 방을 함께 써도 별로 신경 쓰이지 않을 것이라는 의미이다. not too much는 '별로 그렇지 않다'는 표현으로 정답은 (b)이다.

share 함께 사용하다 **bother** 괴롭히다 **make a mess** 어지르다

정답_(b)

3

A Should I apply for the managerial position?

B It _____.

(a) will try not to hurt you
(b) will try to hurt you not
(c) won't hurt to try you
(d) won't hurt you to try

SOLUTION

A 관리직에 지원을 해야 할까?

B 해본다고 손해볼 건 없지.

⊞ **기출 POINT**

조동사 should는 충고를 하거나 받을 때 사용할 수 있다. Should I...? 는 '내가 ~해야 할까?'의 뜻으로 조언을 구하는 말이다. 내용상 '시도해서 손해볼 건 없다'라는 말이 되어야 하므로 to try가 진주어가 되고 won't hurt가 It에 이어져야 한다.

apply for ~에 지원하다 **managerial position** 관리직 **정답_(d)**

4

A The judge didn't seem to believe that the witness was telling the truth.

B I agree. He didn't look _____.

(a) convinced
(b) convincing
(c) to convince
(d) to be convincing

SOLUTION

A 판사는 증인이 진실을 말하지 않는다고 생각하는 것 같더라.

B 맞아. 납득하는 것 같지 않았어.

⊞ **기출 POINT**

look 다음에 오는 형용사 문제이다. 형용사로 쓰이는 현재분사는 능동 또는 진행의 의미로 쓰이고, 과거분사는 수동 또는 완료의 의미로 쓰인다. convince는 '납득시키다'라는 뜻의 동사이고 판사는 '납득당하는' 것이므로 look convinced가 되어야 한다.

judge 판사 **witness** 증인 **convinced** 확신을 가진 **convincing** 설득력 있는 **정답_(a)**

5

A Mary, _____?
B My mother. Her birthday is next week.

(a) you wrote to whom a letter
(b) to whom you wrote a letter
(c) to whom did you write a letter
(d) whom did you write to a letter

SOLUTION

A 메리, 누구한테 편지를 썼니?
B 저희 어머니한테요. 어머니 생신이 다음 주예요.

⊞ 기출 POINT

'누구에게 편지를 썼느냐'는 질문이 되기 위해서는 write a letter to에서 to의 목적어로 의문사 whom이 와야 한다. Whom did you write a letter to? 또는 목적격 Whom 대신 Who를 써도 된다. 전치사가 의문사 앞에 와서 To whom did you write a letter?도 가능하므로 정답은 (c)가 된다. 단 이 경우, whom 대신 who를 쓸 수 없다.

정답_(c)

6

A Do you think Caroline was right to leave her job?
B No, she _____.

(a) shouldn't
(b) shouldn't do
(c) shouldn't have
(d) should have never

SOLUTION

A 캐롤라인이 직장을 그만둔 게 옳았다고 생각해?
B 아니, 그만둬서는 안 됐지.

⊞ 기출 POINT

was로 봐서 캐롤라인이 직장을 그만둔 것은 과거이다. 과거의 일에 대한 아쉬움을 나타낼 때 should have p.p.를 써서 '~했어야 했는데'라는 뜻을 나타내는데, 여기서는 본동사(leave)의 반복을 피하기 위해 조동사만을 쓴 (c)가 정답이다.
leave one's job 직장을 그만두다

정답_(c)

7

A Where can I find some painkillers?
B I'm sorry. I didn't hear you. Could you repeat _____ you said?

(a) that
(b) how
(c) what
(d) which

SOLUTION

A 진통제는 어디 있나요?
B 죄송합니다. 못 들었어요. 다시 한번 말씀해 주시겠어요?

⊞ 기출 POINT

Could you repeat 다음에 들어갈 관계대명사를 찾는 문제이다. 선행사가 없으므로 '~한 것'을 의미하는 what이 들어가야 한다. Where can I find...?는 '~가 어디 있나요?'라는 질문이며 '당신의 말을 못 들었어요'라고 할 때에는 I didn't hear you라고 표현한다.
painkiller 진통제   **repeat** 되풀이해서 말하다

정답_(c)

8

A That's a new cell phone, isn't it?
B Oh, you _____. I got it as a graduation gift.

(a) will be noticed
(b) were noticed
(c) will notice
(d) noticed

SOLUTION

A 그거 새로 나온 휴대폰 아니니?
B 아, 알아봤구나. 졸업 선물로 받았어.

⊞ 기출 POINT

상대방이 새 휴대폰을 알아보고 한 말에 대해 '아, 네가 알아봤구나'라는 응답이 알맞다. notice는 '알아차리다'라는 뜻이므로 과거시제 you noticed가 되어야 한다.
cell phone 휴대폰   **notice** 알아보다

정답_(d)

9

A Where are you staying?
B I _____ in my uncle's apartment since I arrived.

(a) live
(b) am living
(c) was living
(d) have been living

SOLUTION

A 어디에 묵고 있는 거야?
B 도착한 후로 우리 삼촌 아파트에서 살고 있어.

⊞ 기출 POINT

since가 '~한 이래로'라는 뜻의 접속사로 쓰이면 since절에는 주로 과거형(arrived)이, 주절에는 현재완료 시제가 온다. 단, 여기에서는 과거부터 현재까지 살고 있는 경우이므로 현재완료진행 시제(have been living)로 응답하는 것이 더 적절하다.
since ~이후로   정답_(d)

10

A What's all that noise outside?
B They are excavating land for a new building _____.

(a) to our right next
(b) next to our right
(c) right next to ours
(d) ours right next to

SOLUTION

A 밖에 저 소음은 다 뭐야?
B 우리 건물 바로 옆에 새 건물을 짓는다고 땅을 파고 있어.

⊞ 기출 POINT

장소를 나타내는 전치사구가 빈칸에 와야 한다. 장소를 나타내는 전치사 next to를 사용해서 바로 옆은 right next to로, our building은 대명사 ours로 쓴 (c)가 정답이다.
excavate 땅을 파내다   **right next to** 바로 ~옆에   정답_(c)

11

A Have you ever been forced to do something you didn't want to?
B Fortunately no; _____ do that to anyone else.

(a) I would ever
(b) would I ever
(c) nor would I ever
(d) nor I would ever

SOLUTION

A 하기 싫은 일을 억지로 하도록 강요받은 적 있니?
B 다행히 없어. 그리고 나도 다른 사람에게 그런 일은 절대 하지 않을 거야.

⊞ 기출 POINT

Fortunately no는 '다행히도 없어'라는 말이다. '나도 절대 하지 않을 거야'라는 말이 되려면 부정어 nor가 필요하다. 부정어가 문장 앞에 왔으므로 주어와 동사가 도치되어 nor would I가 되고, ever는 수식하는 본동사 do 앞에 위치해야 하므로 (c)가 정답이다.
force 강요하다   **fortunately** 다행히   정답_(c)

12

A I'm thinking of going to the Spiders concert.
B Make sure _____ in advance.

(a) buying your tickets
(b) your tickets you buy
(c) you buy your tickets
(d) tickets you are buying

SOLUTION

A 스파이더스의 콘서트에 가려고 생각 중이야.
B 티켓은 꼭 미리 사둬.

⊞ 기출 POINT

콘서트에 가려고 생각하는 사람에게 미리 표를 사두라는 말이 나와야 적절한 응답이 된다. '~하도록 해'라는 뜻의 Make sure 다음에는 that절이 와야 하므로 that이 생략되고 주어와 동사가 나오는 you buy your tickets가 정답이다.
think of -ing ~할까 생각 중이다   **in advance** 미리   정답_(c)

13

A What happened to your blouse?
B _____ the stairs, I accidentally fell and spilt coffee on it.

(a) To walk up
(b) Walking up
(c) I walked up
(d) To have walked up

SOLUTION

A 네 블라우스 어떻게 된 거야?
B 계단을 올라오다가 실수로 넘어져서 커피를 블라우스에 엎질렀어.

⊞ 기출 POINT

콤마(,) 이하에 완전한 문장이 왔으므로 빈칸을 포함한 절에도 접속사를 포함한 완전한 문장이 와야 한다. 이때 접속사와 반복되는 주어(I)를 생략하고 동사를 분사(Walking up)가 이끄는 분사구문으로 만들 수 있다. 따라서 빈칸에 알맞은 형태는 (b)이다.

stairs 계단 **accidentally** 사고로 **spill** 엎지르다   정답_(b)

14

A Who left the lights on?
B Sorry. I _____ have done it.

(a) will
(b) shall
(c) need
(d) must

SOLUTION

A 누가 불을 켜 놨어?
B 미안. 내가 그랬나 봐.

⊞ 기출 POINT

leave the light on은 '불을 켜 놓다'라는 뜻이다. 빈칸에는 조동사가 쓰여 〈조동사+have p.p.〉 형태로 과거의 일을 나타낸다. '내가 그런 게 틀림없다'는 뜻의 강한 추측이 와야 하므로 (d) must가 정답이다.

leave the light on 불을 켜 두다   정답_(d)

15

A Why do all these Moorish houses have a courtyard?
B Because it's an integral part of a house _____ Moorish architecture.

(a) in
(b) at
(c) to
(d) on

SOLUTION

A 왜 이 무어식 주택들에는 모두 안뜰이 딸려 있는 거죠?
B 무어식 건축에서 안뜰은 주택의 필수적인 부분이니까요.

⊞ 기출 POINT

전치사 in은 '〜에서, 〜에 있어서'라는 소속의 뜻을 나타낸다. 따라서 (a)가 정답이다.

Moorish 무어식의 **courtyard** 정원 **integral** 필수적인
architecture 건축   정답_(a)

16

A Do you have any regrets about your decision?
B Yes. I _____ have accepted the offer.

(a) had to
(b) could
(c) might
(d) ought to

SOLUTION

A 네 결정에 대해서 후회하니?
B 응. 그 제의를 받아들였어야 했어.

⊞ 기출 POINT

결정에 대한 후회가 있다고 응답했으므로 과거의 일에 대한 유감, 후회를 나타내는 ought to have p.p.를 사용한다.

regret 후회 **accept the offer** 제의를 수락하다   정답_(d)

17

A If you have any trouble with the instructions, please come and see me.

B Thanks, but I'm certain _____.

(a) I'm to understand them
(b) of them understanding
(c) I can understand them
(d) understanding them

SOLUTION

A 설명을 잘 모르겠으면 저를 찾아오십시오.
B 고맙습니다만, 전 확실히 이해할 수 있을 겁니다.

⊞ 기출 POINT

I'm certain 다음에는 that절이나 of 전치사구가 와야 한다. 따라서, that을 생략하고 주어와 동사가 나오는 (c)가 정답이다. (b)와 같이 certain of를 쓰려면 I'm certain of their understanding이 되어야 한다.

instructions 설명, 지시　　　　　　　　　**정답**_(c)

18

A What are you going to do with your bonus money?

B _____ it all on books.

(a) I spend
(b) I'll spend
(c) I had spent
(d) I'll have spent

SOLUTION

A 보너스 받은 돈으로 뭘 할 셈이야?
B 책 사는 데 다 쓸 거야.

⊞ 기출 POINT

be going to는 '~할 예정이다'라는 뜻으로 미래의 계획을 말한다. What are you going to do with...?는 '~을 가지고 뭘 할 거니?' 라는 말로 미래에 대한 질문을 나타내므로 미래시제로 답하는 (b)가 정답이다.

spend money on ~에 돈을 쓰다　　　　　　**정답**_(b)

19

A Is it true you have students who are often late to school?

B Yes, some students in my class _____ easy access to transportation.

(a) hasn't had
(b) don't have
(c) haven't had
(d) doesn't have

SOLUTION

A 선생님 학생 중에 자주 지각하는 애들이 있다는 게 사실이에요?
B 네, 저희 반 학생 몇 명은 교통 수단을 쉽게 이용할 수가 없어요.

⊞ 기출 POINT

have access to는 '~에 접근하다, ~을 사용할 수 있다'의 뜻이므로 easy access는 쉽게 접근할 수 있다는 말이 된다. 현재 습관에 대한 내용이므로 현재시제로 묻고 있고 응답 역시 현재 사실을 나타내므로 현재시제로 답해야 한다.

have easy access to ~에 쉽게 접근하다　**transportation** 이동 수단　　　　　　　　　　　　　　　　　　　**정답**_(b)

20

A How was the trip to China?

B It was just fantastic! I loved the scenery, _____.

(a) the food to not mention
(b) not to mention the food
(c) the food not mentioning
(d) not mentioning the food

SOLUTION

A 중국 여행은 어땠니?
B 너무 좋았어! 경치도 좋았고, 음식은 두말할 것도 없었지.

⊞ 기출 POINT

'~은 말할 것도 없고'라는 말로 부가적인 정보나 앞의 말을 강조하는 의도로 쓰는 표현이 not to mention이다. '음식은 말할 것도 없다'는 뜻이 되어야 하므로 (b) not to mention the food가 정답이다.

fantastic 멋진　**scenery** 경치　**mention** 말하다　**정답**_(b)

Actual Test 4

21

Michael brought his books to school, _____ he forgot his pencils.

(a) but
(b) for
(c) as
(d) so

마이클은 학교에 책을 가지고 왔지만, 연필 가져오는 것을 잊어버렸다.

▦ 기출 POINT

접속사를 고르는 문제이다. 연결어 문제는 빈칸 앞뒤의 관계를 파악하는 것이 핵심이다. 앞뒤 두 절의 관계가 상반되므로 역접을 나타내는 연결어는 but이다. **정답_(a)**

22

It is estimated that these days, 300,000 homeless people _____ on the streets of America's big cities.

(a) live
(b) lived
(c) were living
(d) had been living

요즘 삼십만 명의 노숙자들이 미국 대도시 거리에서 사는 것으로 추정된다.

▦ 기출 POINT

시제 문제이다. 현재의 사실에 대해 추정하고 있다. 추정하는 시점도 현재이며 that절도 현재 사실에 대한 객관적인 진술이므로 현재시제가 알맞다.

estimate 추정하다 **homeless people** 노숙자들 **정답_(a)**

23

The possibility that comets and large meteorites could collide with the earth in the future _____ serious consideration.

(a) that requires
(b) to require
(c) requiring
(d) requires

혜성과 큰 운석이 미래에 지구와 충돌할 수 있다는 가능성을 진지하게 고려해야 한다.

▦ 기출 POINT

주어(The possibility)를 수식하는 that절이 길게 in the future까지 이어진다. 빈칸에는 목적어 serious consideration을 연결해 줄 동사가 필요한데 주어가 3인칭 단수이므로 정답은 (d)이다.

possibility 가능성 **comet** 혜성 **meteorite** 운석 **collide with** ~와 충돌하다 **serious** 진지한 **consideration** 고려 **정답_(d)**

24

Omega-3 fatty acids in fish can modify the blood, _____ it less prone to clotting.

(a) make
(b) making
(c) to making
(d) and making

생선의 오메가3 지방산은 혈액이 덜 쉽게 응고되도록 변화시킬 수 있다.

▦ 기출 POINT

주절이 〈주어+동사〉로 이루어진 완전한 문장이므로 콤마(,) 이하는 분사구문이 되어야 한다. 접속사가 생략되고 주어는 주절과 같으므로 생략된 분사구문의 형태로 making이 정답이다.

fatty acid 지방산 **modify** 변화시키다 **prone to** ~하기 쉬운 **clot** 응고되다 **정답_(b)**

25

The group's original plan was to go _____ over the weekend.

(a) skied
(b) to ski
(c) skiing
(d) to skiing

SOLUTION

그 단체의 원래 계획은 주말 동안 스키를 타러 가는 것이었다.

⊞ 기출 POINT

go -ing는 '~하러 가다'라는 뜻이며 go skiing/ go swimming/ go shopping 등으로 사용한다.

original 원래의　　　　　　　　　　　　　　　　정답_(c)

26

Mencius is famous for his argument _____ most humans are inherently good.

(a) that
(b) what
(c) which
(d) whose

SOLUTION

맹자는 대부분의 인간은 선천적으로 선하다는 주장으로 유명하다.

⊞ 기출 POINT

argument와 most humans are inherently good의 관계를 살펴 보면 argument의 내용이 most 이하와 같으므로 동격을 나타내는 that이 와야 한다. that은 명사 뒤에서 동격을 나타내는 접속사로 사용 될 수 있다.

argument 주장　**inherently** 선천적으로　　　　　정답_(a)

27

In the warm, crystal-clear waters of the tropics, coral reefs flourish, _____ vast areas.

(a) covered
(b) covering
(c) have covered
(d) to be covered

SOLUTION

산호초는 열대의 따뜻하고 투명한 바닷물 속에서 자라며 넓은 영역을 뒤덮는다.

⊞ 기출 POINT

문장의 맨 앞에 전치사구가 나오고 주어(coral reefs)와 동사(flourish) 가 뒤에 나온 구조이다. flourish의 상태를 부연 설명하기 위해 빈칸에 는 분사가 와야 하는데, cover의 주체가 coral reefs이므로 현재분사 (b)가 정답이다.

crystal-clear 투명한　**tropics** 열대 지방　**coral reef** 산호초
flourish 번성하다　　　　　　　　　　　　　　　　정답_(b)

28

Poor prospects in the domestic job market have prompted many young people _____ for work overseas.

(a) search
(b) searched
(c) to search
(d) searching

SOLUTION

국내 취업 시장의 어두운 전망으로 인해 많은 젊은이들은 해외에서 일자리를 알아보게 되었다.

⊞ 기출 POINT

prompt는 〈prompt A to+동사원형〉으로 'A가 ~하기로 결심하도록 만들다'는 뜻이므로 정답은 (c)가 된다.

prospect 전망　**domestic** 국내의　**prompt** 촉구하다　**overseas** 해외에서　　　　　　　　　　　　　　　　　　　　　정답_(c)

Actual Test 4

29

Sandra really annoyed me, but I _____ and did not say anything.

(a) control myself managed
(b) managed to control myself
(c) myself controlling managed
(d) controlling myself managed

SOLUTION

샌드라는 나를 정말 짜증나게 했지만, 나는 애써 내 자신을 제어했고 아무 말도 하지 않았다.

⊞ 기출 POINT

and는 대등한 두 가지 문법 요소를 연결하므로 did not say와 같은 과거형이 빈칸에 들어가야 한다는 것을 알 수 있다. manage to는 '애써 ~하다'의 의미이므로 정답은 (b)가 된다.

annoy 짜증나게 하다   **manage to** 애써 ~하다   정답 _(b)

30

Last year, all the profits from the sale of the book _____ donated to a charity.

(a) is
(b) are
(c) was
(d) were

SOLUTION

작년 그 책의 판매 수익 전액은 자선단체에 기부되었다.

⊞ 기출 POINT

주어는 from 이하의 수식을 받는 복수(all the profits)이고 시제는 과거(Last year)이므로 (d) were가 정답이다.

profit 수익   **donate** 기부하다   **charity** 자선단체   정답 _(d)

31

Animals that blend into their environment have the advantage _____ by predators.

(a) to be not easily detected
(b) not to be detected easily
(c) of not being easily detected
(d) of being not to be detected easily

SOLUTION

환경과 섞이는 동물들은 육식 동물들에게 쉽게 발각되지 않는다는 이점이 있다.

⊞ 기출 POINT

'~라는 이점이 있다'는 말로 have the advantage of -ing라는 어구를 사용한다. 동명사의 부정은 동명사 앞에 not을 붙이므로 (c)가 정답이다.

blend 섞이다   **advantage** 이점   **predator** 육식 동물   정답 _(c)

32

People are not certain _____ the economy can improve in the near future.

(a) even
(b) since
(c) unless
(d) whether

SOLUTION

사람들은 경제가 빠른 시일 내에 개선될지 확신하지 못한다.

⊞ 기출 POINT

빈칸에는 certain의 목적어가 와야 하는데 명사절을 이끄는 whether 절이 와서 '~인지 아닌지'의 뜻을 나타낼 수 있다. certain의 목적어 형태: ex) I'm certain of his success./ I was not certain that I closed the door./ I'm not certain what to choose.

certain 확신하는   **improve** 개선되다   **unless** ~하지 않는다면
whether ~인지 아닌지   정답 _(d)

33

Richard said that 25 dollars _____
considerably more than he expected to pay for a
pair of socks.

(a) was
(b) were
(c) is being
(d) are being

SOLUTION

리처드는 25달러는 양말 한 켤레에 지불할 금액으로 자신이 생각했던
것보다 꽤 많은 돈이라고 말했다.

⊞ 기출 POINT
25 dollars는 복수형이지만 금액을 말하는 것으로 하나의 단위로 간주
해 단수 동사가 와야 한다. said와 expected로 볼 때 과거형이 되어
야 하므로 정답은 (a)이다. 금액, 시간, 거리 등을 나타내는 명사는 복수
형이라도 단수 취급한다. ex) Four hours is not enough for me to
finish it./ Two hundred miles is quite a long distance.
considerably 꽤, 상당히 　　　　　　　　　　　　**정답**_(a)

34

It is the responsibility of parents or guardians to
supervise _____ under their care while in
the park.

(a) ones
(b) some
(c) those
(d) them

SOLUTION

공원 내에서는 부모나 보호자가 자신들이 돌보는 사람들을 관리할 책임
이 있다.

⊞ 기출 POINT
those는 관계대명사 who 앞에 쓰여 '사람들'이라는 뜻으로, 특정한
사람이 아닌 일반적인 사람들을 말할 때 사용된다. those 뒤에는 who
are가 생략되었다.
responsibility 의무　**guardian** 보호자　**supervise** 돌보다
　　　　　　　　　　　　　　　　　　　　　　　　　　정답_(c)

35

The professor gave _____ F to each
student who did not turn in his or her term paper.

(a) a
(b) an
(c) any
(d) every

SOLUTION

교수는 기말 보고서를 제출하지 않은 학생 전원에게 F학점을 주었다.

⊞ 기출 POINT
each student에게 F학점을 준다는 의미이므로 빈칸에는 관사가 들어
가야 하며 F는 자음으로 시작하지만 발음은 모음 [ef]이므로 an이 정답
이다.
turn in 제출하다　**term paper** 기말 보고서　　　　**정답**_(b)

36

Conflicts between elephants are communicated
by a display of aggression _____ they twirl
their trunks or throw dust into the air.

(a) what
(b) which
(c) in what
(d) in which

SOLUTION

코끼리들 간의 충돌은 공격성의 표출로 전달되며, 이때 코끼리들은
코를 빙빙 돌리거나 허공에 흙먼지를 집어던진다.

⊞ 기출 POINT
관계대명사를 고르는 문제이다. 선행사인 a display of aggression
은 뒷문장에서 전치사구로 사용된다. 〈전치사+관계대명사〉가 필요하므
로 in which가 정답이다.
conflict 충돌　**display of aggression** 공격성의 표출　**twirl** 돌리다
trunk 코　**dust** 흙먼지　　　　　　　　　　　　　**정답**_(d)

37

Nowadays teachers consider themselves fortunate if they have just a few _____ studying.

(a) enjoying students in their class
(b) in their class students enjoying
(c) students in their class who enjoy
(d) students who enjoy in their class

SOLUTION

요즘 교사들은 한 반에 몇 명이라도 공부를 즐기는 학생들이 있으면 스스로를 운이 좋다고 여긴다.

⊞ 기출 POINT
'반에 몇 명이라도 공부를 즐기는 학생들이 있다'는 내용이 빈칸에 들어가야 한다. 빈칸 앞 a few에 이어지도록 students가 나오고 who enjoy는 선행사인 students를 수식하는 관계대명사절이다. 보통은 선행사 다음에 바로 관계대명사가 오지만, 수식어구인 in their class는 studying 앞에 올 수 없으므로 선행사와 관계대명사 사이에 위치하게 된다.

consider ~로 여기다 **fortunate** 운이 좋은   정답 _(c)

38

There may be some decline in intelligence with age, but this is smaller and more limited in scope than _____.

(a) was once widely believed
(b) once being widely believed
(c) being widely believed once
(d) once widely it was believed

SOLUTION

나이가 들면서 지능이 약간 쇠퇴할 수는 있지만, 이는 한때 널리 믿었던 것보다 그 범위가 더 작고 제한적이다.

⊞ 기출 POINT
관계대명사 기능을 하는 than 이하의 어순을 묻는 문제이다. 절이 와야 하므로 동사가 들어가 있는 (a)와 (d) 중에서 고르도록 한다. than이 주어 역할을 하므로 주어가 빠진 (a)가 정답이다. 목적어나 보어 역할을 하는 than: They gave me more food than I ordered./ She was more nervous than I was.

decline 쇠퇴 **intelligence** 지능 **scope** 범위   정답 _(a)

39

_____ to fit all head sizes, the hat is suitable for anyone.

(a) It is designed
(b) Designing
(c) To design
(d) Designed

SOLUTION

모든 머리 크기에 다 맞도록 제작된 그 모자는 누구에게나 어울린다.

⊞ 기출 POINT
콤마(,) 이하에 완전한 절이 나오므로 연결어 없이 또 다른 절이 오는 (a)는 옳지 않다. the hat과 design은 수동 관계이며, As it is designed to fit에서 접속사와 주어를 생략하고 (Being) Designed만 남은 분사구문이다.

be suitable for ~에게 적당하다, 맞다   정답 _(d)

40

_____ dates from an idea first conceived in the early 19th century.

(a) Computer
(b) The computer
(c) Any computer
(d) Each computer

SOLUTION

컴퓨터는 19세기 초 처음 고안된 아이디어로 거슬러 올라간다.

⊞ 기출 POINT
정관사 the가 단수명사 앞에 쓰여서 일반적인 대상 전체를 가리키는 경우이다. The computer는 특정 컴퓨터가 아니라 컴퓨터라는 일반적인 대상을 말한다. ex) The cellphone has changed everyone's life./ The dog is a faithful animal.

date from ~로부터 시작되다 **conceive** 생각해내다   정답 _(b)

41

(a) A Hey, Iris, take a look at this article on nutrition in today's paper.

(b) B Don't tell me. It's the new National Institute of Health report, right?

(c) A That's right! It's all the latest on low-fat diets! How do you guess?

(d) B I read the article on the way home from work.

(a) 이봐, 아이리스, 오늘 신문에 난 이 영양 관련 기사 좀 봐.
(b) 혹시 그거 국립보건원 보고서 아니니?
(c) 맞아! 저지방 식단에 대한 최신 보고서야! 어떻게 알았어?
(d) 퇴근하고 집에 오는 길에 그 기사 읽었어.

기출 POINT
(c)에서 guess는 '추측하다, 짐작하다'의 뜻이다. A가 언급한 기사를 이미 알고 있는 것에 대해 어떻게 알았냐고 묻고 있으므로 How did you guess?가 알맞다. all the latest는 '최신의'라는 표현이다.
article 기사 **Don't tell me.** 설마. **low-fat diet** 저지방 식단
all the latest 최신의   정답_(c) do → did

42

(a) A Are you going out later?
(b) B I don't think so. I'm such tired.
(c) A Why? Were you up late last night?
(d) B Yes. I didn't go to sleep until 2 a.m.

SOLUTION

(a) 있다가 외출할 거야?
(b) 아닐 것 같은데. 너무 피곤해서 말이야.
(c) 왜? 어젯밤에 늦게 잤어?
(d) 응. 새벽 2시까지 안 잤어.

기출 POINT
(b)에서 '매우'라는 뜻의 such는 명사 또는 〈형용사+명사〉 앞에 사용되어 이들을 수식한다. ex) such a fool/ such good food/ such a lovely person 따라서 형용사 tired를 수식할 수 있는 것은 부사 very나 so이다.
such 매우 **be up late** 늦게까지 깨어 있다
                정답_(b) such → very/ so

43

(a) A I don't think we can finish this project in time.

(b) B I agree, but what can we do about it?

(c) A We just need to tell the boss and explain why.

(d) B Then let's go now and sort things out to him.

SOLUTION

(a) 우리 이 프로젝트 제시간에 못 끝낼 것 같아.

(b) 나도 그렇게 생각해. 그런데 어떻게 해야 할까?

(c) 사장님께 이야기하고 이유를 설명해야지.

(d) 그러면 지금 가서 사장님과 해결해 보자.

⊞ 기출 POINT

(d) sort out은 문제를 '해결하다'는 뜻이며, 사장님께 말하고 함께 문제를 해결하는 내용이므로 전치사 to 대신 with가 와야 한다.

sort out 해결하다　　　　　　　　　　　**정답**_(d) to → with

44

(a) A John, you're a T2 fan—are you going to the concert?

(b) B I don't know yet. I'm supposed you already have your tickets.

(c) A Actually, not yet. I'm going to buy them today.

(d) B Can I go to the concert with you? I don't know anybody else who's going.

SOLUTION

(a) 존, 너 T2 팬이잖아. 콘서트에 갈 거야?

(b) 아직 몰라. 넌 벌써 표를 샀겠구나.

(c) 아직. 오늘 살 거야.

(d) 너랑 콘서트에 같이 가도 될까? 다른 사람 중에 누가 가는지 모르겠어.

⊞ 기출 POINT

(b)에서 '~라고 추측하다'의 뜻으로 쓰는 suppose는 I'm supposed 가 아니라 I suppose that 형태로 써야 한다. 〈I'm supposed to+ 동사원형〉은 '내가 ~할 예정이다'의 뜻으로 전혀 다른 표현이다.

actually 사실은　　　　　　　**정답**_(b) I'm supposed → I suppose

45

(a) A What do you think I should get Vanessa for Valentine's Day?

(b) B How about a card and a red rose?

(c) A Come on. Where's your imagination? All the guys buy flower.

(d) B I don't see anything wrong with that.

SOLUTION

(a) 발렌타인 데이에 바네사에게 무슨 선물을 해줘야 할까?

(b) 카드랑 빨간 장미 한 송이 어때?

(c) 야. 상상력은 뒀다 어디에 쓰냐? 남자들이면 다 꽃은 살 거라고.

(d) 그게 뭐가 잘못됐다는 건지 나는 모르겠는데.

🔲 기출 POINT

(c)에서 flower는 셀 수 있는 명사이므로 앞에 관사가 필요하다. 여기에서 '남자들은 다 꽃을 산다'는 말은 일반적인 내용이므로 flowers가 되어야 한다.

imagination 상상력　　　　　　**정답**_(c) flower → flowers

46

(a) Recently, there have been protests about the cost of prescription drugs. (b) There has also been criticism about not having access to newly developed medicines. (c) Yet people are still not getting the medicines they need to stay healthily. (d) We need to do more to force the government to fix this problem.

SOLUTION

(a) 최근 처방 약품 가격에 대한 시위가 있었다. (b) 새로 개발된 의약품을 구할 수 없다는 데 대한 비판도 있었다. (c) 하지만 사람들은 아직도 건강을 유지하는 데 필요한 의약품을 얻지 못하고 있다. (d) 우리는 정부가 이 문제를 해결하도록 하기 위해 더 많은 일을 해야 한다.

🔲 기출 POINT

(c)에서 '건강을 유지하다'는 stay healthy이다. stay는 remain과 같이 '～한 상태로 있다'라는 뜻의 자동사이므로 형용사 보어를 수반한다.

recently 최근에　**protest** 시위　**prescription** 처방　**criticism** 비판
medicine 약　**fix** 해결하다　　　　**정답**_(c) healthily → healthy

47

(a) You need to be sensible if you intend to exert yourself in hot weather. (b) The hotter it is, the harder it is for you to get rid of excess heat, and the type of clothing you wear can make a big difference. (c) It is logical that if you wore lighter clothing when exercising, you will be cooler. (d) Everyone knows that, but few people realize that light clothing may actually save you from heat stroke and even death.

SOLUTION

(a) 더운 날씨에 몸을 많이 움직일 생각이라면 분별이 있어야 한다. (b) 날씨가 더울수록 잉여 열을 없애기가 더 어렵고, 어떤 종류의 옷을 입고 있는지가 큰 영향을 줄 수 있다. (c) 운동을 할 때 더 가벼운 옷을 입으면 더 시원할 것이라는 것은 논리적이다. (d) 가벼운 옷이 당신을 열사병과 심지어 사망으로부터 구해줄 수도 있다는 것은 모두가 알고 있지만 이를 자각하는 사람은 거의 없다.

기출 POINT

(c)에서 if절에 쓰인 동사(wore)와 주절에 쓰인 동사(is)의 시제가 맞지 않는다. 내용상 It is logical that 다음에 오는 if는 가정법이 아니라 일반적인 조건을 나타내는 문장이므로 현재시제가 되어야 한다.

sensible 분별이 있는 **exert** 움직이다 **get rid of** ~을 없애다
excess 잉여의 **logical** 논리적인 **heat stroke** 열사병

정답_(c) wore → wear

48

(a) Rocks provide clues about the nature and timing of the events that formed them. (b) Layer of rock, for instance, can tell us about an event that occurred millions of years ago. (c) Geologists are able to use this information to develop a larger picture of the processes that shaped the earth. (d) Then, they can better predict what geological events are likely to occur in the future.

SOLUTION

(a) 암석은 그것을 형성하게 된 사건들의 시점과 특징에 대해 실마리를 제공한다. (b) 예를 들면 암석층은 수백만 년 전에 일어났던 사건을 우리에게 알려줄 수 있다. (c) 지질학자들은 이 정보를 사용해서 지구가 형성된 과정의 더 큰 그림을 그려낼 수 있다. (d) 그러면 이들은 미래에 어떤 지질학적 사건이 발생할 것인지 더 잘 예측할 수 있다.

기출 POINT

(b)는 암석이 쌓인 층에 대한 내용이며 layer 앞에는 관사가 필요하다. 불특정한 암석층을 가리키는 말이므로 A layer of rock이 적절하다.

provide 제공하다 **layer** 층 **occur** 발생하다 **geologist** 지질학자
predict 예언하다

정답_(b) Layer → A layer

49

(a) No one ever found out who murdered the old woman. (b) Many people thought it was Mr. Crawshank because he stood to gain the most from her death. (c) Certainly their animosity for each other was well known. (d) But if he be the murderer, surely he would have hidden his delight at the news of her death.

SOLUTION

(a) 누가 그 노년의 여성을 살해했는지 어느 누구도 알아내지 못했다. (b) 많은 사람들은 크로생크 씨가 그녀의 죽음으로부터 가장 큰 이득을 얻을 것 같았기 때문에 그가 범인이라고 생각했다. (c) 이들의 적대감은 분명 잘 알려져 있었다. (d) 하지만 만약 그가 살인범이라면, 그는 틀림없이 그녀의 사망 소식에 대한 자신의 기쁨을 잘 감추고 있는 것이다.

 기출 POINT

(d)에서 주절의 동사(would have hidden) 형태로 봐서 if절에는 가정법 과거(were)나 과거완료(had been)가 와야 한다.
murder 살해하다   **gain** 얻다   **animosity** 적대감   **murderer** 살해자
delight 기쁨   정답_(d) be → were/ had been

50

(a) Modern entertainment magic owes much to Jean Houdin, who opened a magic theater in Paris in the 1840s. (b) His specialty was the construction of machines that appeared to move and act as if were alive. (c) But he also displayed a gift for presentation which would set him apart from his peers. (d) In particular, his practice of appearing in a suit, rather than elaborate robes, has led many to see him as the first "modern" magician.

SOLUTION

(a) 근대 오락 마술에는 1840년대 파리에 마술 극장을 열었던 장 우댕의 공이 크다. (b) 그의 주특기는 마치 살아 있는 것처럼 움직이고 행동했던 기계들을 만드는 것이었다. (c) 하지만 그는 공연으로 이를 보여주는 데도 천부적 자질을 보였으며, 이 때문에 그의 동료들보다 더 돋보이기도 했다. (d) 특히 화려한 마술사복보다는 정장을 입었던 그의 습관 때문에 많은 사람들은 그를 최초의 '근대' 마술사로 여기게 되었다.

기출 POINT

주절의 동사가 과거형일 때 as if 뒤에 〈주어+동사의 과거형〉이 나와 '마치 ~한 것처럼'이라는 뜻으로 쓰이며 과거 사실의 반대를 의미한다. 이때 as if는 사실과 다른 내용을 말하며 일반적으로 가정법의 형태를 취하게 된다. 따라서 (b)의 as if 다음에는 they were alive가 되어야 한다.
entertainment 오락   **specialty** 특기   **construction** 축조
display 보여주다   **presentation** 공연   **set apart** 구분하다
elaborate 화려한   **robes** 예복, 옷

정답_(b) as if were alive → as if they were alive

1

A   I really like your new haircut.
B   Thanks. It's _____ of you to say so.

(a) nice
(b) mild
(c) ideal
(d) pleasant

SOLUTION

A   새로 자른 네 머리 스타일 정말 마음에 든다.
B   그렇게 말해주니 고맙구나.

🔲 **기출 POINT**

칭찬, 감사나 비난의 말을 할 때 형용사 다음에 오는 to부정사의 의미상의 주어는 〈for+목적격〉이 아니라 〈of+목적격〉으로 쓴다. kind, careless, nice, rude, wise, thoughtful, generous 등의 형용사가 이에 해당된다. 여기서는 감사의 말이므로 nice가 가장 적절하다.
mild 온화한   **ideal** 이상적인   **pleasant** 즐거운   정답_(a)

2

A   Can I help you _____ your groceries?
B   Thank you. They are quite heavy.

(a) buy
(b) find
(c) leave
(d) carry

SOLUTION

A   장 본 물건 들고 가시는 걸 도와드릴까요?
B   고마워요. 꽤 무겁네요.

🔲 **기출 POINT**

〈help+목적어+동사원형〉의 형태로 '누가 ~하는 것을 돕다'라는 뜻이다. groceries는 장을 본 물건을 의미하므로 '장 본 물건 옮기는 걸 도와준다'는 말이 알맞다. 따라서, '운반하다, 옮기다'라는 뜻의 (d) carry가 정답이다.
grocery 식료품, 장 본 물건   정답_(d)

3

A   Is your teacher better today?
B   No. He's still not in a very good _____.

(a) sense
(b) mood
(c) manner
(d) standard

SOLUTION

A   너희 선생님 오늘은 기분이 좀 나아지셨니?
B   아니. 아직도 별로 안 좋으셔.

🔲 **기출 POINT**

기분의 상태를 말할 때는 mood를 쓴다. in a good mood는 '기분이 좋은(happy)'이라는 말이다. 반대로 in a bad mood는 '기분이 나쁜(unhappy or angry)'의 뜻이다.
be better (기분이나 건강이) 더 낫다   **sense** 감각   **mood** 분위기
manner 방법   **standard** 기준   정답_(b)

4

A   What should I do if I can't keep my appointment?
B   Let us know as soon as possible, and we'll _____.

(a) repeat
(b) return
(c) respond
(d) reschedule

SOLUTION

A   만약 약속을 지킬 수 없으면 어떻게 해야 하나요?
B   최대한 빨리 저희들에게 알려주시면, 약속을 다시 잡겠습니다.

🔲 **기출 POINT**

appointment는 '약속'을 의미하는 말이므로 만약 약속을 지키지 못할 때에는 연락해서 다시 잡는다는 말이 되어야 한다. 따라서 reschedule이 적절하다.
keep one's appointment 약속을 지키다   **repeat** 반복하다
respond 대답하다   정답_(d)

5

A I hope the hotel you booked has everything we need.

B Don't worry. It has great _____, such as a spa, bar and much more.

(a) outfits
(b) assets
(c) services
(d) facilities

SOLUTION

A 네가 예약한 호텔에 우리가 필요한 것들이 다 있으면 좋겠다.
B 걱정 마. 스파, 바, 기타 등등 시설이 아주 좋아.

🎫 기출 POINT

facilities는 복수형으로 쓰여서 특별한 목적으로 제공되는 설비나 시설 등을 가리키는 말이다. ex) spa, bar, gym, swimming pool
book 예약하다 **spa** 스파 **outfit** 용품; 장비; 의상 한 벌 **asset** 자산
facilities 편의 시설   정답_(d)

6

A I'm very sorry about the other day.

B There's no need to _____ an apology.

(a) use
(b) make
(c) allow
(d) spend

SOLUTION

A 그저께는 내가 너무 미안했어.
B 사과할 필요 없어.

🎫 기출 POINT

'사과하다'는 make an apology로 표현한다. 반대로 '사과를 받아들이 다'는 accept an apology라고 한다.
the other day 일전에 **there's no need to** ~할 필요가 없다
apology 사과   정답_(b)

7

A Why isn't the car moving?

B You have to _____ the parking brake.

(a) start
(b) release
(c) position
(d) accelerate

SOLUTION

A 왜 차가 안 움직이지?
B 주차 브레이크를 풀어야지.

🎫 기출 POINT

주차 브레이크를 풀어야 차가 주행할 수 있는 상태가 된다. 이 경우
release the parking brake라고 쓴다. 주차 브레이크를 거는 것은
apply나 engage라는 동사를 쓴다.
parking brake 주차 브레이크 **release** 풀다 **position** 위치시키다
accelerate 가속시키다   정답_(b)

8

A My skin is really _____ these days.

B You should apply moisturizing lotion right after you shower.

(a) dry
(b) soft
(c) thin
(d) tense

SOLUTION

A 내 피부가 요즘 너무 건조해.
B 샤워하고 나서 바로 보습 로션을 발라야 돼.

🎫 기출 POINT

moisturizing의 뜻을 알아야 풀 수 있는 문제이다. moisture(습기)라 는 명사에서 나온 것으로 여기에서는 '수분을 주는'이라는 현재분사로 사용되었다. 따라서 반대 의미인 dry가 알맞다.
apply 바르다 **moisturizing lotion** 보습 로션 **right after** ~직후에
tense 긴장한   정답_(a)

9

A Could we have a table by the window?

B I'm sorry, but the window tables are all
_____.

(a) served
(b) shared
(c) crowded
(d) occupied

SOLUTION

A 창가 테이블로 할 수 있을까요?

B 죄송합니다만 창가 테이블은 다 찼습니다.

⊞ 기출 POINT

방, 좌석이 '사용 중이다, 다 찼다'는 의미로 be occupied를 쓴다.
음식점과 같은 장소에서 자리를 잡으려는 상황이므로 crowded는
부적절하다.

window table 창가 좌석 **serve** 근무하다 **share** 함께 사용하다
occupy (자리를) 차지하다   **정답_(d)**

10

A I know you're upset, but please don't cry.

B I can't _____ it.

(a) help
(b) keep
(c) ensure
(d) save

SOLUTION

A 화난 건 알겠지만 제발 울지는 마.

B 나도 어쩔 수 없다고.

⊞ 기출 POINT

can't help는 '~하는 것은 어쩔 수 없다'는 뜻으로 I can't help it은 '나
도 어쩔 수 없다'는 말이 된다. can't help -ing/ can't help but+동사
원형: ~하지 않을 수 없다 ex) I could not help crying./ I could not
help but agree with them.

upset 화난 **ensure** 확실하게 하다   **정답_(a)**

11

A Do you know where I should get off for the
Stella Theater?

B Sure, it's the third stop from here.
Actually, I'm _____ there, too.

(a) posted
(b) headed
(c) directed
(d) forwarded

SOLUTION

A 스텔라 극장에 가려면 어디에서 내려야 하는지 아세요?

B 여기서부터 세 번째 정류장입니다. 실은 저도 거기에 가는 중이에요.

⊞ 기출 POINT

사람을 주어로 해서 '~로 가다'는 표현은 선택지 중 I'm headed만 가
능하다. I head로도 쓰이고 I'm headed도 같은 뜻으로 쓴다.

get off (차에서) 내리다 **post** 게시하다 **direct** ~에게 길을 가리키다
forward 발송하다   **정답_(b)**

12

A I thought that I _____ a better grade than
this.

B Well, go talk to the professor if you think it's
too low.

(a) received
(b) intended
(c) deserved
(d) demanded

SOLUTION

A 당연히 이것보다는 더 나은 성적을 받을 줄 알았어.

B 음, 성적이 너무 낮다고 생각되면 교수님에게 말씀드려 봐.

⊞ 기출 POINT

더 나은 성적을 받아야 마땅하다고 생각한다는 내용이 적절하다.
deserve는 '~할 만하다'의 뜻으로 deserve 다음에 명사가 오거나
〈to+동사원형〉이 와서 deserve attention/ deserve to win 등으로
쓴다. received는 '더 나은 점수를 받았다고 생각했다'는 내용이므로
부적절하다.

grade 성적 **intend** 의도하다 **deserve** ~을 받아 마땅하다
demand 요구하다   **정답_(c)**

13

A Can I _____ these trousers?
B Of course. The fitting room's over there.

(a) try on
(b) put away
(c) wear out
(d) make over

SOLUTION

A 이 바지 입어봐도 되나요?
B 그럼요. 탈의실은 저쪽입니다.

⊞ 기출 POINT

'입어보다'라는 뜻을 나타낼 수 있는 관용표현을 묻는 질문이다. try on
은 '~을 입어보다'라는 표현이며 목적어가 명사일 경우 try on these
trousers 혹은 try these trousers on 둘 다 가능하다.
fitting room 탈의실 **put away** ~을 치우다 **wear out** ~을 써서
낡게 하다 **make over** 다시 만들다, 변경하다   정답_(a)

14

A How often do you _____?
B I go to the gym every day.

(a) turn out
(b) take out
(c) work out
(d) figure out

SOLUTION

A 운동을 얼마나 자주 하세요?
B 매일 헬스 클럽에 갑니다.

⊞ 기출 POINT

대답이 go to the gym인 것으로 보아 얼마나 자주 운동을 하는지
묻는 질문이 적절하다. '운동을 한다'는 뜻으로 사용하는 2어 동사는
work out이다. turn out은 '~임이 판명되다'라는 뜻이다.
turn out ~임이 판명되다 **take out** 꺼내다 **work out** 운동하다
figure out 파악하다   정답_(c)

15

A Mount Seorak is breathtaking in the fall.
B That's what I _____.

(a) hear
(b) plan
(c) meet
(d) grasp

SOLUTION

A 설악산은 가을에 장관이지.
B 나도 그렇게 들었어.

⊞ 기출 POINT

산이 장관이라는 말에 동조하는 말로 적당한 것은 '나도 그렇게 들었어'
이다. That's what I hear는 상대방의 말에 동조할 때 쓰는 표현이다.
breathtaking 장관인 **grasp** 파악하다, 이해하다   정답_(a)

16

A Hello. Can I speak to someone about my
   account?
B Everyone's busy right now. I'll have to
   _____ you on hold.

(a) ask
(b) tell
(c) put
(d) give

SOLUTION

A 여보세요. 제 계좌에 대해 상담 좀 할 수 있나요?
B 지금은 모두 통화 중이에요. 잠시 기다려 주셔야 할 것 같습니다.

⊞ 기출 POINT

전화 대화에서 I'll put you on hold는 '전화를 끊지 말고 기다려 달라'
는 말이다. 전화 표현: Hold the line./ Stay on the line./ Hold on a
second . 끊지 말고 기다려 주세요.
account 계정, 계좌   정답_(c)

Actual Test 4

17

A So, what did the judge decide?

B The defendant was _____ and sentenced to 20 years in prison.

(a) acquitted
(b) convicted
(c) suspected
(d) prosecuted

SOLUTION

A 그래서, 판사는 어떻게 판결을 내렸니?
B 피고는 유죄 판결을 받았고 20년 수감형을 선고받았어.

⊞ 기출 POINT

20년 형을 받았다는 내용과 연결되기 위해서는 유죄 판결을 받았다는 말이 나와야 한다. be convicted는 '유죄 판결을 받다', prosecute는 '기소하다'는 뜻이다.

defendant 피고 **acquit** ~을 무죄로 하다 **convict** 유죄 판결하다 **suspect** 의심하다 **prosecute** 기소하다 정답_(b)

18

A Do you have any _____ to check in?

B No, I only have one carry-on.

(a) luggage
(b) burden
(c) pack
(d) load

SOLUTION

A 부칠 수하물이 있나요?
B 아니요, 기내 반입 수하물 하나뿐입니다.

⊞ 기출 POINT

check in은 호텔에서 숙박 수속을 하거나 공항에서 탑승 수속을 한다는 말이다. 여기서는 탑승 수속에서 수하물을 부치는 상황이므로 '수하물'이라는 뜻의 luggage를 check in한다는 말이 된다. carry-on은 '기내에 가지고 타는 짐'을 의미한다.

check in 탑승 수속을 하다, 짐을 맡기다 **carry-on** 기내 반입물 **luggage** 수하물 **burden** 짐 **load** 적재 화물 정답_(a)

19

A I think the office air conditioning is up too high.

B Yeah. Let's go _____ it to the manager.

(a) call
(b) press
(c) lower
(d) mention

SOLUTION

A 사무실 에어컨이 너무 세게 켜져 있는 것 같아.
B 맞아. 매니저한테 가서 얘기하자.

⊞ 기출 POINT

'매니저에게 가서 얘기하자'는 말이 되어야 하므로 목적어인 it과 to the manager를 연결하는 말이 와야 한다. 〈mention+목적어+to+사람〉은 '~에게 …을 말하다'라는 뜻이므로 정답은 (d)이다.

air conditioning 에어컨 **manager** 관리인 **lower** 낮추다 **mention** 말하다 정답_(d)

20

A Hi, Charles. How's everything going?

B Oh, I can't _____.

(a) argue
(b) dispute
(c) disagree
(d) complain

SOLUTION

A 안녕, 찰스. 어떻게 지내?
B 아, 그럭저럭 잘 지내.

⊞ 기출 POINT

I can't complain은 직역하면 '불평할 것이 없다'는 말인데 안부 인사에 대한 답이므로 '별일 없다'는 말이다. argue나 dispute는 '논쟁하다'는 뜻이므로 오답이다.

argue 주장하다 **dispute** 논쟁하다 **complain** 불평하다 정답_(d)

21

A How soon will the curtain _____?
B The performance will start in about five minutes.

(a) come down
(b) move over
(c) roll out
(d) go up

SOLUTION

A 막이 언제 오르니?
B 공연은 5분 정도 후면 시작할 거야.

⊞ 기출 POINT

the curtain goes up이라는 표현을 써서 공연이 '개막된다, 시작된다'라는 의미를 나타낸다. go up 대신 rise를 쓰기도 한다. 반대로 '공연이 끝난다'는 말로는 the curtain comes down을 사용한다.
performance 공연 **move over** 자리를 좁히다 **roll out** ~을 펴다
go up 올라가다   정답_(d)

22

A How are people prevented from sneaking guns into the building?
B Guards at the entrance check everyone to see if they're _____.

(a) armed
(b) loaded
(c) equipped
(d) protected

SOLUTION

A 어떻게 사람들이 건물에 몰래 총기를 숨겨서 반입하지 못하도록 해?
B 입구의 경호원들이 사람들이 총기를 소지하고 있는지 전부 검사해.

⊞ 기출 POINT

sneak guns into the building은 '총을 숨겨서 반입하다'라는 뜻이다.
see if는 '~인지 알아보다'이므로 '총을 소지한'이라는 의미인 armed가 정답이다. loaded는 '탄알을 잰, 장전한'의 뜻으로 답이 될 수 없다.
prevent from ~을 막다 **sneak** 숨기다 **armed** 무장한 **loaded**
장전된 **equipped** 설비를 갖춘   정답_(a)

23

A Cathy is always fashionable, isn't she?
B Yes. She has a(n) _____ for high fashion.

(a) legacy
(b) inkling
(c) penchant
(d) discipline

SOLUTION

A 캐시는 항상 패션 감각이 넘치지 않니?
B 응. 캐시는 최신 유행 패션을 좋아해.

⊞ 기출 POINT

have a penchant for는 '~을 아주 좋아하다'라는 뜻이다. legacy는
'유산'을, inkling은 '암시'를 뜻한다.
fashionable 패션 감각이 넘치는 **legacy** 유산 **inkling** 암시
penchant 경향, 강한 기호 **discipline** 훈련   정답_(c)

24

A Jane isn't very sociable these days.
B Well, she's been _____ with a lot of problems lately.

(a) getting through
(b) making away
(c) broken down
(d) caught up

SOLUTION

A 제인은 요즘 그다지 사람들과 어울리지 않아.
B 그게, 최근 제인한테 문제가 많이 생겼어.

⊞ 기출 POINT

제인에게 많은 문제가 생겨서 사람들과 어울리지 못했다는 내용이다.
단, 전치사 with와 연결을 고려해서 답을 골라야 하는 문제이다.
problems를 목적어로 취해 의미가 통하는 (d) caught up이 정답이다.
sociable 사교적인 **get through** 빠져나가다 **make away** 급히
달아나다 **break down** 고장나다 **catch up with** 나쁜 결과를 가져
오다   정답_(d)

25

A Joseph thinks he's somebody since he got promoted.

B I know. He's had a(n) _____ air about him ever since.

(a) acrimonious
(b) ignominious
(c) pretentious
(d) veracious

SOLUTION

A 조셉은 승진한 이후로 자기가 대단한 사람이라고 생각해.
B 그러게 말야. 그 이후로 잘난 체하지.

⊞ 기출 POINT

have a A air는 'A한 태도를 취하다'라는 뜻이다. somebody는 '대단한 사람'이라는 말이고 반대말은 nobody이다. thinks he's somebody라는 부분에서 자랑하는 태도를 유추할 수 있으므로 '자만하는'이라는 뜻의 pretentious가 적절하다.

somebody 대단한 사람 **get promoted** 승진하다 **acrimonious** 신랄한 **ignominious** 불명예스러운 **pretentious** 자만하는 **veracious** 진실한

정답_(c)

26

Woodwind instruments make sound when air is _____ through a mouthpiece.

(a) opened
(b) drawn
(c) added
(d) blown

SOLUTION

목관 악기는 마우스피스를 통해 공기를 불어넣을 때 소리가 난다.

⊞ 기출 POINT

목관 악기는 부는 구멍으로 공기를 불어넣어 소리를 내는 것이므로 '불어넣다'에 해당하는 blow가 정답이다. 단, 공기는 불어넣어지는 것이므로 수동태를 사용했다. draw는 '끌어당기다'라는 뜻이므로 부적절하다.

woodwind instrument 목관 악기 **mouthpiece** 마우스피스, 입에 대는 부분

정답_(d)

27

Rest and proper care are needed to _____ from the flu.

(a) return
(b) excuse
(c) recover
(d) manage

SOLUTION

감기가 나으려면 휴식과 적절한 치료가 필요하다.

⊞ 기출 POINT

'병에서 회복하다, 병을 이기다'는 동사가 나와야 한다. 전치사 from을 동반하여 이런 뜻을 나타내는 것은 recover from이다. excuse from은 '~을 면제하다'는 뜻이다.

excuse 핑계를 대다

정답_(c)

28

High heels should be _____ since they can cause foot deformities.

(a) muffled
(b) checked
(c) proposed
(d) discouraged

SOLUTION

굽 높은 구두는 발의 기형을 유발할 수 있기 때문에 멀리해야 한다.

⊞ 기출 POINT

발의 모양을 변형시킬 수 있기 때문이라고 했으므로 하이힐을 신는 것을 말리는 내용이 들어가야 한다. '~을 못하게 말리다'는 discourage가 와야 하나 High heels가 사물 주어이므로 수동태 should be discouraged가 쓰였다. 반대말은 encourage이다.

deformity 기형 **muffle** 덮어 싸다 **propose** 제안하다 **discourage** ~을 말리다, 단념시키다

정답_(d)

29

Students can _____ greatly from regular use of dictionaries.

(a) differ
(b) benefit
(c) instruct
(d) motivate

학생들은 적절하게 사전을 활용함으로써 많은 이점을 볼 수 있다.

⊞ 기출 POINT

Students를 주어로 하고 전치사 from을 동반하는 자동사가 온 것에 유의한다. 사전을 활용하는 것과 관계 있는 것은 benefit from이다. benefit greatly from에서 수식어의 위치에 유의한다.
benefit from ~로부터 혜택을 얻다　**instruct** 가르치다　**motivate** 동기를 부여하다　　　　　　　　　　　　　　　　**정답** (b)

30

People who eat a balanced, nutritious breakfast are usually _____ than those who do not.

(a) frailer
(b) denser
(c) greedier
(d) healthier

SOLUTION

균형 잡히고 영양가 있는 아침식사를 하는 사람들은 그렇지 않은 사람들보다 일반적으로 더 건강하다.

⊞ 기출 POINT

비교급과 than을 볼 때 비교하는 내용임을 알 수 있다. 마지막 단어 do not은 do not eat a balanced, nutritious breakfast를 대신한다. 균형 잡히고 영양가 있는 아침을 먹는 사람들이 그렇지 않은 사람들보다 더 건강하다는 내용이 되어야 하므로 healthy의 비교급인 healthier가 정답이다.
frail 약한　**dense** 짙은　**greedy** 욕심이 많은　　　　**정답** (d)

31

Every time your heart _____, blood is pushed through the arteries.

(a) ticks
(b) beats
(c) turns
(d) strikes

SOLUTION

심장이 뛸 때마다 혈액이 동맥을 통과한다.

⊞ 기출 POINT

심장의 운동 원리를 설명하는 내용이다. 심장이 '뛰다, 고동치다'라고 할 때 beat을 쓴다. '심장 박동'은 heartbeat이다.
push through 뚫고 나가다　**artery** 동맥　**tick** 똑딱거리다　**beat** 뛰다, 고동치다　**strike** 때리다　　　　　　　　　　**정답** (b)

32

The house was _____ vacant for three months until a new owner moved in.

(a) left
(b) met
(c) sold
(d) taken

SOLUTION

그 집은 새 주인이 이사해 들어올 때까지 3개월간 빈집이었다.

⊞ 기출 POINT

〈leave+목적어+목적보어〉는 '~을 어떤 상태로 두다'의 뜻을 나타낸다. leave the door open/ leave the phone off/ leave the room empty 등으로 사용하며 여기에서는 left the house vacant라는 문장이 수동태가 되어 The house was left vacant가 된 것이다.
vacant 텅 빈　**move in** 이사오다　　　　　　　　　　**정답** (a)

33

Parents should be _____ and treat every child equally.

(a) biased
(b) obedient
(c) impartial
(d) intolerant

SOLUTION

부모는 공정해야 하고 모든 자녀들을 똑같이 대해야 한다.

⊞ 기출 POINT

접속사 and는 비슷한 내용을 연결하고 있다. treat every child equally를 표현해 줄 만한 단어는 impartial(공정한)이다. 반대말에 가까운 biased는 '치우친, 편견을 가진'의 뜻이며, intolerant는 '옹졸한, 편협한'의 뜻이다.

biased 편향된 **obedient** 복종하는 **impartial** 공평한 **intolerant** 옹졸한, 편협한

정답_(c)

34

Drawing pictures and telling stories were probably the earliest forms of creative _____.

(a) expression
(b) suggestion
(c) application
(d) preparation

SOLUTION

그림을 그리고 이야기하는 것이 아마 창의적인 표현의 가장 초기 형태였을 것이다.

⊞ 기출 POINT

그림과 이야기하기는 창의적인 표현이라고 할 수 있다. expression은 자신의 생각과 감정을 드러내는 것을 의미하므로 가장 적절하다.

suggestion 제안 **application** 응용 **preparation** 준비 정답_(a)

35

At the last soccer game, the _____ called a lot of offsides.

(a) referee
(b) advisor
(c) inspector
(d) supervisor

SOLUTION

지난번 축구 경기에서 심판은 오프사이드 판정을 많이 내렸다.

⊞ 기출 POINT

스포츠 경기의 '심판'은 referee라는 단어를 사용한다. inspector는 '검사관, 검열관'이고 supervisor는 '감독자, 지휘관'을 가리킨다.

offside 오프사이드 **referee** 심판 **advisor** 고문, 보좌관 **inspector** 검사자 **supervisor** 감독자 정답_(a)

36

The court _____ its original decision and freed the man.

(a) conformed
(b) restricted
(c) curtailed
(d) reversed

SOLUTION

법원은 원심 판결을 뒤집고 그 남자를 석방해 주었다.

⊞ 기출 POINT

원심 판결을 뒤집고 석방했다는 내용이 적절하다. reverse는 '결정이나 판결 과정을 뒤집다, 반대로 하다'는 의미이다. reverse a process 절차를 거스르다/ reverse the verdict 판결을 뒤집다 등으로 사용한다. conform은 '따르다, 순응하다'는 뜻이며, '확정하다'라는 뜻의 confirm과 구별해야 한다.

court 법원 **original decision** 원심 판결 **conform** (규율 등에) 맞추다 **restrict** 제한하다 **curtail** 짧게 줄이다 **reverse** 반대로 하다, 뒤집다 정답_(d)

37

Understanding the links between culture and communication is _____ for passing this linguistics course.

(a) vital
(b) fatal
(c) secure
(d) delicate

SOLUTION

문화와 커뮤니케이션의 관계를 이해하는 것은 이 언어학 과정을 성공적으로 이수하는 데 매우 중요하다.

기출 POINT

이 언어학 과정을 이수하는 데 문화와 커뮤니케이션의 관계를 이해하는 것이 극히 중요하다는 내용이 알맞다. '아주 중요한'에 해당하는 단어가 vital이다. 생명과 관련된 이 단어는 be vital to[for]/ It is vital (that) 등의 형태로 쓰인다.

linguistics 언어학   **vital** 중요한   **fatal** 치명적인   **secure** 안전한
delicate 섬세한; 미묘한   정답_(a)

38

Most people _____ a mortgage with a bank before they buy a house.

(a) entrust
(b) confine
(c) arrange
(d) delegate

SOLUTION

대부분 사람들은 주택을 구입하기 전 은행에 담보 대출을 설정한다.

기출 POINT

주택 구입 전에 은행에 '담보 대출을 설정하다'는 arrange a mortgage 라고 한다. entrust는 '~에게 맡기다, 위임하다'의 뜻이다. get[take out] a mortgage 담보 대출을 받다/ pay off a mortgage 담보 대출 금을 갚다

mortgage 담보 대출   **entrust** 위임하다   **confine** 한정하다   **arrange** (미리) 정하다, 설정하다   **delegate** (권한 등을) 위임하다   정답_(c)

39

The World Business Trade course is designed to teach you how to _____ sales deals successfully.

(a) hassle
(b) confer
(c) charm
(d) negotiate

SOLUTION

국제 비즈니스 교역 과정은 여러분에게 영업 거래를 성공적으로 협상하는 방법을 가르치도록 설계되어 있습니다.

기출 POINT

'거래를 협상하는 법을 가르친다'는 내용이 적절하다. 동사 negotiate 는 negotiate with의 형태로도 쓰이지만 with 없이 바로 목적어를 취하여 '~을 협상하다'의 뜻으로 사용되기도 한다. ex) negotiate sales deals/ negotiate a contract/ negotiate an agreement

hassle 괴롭히다   **confer** 수여하다   **charm** 매혹하다   **negotiate** 협상하다   정답_(d)

40

In a(n) _____ and stable family unit, a child develops a sense of personal integrity and security.

(a) fragile
(b) dainty
(c) eligible
(d) affectionate

SOLUTION

사랑이 넘치고 안정적인 가정 안에서 어린 아이는 개인적 성실성과 안전감을 키운다.

기출 POINT

바람직한 가정상에 대한 내용이 들어가야 하므로 stable과 잘 연결될 수 있는 형용사를 찾아야 한다. '사랑이 넘치는'이라는 뜻의 affectionate이 가장 알맞다.

stable 안정적인   **integrity** 성실성   **security** 안전감   **fragile** 깨지기 쉬운   **dainty** 섬세한; 까다로운   **eligible** 적임의, 적합한
affectionate 애정이 넘치는   정답_(d)

41

The protest became violent as demonstrators _____ with police.

(a) clustered
(b) pinched
(c) clashed
(d) raced

SOLUTION

시위대가 경찰과 충돌하면서 시위는 폭력적으로 변했다.

기출 POINT

clash with가 '~와 충돌하다, 싸우다'의 뜻으로 쓰였다. clash는 의견이 맞지 않아 논쟁하는 것과 싸우는 것 모두에 사용할 수 있다. cluster는 '떼를 짓다'라는 뜻이다.

protest 시위 **demonstrator** 시위대 **cluster** 떼를 짓다 **pinch** 꼬집다; 훔치다 **clash** 충돌하다   정답_(c)

42

Body weight usually _____ throughout the day, such that people have different weights at different times of day.

(a) endures
(b) acquires
(c) preserves
(d) fluctuates

SOLUTION

체중은 일반적으로 온종일 변하기 때문에 사람들은 하루 중 다른 시간대에 따라 체중이 달라진다.

기출 POINT

different weights at different times of day에 맞는 내용이 되기 위해서는 '체중은 온종일 변동한다'는 말이 와야 한다. '계속 바뀌다, 변동하다'는 fluctuate라는 단어를 사용한다. fluctuate: 계속 변화하는 상태를 나타내는 말 ex) fluctuate between A and B A와 B 사이를 왔다갔다하다/ fluctuate by A A만큼의 폭으로 변동하다

endure 견디다 **acquire** 얻다 **preserve** 보존하다 **fluctuate** 변동하다   정답_(d)

43

The baby _____ his arms toward his mother because he wanted to be picked up from his crib.

(a) enticed
(b) clutched
(c) stretched
(d) expanded

SOLUTION

아기는 유아용 침대에서 나오고 싶어서 자신의 팔을 어머니 쪽으로 내뻗었다.

기출 POINT

toward와 함께 쓰일 수 있는 단어가 들어가야 한다. wanted to be picked up에서도 힌트를 찾을 수 있다. 나가고 싶어서 팔을 어머니 쪽으로 뻗었다는 내용이 적절하다. stretch는 '쭉 펴다, 내뻗다'는 뜻으로 stretch toward(~쪽으로 뻗다)/ stretch for(~을 위해 내뻗다)/ stretch out(활짝 내뻗다) 등의 표현으로 사용한다.

crib 유아 침대 **entice** 꾀다, 유인하다 **clutch** 붙잡다 **stretch** 뻗다 **expand** 확장하다   정답_(c)

44

The first report on recent human rights abuses _____ in the country has just been published.

(a) crammed
(b) committed
(c) discharged
(d) appropriated

SOLUTION

그 국가에서 자행된 최근 인권 유린에 대한 첫 번째 보고서가 얼마 전 발표되었다.

기출 POINT

human rights abuses를 수식하는 과거분사형을 찾는 문제이다. '저지르다, 자행하다'는 commit를 써서 human rights abuses committed가 되어야 한다.

abuse 유린 **cram** 밀어넣다 **commit** 저지르다 **discharge** 방출하다, 해방시키다 **appropriate** 사용하다, 횡령하다   정답_(b)

45

Electricity, water and other utilities will be
_____ on your monthly bill.

(a) augmented
(b) transcribed
(c) solidified
(d) itemized

SOLUTION

전기, 물, 그리고 기타 공공 요금은 월별 청구서에 항목별로 명시될 것이다.

⊞ 기출 POINT

요금이 월별 청구서에 명세화된다는 내용이다. '항목별로 명시하다'는 뜻으로 itemize를 쓴다. itemize a bill은 '항목별로 청구서를 작성하다'라는 뜻이다. 요금별 명세가 나오는 청구서는 itemized bill이라고 한다.
electricity 전기 **utility** 유용물, 공익 설비 **augment** 증가시키다
transcribe 베끼다; 번역하다 **solidify** 응고시키다; 확정하다
itemize ~의 명세를 쓰다 　　　　　　　　　　　정답_(d)

46

The word "music" _____ from "Muse,"
which is a Greek word for a goddess who presides
over some form of artistic endeavor.

(a) derives
(b) conveys
(c) modifies
(d) formulates

SOLUTION

'음악'이라는 단어는 '뮤즈'에서 유래했으며, 뮤즈는 예술적인 노력의 특정 형태를 관장하는 여신을 뜻하는 그리스어 단어이다.

⊞ 기출 POINT

단어의 유래에 대한 내용이다. '~에서 유래하다'는 뜻으로 derive from을 사용한다. This word is derived from Greek처럼 수동태로도 쓰인다.
preside 통솔하다 **endeavor** 노력 **derive** 유래하다, 파생하다
convey 전달하다 **modify** 수정하다 **formulate** 명확히 말하다
　　　　　　　　　　　　　　　　　　　　　　　정답_(a)

47

Groundwater _____ has led to a national
water crisis.

(a) depletion
(b) allowance
(c) conservation
(d) reinforcement

SOLUTION

지하수 고갈로 전국적인 물 위기가 벌어졌다.

⊞ 기출 POINT

lead to는 '~한 결과로 이어지다'는 의미이다. 따라서 national water crisis가 결과이고 그 원인이 되는 내용이 앞에 나온다는 것을 알 수 있다. 지하수 고갈을 뜻하는 groundwater depletion이 정답이며, depletion of ozone layer 오존층의 고갈/ depletion of oxygen 산소 고갈 등으로 사용한다.
groundwater 지하수 **crisis** 위기 **depletion** 고갈 **allowance** 허용 **conservation** 보존 **reinforcement** 강화 　　정답_(a)

48

The venom of some species of spiders is so
_____ that a victim can die within minutes
if not treated immediately.

(a) lethal
(b) wicked
(c) terminal
(d) obnoxious

SOLUTION

일부 거미종의 독은 너무나 치명적이어서 이런 거미에 물린 사람들은 즉시 치료를 받지 않으면 수분 내에 사망할 수 있다.

⊞ 기출 POINT

so … that 구문에서 that 이하에 대한 이유가 빈칸에 들어갈 수 있다. 금방 죽을 수도 있는 정도의 독은 '치사의, 죽음에 이르는'이라는 뜻의 lethal이 적절하다. ex) lethal weapons 살상 무기/ lethal dose 치사량 terminal은 병과 관련되어 '말기의, 불치의'의 뜻으로 쓰인다.
venom 독 **victim** 희생자 **lethal** 치명적인 **wicked** 사악한
terminal 말기의 **obnoxious** 역겨운, 추한 　　　　　정답_(a)

Actual Test 4

49

British authorities are readying new laws that will give police greater powers toward _____ terror attacks.

(a) debasing
(b) thwarting
(c) immolating
(d) deteriorating

SOLUTION

영국 당국은 테러 공격을 저지하는 데 있어 경찰에 더 많은 권한을 부여할 새로운 법안들을 준비 중이다.

 기출 POINT

경찰에게 더 많은 권한을 주는데 그것은 테러 공격을 저지하는 것을 목표로 한다는 내용이 되어야 한다. '저지하다, 좌절시키다'의 뜻으로 thwart가 정답이고, thwart 다음에는 대상이나 사람 모두 올 수 있다. **authorities** 당국 **terror attack** 테러 공격 **debase** (가치를) 저하시키다 **thwart** 방해하다, 좌절시키다 **immolate** 희생하다 **deteriorate** (질을) 나쁘게 하다 　　　　　　　　정답_(b)

50

Shopping for groceries at discount stores is one way to be _____ and save money.

(a) frugal
(b) scanty
(c) scabby
(d) meager

SOLUTION

할인점에서 장을 보는 것은 검소하게 생활하고 돈을 절약하는 한 가지 방법이다.

 기출 POINT

save money와 대등한 의미로 연결되는 단어는 frugal(검소한)이다. a frugal lifestyle/ a frugal meal 등의 표현으로 사용한다. scanty는 양이나 수가 '부족한'이고, scabby는 '비열한, 경멸할 만한'이라는 뜻이다.

discount store 할인점 **frugal** 검소한 **scanty** 부족한 **scabby** 비열한, 불쾌한 **meager** 빈약한, 메마른 　　　　　　　　정답_(a)

1

Harwood University is an accredited cyber university that offers the atmosphere and environment of a traditional classroom enhanced by the added flexibility of online education. We offer bachelor's degrees in some of the most highly competitive fields, such as business administration, education, human services and information technology. Now you can obtain a diploma even if you work full time or live a busy life. Harwood University can ＿＿＿＿＿＿＿＿＿＿＿.

(a) guarantee a high salary
(b) fit education into your life
(c) train you for a medical career
(d) supply technological assistance

SOLUTION

하우드 대학은 전통적인 교실 분위기와 환경에 온라인 교육의 유연성을 더한 개선된 공인 사이버 대학입니다. 저희는 경영, 교육, 인사 및 정보기술 등 가장 경쟁력 있는 일부 분야에 학사 학위를 제공합니다. 이제 여러분은 정규직으로 직장에 근무하거나 생활이 바쁘더라도 학위를 취득할 수 있습니다. 하우드 대학은 교육을 당신의 삶에 맞추어 드릴 수 있습니다.

기출 POINT
사이버 대학에 대한 소개로 온라인에서 학위를 취득하는 과정에 대한 설명이다. 마지막 문장에서 full time으로 일하거나 생활이 바쁘더라도 학위를 취득할 수 있다고 했으므로 빈칸에 들어갈 내용은 (b)가 적절하다.
accredited 공인된　**atmosphere** 분위기　**enhance** 개선하다
flexibility 유연성　**bachelor's degree** 학사 학위　**competitive**
경쟁력 있는　**business administration** 경영　**obtain** 취득하다
diploma 학위　　　　　　　　　　　　　　　　　정답_(b)

2

Aristotle once said that philosophy begins by ＿＿＿＿＿＿＿＿＿＿＿. If this is so, then children must be the world's greatest philosophers because children are known to ask questions that are not always easy for adults to answer. For example, "Why do people exist? Why was I born a human and not a frog?" or "What was the name of the world's first person?" are questions a child might ask. Although these questions seem simple, they raise some very complex philosophical issues.

(a) reading widely
(b) asking questions
(c) offering criticism
(d) expressing wonder

SOLUTION

아리스토텔레스는 한때 철학의 시작은 질문을 던지는 것이라고 이야기했다. 만약 이것이 사실이라면 아이들은 항상 성인들이 대답하기 쉬운 것들을 질문하는 것은 아니므로 세계 최고의 철학가들임에 틀림없다. 예를 들면, '사람들은 왜 존재해요? 왜 나는 개구리가 아니라 인간으로 태어났나요?' 혹은 '인류 최초의 사람은 이름이 뭐였나요?'와 같은 질문들은 어린 아이가 물어볼 수 있는 것들이다. 이 질문들은 단순해 보이지만 어떤 매우 복잡한 철학적 문제를 제기한다.

기출 POINT
빈칸 다음에 이어지는 내용에서 철학이 시작되는 방법을 찾아야 한다. 필자는 질문을 하기 때문에 아이들이 가장 위대한 철학자이며 그런 질문의 예를 들어주고 있다. 따라서 철학은 질문을 던지는 것에서 시작한다는 말이 도입문이 되어야 하므로 정답은 (b).
philosophy 철학　**exist** 존재하다　**raise** ～을 제기하다　**criticism**
비평　**wonder** 경이로움　　　　　　　　　　　　　정답_(b)

3

In the past, a clearly defined political model existed, whereby it was easy to distinguish whether a political party was left-wing or right-wing. On the left side of politics, you had anarchism, communism and socialism, and on the right you had liberalism, conservatism and fascism. Today, this model _____. Several other ideologies have emerged that do not readily fit into either the left or right side of politics, such as populism, libertarianism and environmentalism.

(a) is the standard used by the media
(b) clearly represents public opinion
(c) tends to be followed too closely
(d) does not reflect current trends

SOLUTION

과거에는 명확하게 정의된 정치 모델이 존재했고, 이에 따라 한 정당이 좌익인지 우익인지 구별하기 쉬웠다. 좌익 정치에는 무정부주의, 공산주의와 사회주의가, 그리고 우익에는 자유주의, 보수주의와 파시즘이 있었다. 오늘날 이 모델은 현 추세를 반영하지 않는다. 인민주의, 자유옹호론과 환경 보호주의 등 좌익 정치에도 우익 정치에도 쉽게 들어맞지 않는 몇몇 사상들이 생겨났다.

⊞ 기출 POINT

In the past와 Today로 시작되는 두 부분으로 나뉘는 구조로 과거와 현대의 정치 모델을 비교하는 글이다. 현대의 사상들은 좌익 우익 어디에도 맞지 않는 새로운 사상들이라는 설명이므로 과거의 좌익과 우익을 가르는 모델은 현대의 추세를 반영하지 않는다는 (d)가 정답이다.
whereby 그것에 의해 **left-wing** 좌익의 **right-wing** 우익의 **anarchism** 무정부주의 **communism** 공산주의 **socialism** 사회주의 **liberalism** 자유주의 **conservatism** 보수주의 **fascism** 파시즘 **ideology** 사상 **emerge** 생겨나다 **populism** 인민주의 **libertarianism** 자유옹호론　　　　　정답_(d)

4

Unemployment in America is on the rise while _____. Employers are hiring fewer workers because they can have their existing employees work longer hours. In the Detroit Metropolitan area, the average employee works 47.5 hours every week. But those working for the auto manufacturer Sazarn have a regular 50-hour week, and in some factories workers are putting in 60 hours a week. The United Auto Workers estimates that 59,000 automobile jobs would be created if the plants were on a recommended 40-hour week.

(a) the hours of those with jobs are growing longer
(b) the dependence on immigrant workers is rising
(c) the number of low-paid auto workers is increasing
(d) the amount of shareholder investment is
    decreasing

SOLUTION

미국에서 실업은 증가 추세인 반면 일자리를 가진 사람들의 업무시간은 점점 더 늘어나고 있다. 고용주들은 현 직원들을 더 오랜 시간 일을 시키면 되기 때문에 직원들을 덜 채용하고 있다. 디트로이트 지역에서 직원들은 매주 평균 47.5시간 근무한다. 하지만 사잔 자동차 제조업체에서 일하는 사람들은 주당 근로시간이 50시간이며, 일부 공장에서 근로자들은 주당 60시간을 일하기도 한다. 전미 자동차 노조는 공장들이 주당 40시간 권고사항을 준수한다면 자동차 업계에 5만 9천 개의 일자리가 생길 것이라고 추산한다.

⊞ 기출 POINT

상반되는 내용을 연결하는 접속사 while이 힌트가 된다. 실업은 증가 추세이고 반면에 기존 근로자들은 더 오랜 시간 동안 일을 하고 있다는 내용이 되어야 하므로 정답은 (a). 두 번째 문장에서는 같은 내용을 부연 설명하고 있다.
on the rise 증가하는 **auto manufacturer** 자동차 제조업체 **estimate** 추산하다 **recommended** 권장된 **immigrant worker** 이주 노동자 **shareholder investment** 주주 투자　　　정답_(a)

5

Although water is the only fluid that we need to stay alive, drinking certain other fluids provides many health benefits as well. Milk, for instance, can provide you with protein and calcium, while fruit juice can give you a little in the way of vitamins and fiber. However, other fluids, such as coffee, tea, beer and soda might be categorized as unhealthy. This is because they _____.

(a) contain few or no calories
(b) contain harmful ingredients
(c) use very little artificial flavoring
(d) give you other kinds of benefits

SOLUTION

비록 물이 우리가 생존하는 데 필요한 유일한 액체이기는 하지만, 다른 액체를 마시는 것도 건강에 많은 도움을 준다. 예를 들면, 우유는 단백질과 칼슘을 제공하고, 과일 주스는 비타민과 섬유질을 제공해 줄 수 있다. 그러나 커피, 차, 맥주와 청량음료와 같은 다른 액체는 건강에 좋지 않은 것들로 분류될 수 있다. 이것은 이들이 해로운 성분을 함유하고 있기 때문이다.

⊞ 기출 POINT
문장 간의 연결 관계를 나타내는 표현을 통해 쉽게 문제를 풀 수 있다.
This is because로 시작하는 문장이므로 앞 문장에 대한 이유이다. 앞 문장은 However라는 접속사로 시작하고 있으므로 빈칸은 우유나 과일 주스가 영양 성분을 주는 것과 상반되는 내용이 되어야 한다. 따라서 정답은 (b).

fluid 액체 **protein** 단백질 **calcium** 칼슘 **fiber** 섬유질
categorize 분류하다 **contain** 포함하다 **ingredient** 성분
artificial flavoring 인공 향료 **정답** (b)

6

In 1829, a man by the name of Louis Braille _____. He developed an alphabet consisting of raised dots which represented letters and punctuation marks. By running their fingertips along the dots, blind people could read. Braille, as it later became known, was not readily accepted at first, but by 1932 it was used in many schools for the blind.

(a) began to work on a new medical treatment
(b) discovered a set of ancient writing systems
(c) started a vocational school for illiterate adults
(d) invented a system of communication for the blind

SOLUTION

1829년, 루이스 브라유라는 이름을 가진 남자는 시각 장애인을 위한 커뮤니케이션 체계를 발명했다. 그는 문자와 문장 부호를 나타내는 점자로 이뤄진 자모를 개발했다. 손가락 끝을 점을 따라 움직임으로써 시각 장애인들은 글을 읽을 수 있었다. 이것은 차후 브라유식 점자로 알려지게 되었는데, 처음에는 쉽게 받아들여지지 않았으나, 1932년에 이르러 여러 시각 장애인 학교에서 사용되었다.

⊞ 기출 POINT
전체 내용에 대해 개략적으로 소개하는 도입문이 들어가야 한다. 이후의 내용이 루이스 브라유가 만든 점자에 대한 사용법과 활용에 대한 설명이므로 도입문으로는 (d)의 시각 장애인을 위한 커뮤니케이션 체계를 만들었다는 내용이 적절하다.

consist of ~로 구성되다 **raised dots** 점자 **punctuation mark** 문장 부호 **fingertip** 손가락 끝 **vocational school** 직업학교
illiterate 문맹의 **정답** (d)

7

African art relics are increasingly valued and coveted for their intrinsic beauty and artistic merit. However, this greater appreciation has _____. Gravesites have been robbed, archaeologically sensitive areas have been plundered, and precious relics have ended up in the hands of wealthy private collectors. The problem is not a new one; ancestral sites have been pillaged and artifacts stolen for decades, despite the bans on the exportation of cultural property that exist in many African states. Now, with the soaring demand for African relics, it is likely that much of Africa's cultural heritage will disappear into private hands.

(a) had a detrimental effect on the African economy
(b) meant that African art is too expensive for tourists
(c) been a windfall for museums displaying the treasures
(d) attracted the attention of a growing number of looters

SOLUTION

아프리카 예술 유적은 그 고유의 미와 예술적 가치로 인해 점점 더 높은 평가를 받고 탐내는 사람들도 많아졌다. 그러나 그 진가에 대한 이해도가 높아지면서 점점 더 많은 약탈자들의 관심도 끌게 되었다. 묘는 약탈당했고, 고고학적으로 섬세한 지역들이 강탈당했으며, 소중한 유적들이 부유한 개인 수집가들의 손에 들어가게 되었다. 이 문제는 어제 오늘의 이야기가 아니다. 여러 아프리카 국가들의 문화 유적 수출 금지령에도 불구하고 수십 년간 고대 유적지는 약탈당했고 유물은 도난되었다. 이제 아프리카 유적에 대한 수요가 급증하면서 아프리카 문화 유산의 대부분은 개인의 주머니 속으로 사라질 것이다.

⊞ 기출 POINT

However라는 접속사가 힌트이다. 빈칸에는 아프리카 예술 유적이 높이 평가받게 되면서 생긴 좋지 않은 결과가 들어가야 한다. 약탈당하거나 개인 수집가의 소유가 되고, 도난당하여 외국으로 수출되는 현실에 대한 서술이 이어지는 것으로 보아 (d)가 가장 적절하다.

relic 유적 **covet** 탐내다 **intrinsic** 고유의 **appreciation** 이해도 **gravesite** 묘소 **archaeologically** 고고학적으로 **plunder** 약탈하다 **pillage** 강탈하다 **ban** 금지 **exportation** 수출 **soaring** 급증하는 **heritage** 유산 **detrimental** 해로운 **windfall** 뜻밖의 횡재 **looter** 약탈자

정답_(d)

8

Dear Mr. and Mrs. Brown,

Since 1980, our organization, Rural Life, has been bringing underprivileged children from their crowded urban homes to a country ranch for two weeks of fresh air and sunshine. Our research shows that _____ enriches the lives of these inner-city children and leaves them feeling healthier and more fulfilled. For only $350, you can bring joy to an underprivileged child with the gift of a rural experience. Please call our number or write to us today.

Sincerely,
Gerald R. Miller
President, Rural Life

(a) working in the inner city
(b) being exposed to rural life
(c) having a good summer job
(d) taking part in outdoor sports

SOLUTION

브라운 씨 내외 귀하,

1980년 이후로 저희 기관 루럴 라이프에서는 혜택받지 못한 어린이들을 이들이 사는 혼잡한 도시의 집을 떠나 2주간 신선한 공기와 햇살이 있는 시골 농장으로 보내주는 일을 했습니다. 저희 연구에 따르면 농촌 생활에 노출되면 이들 도심 빈민가 아이들의 삶이 윤택해지고 이들은 건강함과 충만함을 더욱 느낀다고 합니다. 단 350달러이면 귀하도 혜택받지 못한 어린아이 한 명에게 시골 체험이라는 선물로 기쁨을 선사할 수 있습니다. 지금 저희에게 전화나 편지 주십시오.

루럴 라이프 사장
제럴드 R. 밀러 드림

⊞ 기출 POINT

이 기관에서 하는 일은 혜택받지 못한 아이들에게 시골 농장 체험을 하게 해주는 것이다. 빈칸이 있는 문장은 이 활동에 대한 연구 결과를 요약하는 부분에 해당하고 연구 결과가 enriches 이후에 서술되고 있으므로 빈칸에는 기관에서 하는 일이 들어가야 한다. 따라서 정답은 (b).

underprivileged 혜택받지 못한 **urban** 도심의 **ranch** 농장 **enrich** 풍성하게 하다 **fulfilled** 충만한 **rural** 시골의 **expose to** ～에 노출하다

정답_(b)

9

Body temperature is controlled by the circulation of blood. The production and loss of body heat are balanced out by heat transfer through the bloodstream which is accomplished by _____. When the human body becomes overheated, the vessels dilate and an increased volume of blood flows through the skin. Heat is then able to spread more rapidly through the skin, dropping one's body temperature. When a person is cold, their blood vessels shrink, diverting blood from the skin to reduce heat loss.

(a) either perspiring or shivering
(b) adjusting the body's temperature
(c) varying the width of blood vessels
(d) changing the bloodstream's composition

SOLUTION

체온은 혈액 순환에 의해 통제된다. 체온의 증감은 혈류를 통한 열 전도를 통해 균형을 이루게 되고, 이는 혈관의 너비를 다양하게 조절함으로써 이뤄진다. 인체가 과열되면 혈관은 팽창하고 피부를 통과하는 혈류의 양이 증가하게 된다. 그러면 열이 피부를 통해 더 빨리 확산될 수 있어 체온이 떨어지게 된다. 사람이 추위를 탈 때는 혈관이 수축함으로써 혈액을 피부에서 멀어지게 하여 열 손실을 줄인다.

기출 POINT

빈칸 앞의 is accomplished by에 의해 어떤 작용을 통해 체온 증감이 이루어지는지에 대한 내용이 들어간다는 것을 알 수 있다. 혈관 팽창과 체온 증감 관계에 대한 내용이므로 정답은 (c).
body temperature 체온 **circulation** 순환 **heat transfer** 열 전도 **bloodstream** 혈류 **accomplish** 이루어지다 **vessel** 혈관 **dilate** 팽창하다 **volume** 양 **shrink** 줄어들다 **divert from** ~로부터 떨어지게 하다 **perspire** 땀을 내다 **shiver** 몸을 떨다 **정답**_(c)

10

Toronto will host the first in a series of anti-poverty concerts scheduled for this summer at multiple venues around the globe, which also include Tokyo and Johannesburg later in the summer. The announcement of the remaining host cities is due on Tuesday. Canadian organizers verified that the Toronto concert will be held on July 2 but would not provide any further information. The worldwide series of concerts _____. The events are aimed at those who might not otherwise fully recognize the seriousness of the issue.

(a) is likely to become an annual event
(b) should make a large profit for organizers
(c) has seen decreased attendance numbers
(d) is meant to spread the anti-poverty message

SOLUTION

늦여름에는 동경과 요하네스버그를 포함, 올 여름 세계 각국 여러 장소에서 예정되어 있는 빈곤 퇴치 콘서트 시리즈 중 첫 번째 콘서트가 토론토에서 개최됩니다. 나머지 주최 도시측의 발표는 화요일로 예정되어 있습니다. 캐나다 측 주최자들은 토론토 콘서트가 7월 2일 개최될 것이라고 확인해 주었으나, 추가 정보는 제공하지 않았습니다. 이러한 전세계 콘서트 시리즈는 빈곤 퇴치 메시지를 확산시키기 위함입니다. 이번 콘서트 시리즈는 이런 행사가 아니라면 이 문제의 심각성을 제대로 인지하지 못하는 사람들을 겨냥한 것입니다.

기출 POINT

전체 지문의 주제가 되는 문장을 찾아야 한다. 이 worldwide series of concerts는 빈곤 퇴치 메시지를 확산시키기 위함이라는 문장이 주제문으로 알맞으므로 정답은 (d). 마지막 문장은 이에 대한 부연 설명이다.
anti-poverty 빈곤 퇴치 **multiple** 다수의 **venue** 장소 **announcement** 발표 **host city** 주최 도시 **verify** 증명하다 **profit** 수익 **정답**_(d)

Actual Test 4

11

Improvisation—spontaneous creation of musical passages—has been called "the lifeblood of jazz." Yet this central jazz concept is often misunderstood by laypeople. Often they see improvisation as unrelated to any musical structure or underlying composition as if it were a musical free-for-all, played without rules or any form of restraint. This is far from the truth however. Jazz improvisation invariably involves _____.

(a) more playing from the heart than classical music
(b) following a chord sequence and preexisting melody
(c) radical experimentation beyond set musical patterns
(d) pulsating rhythms derived from African tribal melodies

SOLUTION

악절의 자연스러운 창작인 즉흥연주는 '재즈의 혈액'이라 불리고 있다. 그러나 일반인들은 이 중추적인 재즈의 개념을 오해하는 경우가 많다. 종종 이들은 즉흥연주가 어떤 음악적 구조나 기저에 깔린 음악 작품에도 연관되어 있지 않은 것으로 보고, 마치 이것이 제멋대로의 음악이며 어떤 규칙이나 제약도 없이 연주되는 것으로 생각한다. 그러나 이것은 사실과 거리가 멀다. 재즈 즉흥연주는 반드시 화음 반복 진행과 이미 존재하는 주선율을 따라야 한다.

⊞ 기출 POINT

재즈 즉흥연주의 잘못 알려진 개념에 대해 소개하는 글이다. This is far from the truth, however라는 부분에서 앞의 내용과 상반된 설명이 나올 것을 추측할 수 있다. 재즈 즉흥연주는 아무런 제약 없이 이루어지는 것이 아니라 화음의 진행과 기존 주선율을 따라야 한다는 (b)가 정답이다.
improvisation 즉흥연주 **spontaneous** 임의의 **laypeople** 일반인 **concept** 개념 **unrelated** 관계가 없는 **underlying** 기저에 깔린 **composition** 음악 작품 **free-for-all** 누구나 자유롭게 참가하는 연주 **restraint** 제약 **invariably** 예외 없이 **chord** 화음 **preexisting** 기존의 **radical** 급진적인 **pulsating** 두근거리는 **derive from** ~에서 유래하다
정답 (b)

12

I was naive to have thought that I'd find my "African-American" identity in Paris. But at that time, it seemed like a good idea. America was for me a country divided between black and white, a country that judged me only by the color of my skin. On the other hand, Paris represented liberation and equality—that is, until I got there. What I found was indifference and isolation. It's one thing to be wrongly judged because you are black, but to be completely ignored, well, that seemed somehow even worse. And it wasn't just in Paris. Generally, in Europe, a black American exile seeking freedom soon discovers _____.

(a) much less prejudice and racism
(b) that equality exists in his mind alone
(c) a desire to adopt a European identity
(d) an identity that was not available at home

SOLUTION

파리에서 '아프리카계 미국인'의 주체성을 찾을 것이라고 생각했던 나는 너무 순진했다. 하지만 당시에는 그것이 괜찮은 생각인 것 같았다. 나에게 미국은 흑과 백으로 분열된 나라, 나를 단지 내 피부색으로만 판단하는 나라였다. 반면, 파리는 해방과 평등을 대변했다. 하지만 이것은 내가 그곳에 도착하기 전까지의 얘기다. 내가 발견한 것은 무관심과 고립이었다. 흑인이라는 이유로 부당한 판단을 받는 것과, 완전히 무시당하는 것 중 아무래도 후자가 더 나쁜 것 같았다. 그리고 이것은 단지 파리에서만 그런 것이 아니었다. 일반적으로 유럽에서 자유를 찾아 망명하는 흑인 미국인들은 평등이란 자신들의 머릿속에나 있다는 것을 곧 발견하게 된다.

⊞ 기출 POINT

해방과 평등을 찾아 망명의 길을 떠난 주인공의 절망적인 깨달음은 어디를 가든 흑인이라는 정체성에서 자유로울 수 없다는 사실이므로 (b)가 정답이다.
naive 순진한 **identity** 주체성 **liberation** 해방 **equality** 평등 **isolation** 고립 **exile** 망명 **prejudice** 편견 **racism** 인종주의
정답 (b)

13

The revolution in art that impressionism represented did not arise solely from the artistic skills of key individual painters. Other historic forces were also at play. For one thing, impressionism emerged after half a century of some of the most dramatic innovations in pigment manufacturing that the visual arts had ever seen. This meant that new materials were presenting artists with new possibilities. Impressionist painters could not have produced what they did _____.

(a) without the introduction of new materials
(b) if the wealthy had not purchased their art
(c) without the ingenuity of masters like Monet
(d) if fine arts academies had not supported them

SOLUTION

인상주의로 대변되었던 예술의 혁명은 주요 개별 화가들의 예술적 기술에서만 생겨난 것은 아니었다. 다른 역사적인 힘도 작용했다. 첫째는, 인상주의는 도료 제조에 있어 시각 예술이 경험한 가장 극적인 몇 가지 혁신이 일어난 지 반세기 이후 생겨났다. 이는 새로운 재료들이 화가들에게 새로운 가능성을 열어주었다는 것을 의미했다. 인상파 화가들은 새로운 재료의 도입이 없었다면 자신들의 작품을 창작할 수 없었을 것이다.

🏛 기출 POINT
도입문에서 인상주의는 화가들의 예술적 기술에 의해서만 생겨난 것이 아니라는 측면을 언급한다. 거기에는 Other historic forces가 있으며 그 중 하나로 재료의 혁신적인 변화를 들고 있다. 새로운 재료의 도입이 없었더라면 인상파 화가들의 창작은 어려웠을 것이라는 (a)가 가장 적절하다.
revolution 혁명 **impressionism** 인상주의 **represent** 대표하다
solely 오직 **emerge** 발생하다 **innovation** 혁신 **pigment** 도료
manufacturing 제조 **visual art** 시각 예술 **purchase** 구매하다
ingenuity 창의력   정답 (a)

14

The Food and Drug Administration (FDA) is alerting healthcare experts and patients treated with Ruxate to reports of an increased risk of a fatal central nervous system viral infection. Patients presently being treated with Ruxate, who experience any significant changes in vision, balance or coordination, are advised to promptly consult their physician. While the medication has not yet been recalled, the FDA is working with Healthtech, the drug's sponsor, to gather data on risk potential. In addition, the FDA is also asking all healthcare professionals to _____.

(a) contact Healthtech regarding alternative drug and treatment options
(b) prescribe Ruxate for viruses afflicting the central nervous system
(c) report any adverse events associated with the drug
(d) administer the drug to prevent further complications

SOLUTION

식품의약청(FDA)은 의학 전문가와 럭세이트로 치료를 받고 있는 환자들을 대상으로 치명적인 중추 신경계 바이러스 감염 위험이 증가하고 있다는 보고서에 대해 주의를 환기시키고 있다. 현재 럭세이트로 치료를 받고 있는 환자들 중에 시력이나 균형감각, 혹은 협응에 상당한 변화를 경험한 환자들은 신속하게 담당 주치의와 상담할 것을 권고한다. 본 의약품에 대한 리콜은 아직 시행되지 않았으나, 식약청은 이 약의 후원사인 헬스테크와 함께 잠재적 위험에 대한 자료를 수집 중이다. 추가적으로 식약청은 전 의료 전문가들에 대해 이 의약품과 관련된 부정적인 사건 일체를 보고해 줄 것을 요청하고 있다.

🏛 기출 POINT
럭세이트라는 의약품의 부작용과 위험성에 대한 내용이다. 중추 신경계 바이러스 감염 위험이 있고, 현재 리콜은 하지 않았지만 잠재적인 위험성에 대한 자료를 수집 중이라는 설명이다. In addition 다음에는 앞의 내용과 비슷한 맥락이 될 것을 추측할 수 있으므로 (c)가 정답이다.
alert 경고하다 **fatal** 치명적인 **central nervous system** 중추 신경계
viral infection 바이러스 감염 **significant** 상당한 **coordination**
협응 **promptly** 즉시 **medication** 의약품 **potential** 잠재적인
alternative 대체적인 **adverse** 부정적인 **administer** 관리하다
정답 (c)

15

British ministers have been criticized for "misleading" the public regarding the success of their city academies program. An evaluation of the first 11 privately sponsored academies by consultants at Watson & Company shows that the academies are not functioning as effectively as expected. _____, the government dismisses such accusations, maintaining that academies a indeed bringing about "noteworthy changes" to conventional classroom culture. The academies, costing an average of 25 million dollars to build, were established to raise education levels in impoverished urban areas.

(a) However
(b) Similarly
(c) Therefore
(d) Otherwise

SOLUTION

영국 장관들은 자신들의 도시 학원 프로그램의 성공과 관련, 대중을 '오도'하는 것으로 비난받아 왔다. 최초로 민간 후원을 받은 학원 11개소에 대한 왓슨 앤 컴퍼니 소속 컨설턴트들의 평가에 따르면 이 학원들은 기대했던 것만큼 효과적인 역할을 하지 않고 있음을 알 수 있다. 그러나 정부는 학원들이 실로 재래식 교실 문화에 '주목할 만한 변화'를 일으키고 있다고 주장하며, 이 같은 비판을 일축하고 있다. 건축에 평균 2천 5백만 달러가 소요되는 이들 학원은 빈곤에 허덕이는 도심 지역 교육 수준을 높이기 위해 설립되었다.

🏷 기출 POINT

접속사를 고르는 문제는 앞뒤 문맥의 관계를 파악해야 한다. 학원이 예상만큼 효과적인 역할을 하지 못한다는 내용과 정부는 이러한 비난을 일축하고 학원 프로그램이 주목할 만한 변화를 일으키고 있다고 주장하는 내용은 상반되므로 역접의 However가 들어가야 흐름이 자연스럽다.
minister 장관 **criticize** 비난하다 **mislead** 오도하다 **evaluation** 평가 **consultant** 컨설턴트 **dismiss** 일축하다 **accusation** 비난 **noteworthy** 주목할 만한 **conventional** 재래식의 **impoverished** 빈곤한
정답_(a)

16

The way your goals are picked is as important as the goals themselves. If you allow others to pick your goals for you, your chances of not measuring up will increase greatly. _____, if you take a strong leadership role in setting your goals, you will have a better success rate because you will know better than anyone else what is right for you and what you can conceivably accomplish.

(a) On the other hand
(b) In the meantime
(c) For instance
(d) In any case

SOLUTION

목표를 설정하는 방식은 목표 자체만큼이나 중요하다. 다른 사람이 당신의 목표를 대신 설정할 수 있게 한다면, 목표를 달성하지 못할 확률은 매우 높아질 것이다. 반면, 목표를 설정하는 데 강한 주도적 역할을 한다면, 그 누구보다 당신에게 맞고 당신이 성취할 수 있는 것을 잘 알 것이므로 성공률도 높아질 것이다.

🏷 기출 POINT

자신이 스스로 목표를 정했을 때의 장점을 부각시키기 위한 글이다. 연결어 앞과 뒤는 If로 시작하는 두 가지 내용이 제시되어 있는데 다른 사람이 당신의 목표를 정해 주었을 때와 스스로 목표를 정했을 때를 대조하고 있다. 대조하는 두 내용이므로 On the other hand가 정답이다.
measure up ~에 들어맞다, 부합되다 **success rate** 성공률 **conceivably** 생각할 수 있게 **accomplish** 성취하다 **in the meantime** 그 사이에
정답_(a)

17

One day last May, photographers from across the US—rookies and Pulitzer Prize winners alike—were invited to tell the story of their lives, their communities and what it means to be American through digital photographs. The stunningly compelling images from this historic shoot, alongside essays by prominent writers, are now compiled in *One Day in America*, one of the most anticipated publications of the year.

Q What is the advertisement about?
(a) A tourist guide for America
(b) A book of photos and essays
(c) A guide to good photography
(d) Pictures of celebrated landmarks

SOLUTION

지난 5월 어느 날, 신인, 퓰리처상 수상 작가 할 것 없이 미국 전역의 사진가들은 디지털 사진을 통해 자신들의 인생 이야기, 지역사회 이야기, 그리고 미국인이라는 것의 의미에 대해 이야기하는 자리에 초청을 받았다. 유명 작가들의 수필이 곁들여진 놀랄 만큼 매혹적인 이 역사적 촬영의 산물은 이제 올해 가장 기대되는 출간물 중 하나인 〈미국에서의 하루〉로 편찬되었다.

Q 무엇에 대한 광고인가?
(a) 미국 관광객 가이드
(b) 사진과 수필 서적
(c) 훌륭한 사진술에 대한 지침
(d) 명소 사진

⊞ 기출 POINT
마지막 부분 one of the most anticipated publications에서 출간물임을 알 수 있다. 사진과 유명한 작가들의 에세이가 결합된 책이라는 설명을 볼 때 (b)의 사진과 수필 서적이 광고 대상임을 알 수 있다.
rookie 초보자 **Pulitzer Prize** 퓰리처상 **community** 지역사회
stunningly 놀랄 만큼 **compelling** 흥미로운, 매력적인 **shoot** 촬영
alongside 곁들여진 **prominent** 유명한 **compile** 편찬하다
anticipated 기대되는   정답 _(b)

18

Preschool teachers must be aware of classroom dynamics and the ways children interact at all times. At the preschool level, groups should be small, with children in pairs or trios. In most cases, groups of four or more are too large. Note that group diversity should be maximized. Children of different ability levels, genders, language skills, and ethnic and cultural backgrounds should be mixed together.

Q What is the topic of the passage?
(a) The types of afterschool activities for preschoolers
(b) The ideal size and composition of preschool groups
(c) The need to expose preschoolers to foreign cultures
(d) The problems preschoolers have in new environments

SOLUTION

유치원 교사들은 교실 역학과 아이들이 상호 작용하는 방식을 항상 인지하고 있어야 한다. 유치원 수준에서 그룹의 규모는 작아야 하고, 아이들은 두 명이나 세 명씩 짝지어 주어야 한다. 대부분의 경우 네 명 이상으로 구성된 그룹은 너무 크다. 그룹 다양성을 극대화해야 함에 유의하라. 능력, 성별, 언어 능력, 그리고 인종적·문화적 배경이 다른 어린이들이 함께 섞여 있어야 한다.

Q 지문의 주제는?
(a) 유치생들을 위한 방과 후 활동의 종류
(b) 유치원 그룹의 이상적인 크기와 구성
(c) 유치원생들이 외국 문화에 노출될 필요성
(d) 새로운 환경 속에서 유치원생들이 겪는 문제점들

⊞ 기출 POINT
유치원 교사들은 항상 아이들과 상호 작용하는 방식을 알고 있어야 한다는 도입문으로 시작하여 아이들을 몇 명의 소그룹으로 만들어 주어야 하고 다른 배경을 가진 다양한 아이들이 같이 섞일 수 있는 그룹이 되어야 한다는 내용이므로 (b)가 주제이다.
be aware of ~을 알다 **interact with** ~과 상호 작용하다 **trio** 세 명
diversity 다양성 **maximize** 극대화되다 **gender** 성 **ethnic** 인종적인
                                                          정답 _(b)

19

Trying to figure out which insurance plan is right for you? WowInsurance is a free service that allows you to compare hundreds of the nation's leading life insurance companies in just a few easy steps. We have the nation's fastest and easiest online service to compare insurance rates from the largest pool of life insurance companies available. Just log on to wowinsurance.com and see for yourself. Helping you make a smart and informed decision about your insurance needs is always our biggest priority!

Q   What is being advertised?
(a) An insurance company providing the lowest rates
(b) A company selling life insurance over the Internet
(c) A search tool for locating local insurance
     companies
(d) An online service offering insurance rate
     comparisons

SOLUTION

어떤 보험상품이 적합한지 파악하는 중인가요? 와우 보험은 전국 유수의 생명 보험사 수백 개를 단지 몇 가지 쉬운 절차만으로 비교할 수 있는 무료 서비스입니다. 저희는 가장 방대한 생명 보험사 목록으로부터 보험료를 국내에서 가장 빠르고 가장 쉽게 비교할 수 있는 온라인 서비스를 갖추고 있습니다. wowinsurance.com에 접속하셔서 직접 눈으로 확인하십시오. 여러분의 보험 수요에 대해 현명하고 정확한 정보에 근거한 결정을 내릴 수 있도록 돕는 것이 저희의 최우선 사항입니다!

Q   무엇을 광고하고 있는가?
(a) 최저가를 제공하는 보험회사
(b) 인터넷에서 생명 보험을 판매하는 회사
(c) 지역 보험회사를 찾아주는 검색 도구
(d) 보험료를 비교해 주는 온라인 서비스

기출 POINT
광고하는 것은 국내 유수한 보험회사의 보험료를 무료로 비교할 수 있는 사이트이다. 세 번째 문장 compare insurance rates를 통해 (d)가 정답임을 알 수 있다. easiest online service에만 집중하여 (b)를 답으로 하지 않도록 주의한다.

figure out 파악하다 **insurance rate** 보험료 **pool** 공동 이용 시설, 목록
log on ~에 접속하다 **priority** 최우선 사항 정답_(d)

20

Dear Mr. Kim:

We received details from Mr. Lee, who has recently returned home from your country, stating that you would be interested in our electric fans. The enclosed catalogue will give you information on our complete product line. Please note that for payments we require that all transactions be based on an irrevocable letter of credit. We look forward to hearing from you soon.

Sincerely,
Tina Collins
Manager, Electric Fans Corporation

Q   What is the purpose of the letter?
(a) To return a shipment of a product
(b) To process import taxes and duties
(c) To check on a customer's line of credit
(d) To inform Mr. Kim about products and payment

SOLUTION

김 선생님 귀하

얼마 전 김 선생님이 계신 곳에서 돌아온 이 선생님으로부터 김 선생님께서 저희 전기 선풍기에 관심이 있다는 말을 들었습니다. 동봉한 카탈로그를 보시면 저희의 전 취급 제품에 대한 정보를 얻을 수 있을 것입니다. 결제와 관련해 저희의 모든 거래는 취소 불능 신용장을 기반으로 할 것을 요구하고 있음을 유념하십시오. 곧 김 선생님으로부터 회신을 받을 수 있기를 기대합니다.

전기 선풍기 회사 매니저
티나 콜린스 드림

Q   편지의 목적은?
(a) 발송 제품 반품
(b) 수입세와 관세 처리
(c) 고객 신용 한도 확인
(d) 김 선생님에게 제품과 지불에 대한 정보 제공

기출 POINT
편지를 쓴 의도를 묻는 문제이다. 우선 편지의 수신자와 발신자를 확인하면 내용을 더욱 빠르게 이해할 수 있다. 선풍기 회사에서 고객에게 보낸 편지로 카탈로그를 동봉하면서 제품과 지불에 대한 정보를 주고 있으므로 정답은 (d).

electric fan 선풍기 **enclosed** 동봉한 **transaction** 거래
irrevocable 취소 불능의 **letter of credit** 신용장 **shipment** 발송
import tax 수입세 **duties** 관세 **line of credit** 신용 한도 정답_(d)

21

Due to the easy access to so many images on the Internet, copyright owners' rights to these images are often forgotten. Pursuing offenders can be costly and has often not been undertaken. But now, technology is catching up with image thieves. Some copyrighted images are now encoded with a digital watermark so that it is possible to detect their unlawful use if they are published without the owners' consent.

Q What is the passage mainly about?
(a) A new method for protecting copyrights
(b) The need to be careful about copyrights
(c) The best way to download images free
(d) Software for enhancing image quality

SOLUTION

인터넷상의 너무 많은 이미지에 쉽게 접근할 수 있게 되면서 이들 이미지에 대한 저작권 소유자의 권리는 잊히는 경우가 많다. 위반한 사람들을 추적하는 데는 비용이 많이 들 수 있고, 수사에 착수하지 않는 경우가 많았다. 하지만 이제 기술이 이미지 도둑들을 잡고 있다. 일부 저작권으로 보호된 이미지는 이제 디지털 워터마크가 내장되었기 때문에 소유권자의 동의 없이 유통될 경우 불법 사용을 탐지하는 것이 가능하다.

Q 지문의 주된 내용은?
(a) 저작권 보호를 위한 새로운 방법
(b) 저작권에 대해 신중해야 할 필요성
(c) 이미지를 무료로 다운로드 받는 최선의 방법
(d) 이미지 품질을 향상시키는 소프트웨어

⊞ 기출 POINT
저작권을 보호할 수 있는 새 방법에 대한 지문으로 크게 두 부분으로 나눌 수 있다. 앞 부분은 저작권이 있는 이미지를 사용하는 위반자들이 있다는 내용이고 But now이후에는 digital watermark라는 기술로 불법 사용을 탐지할 수 있게 되었다는 내용이므로 정답은 (a)이다.
access 접근 **copyright** 저작권 **pursue** 추적하다 **offender** 위반자 **encode** 암호화하다 **detect** 탐지하다 **unlawful** 불법적인 **consent** 동의
정답 _(a)

22

The next edition of Channel 10's most acclaimed program, *Insight*, looks at a highly classified spy agency in order to disclose how government organizations use surveillance technologies to monitor dissident citizens. Raw interviews with ex-spies, as well as with scientists who have developed voice recognition software, provide a flabbergasting insight into the new paradigm of "information warfare." Check your local listings for more details and the program schedule.

Q What is the program mainly about?
(a) Personal confessions of former spies
(b) A look at warfare from a spy's point of view
(c) Methods for uncovering government secrets
(d) Technology now being used to spy on people

SOLUTION

채널 텐에서 가장 호평을 받는 프로그램인 〈인사이트〉의 다음 편에서는 정부 조직들이 반체제 시민들을 관리하는 데 있어 감시 기술을 어떻게 활용하는지 보여주기 위해 특급 기밀 정보 기관을 살펴봅니다. 음성 인식 소프트웨어를 개발한 과학자들뿐 아니라 전직 비밀요원들과의 여과 없는 인터뷰는 정보 전쟁의 새로운 패러다임에 대한 깜짝 놀랄 만한 통찰력을 제공합니다. 자세한 정보와 방영 시간은 지역별 방송 시간표를 확인하세요.

Q 프로그램의 주된 내용은?
(a) 전직 비밀요원들의 개인적 고백
(b) 비밀요원의 관점에서 본 전쟁
(c) 정부 비밀을 밝혀내는 방법들
(d) 사람들을 감시하는 데 현재 사용 중인 기술

⊞ 기출 POINT
프로그램의 의도는 in order to 다음에 제시되어 있다. 정부 기관이 반체제 시민들을 통제하기 위해 어떤 감시 기술을 쓰고 있는가에 대한 내용이므로 정답은 (d).
acclaim 호평하다, 인정하다 **classified** 기밀 취급의 **spy agency** 비밀요원 기관 **disclose** 드러내다 **surveillance** 감시 **monitor** (사람·일 등을) 감시, 관리하다 **dissident** 반체제의 **ex-spy** 전직 비밀요원 **voice recognition** 음성 인식 **flabbergasting** 깜짝 놀랄 만한 **insight** 통찰력
정답 _(d)

23

One of the oldest and simplest multi-cell forms of life on earth is worms, of which there are thousands of different kinds. Some worms eat small plants and animals, whereas others feed on decomposing matter. Still others exist as parasites inside various animals and plants, causing a number of diseases. Most types have a well-developed sense of touch and specialized organs that respond to chemicals in their surroundings. Also, many have a sense of sight, with eyes or eyespots on the head.

Q Which of the following is correct about worms according to the passage?
(a) They are difficult to recognize.
(b) There are many kinds of them.
(c) They are poisonous to animals.
(d) They lack specialized organs.

SOLUTION

지구상에서 가장 오래되고 단순한 다세포 생명체 중 하나는 벌레이며, 수천 가지 종류가 있다. 어떤 벌레는 작은 식물과 동물을 잡아먹는 반면, 어떤 벌레는 부패물을 먹고 살기도 한다. 또 어떤 벌레는 여러 동식물 안에 기생충으로 존재하면서 많은 질병을 일으키기도 한다. 대부분의 벌레는 잘 발달된 촉각과, 주변 환경의 화학물질에 반응하는 특화된 기관을 가지고 있다. 또한 많은 벌레들은 머리에 눈 혹은 안점이 있고 시력을 가진다.

Q 벌레에 대해 옳은 내용은?
(a) 알아보기가 어렵다.
(b) 종류가 많다.
(c) 동물들에게 유해하다.
(d) 특화된 기관이 없다.

⊞ 기출 POINT

벌레는 수천 가지 종류가 있고, 잘 발달된 촉각과 특화된 기관을 가진다. 어떤 벌레는 기생충으로 존재하면서 질병을 일으키므로 (c)처럼 동물에게 유해하다고 할 수는 없다. 따라서 종류가 많다는 (b)가 지문과 일치하는 내용이다.

multi-cell 다세포 **whereas** 반면 **feed on** ~을 먹고 살다
decomposing matter 부패물 **parasite** 기생충 **sense of touch** 촉각 **specialized organ** 특화된 기관 **chemical** 화학물질
eyespot 안점 **poisonous** 유해한   정답_(b)

24

A natural athlete, Terry Fox, after developing a form of bone cancer in 1980, had his right leg surgically removed from the knee down. During his recovery, he decided to do a cross-Canada run to boost cancer awareness. Terry began this "Marathon of Hope" on April 12, 1980, but his unyielding march was halted on September 1 of that year, after cancer spread to his lungs. He passed away on June 28, 1981. Today, Terry's heroic perseverance is commemorated through numerous awards, research fellowships and the annual Terry Fox Run, held in 60 nations around the world.

Q According to the passage, why did Terry Fox end his "Marathon of Hope?"
(a) Cancer progressed to his lungs.
(b) His leg was amputated above the knee.
(c) His pace caused him to collapse.
(d) Not enough money was collected.

SOLUTION

천부적 육상 선수인 테리 팍스는 1980년 일종의 골육종에 걸린 후 오른쪽 다리의 무릎 아랫부분을 수술로 절단해야 했다. 회복하는 동안 그는 암에 대한 인식을 높이기 위해 캐나다 횡단 달리기를 하기로 결심했다. 테리는 '희망의 마라톤'이라는 것을 1980년 4월 12일 시작했으나, 그의 불굴의 행진은 암이 폐로 전이됨에 따라 같은 해 9월 1일 중단되었다. 그는 1981년 6월 28일 세상을 떠났다. 오늘날 테리의 영웅적 의지는 수많은 상과 연구 장학금 및 전세계 60개국에서 열리는 연례 테리 팍스 달리기를 통해 기려지고 있다.

Q 테리 팍스는 왜 '희망의 마라톤'을 끝냈는가?
(a) 암이 폐로 전이되었다.
(b) 무릎 위쪽으로 그의 다리가 절단되었다.
(c) 달리는 속도 때문에 그가 실신했다.
(d) 충분한 자금이 모이지 않았다.

⊞ 기출 POINT

세부 정보를 묻는 문제이다. 문제에 해당하는 부분을 우선적으로 읽는다. 세 번째 문장을 보면, 암이 폐로 전이되어서 횡단 달리기를 중단하게 된 것임을 알 수 있다. progress to는 '~로 이동하다'의 뜻으로 spread to와 비슷한 뜻으로 쓰인 것이다.

bone cancer 골육종 **surgically** 수술로 **subsequently** 결과적으로
boost 증대시키다 **unyielding** 단호한 **halt** 멈추다 **pass away** 세상을 떠나다 **perseverance** 의지 **commemorate** 기리다 **progress** (~로) 이동하다 **amputate** 절단하다 **collapse** 붕괴하다   정답_(a)

25

Renovated only six months ago, Sandy Beach Resort now has a viewing deck, a new restaurant and an extra swimming pool. All rooms have been refurbished, and inside each you will find a living room with a large sofa, big-screen TV, DVD player, coffee table and decorative fireplace. Serviced by an executive ferry from midtown Manhattan, Sandy Beach Resort is your own private getaway.

Q Which of the following is correct about Sandy Beach Resort?
(a) It has different types of rooms.
(b) It was first built six months ago.
(c) It has an exclusive private beach.
(d) It provides transportation from Manhattan.

SOLUTION

6개월 전에 새 단장을 마친 샌디 비치 리조트는 전망대와 새 식당, 추가 수영장을 갖추었습니다. 전 객실을 수리했고, 각 객실 내에는 대형 소파와 대형 TV, DVD 플레이어, 커피 테이블과 장식용 벽난로가 설치된 거실이 있습니다. 맨해튼 중심가에서부터 고급 페리를 서비스하는 샌디 비치 리조트는 당신만의 은밀한 휴양지입니다.

Q 샌디 비치 리조트에 대해 옳은 것은?
(a) 여러 종류의 객실이 있다.
(b) 6개월 전에 처음 지어졌다.
(c) 리조트 전용의 사유 해변이 있다.
(d) 맨해튼에서부터 교통편을 제공한다.

⊞ 기출 POINT
6개월 전에 지은 것이 아니라 새 단장을 한 것이고, 최고급 페리를 타고 가는 조용한 휴양지이며, 맨해튼에서 리조트까지 교통편으로 최고급 페리를 제공한다는 내용이므로 (d)가 정답이다.

renovated 새 단장을 한 **viewing deck** 전망대 **refurbish** 개조하다, 수리하다 **executive ferry** 고급 페리 **getaway** 휴양지 **exclusive** 전용의 　　　　　　　　　　　　　　　　　　　　　　　정답_(d)

26

Midsummer's Eve is probably the most popular festival day in Sweden, together with Christmas. Midsummer is an old pagan celebration, dating back to the Viking era, and is celebrated on the longest day of the year (summer solstice), signifying that summer has reached its halfway point. It was originally a fertility rite to promote a good harvest in the autumn. These days it is better known as a national holiday, when family and friends meet to eat herring and fresh potatoes and to drink beer.

Q Which of the following is correct about Midsummer's Eve?
(a) It is intended to promote a high birth rate.
(b) It has been celebrated since the Viking era.
(c) It is more popular than Christmas in Sweden.
(d) It is celebrated on the shortest day of the year.

SOLUTION

하지제 전야는 크리스마스와 함께 스웨덴에서 가장 인기있는 축제일 것이다. 하지제는 오랜 토속종교 축제로 바이킹 시대로 거슬러 올라가며, 연중 낮이 가장 긴 날(하지)에 치러짐으로써 여름의 반이 지났음을 나타낸다. 이것은 원래 가을의 풍성한 수확을 장려하기 위한 다산제였다. 요즘은 가족과 친구들이 모여 청어와 신선한 감자를 먹고 맥주를 마시는 국가 공휴일로 더 잘 알려져 있다.

Q 하지제 전야에 대해 옳은 것은?
(a) 높은 출산율을 장려하기 위함이다.
(b) 바이킹 시대부터 거행되었다.
(c) 스웨덴에서는 크리스마스보다 더 인기가 있다.
(d) 연중 가장 낮이 짧은 날을 기념한다.

⊞ 기출 POINT
하지제 전야는 바이킹 시대부터 그 유래가 시작되었고 성탄절과 함께 가장 유명한 명절이지 성탄절보다 인기가 있다는 언급은 없었다. 연중 낮이 가장 긴 날인 하지에 해당되는 날이며, 원래는 다산제였으나 현재는 가족과 친구가 청어와 감자, 맥주를 함께 하는 공휴일이다. 따라서 정답은 (b).

Midsummer's Eve 하지제 **pagan** 토속종교, 이교 **celebrate** 축하하다 **summer solstice** 하지 **signify** 의미하다 **fertility rite** 다산제 **herring** 청어 　　　　　　　　　　　　　　　　　　　　　　　정답_(b)

27

In 1992, I was amazed to learn that Digitone had sent the first text message. So amazed, in fact, that in 1994 after my graduation, I did everything I could to get a job at Digitone. I was successful, and in two years I rose to become the company's product manager for text messaging. Text messaging was bigger than ever, but Digitone was not going in the direction I thought it should, and I felt confined by such a large organization. That's why in 1998, I left the company to write my book *Messaging for the Masses*. It sold 30,000 copies within a few months.

Q Which of the following is correct according to the passage?
(a) In 1994, the writer became a product manager at Digitone.
(b) The writer did not expect text messaging to be so important.
(c) The writer quit working at Digitone to write about text messaging.
(d) Working for a large organization gave the writer a sense of accomplishment.

SOLUTION

1992년, 디지톤에서 최초의 문자 메시지를 발송했다는 사실을 알고 나는 몹시 놀랐다. 실은 너무 놀라서 졸업 후 1994년 나는 디지톤에 취직을 하기 위해 할 수 있는 모든 일을 했다. 나는 성공했고, 2년 후 디지톤의 문자 메시징 상품 매니저로 승진했다. 문자 메시징은 그 어느 때보다도 큰 인기를 누렸지만, 디지톤은 내가 생각하는 올바른 방향으로 가고 있지 않았고, 나는 큰 조직에 갇혀 있다는 기분이 들었다. 그래서 1998년 나는 〈대중을 위한 메시징〉이라는 책을 집필하기 위해 회사를 떠났다. 그 책은 몇 달 만에 3만 부가 팔려나갔다.

Q 지문에 따르면 옳은 것은?
(a) 1994년에 필자는 디지톤의 제품 매니저가 되었다.
(b) 필자는 문자 메시징이 그렇게 중요해질 것이라고 기대하지 않았다.
(c) 필자는 문자 메시징에 대한 글을 쓰기 위해 디지톤을 퇴사했다.
(d) 대기업에서 일하는 것은 필자에게 성취감을 주었다.

기출 POINT

필자는 1994년 졸업해서 디지톤에 취직한 뒤 2년 후에 제품 매니저가 되었으나 회사의 방향이 자신의 생각과 달랐고 큰 조직에 갇혀 있다는 느낌이 들어서 회사를 떠나 문자 메시징에 대한 책을 쓰게 된다. 따라서 정답은 (c).

text message 문자 메시지   **product manager** 제품 매니저
confined 갇힌   정답 (c)

28

Despite the apparent chaos in the financial markets, authorities say donations are up at Crown University. Walter Knight, the university's chief financial officer and treasurer of the CU Foundation, says almost $214 million was given to the university and the foundation for the fiscal year ending June 30. Total private giving rose 12 percent from 2007, and giving among alumni and friends of the university increased by more than 15 percent—or nearly $13 million—from 2007. The university is in the midst of its largest fundraising campaign ever. The campaign, called Bright Futures, was launched in the summer of 2007 and has a target of $2.25 billion.

Q Which is correct according to the passage?
(a) Private donations to the university rose 12 percent from 2007.
(b) Alumni and friends gave the university $13 million in 2007.
(c) Bright Futures is an institution that gave huge donations to the university.
(d) The university reached the target of $2.25 billion in its donation fund.

SOLUTION

금융 시장의 표면적 혼란에도 불구하고, 당국에서는 크라운 대학에 대한 기부금이 증가했다고 말한다. 대학의 최고 재무 책임자이자 CU 재단의 회계원인 월터 나이트는 6월 30일부로 마감되는 회계연도에 약 2억 1천 4백만 달러가 대학과 재단에 기부되었다고 한다. 총 민간 기부액은 2007년에 비해 12% 증가했으며, 대학 동문과 후원자들의 기부는 2007년에 비해 15% 이상, 즉 거의 1천 3백만 달러가 증가했다. 크라운 대학은 사상 최대의 기금모금 활동을 벌이는 중이다. 밝은 미래로 명명된 이 캠페인은 2007년 여름에 시작되었고, 목표 금액은 22억 5천만 달러이다.

Q 지문에 따르면 옳은 것은?
(a) 대학에 대한 민간 기부가 2007년 대비 12% 상승했다.
(b) 2007년 동문과 후원자들은 대학에 1천 3백만 달러를 기부했다.
(c) 밝은 미래는 대학에 고액 기부를 했던 기관이다.
(d) 대학은 기부금 목표 22억 5천만 달러를 달성했다.

기출 POINT

크라운 대학의 기부금은 개인 기부액이 12% 증가했고, 동문과 후원자들의 모금은 15% 이상, 1천 3백만 달러가 증가했다. 밝은 미래라 명명된 기금모금 캠페인은 목표액이 22억 5천만 달러이고 달성 여부는 언급되지 않았다. 따라서 지문과 일치하는 내용은 (a)이다.

apparent 표면적인   **chaos** 혼란   **financial market** 금융 시장
authorities 당국   **donation** 기부금   **treasurer** 회계원   **foundation** 재단   **fiscal year** 회계연도   **alumni** 동문   **fundraising** 기금모금
launch 개시하다   정답 (a)

29

The following documents are required of minors when applying for a passport: birth certificate, marriage certificate of parents, identification cards of mother and father, and consent form signed by parents or legal guardian(s). Minors 15 or younger must come to the passport office accompanied by at least one parent or legal guardian. Minors over 15 may apply alone for a passport with a letter of consent signed by both mother and father or legal guardian(s).

Q Which of the following is correct according to the requirements?
(a) A 14-year-old need not bring a guardian to apply for a passport.
(b) Minors must bring their parents' marriage certificate with them.
(c) Minors do not need a birth certificate if accompanied by parents.
(d) A 16-year-old can apply for a passport without a letter of consent.

SOLUTION

미성년자가 여권을 신청할 때는 출생증명서, 부모의 결혼증명서, 부모의 신분증 및 부모나 법적 보호자가 서명한 동의서 양식을 반드시 구비해야 합니다. 15세 이하의 미성년자들은 적어도 부모 중 한 명이나 법적 보호자를 동반하고 여권 사무소를 방문해야 합니다. 16세 이상의 미성년자들은 양쪽 부모나 법적 보호자가 서명한 동의서를 지참하면 혼자서 여권을 신청할 수 있습니다.

Q 자격에 대해 옳은 것은?
(a) 14세는 여권을 신청하기 위해 보호자를 동반할 필요가 없다.
(b) 미성년자들은 반드시 부모의 결혼증명서를 지참해야 한다.
(c) 미성년자들은 부모를 동반하면 출생신고서가 필요 없다.
(d) 16세는 동의서 없이 여권을 신청할 수 있다.

⊞ 기출 POINT

미성년자들의 여권 신청 절차에 대한 내용이다. 15세 이하의 미성년자들은 보호자를 동반해야 하고, 반드시 부모의 결혼증명서와 자신의 출생증명서를 지참해야 한다. 16세 이상의 미성년자들은 동의서가 있으면 혼자서 여권 신청이 가능하다는 내용이다. 모든 미성년자들은 출생신고서와 부모의 결혼증명서가 필요하므로 (b)만 일치한다.

document 서류   **minor** 미성년자   **birth certificate** 출생증명서
identification card 신분증   **legal guardian** 법적 보호자
accompany 동행하다   **letter of consent** 동의서   정답_(b)

30

Dear Sir or Madam:

I read your letter yesterday from a woman seeking help for her depressed aging father. Her situation reminded me of my own, and I thought my experience could help her. In his last years, my father became depressed, and I did not know what to do to cheer him up. Then my sister-in-law came up with a wonderful idea. She assembled a collage of pictures from his life. He spent countless hours gazing at the collage with a faraway, happy expression on his face that let us know he was remembering happier times. Perhaps that woman's father would enjoy something like that as well.

Sincerely,
Mark in Westview

Q What does the writer recommend to the woman with an aging father?
(a) Making a picture collage for him
(b) Coming up with a surprise for his birthday
(c) Talking with him for hours to cheer him up
(d) Writing a letter to help him overcome depression

SOLUTION

담당자 귀하

저는 어제 우울증에 걸린 고령의 아버님을 돕고 싶다는 내용이 담긴, 한 여성이 보낸 편지를 읽었습니다. 그 여성의 상황을 읽으니 제 자신의 상황이 떠올랐고, 제 경험이 그 여성에게 도움이 될 수 있을 것이라 생각했습니다. 말년에 저희 아버님도 우울증에 시달렸고, 저는 어떻게 해야 아버님의 기분을 밝게 해드릴 수 있는지 몰랐습니다. 그때 제 처제가 멋진 아이디어를 냈습니다. 처제는 아버님이 살아오시면서 찍은 사진들을 콜라주로 만들었습니다. 아버님은 셀 수 없이 많은 시간을 꿈꾸는 듯한 행복한 표정으로 그 콜라주를 응시하며 보내셨고, 그 표정에서 저희는 아버님이 행복했던 시절을 추억하고 계신다는 것을 읽을 수 있었습니다. 아마 그 여성의 아버님도 그런 무언가라면 좋아할 것입니다.

웨스트뷰의 마크 드림

Q 필자가 고령의 아버지를 모시는 여성에게 권고하는 것은?
(a) 아버지를 위해 사진 콜라주를 만드는 것
(b) 아버지의 우울증을 극복하는 데 도움이 될 편지를 쓰는 것
(c) 아버지의 생일에 뜻밖의 이벤트를 하는 것
(d) 아버지의 기분을 밝게 해드리기 위해 몇 시간이고 이야기를 나누는 것

⊞ 기출 POINT

세부 정보를 찾는 문제는 해당 부분을 빠르게 찾아서 읽는 것으로 시작한다. wonderful idea라고 언급하는 네 번째 문장 이후에서 아버지의 사진으로 콜라주를 만드는 것을 추천함을 알 수 있다.

aging 고령의   **remind of** ~을 생각나게 하다   **cheer up** 기운나게 하다
come up with 제안하다   **assemble** 모으다   **collage** 콜라주
faraway 꿈꾸는 듯한   정답_(a)

31

Although the 5th centennial in 1992 of Christopher Columbus' first voyage to the Indies was viewed as a once-in-a-lifetime occasion to appreciate history and learn new truths, the actual event aroused more contention than enlightenment. Many arguments were discordantly raised and few discoveries were made. Surprisingly, the most controversial disputes were over this deceptively simple question: What was Christopher Columbus really like?

Q What was supposed to happen at the Columbus anniversary?
(a) Columbus' first voyage to the Indies was going to be retraced.
(b) People were expected to celebrate the past and learn new facts.
(c) The event was expected to be more contentious than enlightening.
(d) People were supposed to debate about what Columbus was really like.

SOLUTION

크리스토퍼 콜럼버스가 인도양을 최초로 항해한 지 500주년을 맞는 1992년은 역사를 올바로 이해하고 새로운 사실을 배울 수 있는 일생에 한 번뿐인 기회로 여겨졌음에도 불구하고, 실제 행사는 계몽보다는 언쟁을 불러 일으켰다. 여러 주장들이 뒤죽박죽 제기되었고 발견된 것은 거의 없었다. 놀랍게도 가장 논란이 되었던 논쟁은 크리스토퍼 콜럼버스가 정말 어떤 사람이었는가에 대한, 믿을 수 없을 만큼 단순한 질문을 놓고 벌어졌다.

Q 콜럼버스 기념일에 예정되었던 일은?
(a) 콜럼버스의 첫 인도양 항해를 되새기려고 했었다.
(b) 사람들은 과거를 기념하고 새로운 사실을 배울 것을 기대했다.
(c) 행사는 계몽보다는 논쟁을 불러일으킬 것으로 기대됐다.
(d) 사람들은 콜럼버스가 정말 어떤 사람이었는지를 놓고 토론하기로 했다.

⊞ 기출 POINT
콜럼버스 기념일에 대한 전반적인 개념이 첫 문장에 나타나 있다. 500주년 기념일은 역사를 올바로 이해하고 새로운 사실들을 배우는 것이 원래의 의도였지만 실제 행사에서는 혼란스러운 언쟁과 논란이 많았다. was supposed to로 원래의 계획이나 예정을 묻고 있으므로 (b)가 정답이다.
centennial 백주년 **once-in-a-lifetime** 일생에 한 번 뿐인 **appreciate** 이해하다 **contention** 언쟁 **enlightenment** 계몽 **argument** 논쟁 **discordantly** 뒤죽박죽으로 **controversial** 논란이 된 **dispute** 논쟁 **deceptively** 믿을 수 없을 만큼   정답_(b)

32

As a scientist, Leonardo da Vinci understood the importance of keeping scientific records better than anybody else in his time. So even if he never completed planned treatises on a variety of subjects, his undeveloped theories were contained in numerous notebooks. These were difficult for his contemporaries to comprehend, however, and that meant Da Vinci's findings were not well-known in his own lifetime. Had they been known, they would likely have revolutionized the scientific world of the 16th century.

Q Which of the following is correct according to the passage?
(a) Da Vinci's records were based on scientific experiments.
(b) Da Vinci revolutionized the 16th-century scientific world.
(c) Da Vinci's scientific theories were not easy to understand.
(d) Da Vinci completed most of his planned scientific treatises.

SOLUTION

과학자로서 레오나르도 다 빈치는 과학 기록 보관의 중요성을 당대의 어느 누구보다도 잘 이해하고 있었다. 그래서 비록 그가 다양한 주제에 대해 계획된 학술 논문을 다 완성하지는 못했지만, 수많은 노트에는 그의 미완의 이론들이 실려 있었다. 그러나 그의 동시대인들은 이를 이해하지 못했으며, 이는 곧 다 빈치의 발견이 그의 살아 생전에는 잘 알려지지 않았음을 의미했다. 이것들이 알려졌다면 16세기 과학계에 혁명을 일으켰을 것이다.

Q 지문에 따르면 옳은 것은?
(a) 다 빈치의 기록은 과학 실험에 기초를 두었다.
(b) 다 빈치는 16세기 과학계에 혁명을 일으켰다.
(c) 다 빈치의 과학 이론은 쉽게 이해할 수 없었다.
(d) 다 빈치는 그가 계획했던 과학 학술 논문 대부분을 완성했다.

⊞ 기출 POINT
레오나르도 다 빈치의 과학자로서의 면모를 다루는 내용이다. 미완의 이론들이 다수 기록되어 있었고, 그의 과학적 발견을 동시대인들은 쉽게 이해하지 못했지만 만약 이것이 알려졌다면 16세기 과학계에 혁명을 일으켰을 것이다. 따라서 정답은 (c).
treatise 논문 **undeveloped** 미완의 **contemporary** 동시대인 **revolutionize** 혁명을 일으키다   정답_(c)

33

There are many misunderstandings about Che Guevara's arrest. The US involvement in Bolivian affairs was far-reaching, but the US contribution to the military overthrow of Che's guerilla operations was minimal. To be exact, the US-trained-and-led Bolivian Rangers were responsible for capturing Che and almost routing his small forces in October 1967. However, Che's guerilla operations were already defeated prior to the arrival of the Rangers, so the role of the US was not crucial.

Q What can be inferred from the passage?
(a) The Bolivian government was largely self-sufficient.
(b) Che would not have been captured without US help.
(c) US involvement in capturing Che tends to be exaggerated.
(d) Che had already surrendered before the Rangers intervened.

SOLUTION

체 게바라의 검거를 둘러싼 오해는 많다. 미국이 볼리비아 내정에 널리 개입하기는 했지만, 체의 게릴라 작전을 군사적으로 전복시킨 데 대한 미국의 기여도는 미미했다. 정확하게 말하자면, 미국에서 훈련을 받고 미국이 주도한 볼리비아 특수 부대원들이 1967년 10월 체를 검거하고 그의 소규모 병력을 대부분 소탕한 장본인들이었다. 그러나 체의 게릴라 작전은 특수 부대가 도착하기 전 이미 패색이 짙었기 때문에 미국의 역할은 결정적이지 않았다.

Q 지문에서 유추할 수 있는 것은?
(a) 볼리비아 정부는 충분히 자족할 수 있었다.
(b) 미국의 도움이 아니었다면 체는 검거되지 않았을 것이다.
(c) 체의 검거에 대한 미국의 개입은 과장되는 경향이 있다.
(d) 체는 특수 부대원들이 개입하기 전 이미 투항했다.

🎫 기출 POINT

체 게바라의 검거에 대한 오해를 다루는 글이다. 미국이 볼리비아 내전에 개입했지만 기여도가 미미하다는 측면을 제시하고 있다. 체 게바라를 검거한 것은 사실이지만 미군의 개입 이전부터 그의 작전은 패색이 짙었다고 했으므로 (c)를 유추할 수 있다.

involvement 개입 **overthrow** 전복 **far-reaching** 광범위하게 미치는 **contribution** 공헌 **capture** 체포하다 **rout** 완패시키다 **guerilla operation** 게릴라 작전 **prior to** ~이전에 **ranger** 특수부대 **crucial** 결정적인 **self-sufficient** 지급 자족의 **exaggerate** 과장하다 **surrender** 투항하다

정답_(c)

34

The Portuguese and Spanish were not the only ones pioneering the seas in the 1400s. In 1405 when the Portuguese and Spanish still believed that sailing past Cape Bojador on Africa's west coast meant burning in boiling seas, a Chinese sailor and explorer named Zheng He was sailing far and wide throughout the Indian Ocean. Zheng opened trade routes between China and more than 20 countries, including some in East Africa and Arabia, dealing in rare and foreign merchandise.

Q What can be inferred from the passage?
(a) The Portuguese and Spanish traded with Zheng He.
(b) Zheng He brought many exotic animals back to China.
(c) The Portuguese and Spanish discovered Cape Bojador in 1405.
(d) Chinese sea exploration was once superior to that of the Europeans.

SOLUTION

포르투갈인들과 스페인인들만이 1400년대에 바다를 개척한 유일한 사람들은 아니었다. 포르투갈인들과 스페인인들이 아프리카 서안의 보자도르 곶을 지나 항해하면 끓는 바닷물에 타 죽는다고 믿었던 1405년, 정화라는 중국의 항해사 겸 탐험가는 인도양 도처를 항해하고 있었다. 정화는 동아프리카와 아라비아의 일부를 포함하여 20여 개국과 중국 간에 교역로를 열어서 희귀하고 이국적인 물품들을 거래했다.

Q 지문에서 유추할 수 있는 것은?
(a) 포르투갈인과 스페인인은 정화와 교역했다.
(b) 정화는 여러 이국적인 동물들을 중국으로 들여왔다.
(c) 포르투갈인들과 스페인인들은 1405년 보자도르 곶을 발견했다.
(d) 중국의 해양 탐험은 한때 유럽인들보다 더 앞섰다.

🎫 기출 POINT

인도양을 항해한 중국 항해사 정화에 대한 내용이다. 포르투갈인과 스페인인들이 바다를 개척한 선구자들이라고 알려져 있는데 1405년 그들이 아직 미신에 묶여 아프리카 서안을 가지 못하고 있을 때 이미 중국 항해사인 그는 20여 개국과 중국의 교역로를 열었다는 내용이다. 따라서 중국의 탐험이 유럽인들보다 앞섰다는 것을 유추할 수 있다.

pioneer 개척하다 **Indian Ocean** 인도양 **trade route** 무역로 **deal in** ~을 거래하다 **merchandise** 물품 **exotic** 이국적인 **superior to** ~보다 우세한

정답_(d)

35

Our planet's environment is in a constant state of flux. While gradual natural changes impact species only slightly, rapid changes can endanger a species' existence. And the main cause of rapid changes is invariably some form of human activity. Loss of microbes in tropical forest soils, polluted aquatic habitats and global climate changes—these are all results of human activity, and all of these can lead to the loss of species.

Q What can be inferred from the passage?
(a) Human activities need to be better managed to protect species.
(b) Rapid environmental changes are necessary for human survival.
(c) It is hard to gauge the impact of human activity on other animals.
(d) Industrial development does not affect already endangered species.

SOLUTION

지구의 환경은 끊임없이 변화하고 있다. 점진적인 자연의 변화는 종에게 약간의 영향을 주는 반면, 급격한 변화는 종의 존재를 위험에 빠뜨릴 수도 있다. 그리고 급격한 변화의 주요 원인은 예외 없이 인간 활동이다. 열대 우림 토양에서의 미생물의 상실, 수생 서식지의 오염 및 국제적인 기후 변화, 이 모든 것들은 모두 인간 활동의 결과이며, 종의 소멸을 초래할 수 있다.

Q 지문에서 유추할 수 있는 것은?
(a) 종들을 보호하기 위해 인간 활동을 더 잘 관리할 필요가 있다.
(b) 급격한 환경 변화는 인간 생존에 필요하다.
(c) 인간 활동이 다른 동물에 미치는 영향을 측정하기는 어렵다.
(d) 산업 개발은 이미 멸종 위기에 처한 종들에게는 영향을 미치지 않는다.

⊞ 기출 POINT
지구 환경의 변화 중 점진적인 자연적 변화와 달리 급격한 변화는 종의 존재를 위험하게 만든다는 내용이다. 그런데 이런 급격한 변화는 인간 활동에 의힌 것이기 때문에 환경적인 위험과 종의 소멸을 초래하지 않기 위해서는 인간 활동을 관리해야 할 필요가 있다는 (a)를 유추할 수 있다.

flux 변동 **gradual** 점진적인 **impact** 영향을 주다 **endanger** 위험에 빠뜨리다 **invariably** 예외 없이 **microbe** 미생물 **tropical forest** 열대림 **aquatic habitat** 수중 서식지 **gauge** 측정하다   정답_(a)

36

The Consumer Rights Center has revealed that a change in packaging milk is cheating consumers. Milk Factory's new plastic milk carton, modeled after the obsolete glass bottles, is the same price and height as its one-liter cardboard package, but holds 100ml less milk. Consumer Rights Center president David Russell criticized Milk Factory's packaging change "a cheap commercial trick that intends to deceive buyers" and is urging consumers to "fight back by refusing purchase of the given brand."

Q What can be inferred from the news report?
(a) Old style milk container designs keep milk fresher.
(b) Customers prefer milk in glass than in plastic containers.
(c) People have been tricked into paying more money for milk.
(d) The milk packaged in the new container is lower in quality.

SOLUTION

소비자 권익 센터에서는 우유 포장의 변화가 소비자를 기만하고 있다고 폭로했습니다. 구식 유리병을 본따 만든 밀크 팩토리의 신형 플라스틱 우유갑은 1리터들이 종이팩 포장과 가격과 높이가 동일하지만, 우유 100ml가 덜 들어가 있습니다. 데이빗 러셀 소비자 권익 센터 사장은 밀크 팩토리의 포장 변경은 '구매자들을 기만할 의도인 인색한 상업적 속임수'라고 비난했고, 소비자들에게 '해당 브랜드의 구매를 거부함으로써 맞서 싸울 것'을 촉구하고 있습니다.

Q 뉴스 보도에서 유추할 수 있는 것은?
(a) 구형 우유 용기 디자인이 우유를 더 신선하게 유지해 준다.
(b) 소비자들은 플라스틱 용기보다 유리에 든 우유를 선호한다.
(c) 사람들은 속아서 우유에 더 많은 돈을 지불해 왔다.
(d) 새 용기에 포장된 우유는 품질이 더 낮다.

⊞ 기출 POINT
new plastic milk carton에 든 우유에 대한 소비자 기만 행위를 다루고 있다. 새로운 포장의 우유는 같은 크기와 높이의 기존 포장보다 100ml가 덜 들어가 있다는 사실이 드러난 것이다. 따라서 (c)처럼 새 포장 용기의 우유는 더 많은 돈을 지불하도록 속임수를 쓴 것이라고 볼 수 있다.

reveal 폭로하다 **milk carton** 우유팩 **model after** ~을 본따서 만들다 **obsolete** 구식의 **cardboard package** 두꺼운 종이팩 포장 **criticize** 비난하다 **commercial trick** 상업적인 속임수 **deceive** 속이다 **urge** 촉구하다 **container** 용기   정답_(c)

37

One of the most significant events affecting medieval European culture was colonization. Following Europe's discovery of the Americas, Europeans at first arrogantly regarded the New World as antithetical to all that was deemed civilized. Yet the discovery of other civilizations and cultures gradually provoked debate and self-reflection; European thinkers were forced to reassess Europe's position in the world and to question all Eurocentric assumptions. This reassessment of values influenced every aspect of European culture and effectively changed it forever.

Q What can be inferred from the passage?
(a) The decline of Christianity in Europe began with colonization.
(b) Conquered American cultures regarded Europeans as uncivilized.
(c) The discovery of new cultures undermined Europe's sense of superiority.
(d) European colonization was fueled by the desire for cultural enlightenment.

SOLUTION

중세 유럽 문화에 영향을 미친 가장 중요한 사건들 중 하나는 식민지 건설이었다. 유럽이 미주를 발견하고 나서 유럽인들은 처음에는 거만하게도 신세계를 문명화된 것으로 간주되었던 모든 것과 정반대라고 여겼다. 그러나 다른 문명과 문화의 발견은 점차적으로 토론과 자성을 촉발시켰다. 유럽의 사상가들은 세계에서 유럽의 위상을 재평가하고 유럽 중심적인 모든 가정에 이의를 제기할 수밖에 없었다. 이 가치관의 재평가는 유럽 문화의 전 측면에 영향을 주었으며 유럽 문화를 실상 영원히 바꾸어 놓았다.

Q 지문에서 유추할 수 있는 것은?
(a) 유럽에서 기독교의 쇠퇴는 식민지 건설과 함께 시작됐다.
(b) 정복당한 미국 문화들은 유럽인들을 미개하다고 여겼다.
(c) 새로운 문화의 발견은 유럽의 우월감을 약화시켰다.
(d) 문화적 계몽의 욕구가 유럽의 식민지 건설을 부채질했다.

🏛 기출 POINT

유럽인들은 미개하다고 생각했던 다른 문명과 문화를 발견하면서 기존의 유럽 중심적인 가치관을 재평가하게 되었다고 했으므로 (c)의 추론이 적절하다. 문화적 계몽의 욕구 때문에 식민지 건설이 이루어진 것이 아니므로 (d)는 오답이다.

medieval 중세의　**colonization** 식민지화　**arrogantly** 거만하게도　**antithetical to** ～의 정반대인　**deem** ～라고 간주하다　**civilization** 문명　**provoke** 촉발시키다　**self-reflection** 자성　**be forced to** ～하도록 강요되다　**reassess** 재평가하다　**Eurocentric** 유럽 중심인　**assumption** 가정　**Christianity** 기독교　**undermine** ～을 약화시키다　**fuel** 부추기다
　　　　　　　　　　　　　　　　　　　　정답_(c)

38

People have always used plants to treat diseases and other ailments. (a) Today, botanists continue to search for plants that may provide new medicines, but they do it with care. (b) Botany—the study of plants—was considered to be a branch of medicine until the mid-1800s. (c) Steps are taken to preserve plant species from the risk of extinction as a result of being over-harvested for medicines. (d) Fortunately, the medicinal ingredients of most plants used for medical purposes can be synthesized, which lowers the demand for plants in the wild.

SOLUTION

사람들은 항상 질환과 기타 병을 치료하는 데 식물을 사용했다. (a) 오늘날 식물학자들은 새로운 의약품이 될 수 있는 식물을 계속해서 찾고 있으나, 이에 대해 조심스럽게 접근하고 있다. (b) 식물을 연구하는 식물학은 1800년대 중반까지 의학의 한 분야로 간주되었다. (c) 약용으로 과다 수확되어 식물종이 멸종하는 위험을 막기 위한 조치가 취해지고 있다. (d) 다행스럽게도 의학적 목적으로 사용되는 대부분 식물들의 약용 성분들은 합성이 가능하기 때문에 야생 식물에 대한 수요를 낮춰 준다.

🏛 기출 POINT

약용 식물을 과다하게 채취하여 멸종되지 않도록 조치가 취해지고 있다는 내용이다. (a)에서 with care라는 표현을 통해 약용 식물의 채취가 조심스러운 접근이 필요한 일임을 알 수 있다. 그러나 (b)의 식물학이 과거 의학의 한 분야였다는 내용은 조심스러운 접근법에 연결되는 내용이 아니므로 부적절하다. 따라서 정답은 (b).

ailment 질병　**botanist** 식물학자　**medicine** 의약품　**branch** 분야　**preserve** 보존하다　**extinction** 멸종　**ingredient** 성분　**synthesize** 합성하다　**in the wild** 야생에
　　　　　　　　　　　　　　　　　　　　정답_(b)

39

The idea that humans are the only savagely violent primates that kill their own kind no longer holds. (a) Research has found that other primates also kill their own species. (b) Some primates show "semanticity," or the use of symbols, to signify objects and actions in their communications. (c) Some even demonstrate tool-making skills to design homemade weapons. (d) Others engage in what can only be referred to as warfare-organized, proactive group coercion directed at other populations.

SOLUTION

인간이 유일하게 자기 자신의 종족을 죽이는 잔인하게 폭력적인 영장류라는 생각은 더는 진실이 아니다. (a) 연구에서는 다른 영장류도 자신들의 종족을 죽인다는 것을 발견했다. (b) 일부 영장류는 의사소통에서 목적과 행위를 나타내기 위해 의미성을 보이거나 기호를 사용한다. (c) 어떤 영장류는 수제 무기를 설계하는 도구 제조 기술까지도 보여준다. (d) 또 다른 영장류는 전쟁이라고 일컬어질 수밖에 없는, 즉 다른 개체군에 대한 조직적이고 예방적인 집단 탄압에 참여하기도 한다.

⊞ 기출 POINT

인간 외에 다른 영장류도 종족을 죽인다는 내용으로 잔인함과 무기를 만드는 기술, 전쟁으로 다른 개체군을 탄압한다는 점 등을 들고 있는데 (b)만 의사소통하기 위해 기호를 사용한다는 다른 화제를 다루고 있다.

savagely 잔인하게 **primate** 영장류 **hold** 사실이다, 유효하다 **semanticity** 의미성 **signify** 의미하다 **demonstrate** 보여주다 **homemade** 수제의 **refer to** ~라고 일컫다 **proactive** 예방적인 **coercion** 탄압

정답_(b)

40

Although Constantin Alajalov was born and studied art in Russia, the revolution there forced him to immigrate to the US. (a) During his lifetime, he was overlooked by art historians and considered a non-person by the Soviet Union. (b) He eventually established himself as a magazine cover artist, with drawings appearing on *The Saturday Evening Post* and *The New Yorker*. (c) This is a particularly remarkable achievement, as these magazines never used the same artists except Alajalov. (d) His career continued to thrive, and he became one of the most famous magazine illustrators of the 20th century.

SOLUTION

콘스탄틴 알라자로프는 러시아에서 태어나 미술을 공부했지만, 혁명 때문에 미국으로 이민 갈 수밖에 없었다. (a) 평생 동안 그는 미술 사학자들에게 도외시되었고 소비에트 연방에 의해 사람 대접도 받지 못했다. (b) 그는 결국 잡지 표지 아티스트로 일하게 되었고, 그의 그림은 〈새터데이 이브닝 포스트〉와 〈뉴요커〉를 장식했다. (c) 이들 잡지는 알라자로프를 제외하고는 같은 아티스트를 절대 두 번 기용하지 않았기 때문에 이는 특히 더 놀랄 만한 성과이다. (d) 그의 경력은 계속 번창했고, 그는 20세기 가장 유명한 잡지 일러스트레이터 중 한 명이 되었다.

⊞ 기출 POINT

러시아 태생의 콘스탄틴 알라자로프의 생애를 기술한 내용이다. 러시아에서 태어났으나 혁명 때문에 미국으로 이민 가야 했고, 거기에서 잡지 표지 아티스트로 일하게 되어 20세기 최고의 삽화가가 되었다는 내용이다. 최고의 삽화가가 되었다고 했는데 평생 동안 미술 사학자들에게 무시를 당했다는 (a)는 어색한 문장이다.

immigrate 이민 가다 **overlook** 도외시하다 **non-person** 인간이 아닌 **eventually** 결국 **remarkable** 놀랄 만한 **achievement** 성과 **thrive** 번창하다 **illustrator** 삽화가

정답_(a)

Answer Keys

🎧 Listening Comprehension

1	(d)	2	(d)	3	(a)	4	(c)	5	(b)	6	(d)	7	(d)	8	(c)	9	(d)	10	(a)
11	(d)	12	(c)	13	(b)	14	(a)	15	(d)	16	(c)	17	(a)	18	(c)	19	(b)	20	(b)
21	(c)	22	(d)	23	(c)	24	(d)	25	(c)	26	(b)	27	(a)	28	(d)	29	(d)	30	(b)
31	(a)	32	(a)	33	(d)	34	(a)	35	(d)	36	(a)	37	(b)	38	(a)	39	(a)	40	(b)
41	(a)	42	(d)	43	(b)	44	(c)	45	(b)	46	(c)	47	(a)	48	(b)	49	(c)	50	(d)
51	(c)	52	(b)	53	(c)	54	(b)	55	(c)	56	(d)	57	(c)	58	(b)	59	(d)	60	(d)

📷 Grammar

1	(a)	2	(b)	3	(d)	4	(a)	5	(c)	6	(c)	7	(c)	8	(d)	9	(d)	10	(c)
11	(c)	12	(c)	13	(b)	14	(d)	15	(a)	16	(d)	17	(c)	18	(b)	19	(b)	20	(b)
21	(a)	22	(a)	23	(d)	24	(b)	25	(c)	26	(a)	27	(b)	28	(c)	29	(b)	30	(d)
31	(c)	32	(d)	33	(a)	34	(c)	35	(b)	36	(d)	37	(c)	38	(a)	39	(d)	40	(b)
41	(c)	42	(b)	43	(d)	44	(b)	45	(c)	46	(c)	47	(c)	48	(b)	49	(d)	50	(b)

🖳 Vocabulary

1	(a)	2	(d)	3	(b)	4	(d)	5	(d)	6	(b)	7	(b)	8	(a)	9	(d)	10	(a)
11	(b)	12	(c)	13	(a)	14	(c)	15	(a)	16	(c)	17	(b)	18	(a)	19	(d)	20	(d)
21	(d)	22	(a)	23	(c)	24	(d)	25	(c)	26	(d)	27	(c)	28	(d)	29	(b)	30	(d)
31	(b)	32	(a)	33	(c)	34	(a)	35	(a)	36	(d)	37	(a)	38	(c)	39	(d)	40	(d)
41	(c)	42	(d)	43	(c)	44	(b)	45	(b)	46	(a)	47	(a)	48	(a)	49	(b)	50	(a)

📖 Reading Comprehension

1	(b)	2	(b)	3	(d)	4	(a)	5	(b)	6	(d)	7	(d)	8	(b)	9	(c)	10	(d)
11	(b)	12	(b)	13	(a)	14	(c)	15	(a)	16	(a)	17	(b)	18	(b)	19	(d)	20	(d)
21	(a)	22	(d)	23	(b)	24	(a)	25	(d)	26	(b)	27	(c)	28	(a)	29	(b)	30	(a)
31	(b)	32	(c)	33	(c)	34	(d)	35	(a)	36	(c)	37	(c)	38	(b)	39	(b)	40	(a)

TEPS

Test of English Proficiency
developed by
Seoul National University

TEPS

Test of English Proficiency
developed by
Seoul National University

수험번호 Registration No.

성명 Name
한글
한자

문제지번호 Test Booklet No.

감독관확인란

청해 Listening Comprehension

1~60

문법 Grammar

1~50

어휘 Vocabulary

1~50

독해 Reading Comprehension

1~40

주민등록번호 National ID No.

수험번호 Registration No.

비밀번호 Password

고사실란 Room No.

좌석번호 Seat No.

서약

본인은 필기구 및 기재오류와 답안지 훼손으로 인한 책임을 지고, 부정행위 처리규정을 준수할 것을 서약합니다.

답안작성시 유의사항

1. 답안 작성은 반드시 **컴퓨터용 싸인펜**을 사용해야 합니다.
2. 답안을 정정할 경우 수정테이프(수정액)를 사용해야 합니다.
3. 본 답안지는 컴퓨터로 처리되므로 훼손해서는 안되며, 답안지 하단의 타이밍마크(▮▮▮)를 찢거나, 낙서 등으로 인한 훼손시 불이익이 발생할 수 있습니다.

4. 답안은 문항당 정답을 1개만 골라 ● 외 같이 정확히 기재해야 하며, 필기구 오류나 본인의 부주의로 잘못 표기한 경우에는 답 관리위원회의 OMR판독기의 판독결과에 따르며, 그 결과는 본인이 책임집니다.

Good ●
Bad ◐ ◑ ⊗ ◉

5. 감독관의 확인이 없는 답안지는 무효처리됩니다.

TEPS

Test of English Proficiency
developed by
Seoul National University

성명 (성 · 이름순으로 기재)

성 HONG
명 GIL DONG
EX HONG GIL DONG

응시일자 : 20   년   월   일

성명 | 영문
     | 서명

단체구분

학생	일반
○	○

질문란

1. 귀하의 TEPS 응시목적은?
   (a) 입사지원   (b) 인사정책
   (c) 개인실력측정   (d) 입시
   (e) 국가고시 지원   (f) 기타

2. 귀하의 영어권 체류 경험은?
   (a) 없다   (b) 6개월 미만
   (c) 6개월 이상 1년 미만   (d) 1년 이상 3년 미만
   (e) 3년 이상 5년 미만   (f) 5년 이상

3. 귀하께서 응시하고 계신 고사장에 대한 만족도는?
   (a) 0점   (b) 1점
   (c) 2점   (d) 3점
   (e) 4점   (f) 5점

4. 최근 1년간 TEPS 응시횟수는?
   (a) 없다   (b) 1회
   (c) 2회   (d) 3회
   (e) 4회   (f) 5회 이상

직업

직업	전공	학력
공무원	인문	(재학/졸업)
교사/교수	사회과학·법학	초등학교
군인	경제학·경영학	중학교
의료인	자연과학	고등학교
자영업	의학·약학·간호학	전문대학
학생	교육	대학
회사원	예술·미술·체육	대학원
무직	기타	
기타		

직책

직책	종	직종
임원	마케팅	기관/의료직
부장	외환	전문직(과학/공학)
차장	금융	전문직(법/의약)
과장	자재구매	전문직(예술/회계/금융)
대리	공정관리	기술/정비
계장	영업관리	경영/사무직
사원	품질관리	홍보/광고
인턴	전산	종교인
기타	생산	생산/서비스
	섭외	기타
	기타	

<부정행위 및 규정위반 처리규정>

1. 모든 부정행위 및 규정위반 적발 및 이에 대한 조치는 TEPS관리위원회의 처리규정에 따라 이루어집니다.

2. 부정행위 및 규정위반 행위는 현장 적발 뿐만 아니라 사후에도 적발될 수 있으며 모두 동일한 조치가 취해집니다.

3. 부정행위 및 적발 시 당해 성적은 무효화되며 사안에 따라 최대 5년까지 TEPS관리위원회에서 주관하는 모든 시험의 응시자격이 제한됩니다.

4. 문제지 이외에 메모를 하는 행위와 시험 문제의 일부 또는 전부를 유출하거나 공개하는 경우 부정행위로 처리됩니다.

5. 각 파트별 시간을 준수하지 않거나, 시험 종료 후 답안 작성을 계속할 경우 규정위반으로 처리됩니다.

TEPS

Test of English Proficiency
developed by
Seoul National University

청해 Listening Comprehension

문법 Grammar

어휘 Vocabulary

독해 Reading Comprehension

수험번호 Registration No.
성명 Name 한글 / 영어 / 한자

문제지번호 Test Booklet No.

감독관확인란

주민등록번호 National ID No.

수험번호 Registration No.

비밀번호 Password

좌석번호 Seat No.

고사실란 Room No.

서약

본인은 필기구 및 기계오분외 답안지 훼손으로 인한 책임을 지고, 부정행위 처리규정을 준수할 것을 서약합니다.

TEPS

Test of English Proficiency
developed by
Seoul National University

응시일자 : 20   년   월   일

성 명	영문	
	서명	

학력

학력	졸업 재학 휴학				
초등학교	◯				
중학교	◯				
고등학교	◯				
전문대학교	◯				
대학교	◯				
대학원	◯				

전공

학인문·어학
사회과학·법학
경제학·경영학
자연과학
의학·약학·간호학
공학
교육학
음악·미술·체육
기타

직업

공무원
교사·교수
군인
의료인
자영업
학생
회사원
무직
기타

직종

임원
부장
차장
과장
대리
계장
사원
인턴
기타

업종

무역
외환
자금
금융
국내영업
품질관리
생산관리
전산
행정
신용
서비스
기타

직위

고위직
전문직 (과·차장급)
전문직 (과·차장급)
전문직(부·차장급)
기능직
영업
일반직
기타

단체구분

| 학생 | ◯ |
| 일반 | ◯ |

질문란

1. 귀하의 TEPS 응시목적은?
   ⓐ 입사지원 ⓑ 인사·성적
   ⓒ 개인실력측정 ⓓ 입시
   ⓔ 국가고시자격 ⓕ 기타

2. 귀하의 영어권 체류 경험은?
   ⓐ 없다 ⓑ 6개월 미만
   ⓒ 6개월 이상 1년 미만 ⓓ 1년 이상 3년 미만
   ⓔ 3년 이상 5년 미만 ⓕ 5년 이상

3. 귀하께서 응시하고 계신 고사장에 대한 만족도는?
   ⓐ 0점 ⓑ 1점
   ⓒ 2점 ⓓ 3점
   ⓔ 4점 ⓕ 5점

4. 최근 1년내 TEPS 응시횟수는?
   ⓐ 없다 ⓑ 1회
   ⓒ 2회 ⓓ 3회
   ⓔ 4회 ⓕ 5회 이상

성 명 (성 · 이름순으로 기재)

성   명 (성 · 이름순으로 기재)

E X | H O N G | G I L | D O N G

| | A | B | C | D | E | F | G | H | I | J | K | L | M | N | O | P | Q | R | S | T | U | V | W | X | Y | Z |

(성명란의 각 칸에 A부터 Z까지 알파벳 마킹란이 세로로 배열되어 있음)

〈부정행위 및 규정위반 처리규정〉

1. 모든 부정행위 및 규정위반 적발 및 이에 대한 조치는 TEPS관리위원회의 처리규정에 따라 이루어집니다.

2. 부정행위 및 규정위반 행위는 현장 적발 뿐만 아니라 사후에도 적발될 수 있으며 모두 동일한 조치가 취해집니다.

3. 부정행위 적발 시 당해 성적은 무효화되며 사안에 따라 최대 5년까지 TEPS관리위원회에서 주관하는 모든 시험의 응시자격이 제한됩니다.

4. 문제지 이외에 메모를 하는 행위와 시험 문제의 일부 또는 전부를 유출하거나 공개하는 경우 부정행위로 처리됩니다.

5. 각 파트별 시간을 준수하지 않거나, 시험 종료 후 답안 작성을 계속할 경우 규정위반으로 처리됩니다.

TEPS

Test of English Proficiency
developed by
Seoul National University

수험번호 Registration No.

성명 Name
안글
한자

문제지번호 Test Booklet No.

감독관확인란

청해 Listening Comprehension

(문항 1–60)

문법 Grammar

(문항 1–50)

어휘 Vocabulary

(문항 1–50)

독해 Reading Comprehension

(문항 1–40)

주민등록번호 National ID No.

수험번호 Registration No.

비밀번호 Password

좌석번호 Seat No.

고사실란 Room No.

뒷면 (Side 2)

TEPS
Test of English Proficiency
developed by
Seoul National University

응시일자 : 20 년 월 일

성명 / 서명

성명 (성 · 이름순으로 기재)
성: HONG
명: GIL DONG

단체구분

학생	일반

질문란

1. 귀하의 TEPS 응시목적은?
   ⓐ 입사지원　ⓑ 인사정책
   ⓒ 개인실력측정　ⓓ 입시
   ⓔ 국가고시지원　ⓕ 기타

2. 귀하의 영어권 체류 경험은?
   ⓐ 없다　ⓑ 6개월미만
   ⓒ 6개월이상 1년미만　ⓓ 1년이상 3년미만
   ⓔ 3년이상 5년미만　ⓕ 5년이상

3. 귀하께서 응시하고 계신 고사장에 대한 만족도는?
   ⓐ 0점　ⓑ 1점
   ⓒ 2점　ⓓ 3점
   ⓔ 4점　ⓕ 5점

4. 최근 2년내 TEPS 응시횟수는?
   ⓐ 없다　ⓑ 1회
   ⓒ 2회　ⓓ 3회
   ⓔ 4회　ⓕ 5회 이상

〈부정행위 및 규정위반 처리규정〉

1. 모든 부정행위 및 규정위반 적발 및 이에 대한 조치는 TEPS관리위원회의 처리규정에 따라 이루어집니다.

2. 부정행위 및 규정위반 행위는 현장 적발 뿐만 아니라 사후에도 적발될 수 있으며 모두 동일한 조치가 취해 집니다.

3. 부정행위 적발 시 당해 성적은 무효 화되며 사안에 따라 최대 5년까지 TEPS관리위원회에서 주관하는 모든 시험의 응시자격이 제한됩니다.

4. 문제지 이외에 메모를 하는 행위와 시험 문제의 일부 또는 전부를 유출 하거나 공개하는 경우 부정행위로 처리됩니다.

5. 각 파트별 시간을 준수하지 않거나, 시험 종료 후 답안 작성을 계속할 경우 규정위반으로 처리됩니다.

성명 / 서명

학력

학	력	졸업	재학중
초등학교			
중학교			
고등학교			
전문대학			
대학교			
대학원			

전공

| 인문 |
| 사회과학 · 법학 |
| 경제학 · 경영학 |
| 자연 |
| 어학 · 어학 · 교육 |
| 교육 |
| 음악 · 미술 · 체육 |
| 기타 |

직업

| 공무원 |
| 교사 / 준비 |
| 회사원 |
| 군인 |
| 의료인 |
| 자영업 |
| 학생 |
| 회사원 |
| 무직 |
| 기타 |

직종

| 고위임직원 · 관리자 |
| 전문직 (과학/공학) |
| 전문직 (보건/의료) |
| 전문직 (법률/회계/금융) |
| 기술공 |
| 사무 |
| 서비스 |
| 판매 |
| 농림어업 |
| 기능원 |
| 기타 |

직책

| 임원 |
| 부장 |
| 차장 |
| 과장 |
| 대리 |
| 계장 |
| 사원 |
| 인턴 |
| 기타 |

서울대
텝스 관리위원회
최신기출
1000

청해 Part 1&2 기출 빈출표현 50

기출 빈출어휘 500

유형 1 인사, 안부

01
M So, what have you been doing lately?
W I've been busy at work.

M 그래서, 요즘 어떻게 지내셨어요?
W 회사 일이 바빴어요.

02
M How's the new professor doing?
W She seems to get along well.

M 새 교수님은 어떻게 지내시니?
W 잘 지내고 계시는 것 같아.

03
M Hi, Janice. What have you been up to these days?
W Not much, just staying warm indoors.

M 안녕, 재니스. 요즘 뭐 하고 지냈어?
W 별로 한 것 없었고, 그냥 따뜻하게 집안에서 보냈어.

04
M Hey, Jennifer! I haven't seen you in a while.
W Yeah. It's been months.

M 이봐, 제니퍼! 못 본 지 꽤 됐다.
W 응, 몇 달 됐지.

05
M I'm really glad to have met you tonight.
W Me, too. Let's get together again.

M 오늘 밤 너를 만나서 정말 반가웠어.
W 나도, 또 보자.

06

M **How was your vacation?**

W I had a very relaxing time.

M 휴가는 어땠어?

W 굉장히 느긋한 시간을 보냈어.

07

W Hey, Ted! **I haven't seen you in ages.**

M Hi, Kathy. Yes, I've been really busy at work.

W Well, don't work so hard that you neglect your friends.

M I don't intend to.

W 이야, 테드! 너 한참 안 보이더라.

M 안녕, 캐씨. 그래. 회사 일이 엄청나게 바빴어.

W 음, 일 너무 열심히 하다가 친구들한테 소홀하지는 마라.

M 일부러 그러는 건 아니야.

08

W Hi, Philip. **How was your weekend?**

M Fine. How about yours?

W Relaxing. I just watched some movies.

M That must've been nice.

W 안녕, 필립. 주말 어떻게 보냈니?

M 좋았어. 너는?

W 느긋하게 보냈어. 영화 좀 봤지.

M 좋았겠다.

09

W Hi, Mark. **How have you been?**

M Very well. What about you?

W Oh, work has been keeping me busy.

M It's been the same with me.

W 안녕, 마크. 어떻게 지냈니?

M 아주 잘 지냈어. 넌 어때?

W 아, 회사 때문에 바빴어.

M 나도 마찬가지였어.

10

M   How long have you been here in New York?

W   Umm, nearly a week.

M   And are you enjoying it?

W   It's been fantastic so far.

M   여기 뉴욕에는 얼마나 오래 있었어?

W   음, 거의 일주일.

M   좋은 시간 보내고 있어?

W   지금까지는 환상적이었어.

11

M   I hate to leave the party, but it's getting late.

W   Thanks for coming. It was good to see you.

M   I had a good time, too.

W   I'm glad you enjoyed yourself.

M   파티를 떠나기는 싫지만, 시간이 늦어서요.

W   와 주셔서 감사합니다. 뵙게 되어 반가웠습니다.

M   저도 좋은 시간 보냈습니다.

W   즐거우셨다니 다행이네요.

유형 2   격려, 유감

12

W   Ugh! I have a terrible headache.

M   Sorry to hear that.

W   아휴, 두통이 너무 심해요.

M   안됐네요.

13

M   It's a shame Bob injured his leg. He'll miss weeks of football.

W   It's not too serious, so he may not.

M   밥이 다리를 다쳤다니 유감이다. 몇 주 동안 축구를 못할 거야.

W   아주 심각하지는 않으니까 그렇지 않을지도 몰라.

14 M It's a pity we have to work on such a sunny day.

W I couldn't agree more.

M 이렇게 화창한 날 일을 해야 하다니 애석하군.

W 내 말이 바로 그 말이야.

15 M Have you noticed the attention Peter has been paying to Janet?

W I have. It's really too bad for Sally, though.

M What do you mean?

W She was hoping to date Peter.

M 피터가 재닛한테 신경 쓰는 거 눈치챘어?

W 그럼. 그런데 샐리는 정말 너무 안됐어.

M 무슨 말이야?

W 샐리가 피터랑 데이트하기를 바라고 있었거든.

16 W It's a nice picnic, isn't it?

M It sure is. But my son seems bored.

W That's a shame. Doesn't he like picnics?

M Not really, he likes to play alone.

W 좋은 소풍이네요. 그렇죠?

M 그러게요. 그런데 우리 아들은 좀 지루한가 봐요.

W 유감이네요. 아드님이 소풍을 안 좋아하나요?

M 별로요. 혼자 노는 걸 좋아해요.

17 M How are you enjoying business school?

W Well, the truth is, I'm not. It's really hard.

M I'm sure it is. But don't give up.

W Don't worry. I won't.

M 경영 대학원 생활은 재미있니?

W 음, 그게 말이야. 실은 재미없어. 정말 힘들어.

M 물론 그렇겠지. 하지만 포기하지 마.

W 걱정 마. 포기 안 할 거야.

5

유형 3 칭찬, 감사

18
W Guess what? I was promoted to office manager.
M I'm happy for you.

W 있잖아요, 저 사무실 관리자로 승진했어요.
M 잘됐네요.

19
W Excuse me. You dropped your wallet.
M Oh, so I did. Thank you.

W 저기요, 지갑 떨어뜨리셨는데요.
M 이런, 그랬군요. 감사합니다.

20
M I wish I could draw well, like you.
W Thanks for the compliment.

M 나도 너처럼 그림을 잘 그리면 좋을 텐데.
W 칭찬 고마워.

21
M Thanks for treating me to a great dinner.
W I'm glad you liked it.

M 멋진 저녁 대접해 줘서 고마워.
W 마음에 들었다니 다행이야.

22
W Did you know that Sam got a university scholarship?
M Yes, I'm so happy for him.

W 샘이 대학 장학금을 받았다는 거 알고 있었니?
M 응, 너무 잘됐어.

23

M You look different today.

W You've noticed. I've had my hair colored.

M Oh, yes. It makes you look much younger.

W **That's nice to hear.**

M 오늘 달라 보이네요.

W 알아보셨네요. 머리를 염색했어요.

M 아, 그래요. 훨씬 더 어려 보여요.

W 듣기 좋네요.

24

W **The presentation you prepared looks great.**

M Thanks. I hope it helps in getting our proposal accepted.

W Well, it'll definitely boost our chances.

M A lot went into it, so I hope you're right.

W 네가 준비한 발표, 훌륭해 보인다.

M 고마워. 우리 제안이 받아들여지는 데 도움이 되면 좋겠어.

W 음, 그럴 가능성을 분명 높여줄 거야.

M 거기에 많은 걸 투자했으니까 네 말대로 됐으면 좋겠어.

25

W I've decided to volunteer at the hospital.

M Why did you decide to do that?

W I wanted to give something back to the community.

M **That's very noble of you.**

W 병원에서 자원 봉사하기로 했어.

M 왜 그러기로 한 거야?

W 지역 사회에 뭔가 되돌려주고 싶었어.

M 너 정말 훌륭하다.

유형4

26 M **Congratulations on completing the project!** It's a real achievement.
W Thanks, but I was only part of a team.
M Don't be modest. Your vision led the way.
W True, but many people made it a reality.

M 프로젝트 완료한 것 축하해요! 정말 큰 성취네요.
W 고마워요. 하지만 저는 그저 팀의 일원이었을 뿐인데요.
M 겸손하시긴요. 당신의 비전이 방향을 이끌었는데요.
W 그렇기는 하지만, 많은 사람들이 그걸 현실로 만든 거니까요.

유형 4 불만, 걱정

27 M I can't believe we have to work this Saturday.
W **We have no other choice.**

M 이번 주 토요일에 일을 해야 하다니 믿을 수가 없어요.
W 별 수 없잖아요.

28 M You're late! I always end up waiting for you!
W **That's not always the case.**

M 늦었잖아! 나는 항상 너를 기다리게 된다고!
W 항상 그런 건 아니지.

29 W You're late again. **What's your excuse this time?**
M My car broke down on the way.

W 또 늦었구나. 이번 변명거리는 뭐니?
M 오는 길에 차가 고장났어.

30 W I don't think we can trust the salespeople at this dealership.
M **I've got a bad feeling about them, too.**

W 이 대리점 영업 사원들은 신뢰가 안 가는 것 같아요.
M 저도 이 사람들에 대해 안 좋은 느낌이 들었어요.

8

31

M **Excuse me waitress, but my food is cold.**
W I'm sorry, sir. I'll warm it up for you.

M 아가씨, 제 음식이 차갑네요.
W 손님, 죄송합니다. 다시 데워 드리겠습니다.

32

W Excuse me, but when can I see Dr. Ashley?
M I'm afraid he's with a patient.
W **But my appointment was an hour ago.**
M I know, but we're really backed up.

W 실례지만, 애슐리 선생님을 언제 뵐 수 있는 거죠?
M 죄송하지만 진료 중이십니다.
W 하지만 한 시간 전으로 진료 예약을 했는데요.
M 압니다만 환자가 많이 밀려서요.

33

W How was the little league baseball game?
M **Awful! A terrible thunderstorm spoiled everything.**
W Oh, no. What did you do?
M We ran for cover and waited till it stopped.

W 어린이 야구 리그 경기는 어땠어?
M 끔찍했어! 엄청난 폭우가 모든 걸 망쳤지.
W 어머 저런, 너는 어떻게 했니?
M 우리는 급히 비를 피하고 나서 비가 그칠 때까지 기다렸어.

34

W What is the most serious problem in this country?
M I'd say air pollution.
W Isn't that just an urban problem?
M **Actually, it's a nationwide problem.**

W 이 나라에서 가장 심각한 문제가 뭐니?
M 대기 오염이겠지.
W 그건 그냥 도시의 문제 아니니?
M 사실 전국적인 문제야.

35

W Could you check my car?

M What seems to be the problem?

W I can't get the engine to start.

M Okay, I'll have a look.

W 제 차 좀 검사해 주시겠어요?

M 어디에 문제가 있는 것 같아요?

W 시동이 안 걸리네요.

M 알겠습니다. 제가 살펴보죠.

유형 5 의견

36

W Oh, no! Judy hasn't shown up for the audition yet!

M I'm sure she's on her way here.

W 앗, 이런! 주디가 아직 오디션에 안 나타났어!

M 오는 중일 거야.

37

W Just be yourself, and you'll do fine in the interview.

M But you know I can't take stress well.

W 평소대로 하면 면접에서 잘할 거야.

M 하지만 내가 스트레스에 약한 거 너도 알잖아.

38

M You should get your brakes checked. They're squeaking.

W I'll take it to the garage tomorrow.

M 너 브레이크 검사해 봐야겠다. 끽끽 소리가 나는데.

W 내일 정비소에 가 볼게.

39

W What's the best way to get downtown?

M You're better off grabbing a cab.

W 시내로 가는 가장 좋은 방법이 뭐죠?

M 택시를 타는 편이 나을 거예요.

40

M Look at the long line at the ticket booth.

W Maybe we should come back another day.

M 매표소에 길게 줄 늘어선 것 좀 봐.

W 다른 날 다시 와야 할 것 같다.

41

W Would you like to join me for tea sometime?

M Sounds great. Let's do that.

W 언제 저랑 차 한잔 하시겠어요?

M 좋죠. 그렇게 합시다.

42

M Do you want to go out tonight?

W Sure. We could go to our favorite restaurant.

M Actually, I'd like to do something different.

W I'm up for whatever you suggest.

M 오늘 밤에 외출할래?

W 좋아. 우리가 제일 좋아하는 식당에 가면 되겠다.

M 실은 뭔가 다른 걸 해보고 싶어.

W 네가 제안하는 거라면 난 뭐든 좋아.

43

W How do you take your coffee, Steve?

M Cream and sugar, please.

W How about Caroline?

M She likes it black.

W 스티브, 커피를 어떻게 드세요?

M 크림과 설탕을 넣어주세요.

W 캐롤라인은요?

M 그녀는 블랙으로 마시는 걸 좋아해요.

44

M Are you busy?

W No. Why?

M Let's step out for some fresh air.

W I'd love that.

M 바쁘니?

W 아니. 왜?

M 바람 좀 쐬러 밖에 나가자.

W 좋은 생각이야.

45

M How are the job applicants this time?

W Not as good as we'd like them to be.

M You aren't thinking of rejecting them all, are you?

W I can't do that. We're shorthanded at the moment.

M 이번 지원자들은 어때?

W 우리가 원하는 만큼 훌륭하지는 않아.

M 지원자들을 다 퇴짜 놓을 생각은 아니겠지?

W 그렇게는 못하지. 지금 일손이 모자라는데.

46

M How would you like your hair done?

W I'd like a trim.

M No perm or coloring?

W Nothing too fancy.

M 머리를 어떻게 해 드릴까요?

W 살짝 다듬어 주세요.

M 펌이나 염색은 안 하시고요?

W 너무 화려한 건 안 하려고요.

47

M That was a wonderful meal!

W It sure was. What did you like best?

M The smoked salmon.

W Me, too. It was delicious.

M 훌륭한 식사였어요!

W 정말 그랬어요. 제일 좋았던 음식이 뭐였어요?

M 훈제 연어요.

W 저도요. 훈제 연어가 맛있었죠.

48

M What are your career plans for after college?

W I want to get a job in a large corporation.

M Do you have any specific one in mind?

W No, I'm planning to apply to several.

M 대학 졸업 후 진로 계획이 어떻게 되니?

W 대기업에 일자리를 얻고 싶어.

M 구체적으로 마음에 두고 있는 곳이 있어?

W 아니, 몇 군데 지원해 볼 계획이야.

49

M Do you have plans for winter vacation?

W I'm thinking about going someplace warm.

M How about Phuket? The weather is nice, and it's not that expensive.

W Sounds like the kind of place I'd enjoy.

M 겨울 휴가 계획은 있으세요?

W 어디 따뜻한 곳으로 갈까 생각 중이에요.

M 푸켓은 어때요? 날씨도 좋고, 그렇게 비싸지도 않아요.

W 제가 좋아할 장소 같네요.

50

W I'm thinking of buying a treadmill.

M Don't. You'll be wasting money.

W No, I won't. I'll use it every day.

M I doubt it. You'll quit after a month.

W 러닝 머신을 살까 생각 중이야.

M 사지 마. 돈만 낭비할 거야.

W 아니, 낭비하지 않을 거야. 매일 사용할 건데.

M 글쎄, 너 한 달 후면 그만둘 거야.

☐ **What have you been doing lately?** 요즘 어떻게 지내셨어요?

☐ **She seems to get along well.** 잘 지내고 계시는 것 같아.

☐ **What have you been up to these days?** 요즘 뭐 하고 지냈어?

☐ **I haven't seen you in a while.** 못 본 지 꽤 됐다.

☐ **Let's get together again.** 또 보자.

☐ **How was your vacation?** 휴가는 어땠어?

☐ **I haven't seen you in ages.** 너 한참 안 보이더라.

☐ **How was your weekend?** 주말 어떻게 보냈니?

☐ **How have you been?** 어떻게 지냈니?

☐ **It's been fantastic so far.** 지금까지는 환상적이었어.

☐ **It was good to see you.** 뵙게 되어 반가웠습니다.

☐ **Sorry to hear that.** 안됐네요.

☐ **It's a shame Bob injured his leg.** 밥이 다리를 다쳤다니 유감이다.

☐ **It's a pity we have to work on such a sunny day.**
   이렇게 화창한 날 일을 해야 하다니 애석하군.

☐ **It's really too bad for Sally.** 샐리한테는 정말 너무 안됐어.

☐ **That's a shame.** 유감이네요.

☐ **Don't give up.** 포기하지 마.

☐ **I'm happy for you.** 잘됐네요.

☐ **Oh, so I did. Thank you.** 이런, 그랬군요. 감사합니다.

☐ **Thanks for the compliment.** 칭찬 고마워.

☐ **Thanks for treating me to a great dinner.** 멋진 저녁 대접해 줘서 고마워.

☐ **I'm so happy for him.** 너무 잘됐어.

☐ **That's nice to hear.** 듣기 좋네요.

☐ **The presentation you prepared looks great.** 네가 준비한 발표, 훌륭해 보인다.

☐ **That's very noble of you.** 너 정말 훌륭하다.

☐ Congratulations on completing the project! 프로젝트 완료한 것 축하해요!

☐ We have no other choice. 별 수 없잖아요.

☐ That's not always the case. 항상 그런 건 아니지.

☐ What's your excuse this time? 이번 변명거리는 뭐니?

☐ I've got a bad feeling about them, too.
저도 이 사람들에 대해 안 좋은 느낌이 들었어요.

☐ Excuse me waitress, but my food is cold. 아가씨, 제 음식이 차갑네요.

☐ But my appointment was an hour ago.
하지만 한 시간 전으로 진료 예약을 했는데요.

☐ Awful! A terrible thunderstorm spoiled everything.
끔찍했어! 엄청난 폭우가 모든 걸 망쳤지.

☐ Actually, it's a nationwide problem. 사실 전국적인 문제야.

☐ What seems to be the problem? 어디에 문제가 있는 것 같아요?

☐ I'm sure she's on her way here. 오는 중일 거야.

☐ Just be yourself. 평소대로 해.

☐ You should get your brakes checked. 너 브레이크 검사해 봐야겠다.

☐ What's the best way to get downtown? 시내로 가는 가장 좋은 방법이 뭐죠?

☐ Maybe we should come back another day. 다른 날 다시 와야 할 것 같다.

☐ Would you like to join me for tea sometime? 언제 저랑 차 한잔 하시겠어요?

☐ I'm up for whatever you suggest. 네가 제안하는 거라면 난 뭐든 좋아.

☐ How do you take your coffee? 커피를 어떻게 드세요?

☐ Let's step out for some fresh air. 바람 좀 쐬러 밖에 나가자.

☐ How are the job applicants this time? 이번 지원자들은 어때?

☐ How would you like your hair done? 머리를 어떻게 해 드릴까요?

☐ What did you like best? 가장 좋았던 것이 뭐예요?

☐ I'm planning to apply to several. 몇 군데 지원해 볼 계획이야.

☐ Do you have plans for winter vacation? 겨울 휴가 계획은 있으세요?

☐ I'm thinking of buying a treadmill. 러닝 머신을 살까 생각 중이야.

A

- abandon 버리다
- abhorrence 혐오
- abrupt 갑작스러운
- absorb 흡수하다
- abstract 추상적인
- abundant 풍부한
- abuse 남용; 학대하다
- acclaim 호평; 인정하다
- accommodate 배려하다; 수용하다
- accredited 공인된
- accuse 비난하다; 고발하다
- acrimonious 신랄한
- acute 급성의
- adamantly 철저히
- adaptation 각색; 적응
- adherent 신봉자
- adjust 조정하다
- administration 행정부
- adorn 꾸미다
- adverse 부정적인
- advocate 옹호자

- aesthetic 미학적인
- ailment 질병
- airlock 기밀구역
- alongside 곁들여진
- alter 바꾸다
- alteration 변경
- altercation 언쟁
- alumnus 동문(pl. alumni)
- amicable 우호적인
- ample 풍부한
- amputate 절단하다
- anguish 고충
- annex 첨가하다
- anonymity 익명성
- antibiotic 항생물질
- ape 유인원
- apparently 분명히
- appeased 진정된
- application 응용
- appreciation 이해도; 감사
- appropriate 횡령하다; 적절한
- archaeology 고고학

□ **architecture** 건축학

□ **armed** 무장한

□ **arrogantly** 거만하게

□ **artery** 동맥

□ **assert** 주장하다

□ **assess** 평가하다

□ **asset** 자산

□ **assign** 배정하다, 할당하다

□ **attendant** 수행원; 참석자

□ **authenticity** 진실성, 신뢰성

B

□ **bewildering** 당혹스러운

□ **biased** 편향된

□ **blur** 흐려지다

□ **boost** 후원하다; (사기를) 돋우다

□ **botanist** 식물학자

□ **brandish** 휘두르다

□ **brash** 건방진

□ **breakthrough** 돌파, 큰 발전

□ **brink** 직전, 가장자리

□ **browse** 둘러보다

□ **brutally** 잔인하게

□ **budding** 신생의; 싹트는

C

□ **carnivorism** 육식주의

□ **censor** 검열하다

□ **chemotherapy** 화학요법

□ **circumvent** 피하다, 우회하다

□ **coercion** 강압

□ **commitment** 의무, 책임; 헌신

□ **communism** 공산주의

□ **compelling** 흥미로운; 매력적인

□ **compensate** 보상하다

□ **compile** 수집하다, 집필하다

□ **comprise** 차지하다

□ **compromise** 타협하다

□ **compulsory** 의무적인

□ **conceive** 구상하다; 잉태하다

□ **condensation** 응축

□ **condolence** 조의

□ **confer** 수여하다

□ **confine** 한정하다

□ **consent** 동의(하다)

□ **consequence** 결과

□ **conservative** 보수적인

□ **consistently** 꾸준히

□ **contamination** 오염

D~E

□ **contend** 겨루다

□ **contention** 언쟁

□ **contraption** 고안물

□ **contravene** 위반하다

□ **conversion** 전환

□ **convert** 개조하다, 전환하다

□ **convey** 전달하다

□ **convict** 유죄 판결하다

□ **coordination** 협응

□ **cordially** 정성껏

□ **corporal** 신체적인

□ **correlation** 상관관계

□ **corruption** 부패

□ **counterpart** 대응물, 상응물

□ **courteously** 정중하게

□ **covet** 탐내다

□ **cram** 밀어넣다

□ **crass** 우둔한

□ **culminate** 절정에 달하다

□ **culprit** 범인

□ **cultivate** 배양하다

□ **cumbersome** 번거로운

□ **cumulative** 누적되는

□ **curtail** 짧게 줄이다

D

□ **dainty** 섬세한; 까다로운

□ **dampen** 무디게 하다

□ **debase** (가치를) 저하시키다

□ **debunk** 폭로하다

□ **decadence** 퇴폐

□ **deceive** 속이다

□ **decline** 쇠퇴, 침체

□ **dedicate** 헌신하다

□ **deduce** 추론하다

□ **deduct** 빼다

□ **defendant** 피고

□ **defense** 국방; 방어; 변호

□ **deficient** 부족한

□ **defining** 뚜렷한

□ **definitive** 한정적인; 완성된

□ **deformity** 기형

□ **defy** 도전하다

□ **delegate** (권한 등을) 위임하다

□ **depict** 묘사하다

□ **depletion** 고갈

□ **depression** 침체

□ **derive** 유래하다, 파생하다

□ **designate** 지정하다

18

□ **desirable** 바람직한

□ **desolate** 황량한

□ **despotism** 횡포

□ **destitute** 궁핍한

□ **detect** 찾다, 탐지하다

□ **detrimental** 해로운

□ **diabolical** 사악한

□ **diagnose** 진단하다; 원인을 밝혀내다

□ **dictate** 명령하다

□ **dignity** 존엄성

□ **dilate** 팽창하다

□ **dilatory** 행동이 느린

□ **diplomacy** 외교

□ **diplomat** 외교관

□ **dire** 비참한

□ **disciplinary** 징계의

□ **discipline** 규율; 학문; 훈련

□ **dismiss** 일축하다; 해산시키다

□ **dispersion** 확산

□ **disposition** 기질

□ **dissident** 반체제의

□ **dissociation** 분리

□ **distortion** 왜곡

□ **divulge** 폭로하다

□ **drain** 부담

□ **drastic** 극적인

□ **drought** 가뭄

E

□ **electrical plant** 전력 발전소

□ **electromagnetic** 전자기의

□ **elegant** 우아한

□ **embed** 파묻다

□ **embezzlement** 횡령

□ **emerge** 나타나다

□ **emit** 방출하다

□ **enact** 제정하다

□ **endeavor** 노력

□ **endemic** 만연한

□ **enigmatic** 불가사의한

□ **enlist** 참여하다

□ **entail** 수반하다, 포함하다

□ **entice** 꾀다, 유인하다

□ **entrancing** 매혹적인

□ **entrust** 위탁하다

□ **envisage** 상상하다

□ **equitable** 형평성이 있는

□ **equivalent** 동일한

□ **erode** 침식하다

□ **erroneous** 잘못된

□ **evaporation** 증발

□ **exclusively** 독점적으로

□ **excursion** 유람

□ **execute** 처형하다

□ **exile** 망명

□ **exonerated** 면제된

□ **exorbitantly** 턱없이

□ **expectant** 임신한

□ **expedite** 진척시키다

□ **exploitative** 착취적인

□ **exponent** 해설자; 설명적인

□ **exposure** 노출

□ **expunge** 삭제하다

□ **extent** 넓이; 범위; 정도

□ **extract** 발췌하다, 추출하다

□ **extravagant** 화려한

□ **exude** 스며 나오다

📁 **F**

□ **fabricate** 조작하다

□ **facet** 측면

□ **fallible** 틀리기 쉬운

□ **falsified** 왜곡된, 위조된

□ **felicitous** 적절한, 타당한

□ **fermented** 발효된

□ **fiber** 섬유질

□ **fluctuate** 변동하다

□ **flux** 변동, 유전

□ **fraternize** 친화하다

□ **frugal** 검소한

□ **fuel** 연료; 부추기다, 자극하다

📁 **G**

□ **gauge** 계량기; 측정하다

□ **generated** 생성된

□ **genocide** 인종학살

□ **glide** 미끄러지다

□ **glimpse** 흘끗 봄

□ **glitch** 결함

□ **glutinous** 접착성의

□ **greedy** 욕심이 많은

□ **guileless** 교활하지 않은

□ **guilt** 과오

📁 **H**

□ **halt** 멈추다, 중지하다

□ **hardy** 튼튼한; 대담한

□ **hassle** 골칫거리; 괴롭히다

□ **hiatus** 공백기

□ **hibernation** 동면

□ **hominid** 원시 인류

I

□ **identification** 식별

□ **identity** 주체성

□ **ideology** 사상

□ **idle** 공회전하다

□ **ignominious** 불명예스러운

□ **immolate** 희생하다

□ **immune system** 면역 체계

□ **impartial** 공평한

□ **imperative** 필수적인

□ **implant** 이식물

□ **implement** 시행하다, 이행하다

□ **implication** 함축

□ **inadequate** 부적절한

□ **incoming** 신임의

□ **incorporate** 통합하다, 결합하다

□ **indulge** 빠지다, 탐닉하다

□ **inertia** 관성

□ **infectious** 전염성의

□ **influx** 유입

□ **infrastructure** 기반 시설

□ **infringement** 침해

□ **infusive** 고취시키는

□ **ingenious** 독창적인

□ **ingenuity** 창의력

□ **inherit** 유전되다

□ **initiative** 주도권, 추진계획

□ **inkling** 암시

□ **innovation** 혁신

□ **inspirational** 영감을 주는

□ **insurgent** 반란군

□ **integrate** 통합하다

□ **intergalactic** 우주적인

□ **interim** 임시의

□ **intern** 억류하다

□ **intervene** 개입하다

□ **intolerant** 옹졸한, 편협한

□ **invariably** 예외 없이

□ **invert** 역전하다

□ **irritation** 염증; 짜증

J

□ **jeopardize** 위태롭게 하다

□ **jolt** 세계 흔들다

□ **justice system** 사법 제도

□ **juvenile delinquency** 청소년 범죄

K

□ **kennel** 애견상

□ **kidney** 신장

□ **kin** 친척

L

□ **legacy** 유산

□ **legislate** 법률로 제정하다

□ **legislation** 법안

□ **lenient** 관대한

□ **lethal** 치명적인

□ **lethargic** 무기력한

□ **liberal arts** 인문과학

□ **liberalism** 자유주의

□ **liberation** 해방

□ **libertarianism** 자유옹호론

□ **lofty** 고매한

M

□ **maintenance** 유지 보수

□ **malleable** 유순한

□ **maneuver** 책략, 조치

□ **mediate** 중재하다, 조정하다

□ **menace** 위협

□ **merge** 결합하다

□ **methodology** 방법론

□ **mineral substance** 광물질

□ **miscreant** 사악한

□ **modification** 변경

□ **modify** 수정하다

□ **moral conscience** 도덕적 양심

□ **morale** 사기

□ **morbid** 병적인

□ **mortgage** 담보 대출

□ **muffle** 덮어 싸다

□ **mutate** 변이하다

N

□ **normalize** 정상화하다

□ **notable** 주목할 만한

□ **novice** 초심자

□ **nutritious** 영양가 높은

O

□ **obedient** 복종하는

□ **obnoxious** 역겨운, 추한

□ **obscurantist** 반계몽주의자

□ **obsolete** 구식의

□ **obstacle** 걸림돌, 장애(물)

□ **obtrusive** 눈에 띄는

□ **obtuse** 무딘

□ **offender** 위반자

□ **operation** 운영; 효능; 수술

□ **opinionated** 독선적인

□ **opportunistic** 기회주의적인

□ **oppressive** 억압적인

□ **overcast** 찌푸린; 흐리게 하다

□ **override** 우선하다

📁 **P**

□ **pagan** 토속종교, 이교

□ **painstakingly** 공들여

□ **pandemic** 유행

□ **panicky** 겁에 질린

□ **parasite** 기생충

□ **patent** 특허를 얻다

□ **peasant** 소작인

□ **penchant** 경향; 강한 기호

□ **permanent** 영구적인

□ **permeate** 스며들다

□ **persecute** 박해하다

□ **perseverance** 의지

□ **persistent** 완고한

□ **pertinacity** 끈기

□ **pervade** 팽배하다

□ **petition** 탄원(하다)

□ **pillage** 강탈하다

□ **pioneer** 개척하다; 개척자

□ **plunder** 약탈하다

□ **poach** 밀렵하다

□ **poised** 침착한

□ **poisonous** 유해한

□ **polemic** 논쟁

□ **polish** 연마하다

□ **posh** 고급의, 호화로운

□ **posturing** 가식적인 태도

□ **preclude** 방해하다

□ **preexisting** 기존의

□ **prestigious** 고급의; 유명한

□ **primate** 영장류

□ **prime minister** 국무총리

□ **prized** 가치 있는, 중요한

□ **proactive** 예방적인

□ **procedure** 절차

□ **proclaim** 선포하다, 주장하다

□ **prodigy** 천재

□ **prominent** 유명한

□ **propagate** 전파하다

□ **propulsion** 추진

□ **prosecute** 기소하다

□ **protest** 시위; 항의(하다)

□ **provincial** 지방의

□ **provision** 설비, 준비

□ **provoke** 촉발시키다

📁 **Q**

□ **qualification** 자격요건, 조건

□ **questionable** 의심스러운

📁 **R**

□ **radiate** 방출하다, 방사하다

□ **raffle** 추첨

□ **rampant** 성행하는

□ **rationale** 이론적 근거

□ **raunchy** 초라한

□ **readily** 선뜻, 쉽사리

□ **redundant** 과다한, 남아도는

□ **referee** 심판

□ **refine** 정제하다

□ **refurbish** 개조하다, 수리하다

□ **refute** 반박하다

□ **regimen** 계획

□ **register** 등록하다

□ **regulate** 통제하다

□ **regulation** 규정

□ **rehabilitation** 재활

□ **reign** 집권

□ **relic** 유적

□ **remit** 송금하다

□ **rendition** 번역

□ **renege** 손을 떼다, 취소하다

□ **repository** 보고, 저장소

□ **repossess** 회수하다

□ **reproduction** 번식

□ **rescind** 무효화하다

□ **resignation** 사직

□ **resistance** 내성; 저항

□ **retribution** 보복

□ **retrieve** 회수하다

□ **revitalization** 활성화

□ **revoke** 취소하다

□ **rift** 균열, 격차

□ **rivalry** 경쟁

□ **rural** 전원의

📁 **S**

□ **salutation** 인사

□ **sane** 정상인; 멀쩡한

□ **satirical** 풍자적인

□ **saturate** 적시다

□ **savor** 음미하다

□ **scabby** 비열한, 불쾌한

□ **scanty** 부족한

□ **scenic** 아름다운

□ **seductive** 매혹적인

□ **seedy** 누추한

□ **seep** 스며 나오다

□ **segregation** 인종 차별; 분리

□ **seizure** 발작

□ **self-evident** 자명한

□ **semblance** 유사함

□ **severe** 극심한, 심각한

□ **shabby** 초라한

□ **shiver** 몸을 떨다

□ **siege** 포위, 공격

□ **significant** 상당한; 중요한

□ **signify** 의미하다

□ **simulate** 흉내내다

□ **simultaneously** 동시에

□ **skepticism** 의심

□ **slack** 늘어진

□ **sneak** 숨기다

□ **soaring** 급증하는

□ **sobriety** 절제

□ **solely** 단지, 오직

□ **solidify** 응고시키다; 확정하다

□ **sophisticated** 능란한; 세련된

□ **sort out** 해결하다

□ **speculate** 생각하다

□ **spontaneous** 임의의

□ **spurious** 가짜의

□ **stark** 극명한, 뚜렷한

□ **statistic** 통계치

□ **steer** 향하다

□ **stifle** 참다, 억제하다

□ **strain** 변종, 변형; 부담

□ **stratification** 계층

□ **subsequently** 결과적으로

□ **substantial** 상당한

□ **substantiate** 실증하다, 입증하다

- substitute 대신하다
- subsume 포함하다
- subtle 미묘한
- subtract 빼다
- surge 급증; 돌진
- surrender 투항하다; 항복(하다)
- surveillance 감시
- sycophancy 아첨
- symmetry 대칭
- synchronize 동시에 일어나다
- synonymous 동일한
- synthesize 합성하다

T

- tackle 다루다
- tactic 전법, 전술
- tailor 맞춤화하다
- taint 더럽히다
- tenaciously 끈질기게
- terminate 종결시키다, 종결하다
- texture 질감
- thrive 번영하다, 번창하다
- throne 왕위
- thwart 방해하다, 좌절시키다

- torture 고문하다
- tract 지대
- transparent 투명한
- treatise 논문
- trigger 유발하다

U

- umpire 심판
- underestimate 과소평가하다
- underlying 기저에 깔린
- undermine 해치다, 손상시키다
- undo 원상태로 돌리다
- unruly 버릇 없는
- unyielding 단호한
- urge 권유하다; 촉구하다

V

- vacillate 흔들다
- vandalize 파손하다
- vapor 수증기
- variation 변동
- vault 금고
- venom 독
- vent 새어나오다

☐ **veracious** 정직한, 진실한

☐ **versatility** 융통성

☐ **vertical** 수직의

☐ **vessel** 혈관

☐ **vice versa** 거꾸로, 반대로

☐ **vigorous** 박력 있는

☐ **viral infection** 바이러스 감염

☐ **virility** 남성성

☐ **vital** 중요한

W

☐ **ward** 병동

☐ **warranty** 보증

☐ **wastage** 소모

☐ **windfall** 뜻밖의 횡재

☐ **worsen** 악화되다

TEPS

Test of English Proficiency
developed by
Seoul National University